Early Childhood Education, Birth–8

Early Childhood Education, Birth–8

The World of Children, Families, and Educators

Amy Driscoll
Portland State University

Nancy G. Nagel
Lewis and Clark College

Allyn and Bacon
Boston ■ London ■ Toronto ■ Sydney ■ Tokyo ■ Singapore

Series Editor: *Frances Helland*
Editorial Assistant: *Bridget Keane*
Director of Education Programs: *Ellen Mann Dolberg*
Marketing Manager: *Brad Parkins*
Production Administrator: *Annette Joseph*
Production Coordinator: *Holly Crawford*
Editorial-Production Service: *Lynda Griffiths, TKM Productions*
Text Designer: *Carol Somberg/Omegatype Typography, Inc.*
Composition Buyer: *Linda Cox*
Electronic Composition and Art: *Omegatype Typography, Inc.*
Manufacturing Buyer: *Suzanne Lareau*
Cover Administrator: *Linda Knowles*

Copyright © 1999 by Allyn & Bacon
A Viacom Company
160 Gould Street
Needham Heights, MA 02494
Internet: www.abacon.com

Library of Congress Cataloging-in-Publication Data

Driscoll, Amy.
    Early childhood education, birth–8 : the world of children,
families, and educators / Amy Driscoll, Nancy G. Nagel.
        p.   cm.
    Includes bibliographical references and index.
    ISBN 0-205-19984-4
    1. Early childhood education—Case studies.   2. Child development—
Case studies.   I. Nagel, Nancy G.   II. Title.
LB1139.23.D77   1998
372.21—dc21   98-26472
                                                                 CIP

Printed in the United States of America
10 9 8 7 6 5 4 3 2 1   RRDV   03 02 01 00 99 98

Photo credits: pages 10, 27, 34, 66, 148, 180, 195, 219, 410, 424, 436, 451, and 472:
Will Hart; pages 15, 39, 56, 85, 114, 118, 129, 138, 158, 205, 292, 298, 446, and 456:
Will Faller; pages 50, 198, 300, 480, and 491: Robert Harbison; page 170: AP/Wide
World Photos.

Permission acknowledgment: Figure 6.2, page 206, and Figure 6.3, page 216: From *Child,
Family, Community,* Third Edition by Roberta M. Berns, copyright © 1993 by Holt, Rinehart and
Winston, reprinted by permission of the publisher.

CONTENTS

chapter **3**   *Theories of Development: Foundations for Practice*   *74*

chapter **4**

Children's Play: A Source of Development and Learning   *114*

chapter **5**

Early Childhood Curriculum: Thinking and Practices **158**

chapter 6 *Families and Communities: Context for Understanding Children* 198

chapter **7**   *Infant Care Programs and Practices: Luke's Story*   *244*

chapter **8**

chapter **9**

Head Start: Felipe's Story *332*

chapter **10**

Kindergarten: Keeley's Story   *372*

chapter **11**

The Primary Grades: Jodie's Story of Special Education **410**

chapter 12

The Changing World of Early Childhood

PREFACE

This book will introduce you to the profession of early childhood education. You will meet children in their early years (birth through age 8); their families, who play important roles as educators and caregivers; and professional educators, who support the children in their development and learning as well as assist the families in their roles. These introductions take place in the homes of children and families and in the kinds of programs in which young children spend their days. We have attended to the diversity of children's and families' ethnic and cultural heritages, to varied family configurations, and to the differences in early childhood education programs and settings.

Throughout the chapters, we encourage you to observe children, families, and early childhood professionals and to learn from them. Observations take the form of brief vignettes in the beginning chapters and extended cases in later chapters. The cases and vignettes provide a shared observation for you to process together with your peers, through class discussions and varied course assignments. In the constructivist tradition, we nudge and encourage you to create your own knowledge and understanding of early childhood education by processing the observations. A very important message we hope to communicate is that children and families are the most important source of information for the thinking, planning, decision making, and teaching in which you will engage in the future.

We pause frequently throughout the chapters and ask you to reflect on what you have just observed or what we are discussing. Those **reflections** take multiple forms to assist you in "making meaning" of the text. Some of the processing includes:

Clarifying sophisticated concepts
Generalizing from an example
Promoting the application of ideas to practice
Engaging in decision making
Connecting to your personal life and experiences
Probing for multiple and alternative views
Encouraging perspective taking
Developing professional responses to issues

Those processes, identified by the journal symbol and the word **Journal,** can be used for individual reflections (written or unwritten), group discussions, and peer reflections. Our hope is that you will develop the habit of reflection in the early stage of your professional preparation. We also hope that you will expand your experiences with children and families beyond what you read in this book, so we suggest additional **Field**

Experiences at the end of each chapter. As part of your professional development, we also encourage you to begin assembling a **Professional Portfolio** to document your understandings and skills and a **Professional Library** of resources (books, articles, web sites, and Internet addresses).

In the process of preparing this book, we carefully selected early childhood settings that exemplified best practices. Some may contend that the settings in our chapters are ideal, and that is exactly our intention. We believe that you, as a beginning professional, need to observe and study the very best programs available so that you build your knowledge and understandings from excellent examples. Soon enough in your professional development you will realize that there are plenty of examples that contradict what you are learning about children and families. In our combined years of working with preservice teachers, we have never heard them ask for an example of what not to do. Instead, our students typically ask where they can observe the kind of programs and practices they read and hear about. We had those questions in mind as we wrote this book. We describe the curriculum and guidance strategies used by some of the best professionals. To show you the best examples, these curriculum and guidance symbols appear in the margins alongside the cases: *C* , *G* . We have visited the

kind of places our students have longed to observe and have described what we saw and heard as authentically as possible. We have selected programs and professionals that modeled what we are trying to teach through this text. We have listened for the kind of thinking and decision making that we encourage you, a beginning professional, to prepare to do. Our hope is that you will learn from the modeling of excellent practices found in the cases and stories presented here.

Each of the families in our cases is quite different from one another, but they only begin to represent the diversity awaiting future early childhood professionals. Many beginning students have experienced only the diversity of their own neighborhoods, and it is often a limiting experience. We intend for our stories and cases to broaden those experiences and perspectives by introducing you to families that might be different from those in your neighborhood. The same is true for the different kinds of programs that exist for children and families. It is so important that in your preparation to work in those settings, you observe a broad range of programs and professional roles in which to seek employment when your preparation is complete. Throughout the chapters, we urge you to take an active role in your own professional development and to begin the reflection and decision making that characterize a professional. We sincerely hope that after reading this book, your preparation will continue to build on and expand a range of experiences.

Finally, *Early Childhood Education, Birth–8* is designed to provide a comprehensive overview of the professional content to be studied by an early childhood professional. It is important to note that many of the content areas need further and intensive development. The best example is the study of child development. This book contains a chapter that describes typical development from infancy to age 8, a chapter that explains major theories of development, and various cases of children of different ages to highlight the development typically observed at each age. We do not consider those chapters and cases sufficient content for the extensive study of child development that is critical for the early childhood professional. We strongly urge you to use the content of this text as foundational information and to build on the ideas and concepts in future courses and experiences.

Acknowledgments

We wish to acknowledge those early childhood professionals who assisted our writing by welcoming us to their centers and schools, by interpreting their programs, by discussing their beliefs and practices, and by introducing us to the children and their families. We are grateful to the following families and early childhood professionals: Robin Lindsley, Francis and Akosa Wambalaba and family, Luke and George Kolln, Margaret Browning, Sue Patterson, Kristine Digman, Faridah Haron and Ibrahim, Ellie Noland and staff of Helen Gordon Child Development Center, Carolyne Westlake, Susana Grandjean, Lynn Reer, Vicki Lawry, Tim Lauer, Candace Beck, Vineeta Pahalad, Ann Gray, Nancy Johnson-Dorn, Jana Patterson, and Nancy Anderson.

We also acknowledge the careful and productive support of our students and assistants: Kristin Engelbretson, Kari Grosvold, Robert Halstead, M. J. Longley, Anita Bilbao, and Bonnie Larsen. In addition, we appreciate our excellent reviewers who contributed to the clarity, organization, and comprehensive quality of this text: Nancy File, Santa Fe Community College; Shelia Hendershot, Garden City Community College; Joan P. Isenberg, George Mason University; Penny Luken, Broward Community College; Frank Miller, Pittsburg State University; Colleen Olson, Cuyahoga Community College–Metro Campus; and Mary Rivkin, University of Maryland, Baltimore County.

Frances Helland, our editor at Allyn and Bacon, was a vigilant mentor and friend through our years of work. Her e-mails of encouragement, critique, and celebration were a consistent source of support. Nancy Forsyth, Editorial Director, was instrumental in the early stages of this book. She nurtured its initiation with Allyn and Bacon, and we thank her.

Both of us must mention our families and express appreciation for their interest in our work and their encouragement and support. We thank Kerry, Kelly, Katy, Keenan, and Keeley Driscoll, and Ralph, Marc, and Scott Nagel.

Early Childhood Education, Birth–8

chapter

1

What Is Early

Childhood Education?

When you finish reading and reflecting on this chapter, you will be able to:

1. Describe a range of diverse early childhood education settings for young children and varied professional roles for working with those children and their families.

2. Describe some of the qualities possessed by an early childhood professional and conduct a self-assessment related to the professional role.

3. List the basic competencies needed by an early childhood professional.

4. Develop an initial plan for your own professional development of knowledge and skills.

"Individuality is a concentration of the whole world at the site of a individual" (Sewell, 1995, personal communication). The concept of individuality guides us as we begin this writing. Our hope is that it guides you as you prepare to care for children and their families. As we listen to the voices of our society, we hear a yearning for community, a hope for relationships, and a sigh of isolation. In our work with young children and their families, we have the opportunity to respond to the yearning—to provide loving support, to model cooperation, and to build partnerships. As we participate in your professional development with this writing, we have similar opportunities and we will work to build a relationship with you as you read.

Building a Community of Early Childhood Professionals

We hope to interact with you to develop an early childhood education community. We welcome you to a profession of committed, caring, and competent individuals. This text is possibly different from other books you are using or have studied in the past, so we will describe how we intend to teach and mentor you as you begin your professional development.

A Text of Stories

We have chosen to tell stories. As Marchant and McBride (1994) remind us, "Stories have a unique and captivating power over us." Most people love to tell and to listen to stories. For us, it is important that stories or narratives have the power to build community. They are a traditional form of sharing culture. Storytelling has the potential to build bonds of understanding. As a rule, people feel closer to a friend when they have heard his or her stories. Most people also remember stories better than other forms of discourse (Shulman, 1990), so we hope that you will remember the ideas in this book by recalling the narratives. We believe that stories will make the content of this book more interesting and relevant and that they will draw you into the community of early childhood education professionals.

We urge you to listen to our stories and picture yourself meeting the children and families, listening to their conversations, and feeling the spirit of their activities. Leave your surroundings and put your issues aside when you read. Put yourself into the homes and neighborhoods and schools so that your senses can experience the sights and sounds and scents. You will meet an infant named Luke and his dad, and will learn about Luke's family's concerns regarding his time in child care. A toddler named Ibrihim, whose parents are from Malaysia and Egypt, will stun you with his trilingual abilities. At a rural Head Start center, you will enjoy Felipe and his preschool activities. You will also visit his home and get acquainted with his mom and grandmother, who take such good care of him. You will fall in love with Keeley, who attends kindergarten in a public school for the arts. You will find yourself empathizing with her single mom and beginning to understand the challenges of raising a child alone. Finally, you will delight in Jodie, a 6-year-old who was diagnosed with Down syndrome at birth and who has tremendous ability to care for others. She also attends a public school and spends her day in an inclusive classroom that blends first and second grades. Her family will welcome you to their home and you will have the opportunity to hear their stories. You will also become acquainted with three brothers, Chimieti (7 years old), Otioli (5 years old), and Wamalwa (2 years old), and their parents from Kenya, as well as Angela Russo and her mom in Brooklyn, New York, who will introduce you to the community of professionals who help raise Angela. In addition to these children, you will meet the many children that we have encountered and observed during our combined 50 years of experience in classrooms and programs of all types.

Jodie, Keeley, Felipe, Ibrihim, and Luke are all real children, and their families were kind enough to let us share their stories with you. In a way, their conversations provide an opportunity for you to get to know them and us and our experiences with children. As you read the chapters, think about the children and families that you know and apply the ideas to their situations. That's just one suggestion for how to read our text.

Your Role in Reading This Book

As we tell the stories of this book, we promise to let you in on our thinking—what is going on in our heads. Since we won't be able to talk face to face, our intent is for our communication to be as clear as possible. We also want to interact with you. Get yourself a journal to use with this book—keep it nearby whenever you read these chapters. We will be posing questions, asking you to list ideas, urging you to write what comes to mind when you hear or see the situations described in these chapters. Whenever you see the symbol , we expect you to think about and write your ideas before going on with your reading. If learning is active, understanding and memory are enhanced.

Your participation (writing your thoughts) when you see the journal symbol will help you take an active learner role.

We do not intend to provide information for you to memorize or to answer every question we ask. When we tell stories or describe classroom situations, we often focus on curriculum and guidance. When you see this symbol [C], it means that the story is about curriculum. When you see this symbol [G], it means that the story is about guidance stategies. We will tell stories, describe situations, and observe children and adults with you. We might ask you questions about topics that will require you to draw from your lifetime of experiences. We will provide as many options as possible rather than tell you the "right" way to do things. Then we will ask you to **respond**—to predict, to analyze, or to make recommendations. Sometimes we will ask you to **reflect**—to feel, to integrate ideas with your own experiences and beliefs, or to consider multiple perspectives or varied issues. We want you to make choices and to construct your own understanding, That is exactly the way we believe in teaching children, and we feel strongly that you should have the same kind of learning experience.

Teaching is a decision-making role, and we hope you will begin forming opinions and making decisions now, as you read this book and start your own professional development. In order to make all the decisions that teaching demands, you must first become a **reflective observer**—someone who watches and listens well and then questions what was seen and heard. In a classroom where teachers truly guide children's development and learning, there is constant action and interaction, and in the midst of it all, attention is paid to what is happening for each individual (Jones, 1993). In such a classroom, the teacher is not someone who tells and corrects, but someone who watches and asks, "What happened? What did you notice?" and reflects, "I noticed . . ." (Wasserman, 1990). An effective teacher never stops observing and asking.

Meet an Early Childhood Professional

We will begin by introducing you to a friend who is an outstanding early childhood education professional. It might be helpful for you to meet a real person who has the professional qualities we encourage you to develop. Robin, who is pictured at the opening of this chapter, is definitely a decision maker and a reflective observer—the ultimate early childhood professional. When you meet her later in this chapter, you will see her in a blended first/second-grade classroom in a public school.

Robin can be seen at every workshop or professional meeting that is scheduled—mostly in a very involved role. She questions her practices frequently and publicly. We still remember when she began questioning her morning calendar routine and the developmentally appropriateness of it for her first-graders. Morning calendar routines have been done by early childhood teachers for years and years, and most everyone just unhesitatingly accepted the practice. Not Robin! She questioned others about the value of the routine and asked herself about how well it matched the development of her children, then she made her decision. She decided to abandon the morning calendar routine, with its rote chorus of month, day and year, because it had little meaning for her children. Robin is a risk taker in her work with children. She had 14 literacy centers in her classroom and was practicing *whole language* approaches long before we heard of the term. She blended her first-graders with the previous class of first-graders (now second-graders) after much studying and thinking, but before it became popular to mix different-aged children in groups.

The dining room table in Robin's home is never free of the most current children's books, latest curriculum materials, or stacks of recycled materials (for her construction center) she collects with a passion. If you talk with her, you find that she has read the latest book or journal about early childhood education. Most of us would like to slow her down a little—we worry about her burning out. Her human side is strong and her energy is boundless. Robin connects with others in a variety of other contexts—music, theater, antiqueing, cooking, walks, and dancing. She also is a Big Sister and a member of her local church women's group.

The important quality we see in Robin is that she never finishes learning. She questions and probes all of the time. She does not accept every new approach that comes along, but she is curious. She consistently seeks improvement in what she does with children. Robin also serves as an advocate for children and families as well as for teachers. She has spoken to the legislature on behalf of children and teachers, and she has held offices in all of the major professional associations.

Recently, Robin received a prestigious national award for being an outstanding teacher. The award came with a generous amount of money, and with those funds, Robin opened *A Teacher's Space* in collaboration with her many early childhood educator friends. It is a storefront space with commercial materials for sale, a library, a workroom for laminating and producing materials, bins and bins of free recyclable materials, a meeting room for workshops and classes, and a place to relax and talk with other teachers.

Robin is exceptional but she is not the exception. You will meet many exciting early childhood professionals as you prepare to be one yourself. Some of them will be introduced to you in this book.

Journal 1.1: Before joining our community, stop and think about your decision to take this course or begin your study in education. What are you thinking? How do you feel about making this decision? Why have you decided to study early childhood education? ■

Make a commitment right now to read this text with a questioning approach. Read the stories and practice being a reflective observer. Be actively involved in your learning. As we describe your options in early childhood education, try to visualize yourself working in the different programs—in other words, do some personal roleplaying!

Exploring the Options in Early Childhood Education: Programs and Roles

We are about to take you on a tour of early childhood education (ECE) programs, where you will be introduced to the many career choices available to you as an early childhood professional. There is a wide range of roles and responsibilities undertaken by early childhood professionals and there are many variations in ECE programs. Our first story, similar to a travelogue, takes you on a trip through the community in which we live. We will introduce you to early childhood professionals and give you the opportunity to observe some of the varied programs for children here in our part of the country. We will also share our stories of programs around the country that we have visited, so that you will have a broad picture of the range of programs waiting for you.

A Downtown Child Care Center

Our community—Portland, Oregon—is a medium-sized city with all the advantages and disadvantages of an urban area. With respect to the early childhood education profession, Portland represents a typical metropolitan setting for viewing professional roles and programs. We begin downtown, amidst the city's office buildings and busiest traffic, where we find a very large child care center named Little Peoples. It is an example of a **proprietary care center,** meaning that it provides care and education for children and is designed to make a profit. Little Peoples fills an entire block at the street level. The floor-to-ceiling windows across the front and sides of the center allow the children to observe the downtown activity. On the outside, we see pedestrians observing the children. The center is bright with massive amounts of natural light (when it isn't one of Portland's famous rainy days) and the space is arranged with large play areas. Little Peoples opens at 7:00 A.M. to accommodate working parents and it closes at 6:00 P.M., when most downtown workers are getting on the freeways to go home.

As we pass the center, two caregivers, Natasha and Jill, push the double doors open and emerge with six toddlers in strollers. The specially made strollers accommodate three children at once. A cool wind is blowing, so the children are wearing light sweaters and jackets. We hear the caregivers talking to the children: "Look at the big bus! There's lots of people in the bus. Listen to the bus." Soon, half the toddlers are pointing to the bus and communicating in their own way about the scene. Angela is shouting quite clearly, "Bus—beep beep, beep." Jill responds to the toddler, "Yes, the horn

on the bus goes beep, beep, beep." She urges the children to wave back to the occupants on the bus who are now waving at the children.

At the intersection, the caregivers stop to discuss what direction to take for today's walk. Natasha reminds Jill that they planned to walk past the produce market because pumpkins and apples are in season. She steps in front of the strollers and tells the children, "We're going to see pumpkins and apples today. Can you make a pumpkin with your arms?" Angela and Dexter both lift their arms into a circle immediately, and others follow. Natasha also makes the pumpkin shape with her arms and begins singing a pumpkin song. She and Jill push the strollers for four blocks to the produce market.

We return to the center and watch the indoor activities. Preschool-aged children are involved in many different activities in one large room: Two children are painting at an easel, two others are sitting at a table with puzzles and Legos, several children are dressed up and playing in a dramatic play area, and a small group is cutting and pasting at a table with an adult who assists with the cutting and distribution of small mounds of paste. One child is wandering around and watching everyone else, and two boys are quietly wrestling on the rug. We look around the room and notice another adult who is comforting a child who appears to have a problem. In general, there's a calm about this place—only a slight hum of activity.

Everything in this place feels so new and shiny, so orderly. It is obvious that the facility was carefully designed and built for the child care activities we observe here. Wondering how old it is, we stop in at the office and are told that the facility is 6 years old, and that it is part of a commercial chain of centers. We also learn that the caregivers have a wide range of qualifications. Natasha has a bachelor's degree in child development, and several of the other caregivers have associate degrees in early childhood education from community colleges. Some have had experience at other centers. Others have some college credits, and many of the caregivers are attending the nearby university.

Professional requirements.   Little Peoples is not unique in its staff qualifications. The National Child Care Staffing Study (Whitebrook, Phillips, & Howes, 1993) surveyed 227 child care centers in four major cities and found that only 12 percent of the respondents held bachelor's degrees or graduate degrees in a field related to early childhood education, only 19 percent had some college education related to ECE, and 38 percent had no education at all related to the field. Most requirements governing child care programs are inconsistent when it comes to staff qualifications, so there is huge variation in the training backgrounds of child care personnel (Phillips, 1994). You could probably stop reading now and find yourself a job as a child care provider. You would definitely start learning on the job, but you would have few options regarding your future in ECE and you might not always be able to serve children well. We sincerely hope that you will not stop reading and that you will make a commitment to learn as much as you can about children and their families. We urge you to become an early childhood *professional.* Come with us and look at some other programs for children so that you will be able to make choices and decisions.

A Downtown Child Care Center for Children with Disabilities

This time, we are in the middle of Montreal, Quebec, Canada, and the downtown center is called Papillon (French for *butterfly*). It is an unusual child care center because Papillon is intentionally structured to serve an equal number of children with and without disabilities. It is also quite different from Little Peoples because Papillon is operated as a nonprofit center and sponsored by the Quebec Society for Handicapped Children. Papillon's location in a large metropolitan city and its reputation for excellent child care attracts a diverse population of families, thus children of many ethnic backgrounds attend the center. There are two official languages spoken by the children and adults of Montreal: French and English. However, there are many other languages spoken informally at Papillon. It will be interesting to listen and observe for just a few minutes.

We enter Papillon through a wide hallway bordered on each side by larger-than-usual cubbies for children's belongings. The floor is full of children struggling with boots and snowsuits. Several parents are helping their children and providing the usual encouragement ("Don't forget to bring your mittens home"). We hear French, English, Spanish, and Japanese spoken.

We notice a smiling 5-year-old, Teresa, arriving in a wheelchair. She is greeted by several teachers and she looks at us with an inquiring expression. *"Bonjour, comment ça va?"* she asks. We respond with our best French, telling her that we are fine, and she smiles. Her friend Natalie begins to remove Teresa's jacket, talking softly to her in French. When Natalie finishes, she places Teresa's belongings in Teresa's cubby and puts soft slipperlike shoes on her friend.

Natalie wheels Teresa into the classroom and pushes her chair up to one of the amoeba-shaped tables. She then gathers paper and markers and seats herself at the table next to her friend. She places several colored markers and a paper on a raised stand in front of Teresa at the table. As we watch the two friends, we are touched by the opportunity that both of these children have for learning about differences. Later, we realize that this is the first of many advantages of **inclusion,** the integration of children with varying needs and abilities.

Back in the hall, we hear "Ooh la la" from adults in response to the children's efforts and successes in removing their difficult, bulky, winter clothing. We also hear Gaby, one of the teachers, greet Robert, who is sitting on the floor fully clothed in his winter wear, and ask him, "Is anyone undressing you?" He shakes his head to indicate that no one is assisting. Gaby follows with, "OK, which leg is your prosthesis?" He points to his right leg and she carefully removes a boot from his right foot. She insists that he help by indicating where his clothes go. "Show me where your hook and your cubby are." Once Robert is ready for the day, Gaby encourages him to use the side

In an inclusive setting, children learn to appreciate differences.

rail, and he scoots down the hall to his classroom. As we reflect on this brief episode, we are aware of Papillon's goal of building self-confidence. Gaby provided Robert a chance to "be in charge," even while helping him (Driscoll, 1995).

Papillon is the kind of place where you could learn a great deal about how to be an early childhood educator. That is also true of our next stop in Portland, because we are going to visit a university laboratory preschool.

A University Laboratory School

Our next stop, the university campus, is just five blocks away. There, we will visit the Helen Gordon Child Development Center, a university **laboratory school.** The center is in a lovely old home, now a historic site. Upon entering, there is the feeling of comfort and warmth that one gets when entering an old home. Two floors of large classrooms accommodate children aged 2 to 5. At

least four adults are in each of the rooms—practicum students from the university and two preschool teachers per group. The center's status as a *laboratory school* means that there are always students engaged in fulfilling practicum or student-teaching requirements and faculty engaged in supervision or research projects. Also, there is a happy mix of children's conversations, singing, story reading, and laughter, and it carries through the halls of this center.

The activities are not very different from what we saw at the Little Peoples and Papillon, but there appears to be extensive adult/child interaction. The rooms feel different, too. The equipment looks old and very well used. There is an abundance of materials and well-defined **centers** (areas in which one kind of play is focused, such as a dramatic play center or a block center). The most noticeable difference is the presence of lots of blocks—and most of them on the floor, not on the shelves.

Several 4-year-old children are at a table, working with recyclable materials (paper-towel rolls, yarn, empty boxes, and so on). We hear Adam shout, "Look, Maya, I made a cage for my spider." Maya, the teacher responds, "I can see that you worked hard on that. Tell me how you made it." Adam responds with descriptions of much cutting and gluing and "I used lots of tape" as Maya and some of the children listen. Bryna and Matt decide that they are going to make cages, too. Maya poses the question, "What other creatures could be in a cage like that?" The table erupts into a lively discussion of different insects and animals.

We take a peek outside the child development center and see that the entire yard is converted to a playground. There is a huge sand region, an area of tire swings and a slide, tricycles and a smoothly paved area for riding, and some space devoted to gardens. Beyond the tall fence surrounding the playground is the traffic of the city and the talk of students going to university classes. This outside area has that same well-used look that we saw inside the center.

Journal 1.2: How do you feel when you come into a center that is sparkling new and very neat? What questions do you have? How do you feel when you come into a center that is worn but appealing, with materials that look used but abundant? What questions do you have? What types of environments make children feel welcome and supported? What kinds of environments do not feel that way? ■

Professional requirements.   The university context and the use of the Helen Gordon Child Development Center for demonstration purposes has an influence on the qualifications of the staff. All the head teachers have degrees in early childhood education and many of them are pursuing master's degrees. Their assistants have two-year associate's degrees in early childhood education. The center pays well and attracts such qualified personnel. The program quality observed at the center is in direct relationship to the preparation of its staff (Goelman, 1992) and its reputation attracts long waiting lists of children. Most of the parents feel that their children are challenged and are developing well, both cognitively and socially. There is ample evidence that high-quality early childhood programs benefit children in terms of school success, social and emotional competence, and improved opportunities for health (NAEYC, 1990c).

The tradition of laboratory schools.   Laboratory schools began as nursery schools in the 1920s, with the same purpose as they currently have. The Helen Gordon Child Development Center is very much a part of university life, as are many laboratory schools on campuses of universities, colleges, and community colleges. Some are associated with schools of education, some with departments of child and family studies, and others with departments of psychology, child development, and related disciplines.

All our local laboratory schools have a reputation for providing very high quality early childhood education programs. You probably have access to a laboratory school on the campus where you are studying. If you have not already visited the program, make it a priority for your beginning professional development as you study with us. Laboratory schools are ideal places to observe and begin learning about the profession. In our city, they are one of many good examples of early childhood education programs. Now it is time to see another example. Let's get ready to travel.

A Public School Early Childhood Education Center

Portland is a city divided by a river. We now cross one of the city's many bridges to see more examples of what is available for young children and their families. Close to the edge of a commercial area, in a section of the city marked by poverty, is an exceptional public school: Boise Eliot Elementary. It is one of Portland Public Schools' Early Childhood Education Centers, with classes for preschool children through third grade. The school is in a very large—almost imposing—old brick building. When we enter, the hallways feel familiar, much like they were when we went to school. However, once we enter the classroom area, there is a dynamic difference.

The hallway widens and is filled with equipment for woodworking, cooking, large motor activities, and so on. We learn that these areas are called the *commons* and that children in all of the adjoining classes use them. There is a distinctive smell of applesauce in this area. Children of different ages are in this common area engaged in varied activities. One teacher seems to be supervising them. She moves about, watching, commenting, or interacting with children, scanning their activities frequently. Adjoining this common area is a preschool classroom. Let's go and observe.

A preschool class.   Inside the preschool room, children are gathered around a teacher as she writes their ideas about making applesauce. They have just come back to the room from the commons, where they washed and peeled apples, cut them into tiny pieces (very tiny), then mashed and cooked them into sauce. No wonder it smelled so good! We hear, "We squashed the apples" and "I'm a good peeler." Mac asks, "Is it cool yet, Miss Sabrina?"

Two children go back to the commons area and get bowls of applesauce from the refrigerator. Soon, children are excitedly tasting their success.

Looking around the room, we notice that it is very similar to the one at the Helen Gordon Center. There are lots of centers: a block area, a dramatic play area, tables and shelves of art materials, a science corner, and a reading center. The room is cozy, with a little lamp and colorful pillows in the reading center. The dramatic play area offers many inviting accessories: a telephone, a typewriter, dishes and pots, dress-up clothes, child-sized furniture, and dolls. When the children finish eating, they scatter around the room and become quickly involved in play. Several children call out, "Grandpa's here," when they see a grey-haired man come into the classroom. He is immediately coaxed and pulled into the reading center and children bring books for him to read.

While keeping one eye on the children with Grandpa in the reading center, we browse the walls of this preschool classroom. We believe that a person can learn a lot about a program by studying the walls. Lots of examples of children's art, many of which look like they were hung by the children, decorate the walls. Sheets of photographs of the children engaged in activities are mounted with captions that sound like they were dictated by the children. We recall now that Miss Sabrina took some pictures of the children eating their applesauce. Now we know why. This is a room where we could spend a lot of time, but we must move on.

A kindergarten class.   The next classroom is a kindergarten with one teacher and a teacher's aide. We also see a parent reading a book to a small group of children on an old sofa. Several children are drawing and writing in journals, some are "writing" with computers, and others are listening to story tapes. The teacher's aide, Jeremy, is sitting on the floor with five children looking closely at a basket of squash. They take turns touching the squash and describing its textures as Jeremy records their vocabulary on a large sheet of paper: *bumpy, ridges, rough, like little hills.*

The children's writing is hung in places all around the room. We see that some of it has been dictated to the adults and some of it is **invented spelling.** The kindergartners are encouraged to spell words as they sound, so the children invent their own spellings. Many displays are around the room: on window sills, small tables, shelves, and hanging from the ceiling in mobile form. Those displays tell us that the children engage in projects, or in the **project approach,** in this classroom. Projects are focused studies of topics in which all of children's learning is integrated into the study. For example, there is evidence of a project about windows, with children's paintings of stained glass windows, photos of windows around the neighborhood and around the world, measurements of windows, and window-washing equipment in the display area.

Once again, the environment in this kindergarten tells us much about the activities of this class. As we prepare to leave, we see the children go into small groups (of three or four) and begin to have **Show and Tell time.** Some of the children have bags or boxes of items they have brought from home to show, while others tell about an event at home or an adventure in the neighborhood. Adults are in some of the groups but not in all. The children appear quite capable of conducting their own group activity, and we notice that they listen intently to each other. We would love to stop and listen to those conversations, but there is one more classroom to visit before leaving Boise Elliot School.

A blended class. The next classroom is a blended class of first-grade and second-grade children. Their teacher is Robin, whom you met at the beginning of this chapter. About half of the 23 chil-

When topics are relevant to their lives, children are engaged and enthusiastic.

dren are sitting with Robin, talking about today's edition of the *Oregonian,* the local newspaper. They are especially interested in a story about children at another school. The children clamor to see the photos of the other children planting tiny trees. "Read what it says, please," asks Micah. Robin shows them the headline and asks if anyone can read it. Several children shout out the words *trees* and *children* and *school.* Robin assists them with the words *learn* and *neighborhood,* then asks the group to predict what the story is about. She guides them to see that the headline and the photos help them begin reading the story. Then she reads the news story to the group. During this time, the other children are at centers for painting, construction, card making, and block building.

Thuy, one of the children in Robin's class, is sitting with her mother. Thuy and her family are recent refugees from Viet Nam. After the newspaper discussion, Robin comes to Thuy and her mother and guides them around the room. She shows them examples of children's work or activity in each of her many centers, and Thuy's mom nods her head, acknowledging her understanding of what Robin is showing her. When they stop at the easels, Thuy shows interest, so her mother puts a painting apron on Thuy and encourages her to paint, speaking to her in Vietnamese. Thuy seems a little hesitant but proceeds to paint. Soon, one of the other children is chatting with her and encouraging her painting.

It looks like Thuy's mother is preparing to leave, and we see Robin packing a canvas bag of books for her to take home. She has selected simple children's books with little text, and adds some drawing paper and colored pens. They shake hands good-bye, and Robin goes immediately to Thuy's side, puts her arm around her, and talks about her painting. Just listening to her is com-forting, and we predict that Thuy and her family will make a smooth transition to her new school.

Journal 1.3: Many teachers and caregivers are facing the situation we just described—that is, the entry of a child who speaks no English and who is probably making a transition from one culture to another. When you put yourself in Robin's role, what would that be like for you? Have you ever been in a similar situation of trying to communicate with someone who couldn't understand you? What did you do and how did you feel? ■

Professional requirements. All the teachers at Boise-Eliot school have elementary teaching certificates, some with early childhood endorsements. Many of the teachers, like Robin, have master's degrees and years of experience. The teacher's aides have degrees in related programs—psychology, child and family studies, social work, and so on. Public school requirements for full-time teachers of young children are different depending on where you live. States vary tremendously in terms of certification requirements and the kind of preparation required for teaching young children. Some states require special certification and others require only an elementary teaching certificate.

Another kind of early childhood education program with varied requirements for its personnel is Head Start. Head Start programs are federally funded comprehensive programs that began in the 1960s during the War on Poverty. They were designed to counter the negative effects of poverty on young children and their families, and to offer high-quality early childhood education experiences for the children. Early in Head Start's history, it was realized that if parents weren't involved, the program would not be very successful. Head Start, then, is well known for its serious commitment to parent and family involvement. Our next stop is a Head Start center.

A Head Start Program

About 10 blocks from Boise-Eliot school is a rambling, dark brown house with multiple extensions—the site of a Head Start program. As we enter, we are once again greeted by the sounds of children. One group of 4- and 5-year-old children is approaching us and singing "This Old Man" as they climb the stairs. They gather just outside the building, sit on the grass, and listen as their teacher reminds them, "We're going to walk around our neighborhood today. What are we looking for?" Several children say, "Houses." Their teacher, Jonah, probes, "What do we want to notice about the houses?" Kim raises her hand and contributes, "We are looking for brick houses, wood houses, stone houses, and . . ." Joseph shouts, "And plastic houses." Jonah agrees and asks for volunteers to be recorders. Many children volunteer, so four recorders are easily available. Jonah gives each recorder a sheet with a picture of a different kind of house. He reminds the children that the recorders will make a mark every time the group sees a certain kind of house. "Then we will count the marks to see what is the favorite kind of house in our neighborhood. Which kind do you think will be the favorite?" he asks. After the predictions, Jonah nods to his teaching assistant, Melissa, indicating he is ready to leave. She gathers half of the group to walk with her, and the rest of the children leave with Jonah.

Back inside the Head Start center, we see a group of parents in a lounge area talking about their children and about the center. As members of the parents' advisory group, these individuals are responsible for policy decisions and recommendations to the center. Today, they are planning a transition program for children and families who will be moving on to kindergarten programs. We hear, "My older son had a terrible time when he left Head Start. I don't want that to happen to Tyrone." Another parent responds, "I think that we should spend some time visiting those kindergartens before we can decide what the children will need." Lots of head nodding and verbal agreement follow the suggestion.

Professional requirements. Most Head Start programs are not associated with public schools and have different requirements for teaching positions. In fact, most of the program's 109,345 paid staff begin their Head Start employment without baccalaureate degrees in early childhood education (Wolfe, 1994). Many Head Start teachers have or are working toward the Child Development Associate (CDA) credential, which will be described in Chapter 12. Orientation, in-service, and other forms of on-the-job training and learning are a critical part of the structure of Head Start programs.

This is a good time to look at the different staff positions for professional roles in early childhood education and the educational qualifications desired for quality programs for children. Figure 1.1 displays a sample of some of the major roles in early childhood education. It would be ideal if we could tell you that you need specific qualifications for specific roles, but there is great flexibility in the profession at this time. Head Start has a number of the specialty roles described at the bottom of Figure 1.1 and the qualifications for those roles may depend on the community of children and families, the availability of qualified professionals, and the program emphasis.

One of the major characteristics of Head Start programs is their **integration of services** for families. Many kinds of services (medical, dental, counseling, and housing assistance) are blended into the educational program. Let's visit another Head Start program. This one, in Alachua County, Florida, epitomizes service integration.

A comprehensive program for families. The Family Services Center of Alachua County, Florida, is conceptualized as a "one-stop-shop" of family services. Through its on-site services and connections with other nearby facilities, over 750 preschool children and their families are served. It began in a complex of portable buildings with stairs and walkways connecting the units. In each of the buildings is a different kind of service for families.

The center has a Head Start program and its resources and services are shared with subsidized child care centers in the surrounding neighborhood housing projects. The nearby elementary school also has Head Start classrooms. Head Start is part of a huge collaboration between state-funded

■ **FIGURE 1.1**   Sample Differentiated Staffing Structure for Educational Personnel with Suggested Educational Qualifications

Staff Role	Relevant Master's	Relevant Bachelor's	Relevant Associate's	CDA Credential	Some Training	No Training
Director	←	Degree and 3 years' experience				
Master Teacher	←	Degree and 3 years' experience				
Teacher	←					
Assistant Teacher		←				
Teaching Assistant			←			

Note: This figure does not include specialty roles such as educational coordinator, social services director, or other providers of special services. Individuals fulfilling these roles should possess the knowledge and qualifications required to fulfill their responsibilities effectively.

Source: Reaching the Full Cost of Quality in Early Childhood Programs by B. Willer, 1990, Washington, DC: NAEYC. Copyright 1990 by NAEYC. Reprinted with permission from the National Association for the Education of Young Children.

prekindergarten programs, early intervention classes, private child care and preschools, and public kindergartens and primary grades. Children benefit from the arrangement because there are more resources, easier transitions between programs, and high-quality programs due to combined expertise and consultation.

Back at the center there is also a health clinic with a nurse practitioner and a doctor. Their services include physicals, immunizations, well child care, family planning, and general medical care. In another building are adult education classes for fam-

ily members. Many of the adults are working toward their general equivalency diplomas (GEDs) by fulfilling requirements and preparing to take exams. There are also technology classes and seminars in various topics such as nutrition, family finances, and music appreciation.

We listen to the conversations between Dr. Shelton Davis and a group of parents sitting in a semi-circle around him. We hear a parent share, "Eddie is 6 years old now and he's very complicated. He was two weeks overdue and when he was born, he looked old. He was so wrinkled, he just looked old. He was a baby that was always moving, like he does now. Sometimes it was like he was shaky, and he got frustrated easily. If I woke him up to feed him, he acted frustrated. If I stopped what he was doing to change him, he acted frustrated. Mostly, I just remember him as so active."

At this point, Eddie's mom and Dr. Davis talk about hyperactivitiy and its connection to nutrition and the need for fresh fruits and vegetables. Dr. Davis reminds the group, "You remember when you roleplayed hyperactivity and we had our bodies wiggling and moving?" Lots of heads nod, and another parent says, "I remember that it

was impossible to notice or hear anything else but my own movement." The discussion continues and gets quite lively. It's obvious that there is mutual trust and caring among this group (Driscoll, 1995, p. 199).

Journal 1.4: Think for a minute what it might be like to be very poor, to be a single parent with two young children, without transportation, and feeling isolated. What would be your major concerns? If representatives of a program like Head Start approached you, what would you want them to provide? ■

Just as the Portland Head Start program and the programs in Alachua County are quite different in the way they go about serving children and families, so are Head Start programs all over the country. Much depends on the community. Whether it is a tiny rural town or a crowded major city, you will consistently find that Head Start programs reflect the community of families in which they are located. When you meet Felipe and his family, you will visit his Head Start preschool and meet many of the professionals who make the program a success. For now, it's time to meet another professional and visit another setting.

A Family Child Care Facility

It's time to experience family child care, often called **day home,** so we leave the city. We get on the freeway and drive to one of the many suburban communities encircling the downtown area of Portland. In these sprawling neighborhoods, there are many family day homes for children. This alternative child care arrangement is another option for families. We park in the driveway of a family day home and it looks just like the other homes in this neighborhood. Once inside the front door, it is obvious that this home is different from most others in the neighborhood. Rather than the usual home furnishings, there is an abundance of toys

and materials for children. There is even an easel set up in the kitchen. Two young children are sitting at the kitchen table, coloring on large white sheets of paper, and a child of 10 months is sitting in a highchair next to the table. One of the children, Xavier, tells us immediately, "These are our placemats for lunch" as he colors his sheet. The family child care provider, Harriet, is also at the table, cutting apples on a wooden board. The wonderful smell of fresh bread baking in a bread maker on the counter fills the house. Harriet converses with the children and places small slices of apple on the highchair tray. She tells us that two children will be arriving for lunch from the kindergarten at the end of the block.

We wander through her home and see a number of accommodations that she has made for the children in her home. The bathroom has a little step stool at the sink, a stack of paper cups, and a rack of towels with children's names on them. Her living room has only a couch, a chair, and a TV wall unit. A large rug covers the floor and we see an assortment of colorful boxes of plastic blocks, Tinker Toys, puzzles, and Legos. In the adjoining dining room, there are no usual furnishings, only children's materials, a rocking chair, a book shelf, and large pillows. On the wall are colorful creations by Xavier and Jesse, who are sitting in the kitchen. As we leave, we hear them singing a finger-play about apples and passing the apple slices around the table.

A very important component of Head Start is parent involvement. What are the advantages of this dad spending time in his daughter's class?

Professional requirements. As family child care gains recognition and regulation, the qualifications required for this child care arrangement are demanding attention. With more than 11 percent of children in child care being cared for in family child care settings, the staff is becoming increasingly important. Staff qualifications will vary greatly, depending on whether the home is regulated, licensed, or associated with a state or local agency. Licensing standards often specify staff qualifications, and training for family child care staff is offered by a variety of agencies and professional associations. It is difficult for family child care providers to take time off to attend workshops and other training sessions because they cannot leave parents without the needed care. Some providers seek weekend and evening training opportunities. Many of the providers are committed to the professionalization of their child care arrangements.

Professionalization of family child care. Not so long ago, family child care was unregulated and invisible (Whitehead, 1994). Those who provided care in their homes were usually referred to as babysitters and viewed simply as custodial caregivers. Today, family care has become increasingly visible due to regulations, support from child care resources and referrals, and the connections of parents to family child care. Families have come to appreciate the benefits of family child care: proximity of care in one's neighborhood, small groups of children, a home environment, and a familylike structure. In addition, family home care providers have a very committed professional organization, the National Association for Family Child Care, with extensive offerings of workshops and classes in child development, developmentally appropriate practice, guidance and discipline, health and safety issues, and so on. For many of the experienced professionals in this type of arrangement, family child care represents an important alternative for children and families. Another alternative for families is parent cooperative programs, which we will look at next.

A Parent Cooperative Preschool

Our destination is a large church with an adjoining building that houses a **parent cooperative preschool, or nursery school,** a program in which the parents fulfill many of the planning and teaching responsibilities and the administration of the program. The two classrooms are filled with colorful and attractive play materials, many of which appear to be home made rather than commercially produced. The place has a comfortable feeling and there is a quiet hum of children at work. Two fathers and three mothers are working with the children at this time. On one large table there are several large tubs of home-made play-dough and lots of kitchen and cooking utensils for molding and shaping the dough. The two adults and seven children sitting around the large table are very occupied with their play-dough creations, and the conversation is completely focused on their work. "Try rolling it," someone advises. "Look what I made," a child announces. Many play-dough snakes and cookies adorn the table.

Across the room, one of the mothers is reading to a small group of children. Another mom is guiding four children hard at work in the exploration center, filled with a variety of scales, rulers and measuring tapes, and very compelling objects to weigh and measure. One of the dads, Mr. Margolin, is sitting at the snack table, encouraging Alex as he spreads cream cheese on his bagel. He asks Alex if he knows what cream cheese is made of, and Alex shakes his head no. Mr. Margolin asks Alex if he likes other kinds of cheeses, and soon they are discussing swiss and cheddar, referring to "that white cheese with all the holes," and "the bright orange one we have on our tacos." It becomes obvious to us that the two are very comfortable together, and that Mr. Margolin spends a lot of time at the preschool.

Professional requirements. There are no professional requirements for the parents working at this center, but cooperative programs generally schedule workshops and classes for the parents. The teacher requirements vary from one program to another and are often determined by the parents. Parent cooperatives reflect the neighborhood in which they are situated. The socioeconomic status of families influences the budgetary aspects of the program and, consequently, the salary and staff requirements. It's time now to drive to the outer limits of Portland to visit yet another type of child care center.

An Employer-Sponsored Child Care Center

We arrive at an area of business and industrial complexes—mostly newly constructed office buildings, manicured lawns and shrubbery, and huge parking lots. One complex is that of Mentor Graphics Corporation. The corporation has invested in quality child care for the children of those who work there. Such investments may be the way of the future.

We approach the Child Development Center building and are immediately impressed by the dynamic architecture, the festive quality of the building's design, and the convenient location for parents. We note the walking paths from the center leading to various office buildings. They are well used.

The entrance of the Child Development Center is not like most of the places we have visited so far. It is definitely part of a business—streamlined in furnishings and space. Just inside the door where we sign in is a large window. We hear the

Why do you think it is so important for infant caregivers to be well prepared for their role?

usual sounds of children's play but the sounds are muffled. The volume increases as we approach the classrooms and peek in the large circular windows that allow those in the hallway to watch the classroom events.

An infant program.   The Mentor Graphics center offers excellent care for infants, a rarity in available child care in most places. We decide to visit the infant room so that we can see what it takes to offer quality care to such young children.

Sue, the head teacher, greets us and introduces her assistant, Caryl, and to the babies. Noah is on his stomach in front of a mirror, and Ivy is nearby, also on her stomach, reaching for a soft colorful ball. Two of the babies are in Caryl's lap listening to a story. Sue leaves me and takes Seth to a table for a diaper change. On the way, she stops and speaks to Luke, saying, "Look at Luke. See that

happy face." Luke responds with a grin for Sue and for himself in the mirror. As Sue changes Seth's diaper, she talks softly to him. She hands him the fresh diaper to hold and continues to talk.

Sue is an outstanding professional and is really the norm at Mentor Graphics. She has a master's degree in ECE, and Caryl has an associate's degree in ECE from a nearby community college. The staff is very committed and professional. They participate in many state and national workshops and are often the presenters for such sessions. The Mentor Graphics Center is able to maintain such qualified staff because the pay is better than most centers and the benefits are quite attractive. Other corporate-sponsored child care centers will vary in terms of staff qualifications and corresponding quality.

Many educators in our community consider the Mentor Graphics center a kind of laboratory school. The environment, the curriculum, and the practices of the professionals are often called *state of the art,* meaning that they represent educators' best knowledge about early childhood education. You will get to spend much more time at this center in Chapter 7, but for now, let's focus on some obvious qualities of the program. For example, now that you have been in a variety of centers for children, have you noticed the number of adults in the classrooms, especially in the rooms with very young children (infants and toddlers)? When you count the adults and children, you come up with 1 adult for every 3 infants and 1 adult for every 4 toddlers. The Mentor Graphics center follows the recommendations of the National Association for the Education of Young Children (NAEYC), a group that you will come to know well. Table 1.1 on page 18 displays those recommended child/staff ratios and group sizes. Notice how the ratio changes when the group is larger.

Journal 1.5: Think about group size and why more adults would be needed if a group was larger. Describe some reasons, both from the child's perspective as well as from the adult's perspective. ∎

■ **TABLE 1.1   Recommended Staff/Child Ratios within Group Size***

| | GROUP SIZE | | | | | | | | | | |
AGE OF CHILDREN	6	8	10	12	14	16	18	20	22	24	28
Infants (birth to 12 mos.)	1:3	1:4									
Toddlers (12 to 24 mos.)	1:3	1:4	1:5	1:4							
2-year-olds (24 to 30 mos.)		1:4	1:5	1:6							
2½-year-olds (30 to 36 mos.)			1:5	1:6	1:7						
3-year-olds					1:7	1:8	1:9	1:10			
4-year-olds						1:8	1:9	1:10			
5-year-olds						1:8	1:9	1:10			
6- to 8-year-olds								1:10	1:11	1:12	
9- to 12-year-olds										1:12	1:14

*Smaller group sizes and lower staff/child ratios have been found to be strong predictors of compliance with indicators of quality such as positive interactions among staff and children and developmentally appropriate curriculum. Variations in group sizes and ratios are acceptable in cases where the program demonstrates a very high level of compliance with criteria for interactions (A), curriculum (B), staff qualifications (D), health and safety (H), and physical environment (G).

Source: Accreditation Criteria and Procedures of the National Academy of Early Childhood Programs, 1991, Washington, DC: NAEYC. Copyright 1991 by NAEYC. Reprinted with permission from the National Association for the Education of Young Children.

Other forms of employer-sponsored support.   Although employer-sponsored child care is a hot topic in the corporate world and the early childhood education profession, it continues to be the least frequently provided employee benefit. Besides setting up an on-site center, employers can provide support for families and their child care needs in varied forms:

- Financial supplements or subsidies may be granted to help employees pay the cost of child care.
- Employers may issue vouchers to employees, who use them to purchase child care services.
- Contributions may be made to local child care centers that provide care for large numbers of employees' children. The contributions reduce the rates for families, so they are a kind of subsidy.
- Employers purchase child care services at nearby centers and make such services available to employees free or at reduced rates.
- Services that include information and counseling for families in need of child care may be provided.

All these forms of support ultimately make child care arrangements easier and more accessible for families. Other ways that employers can help is to provide flexible schedules, maternity and paternity leaves, and parent education programs. Many businesses and corporations have learned that their employees will be more satisfied and productive in their work if their children are well cared for.

Other Early Childhood Education Programs and Options for Families

We will return to the Mentor Graphics Center when we study about infants later in this book, so you will get to know Luke and the center very well. In the meantime, we need to move on before we run out of time for our travels. For efficiency reasons, we will simply describe some of the child care and preschool alternatives that you will find in the middle-class suburban neighborhoods in which we are traveling. In a number of the homes nearby, **nannies** live with families to take care of children. Nannies, which represent about 5 percent of the child care options, are usually trained in short-term programs for their work. Some nannies, referred to as *au pairs,* come from Europe and usually stay for a year. This particular child care alternative is especially appropriate for parents who work flexible schedules or extensive hours. Often, nannies help with transportation to school and to activities such as scouts and lessons, and with a few household chores.

The other options you will find in these neighborhoods are preschool programs: a school with a Montessori curriculum and a church-related school. We will describe Montessori ideas in detail in Chapter 4, so our discussion here will focus only on **church-based or church-related preschools.** Some claim that churches are the largest single provider of child care in the United States (Neugebauer, 1991). They generally offer toddler groups, full- and part-time preschool classes, full-day child care programs, and after-school care for elementary-aged children. In many of these programs, religious or spiritual development is subtly integrated into a traditional ECE curriculum. Staffing structures vary in church-related schools and the criteria for hiring is often influenced by program goals. A tremendous variation exists in this category of programs, but there is a common quality of providing a warm and loving environment for children.

A Community-Based Program for Homeless Children and Families

We return now to the downtown area because we want to show you one more program for children and families. This fairly new kind of program reflects some of the societal issues we posed at the beginning of this chapter. In downtown Portland, the YWCA offers a school for homeless children. These children often move from shelter to shelter, changing schools with every move. Having a school right in the shelter encourages a family to stay in one place and provides some stability for children. This school has been supported by extensive volunteer efforts and resources shared by other agencies. University students also assist here to help stretch the minimal budget available for this program. The shelter location supports an integration of services for the whole family—that is, some health services, parent education, assistance with housing, and school for the children. In Portland and in other cities, these schools have been successful in providing full and equal educational opportunities for homeless children.

As we look into the large living room, we see children snuggled on the couch with a young woman who is reading a story and asking questions about the characters. Three children are sitting on the floor around a coffee table with a dad. They have plastic poker chips and are using them to figure out math problems. A mom and her son are working with another adult on a project to weigh and measure the children in the group. Billy is recording the weight and height of each child. In a little side room, children are sorting clothes into piles for summer and winter. There is conversation about the color of the garments, the buttons, whether certain items will keep someone warm or not, and the children's likes and dislikes.

In 1996, it was estimated that 300,000 children were homeless (Children's Defense Fund, 1996). That is probably a conservative estimate, but nonetheless, the problem exists with enough significance that it must be addressed by educators at all levels. We will discuss more about the issues of homelessness when we describe families and communities in Chapter 6. For now, it is important for you to reflect on this and other societal problems that seriously affect the quality of life for children and families.

JOURNAL 1.6: Make a list of societal problems and issues that you think influence children and families. When you review your list, how do the issues make you feel about your future professional role with children and families?

Summary of Professional Roles and Programs

Professional roles.   As we visited Portland's early childhood education programs, you encountered a variety of professional roles. We advocate calling all who work with young children and their families *early childhood professionals.* The term reflects a concerted effort to recognize the status of those who work with young children. Although there are still some who regard these individuals as mere babysitters, there is an increasing recognition that these individuals deserve the respect, the rewards, and the responsibilities that accompany professional status. As you prepare for the profession and as you begin your career, you will encounter both kinds of thinking. It is important for you to be able to represent the profession by being able to describe why it is a profession. Keep that in mind as you read the stories to come and as you respond to the journal questions.

From the broad term *early childhood professional,* we move to the varied roles associated with the kind of programs in which individuals work and with the kind of preparation individuals have. You may see yourself becoming an early childhood teacher, a preschool or nursery school teacher, or a kindergarten or a primary grade teacher. If you intend to pursue one of those roles, you will need specialized preparation for your work and possibly a certification of your competencies. You will have responsibility for planning and implementing a developmentally appropriate program for children. Perhaps you will begin by working with a teacher as an assistant or associate teacher. Again, you will need some specialized training, but you will be in a supportive role of helping teachers. Maybe you will begin as a teacher's aide in classrooms, helping teachers and assistant teachers. You will not be required to have as much preparation, but you will be able to use your position to learn more about early childhood education. Another category of early childhood professionals are caregivers and their aides. These individuals have a variety of preparation, depending on the kind of program in which they work and the criteria for hiring. They have responsibility for basic care, protection, education, and guidance of young children; support for their families; and, in most cases, planning and implementing a developmentally appropriate program for children. In administrative roles in early childhood education, we find directors of child care and preschool programs, as well as principals of schools in which there are kindergartens and primary grades.

On a national level, there is a continuum of early professional development that starts with where you are at this time—"starting on a professional path." The continuum is a system of levels that reflect a program of study and the kind of competence to be achieved. The continuum of professional development in Figure 1.2 on page 22 is a beginning attempt to reach agreement on what kind of competencies you will need for which professional role. At this time, many of the areas of specialization within the early childhood profession (family child care, child care directors) are working to make those decisions. You will be part of that process as you proceed on your professional path. What most professionals do agree on is the idea that professional development is an ongoing process. No matter how qualified you are, there will always be new knowledge and new skills you will need as you work with children and families.

Although the work of early childhood professionals varies significantly, many feel that there are some common roles shared by all (Kostelnik, Soderman, & Whiren, 1993). "They all provide instruction to children, nurture and comfort children, offer medical assistance, keep records, work with parents, and cooperate with support staff" (p. 27) in the settings in which they work. Most of us would also agree that all early childhood professionals contribute to the general growth and development of children, and especially to their socialization and moral development.

Journal 1.7: Think of all the professional roles you observed. What kind of early childhood educators do you know in your community? At this time, what role(s) appeals to you? ■

Range of programs. As you observed in our travels through the city, our profession, that of early childhood education, encompasses an enormous range of program options. That range of programs has often been simplified into five program types:

1. Family child care for children from 6 weeks to kindergarten entry age
2. Group care for infants, toddlers, preschoolers, and school-age children
3. Preschool or nursery school programs for children from 3 to 5 years old
4. Kindergartens for 5 and 6 year old children
5. Elementary school grades 1 through 3 (Day & Goffin, 1994, p. 5)

Within these program types, there is much diversity, especially in child care and preschool/nursery school programs. That diversity has implications for you as you prepare to work with young children. You have many choices in your chosen career. Will you select a public or private faculty? What size program interests you? Private

■ **FIGURE 1.2** Definitions of Early Childhood: Professional Categories

Early Childhood Professional Level VI

Successful completion of a Ph.D. or Ed.D. in a program conforming to NAEYC guidelines; OR

Successful demonstration of the knowledge, performance, and dispositions expected as outcomes of a doctoral degree program conforming to NAEYC guidelines.

Early Childhood Professional Level V

Successful completion of a master's degree in a program that conforms to NAEYC guidelines; OR

Successful demonstration of the knowledge, performance, and dispositions expected as outcomes of a master's degree program conforming to NAEYC guidelines.

Early Childhood Professional Level IV

Successful completion of a baccalaureate degree from a program conforming to NAEYC guidelines; OR

State certificate meting NAEYC certification guidelines; OR

Successful completion of a baccalaureate degree in another field with more than 30 professional units in early childhood development/education including 300 hours of supervised teaching experience, including 150 hours each for two of the following three age groups: infants and toddlers, 3- to 5-year-olds, or the primary grades; OR

Successful demonstration of the knowledge, performance, and dispositions expected as outcomes of a baccalaureate degree program conforming to NAEYC guidelines.

Early Childhood Professional Level III

Successful completion of an associate degree from a program conforming to NAEYC guidelines; OR

Successful completion of an associate degree in a related field, plus 30 units of professional studies in early childhood development/education including 300 hours of supervised teaching experience in an early childhood program; OR

Successful demonstration of the knowledge, performance, and dispositions expected as outcomes of an associate degree program conforming to NAEYC guidelines.

Early Childhood Professional Level II

II. B. Successful completion of a one-year early childhood certificate program.

II. A. Successful completion of the CDA Professional Preparation Program OR completion of a systematic, comprehensive training program that prepares an individual to successfully acquire the CDA Credential through direct assessment.

Early Childhood Professional Level I

Individuals who are employed in an early childhood professional role working under supervision or with support (e.g., linkages with provider association or network or enrollment in supervised practicum) and participating in training designed to lead to the assessment of individual competencies or acquisition of a degree.

Source: The Early Childhood Career Lattice: Perspectives on Professional Development by J. Johnson and J. B. McCracken (Eds.), 1994, Washington, DC: NAEYC. Reprinted with permission from the National Association for the Education of Young Children.

home? Small group center? Large school? What about the length of your workday? Your choices range from full day to half day, every day to some days, and combinations thereof. For a more expansive overview, Table 1.2 gives you a look at every possible early childhood program with a description of the purpose and the age of the target population.

■ TABLE 1.2   Types of Early Childhood Programs

Program	Purpose	Age
Early childhood program	Multipurpose	Birth to grade 3
Child care	Play/socialization; baby-sitting; physical care; provides parents opportunities to work; cognitive development; full-quality care	Birth to 6 years
High school child care programs	Provide child care for children of high school students, especially unwed parents; serve as an incentive for student/parents to finish high school and as a training program in child care and parenting skills	6 weeks to 5 years
Drop-off child care centers	Provide care for short periods of time while parents shop, exercise, or have appointments	Infancy through the primary grades
After-school care	Provides care for children after school hours	Children of school age; generally K to 6
Family day care	Provides care for a group of children in a home setting; generally custodial in nature	Variable
Employer child care	Different settings for meeting child care	Variable; usually as early as 6 weeks to the beginning of school
Corporate child care	Same as employer child care	Same as employer child care
Proprietary care	Provides care and/or education to children; designed to make a profit	6 weeks to entrance into first grade
Nursery school (public or private)	Play/socialization; cognitive development	2 to 4 years
Preschool (public or private)	Play/socialization; cognitive development	2½ to 5 years
Parent cooperative preschool	Play/socialization; preparation for kindergarten and first grade; baby-sitting; cognitive development	2 to 5 years
Baby-sitting cooperatives (co-op)	Provide parents with reliable baby-sitting; parents sit for others' children in return for reciprocal services	All ages
Prekindergarten	Play/socialization; cognitive development; preparation for kindergarten	3½ to 5 years
Junior kindergarten	Prekindergarten program	Primarily 4-year-olds
Senior kindergarten	Basically the same as regular kindergarten	Same as kindergarten
Kindergarten	Preparation for first grade; developmentally appropriate activities for 4½ to 6-year-olds; increasingly viewed as the grade before first grade and as a regular part of the public school program.	4 to 6 years
Pre-first grade	Preparation for first grade; often for students who "failed" or did not do well in kindergarten	5 to 6 years

(continued)

■ **TABLE 1.2** *(continued)*

Program	Purpose	Age
Interim first grade	Provides children with an additional year of kindergarten and readiness activities prior to and as preparation for first grade	5 to 6 years
Transitional or transition classes	Classes specifically designed to provide for children of the same developmental age	Variable
Developmental kindergarten	Same as regular kindergarten; often enrolls children who have completed one or more years in an early childhood special education program	5 to 6 years
Transitional kindergarten	Extended learning of kindergarten preparation for first grade	Variable
Preprimary	Preparation for first grade	5 to 6 years
Primary	Teaches skills associated with grades 1, 2, and 3	6 to 8 years
Toy lending libraries	Provide parents and children with games, toys, and other materials that can be used for learning purposes; housed in libraries, vans, or early childhood centers	Birth through primary years
Lekotek	Resource center for families who have children with special needs; sometimes referred to as a *toy* or *play library* (*lekotek* is a Scandinavian word that means play library)	Birth through primary years
Infant stimulation programs (also called parent/infant stimulation and mommy and me programs)	Programs for enhancing sensory and cognitive development of infants and young toddlers through exercise and play; activities include general sensory stimulation for children and educational information and advice for parents	3 months to 2 years
Multiage grades or groups	Groups or classes of children of various ages; generally spanning 2 to 3 years per group	Variable
Dual-age classroom	An organizational plan in which children from two grade levels are grouped together; another term for multiage grouping and for maintaining reasonable student-teacher ratios	Variable
Learning families	Another name for multiage grouping. However, the emphasis is on practices that create a family atmosphere and encourage living and learning as a family. The term was commonly used in open education programs. Its revival signifies the reemergence of progressive and child-centered approaches	Variable
Junior first grade	Preparation for first grade	5 to 6 years
Split class	Teaches basic academic and social skills of grades involved	Variable, but usually primary
Head Start	Play/socialization; academic learning; comprehensive social and health services; prepares children for kindergarten and first grade	2 to 6 years

■ TABLE 1.2   *(continued)*

Program	Purpose	Age
Follow Through	Extended Head Start services to grades 1, 2, and 3	6 to 8 years
Private schools	Provide care and/or education	Usually preschool through high school
Department of Children, Youth, and Families	A multipurpose agency of many state and county governments; usually provides such services as administration of state and federal monies, child care licensing, and protective services	All
Health and Human Services	Same as Dept. of Children, Youth and Families	All
Health and Social Services	Same as Dept. of Children, Youth and Families	All
Home Start	Provides Head Start service in the home setting	Birth to 6 or 7 years
Laboratory school	Provides demonstration programs for preservice teachers; conducts research	Variable; birth through senior high
Child and Family Resource Program	Delivers Head Start services to families	Birth to 8 years
Montessori school (preschool and grade school)	Provides programs that use the philosophy, procedures, and materials developed by Maria Montessori	1 to 8 years
Open education	Child-centered learning in an environment characterized by freedom and learning through activities based on children's interests	2 to 8 years
British primary school	Implements the practices and procedures of open education	2 to 8 years
Magnet school	Specializes in subjects and curriculum designed to attract students; usually has a theme (e.g., performing arts); designed to give parents choices and to integrate schools	5 to 18 years

Source: Early Childhood Education Today, Sixth Edition by G. Morrison, © 1994. Reprinted by permission of Prentice-Hall, Inc., Upper Saddle River, NJ.

The core of your preparation will be consistent, no matter what kind of program you choose to pursue for employment. Some additional skills or knowledge may be required, depending on your choice. That is our next and possibly our most important question. What do early childhood professionals need to know and be able to do? It is important to answer that question in this first chapter to give you some direction and to frame the remaining chapters. It is also important that we make certain to guide and support your development toward that knowledge and those skills. You must direct your efforts so that you are ready to fulfill the early childhood educator role.

What Do Early Childhood Educators Need to Know and Be Able to Do?

To answer the question of what you need to know and be able to do, we looked at two categories of information: competencies and characteristics. The competencies are simpler to address. They are straightforward lists of what you must know and be able to do. The characteristics are more complex because they begin to describe who you must be. They are not direct—we will have to interpret them together. That is where your individuality will come in. We can only guide—it is you who will be making the decisions.

Qualities and Characteristics of an Early Childhood Educator

A wealth of qualities and characteristics exist among early childhood educators. The diversity reflects the wide range of opinions represented within the profession. We begin with a set of recommendations about what makes a good preschool teacher, because we think that the statements apply to all early childhood professionals. Those qualities include:

Good teachers are able to view themselves as learners.

Good teachers are willing and able to grow.

Good teachers are keen observers.

Good teachers know the community in which they teach.

Good teachers have something they care to teach.

Good teachers have lots of energy.

Good teachers are able to take risks.

Good teachers possess a willingness to "mess around" and explore.

Good teachers are flexible.

Good teachers are filled with a sense of wonder. (Kramer, 1994, pp. 31–33)

Kramer concludes with, "In order to be a good teacher, one must love teaching." We do not expect you to know whether you love teaching at this time; in fact, we are not sure that good teachers love teaching all the time. However, as you learn about the profession and begin practicing the professional roles, pay attention to your feelings. You will need to feel passionate about your future role; otherwise, you might want to reconsider and pursue other career options. Spend some time thinking about your po-

Can you see yourself as one of these early childhood professionals? They're happy, dedicated, patient, confident, and full of insight.

tential for taking risks, or being flexible, or having enough energy. Our book cannot have any impact on these characteristics, but we do plan to address the first two qualities on Kramer's list. We care about how you see yourself as a learner and we will put our energy into nurturing you in your learner role. We hope to motivate your willingness to learn and grow by the kind of conversations we have in this book.

Another quality must be added to the preceding list of qualities and characteristics. Olson (1994) thinks that an effective early childhood professional must be an active decision maker. She suggests that the knowledge you gain about children and curriculum leads to the decisions you make about children's learning and your teaching. She believes that those decisions are essential if you are going to respect the differences among children and their families and if you are going to become a true professional.

Other qualities of good teachers include dedication, responsibility, compassion, insight, patience, and self-confidence. "Teachers should also be happy people who can laugh and use their sense of humor wisely" (Gordon & Browne, 1993). Emphasis is on the human qualities of teachers—their potential to connect education with life, to connect with children and families, and to connect with other professionals. This may sound overwhelming! You are likely immersed in assessing your own qualities at this point.

Journal 1.8: We hope that you have already begun to consider who you are in relation to the professional role of early childhood educator. We urge you to consider yourself, your personality, your previous experiences, and your strengths and limitations, especially in your interactions with others. Stop now and write about those qualities. Don't worry about format or sentences—just write everything that comes to mind about who you are. Describe how you feel about yourself. Later, take some time to assess your thoughts with friends. Ask someone you trust to describe your personal qualities.   ■

A Common Core of Knowledge and Skills

Back to answering the questions! To begin with competencies, we turn to the common core of knowledge and skills needed by all early childhood professionals (Bredekamp, 1995) identified by the National Association for the Education of Young Children. To be prepared as an early childhood professional, you must have the knowledge and abilities to:

1. Demonstrate and apply a basic understanding of child development, including observation and assessment of individual children.

2. Establish and maintain an environment that ensures children's safety and their healthy development.

3. Plan and implement developmentally appropriate curricula.

4. Establish supportive relationships with children and implement appropriate guidance and group management.

5. Establish positive and productive relationships with families.

6. Support the uniqueness of each child, recognizing that children are best understood in the context of their family, culture, and society.

7. Demonstrate basic understanding of the early childhood profession and make a commitment to professionalism. (Bredekamp, 1995, p. 68)

This basic set of competencies is echoed in most sets of early childhood teacher education standards. When you read them, you can see that they are competencies that you can strive for by reading, studying, observing, and practicing. We will give you opportunities to do all of those activities as you work through this book. The competencies are broad enough for you to construct their meaning yourself. They are definitely one set of goals for this book. Reflect on your capacity to fulfill this very complex and demanding role of an early childhood professional. If you are still interested and willing to learn and adapt, then continue reading. We will suggest some other personal experiences for your reflection.

Those competencies represent years of study and preparation, even though they may not appear that complex. Do you remember back in the beginning of this chapter when we were visiting the downtown child care center called Little Peoples? We described the frequent lack of qualifications for caregiver positions; that lack often accompanies other early childhood roles, as well. For a long time, we had no evidence that training and preparation—taking a course such as this one—could make any difference in the care and education of children. Fortunately, at this time, we have many studies and solid evidence that your preparation *will* make a difference. Take

■ **FIGURE 1.3** Relationships between Caregiver/Teacher Characteristics, Program Quality, and Child Outcomes

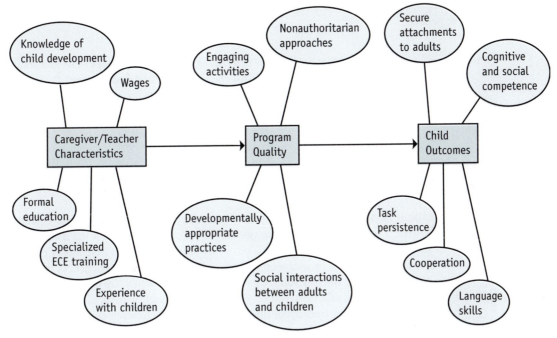

a look at the evidence in Figure 1.3 to understand what difference it will make if you take classes, go to workshops, read professional material, and participate in professional organizations.

Professional Reflection

Our final answer to the question of what early childhood educators need to know and be able to do concerns professional reflection. It is important that professionals be reflective about their work with children and about their professional development. This is the time to start professional reflection, so that by the time you embark on your career, it is a habit.

Some of the staff development that has been done in Head Start programs has shown that teachers can make changes in their professional practices and their personal lives when they get in touch with their own childhood experiences and relate those experiences to their present lives (Jones, 1984, 1986). In Head Start programs, teachers often reflect on their own childhood experiences with respect to the goals and activities that they promote for children. We ask you to do some of that same reflection—to think about how you were treated, taught, and talked to with respect to health and safety issues. Those issues are a priority for Head Start and early childhood education in general.

Journal 1.9: What do you remember about your own creative pursuits as a child? How did others respond to you? What about your physical development? Do you remember learning to ride a bike? Skip? Jump? Cut with scissors? Do you remember how you learned these things? ■

Before you go on to the next chapter, we have a final activity for you. It is an opportunity to reflect on your future as an early childhood professional. We will ask you to do some things that are a bit unusual—but stay with us and follow the directions.

Journal 1.10: First, draw a picture of yourself as a teacher teaching young children. Even if you are a great artist, use stick figures. Use a large sheet of paper instead of your journal and use crayons. Try to get a box of 64 colors so that you have lots of choices. The next task can be done in your journal. Make a list of people and experiences that have been most influential in the way you see yourself as a teacher. When you have done that, we have a final task. Think of a metaphor (a comparison of yourself with an object, a place, or a person) for yourself as a teacher, for the classroom you hope to teach in, and for the children you hope to teach. To help get you started, here is a metaphor one of us came up with: "I see myself as a gardener, the classroom as a garden, and the children as plants of all kinds." Do you get the idea? ■

The tasks you just performed come from Suzanne Krogh and Anneli Nikko (1994) at Western Washington University, who work with students just like you, who are beginning their teacher preparation. They and their students have learned a lot about the kind of images of teaching that we all bring into our preparation. You will, too. When you finish these tasks, study your picture and see what it tells you about your vision of teaching. Your beginning philosophy will be evident in the way the environment looks, in your interactions with the children, and the style of teaching you see in your picture. What do the children look like? Are they the same or different? Spend some time with your drawing. Now reflect on your list. Those influences have probably shaped your philosophy and your priorities as you prepare to teach. Be aware of them. Finally, what does your metaphor tell you about yourself? Your emerging philosophy? How you feel about children?

Our reason for the preceding tasks comes from a belief that your past experiences, the influences of others, and your current ideas about teaching are a foundation for the preparation you are beginning. Bullough and Gitlin (1995; Bullough, 1994) have studied teachers and found that their personal biographies, or stories of their lives, reveal insights about their teaching. They say, "Who you are is important because it is through your prior experience that you will make sense of teaching and of children's backgrounds and abilities, formulate curriculum, frame problems for study, and ultimately negotiate a teacher role" (1995, p. 14). The events of your life will probably influence the decisions you make in your future work with children. This is an important time to bring those ideas and influences to the surface and reflect on them. When you finish this chapter, spend some time reflecting on your life thus far, or, better yet, write about your life history. See if you can pull out some themes that may have an effect on your future professional role. We encourage you to share those themes with your peers and with your instructor, because they are integral to how your preparation is planned. Remember that your stories are also important contributions to building that professional community that we are striving for in this journey together.

PRINCIPLES AND INSIGHTS: A Summary and Review

We wrote this chapter to show you the diversity of professional roles ahead of you and the range of professional settings in which you could choose to work with young children. It would be repetitive to summarize each type of program or to review the level of professional roles. Instead, we will emphasize the insights we want you to take into the next chapter and into your professional thinking. First, *you have choices* in early childhood education. That is part of the richness of the profession, as well as part of the complexity. Think of this feature as one of the main attractions to the profession and stay open to its diversity. Second, *preparation and education* are critical to the early childhood education profession and to your own professional development. You saw the differences that preparation and training can make. Be committed in your own thinking to lifelong learning and advocate for others to do the same. You can make a difference in the lives of children and in the profession. Finally, *know yourself.* As you observe children and adults, notice your reactions, your thinking, and your feelings. Maintain that reflective stance that you began in this chapter as you responded to the journal entries. Reflect on your life story, tell your stories to others, and begin building community.

In sum, you have many options ahead of you: varied professional roles, varied settings in which to work, varied models and mentors from which to learn, and varied ways to prepare for the profession. We look forward to this path we are taking together and we wish you well. Welcome to the community of early childhood professionals!

Becoming an Early Childhood Professional

At the end of each chapter we will suggest opportunities for your professional development that are related to the content of the chapter. The reflection in which you engage in each chapter needs to be extended beyond our stories. We encourage you to get out and observe in your community and to pursue situations in which you can practice. You can design your own informal practicum experiences to extend the ones you will complete as part of your formal program of studies. Seek advice from your instructor about appropriate experiences to determine your readiness.

As you reflect, observe, and practice, we recommend documenting your experiences in a professional portfolio. That portfolio will be useful for self-reflection and assessment as well as for representing yourself when you begin your career. It is a very good professional practice to begin now. Our final recommendation is to develop a professional library. No matter how well you learn to be an early childhood educator, you will continue to encounter situations or problems for which you need new ideas or solutions. You will want to have books and other resources to browse for information or to be refreshed. Remember Robin? We hope that you will follow her example and read and study constantly to keep improving your practice. One of the most important qualities of an early childhood professional is that of being a lifelong learner. Developing your own professional library is a good step in that direction.

Your Field Experiences

1. Begin this first experience by browsing the Yellow Pages of your phone book. Notice what kind of preschools and child care centers are available in your community. Simply by driving by some of them, you will be able to gather information: Check the outdoor play space. What kind of entrance do the children first see? What is in the surrounding environment?

2. Look in the phone book for family day homes or family child care. Call one of them and ask if you may observe for a few hours, or an entire day if you can schedule it. Observe the activities, the children's routines, the environment, and the health and safety features. Reflect occasionally about how the day must feel to the children as well as to the adult(s).

3. Ask your instructor about the local professional associations for early childhood teachers and attend a meeting or workshop. You will find that your time is well spent and that affiliations will be rich learning experiences. This is definitely part of your professional development and lifelong learning. Be sure to document your attendance and participation at meetings and workshops in your professional portfolio.

Your Professional Portfolio

1. An assessment of your personal qualities and capacity to fulfill the role of an early childhood educator would be an excellent first entry for your professional portfolio.

2. We encourage you to set some goals for your professional development. At regular intervals, return to those goals to assess your progress or to set new direction.

Your Professional Library

Some suggestions for books and other resources for this beginning stage of your professional development include the following books, articles, and Internet and World Wide Web addresses:

Books and Articles

Driscoll, A. (1995). *Cases in early childhood education: Stories of programs and practices.* Boston: Allyn & Bacon.

Johnson, J., & McCracken, J. (Eds.). (1994). *The early childhood career lattice: Perspectives on professional development.* Washington, DC: National Association for the Education of Young Children.

National Association for the Education of Young Children (NAEYC). (1990). *What are the benefits of high quality early childhood programs?* Washington, DC: NAEYC.

Internet Addresses and World Wide Web Sites

goodstuff.prodigy.com/ig/earlych.htm
  *Early Childhood Education Interest Groups
  (S. Needleman, Prodigy Services, 1996)*

members.aol.com/aactchrday/links/links.htm
  *The Perpetual Preschool: Early Childhood Education
  Links (Commonwealth Network)*

www.cas.psu.edu.docs/pde/teachers.html
  *Places for Teachers: Directories/Indexes to
  Resources/Grants/Lesson Plans/Teachers Helping
  Teachers/etc. (1997)*

The Wonder of Children

DEVELOPMENT AND

DISPOSITIONS

When you finish reading and reflecting on this chapter, you will be able to:

1. Describe major aspects of the development of an infant, a toddler, a preschooler, a child in kindergarten, and a child in the primary grades.

2. Draw implications from the development of each of the above children and plan a play activity or select a play material (toy) for each.

3. Define *disposition* and give a rationale for studying children's dispositions.

4. Recommend developmentally appropriate practices for each age group of young children based on those children's physical, cognitive, emotional, and social development.

5. Make an initial choice of an age group with which you would like to work and give a developmental rationale for your decision.

This chapter is about development and dispositions—two critical concepts for our study of children and the planning we do for their care and education. When we focus on the development of children, we learn what they are able to understand, do, feel, and be. With that understanding, we can set appropriate goals of knowledge, skills, and feelings and involve children in suitable activities. In addition to the learning goals that are typical for most early childhood education programs, we encourage you to include children's dispositions when planning for their education. You have probably heard the word *disposition* used in a context of describing someone you know. "She's got a sunny disposition" or "What a miserable disposition!" is commonly used. Based on those expressions, take a minute to think about what *disposition* might mean. In our conversations about children in this chapter, we will focus on both development and dispositions.

Introduction to Development and Dispositions

To begin to understand the concepts of *development* and *dispositions,* we are going to spend time observing a group of children. Unlike the groups we have observed thus far, this group is a mixed-age group—that is, the children are not all the same chronological age. It is a class at the laboratory preschool we visited in chapter 1, where we will see children from 3 to 6 years old. For a variety of reasons that include personality, social skills, play patterns, development, disposition, and age, these children work and play individually and together each day.

As you watch these children, keep in mind that you will see differences in their development and dispositions. Even if you have only a vague idea of what those concepts mean, we expect that you will begin to understand them by observing the differences in children. Remember: Children have a lot to teach us, if only we will pay attention.

Studying Children to Learn about Development and Dispositions

It is 8:12 A.M. and a sleepy-looking Adam, age 4, arrives at preschool, with his dad encouraging him to "have a good day" at the door. Adam hesitates at the door and waits for his teacher, Elena, to welcome him. Even with her cheerful, "Adam, we're so glad to see you," he remains at the door until she goes to him and takes his hand. Keeley, who is 5 years old, spots Adam and immediately begins organizing his play: "Adam, you're going to be the kid and I'm the bus driver. Pretend that you're waiting here for me to pick you up." Just moments before, Keeley brought 4-year-old Amanda into the bus play and resisted Amanda's attempt to be the bus driver. Not only has Keeley lined up six chairs in a row to create her bus but she also has a steering wheel and a hat for her accessories.

As the children are riding along, we hear Keeley ask, "Where do you want to get off?" Adam says, "Home," rather softly, but Amanda says, "Broadway Drive, please." Adam looks a bit unhappy and says that he does not want to play. He continues to sit in his bus seat, however, as Keeley engages other children in the bus play. After another two minutes, Amanda steps out of the bus and says emphatically, "I don't want to play any more." When the bus play ends, Keeley arranges the chairs in front of the puppet theater, then looks about the room. She approaches 5-year-old Olivia and 4-year-old Andrew, who are completing puzzles. "Those are easy puzzles," says Keeley. Andrew returns the boast: "I can do puzzles with a hundred pieces." "So can I," echo Keeley and Olivia.

"Would you like to help me make a puppet show?" asks Keeley. "You can be the prince and princess and live in a castle with a gatekeeper," she continues. "Who will be our audience?" asks Olivia. "I'll get Miss Elena to watch us," Keeley responds as she looks for her teacher. Later, we learn that Keeley's puppet character is Merlin the royal magician. The other two children don't seem to know about Merlin, so she explains his role in the royal palace.

During this time, Adam has been sitting near the block area, playing with a few small blocks but mostly watching Leandra, age 4, and Ronald, age 3½, build a large structure. When their building looks like it is spreading in his direction, Adam scoots back away from it. When Miss Elena sits down on the floor next to him and asks him what he would like to do, he mumbles that he doesn't know. Together, they watch Leandra and Ronald drive little cars all over the block area and into their recently constructed parking garage. "Now we're parking and going to work" and "It's time to go home from work" are the dominant themes for about 10 minutes. Soon the two children begin playing independently of each other, building other structures and driving their cars.

Journal 2.1: After watching these preschool children for just a few minutes, you can begin to predict and make assumptions about development and dispositions. Consider Keeley. How would you describe her disposition? What about Adam? Does Keeley's development seem to be what you would expect for a 5-year-old? Write your thoughts in your journal. ■

If you could watch Keeley and Adam for several days—which would be appropriate before coming to any conclusions about them—you would see that Keeley consistently is a "take charge" kind of child. She is an organizer, she is self-assured, and she is very social. These are some *dispositions* we would attribute to Keeley. However, if you watched Adam for several days, you would see a child quite different from the one you saw in the brief episode. On the morning we watched, Adam was just recovering from being ill and had returned to his class with some uncertainty. Generally, he is independent and energetic. You would likely describe Adam's dispositions as curious and sensitive if you could watch him on a day when he feels well. Now you are probably coming up with some understanding of the term *disposition*.

Defining disposition. A *disposition* is a tendency to exhibit frequently, consciously, and voluntarily a pattern of behavior that is directed to a broad goal (Katz, 1993). Another way of referring to a person's disposition is her *temperament*. In addition to promoting children's development in our work, dispositions are important goals for our efforts. Adam's parents have nurtured his disposition to be curious by providing a stimulating home environment and interesting experiences. From the time he was an infant, they gave him a lot of freedom to explore and ask questions. If you were to observe Keeley in her home, you would see that her disposition to take command and be self-assured has also been nurtured by her mother, who supports Keeley's control over her environment, her decision making, and her activities. Keeley helps plan the week's menus and determines how the furniture is arranged in her room. These individual dispositions of Adam's and Keeley's are further nurtured in their preschool program.

Defining development. What did you notice about Keeley's development? Consider her language. Think about what she was able to do—that is, her physical and social skills. How does she handle situations emotionally? Over a period of time, you would see Keeley's consistent creation of dramatic play situations, her flexibility with changing conditions in the class, her ease in initiating conversations and activity with adults and children, her understanding of concepts and information, her frequent attempts to read, and her application of skills in puzzle making, painting, writing, climbing, and skipping. When you watched Keeley, did you notice her physical development, her cognitive development, her social development, and her emotional development?

Observing children's development guides our decisions about how to create their environments, select their instructional and play materials, plan their activities, and provide guidance when needed. What is **development**? A simple definition is the series of changes that occur in humans from birth to death. The most exciting aspect of being an early childhood professional is that you have the opportunity to observe and support those changes in young children.

Basic Principles of Development

With a reminder to attend to children's individuality, we move now to the basic principles of development. Many of the principles refer to *development* as *learning,* so we will use those words interchangeably. Each of the principles will be discussed before we describe the developmental characteristics of children at specific ages. The descriptions have been developed from years of observations by early childhood educators who have extensive experiences and expertise. As we continue observing children throughout this book, developmental characteristics will provide a beginning framework for what you will someday plan and provide for children. As you meet Luke, Felipe, and Jodie in later chapters, you will add detail to the framework and better understand their development.

Even with the constantly changing body of knowledge about child development, there is wide agreement about a few principles that help explain how children develop and learn. Later, in Chapter 3, we will talk about more sophisticated ideas and theories from important thinkers in our profession, but for now, let's look at six basic principles of development:

1. *Development and learning are characterized by individual variation.* This principle is the foundation of any theory of development. Children have different genetic makeups, they come from different home environments, they have different experiences, and they will grow and learn at different rates and in different ways. In Chapter 4, you will meet three brothers, Chimieti, Otioli, and Wamalwa. Even though they have been raised by the same parents in the same home, they are vastly dissimilar. Their dispositions are different and their development has been different. "Each of them has been so individual—it certainly makes parenting interesting," said Francis, their father.

2. *Development occurs in a fairly predictable sequence.* Some say that development moves from awareness to exploration to inquiry to utilization (NAEYC, 1991). Others describe the progression as moving from simple to complex, whether it be physical development or cognitive development. The progression has also been described as moving from general to specific. The word *predictable* does not mean that children do not move through the sequence in individual ways. For example, Chimieti and Otioli both liked to climb at a young age, but Wamalwa is far more adventurous and creative in his climbing pursuits than either of his brothers ever were.

3. *Children learn and develop well when their needs are met.* Those needs include physical and emotional needs as well as social needs. Maslow's hierarchy of needs reminds us that basic needs of food and shelter, as well as emotional safety and a sense of belonging, must be met before humans can begin to attain other needs. You will read about other ideas from Maslow in the next chapter. Ideally, children's needs would be met consistently at home and in schools or other programs, but we live in a society that does not assure that those basic needs are being met for all children. Consequently, those of us in the early childhood profession must often take care of hunger, fears, and loneliness in children before we can begin to teach or facilitate development. Remember when Adam came to his preschool after being ill? His insecurity kept him from joining in the play. He needed a lot of reassurance before he could truly participate.

4. *Children learn from interacting with the environment and with other children and adults.* The physical interactions children have as they touch, explore, manipulate, and experiment with the physical world around them promotes their physical and cognitive development. The social interactions children have as they watch, play, and work with others, and as they gradually cooperate with others promotes their cognitive, social, and emotional development. All the toys and materials you see in a preschool or child care cen-

Observing children even briefly can reveal much about their development. What might you learn from watching this girl?

ter contribute to each child's development. The adults and the child's peers are major contributors to development.

5. *Children learn from play.* Children's play, sometimes called "work" by them, promotes development in all aspects of growth. Play is the best context for children's learning and development in that it is open ended and free, children have control over it, it can be done alone or with others, it can even occur without any materials or equipment, and it can take place in many settings. Play comes naturally to children, so it makes sense that they learn from it.

6. *Children construct their own knowledge.* This idea is a fairly recent one. In the past, educators talked about children making discoveries as they played and interacted with others, but only recently have educators described what happens as children construct their own knowledge. It is what we are asking you to do in this book—that is, construct your own knowledge. In the beginning of this chapter, we did not define *disposition* for you. We hinted at its meaning, then we had you observe Keeley and see if you could describe her disposition. In other words, we left it to you to create your own definition, your own understanding. This principle is exemplified in our request to you to reflect on and respond to the journal entries every so often in each chapter. We're encouraging you to construct your own knowledge.

Journal 2.2: Return for a minute to the scene in the mixed-age class and watch Keeley and Adam again. See if you can find evidence of the basic principles in their play and interactions. Did you see them construct their own knowledge? What did they do? If Keeley and Adam did not have their basic needs met, what might you have seen them doing? If you are involved in a practicum while using this book, watch the children in your practicum setting for these principles, or think about your own children or those of a friend or neighbor. ■

The basic principles we've listed are very broad; we will elaborate on them later. For now, we ask you to keep them in mind as we describe characteristics of each of the ages of children included in this book. We will be looking at children from birth to age 8, because those are the typical parameters of early childhood education. That is not to say that there are not some 10- and 11-year-olds out there who can be described with similar developmental descriptions. For our purposes of creating some generalizations about development, we will look at infants (birth to 24 months), toddlers (12 months to 36 months), preschoolers (3 to 5 years), kindergarten learners (5 to 6 years), and primary grade learners (6 to 8 years). You may have noticed an overlap between infants and toddlers, and that was intentional. Because children develop so differently, some children are considered an infant at 18 months and others are considered a toddler at 18 months. The variety of early childhood programs classifies those two groups differently, so we tried to encompass all the possibilities.

Why Study Development?

Educators have been interested in children's development since the early 1900s. At that time, the child study movement focused on the characteristics of young children at each age and the influence of heredity and environment. In Chapter 3, we will look at some of the theories about development that emerged from early study of children, but for now, it is important to know that the information we have today about child development comes from a wide variety of sources. It has been said that the body of knowledge about children's development doubles every three years. Today's knowledge comes from studies in psychology, sociology, linguistics, health, anthropology, history, and education. This may sound overwhelming, but it serves as a reminder of how important it is to be constantly watching children to learn about their development. Many research studies and significant theories about development will guide us as we observe children and make decisions about their learning. Why study development? The answer is decision making. Using what we know and observe about children's development guides our decisions about their environment, their activities, and how we interact with them.

Using developmental guides.   To assist us in understanding what we see when we watch children, there are normal **developmental guides**—indicators of what a typical 4-year-old or toddler looks like. Descriptions of **normative development**—what we know about so-called typical 4-year-old or 18-month-old children—are sort of an average developmental level. Talking about normative development comes with a caution to remember that each child is different. We must observe children with constant attention to the individuality of humans. There really is no such thing as a *typical* toddler or a *typical* 4-year-old. With young children especially, we know that development is happening so fast that their understandings and their skills change from day to day. For example, Keeley's language is expanding rapidly and her coordination is smoothing out right in front of her teacher's eyes. Her development may slow down for a few months and then suddenly accelerate. Children's rates of growth and development vary tremendously, so any developmental guidelines must take individuality into account.

Preview of developmental profiles. To begin, we will provide a developmental snapshot of each of the age groups we listed for early childhood education. The profiles will not be detailed. Perhaps you have been around children of all the ages described by early childhood. If so, you have a beginning understanding of what each age is like. If not, begin to take notice of children in your community—in the grocery store or library, on the bus, or in the center where you work.

In the chapters that follow, you will meet children of each age and observe them intensely at home and in a program or class where they spend their days. Those chapters will develop a more in-depth understanding of normative development of each age, while introducing the individual differences of the children in our stories. You will notice and describe their developmental characteristics, draw conclusions about them, and mentally plan environments and activities for them (constructing your own learning). We will also have in-depth conversations about the development of Ibrahim (Chapter 8), and Keeley (Chapter 10), and Jodie (Chapter 11) to get you ready for your role as an early childhood professional.

Studying Infants

Before describing infant development, it is appropriate to think about what happens before an infant is born. In today's society, with multiple stresses on families, with many teens giving birth, and with children born to adults who do not receive good prenatal care, your understanding of infant development would be incomplete without a look at the situation before birth.

Before Birth

The following factors help us focus on the situation before, during, and after birth that directly influence how a child will develop. They include:

Family economics (resources, needs, and limits)

Family support system

Family health (physical, emotional, and social)

Community and dominant themes within

Educational levels of family members

Cultural background of family

Family size

Family attitudes toward pregnancy, children, education

Journal 2.3: Reflect on how you think each of these factors will affect a newborn. Make notes in your journal about what you know about family health and attitudes, what concerns you may have, and what questions you want to ask about those and other factors. Be sure to consider your own experiences as an infant or as a parent. This is a good time to talk to others—your parents, your friends, your instructor, a teacher that you know, or a doctor. ■

The behaviors and attitudes of parents directly influence the growth and development of a child before birth (Black & Puckett, 1996). Today's infants may be born to a homeless couple, to a drug-addicted family, or to a violent home. Birth may follow a pregnancy characterized and influenced by undernutrition, alcohol abuse, or depression about having an unwanted child. All of these factors will have an effect on how babies develop. In contrast, babies are also born to healthy parents as you will see in many of our chapters. In most cases, babies are wanted and cherished. Their environments are often nurturing, stimulating, and secure. So what are infants like? How can we describe them in terms of development?

Infant Development

In the past, infants were not given credit for being able to do much, but today, people are aware of infants' incredible capacities. From the moment they are born, they must make a number of physiological adjustments that begin with breathing, eating, and eliminating. They adjust from a very secure, warm, and sheltered environment within their mothers to one of varied stimuli, with less security, and different temperatures. For these reasons, the first four weeks, the **neonatal period,** is a critical period in infant development.

By the end of the neonatal period, the infant displays a number of inborn movements called **reflexes.** If you watch a newborn, you may see survival reflexes—such as breathing, rooting, sucking, and eye blinks—or primitive reflexes—such as grasping and the startle reflex (which occurs when a loud noise or sudden movement causes the arms to thrust out from the body).

Physical and motor development.   An infant's physical development is marked by observable changes in weight and length as well as internal changes of the central nervous system, bones, and muscles. As the nervous system matures, the bones and muscles grow and become coordinated. Consequently, the first year of life is one of exciting motor development—that is, physical development focused on movement. Table 2.1 shows the changes, or developmental milestones, of motor development during the infant's first year. These changes in the infant's ability to move and manipulate his environment have many implications for the kind of environment he needs, the appropriate play materials, and the types of activities from which he can learn and enjoy.

Journal 2.4: When you read the list of milestones in Table 2.1, what comes to mind in terms of what an infant will need? What play materials would you provide? What activities would you do with the infant? ■

You may have written *a safe place, soft surfaces,* and *carefully selected objects that can be held and tasted by the infant.* Each characteristic of infant development will give you an indication of what kind of setting and what sorts of activities and interactions are appropriate.

■ **TABLE 2.1 Developmental Milestones in Motor Control during the First Year**

Age	Motor Development
Birth to 3 months	Supports head when in prone position Lifts head Supports weight on elbows Hands relax from the grasping reflex Visually follows a moving person Pushes with feet against lap when held upright Makes reflexive stepping movements when held in a standing position Sits with support Turns from side to back
3 to 6 months	Slaps at bath water Kicks feet when prone Plays with toes Reaches but misses dangling object Shakes and stares at toy placed in hand Head self-supported when held at shoulder Turns from back to side Sits with props Makes effort to sit alone Exhibits crawling behaviors Rocks on all fours Draws knees up and falls forward
6 to 9 months	Rolls from back to stomach Crawls using both hands and feet Sits alone steadily Pulls to standing position in crib Raises self to sitting posture Successfully reaches and grasps toy Transfers object from one hand to the other Stands up by furniture Cruises along crib rail Makes stepping movements around furniture
9 to 12 months	Exhibits "mature" crawling Cruises holding on to furniture Walks with two hands held Sits without falling Stands alone May walk alone Attempts to crawl up stairs Grasps object with thumb and forefinger

Source: The Young Child: Development from Prebirth through Age Eight by J. Black and M. Puckett, © 1996. Reprinted by permission of Prentice-Hall, Inc., Upper Saddle River, NJ.

Social and emotional development.   Normal social and emotional development of infants is characterized by the beginnings of trust and attachment, an array of emotions, crying and other forms of communication, and the start of social cognition. Each of these developments has important implications for the adults who interact with infants. Trust is learned by infants when their care is nurturing and predictable. The youngest infant soon realizes if she can depend on being comforted when upset, or changed when wet, or fed when hungry. This is the beginning of trust. In addition to trusting adults, infants learn to trust themselves. They learn that they have the capacity to get what they need by communicating with others. For example, an infant soon realizes that when she cries, one of the parents will comfort her; thus begins the baby's awareness of her ability to get what she needs.

Attachment is a complex kind of bonding and an emotional relationship between an infant and a significant adult (mother, father, or caregiver). The observable characteristics are mutual affection and the desire or need for proximity of each other. Emotionally healthy infants form attachments gradually during their first year. Bowlby (1962/1982) describes a sequence of four phases that characterize the development of attachment (Figure 2.1).

During phase 3, two related developments occur. Infants develop separation anxiety and stranger anxiety. For your work with young children, it will be important to understand these fears. **Separation anxiety** occurs when the attachment between infant and adult becomes quite intense. It is understandable, then, that the infant becomes very upset when separated from the adult. For a caregiver or other early childhood professional, the onset of separation anxiety means that the infant will need extra reassurance and support, gradual separations from the important adult, and well-established routines and rituals. **Stranger anxiety** is actually a healthy indication that the infant recognizes familiar adults and is insecure around those who are unfamiliar. Again, there are ways to ease the anxiety. Infants need long periods of unhurried time to get used to someone new. The security of a familiar object (blanket, stuffed animal, or toy) and familiar people (sibling, parent, or caregiver) help the infant become comfortable with someone new.

Development in an unhealthy beginning.   We have been describing what happens as healthy infants develop, but what occurs for those who do not have healthy beginnings? One characteristic that is in contrast to attachment is disorganization or conflicted feelings and behaviors expressing stress or anxiety. Not surprisingly, there is a connection between infant disorganization and parental neglect and abuse, maternal depression, low socioeconomic status, and no family support. In addition to the stress and anxiety observed in some infants, a **failure to thrive** characterizes some babies. Infants who are neglected or deprived of parental nurturance and stimulation fail to grow and develop normally. When you look back at those factors that influence how a child will develop, you can understand how those factors could result in deprivation or neglect. For instance, if family economics are drastic, and there is little food or heat in a home, it will be difficult to provide for a baby's needs. Likewise, if the family does not have a support system, new parents may become stressed by an infant's cry and not respond in healthy ways. Caring for an infant often requires 24-hour care and good physical and

■ **FIGURE 2.1**   Bowlby's Sequence for the Development of Attachment

Phase 1 (Birth to 8–12 weeks) Indiscriminate Responsiveness to Humans

During this phase, infants orient to persons in their environment, visually tracking them, grasping and reaching for them, and smiling and babbling. The infant often ceases to cry upon seeing a face or hearing a voice. These behaviors sustain the attentions of others and thus their proximity to the infant, which is the infant's goal.

Phase 2 (3 to 6 months) Focusing on Familiar People

The infant's behaviors toward others remain virtually the same except that they are more marked in relation to the mother or perhaps the father. Social responses begin to become more selective, however, with the social smile reserved for familiar people. Strangers receive a long, intent stare. Cooing, babbling, and gurgling occur with familiar people. A principal attachment figure begins to emerge, usually the mother.

Phase 3 (6 months to 3 years) Active Proximity Seeking

Infants show greater discrimination in their interactions with people. They become deeply concerned for the attachment figure's presence and cry when that person starts to leave. Infants will monitor the attachment figure's movements, calling out to them or using whatever means of locomotion they have to maintain proximity to them. The attachment figure serves as a base from which to explore and is followed when departing and greeted warmly upon return. Certain other people may become subsidiary attachment figures; however, strangers are now treated with caution and will soon evoke alarm and withdrawal.

During phase 3, two very predictable fears emerge. *Separation anxiety* occurs as the relationship between the infant and the attachment figure becomes more intense and exclusive. The infant cries, sometimes quite vociferously, upon the departure of the attachment figure and exhibits intense joy upon their reunion.

Stranger anxiety is another characteristic fear of phase 3. Occurring around 7 to 8 months, the infant's stranger anxiety is characterized by lengthy stares and subsequent crying at the sight of an unfamiliar person. Alarmed, the infant will cling tightly to the attachment figure and resist letting go.

Phase 4 (3 years to the end of childhood) Partnership Behavior

Prior to this phase, the child is unable to consider the attachment figure's intentions. For instance, the suggestion that "I'll be right back" is meaningless to the child, who will insist on going along anyway. By age 3, the child has developed a greater understanding of parental intent and plans and can envision the parent's behavior while separated. The child is now more willing and able to let go and can be more flexible.

Source: The Young Child: Development from Prebirth through Age Eight by J. Black and M. Puckett, © 1996. Reprinted by permission of Prentice-Hall, Inc., Upper Saddle River, NJ.

emotional health on the part of the adults. When the situation is supportive of infant development, babies are capable of rapid growth and development. They are able to accomplish so much in a short time.

Capacities of infants.   At a recent baby shower, the favorite gift was a large mirror. On the other side of mirror was a series of very distinctive black and white patterns. Several young parents who were attending the event raved about the gift and told stories of their children. "When Ben was 3 months, he stared at those patterns all the time, and he loved looking at himself in the mirror," said one mom. Another talked about her daughter Tory (10 months) watching their family Dalmatians constantly. As recent as two decades ago, such gifts did not exist because people were not aware of infants' abilities. As we described earlier in the chapter, we are learning more about human development every day. One area of expanding knowledge is the capacity of infants. By watching them, we are learning that they are able to do so much more than we ever imagined. We encourage you to learn from them, too.

Infancy and Dispositions

Although infants go through rapid changes in some aspects of their development, their dispositions begin to emerge slowly. Individual temperaments might seem evident at birth, but a number of factors (feeding, mood of parents, comfort, order of birth) will probably influence a baby's true disposition. If you were to watch an infant for a period of time, you could probably predict her disposition. Recently, one of us observed a young adult with a very relaxed and accepting disposition. When we commented on her disposition, her mother recalled, "Even as a baby, she was like that."

Babies grow and develop so rapidly that those around them are usually amazed that the babies have become toddlers in such a short time. This fact is a great reminder to stop and watch babies now, for they will make tremendous changes rapidly.

Studying Toddlers

It is difficult to say when infancy stops and toddlerhood begins; in fact, it is different for every child, which is why we gave it a range of 12 to 24 months. For our purposes, let's say that a **toddler** is one who begins walking and talking. Some call **toddlerhood** a transition between infancy and childhood. It is a very exciting time to observe and care for a child, because so many major changes occur and growth is so noticeable. Certainly, you will never get bored around a toddler. When you meet Ibrahim and his toddler friends in Chapter 8, you will be amazed at the energy of their parents and teachers.

Toddler Development

During toddlerhood, children move from almost complete dependence on adults and others to the beginnings of self-reliance. They can move fairly well, do things for themselves, and express what they want. In addition to becoming self-reliant, toddlers begin to learn and comply with the rules and values of society; that is, they become socialized.

Socialization. As children show that they can understand, social rules and values are actively imposed on them by parents and others. Learning theorists suggest that young children comply because they want to maintain closeness with parents and have their needs met. Some educators think that very young children comply with adult expectations and requests because they are born with the desire to please. This is especially reasonable if a child is in a pleasant and supportive environment and has loving caregivers. Elkind (1987) expresses concern about the tendency of adults to mistake the compliance for readiness on the part of the toddler. He refers to some adult attempts as the "miseducation of young children"—those attempts to teach children skills for which they are not ready.

Journal 2.5: Make a list of situations in which adults try to get children to do things for which they are not ready. Now make another list, showing the reasons why adults expect and request such behaviors. ■

As they grow more sociable, toddlers become more competent in their interactions with adults and with other children (Howes, 1988). They can observe and interpret the actions of others, imitate them, and maintain a sequence of interaction with others. Most of the interactions of toddlers are **object centered,** meaning that they focus more on an object (such as a toy) rather than on an activity. One of the most obvious developmental changes in a toddler is his ability to separate from his parent or caregiver and go off to play or explore elsewhere. The toddler will often check to see if mom or dad is still in the room or will call out to her caregiver from across the room, but the distance appears to be comfortable. During toddlerhood, children also develop an ability called **social referencing.** This is the ability to "read" facial expressions and tones of voice as cues for what to do. Many a young child has looked up at a parent's face and expressed dismay at the parent's sad or angry facial expression.

During this stage, most toddlers begin talking; therefore, language development will demand much of our attention as we study this age group. In addition to learning words, toddlers begin to learn the rules, or conventions, for combining sounds into words and words into sentences. This is a fairly sophisticated process by itself, but it must be developed in the complexity of social situations that can change the rules, so it is an amazing accomplishment. Starting with the youngest toddler, we will look at the major tasks of language learning in a progression of typical development.

Language development. The first task in language development is learning sound patterns. In infancy, we hear babies cry and coo and babble, and toward the end of the first year, we hear **patterned speech.** It sounds like babbling but it has a pattern to it, that resembles the intonation and form of the language that the child is hearing from those around him. Once the toddler recognizes and can produce a small number of *phonemes* (groups of sounds, the smallest speech units), he begins to say his first words and to recognize words.

Toddlers quickly develop **expressive language**—that is, the ability to produce language forms. That development follows a sequence. The child begins with a big language learning task—learning words and their meanings. The first words are, of course, the names of familiar people and items. Can you think of a list of predictable first words?

Early vocabulary also includes social commands, such as "Me"; movement, such as "Go bye bye"; and expressions of "No." During this learning period, parents and others who interact with the toddler influence the range of vocabulary and how it is used. Adult language patterns will often determine the toddler's language patterns. For example, if a parent asks a great number of "What?" questions of the toddler, the toddler will develop extensive vocabulary to label things.

The average toddler develops vocabulary slowly until about age 18 months, then the acquisition of new words increases dramatically. Between 1 and 2 years of age, the range of new words learned is between 100 and 1,000 words. That wide range is another reminder of individual differences. During this phase of toddlerhood, we hear young children attempting to make plurals of their words, or changing the tenses. They make a lot of mistakes in the process, often causing adults to chuckle at the attempts.

For most of toddlerhood, children are in a one-word stage, meaning that their speech is limited to using one word at a time. With their use of single words, however, toddlers may be communicating more than a simple label. For example, when a toddler points to her mother and says "Momma," she may simply be acknowledging her mother. But when she holds up her mother's scarf, and says "Momma," she may be saying "Momma's scarf," or when she tugs at her mother's hand and says "Momma," she may be saying "Momma, come." This is an example of a **holophrase,** and toddlers soon have a number of holophrases that communicate their needs and wants as well as enable them to hold a conversation with others. What you will learn about toddlers' speech is that you must not only listen well but you must also notice the situation, observe the toddlers' gestures, and be ready to guess. They want to talk with you, and their language development will be enhanced if you are able to respond appropriately to their early attempts at conversation.

At around 18 to 24 months of age, toddlers begin to put two words together into *two-word sentences.* They are usually very simple ideas and are generally expressed with a noun and a verb, and occasionally an adjective. Such sentences capture the gist of what the toddler wants to say, and adults again must maintain an awareness of the entire situation in order to interpret them appropriately. When you meet Ibrahim in Chapter 8, you will notice how his mother pays close attention to his talk in order to more accurately understand Ibrahim's ideas and needs. As an early childhood professional, you will need to follow her example and be a very good listener.

The stages of language development in Figure 2.2 go beyond two-word sentences, because some toddlers continue to develop their language and use **telegraphic sentences, joined sentences,** and even occasionally **overgeneralizations.** The figure shows the sequence of language development that you will observe when you spend time around toddlers and preschoolers.

Along with the development of language that has such dramatic growth during toddlerhood, there is also the beginning of a capacity for representation. The children begin to use symbols to represent things. Language use is one example of this capacity, but another is seen in pretend play. For example, toddlers will pretend to ride a large rectangular block or to drink out of a cylinder block. Young toddlers will play with actual objects such as dolls, cars and trucks, and animals. Older toddlers (near 2 years) represent other things in their play—blankets and kitchen objects, for instance. When Keeley was 20 months old, she rolled up a cloth and carried it as a baby, and she expected everyone else to treat it like a baby.

■ **FIGURE 2.2**   Stages of Language Development

Sounds

From birth infants make and respond to many sounds. Crying, gurgling, and cooing are important first steps in the language-learning process.

Babbling

All of the sounds found in all languages are encompassed in children's first babbling. Gradually, babbling becomes more specific with native language syllables being consistently practiced. Before the end of their first year, children engage in pseudo-language, babbling that mimics the native language in its intonation and form.

Holophrases

The first word evolves to many single words or syllables that stand for a variety of meaningful sentences or phrases in different situations. *Car* said while looking out the window may mean, "Look at the car outside"; *car* said while standing next to the toy shelf may mean, "I want my toy car." A vocabulary of holophrases enables children to communicate with familiar caregivers. Children use successive holophrases to increase their communicative power: *Car* (pause) *go* to indicate "I want to go for a ride."

Two-Word Sentences

Two-word sentences appear between eighteen and twenty months of age and express ideas concerning relationships: "Mommy sock" (possessor-possession), "Cat sleeping" (actor-action), "Drink milk" (action-object), and so on. A vocabulary of about 300 words is typical.

Telegraphic Sentences

The next stage of language are sentences that are short and simple. Similar to a telegram, they omit function words and endings that contribute little to meaning: "Where Daddy go?" "Me push truck."

Joined Sentences

As language development proceeds, children join related sentences logically and express ideas concerning time and spatial relationships. They come to understand social expectations for language use and begin to use adult forms of language. Vocabularies expand rapidly, the ability to use words increases, and children intuitively acquire many of the rules of language. By age three children have vocabularies of nearly 1,000 words.

Overgeneralizations

As children become more sophisticated in their language, they overgeneralize rules in ways that are inconsistent with common usage; for example, "I comed home" for "I came home" (sometimes called *creative grammar*). Correct forms are temporarily replaced as rules are internalized.

Source: Who Am I in the Lives of Children? 5th Edition by S. Feeney, D. Christensen, and E. Moravcik, © 1996. Reprinted by permission of Prentice-Hall, Inc., Upper Saddle River, NJ.

Physical and motor development.   Physically, toddlers do not grow as rapidly as they did during infancy, but their motor development is impressive. A young toddler walks unsteadily, partly because he still has some baby fat and because his legs make up only about 30 percent of his height. An early childhood classroom for toddlers often has furnishings that can be used for purposes of steadying and gaining balance. As a toddler develops and gains experience, his walking becomes well coordinated. From there, the toddler jumps, runs, and climbs. His large motor skills increase dramatically because his large muscles (in the arms, trunk, and legs) are maturing. He becomes more coordinated and can use wheel toys, and climbing structures, and can throw and kick balls.

During toddlerhood, small muscles also develop and mature. A toddler learns to manipulate objects well and begins building with blocks and other toys. His abilities to reach, grasp, manipulate, and release toys and other items become more precise dur-

Toddlerhood is a time for rapidly developing motor skills and enormous amounts of determination.

ing this developmental period. It takes a great amount of experience or practice, so it is important to provide appropriate materials and activities for children at this age. At this time, the coordination of eyes and hands improves greatly, and the toddler begins to master tasks such as assembling simple puzzles, matching faces, and so on. Figure 2.3 summarizes some of the typical large and small motor skills that you will see when you watch the toddlers in Chapter 8.

Toddlers do not have well-developed **perceptual motor skills**—that is, the combination of what they see and the body movements to match what they perceive. They often bump into furniture or each other, or they try to stuff large toys into bags that are smaller than the toy. When they move to music, most toddlers do not really move to the rhythm or beat; they just move their bodies. At this age, children simply are not ready to process the information that they are taking in with their ears or eyes or touch. There is, however, one aspect of their experience that toddlers begin to organize and acknowledge: awareness of body and gender.

■ **FIGURE 2.3**   Typical Large and Small Motor Skills of Toddlers

---

Young Toddlers (12–24 months)

Exercises physical skills
Likes to lug, dump, push, pull, pile, knock down, empty, fill
Enjoys pushing or pulling while walking
Likes to climb and can manage small indoor stairs
Manipulates in a more exploratory than skillful fashion
Shows interest in multiple small objects
Carries play materials from place to place
(by 2 years) Kicks and catches a large ball
(by 2 years) Strings large beads, turns knobs, uses twist motion

Older Toddlers (2 years+)

Shows skill in most simple large muscle activities
Engages in lots of physical testing: jumping from heights, climbing, hanging by the
     arms, rolling, galloping, doing somersaults, rough-and-tumble play
Throws and retrieves all kinds of objects
Pushes self on wheeled objects with good steering
Demonstrates good hand and finger coordination by 2½ to 3 years
Engages in lots of active play with small objects and explores different qualities of
     play materials

Source: Reprinted by permission, from M. B. Bronson, *The Right Stuff for Children Birth to 8—Selecting Play Materials to Support Development* (Washington, DC: NAEYC, 1995), 47. Copyright by the National Association for the Education of Young Children.

Gender awareness.   It is not surprising that toddlers develop **body awareness** as they acquire and repeat new motor skills. From the time they are in the crib and discover that they can bang their bed against the wall by rocking back and forth, they become aware of their power and their ability to make things happen. As their motor activities increase, toddlers begin to form mental images of themselves. They also begin to touch body parts and later name those parts. This is the time when toilet training may begin, so there is much opportunity for the interest in body parts to heighten.

Toddler body awareness usually extends to curiosity about the body parts of others, such as their parents, siblings, and others in their lives. This is also a time when a toddler is able to tell you whether she is a boy or a girl; however, the toddler also thinks that she can change her gender identity. According to a female toddler, for example, putting on a man's hat changes her into a male. One of us still remembers a 3-year-old's drawing of himself as a girl, accompanied by his description of "I'm going to be a girl when I grow up."

The people around a toddler, both males and females, communicate messages about the child's **gender identity.** A great deal of the environment of a young child sends out information about what is expected of boys and girls, and those expectations are often different. By the second year of life, the play behaviors of children begin to display those different expectations. During this time, children's attention to body parts and comfortable responses from adults who use correct terms to name body parts and functions eventually lead to curiosity about why girls and boys are different. Toddlers are not ready for very elaborate or technical explanations—just simple answers given in a matter-of-fact manner.

Journal 2.6: This is a time to check your sensitivities and comfort with children's bodies and gender awareness. Compose a response to a 2-year-old girl who asks you why her male toddler peer has a penis and she doesn't. What would you say to a 2 ½-year-old who asks, "How did the baby get in my mommy's tummy?" ■

Even if you are completely comfortable in giving answers to these questions, be sure to check with your class peers and instructor. You will probably hear an array of diverse responses and you may find that some feel much better and more appropriate for toddlers to hear than others.

Entire books are devoted to the developmental achievements of toddlerhood, but this brief section gives you a beginning glimpse of what a toddler is like. When you read about Ibrahim and his friends in Chapter 8, you will develop many more insights about this fascinating period as well as direction for how to promote toddler development in your early childhood professional role.

Implications of Toddler Development

All the developmental changes that occur during toddlerhood have implications for the adults who support these young children. Toddler curiosity and the beginnings of independence require specific environments and behaviors on the part of adults. First, there are issues of safety. The physical safety of toddlers demands constant watchfulness and an environment that protects yet stimulates exploration. The National Association for the Education of Young Children (NAEYC, 1997a) demonstrates some of the important characteristics of that environment:

> Floor coverings are appropriate for the activities that occur there—shock-absorbent tiles for open areas where toddlers push and pull toys around and for art, eating, and water and sand play areas. Low-pile, easy-to-clean carpeting or nonslip area rugs cover areas for quiet play. (p. 86)
>
> The environment contains private spaces with room for no more than two children and that are easily supervised by adults. (p. 87)
>
> Care givers directly supervise toddlers by sight and sound, even when they are sleeping. (p. 89)
>
> Adults do safety checks of all areas both indoors and outside several times a day to assure that they are safe (e.g., electric outlets are covered, no objects are on the floor that a toddler could choke on, no splinters or nails are exposed on furnishings and equipment). (p. 89)

Another kind of safety for toddlers is the issue of emotional security. These children are forming relationships, and their relationships with caregivers and educators is a critical one. The adults in the lives of toddlers need to be constant and committed to these youngsters. Toddlers are not yet good communicators, so adults need to know them well and be able to determine and respond to their needs and cues.

The second implication of toddler development is one of balancing opportunities for them to develop initiative, autonomy, and self-reliance with the routines, schedules, and rules that they seem to need. Toddlers want to try everything themselves, to do everything themselves, and to be in charge. At the same time, they have a limited capacity to communicate to others, to share or cooperate with others, and to take care of themselves. Bredekamp and Copple (1997) remind us, "A healthy toddler's inner world is filled with conflicting feelings—independence and dependence, pride and shame, confidence and doubt, self-awareness and confusion, fear and omnipotence, hostility and intense love, anger and tenderness, initiative and passivity" (p. 68). Those contrasts are a real challenge to the adults who intend to support the toddler. When toddlers feel that support, and know that they can count on those adults, they are able to face their own frustrations, struggles, and disappointments. Those adults need to make wise decisions about routines, schedules, and rules, so that they are a source of support to the toddler rather than a source of defeat. Listen to an early childhood professional who provides such support to toddlers:

Ethan: Testing limits

Two-year-old Ethan has brought a wheelbarrow in from the playground and is pushing it around the room, banging into furniture and other children. He seems to have a lot of energy and is quite thrilled with his new skill with the wheelbarrow. After watching him for a brief time, Mimi, his caregiver, approaches him with, "Ethan, you are pushing the wheelbarrow so well, but we don't have enough room inside for the wheelbarrow." She quickly explains that the wheelbarrow may hurt his friends, and gives him a choice of taking it back outside or pushing a truck in the block area. She adds, "I would like to watch so you can show me how strong you are." Ethan pauses, holding tightly to the wheelbarrow, and tries to push it again. Mimi repeats his choices and says, "It's your choice, Ethan." He decides to go back outside, and he takes Mimi's hand, indicating that he wants her to accompany him.

That is the delicate balance of limitations and freedom that toddlers need from the adults in their lives in order to develop autonomy and initiative. It is the challenge of nurturing and supporting normative toddler development. You can begin to understand how important it is to prepare well if you are going to work with this age group. When you meet Darren and Jennifer, two early childhood professionals who are committed to toddlers, you will expand that understanding. Unfortunately, their toddler program is not the norm. "Mediocre and inadequate care" is commonplace for both infants and toddlers (Cost, Quality, & Child Outcomes Study Team, 1995), because their care requires a high level of quality staffing and a large quantity of adult supervision and support. This is a worrisome statistic when you consider the importance of the development that is happening at this time. Fortunately, the next stage of development, the preschool years, has many excellent care and educational programs to meet the needs of children from ages 3 to 5.

Studying Preschool-Age Children (Ages Three to Five Years)

We are now talking about a much wider age span, so we will see a great deal of development and growth. Children of ages 3 to 5 are grouped together because their growth and development is so fluid. Often, you can see a group of 3- to 5-year-olds and be unable to tell who is what age. The individual differences are so prominent by then that it is impossible to describe a typical 3-, 4-, or 5-year old. We will provide a brief profile because you will be meeting a group of preschool-age children in Chapter 9. By then, you will have to have developed a better understanding from watching and listening to them. We begin with their physical and motor development because it's so prominent.

Physical and Motor Development

Large motor development. Some 3-year-olds are still developing the skills we described for toddlerhood, but others are well developed and have the capacity to run and jump. Age 3 is a time when fine motor skills such as cutting with scissors and drawing with crayons or markers are developing rapidly. Many 3-year-olds can copy simple shapes, draw faces, construct simple puzzles, and build with blocks. This is also a time for becoming independent or self-sufficient. These children need less help from the adults in their lives because they are developing the coordination and fine motor skills to do many tasks and because they have the motivation to try. By the end of age 3, children are ready for complex tasks that require extensive movement and coordination. In terms of motor development, preschoolers are ready for limitless physical activities. Their energy is overwhelming and their motor development is related to their abilities in other aspects of development.

By 4 and 5 years of age, the physical development of children is quite advanced, both in terms of skills and growth. These children are skilled at skipping, riding tricycles or bicycles, jumping, climbing, turning cartwheels, and throwing and catching balls. The body proportions of preschool children change significantly and that change contributes to these new skills. Their legs have lengthened and their bones have become harder and stronger. Consequently, they have increased body strength and coordination that enables them to perform various large motor skills. Gallahue (1982) describes the advances of motor development during preschool years with the following characteristics:

1. *Coordination.* The rhythmical integration of motor and sensory systems into a harmonious working together of body parts
2. *Speed.* The ability to move from one point to another in the shortest time possible over a short distance
3. *Agility.* The ability to move from point to point as rapidly as possible while making successive movements in different directions
4. *Power.* The ability to perform one maximum explosive force
5. *Balance.* The ability to maintain one's equilibrium in relationship to the force of gravity in both static and dynamic movement situations (p. 96)

■ TABLE 2.2 Age at Which a Given Percentage of Children Perform Locomotor Skills

	25%	50%	75%	90%
Rolls over	2.3 mo	2.8 mo	3.8 mo	4.7 mo
Sits without support	4.8 mo	5.5 mo	6.5 mo	7.8 mo
Walks well	11.3 mo	12.1 mo	13.5 mo	14.3 mo
Kicks ball forward	15 mo	20 mo	22.3 mo	2 yr
Pedals trike	21 mo	23 mo	2.8 yr	3 yr
Balances on one foot 10 seconds	3 yr	4.5 yr	5 yr	5.9 yr
Hops on one foot	3 yr	3.4 yr	4 yr	4.9 yr
Catches bounced ball	3.5 yr	3.9 yr	4.9 yr	5.5 yr
Heel-to-toe walk	3.3 yr	3.6 yr	4.2 yr	5 yr

Source: Developing Motor Behavior in Children: A Balanced Approach to Elementary Physical Education by D. D. Arnheim and R. A. Pestolesi, 1973, St. Louis: C.V. Mosby. Reprinted by permission of the author.

Small motor development.   Just as the large muscles become stronger and more coordinated, the small muscles also develop so that fine motor skills become more controlled and precise. The fine motor development of preschoolers improves rapidly, enabling them to write letters and draw shapes with pencils. Some of the precision and coordination evident during this time is called **dexterity.** It can be seen as the children handle small puzzle pieces, master buttons and zippers, and use many adult tools such as tweezers, tongs, and screwdrivers. Table 2.2 shows you the age when a given percentage of children perform some common locomotor skills.

Perceptual-motor development.   Another aspect of motor development that becomes obvious during this time is **perceptual-motor development.** We are born with sensory abilities (sight, touch, hearing, smell, and taste) but our ability to interpret the information our senses provides takes some time to develop. **Perceptual-motor movements** are a combination of what the child sees or perceives though her senses and the body movements that respond to those perceptions. The beginning of perceptual-motor development is the use of senses. Beginning at infancy, the capacity to take in sensory input is developing. It becomes well refined by the time children are preschoolers.

Two other aspects of perceptual-motor development are beginning during this time: body/spatial awareness and temporal awareness. Preschoolers are getting better about avoiding objects and furniture when they are on the move (referred to as **body/spatial awareness).** By age 4 or 5, they can run through an area and miss all of the obstacles, evidencing that they are better aware of their bodies and of the space surrounding them. In terms of **temporal awareness,** preschoolers begin to get a sense of time and sequence through the routines of their day. Most preschoolers will let you know if you skip an activity that is part of their usual sequence of events.

Preschool children take pride in their growing independence and motor skills. How might you respond to this child's accomplishments with the pegs?

Journal 2.7: Think about your day and identify some perceptual-motor experiences of your own. Consider how many times a day you use those perceptual-motor abilities. ■

Independence. Motor development enhances the growing independence we see in a preschool classroom. The move toward independence or self-sufficiency continues rapidly with increased ability as preschoolers dress themselves, serve and eat meals, wash their hands and brush their teeth, and organize their own spaces (bedrooms, cubbies, toy shelves, etc.). This same independence means that preschoolers can begin taking more responsibility for themselves. In terms of health and safety, they are able to begin to understand concepts of nutrition and danger, and they can follow simple rules for their own well-being. Later, when we visit Felipe in his preschool, you will see that children of this age can get very involved in rules and quite demanding about their observance.

Social Development

Although preschoolers are still quite egocentric (involved in themselves), they are also quite social. A wonderful scene on a soccer field with a team of 4- and 5-year-old children illustrates these contrasts in development. The soccer game is underway and the children are running down the field toward one of the goals. Five-year-old Tony stops in the middle of the field and calls out to his parents on the side, "Can Eric come over to play today?" The game continues as Tony's parents urge him to "watch the ball" and he remembers that he is part of a group effort, at least temporarily.

The preschool years are characterized by the beginning of friendships. Generally, by age 4, children can maintain friendships. Teachers and caregivers have noticed that children behave differently toward those children that they consider a friend and those that they do not consider a friend. With friends, young children often are more patient, more cooperative, more positive, and less disagreeable (Stroufe, Cooper, & De-

Hart, 1992). Preschoolers' abilities to begin and maintain friendships tell us that they have *social preferences*.

Another significant development that we see in preschool-age children is *social competence*. Social competence is related to the abilities we just described for children's friendships. Simply defined, it is the ability to engage with peers, to be liked and desired as a playmate, and to be able to interact with peers in mutually satisfying ways. Remember Keeley, who you met earlier in this chapter? She is a good example of a socially competent preschooler. She is liked and even admired by her young friends. Her mom constantly hears from other parents that their children "talk about Keeley all the time" and "want Keeley to come over." Keeley is friendly and emotionally positive. She gets a lot of attention from other children in her class and she wins struggles with her peers without ever being hostile. Her mom remembers well the first parent/teacher conference when Keeley's teacher said, "This is the most caring child I have ever encountered." When you watch Keeley with her mixed-age group, you will see that she has fun and is enthusiastic and that she can share that fun and enthusiasm with others. Some of what you observe in Keeley is developmental and some of what you see is her disposition. The two can be highly integrated in areas such as social development.

Cognitive Development

The intellectual development of 4- and 5-year-old children is marked by huge gains in understanding their world. Their use and understanding of symbols that began in toddlerhood is quite advanced. They write and draw symbols, as well as create and use symbols in their play. This is important development for understanding math and science literacy, which children of this age are beginning to pursue. This is a time of extensive "Why?" questions, as children explore their world and try to make meaning of their experiences. Many of the ideas expressed by preschoolers will strike us as humorous or strange, but these children are operating from a lack of information or misinformation. However, from ages 3 to 5 years, it seems that they are determined to gather as much information as possible. Preschoolers are active learners in ways that are different from the active learning of infants and toddlers. Although they maintain the physical and sensory aspects of their learning, they add concepts, vocabulary, and representation to the process. Thus, they actively construct meaning as they explore the world around them. Instead of just observing and describing events around them, preschoolers try to explain the events.

Cognitive limitations.   Although preschool cognition is becoming quite advanced, it is limited developmentally by three characteristics of preschool thinking. The first characteristic is **centration,** the tendency to consider only one piece of information when multiple pieces are relevant. Second is the preschoolers' lack of differentiation between reality and appearance, sometimes between pretend and real. Preschool teachers and caregivers are often asked, "Is it real or pretend?" when a story is read. The third characteristic is the lack of memory strategies. Some 4- and 5-year-olds begin to show some simple approaches to remembering. Keeley, for example, can be heard repeating to herself as she descends the stairs in her house, "Don't forget the backpack."

Cognitive changes.   One aspect of children's thinking that develops during preschool age is **causal reasoning.** This reasoning begins with children making explanations based on their observations—that is, by appearance. If it gets dark when the child goes to bed, then the reason it gets dark is so that people can go to bed. Later, this reasoning is influenced by an acknowledgment of powerful others (e.g., parents, sun, etc.). You may hear a child explain that the "sun made it get dark by going away." As children develop more concepts and vocabulary, their causal reasoning becomes more advanced and they are able to offer reasonable cause-and-effect explanations. When you observe preschoolers, you will notice that when they don't know the reason for something, they will invent one.

Other cognitive changes have been described by Piaget as he observed and discussed children's cognitive development. In the next chapter, you will read about preschoolers' abilities in the areas of conservation, serration, and classification. These are major developments in cognition and are especially relevant to the development of preschool-age children.

Language Development

The language development of 4- and 5-year-olds is amazing. They can comprehend extensive vocabulary and concepts: spatial concepts such as *beside* and *behind;* plural and singular forms of nouns such as *mice* and *mouse* and passive-voice sentences, *The plant was watered by Mary.* Their ability to follow directions continues to improve. Children of this age are curious about reading and are developing many of the skills necessary for reading. For instance, they can repeat stories after hearing them and they know that groups of letters represent words. The vocabulary of the preschooler is extensive—from 1,500 to over 2,000 words.

One of the most fascinating developments you will observe in a preschool class is the playing out of scripts. Children of preschool age have become familiar with scenes and accompanying dialogue of everyday activities, such as grocery shopping, going to the doctor's office, doing laundry at the laundromat and so forth. You will hear them playing the roles with adult dialogue. Their language development comes through in these scenes; in fact, you can learn a great deal about their language by listening to their scripts. Listen to a pair of preschoolers playing out the family's morning:

Angela: "Honey, don't forget your briefcase for work. What time will you be home?
George: "I have to go to work. Don't forget to make supper."
Angela: "Let's go out to dinner. I don't want to cook."
George: "I'm going to catch the bus. Bye."

Does any of this sound familiar? Most preschoolers' scripts are quite realistic and their use of language is accurate. Notice, however, that George wasn't working from the same script that Angela was using. Preschoolers may not listen to each other well but they definitely are paying attention to the adults and world around them.

Another aspect of language development that you will notice is the development of humor. Preschoolers enjoy jokes and riddles. They create jokes of their own and laugh hilariously at them. We adults go along with their jokes and usually laugh at the fact that the jokes are not funny. This ability is one of the enjoyable aspects of working with preschool-age children.

Gender Development

Do you remember in our discussion about toddlers that they can tell you if they are a boy or a girl? You may also remember that gender isn't a constant for them. By age 5, however, children begin to realize that their gender is going to stay the same, no matter what hairstyle, clothing, or preference they have. With their **gender constancy** comes an increased interest in the differences between males and females. Their interest continues to focus on the human anatomy but also takes in differences in roles and

---

A Closer Look

BOX 2.1 ■ Research on Racial Preference, Racial Differences, and Racial Self-Identification

While observing in a second-grade classroom, an early childhood professor overheard some children telling ethnic jokes (Boutte, LaPoint, & Davis, 1993). When the children were questioned, the professor discovered that they did not understand the subtle racial messages of the jokes. Some may think that making an issue of ethnic jokes is not necessary, but evidence shows that lack of attention or failure to challenge such bias will only "perpetuate oppressive beliefs and behaviors" (Derman-Sparks, 1992).

Adult reaction, especially that of teachers and caregivers, to a child's racial or ethnic background will have a significant effect on that child. Her cultural background is an intimate part of her self-esteem. As early childhood educators, we are faced with years and years of powerful research that tells us that young children notice race and other differences. Kenneth and Mamie Clark used brown and white dolls to conduct numerous studies of children. Their work and that of 50 years of study has consistently established that not only are young children aware of racial and ethnic differences but they also have internalized the dominant society's norms regarding the status of different racial and ethnic groups (Katz, 1982a; Goodman, 1946; Ramsey & Myers, 1990).

The Clarks (1947) studied a large sample of African American children ranging in age from 3 to 7. The researchers determined that approximately 93.5 percent of the children studied had an accurate knowledge of racial differences based on their ability to choose the "white doll" or the "colored doll." Most of the African American children identified with the colored doll—that is, they saw the doll

like themselves—whereas 33 percent identified with the white doll. When asked which doll they liked better, the majority preferred the white doll and rejected the colored doll. They said that they liked the white doll the best and wanted to play with the white doll rather than the colored doll. Those preferences decreased with the age of the children.

Later studies documented children's perceptions of the social roles of African Americans and Whites, with children in first- and second-grade ascribing inferior roles to black dolls (Radke & Trager, 1950). Morlund (1966) studied preschool-age children and documented that almost half of his sample of African American children identified their racial group incorrectly. He also noted that those children who correctly identified themselves as Black did so "reluctantly and with emotional strain" (p. 137). A study of Chicano, African American, and Anglo children in preschool and third grade found that Chicano children showed a clear preference for their own ethnic group, and that African American and Anglo children occasionally prefered other races (Rice, Ruiz, & Padilla, 1974).

Studies in the 1980s added sophisticated interpretation to the growing body of research with distinction between children's personal identity (self-esteem) and group identity (reference group). The debate continues among researchers about young children's racial preferences, attitudes, and identifications, but most early childhood educators would agree that it is important to help young children of color develop in-group racial preferences and to promote positive attitudes toward racial and ethnic groups.

behaviors. The adults who are in the life of a preschool child will be communicating information about gender by the way they live their lives. Here again, the way adults respond to questions about gender will send important messages to children who are forming their own gender identities and taking on the beginnings of their own gender roles. Another aspect of development that begins during preschool years is related to awareness of racial differences. Box 2.1 describes what research tells us about how young children respond to racial differences.

An entire book could be written about the development of 3-, 4- and 5-year-olds because so much growth and development is happening during this time. For now, however, you have a beginning sketch of some characteristics of this age. When you meet Felipe and his friends in Chapter 9, you will learn more about this age group. You will also observe how a preschool program accommodates the rapid development of children of this age. Considering the multiple facets of development that characterize the growth and learning of a preschool-age child, you can understand why there are so many preschools with so many different kinds of programs.

Studying Children in Kindergarten and Primary Grades (Ages Five to Eight Years)

Children of 5 to 8 years of age are beginning to make the transition to what is called *middle childhood*. These years are sometimes referred to as the *school years* because children of this age spend so much of their time in school. The physical growth during this period is not as dramatic as in the earlier years, but children in kindergarten and primary grades make exciting gains in terms of motor abilities. It is also a time of spectacular cognitive growth in the ability to handle complex mental tasks. Socially and emotionally, children of this age are developing the capacity for long-term relationships and secure adulthood. Most educational programs for this age begin to focus primarily on the cognitive aspects of learning, so let's begin with cognitive development. No less important will be our discussions of that social, emotional, and physical development.

Cognitive Development

If you remember our description of preschoolers' lack of memory strategies, it won't be surprising to you that from ages 5 to 8 years, memory abilities exhibit significant change. Children nearing middle childhood develop a variety of memory strategies that are increasingly effective. They also become aware of memory and its use. We saw that awareness beginning when Keeley was trying to remember her backpack.

Changes in memory skills. The first change we see in middle childhood is the development of **basic memory processes**—that is, the routine acts of storing and retrieving information. These processes begin in infancy and continue through toddlerhood, but the capacity to remember is limited. By this age, the capacity increases enormously and children are accumulating knowledge—that is, processing information and storing it in memory, both recalled and constructed. When you ask a 6-year-old a complex question, his answer may be partly what he remembers and partly what he is inferring based on what he knows. As adults, we infer a great deal of our knowledge. To give you a better idea of what we're talking about, read the following paragraph:

> Linda was playing with her new doll in front of her big red house. Suddenly she heard a strange sound coming from under her porch. It was the flapping of wings. Linda wanted to help so much, but she did not know what to do. She ran inside the house and grabbed a shoe box from the closet. Then Linda looked inside her desk until she found eight sheets of yellow paper. She cut up the paper into little pieces and put them in the bottom of the box. Linda gently picked up the helpless creature and took it with her. Her teacher knew what to do. (Paris, 1975)

Now try answering these questions without looking back at the paragraph:

1. Was Linda's doll new?
2. Did Linda grab a match box?
3. Was the strange sound coming from under the porch?
4. Was Linda playing behind the house?
5. Did Linda like to take care of animals?
6. Did Linda take what she found to the police station?
7. Did Linda find a frog?
8. Did Linda find a pair of scissors? (p. 233)

Now you can look back. See which answers came from the information in the paragraph.

Some of your answers were inferred based on information you have about children, teachers, winged animals, and how paper is generally cut into pieces (answers to questions 5 through 8). Scott Paris, who developed this paragraph, studied children approaching middle childhood and showed that these children automatically make the same kind of inferences that you did. We call this kind of recall **constructive memory,** it is a good indicator of how well children will remember information.

Earlier in this chapter, you heard Keeley using a memory strategy—repeating her mother's reminder to herself. At ages 5 to 8, children are able to use sophisticated memory strategies called **mnemonics.** The most common mnemonic is rehearsal, deliberately repeating over and over. We hear kindergarten children repeating their phone numbers and their addresses—an example of rehearsal. By ages 7 and 8, children use a great deal of rehearsal in their school learning and are ready for more advanced mnemonics. One of us still remembers the rhyme "Thirty days has September, April, June, and November . . . " and uses it for remembering how many days are in each month.

Journal 2.8: Think of a mnemonic that you learned early in your learning experiences. Think of one that you use currently. When you study, what are some memory strategies that you use? Be sure to discuss your answers with your classmates, for you will find a great deal of variation in the kind of mnemonics that work for individuals. ■

Significant achievements in thinking. One of the most impressive achievements of children of this age is their increasing ability to understand the views or perspectives of

Children in kindergarten begin to understand the views of their friends and are able to get along well with one another.

others. One welcomed effect of this new ability in their social interactions is they get along better. With this ability to see a situation from two perspectives comes the ability to focus on several aspects of a problem at the same time. These children are also able to reverse their thinking; that is, go through a series of steps and reverse them or realize that one step can undo another. In the next chapter, you will learn about Piaget's theories related to these achievements in thinking. Piaget explained for us how children's thinking changes as they mature during this time. Their achievements in thinking are very influential in their abilities to learn math and science in kindergarten and primary grades, so it is important to be aware of their thinking capacities.

Another significant achievement of this age group is **concept acquisition.** Woolfolk (1995) defines **concepts** as categories used to group similar events, ideas, objects, or people, and states that "most of what we know about the world involved concepts and relationships among concepts" (p. 286). What is significant about the achievement of concept acquisition is that children of this age are able to work with abstractions (concepts). Concepts are vague and unlike the concrete learning that preschool children do so well. So, children in kindergarten and primary grades begin to move from physical examples to an understanding of complex concepts such as numbers and time. Preschoolers often recite numbers and can count from 1 to 10 or more, but it doesn't mean that they understand what 1 is or what 10 is. By age 6 or 7, children's understanding of one-to-one correspondence and number is complete, but not until after age 8 are children reasonably accurate in placing events in a time sequence (Bredekamp & Copple, 1997). Concept acquisition means that children are moving beyond memorization to understanding. Gardner (1993a) says that they then have the capacity to "take knowledge, skills, and concepts and apply them appropriately in new situations" (p. 2). You can now see why we called this section Significant Achievements in Thinking.

Classification—the ability to group objects by common attributes—is another exciting capacity of this age. Children begin this ability by using one attribute, such as color or size, to classify objects and then extend the ability to classify using more than one attribute. For instance, in kindergarten, Matt sorts the blocks by shape, but in first grade, he may sort the large rectangles or the small red triangles, thus combining attributes. While in the primary grades, he may also master seriation, which is the ability to place objects in order of length, weight, or size. One of us observed a kindergarten/first-grade class in Victoria, British Columbia, in which the teacher asked the children to line up by height. Listen to what happened as the children struggled with a challenging task of seriation:

> The teacher, Mary, began, "I've been observing many of you measuring lately. You've been measuring your castles and measuring yourselves on our growth chart. We have an activity today to get you started using measurement. I want to see if you can form a line all together with the smallest child on this end and the tallest child on that end. You can do this any way you want."
>
> The children immediately began with ideas:
>
> "If you're not sure, you can stand back to back to measure."
>
> "Start with the smallest ones."
>
> "Start with three people and then get two more."
>
> For the next 10 minutes, three different children tried organizing the children into a line. They succeeded in arranging only four children. Then, one of the kindergarten children, a very petite girl named Sandy, loudly said, "I know what to do." The group allowed her to take over and she began adding children to the line of four children already arranged. Children followed her directions and stood still in their places. Sandy got lots of coaching from the other children as she estimated the "right spot" for each child, measuring with her hand on heads, and stepping back to verify her placements for each child. She succeeded in completing the line of children, then placed herself at the end as the shortest child, which she was. Mary clapped her hands with delight, "You did it all by yourselves." She grabbed a camera and took several pictures, encouraging children to talk about their experiences. Children stepped forward to look at the line of their classmates, and Sandy smiled to herself. (Driscoll, 1995, pp. 198–199)

As you will learn in the next chapter, a great deal of the cognitive development in middle childhood is influenced by children's social interaction. Both Piaget and Vygotsky (whom you will meet) have theorized about the effects of children learning from other children and from adults. Another great thinker, Jerome Bruner, adds discussion to the notion that others contribute to our individual learning processes, indirectly and directly. After reading more about cognitive development, you will be ready to be reacquainted with Keeley, who is now in kindergarten (Chapter 10), and to meet Jodie, a first-grade student, in Chapter 11. Jodie and her friends will help you understand the wide range of children's cognitive development in the primary grades. You will also observe their social and emotional development and see some distinctive differences and changes from the preschool children in Felipe's Head Start class (Chapter 9).

Social Development

This is a time for advances in self-understanding for children of ages 6 through 8 years. These children are able to assess their own personal abilities by making comparisons with peers. They are also able to see themselves in a social context—that is, as a member of a group. You will hear Keeley describing herself as, "I am friendly and nice to my friends." She refers to herself as a kindergartner. She might also say, "I'm Dani's friend" or "I'm the best writer in my class."

In addition to social comparisons and self-evaluation, children in kindergarten and primary grades are continuing their development of gender roles. Parents and other significant adults in children's lives continue to have a significant influence on children's understanding of gender roles. Keeley insists that "girls can't play basketball or baseball" because she is surrounded by a group of adult males who play sports. None of the females in her life do so, so she is certain that girls can't play those sports. Some children arrive in preschool with already developed gender roles, such as boys playing with the blocks and girls playing with the dolls.

Children of this age group begin to play, interact with, and prefer same-sex friends, but demonstrate the beginnings of attraction to the opposite sex. A great deal of kidding takes place about such topics as kissing and boyfriends and girlfriends. During this time, peer relationships begin to move into importance in competition with the family. Once children are in school all day, it makes sense that peers become so important. Many children spend as many hours with friends as they do with family members. Children learn from other children cooperation, relationships and friendships, and how to work and play in groups. By first and second grade, youngsters develop a sense of "groupness"—a beginning feeling of *we* and a collective identity. You often hear a preschooler or a kindergartner say, "I'm not inviting you to my birthday party." Social groups are already forming in kindergarten, but by first grade, they are more stable. It is easy to distinguish between those inside and outside the groups. When you watch Jodie in her class, you will meet some of the children in her group.

Emotional Development

We can learn much about a child's emotional development by watching his or her social interactions. Personality characteristics and dispositions are quite visible when children are working or playing with others. What you also see is how those qualities affect peers and how peers respond to those qualities. Another aspect of a child's emotional development is reflected by a metaphor about children who are 6 to 8 years of age. They are described as a "commuter traveling back and forth between the outside world and the smaller more personal one of the family" (Chilman, 1966, p. 5). With such a context for their emotional development, it is not surprising to note that middle childhood is a time of emotional extremes. Children can be deliriously happy and excited one minute and miserably sad and morose the next.

Attachments.   This is a confusing time! The 6-, 7-, and 8-year-old wants constant attention and affection from parents and other adults and will regularly display exaggerated dependence. Simultaneously, that same child wants independence from those adults. To make things even more confusing, this child will use fairly negative behaviors to get attention and affection; thus, the interpretation of her development may be opposite of what she is actually communicating. To be specific, a 7-year-old may argue or use shocking language to get her mother to pay attention to her. Elkind (1994) thinks that some of this behavior may also be a kind of rebellion against the inequality of the parent/child relationship.

Fears.   The development of new fears and the disappearance of old fears go hand in hand with changes in cognitive development. As children begin to understand things, some fears are released. With new understanding and new information, however, come new fears. Children of this age won't express fears loudly or with intense emotion like toddlers or preschoolers, but they will exhibit **fear responses.** Those responses are characterized by anxiety, discomfort, and repression of the fear. You will see these children bite their nails, stop eating or sleeping, become very dependent, and even show signs of illness. Children in middle childhood boast of not being afraid and they become inattentive or distracted when they are afraid. There's that confusion again between what they really want and what they communicate.

Journal 2.9: Reflect on your childhood. What fears do you remember? Can you attribute them to experiences, the influence of your family, conversations, or lack of understanding? ■

Self-reflection will help you understand the many sources and influences on children's fears. Reflecting on your own experiences is often a way to understand others.

Self-concept.   This is a time of stability of self-concept, and self-concept is greatly influenced by what children believe others think about them. Remember the importance of peers! Children approaching middle childhood are self-critical and they compare themselves with others frequently. They need help in accepting their own feelings and in seeing how those feelings affect their relationships. Adults can provide support for emotional development by engaging in a healthy relationship with the children. If that relationship is characterized by mutual support, acceptance, empathy, and genuine understanding, the children will also develop those qualities.

During this time, children often engage in organized games and sports and those activities can have a significant influence on the children's emotional development, especially self-worth. If those activities are not characterized by acceptance and sensitivity, a child's sense of self may be damaged. Most of us have observed too many Little League games and ballet recitals that satisfied adults but didn't respect children. Those experiences bring us to the final aspect of development: physical and motor development.

Physical and Motor Development

Children who are ages 5 to 8 advance in motor skills partly because of development and partly because they have many opportunities to use those abilities in games and

Consider all of the benefits of these children's physical play and time out of the classroom.

sports. Think of the complexity of playing soccer, skiing, gymnastics, and so on. Many children of this age are physically ready and very enthusiastic and they develop coordination and complex motor skills. Gallahue (1982) recommends, however, that children should not be pushed into advanced sports activities or formalized participation before they are ready or interested.

In terms of small motor development, dexterity has increased and eye-hand coordination is enhanced. Small motor skills greatly influence school success. Making a variety of writing and drawing tools available to children will enhance their interest in these tasks. Children also need a balance of guided and unguided writing and drawing activities. This is an aspect of development in which you will observe enormous variation among a group of children who are exactly the same age.

The final aspect of physical and motor development to be considered is the perceptual-motor development we discussed during our focus on preschool children. Perceptual motor abilities are well developed for kindergarten and primary grade children, and the level of refinement is dependent on the experiential opportunities the children have. Children of this age develop spatial and directional awareness as they participate in games and sports.

Physical development and motor abilities are not a priority in many elementary school programs, especially when the children move beyond kindergarten. This is partly due to dwindling resources in education. At the same time, educators will confirm the relationship between school success and those abilities (Black & Puckett, 1996). It is an aspect of child development that deserves much more attention and programming.

Often, children of this age are expected to sit for long periods of time because they have greater control of their bodies and longer attention spans, but long periods of sitting fatigue these children more than running, jumping, or bicycling does (Bredekamp & Copple, 1997). Programs and time set aside for physical action are essential in kindergarten and primary grades because children are refining their physical skills and expressing their physical power and control. Remember, too, that those physical activities can enhance self-confidence.

Individual Differences in Kindergarten and Primary Grades

All domains of development—physical, social, cognitive, and emotional—are connected or interrelated. So, when a 6-year-old develops new motor skills, it may result in changes in his social development. Especially during these early school years, development in one domain influences and is influenced by development in other domains (Bredekamp & Copple, 1997). Too many of the programs for kindergarten and primary grades focus on cognitive development and ultimately defeat the children's efforts to succeed.

Because children of this age have accumulated five to six years of varying experiences and have been progressing in their development at very different paces, there is huge diversity among children in kindergarten and primary grades. One response to this is the mixed-age class that you encountered earlier in this chapter. Whether you work in a mixed-age class, a class of kindergarten-age children, a first-grade class, or a second-grade class, it's important to remember is that those differences are a primary consideration for all of your decisions. The language of "developmentally appropriate practice" (Bredekamp & Copple, 1997) for 6- through 8-year-olds from the National Association for the Education of Young Children states our reminder well:

> Teachers have high (challenging but achievable) expectations and standards for every child's learning and development. To foster children's self-confidence, persistence, and other positive dispositions as learners, teachers adjust the rate and pace of the curriculum as well as the content so that all children engage in learning experiences in which they can succeed most of the time and yet are challenged to work on the edge of their developing capabilities.
>
> Teachers know each child well. As they plan learning experiences and work with children, they take into account individual differing abilities, developmental levels, and approaches to learning. Responsiveness to individual children is evident in the classroom environment, curriculum and teaching practices. Teachers make sure that every child has opportunities to actively participate and make contributions. (p. 162)

The implications of the wide range of development that occurs when children are in kindergarten and primary grades and of the individual differences in development offer a challenge to the way we prepare to teach or care for these children. The decisions that we have been urging you to get ready for will be complex. Again, the more you know about and understand young children, the better you will be prepared to make those decisions. Our final topic, dispositions, is another individual aspect of development that will help you appreciate the uniqueness of each child.

Dispositions

As we described very early in this chapter, *dispositions* are inclinations and preferences. Only recently have teachers talked about dispositions as a consideration for their work with children and families. Dispositions will offer you greater insight to help you broaden that lens with which you view children. Often, a child's disposition may be his most obvious characteristic—the quality we first encounter. If someone like Adam has the disposition to be curious, his curiosity may be what we notice about him. It may even keep us from noticing other aspects of his development. So, our awareness of the presence of dispositions will help us see a more complete picture of a child.

Before talking about how to use insights about dispositions, it is important to extend your understanding of what dispositions are. Some of the definitions of *disposition* from psychological literature suggest that it is an internal characteristic and that it is somewhat permanent. Katz and Raths (1985) think that disposition is connected to acts that may be so habitual and automatic that they seem intuitive and spontaneous. For instance, Keeley doesn't have to think about "taking charge" of her preschool peers—it seems to be intuitive and it definitely looks spontaneous. Others (Perkins, Jay, & Tishman, 1993) define dispositions as "people's tendencies to put their capabilities into action." Therefore, Keeley's "taking charge" in her preschool is a matter of using her ability to lead (her management skills, her social skills, and her creativity).

Finally, Katz and Raths (1985) suggest that dispositions are "patterns of action that require some attention to what is occurring in the context of the action, that is in a particular context and at particular times" (p. 10). Again, if we had observed Keeley over a period of time, we would see that her pattern had developed over time. We would currently see that pattern of "taking charge" occurring at particular time (during free play and center times) and in particular contexts (on the playground and at home with another child). We would see that she scans the room to find children who are not engaged or who will be open to her planning. We would also see that she often "takes charge" when others are having difficulty, so she is paying attention to what is happening and behaving accordingly. Dispositions are clearly an important aspect of who Keeley is and of each child's individuality.

Why Study Dispositions?

A number of psychologists and, more recently, early childhood educators think that dispositions are a critical goal of education, along with knowledge, skills, and attitudes. Their rationale is that without the disposition to do so, a child will not use all the knowledge and skills that we teach. Cantor (1990) says that "having" is not necessarily "doing." This argument implores us to promote certain dispositions in the way we work with children. If we truly want children to be learners, to be listeners, to be readers, and to be caring individuals, they will need the dispositions to be all these things. Teaching them how to read or how to listen will not be enough. If you agree with the notion that dispositions are essential for learning, then you will need to begin thinking about how to encourage and support dispositions.

Many of us in the early childhood profession are interested in the disposition of caring or being generous or helpful. That interest and commitment comes from concern about our society in general and about children's development. We know from research that humans are born with the capacity to be caring, and that even very young children demonstrate concern and comforting behaviors when other children are distressed. Research has documented that infants as young as age 10 months respond to another child's distress with sad looks and crying themselves (Zahn-Waxler & Radke-Yarrow, 1984). A 12-month-old was observed gently touching another child in distress and then touching himself (Zahn-Waxler, Radke-Yarrow, & King, 1979). By children's second year, they tend to help and comfort other people frequently, but some children are much more inclined to do so than others. By preschool years, children become even more helpful, caring, and generous. If you observe a preschool class, you will likely see some children who are always caring for others and some children who do not seem to notice that others have any needs. For example, it appears to be automatic for Joely to respond whenever anyone else gets hurt or is upset, but we never see Adrian do so.

When caring behaviors are studied, it is clear that there are individual differences in young children's capacities to care and to demonstrate caring. Research also suggests that a number of factors explain or cause that variation among individuals: biological factors, cultural factors, and socializing effects of family, teachers, peers, and media (Eisenberg, 1992). In Chapter 6, we will discuss families and how they socialize children with direct and indirect messages about values. If a child grows up in a family that values caring and demonstrates caring behaviors, that child will probably have a caring disposition. (We say *probably* because some individuals don't become caring people even when they are raised in such an environment.)

Our Role in Children's Developing Dispositions

As a teacher, you will play a role in children's developing dispositions. This is not surprising, considering that many children will spend a significant amount of their day in your class or program. You, as a significant adult in their lives, will be a model for various dispositions. You will also be capable of promoting certain dispositions.

Journal 2.10: Pause for a moment and think about the dispositions that you value. You may find them in your closest friends and family members. List them and then ask yourself if these are the dispositions you will want to nurture in young children. After some reflection, you may add a few to the list or take some off the list. ◼

Whether you are aware or not, you will be promoting certain dispositions in the young children you teach or care for, so it is important to acknowledge those values. Let's

■ **FIGURE 2.4**   Ways to Encourage Caring Behaviors in Children

1. Draw your child's attention to people's feelings. Ask him to imagine how he would feel in their place.
2. Let him know what the impact of his actions is on the feelings of others, including yourself.
3. Explain why people feel the way they do.
4. Make clear (or encourage him to discover) what actions he can take that would be more considerate.
5. Let him know that you expect him to be considerate, that it is important to you.
6. Let him know that you understand and care about *his* feelings and try to offer him a way to get at least some of what he wants—if not now, then in the future.
7. Don't expect him to read minds. Take the time to explain.
8. Help him understand other people's feelings by reminding him of similar experiences in his own life.
9. Help him resist the influence of people who discourage or ridicule his empathic feelings.
10. Give him approval when he is considerate. Show disappointment when he isn't.
11. Use self-control empathy training to teach him to imagine himself in someone else's place whenever he is inclined to hurt that person.
12. Share your own empathic feelings with him.
13. Point out examples of people who are empathic and those who are not, and communicate your admiration for kindhearted people.
14. Stress the good feelings that come from caring about other people.
15. Encourage him to consider a person's capacity for empathy when selecting friends.

Source: Bringing Up a Moral Child by Michael Schulman and Eva Mekler. Copyright © 1985, 1994 by Michael Schulman and Eva Mekler. Used by permission of Doubleday, a division of Bantam Doubleday Dell Publishing Group, Inc.

use as an example the disposition of being caring. If you want children to be caring individuals, there are many ways to promote that disposition. In Figure 2.4, Schulman and Mekler provide a list of ways to encourage children to develop empathic responses to the distress or hurt of others. They give you an idea of how easily you can promote the disposition to care about others.

The important message we are sending to you is that you will play a key role in developing children's dispositions. Your example will contribute to their dispositions and the way you guide children's behavior will promote or discourage certain dispositions. Your first step is awareness. Respond to the reflection we prompted in Journal 2.10 often to maintain that awareness. Notice your behavior with children so that you are aware of your capacity to promote or discourage dispositions. That takes us back to your decision-making role, because you can make the decision to promote certain dispositions and to discourage others, but it will take watchfulness on your part. Begin now by noticing your responses to children, even as you observe them with us. Notice how you feel about the adults in our stories and what you value in their interactions with children.

PRINCIPLES AND INSIGHTS: A Summary and Review

We hope that the glimpses of children throughout this chapter have prompted enthusiasm for your future professional role. Our intent was to begin the process of understanding young children and their development. As you meet the children in the chapters that follow, they will teach you much more about development and individual differences, and you will learn about how to teach and guide children.

In addition to contributing to your knowledge of children and some beginning skills to use when working with them, we hope we have inspired you. Childhood is a time of wonder. We ask you to celebrate with us—celebrate childhood, child development, and the rich differences each of us brings to this world and to each other.

As promised, we provided only profiles of development for each of the age groups. To show you the whole and complete picture, it would have taken entire books about infant development and preschool development, but we wanted simply to begin your "picture" of each age group. What you can take from our descriptions is the certainty that there is a great deal of change occurring at each age, and those changes influence each domain of development—physical, social, emotional, and cognitive. We have already cautioned you about the individuality of children, so keep in mind that those characteristics we just described may not fit every child. We have another caution to describe for you. It's at the heart of a current and significant controversy that is drawing attention within the profession you are about to enter.

One of the dominant beliefs in the ECE profession is that knowledge of child development is the source of decisions for teaching and guiding young children. By *knowledge of child development,* we are referring to an individual child's development as well as child development in general. Stott and Bowman (1996) call this a "slippery base" for practice. Their concern is twofold. First, knowledge of child development is changing rapidly. Second, there are other rich sources of information that offer guidance to our professional practices. Consider the disciplines of sociology, anthropology, history, and public health as just a few possibilities for concepts and skills with which to work with children and families. If you are studying any of those disciplines in other courses, study them for insights about early childhood education. The complexity of our society, and consequently children and families, demands multiple perspective for understanding them. In the chapters to come, we will integrate ideas from these disciplines to encourage you to broaden your thinking beyond child development.

The second discussion that is occurring in our profession centers on the concept of child development being both universal and cross-cultural in nature. This notion of cross-cultural development suggests that children's social, cognitive, physical, emotional, and language development are culturally influenced and constructed in important ways. We just described in this chapter characteristics of children at different ages that were culture free. Many of those characteristics would have looked or have been interpreted differently in some cultures. Cross-cultural child development takes into account not only the lives of children and the course of their development but also the lives of adults and the cultural and societal contexts in which those children and adults interact (New, 1994). An example of that wide lens for looking at children comes with our description of Keeley, the only child of a single working mom, who is being raised with an extended family of adults (Chapter 10). In Chapter 9, you will meet Felipe, one of three children in a Hispanic family that lives in a community in which the majority of residents speak Spanish. Our intent is to encourage you to see children in those cultural and societal contexts in which they are developing. If you truly become an observer (watching and listening) of children, you will begin to comprehend each child's ethnic and family characteristics and background.

You will need to accompany your sharp eyes and ears with basic knowledge of ethnic characteristics and individual family culture as a framework for your observations and questions. With broad perspectives of multiple disciplines and cross-cultural child development insights, you will be ready to make the decisions of an early childhood educator. You will truly be able to notice individual differences and accommodate those differences in the environment you provide, the activities you plan, and the interactions you have with children and families.

Becoming an Early Childhood Professional

This chapter is about child development and dispositions, which is a broad topic. There are volumes and volumes of research, theory, and information on child development. For your professional development, we have selected just a few resources and experiences so that you won't feel overwhelmed.

Your Field Experiences

1. Contact a family member or a friend who has an infant and ask to observe for a few hours. Use the characteristics of infant development from this chapter as a type of checklist to record what you see. Add other characteristics as needed. Continue your development by observing a toddler, a preschool-age child, a kindergarten-age child, and a child attending primary grades.

2. Visit a toy store and make a list of toys suitable for an infant, a toddler, a preschooler, and a child in kindergarten or primary grades. For each of your choices, give a developmental rationale (a reason based on developmental characteristics).

Your Professional Portfolio

1. Your observational records of different ages will be a suitable example of your beginning knowledge of child development. You could also include your toy selection list and rationale.

2. Another item for your portfolio is a set of goals directed to building a solid foundation to your understanding of child development.

Your Professional Library

Books and Articles

Black, J. K., & Puckett, M. B. (1996). *The young child: Development from prebirth through age eight.* Englewood Cliffs, NJ: Merrill.

Bredekamp, S., & Copple, C. (1997). *Developmentally appropriate practice in early childhood programs.* Washington, DC: NAEYC.

Bronson, M. B. (1995). *The right stuff for children birth to 8: Selecting play materials to support development.* Washington, DC: NAEYC.

Internet Addresses and World Wide Web Sites

www.exnet.iastste.edu/Pages/ nncc/ Child.Dev/child.dev.page.html
  Intellectual Development of Toddlers (Marilyn Lopes, University of Massachusetts, 1994)

www.healthysteps.org/ index.html
  Healthy Steps for Young Children

www.exnet.instate.edu/pages/famil . . . nncc/Diversity/fc43_activ.rac.aware.html
  Activities That Promote Racial and Cultural Awareness (B. Biles, No. Central Regional Lab, 1996)

www.exnet.instate.edu/Pages/nncc/Child Dev/child.dev.page.html
  Child Development (National Network for Child Care, 1997)

www.exnet.iastate.edu/pages/nncc/Child.Dev/sp.child.dev.page.html
  Child Development Spanish Resources (National Network for Child Care)

www.ed.ac.uk/webscre/Spotlight54.html
  "No Problem Here?" Children's Attitudes to Race in a Mainly White Area (Donald, Gosling, & Hamilton)

Theories of Development

FOUNDATIONS FOR PRACTICE

When you finish reading and reflecting on this chapter, you will be able to:

1. Define four areas of early childhood development: cognitive, language, social, and emotional.

2. Describe the major contributions associated with each developmental theorist.

3. Create an activity that supports growth in each developmental area.

4. Identify *theories in action* while you observe a preschool in the chapter.

When you spend much time in an early childhood setting, you soon notice that the teachers or caregivers interact with children in ways that create a recognizable pattern of responses, questions, and behaviors. These interactions grow out of specific developmental and learning theories. The environment, including activities and interactions, is based on understanding and interpreting theories of development.

Theories of Development at a Preschool

Jasmine, Scott, and Samantha are enrolled in the 4-year-olds class in the Creative Learning Cooperative Preschool. As in most cooperative preschools, parents work as teaching assistants or assist with other functions several times a month for the preschool. They also hire the teacher and elect a school board.

As you enter the preschool early in the morning, you see Jasmine, Scott, and Samantha near the sink, mixing apple juice with water for the morning snack. Keith, the preschool teacher, is talking about changes in the taste of juice when water is added. Each child tastes a spoonful of juice

from the juice can. "Yuk," says Scott. "I like it this way," shares Jasmine. "Would we have enough for everyone if we only use the juice in the can?" asks Keith. "And what if we used this one tall container instead of these two short ones?" Keith was thinking about Piaget's theory of conservation, or understanding that the same amount can be represented in different containers (two short 32-ounce pitchers or one tall 64-ounce pitcher, in this case). He also was thinking about the use of language when children described the taste of the concentrated juice and their social interactions as they worked together on this task. Knowing that Scott was hungry, he paid attention to the children's emotional needs.

Why Study Theories of Development?

Keith, the teacher in the preschool you just visited, bases his curriculum planning, activities, and interactions with the children on his interpretations of theories of development. Early childhood professionals look to these theories as a foundation for their own belief systems and personal philosophies of early childhood education. These beliefs and philosophies are then translated into practice, resulting in the environment and interactions created for young children.

Theories come from many different disciplines of knowledge. As mentioned earlier, psychology, anthropology, sociology, physical development, health, linguistics, history, and education provide a knowledge base for planning programs for young children. Theorists and scientists in each of these fields have contributed their work and findings. Their theories are analyzed and compiled into the growing body of knowledge about young children and their development.

From this knowledge base, early childhood professionals make numerous decisions about children and the type of environment that will nurture young children. For example, you might plan an activity in which the young children in your care have frequent opportunities to explore through music, art, books, tapes, manipulative activities, and talking and listening experiences. You would be including learning situations drawn from the theory of multiple intelligences, as discussed by Howard Gardner. Planning an experience where toddlers engage in guided verbal interactions around their activity facilitates their language development and supports the work of Lev Vygotsky, with his emphasis on spoken language.

This chapter describes major theorists from each of the developmental areas. We selected these theorists based on their influence in their respective fields and in early childhood education. As you continue with your study of child development, you will note that some theories may conflict with each other, as if saying the opposite about children. You may also notice that even the most respected theorists are criticized or ignored at times. Time spent learning from major theorists will assist you in clarifying the rationale for expectations for appropriate early childhood programs. An understanding of these theories will help you develop your own personal philosophies of what works best (and why) for the children in your care.

Integration of Developmental Theories

Observing a group of young children at play, you will see that cognitive, language, social, and emotional development are integrated throughout their activities. Seldom do children use only one developmental area in isolation. For instance, 4-year-old Marc is busy at the dress-up center, talking to himself about putting his arms into a large coat. He is wearing a firefighter's jacket and hat and tells Samantha, "Let's hurry and put out the fire at the grocery store. We need to find a hose and water fast!" Samantha finds her raincoat and hops on a wooden truck with Marc. Off they go to put out the fire, which is actually the climbing structure outside. Their conversation continues about the fire and looking for a hose (a jump rope).

During this interaction, Marc was sharing his thoughts about the fire, looking around to see who might help put out the fire, and intent on the task at hand. Although this might be described as a social activity, there were many areas of development interwoven in the activity. Marc used language to describe the fire and the equipment needed to put out the fire, including self-talk. He was thinking about the organization and tools needed for fire fighting. At the same time, Marc worked cooperatively with Samantha to put out the fire, and certainly appeared to be enjoying this activity. Each of these behaviors might be classified separately as language development, cognitive development, social development, and emotional development. They were all obviously integrated throughout Marc's activity of fire fighting. When we present the theories that follow, they may appear isolated as you examine one set of ideas, but the major intent is learning how these theories can be applied coherently in your work with young children.

Before you take your next trip to observe in a preschool, you will examine the developmental areas within cognitive, language, social, and emotional domains. Highlights of major contributors to the different developmental fields will be discussed. These theorists will then travel with you to the preschool as you observe their theories in practice.

Cognitive and Language Development

Cognitive development refers to the process of developing thinking and reasoning skills as children acquire language skills (Spodek & Saracho, 1994b). **Language development** requires an understanding of words (meaning) and the structure of word groups (creating sentences), and is a tool for thinking. Cognitive development and language development are closely connected. Early childhood is a time of exploding use of language, both **receptive language** (what children hear) and **expressive language** (what children say). When a toddler begins to talk and express herself through words and phrases, new words seem to be added to her vocabulary each day.

Language shapes our thoughts and thinking. Jerome Bruner finds language and cognition to be intertwined, as did Lev Vygotsky, who saw language as "a logical and analytical tool in thinking" (Vygotsky, 1962). As an early childhood professional, you will need to know how children develop in these two areas and how you can support their development in your program. Many early childhood educators agree that the work of Jean Piaget has influenced the current thinking in child development and early childhood education more than any other theorist or scientist. Let's start with his work as you explore theories of development.

Piaget's Theory of Cognitive Development

Jean Piaget's (1896–1980) background was in biology and intelligence testing. He worked at Alfred Binet's experimental laboratory, where the first intelligence test was developed. While conducting intelligence tests with young children, Piaget became very interested in the children's responses, particularly the wrong answers (Crain, 1980). The pattern of incorrect responses seemed to correlate with the age of a child, which led to Piaget's hypothesis that young children think in an entirely different way than older children and adults (Ginsburg & Opper, 1988). Piaget became interested in the child's view of environment and began to test his own three children to confirm his hypotheses about levels or stages of development. For example, Piaget believed that children younger than age 7 would not believe that a vertical stack of five books were the same five books when spread out over the rug area. Changing the layout of the books seemed also to change the number of books (physical property), according to children who have not yet reached an advanced stage of thinking. This concept, called **conservation,** is considered by Piaget as evidence of higher-level thinking. (Recall, from earlier in this chapter, Keith asking the children about the amount of juice in the different-sized pitchers as he thought about their interpretations of conservation.)

Through his research, Piaget found that people's needs for creating order in their lives is a central drive (Piaget, 1952). He called this the drive for **equilibrium,** or a state of balance. To reach equilibrium, people have biological tendencies to organize and adapt.

Tendency toward organization. Piaget proposed that each person is born with the ability to organize her thinking processes into structures and that the tendency to adapt to the environment is inherited. For example, **organization** allows you to represent your thinking into categories in order to make sense of your world. It would be impossible to deal with every encounter or object as an entirely new experience without drawing on your prior knowledge, which you previously categorized according to certain characteristics.

Let's say you are watching a 5-year-old at the zoo. Earlier, this child had been watching the bears; he has now moved on to the lion area. He keeps talking about the four-legged animals at the zoo. His experience has helped him organize these animals as four-legged creatures. Next, he encounters the parrots. Seeing only two legs, he asks you where the other two legs are. His organization of animals at the zoo was built on the structure that the animals have four legs, so this new experience (the parrots) does not fit his organization, until he learns that parrots are classified as birds and have two legs. Thus, the child expands his thinking, but still uses his organization system based on the number of legs.

The structure or organizational system discussed here is called a **schema** (or *scheme*) and represents the way a person thinks about the world. An example of a simple schema would be when all flowers that are red are grouped into one category. A more complex schema would be built around the classification of flowers according to plant families. A schema assists you in organizing your thinking and provides a foundation or framework for your future experiences.

Tendency toward adaptation. **Adaptation** refers to the way people adjust to their environment. As a biologist, Piaget brought ideas from the science world to educators. His thinking about adaptation prompted a look at the relationship humans have with their environment. Ongoing interactions with the environment constantly change people, as they change the environment. For example, when an infant tries to touch an object that is out of reach, she must adapt by moving toward the object or fussing until someone helps her as she is reaching. When she moves toward the object, she is adapting to the environment by changing her location. New experiences are added to the infant's repertoire and her organization schema. Adaptation becomes more refined and complex as she gains knowledge and skills.

Piaget's research on children's thinking led to his theory based on four stages of cognitive development, as shown in Table 3.1. He proposed that all children proceed

■ TABLE 3.1 Piaget's Stages of Cognitive Development

Stage	Approximate Age	Characteristics
Sensorimotor	0–2 years	Begins to make use of imitation, memory, and thought. Begins to recognize that objects do not cease to exist when they are hidden. Moves from reflex actions to goal-directed activity.
Preoperational	2–7 years	Gradually develops use of language and ability to think in symbolic form. Able to think operations through logically in one direction. Has difficulties seeing another person's point of view.
Concrete operational	7–11 years	Able to solve concrete (hands-on) problems in logical fashion. Understands laws of conservation and is able to classify and seriate. Understands reversibility.
Formal operational	11–15 years	Able to solve abstract problems in logical fashion. Becomes more scientific in thinking. Develops concerns about social issues, identity.

Source: Adapted from *Piaget's Theory of Cognitive and Affective Development* by Barry J. Wadsworth. Copyright © 1971, 1979, 1984, 1989. Reprinted by permission of Addison-Wesley Educational Publishers Inc.

sequentially through each of the stages of development, although at individual rates. Cognitive development is an active construction process, created by each child according to her experiences (Crain, 1980).

Sensorimotor stage. The first stage, **sensorimotor,** includes children from birth to 2 years of age. Infants primarily interact with their immediate environment and learn through sensory actions, such as hearing, grasping, tasting, or seeing. Objects are real only when they are in sight of or touched by the infant. During the first months of life, an infant has not yet developed the ability to mentally represent an object by thinking about it; the object must clearly be present and be seen, touched, smelled, heard, or tasted in order to be "thought of" by the infant.

By the end of the sensorimotor stage, the child gradually begins to think of objects and processes as she moves into using prior knowledge and experiences to solve new situations. An example can be found in the following situation: An 18-month old-infant sitting in her high chair is picking up different crackers from the tray and placing them in her mouth, one by one. Whenever she picks up a goldfish-shaped cheese cracker, she chews it and then swallows. The round crackers, however, are spit back out onto the tray or floor. After a few minutes of trial and error with the crackers, the toddler begins to throw the round crackers onto the floor and eat the goldfish-shaped crackers, without needing to taste them first. She learned to discriminate between the two types of crackers and eventually used her prior knowledge to discard the crackers she did not like.

Preoperational stage.   During the second stage of cognitive development, Piaget proposed that children from 2 to 6 or 7 years of age are at the **preoperational** level. Children have gained the ability and skills to represent images and objects without the object actually present. In other words, children at this stage will use objects during their play as symbols to represent objects that are not available. A 3-year-old might find a Frisbee outside on the playground and turn it over to offer friends a piece of pizza, while another playmate might be sitting on a log and yelling, "Giddy-up horsee!" These children are involved in symbolic representation—using language to name their symbolic representations and inventing their own symbolic meaning for the object at hand.

Other aspects of the preoperational stage include the development of beginning reasoning and **egocentricism** (the world revolves around one's self). Reasoning at this stage tends to be based on actual experiences and may not reflect logical rationale. For

Scott and Marc are utilizing several objects in their play as symbolic representations. What is one symbolic object you notice in the photo?

instance, Jason, a 4-year-old child, encounters a puddle of water near the sink in the playroom. Since it is raining outside, with puddles forming on the sidewalk, he decides that it must also have rained on this floor. Jason's reasoning is derived from his experience of walking in the puddle outside and watching the rain make puddles on the sidewalk. He then transferred this outdoor experience to inside, when he determined the cause for the puddle on the floor.

Egocentricism could also be reflected in this related example. If another child told Jason that the water in the room came from spilling a glass of water, and Jason did not see anyone spill water, he might decide to hold on to his prior reasoning, and explain the puddle from his own point of view. Children at the preoperational stage are not yet able to understand other people's viewpoints. This does not mean that the young child is selfish or self-centered, but rather that the child is firmly grounded in her own perspective, as this is what makes sense to her. Understanding that the child is relating to her personal perspective and experiences helps teachers and caregivers realize that explaining in length about sharing toys may not be as fruitful as short discussions and demonstrations of guidelines for sharing.

As the child progresses through the preoperational stage, she also becomes more **decentered** (and less egocentered), meaning she is able to look farther and farther beyond her own perspective. You might observe some 6-year-olds playing with younger children and talking to these children in shorter sentences, emphasizing certain words to help younger children understand. This is an example of decentering—that is, understanding the other person's perspective and acting on it.

Concrete operations stage. From ages 6 to 12, the child enters the period of **concrete operations.** This stage is characterized by the child gaining the skills and concepts to understand conservation, reversibility, classification, seriation, and the ability to understand someone else's viewpoint. **Conservation** occurs when the physical elements of an object change, yet the object conserves most of its original property. A common example of conservation is found in holding up two identical balls of clay in front of a child. When you ask the child if these balls have the same amount of clay, he responds, "Yes." You then flatten one ball of clay and repeat the question. Typically, the child will decide that the flattened ball of clay is larger because it spreads out over a larger area. Thus, the shape of one of the identical balls of clay changed, but, until he grasps the concept of conservation the child thinks of them as different amounts.

Reversibility is found in the logic that what is done with objects can also be undone or reversed. Reversibility can be represented with beginning addition. A 7-year-old child who understands reversibility would be able to show the relationship between $2 + 4$ and $4 + 2$ with blocks and discuss how they add up to the same amount. This same concept would also be introduced in subtraction, where children find that the $6 - 4$ uses the same amount of blocks as $4 + 2$ and that one equation "undoes" the other.

Classification begins with grouping objects according to one specific characteristic and then expands into a more complicated rationale for classifying. Young children often enjoy sorting like items into separate containers, which provides a structure for their beginning concepts of classification. Objects can be sorted according to shape, color, size, or use. This first step of organization helps children make sense of their world and promotes the understanding of connections and relationships. As children progress through this stage, they are able to increase the difficulty of their classification systems and use their own rationale for the classifications.

When objects are arranged in a sequential order based on one characteristic—such as age, length, or dates—we call this **seriation.** Our number system is a serial system, as it occurs in a specific order representing increasingly larger amounts. A group of 6- and 7-year-olds might make a chart that lists the months of the year according to their birth months, starting with the month with the most birthdays and moving in sequence to the month with the least number of birthdays. The chart represents seriation, with the months arranged according to the organizational schema of the number of birthdays per month.

Another change that occurs during the concrete operational stage is the child's beginning **understanding of other people's perspectives.** Children can now participate in a discussion about their favorite ice cream flavors and recognize that other people might have an opinion (or favorite flavor) that differs from their perspective. This is a wonderful age at which to discuss cultures and express appreciation for diversity in our world.

Formal operations stage.   The fourth and final stage of development, according to Piaget, occurs from age 12 through adulthood and is called **formal operations.** Here, people are dealing with abstract ideas, concepts, and issues. Much of the foundation for this stage was built throughout the prior three stages and is now expanded through the use of formal operations. Hypothetical situations and questions help older children sort their world and solve new problems that move beyond concrete thinking. The examination and exploration of important issues and concepts are teaching strategies that assist adolescents as they construct their attitudes and beliefs.

Applying Piaget's theory.   If you use Piaget's ideas when you set up your early childhood setting, you would include numerous opportunities for children to explore objects and their environment. When presenting the concept of *big* and *little* with a class of 3-year-olds, for example, you would make sure there were many concrete experiences available, such as objects, roleplaying, and pictures. Children learn from exploring their environment and from engaging in activities that allow them to make sense of their world. Simply telling a child what is *big* and what is *little* would produce very different learning. A learning environment where children are actively involved with materials helps them feel, see, draw, and categorize objects that are big or little. The involvement with materials is congruent with Piaget's belief that children learn through interacting with their environment.

Activities would also be designed to enhance the current cognitive development stage of the child. When a child is at the preoperational level, you would encourage her use of objects as symbols for objects that might not be available. For example, two children making a "pretend" breakfast on the play stove talk about the hot stove and remind each other not to touch the pan. They are using the play stove and pans as symbols of a real stove and cooking, and are engaging in language and activities built on symbolism.

Symbolic play is critical to learning, and activities should reflect the children's interests and developmental levels. When you listen to children at play and observe their approaches to problem solving, you are observing important information that helps you determine their current stage of development. This knowledge helps you plan a variety of activities that correspond to this level. While you watch students, you also realize that within a group of children of the same age, there will be differences among their levels of development. Planning developmentally appropriate activities for small groups and individuals shows your awareness of meeting the individual learning needs of each young child. You will visit a preschool later in this chapter and see how one early childhood educator applies Piaget's theories in his classroom.

Journal 3.1: Think of some activities you might plan for a 3-year-old at the preoperational stage. This child demonstrates interest in symbolic play by using a doll to represent a new baby sibling. What activities might you make available for this child that would match her developmental level and interests? ■

Piaget's contributions and limitations.   Piaget's theories about children and their thinking and development shifted educators' emphases on what children already know to examining how children come to know or learn. This shift greatly affected early childhood settings and interactions with children. The belief that acquisition of knowledge and true understanding in learning could be enhanced through activities and experiences had an impact on the curriculum of early childhood programs.

Piaget's ideas produced a schema or organizational structure of developmental levels useful for thinking about cognitive development of children. His work also challenged educators and psychologists to examine the origins of children's knowledge. Prior to Piaget's theories of cognitive development, much of the emphasis in early childhood learning had been based on what children already knew and building programs around their current knowledge. Piaget opened the way to explore how children come to learn new knowledge, which translates into providing activities and an environment that supports growth corresponding to the developmental levels.

Several limitations to Piaget's work have arisen recently. New research finds that infants exhibit behaviors earlier than Piaget established in his work. After all, Piaget did not have access to sophisticated experimental techniques that researchers of today use to determine ages when cognitive stages are reached (Flavell, Miller, & Miller, 1993). Other researchers have suggested that Piaget underestimated young children's cognitive abilities. Work by Miller and Gelman (1983) found that preschool children are able to demonstrate they understand much more about numbers than was previously thought by Piaget. By reducing the amount of objects the children worked with and simplifying the directions, children were able to display that the number (amount) of objects stayed the same, whether the objects were spaced close together or moved apart from each other.

Important applications of Piaget's theory led to the acceptance of discovery learning, which is the role of play in early childhood, and to an increased awareness of the individual nature of learning and development. Piaget's work also laid the foundation for other cognitive developmental theories, such as the work of Jerome Bruner.

■ **TABLE 3.2   Bruner's Three Stages of Cognitive Development**

Stage	Approximate Age	Characteristic
Enactive	0–1½ years	Knows his or her world through senses
Iconic	1½–6 years	Knows his or her world through concrete images
Symbolic	6+ years	Knows his or her world through abstractions

Bruner's Theory of Cognitive Development

In his early work, psychologist Jerome Bruner (born in 1915) studied perception (1951) and thinking (Bruner, Goodnow, & Austin, 1956). His research in these areas led him to propose that children learn as they seek meaning and make discoveries. As Bruner continued his study of cognitive development, he identified three stages of cognitive growth: the enactive, iconic, and symbolic stages (1966, 1971). These stages are outlined in Table 3.2.

Enactive stage.   During the **enactive stage,** the infant comprehends his world through actions, similar to the sensorimotor stage in Piaget's developmental levels. The infant responds to actions and objects through touch, taste, feel, smell, and sound.

Iconic stage.   When the child moves into the **iconic stage** (approximately 18 months to 6 years of age), he now views the world in concrete images. Whatever he sees must be true and real. A scary puppet looks real to a child in this stage.

Symbolic stage.   The final stage is the **symbolic stage,** where the child is able to draw from abstractions, language, and thinking to construct his world. He uses his knowledge gained through actions and images, but is able to move to higher levels of thinking and understand abstract ideas and concepts. You might notice this in a primary-level classroom, where children begin to read, write, and tell stories and remind each other what is real and what is "make believe." In their own imaginations, they are able to relate abstract ideas and share them with others.

Discovery learning and inductive reasoning.   Bruner emphasized discovery learning and inductive reasoning as important instructional approaches for young children throughout all three stages of cognitive development. In Bruner's model of **discovery learning,** the child is an active player in discovering key principles of knowledge through her interaction with examples, materials, and/or problems. For example, a teacher or caregiver presents examples of pennies and other coins to a 5-year-old child. The child works with the coins, making connections and drawing her own meaning from the materials. She sorts the coins into different piles, discovering from another child the name of the brownish coins. She makes the generalization that all brownish coins are called pennies and the other coins are not pennies. When involved in discovery learning, the child builds her own structures and organizes her knowledge instead of passively accepting the teacher's reasoning or answers (Bruner, 1966, 1971).

These children are reading different books. They will then interpret the books and share their stories with their classmates.

If 5-year-old Anthony wants to find out what will float on water, the role of the teacher is to assist Anthony in gathering materials needed to test his hypothesis. He might also want assistance in designing an experiment that will help him discover if rocks, pencils, sticks, or a cookie will float. Anthony is actively exploring and experimenting to find answers to his question.

The teacher wants Anthony to discover the principle of gravity, weight, and buoyancy on his own, so she stops by to ask him about his findings. Through **inductive reasoning,** or drawing from specific examples to develop his own more general principles, Anthony talks about the heavy objects dropping to the bottom right away and the wood things staying on top of the water. Before he places a penny into the water, his teacher asks him to guess, or hypothesize, what will happen: "Will the penny float or sink?" She is encouraging Anthony to use his intuition based on his research, to think intuitively about the next step of his experiment, and to predict outcomes.

Applying Bruner's theory.   An environment that reflects Bruner's ideas would find children actively pursuing their interests and testing ideas to find answers and solutions. The teacher or caregiver would ask questions that require investigations and hands-on learning by the children. You would see lots of equipment and materials available for children to use in a variety of ways. For example, Anthony used a small tub to test his floating theory. Later in the morning, Samantha was curious about the blocks in the play area and started drawing their shapes. She then used the same tub to sort a box of blocks into two piles, one that contains shapes with four sides and one for shapes with more or less than four sides.

In an environment that support's Bruner's theory of learning, children expect to come up with their own answers and to share answers with others. They also expect to make mistakes, as they predict outcomes of their experiments based on their initial investigations and incomplete evidence. As an adult in this setting, you would ask many questions. Many of these questions will be **open ended,** with several possible answers. You would also expect the children to come up with ways to test their ideas and then connect their new learning with previous experiences.

Now we'll look at Vygotsky's work, which strongly supports the theory that children construct language and meaning from experiences with language through social interactions. Vygotsky stressed the importance of children's interactions with their environment to promote learning, as did Piaget and Bruner.

Vygotsky's Theory of Language Development

Lev Vygotsky (1896–1934) was a Russian psychologist whose contributions to early childhood study were in the field of the sociocultural aspects of learning. His work was based on the idea that society and culture influence what and how children learn (Bodrova & Leong, 1996). According to Vygotsky, human behavior must be studied within the social and historical context of the child (Dixon-Krauss, 1995). Teachers and caregivers need to include the social and cultural backgrounds of the children when making educational decisions that reflect their learning.

As a caregiver or teacher, it is important for you to move beyond your own culture and background and become knowledgeable of other cultures of the children with whom you work. For example, some Native American children may have been taught at home to support others, even if there are personal costs for doing so. Such a child in your care might not volunteer to give a correct answer if this made others in the group look as if they do not know as much. Awareness of cultural influences will help you in your interactions with children and their families and in your planning for learning activities (Bodrova & Leong, 1996).

Vygotsky presented the theory that children learn through their interactions with others, thus the people in their world hold great influence on their learning. Language is a cultural tool, reflecting the child's physical and social environments (Bodrova & Leong, 1996). The use of language is critical for cognitive development. Children begin to develop higher levels of thinking when expressing their thoughts and ideas.

Older children and adults play a key role in the cognitive development of a child, often guiding the child to move to more complex ideas, concepts, or skills. When a child is working with others near the limits of her ability, support and guidance from others can help the child solve a new problem. This is called learning in the *zone of proximal development.*

BOX 3.1 ■ Does Cultural Context Influence Child Development?

A Closer Look

If you were to observe a toddler in her home in San Pedro, Guatemala, and another toddler of the same age in Salt Lake City, Utah, you would note similarities and differences in their activities, behaviors, and development. "Each culture has its own system of norms and values in which the development and interactions of the children evolve" (Rogoff et al., 1993, p. 162). Rogoff and colleagues studied toddlers and their interactions with caregivers in four different cultural communities. Two of these communities included Salt Lake City and San Pedro. In this study, the researchers were attempting "to understand development in the context of children's everyday activities and culturally valued goals of development" (p. 9).

Expectations of the children led to variations in their development from culture to culture. For example, in San Pedro, where it is expected that young chil-

dren will assist with household chores, 3 of the 14 toddlers helped their family by running errands, such as purchasing bread at a nearby store. None of the toddlers in Salt Lake City assumed such responsibility. In Salt Lake City, 10 of the 14 mothers of toddlers reported that they had instructed their child in walking or talking, whereas only 2 of the San Pedro mothers reported that they taught these skills. The mothers of the 14 toddlers in San Pedro indicated that their children learned to walk and talk by observing others or with parental encouragement. In San Pedro, 4 of the toddlers were toilet trained, whereas none of the Salt Lake City toddlers were toilet trained.

The differences in reaching developmental milestones seem to be related to values and expectations expressed by the child's social and cultural community. According to Rogoff and colleagues (1993), "Goals of development vary according to local practices and values" (p. 151).

The zone of proximal development. In his theory of the **zone of proximal development (ZPD)**, Vygotsky believed that an educator could assist young children in moving to higher levels in their development by encouraging their involvement in activities that are slightly more difficult than those the child can master alone (Bodrova & Leong, 1996). By working with capable peers or with adults who support them, children successfully complete more complicated activities and thus work at the level of potential development (Vygotsky, 1978). The ZPD theory is most often applicable to cognitive development, although it is certainly connected to language development. For example, when 2-year-old Kendra wanted more apple, she said, "More." Her older brother replied, "You want more apple?" and Kendra answered, "More apple." Through this shared interaction, Kendra put two words together to make a phrase that communicated her request. Her brother's assistance to help her move beyond her current level of language use to a more complex level expanded her development, showing that Kendra was in a zone of proximal development. Vygotsky finds language to be the foundation for all higher cognitive processes (Berk, 1996a).

Journal 3.2: What is the difference between Kendra's language experience with her older brother, compared to an adult correcting Kendra's language by telling her, "No, you mean 'More apple'?" ■

Wood, Bruner, and Ross (1976) studied Vygotsky's zone of proximal development and used the term **scaffolding** to describe the assistance provided by the expert that helps the child move to a higher level of learning. The task itself is not changed, but the level or amount of assistance is gradually decreased until the child is able to perform the task independently. Bruner (1985b) finds the scaffolding provided by the expert (e.g., teacher, caregiver, or older child) to be important to the learning process. The scaffold provides a stable structure that enables a child to try out new knowledge with assistance, with the supports gradually decreased as the child becomes more capable. Scaffolding takes the form of directions, cues, modeling, or demonstrating, as well as many other learning guides. A young child learning to repeat a favorite nursery rhyme starts saying a few words along with his caregiver. After repeating the rhyme, he begins to say more and more words independently, while his caregiver leaves pauses in the rhyme to allow the child to "fill in the blanks." This is an example of scaffolding, where the support is gradually withdrawn as the child becomes more independent with his task.

Expressive language. A second major contribution attributed to Vygotsky is the emphasis on expressive language as a child interacts with her environment. Children use the tool of language to master themselves and gain independence of behavior and thought (Vygotsky, 1986). If you listen to young children at play, you will often hear them talking to themselves, whether explaining what will happen in their play or directing their own actions. According to Vygotsky, young children use their **self-talk** (private speech) for self-guidance and self-direction. We all use self-talk; in fact as I am sitting at the computer, I often read sentences out loud to check for comprehension.

Language development and cognitive ability are affected by interactions children have with others. Infants begin responding to language at birth, and by 3 or 4 months of age, they will smile or turn toward the sound of a familiar voice. The interaction with the environment has a profound impact on language development, as children connect words to concrete objects and activities and form a framework for their thinking and communicating. Table 3.3 highlights the language development of young children.

Applying Vygotsky's theory. A classroom or environment set up around Vygotskian thinking would find the adult planning many activities around guided or assisted discovery. Both Piaget and Vygotsky support discovery learning. The major difference is Vygotsky's incorporation of **guided learning;** that is, an adult or older child assists the child in the learning process. Piaget would have suggested that children learn through their individual interactions with the environment, choosing not to emphasize the roles of others as having an impact on learning, as Vygotsky proposed.

Language plays an active role in guided discovery, with the adult talking about the activity, asking questions, and encouraging the child to describe what he is doing throughout the activity. A rich context for language development would include time for reading, storytelling, sharing and discussions, and, when developmentally appropriate, introducing written symbols of language. There would also be many opportunities to interact with others and become involved in cooperative learning experiences. Children would be working together, sharing ideas and skills to help each other. The voices of many children would be heard as they talked about their interactions and explained their activities to themselves, each other, and adults.

■ **TABLE 3.3 Development of Language**

Age in Months	Characteristics of Vocalization and Language
4	Coos and chuckles
6–9	Babbles; duplicates common sounds; produces sounds such as "ma" or "da"
12–18	A small number of words; follows simple commands and responds to no; uses expressive jargon
18–21	Vocabulary grows from about 20 words at 18 months to about 200 words at 21; points to many more objects; comprehends simple questions; forms 2-word phrases
24–27	Vocabulary of 200 to 400 words; has 2- or 3-word phrases; uses prepositions and pronouns
30–33	Fastest increase in vocabulary; 3- to 4-word sentences are common; word order, phrase structure, and grammatical agreement approximate the language of surroundings, but many utterances are unlike anything an adult would say
36–39	Vocabulary of 1,000 words or more; well-formed sentences using complex grammatical rules, although certain rules have not yet been fully mastered; grammatical mistakes are much less frequent; about 90 percent comprehensible

Source: "Adults Talk and Children's Language Development" by F. F. Schacher and A. A. Strage from *The Young Child: Reviews of Research* (vol. 3) by S. G. Moore and C. R. Cooper (Eds.) (p. 83), 1982, Washington, DC: NAEYC. Copyright 1982 by NAEYC. Reprinted with permission from the National Association for the Education of Young Children.

The teacher or caregiver would also be aware of each child's zone of proximal development and provide activities to engage the child in an activity that required assistance (scaffolding) from a peer or adult. To meet the children's learning needs, many small group activities would be arranged according to the children's current level of development and their zone of proximal development.

Both cognitive development and language development have an impact on children's social and emotional development. Children need emotionally healthy lives in order to fully develop their cognitive and language skills. They also need frequent opportunities to interact with others as they grow socially. Let's turn our attention to social and emotional development and how you could support a young child's development in these areas.

Social and Emotional Development

Social and emotional development are at the heart of effective early childhood programs. Early childhood professionals acknowledge the importance of creating an environment that truly supports and encourages healthy social and emotional growth. **Social development** of a child reflects the standards and values of her family and of her

What are some emotions this child might be experiencing?

society. The child begins to learn acceptable or appropriate behaviors at birth and continues to learn behavior patterns through her relationships with others, adapting these behaviors to her unique personality (Gordon & Browne, 1993). These behaviors are established by the society within which the child lives and become the social expectations that guide social development and the child's interactions with others. **Emotions** are feelings, some of which are complex. At some time in your life, you have felt anger, fear, pride, satisfaction, sorrow, frustration, joy, confidence, hate, or love. Even as an adult, perhaps you have found it difficult to communicate some of these feelings. Young children's feelings grow out of their interaction with their environment and their responses to these interactions. Early childhood is the time when children learn to notice, accept, and express their feelings as they develop emotionally. The child is forming a sense of self.

The foundation for healthy social and emotional growth is established in a child's early years. As an early childhood professional, you have a great responsibility to understand theories of social and emotional development and to be able to translate these theories into sound practice. Many social and emotional behaviors are learned through responses to an individual's behavior, observations of adult or peer behaviors, trying out different roles through play, and opportunities for social interaction. The term **socialization** describes the process of learning which behaviors are appropriate for specific situations. Let's learn more about social development through Erik Erikson's theory of psychosocial development.

Erikson's Theory of Psychosocial Development

Erik Erikson (1902–1994) is considered to be a **psychosocialist,** one who believes that how individuals respond to the demands of society at different stages of life affects development and acquisition of skills and abilities to become contributing members of society (Berk, 1996a). Erikson focused his attention on children's behavior. According to him, interpersonal relationships reveal the core of a person's makeup or personality (Maier, 1978). Based on specific behaviors, Erikson placed a child at a certain stage or level of development according to the description of that level and the match between the child's behavior and the level of development. Erikson's theory of human development is based on the concept that individuals move through development stages as they face problems or crises throughout their lives. When a person successfully solves conflict at earlier stages, then the person moves to the next of the eight life stages, as seen in Table 3.4. Achievement at each stage is dependent on learning and development at prior levels.

■ TABLE 3.4 Erikson's Eight Stages of Psychosocial Development

Stage	Approximate Age	Description
1. Basic trust vs. basic mistrust	Birth to 12–18 months	The infant must form a loving, trusting relationship with the caregiver, or develop a sense of mistrust.
2. Autonomy vs. shame/doubt	18 months to 3 years	The child's energies are directed toward the development of physical skills, including walking, grasping, and sphincter control. The child learns control but may develop shame and doubt if not handled well.
3. Initiative vs. guilt	3 to 6 years	The child continues to become more assertive and to take more initiative, but may be too forceful, leading to guilt feelings.
4. Industry vs. inferiority	6 to 12 years	The child must deal with demands to learn new skills or risk a sense of inferiority, failure, and incompetence.
5. Identity vs. role confusion	Adolescence	The teenager must achieve a sense of identity in occupation, sex roles, politics, and religion.
6. Intimacy vs. isolation	Young adulthood	The young adult must develop intimate relationships or suffer feelings of isolation.
7. Generativity vs. stagnation	Middle adulthood	Each adult must find some way to satisfy and support the next generation.
8. Ego integrity vs. despair	Late adulthood	The culmination is a sense of acceptance of oneself as one is and of feeling fulfilled.

Source: Lester A. Lefton, *Psychology* (4th ed.) (p. 350). Copyright © 1991 by Allyn and Bacon. Adapted by permission.

This infant is able to enjoy a new experience with someone he trusts.

Trust versus mistrust.   In the first stage of psychosocial development, **trust versus mistrust,** an infant is dependent on adults to meet all of her needs. When an adult responds to the cries or discomfort of the infant in a consistent manner, the infant develops trust for the world around her. Infants need consistent care provided by warm, responsive adults who attend to the infant when she is uncomfortable or in need, as well as times when she may want company or interaction with others. When the infant learns that she can depend on others for predictable care, she will then be able to develop trust. At this point, she has resolved the conflict of discomfort by trusting that an adult will help her. At approximately 12 to 18 months of age, she will then move into the second stage.

Autonomy versus doubt and shame.   During the **autonomy versus doubt and shame stage,** children are generally from 18 months to 3 years of age. Children are now testing their independence by assuming more self-responsibilities. This is a busy time, when toddlers explore a rapidly expanding world as they begin to walk and talk. They are also learning to dress and feed themselves, and begin toileting skills. Children at this age are also finding out what they like and do not like, and they will clearly let others know their opinions, even as those opinions change frequently throughout the day.

Erikson believes that adults must provide guidance through support for the child's efforts at independence. If not, the child begins to doubt her own ability to master important tasks and skills, which would lead to lower self-confidence and self-esteem and result in shame and doubt. The role of the adult is critical in supporting and supervising this new independence, and in helping the child feel that she is responsible and capable.

Journal 3.3: Have you ever seen a 2-year-old at the grocery store who wants to put the cereal box into the grocery cart? The child might say, "Me do." Even though the cart may be too high for the child to reach over, with a little help from an adult, the box can go into the cart. What might happen if the adult decides to take the cereal box away and put it into the cart himself? What might the child do and say? Describe what this could mean to the child in terms of Erikson's autonomy versus doubt stage. ■

Initiative versus guilt.   From 3 to 6 years of age, the young child is in the **initiative versus guilt stage.** Now that the child has resolved the crises during his time of growing autonomy, the child is ready to take initiative in planning some actions. He is interested in developing an idea and seeing it take place in action. Adults can encourage this curiosity and desire to take charge and help channel these activities into positive experiences. Erikson points out that if the child continually finds his actions result in "unhappy" events, he will develop guilt feelings.

Nurturing the child's independence and listening to his plans helps the adult head off major problems and guide the child to successful ventures. For instance, a 5-year-old brings his favorite book to day care and wants to take it to the sandbox outside. Because of rain earlier in the day, the sand is wet. Wet sand is great for trucks and road building, but not so great for favorite books. You talk to the child about leaving the book in a special place and finding a construction truck or shovel to take to the sandbox. He agrees and makes sure his book is in a safe place before going outside to play. This exchange helped the child "save" his book and still take the initiative in bringing something out to the sandbox. It also helped avoid the guilt that could develop from ruining a favorite book.

Industry versus inferiority.   During the elementary school years, from age 6 to 12, children enter the crisis of **industry versus inferiority** stage. This period is characterized by many new challenges and the introduction to learning the laws and expectations of society. Children are learning to read, to engage with a larger group of peers, and to master more and more complex skills. Productivity is necessary to complete assignments at school.

Children who find they are successful in their schoolwork and in their activities learn that industry and productivity are pleasant. When children find themselves repeatedly failing at school or in other settings, they begin feeling inferior and decide that they are inadequate. Helping children establish reasonable goals for themselves is an important learning tool. You want children to set realistic goals and maintain the motivation needed to reach these goals. Success must also be seen through the child's eyes in order for it to be believed. Helping children deemphasize their mistakes and focus on the steps needed to progress forward helps them learn to solve problems and gain satisfaction from their accomplishments.

The final four stages of psychosocial development include identity versus role confusion, intimacy versus isolation, generativity versus stagnation, and ego integrity versus despair. These stages begin at puberty and continue through late adult life.

Facing conflicts and crises.   Throughout each of Erikson's eight stages of psychosocial development, people face conflicts and **crises.** In Erikson's theory, crises occur when one needs to respond to a psychological challenge, which may mean adjusting behavior to meet society's expectations. The reaction to and resolution of these conflicts constructs an individual's social development. According to Erikson, each person learns how to interact with others based on personal experiences with conflict, crises, and resolution of these problems. You form who you are and how you relate to others and to society by your experiences and responses to crises throughout these eight stages of development. Difficulties may arise when the negative aspects are more prevalent than the positive for any given stage (Newman & Newman, 1991).

Gender and social development.   Moving through crises and stages of social development lead to the establishment of an individual identity. According to Erikson (1968), "Identity . . . is experienced merely as a sense of psychological well-being. Its most obvious concomitants are a feeling of being at home in one's body, a sense of 'knowing where one is going' and an inner assuredness of anticipated recognition of those who count" (p. 165). A major aspect of identity formation comes from the recognition of gender roles in one's life. Gender roles vary from society to society, which again points to the importance of studying child development within the context of social and cultural contexts.

In the United States, many adults are surprised to find that young children are still treated with different expectations according to their gender, even at a very young age. The perception of gender-typed behavior traits of women and men (e.g., women are warm and communicative, whereas men are assertive and rational) was studied in this country (Bergen & Williams, 1991) and in Europe, Africa, Asia, and Australia (Williams & Best, 1990). These studies showed that these stereotypes are still prevalent. Other studies found that parents of preschool children were unaware that they respond differently to boys and to girls (Fagot, 1978). Caregivers and teachers have a great impact in this area; for example, girls who have gone on to careers in science-related fields report that encouragement received from a teacher influenced their career choice (American Association of University Women, 1992). In his later work, Erikson (1974) noted that changes in society regarding gender roles have occurred since his earlier writing and he predicted that "modern life may come to permit a much freer inter-identification of the sexes in everyday life" (p. 333).

Applying Erikson's theory.   Erikson's theories bring important messages to your work with young children. Your understanding of the four stages or levels of development associated with early childhood and of the major crises associated with each stage will assist you in nurturing the social growth of young children in your care. Realizing that a toddler is attempting to establish her independence and take initiative in her activities helps you support her in reaching her goal. Recognizing that an infant is learning to trust others when you provide consistent and warm care lets you think about the far-reaching consequences of your interactions with this infant.

Erikson also emphasizes the significance of play and opportunities for children to take the initiative and to make choices in their play. Often, the primary role of the adult is to observe children at play and allow them to experience the consequences of their actions (of course, within safety limits). For example, establishing a time for "free play" helps young children learn to make their own choices of activities within their day. They might also learn that other children choose this same activity and consequently toys or play space may need to be shared. Learning the social skills necessary for sharing through their own initiative is much more valuable than being told to share by an adult. You provide the support by establishing clear boundaries within which the children learn social expectations of different situations.

Play is also considered to be an environment where gender roles are acted out. We want to pay close attention to avoiding stereotyping of gender roles. All children should have access to dolls, trucks, science kits, balls, dress-up clothes and quiet time activities. The language of the adult can affect a child's interest in an activity. For instance, telling a girl that she should be a nurse instead of the doctor would be a flagrant example of gender typing that must be avoided. Many responses to children are made without recognizing the bias of gender typing. Gender fair practices and encouragement to try out different roles in play activities must be a conscious effort made by caregivers and teachers, with tremendous implications in social development and the formation of identity. The environment and activities that caregivers and teachers create plays a major role in social development; learning how to relate to others.

Social and emotional development are closely related. In order to interact positively with others, a child needs a healthy self-image. Maslow developed a hierarchy of emotional development that will be helpful as you create an environment that supports and promotes the social and emotional development of young children.

Maslow's Theory of Humanism

The work of Abraham Maslow (1908–1970) has presented important implications for the emotional development of children. Maslow's theory is considered **humanistic** because its core is based on the belief that all people are motivated by fulfilling certain needs. Maslow studied the needs, goals, and accomplishments of successful people and used this information to construct a hierarchy, or ladder, of needs. In order for people to reach the highest level of self-actualization, all physiological needs and social-emotional needs must first be met. **Physiological** needs refer to what you need in order to be physically comfortable (e.g., food when hungry or a warm place to be when it is snowing outside). **Social-emotional** needs include feeling as if you belong to a group and are loved. When these needs are met, you may then move to higher levels toward **self-actualization,** where you realize your individual potential.

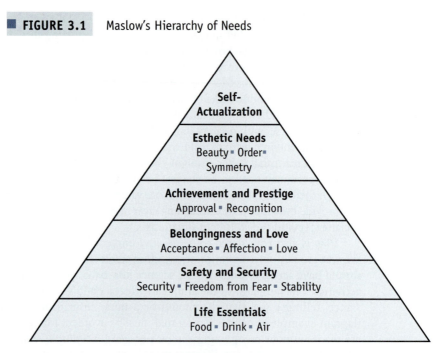

■ **FIGURE 3.1** Maslow's Hierarchy of Needs

Source: "Maslow's Hierarchy of Needs" from *Motivation and Personality,* 3rd Edition by Abraham H. Maslow, Revised by Robert Frager et al. Copyright © 1954, 1987 by Harper & Row, Publishers, Inc. Copyright © 1970 by Abraham H. Maslow. Reprinted by permission of Addison-Wesley Educational Publishers, Inc.

Maslow's self-actualization pyramid. According to Maslow (1987), people move through these six levels in a pyramid sequence as their needs are met, as shown in Figure 3.1. Each person begins at the bottom level, with the most basic needs of food, shelter, and clothing, and then progresses to the sixth level. The sixth level represents self-actualization, where one focuses on attaining meaningfulness or goodness. Maslow claimed that a person moving through the levels will stop trying to meet a high-level need if the person becomes deprived of a lower-level need. The focus is then on satisfying the lower-level need first (Maslow, 1987).

Motivation to move to higher levels occurs after the basic needs are met at prior levels. For example, you may recall a time when you were extremely hungry—perhaps your busy schedule forced you to miss a meal. At that time, it was difficult to think about the beauty in the scenery outside your window as your stomach was growling. You were most concerned with taking care of your hunger. The same situation occurs with young children, and they often do not have the ability to figure out how or where they will obtain food. When a young child is hungry and frustrated, you can imagine how difficult it would be for that child to be fully engaged in a learning activity.

Applying Maslow's theory. Maslow's theory brings helpful insights to those working with young children. For instance, when an infant is uncomfortable with a wet diaper, she lets you know by crying and squirming. This child would have difficulty focusing

These children are content with a picnic on a summer day. Which of their needs, according to Maslow's hierarchy, appear to be met in this scene?

on the different objects in her mobile hanging above her play area. What she really wants is to get rid of the terrible feeling of a wet diaper. Once the diaper has been changed and the baby is comforted, she might then be interested in looking around and reaching out for nearby objects.

The same is true with a child in a kindergarten setting. Think of a child entering a new school and not knowing any of the other children or the teacher. He probably doesn't feel too safe or secure; in fact, he may want his parent, sibling, or caregiver to stay at school for a while to provide the needed security and safety. His teacher might spend some time showing him around the room and introducing him to a few children, watching to see if he begins to feel more comfortable. Again, the child needs to have his basic needs met (in this case, security and safety) before moving into a new and unfamiliar situation where he feels ready to explore and learn in his new classroom.

Caregivers and teachers working with young children find it critical to be attuned to these needs and to provide the support needed. This might mean finding a snack for a hungry child, keeping several warm sweatshirts available for cooler days, or spending some extra time with a child who seems to need extra attention. Maslow's theory proposes that children who have their basic needs met are more likely to achieve positive self-images. Children who feel good about themselves are also more apt to be interested in socializing with others.

Within social and emotional development is the critical area of moral growth and development. Moral development is included within the broader category of social and emotional development, as moral development and reasoning strongly influence social and emotional interactions.

Kohlberg's Theory of Moral Development

Moral development influences understanding the impact of an individual's actions and decisions on others within society. Have you ever wondered how young children perceive what is right or wrong? Or how they make a decision about what is wrong or bad?

■ **FIGURE 3.2**   Kohlberg's Stage Theory of Moral Reasoning

---

Level 1: Preconventional Moral Reasoning

Judgment is based on personal needs and others' rules.

Stage 1   *Punishment-Obedience Orientation*
               Rules are obeyed to avoid punishment. A good or a bad action is determined
               by its physical consequences.

Stage 2   *Personal Reward Orientation*
               Personal needs determine right and wrong. Favors are returned along the
               lines of "You scratch my back, I'll scratch yours."

Level 2: Conventional Moral Reasoning

Judgment is based on others' approval, family expectations, traditional values, the laws
of society, and loyalty to country.

Stage 3   *Good Boy–Nice Girl Orientation*
               Good means "nice." It is determined by what pleases, aids, and is approved
               by others.

Stage 4   *Law and Order Orientation*
               Laws are absolute. Authority must be respected and the social order
               maintained.

Level 3: Postconventional Moral Reasoning

Stage 5   *Social Contract Orientation*
               Good is determined by socially agreed-upon standards of individual rights.
               This is a morality similar to that of the U.S. Constitution.

Stage 6*   *Universal Ethical Principle Orientation*
               Good and right are matters of individual conscience and involve abstract
               concepts of justice, human dignity, and equality.

---

*In later work, Kohlberg questioned whether Stage 6 exists separately from Stage 5.
Source: "The Claim to Moral Adequacy of a Highest Stage of Moral Judgment" by L. Kohlberg,
1973, *Journal of Philosophy, 70,* pp. 631–632. Adapted by permission.

Or why they might choose to go ahead and do something that they know might be considered wrong? These questions lead to thinking about the development of morals.

Piaget and Kohlberg have contributed to knowledge of children's moral development. Both theorists propose that children go through a sequence of levels as they develop more reasoning power and understand consequences for specific behaviors. The development progressing through more advanced stages indicates that cognitive reasoning and social experiences influence progression through levels of moral development (Damon, 1988).

Kohlberg's stages of moral reasoning.   Perhaps the most widely accepted hierarchy of stages of moral development is the one developed by Lawrence Kohlberg (1927–1987), as shown in Figure 3.2. Kohlberg conducted his studies on moral reasoning by presenting a child with **moral dilemmas,** or situations where a child has to decide the best outcome for a problem situation and where the situation has no seemingly right or wrong answer. The children participating in the study were asked to decide what a person involved in the dilemma should do and why. The child's response would then indicate at which level the child was functioning: Level 1—Preconventional Moral Reasoning, Level 2—Conventional Moral Reasoning, or Level 3—Postconventional Moral Reasoning.

Similar to the descriptions of development in other domains, children and adults do not always reach the highest levels of development. Although the stages are loosely connected to age ranges, individuals move through stages at different times in their lives (Kohlberg, 1976). In early childhood settings, you will find most of the children operating at preconventional reasoning in level 1, according to Kohlberg's model.

Moral development is closely related to cognitive and emotional development. It would be difficult for a child who has not developed her ability to think at abstract levels to make moral decisions based on higher-level thought. Kohlberg recognized that thinking is required to make moral decisions. His work expressed the need to increase awareness of moral reasoning, both in one's own thinking and in that of others (Hersh, Paolitto, & Reimer, 1979). At the same time, Kohlberg was cognizant of the role of moral reasoning within a democracy and the important role teachers play in facilitating the development of moral reasoning.

How do children learn moral reasoning? Witherell (1991) suggests that promoting genuine dialogue in the classroom or child care setting is a format to help children make sense of their world. Witherell also feels that sharing stories serves as a springboard for discussing moral or ethical action. Other educators also see communication and dialogue about events occurring in the classroom, both within the curriculum and within the daily life of school (e.g., situations that arise during play), as important opportunities for discussions about moral reasoning. According to Kohlberg's stage model, young children make moral decisions based on avoiding punishment and an expectation of a reward for good behavior. However, children need more than a "Yes, that's right" or a "No, that's wrong." To develop their moral reasoning, children need opportunities to stretch beyond their current abilities to reason and learn the rationale for the rules and the perspective of others (Hersh, Paolitto, & Reimer, 1979). Children begin to develop an awareness of moral standards and empathy generally in their second year of life (Lamb, 1991). This suggests to early childhood professionals that very young children are attending to issues of right and wrong, which supports the rationale to respond to young children with their level of moral reasoning in mind.

Applying Kohlberg's theory.   Some people feel that schools or other public settings should not include moral education in their curricula. In reality, caregivers and teachers continually communicate moral messages to children. The interpretation of rules and children's behaviors reflect moral judgments (DeVries & Zan, 1994). Young children grapple with moral issues based on observable behaviors and immediate consequences. A close look at the interactions and realities of a day-to-day life in a school or child care situation reveals the inherent inclusion of moral development and the need to attend to learning how to support moral development.

Perhaps the most important consideration for adults working with young children is to respect each child and her individual values. Children at a young age are aware of justice and fairness in their environment and recognize when they are treated with respect or disrespect. Each child brings her own value system and stage of moral development with her to the child care setting or classroom and needs to know that her beliefs are honored.

When an adult understands that children might have a different perspective of right and wrong, they are better able to help a child learn to distinguish from acceptable and unacceptable actions. Learning from Kohlberg's theory of moral development will assist you in recognizing the stage in which a child might be currently operating. For example, when a 2-year-old takes another child's toy that was brought from home and runs to the other side of the room to examine the toy, you would not consider this "stealing." If a similar action occurred with an 8-year-old child in a store, then this probably would be considered taking an item that did not belong to him. In the case of the 2-year-old, you might briefly explain, "This is Trina's toy. Let's check with Trina to see if you can look at it, perhaps with her." Children develop their personal value system through their experiences and observing the modeling of others—rarely from being told what to do or what not to do.

Within the early childhood setting, there must also be room for children to make decisions and learn from the results of their own decision making. When situations a 5-year-old child worked through did not seem to turn out quite right, brief discussions or sharing a story about a similar incident might be helpful. The focus of the discussion might be to look at possible alternative behaviors that the child might select if he is in a similar situation again.

The caregiver or teacher's role is also one of noting when actions, incidents, or behaviors occur that reflect conflicts in moral reasoning. Name calling, pushing, taking toys, and not sharing are behaviors that occur in all early childhood settings. The response to these behaviors is how children reason about right and wrong. These conflicts become rich learning tools when used as discussion and reflection opportunities.

Journal 3.4: In Frannie's backyard, a group of 2- and 3-year-olds are playing together in a small wading pool. Renee reaches over and grabs the boat from Franklin's hand. He starts to fuss and wants the boat back. What might Frannie say or do that reflects Renee's level of moral reasoning and also responds to this situation? ■

Another theory of social learning is behaviorism. Behaviorists consider interactions in the social environment an essential aspect of learning. According to behaviorists, a child's behavior is shaped by responses encountered in the child's environment.

Skinner's Theory of Behaviorism

The theory of **behaviorism** is based on the belief that learning is a change in observable behavior occurring as a result of experience (Mazur, 1994). Theorists in this field were interested in changes in behavior as a result of consequences from a child's interactions with his environment. B. F. Skinner (1904–1990) was a behavioral psychologist who developed the theory of operant conditioning (learning through responses and consequences).

Operant conditioning.   Have you ever found a piece of chocolate in the kitchen cupboard, bitten into it, and been unpleasantly surprised to find it was unsweetened chocolate meant for baking? You experienced an immediate consequence for your behavior. It is likely that you changed this behavior by reading labels or asking others about the chocolate before taking a large bite next time. This is an example of **operant conditioning,** where an unpleasant consequence for behavior leads to changes in subsequent actions.

Skinner began his research with rats, which he placed in a Skinner Box and rewarded with food pellets when the rats touched a bar in the box. After a rat learned to press the bar for food, changes were implemented in the procedure. For instance, the rat may need to press the bar three times in succession to receive the food pellet, or the rat may have to listen for a tone before pressing the bar to receive food. To **extinguish** (or terminate) the behavior, food was not given when the bar was pressed and the rat no longer bothered to press the bar. By controlling the environment, Skinner was able to prove that **reinforcing** (providing a desirable consequence following a behavior) the rat's behavior led to changes in behavior. These experiments were the basis of his theory of operant conditioning, where behavior is influenced by the consequences following the behavior (Woolfolk, 1998).

Consequences, the events that follow an action, lead to changed behavior. The use of **reinforcement** (use of consequences to alter behavior) or **punishment** (action that decreases the likelihood of the behavior occurring again) is purposely implemented to create change in behavior. Returning to the scientific experiments with the Skinner Boxes and rats, you will recall that the behavior of pressing the bar in the box resulted in food. The behavior (pressing the bar) resulted in a consequence that was reinforcing (food).

Operant conditioning is one form of behaviorism, with a focus on observable behavior. Each day, you knowingly and unknowingly experience principles of behaviorism. A mother working with her toddler son on toilet training hugs him and gives him a cookie when he uses his potty chair. They both are delighted. This is an example of reinforcing behavior with a reward. The scientific application model of behaviorism (e.g., the rat experiment) might be construed as manipulative on the far end of the continuum of the use of behaviorism. It helps to remember that there is a continuum, or range, of behaviorism, with applications that may be appropriate in certain situations.

Applying Skinner's theory.   In a preschool setting, you might notice Stewart showing his painting to the teaching assistant, Marion. Marion responds, "What a beautiful sun you made." This response might be considered reinforcement by Stewart, who returns to the painting easel and continues painting suns. The child continues a behavior that is praised.

 Journal 3.5: What might be another reinforcement typically used in a preschool setting? How do you feel about the use of reinforcement in promoting learning? ■

In a different scenario at this preschool, Tracy keeps poking Brad. Marion walks over to Tracy and asks her to sit in the corner or to take a time-out. The time-out would be a punishment for the behavior of poking, with the plan that this consequence will decrease the behavior. Marion wants Tracy to eliminate, or extinguish, this behavior, so she creates a punishment (e.g., time-out).

One limitation in using operant conditioning with children is identifying reinforcements and punishments that matter to the child. Some children might be dissatisfied with the response Stewart received about his painting—perhaps they wanted Marion to notice the boats they had painted—so the comment on the suns would not be a reinforcement that would increase the likelihood of the behavior occurring again. With the poking incident, Tracy might like some quiet time, so time-out for her is not a punishment. She might also like to attract Marion's attention, so she might have seen that consequence as a reinforcement.

An even greater limitation is found in looking only at observable behavior and consequences. This approach to working with children minimizes the child's thinking and understanding of the situation. Making decisions based only on observable behavior and not on a child's interpretation of events or your interpretation of the child's reasoning raises some concerns about control and imposing one's judgments on the children in your care. Understanding the effects of praise, reinforcement, and punishment helps bring into focus a larger picture of working with young children. Recognizing the impact of one's statements—as simple as "Great work"—on a child's behavior helps the early childhood professional make decisions about the use of reinforcement and punishment in her setting. Children might come to expect reinforcement for their learning, which would affect learning if an adult were not present (Kohn, 1993).

By understanding the principles of behaviorism and operant conditioning, an early childhood professional can make decisions about when it is appropriate to use consequences, reinforcement, or punishment. Let's explore another important theory that influences early childhood education programs and the curriculum design within programs. Components from prior theories discussed in this chapter are incorporated into the model of multiple intelligences.

Multiple Intelligences Theory

The theory of **multiple intelligences (MI theory)** draws from each developmental domain and proposes there are at least eight separate human capacities that compose the plurality of intellect (Checkley, 1997). Instead of thinking of intelligence as a narrow measure, Gardner presents eight different intelligences, within which each person is capable of further development and growth.

Gardner's Theory of Multiple Intelligences

Howard Gardner (born in 1943) refers to **intelligence** as having more to do with solving problems and fashioning products within a naturalistic setting (Armstrong, 1994) than the artificial setting posed by most intelligence tests. The definition of intelligence as defined by an intelligence test is far more artificial than that posed by Gardner. Intelligence, as scored on tests, basically refers to what a person is born with; it is measurable and can be tested. Gardner's definition examines what a person does with an ability. In addition to the ability to solve problems and create products, a specific intelligence must also meet the following three criteria:

1. Is there a particular representation for this ability in the brain?

2. Do we know of populations that are particularly talented or particularly deficient in this ability?

3. Is there an evolutionary history of this intelligence that can be found in animals other than human beings? (Checkley, 1997)

Every human being has the capacity for developing within each of the eight intelligences, but varying degrees of expertise are displayed with the different intelligences. In order to develop a program for young children based on MI theory, you would want to know more about the children's abilities, interests, and accomplishments within each of the eight intelligences, as outlined in Table 3.5.

■ **TABLE 3.5** Gardner's Multiple Intelligences

Intelligence	Processing Operations	End-State Performance Possibilities
Linguistic	Sensitivity to the sounds, rhythms, and meanings of words and the different functions of language	Poet, journalist
Logico-mathematical	Sensitivity to, and capacity to detect, logical or numerical patterns; ability to handle long chains of logical reasoning	Mathematician, scientist
Musical	Ability to produce and appreciate pitch, rhythm (or melody), and aesthetic-sounding tones; understanding of the forms of musical expressiveness	Violinist, composer
Spatial	Ability to perceive the visual-spatial world accurately, to perform transformations on those perceptions, and to recreate aspects of visual experience in the absence of relevant stimuli	Sculptor, navigator
Bodily-kinesthetic	Ability to use the body skillfully for expressive as well as goal-directed purposes; ability to handle objects skillfully	Dancer, athlete
Interpersonal	Ability to detect and respond appropriately to the moods, temperaments, motivations, and intentions of others	Therapist, salesperson
Intrapersonal	Ability to discriminate complex inner feelings and to use them to guide one's own behavior; knowledge of one's own strengths, weaknesses, desires, and intelligences	Person with detailed, accurate self-knowledge
Naturalistic	Ability to recognize, discriminate and classify living things as well as sensitivity to other features of the natural world	Botanist, farmer

Sources: The first seven intelligences: "Gardner's Multiple Intelligences" adapted from *Frames of Mind* by Howard Gardner. Copyright © 1983 by Howard Gardner. Reprinted by permission of BasicBooks, a division of HarperCollins Publishers, Inc. The eighth intelligence: K. Checkley, "The First Seven . . . and the Eighth," *Educational Leadership 55,* 1: 8–13. (excerpt p. 12). Used by permission of the Association for Supervision and Curriculum Development. Copyright © 1997 by ASCD. All rights reserved.

The eight intelligences. Let's now take a closer look at each of the eight intelligences, according to descriptions by Gardner (1993a), Checkley (1997), and Armstrong (1994). At the same time, teaching strategies that promote learning in each intelligence will be discussed.

Linguistic intelligence, the use of language, is seen in the ability to read, write, or talk to others. Obviously, this intelligence is highly valued in schools. The primary focus in the early years of elementary school is on literacy development, which demonstrates linguistic intelligence. Storytelling is a teaching strategy that allows the caregiver or teacher to weave in concepts, details, or goals that are appropriate to the children. Storytelling has been used for centuries as a medium to share knowledge.

Logico-mathematical intelligence refers to logic and mathematical ability. The ability to use numbers, understand patterns, and exhibit reason are the key characteristics of logical-mathematical intelligence. Certainly, mathematical learning is valued, as evidenced in school curriculum. *Categorization,* for instance, is a teaching strategy that is developmentally appropriate for young children and supports logical learning. Children as young as 3 and 4 years old enjoy sorting materials according to categories, some that they create and others created by those around them. A 4-year-old might sort items by color, then by size, and then according to use. Older children could also record their findings, creating charts and displays of their categorization findings.

Musical intelligence is the ability to perform musically or to produce written music. People who are highly skilled in musical intelligence think in music patterns or see and hear patterns and are able to manipulate these patterns. Do you remember singing your ABCs? This is an example of a teaching strategy that helped you learn the alphabet. Songs for counting, colors, names, and other familiar objects promote learning through musical intelligence.

Spatial intelligence is the ability to create a visual image of a potential project or idea and then act on this visualization. Think of a bridge engineer or an interior decorator who must be able to "see" their ideas before creating them. *Visualization* is a powerful teaching strategy in spatial intelligence. A kindergarten teacher might ask a young child to close her eyes and see a gingerbread man running from the fox before she begins to draw a picture to represent the scene. Visualization can also be used to rehearse the steps or sequence of a task before starting the activity.

Bodily-kinesthetic intelligence refers to the ability to use one's own body or parts of the body as a medium of expression or to solve a problem. A ballet dancer and an Olympic athlete are examples of people who have refined their bodily-kinesthetic skills or intelligence. The use of *manipulatives* in teaching math is an excellent example of the combination of bodily-kinesthetic intelligence with other intelligences. Many young children touch their fingers as they count, using their own teaching strategy for learning the sequence of numbers.

Interpersonal intelligence is the sensitivity one has toward others, along with the ability to work well with other people, understand others, and assume leadership roles. *Sharing* is a way for young children to learn from each other and use their interpersonal intelligence. All ages benefit from sharing and interacting—children can share with peers as well as with children older or younger than them. Depending on the age

This preschool age child is using several senses to note the characteristics of a plant he found in his yard.

of the child, caregivers or teachers should adjust their amount of involvement in the directions and guidance of the sharing situation.

Intrapersonal intelligence is the accurate understanding of one's self (who one is, what one wants, and a realistic sense of what one can do) and the ability to act according to this knowledge. *Modeling* true-felt emotions with young children provides an avenue for children to observe the range of emotions of others. Once a child reaches school age, curriculum is typically presented in a neutral format, with little emotion shown by the teacher. Expressing joy, passion, disappointment, or other emotions sends a message that emotions are part of learning and are welcome in this setting.

Naturalistic intelligence is used to discriminate among living things, such as plants or animals, as well as an understanding of other features of the natural world, such as weather or geology. Farmers, botanists, and hunters are examples of roles where this intelligence is used. Spending time outside on a regular basis facilitates naturalistic intelligence. Touching, seeing, and smelling plants outdoors is far different from looking at pictures of the same plants. Asking questions about the differences and similarities between the plants is appropriate for children as young as age 3 or 4. Young children are very observant and can use their categorization or classification abilities with the abundance of natural materials outside their setting.

Armstrong (1994) outlined four key points in MI theory: (1) People possess all of these intelligences, (2) most people have the potential to develop further in each of the intelligences, (3) the intelligences work together, and (4) there are numerous ways intelligence can be interpreted within each category. Gardner's work with multiple intelligences led educators to a new way of looking at intelligence and learning.

Journal 3.6: In which of these eight intelligences do you feel you are strongest? What might have led to your development in this intelligence? In which area are you most challenged? What might you do to improve in this area? ■

Applying Gardner's theory. When you nurture children's individual abilities and build rich learning activities, you provide experiences in multiple disciplines. You also provide different ways to learn the same material or knowledge. Some children might learn the names of colors best by sorting colors, others by classifying their crayons, others by painting and drawing, others by memorizing colors according to familiar objects (e.g., school bus yellow or stop sign read), and others by singing a song about colors. Your role is to ensure that you use different teaching strategies to reach all your learners.

Gardner (1993b) proposes that an individual-centered school should assess an individual child's abilities, goals, and interests to match to particular curricula and to the ways of learning that prove comfortable for that child. Children should also be involved in experiences that continually stimulate them as they develop within each of the intelligences. There are multiple ways to learn and a variety of ways to show what each child has learned.

With this approach to curriculum, you would plan different activities that involve several of the multiple intelligences in a setting that includes hands-on learning and opportunities for children to explore their environment. An example of stimulating multiple intelligences would be when young children listen to a story about making musical instruments (linguistic intelligence), play musical instruments (musical intelligence), dance to the music (bodily-kinesthetic intelligence), make one of several instruments (spatial intelligence and logical-mathematical intelligence), work together to create a band to play the grand finale (interpersonal and intrapersonal intelligence), and create instruments selected from the natural environment, such as reeds (naturalistic intelligence), differentiating which types and sizes of plant make the best sound and why. Of course, not all activities would include all eight intelligences, but planning around the eight intelligences prior to an activity will help you incorporate multiple intelligences throughout a project.

In the next section of this chapter, you will have an opportunity to watch these theories in an early childhood classroom setting. Get ready to observe a group of preschoolers involved in learning!

Theory into Practice: A Visit to Preschool

Now that you have some beginning ideas about theories of development that influence early childhood education today, you are going to resume your visit to the Creative Learning Cooperative Preschool and observe this group of 4-year-old children. This is your time to examine the major developmental theories "in action." You will also explore what the different theorists might be interested in while observing the same activities along with you.

Starting the Day

As the children enter the preschool, their teacher, Keith, begins the morning by greeting each child with a personal comment. He tells Samantha, "I am so glad you shared your painting with 'new colors' with us. Today, we will all get a chance to try this out." The children also have news to share with Keith. Maria says to Keith, "My baby brother has a new tooth this morning." Maria's mother quietly tells Keith, "Maria was worried if you would be here today for some reason. She wanted me to come in the door with her, but then paid no attention to my presence."

Journal 3.7: Erikson suggests in the initiative versus guilt stage that young children are trying to be independent, yet may be too forceful in asserting their independence. What steps toward independence might Maria be testing? What supports might assist her in taking more initiative? ◼

Keith had placed some cups of juice and plates of graham crackers on the counter for anyone who was hungry for a morning snack. Gabriel, Jasmine, and Michael head straight for the crackers, talking about how hungry they are.

Journal 3.8: Which theorist would be nodding his head when he noticed the teacher taking time to greet each child and placing snacks on the counter? According to this theorist, why are these important actions to take place in the classroom? ◼

Making New Colors

Today, this class of 4-year-olds is exploring the principle of creating new colors by combining two primary colors. Their interest came about when Samantha was finger painting and mixed several colors together and excitedly told the children that she made "new colors." The other children started talking about making "new colors" and were eager to try out some of their ideas.

Journal 3.9: What might Piaget have to say about where the idea for this activity originated? ◼

Several learning centers are set up around the room, with a parent at each center. There are also some materials available on the counter, where children work independently and create their own activities. Some of these materials include transparent, colored pieces of plastic squares; food coloring and small jars of water; as well as crayons, chalk, paper, and some movable color wheels with primary colors.

Journal 3.10: Which theorists would be pleased to see the materials set out on the counter and available for children to use without adult direction? Why? ◼

You see that right inside the door, Marc and Jamie are working together with felt marking pens. They are sharing a large piece of paper clipped to an easel. Both boys have a set of markers and are making little circles, then coloring the circles in with the same marker. Two days ago, Keith read a story about painters who mixed paint together and made a new color from two old colors. The boys were following this theme with their marking pens and were trying out different color combinations by making a new colored circle on top of the first colored circle. Keith walks over, noticing their colors, and talks about the old colors and the new colors with the boys. They all named the new colors together.

Journal 3.11: What might Vygotsky say about the use of language in this color activity? ◼

As Keith moved toward another group of children, Marc and Jamie were heard talking about mixing three or more colors on top of their circles to see what would happen. After trying a few more combinations and getting muddier "new" colors, the boys began scribbling with the pens and chasing

An outdoor art activity creates an enjoyable learning experience.

each other's marker pen lines around the paper. They then put the pens down and began looking for something else to do.

Samantha and Jamil are at the painting area right outside the door. They helped each other put on paint aprons and asked a parent for paints and new paper on the easels. The parent brought over cups of finger paint and asked the children if they wanted to start by putting just one color on the paper. Samantha and Jamil both choose yellow paint, making large swoops on their paper. Jamil starts to paint on Samantha's paper and she tells him, "No." Samantha walks away to find Keith. Jamil then takes Samantha's cup of yellow paint away from her easel. Keith walks over and begins to talk quietly with Jamil.

Journal 3.12: What might Keith say to Jamil in light of Kohlberg's preconventional moral reasoning stage? ■

Jamil gives the yellow paint back to Samantha and they continue painting. The incident seems to be

forgotten. Samantha says, "This looks like a big banana." They then put their fingers into the container of red paint and add red on top of the yellow. Jamil exclaimed, "Wow! We made pumpkin orange!"

Outside in the Play Area

You hear many children's voices, happily calling out to each other somewhere around the corner of the building. As you wander over to the side of the building, you see a large play yard with a climbing structure and an area where children are playing with balls. You notice two parents outside with the children. Sandy is watching the children at play while visiting with several children in a sandbox, and Rudy is playing a game with a soccer ball and four children. The game involves saying the name of another child and kicking the ball to that child across the circle. Lots of giggles erupt when the ball heads to someone else other than the intended receiver.

In the sandbox, Scott, Tanisha, and J. R. are making tunnels, roads, and parking lots with scoops and small shovels. There are several yellow construction trucks moving through their building area, as they try out their highway system. They seem to be especially fond of the curves they made, as they go over and over the curves with small cars and trucks. Scott and Tanisha are talking about the roads and planning to add hills so they can try racing their cars around the curves and hills. You notice that Sandy is watching them, ready to help out if there are conflicts or "sandstorms."

Journal 3.13: Skinner is sitting with you outside watching the play in the sand box. What would he suggest Sandy do or say to increase the likelihood that the sand box play continues in a positive fashion? What would Skinner prompt Sandy to do if Tanisha started throwing sand on Scott and J. R.? ■

Colors and Music

Near the windows, a parent, Ralph, is playing a guitar while Roberto, Danny, and Jessie are composing a song about colors in the rainbow. The beginning of their song starts off with, "Blue is blue, yellow is yellow, but yellow with blue makes green!" The children are singing and dancing to their song, while Ralph follows their lead in creating their tune on the guitar. Marc and Jamie are drawn to the music and walk over to listen.

They begin swaying to the music and join in the singing.

Journal 3.14: Briefly describe several different intelligences you observed in the color and music activity, noting which activities connected to a specific area of intelligence. ■

Revisiting the Morning

Let's take a moment to reflect on some of our observations. In the first scenario, Marc and Jamie used the colored felt pens to make colors on the paper, and continued to draw circles and add new colors on top of the old colors. Because they were adding more and more colors, each combination created a brownish hue and they soon became bored with the activity. When Keith walked by and interacted with them about their two color combinations and named the colors with them, you observed their language use in color identification and an increased interest in the activity. You also observed that without new direction or guidance, they soon became bored with the activity and were ready to move to something different.

Both Piaget and Vygotsky would note that the children were interacting with their environment by experimenting with colors in various media, which supports both men's theories of discovery learning. Erikson would appreciate the choices of activities for the children, as well as the opportunities for interesting interactions among the children and adults in the setting. Bruner would agree with Erikson—that the children learn best when they choose their materials and discover principles independently. The materials available on the counter would enable the children to choose what they needed to "prove" their ideas. Also, open-ended questions from adults would help the children move toward proving their hypotheses or predicted outcomes of their experiments, again in alignment with Bruner's theory of discovery learning.

During the second scenario, the finger-painting activity, you saw guided direction provided by a parent. The results were interesting, and Samantha and Jamil expressed pleasure at creating a "new" color. Vygotsky would view this social interaction with a more knowledgeable adult as helping the child in the child's zone of proximal development, where the guidance supported new learning. He would also appreciate the use of language throughout the activity, along with the many opportunities for children to name their colors and shapes. Skinner might suggest a consequence or punishment, such as a time-out, when Jamil took Samantha's cup of paint. In this case, Keith chose to discuss with Jamil the feelings of others and to assist Jamil in moving toward an understanding of empathy or caring about the feelings of others.

As you continued to observe, you noticed that the children appeared engaged in their activities and felt free to leave one center and move to other sections of the room. They asked questions of the adults and of each other. You heard many conversations going on around the classroom. There was a sense of safety and security, with boundaries shared by the adults in relation to treating each other with respect. Maslow would find this atmosphere supportive of emotional growth, as indicated through the awareness of the teacher to the children's needs by welcoming them in the morning, offering snacks, and continually scanning the classroom to assure that children are safely engaged in interesting activities.

Journal 3.15: Nalani, Scott, and Jeremy are busy mixing colored water in different clear containers. A parent is working next to them, making his own colored creations and listening to their talk. He occasionally identifies his discovery by saying, "Oh, I mixed red and blue water and now I have purple." The children watch him and then try out their own combinations. Nalani also talks about her experiment. She says, "My blue and red makes pretty purple water. Be careful, Nalani, keep your water from spilling." What do you think Vygotsky might comment on regarding this observation? ■

The children continue to paint and watch each other's new colors appear. After a few minutes, Scott leaves to play with the blocks. Nalani is intent on making lots of new colors. She seems to be expending a lot of energy and, as a result of her efforts, is getting tired. After mixing the colors into her container, Nalani quickly pours her colored water onto the floor. She looks around to see if any adult has noticed the puddle she just made. Now she begins talking to herself, "Nalani, no, no, bad to put water on the floor. Uh oh!" She then hurries away from the puddle.

Journal 3.16: What type of moral reasoning might Nalani be applying in this situation and which of Kohlberg's stages seem to match her behavior? What would you do if you were the adult nearest to her? ■

It is the end of the morning now. The children and adults work together to clean up the different play areas. They had quite a busy morning, filled with many activities. The varied experiences involved colors and mixing colors. Gardner's theory of multiple intelligences was clearly attended to through the variety of activities around the theme of new colors, which supports the growth of intelligence in multiple ways.

Many of the theorists' major ideas and each of the different developmental areas discussed throughout the chapter were represented in this brief snapshot of a preschool morning. Keith, the teacher, had planned the curriculum for this morning to reflect the children's interests as well as their developmental levels. The curriculum also reflected Keith's personal philosophy of theories of development.

PRINCIPLES AND INSIGHTS: A Summary and Review

Whether looking at cognitive, language, social, or emotional development, theorists tend to agree that humans develop in a gradual and sequential process. Theorists also agree that individuals vary in the rate of their developmental growth. Culture and society play a role in the context of development, with some cultures emphasizing certain skills or accomplishments that guide a child's learning.

Each of these areas of development overlap, with growth in one area affecting the learning occurring in another developmental area. As the caregiver or teacher working with young children, you have the responsibility to create a rich learning environment based on the principles presented by theorists from each of the developmental domains. Gaining an understanding of these theories and approaches to learning will help you develop your own philosophy of working with young children, which then translates into the daily activities and experiences you create with and for them.

Piaget's work altered the way adults view the learning of young children. According to Piagetian thinking, children move through four stages of cognitive development, acquiring new knowledge, skills, and abilities in each stage. Piaget's work introduced the notion that children think differently at different ages. His theories led to the idea that experiences in early childhood programs can promote growth within a developmental stage and support movement to a more advanced stage.

Bruner followed Piaget's work, extending the theory of cognitive development. He identified three stages of cognitive development and supported the stance that learning occurs in these stages as children make meaning of their experiences. Discovery learning, as described by Bruner, is a powerful learning model. Through discovery learning, children interact with materials or examples and draw their own conclusions or general principles based on their investigations.

Vygotsky agreed with Piaget and Bruner about the impact that a child's interaction with the environment makes in learning. His work emphasized the importance of interactions with others and the connection between language and cognitive development. Vygotsky developed the theory of the zone of proximal development (ZPD), which illustrates the zone or space within which a child is learning. With assistance from an older child or adult, a child can achieve more or accomplish higher-level skills than if working alone. Gradually, less help is needed from others (scaffolding) as the child becomes more skilled or able to complete the task independently.

In the area of social development, Erikson identified eight stages of psychosocial development. The core of a child's personality is revealed through her interpersonal relationships (Maier, 1978). A child's personality is also shaped by the crises she encounters and her reactions to each crisis. The four stages of psychosocial development in early childhood present a framework that will help you understand the actions of children at different ages and stages of social development. For example, as you observe a toddler asserting her independence, you might draw on Erikson's theory that the child is testing her autonomy. Paying attention to these stages and the behaviors associated with each stage will help you plan activities and curriculum to support social growth in each stage.

Social and emotional development are closely related. Social development can be thought of as growth in interactions with others, whereas emotional development is the growth of a sense of self. Maslow's self-actualization pyramid reminds you that a child's basic needs must be met before she is ready to learn and to interact joyfully in her environment. Children's physiological needs—such as hunger, thirst, or rest—must be attended to before they willingly engage in learning activities.

Moral development falls within both social and emotional developmental areas. An understanding of Erikson's and Maslow's theories will assist you in understanding the social and emotional nature of moral reasoning. In order to make wise decisions about what is wrong or right, a child needs a stable sense of self and the ability to interact socially with others. Kohlberg developed a stage model of moral development, where children move from moral decisions based on following the rules to moral reasoning about different situations based on the specifics of that situation. Listening to stories and having discussions about everyday events (including conflicts in the child's setting) will help children reflect on other's decisions and think about how they might respond in a similar setting.

Each theorist discusses the impact of the child's interaction with her environment as part of the learning process in each developmental area. Behaviorists propose that altering the environment can change a person's behavior. Skinner's work with operant conditioning showed that the behavior of rats was shaped by changing the consequences or feeding schedule of the rats. With humans, applying a reinforcement or punishment following a behavior will strengthen or extinguish the behavior. Although behaviorism is used in everyday interactions, early childhood educators are encouraged to examine the practice and make purposeful decisions about when and how to use this model of social learning.

Gardner's work in multiple intelligences presents a learning model that acknowledges and supports the growth of learning in different formats. It is easy to assume that others learn like you, which might lead you to plan most activities to emphasize this area of intelligence. Becoming familiar with the eight intelligences, however, will assist you in planning activities that support learning in each of these areas. Diversity of varied types of experiences enables the young children in your care to grow and develop in multiple intelligences.

As you read the case studies in this book, take time to come back to this chapter and revisit the developmental theories. You will want to bring your new knowledge with you into the different early childhood programs presented in the case studies. Doing so will enable you to assess your emerging philosophy of early childhood education and ground your beliefs in the work of these notable theorists. Your understanding of these developmental theories will continue to increase and expand as you work with young children and observe the theories in practice.

Becoming an Early Childhood Professional

Your Field Experiences

1. Schedule an observation of young children in an early childhood setting. Select a theory of social or emotional development and a theory of cognitive or language development presented in this chapter. Look for practices that support each of these models of development as well as application of the models. Record your observation findings in a short paper, drawing from the theorist's perspective as you discuss the activities you observed.

2. During an observation, watch how the integration of developmental areas looks in reality. Knowing that children learn across developmental areas in most activi-

ties, select one activity that you observed and discuss the growth that might be occurring in different developmental areas.

Your Professional Portfolio

1. Thinking of an age group or developmental level of children that you are interested in working with, develop an activity that would address learning in four or more of the different intelligences. Identify each intelligence and discuss how the activity promotes learning in that area of intelligence. Create a chart that shows the relationship of an activity to multiple intelligences, and place it in your portfolio.

2. In a kindergarten class, children are using solid objects to explore the concept of conservation, as described by Piaget. The teacher stacked five books in one pile and the children talked about the characteristics of the books as well as the set of books. The teacher then moved the books into single spaces, essentially spreading out the five books on the rug. The children discussed what is different and what is the same between the two sets of five books. Now it's your turn to develop an activity about conservation, using solid objects. Develop a plan and use it to teach someone else in your class or a young child. The plan and your written reflection about the success and challenge of teaching this activity will become part of your portfolio.

Your Professional Library

Books

Berk, L., & Winsler, A. (1995). *Scaffolding children's learning: Vygotsky and early childhood education.* Washington, DC: NAEYC.

Charney, R. (1997). *Habits of goodness: Case studies in the social curriculum.* Greenfield, MA: Northeast Foundation for Children.

DeVries, R., & Zan, B. (1994). *Moral classrooms, moral children: Creating a constructivist atmosphere in early education.* New York: Teachers College Press.

Gardner, H. (1983). *Frames of mind: The theory of multiple intelligences.* New York: Basic Books.

Hyson, M. (1994). *The emotional development of young children: Building an emotion-centered curriculum.* New York: Teachers College Press.

Kohn, A. (1994). *Punished by rewards: The trouble with gold stars, incentive plans, A's, praise, and other bribes.* Boston: Houghton Mifflin.

Lickona, T. (1991). *Educating for character: How our schools can teach respect and responsibility.* New York: Bantam Books.

Internet Addresses and World Wide Web Sites

129.7.160.115/inst5931/piaget1.html
Jean Piaget—Intellectual Development

www.koyote.com/personal/hutchk/piaget2.htm
Piaget's Stages of Cognitive Development

129.7.160.115/INST5931/Vygotsky.html
Vygotsky's Thought and Language, Review and Analysis

www~students.biola.edu/~jay/erickson.html
Erikson's Psychosocial Stages of Development

syncorva.cortland.edu/~ANDERSMD/KOHL/CONTENT>HTML
Woolfolk, Criticism's of Kohlberg's Theory

klingon.util.utexas.edu/bt/Howard Gardner.html
Howard Gardner and Multiple Intelligences

chapter

4

Children's Play

A SOURCE OF DEVELOPMENT

AND LEARNING

When you finish reading and reflecting on this chapter, you will be able to:

1. Articulate the importance of play and describe the contributions that play makes to children's development.

2. Describe the differences between the play of infants, toddlers, preschoolers, and children in kindergarten and primary grades, and draw implications for curriculum from those differences.

3. Begin preparing for your adult role in children's play and contemplating the decisions you will make to prepare for, participate in, or intervene in their play activities.

4. Describe children's physical, emotional, social, and cognitive development when observing their play activities.

"I think that play is the most serious thing in the world. I was playing when I invented the aqualung," said underwater pioneer Jacques Cousteau. Unfortunately, not all adults share the sentiments of Cousteau. They do not always appreciate the value of play; for example, you will hear adult comments such as:

"They're just playing but they're not learning anything."

"It's alright for young children to play but by kindergarten there's a lot to learn."

"Their playtime is so free—how can you tell what they're learning?"

"Play is a mere time filler."

Parents and other adults frequently express their concerns about the time children spend in play and generally they believe that playtime should decrease as children get older (Rothlein & Brett, 1987). When children respond to the age-old question of What did you do in school (or preschool or child care) today? with, "We just played," some parents feel anxious or even angry. Many parents do not fully understand or value the role of play in children's development and in early childhood education's curriculum (Brewer & Kieff, 1996/1997).

In contrast to those adult observations, educators who have observed children for long periods of time can describe the serious quality of children's play and can list impressive learning outcomes from play activities. Research studies continue to document the learning that happens when children play (Berk, 1994; Isenberg & Jalongo, 1993).

115

Recognition of the value of play isn't a new insight. In 1948, Pratt passionately defended play as she wrote about children's work:

> Children have their own meaning for the word play. To them it does not, as it does to adults, carry the ideas of idleness, purposelessness, relaxation from work. When we began our school, we had it named a "play school," as a way of saying that it was our teaching. It was the children who made us, early in the school's history, delete the word from the school's name. To them, it was not a "play school" but a school and they were working hard at their schooling. How hard they work, only we who have watched them really know. They do not a waste precious moment. They are going about their jobs all the time. No father in his office or mother in her home [remember—this was written in 1948] works at such a pace. For a long time I was principally afraid that they would exhaust themselves in this strenuous new kind of school. (p. 9)

Definitions and Thinking about Play

To help you begin to appreciate and understand play, we have gathered some definitions of *play*. We also describe some of the qualities to observe when you watch children at play. The thinking of theorists, researchers, and well-known early childhood educators is quite convincing regarding the importance of play in the lives of children. Here are some of their thoughts:

> "Play is that absorbing activity in which healthy young children participate with enthusiasm and abandon" (Scales et al., 1991).

> "Play is the essential ingredient, the vehicle by which children communicate, socialize, learn about the world around them, understand themselves and others, deal with their problems, and practice some of the skills they will use in the future" (Hartley, 1971).

> "Play is the fundamental means by which children gather and process information, learn new skills, and practice old ones" (Spodek, 1986).

> "Play is the ultimate realization of learning by doing" (Feeney, Christensen, & Moravcik, 1996).

> "Play is the need of every child. . . . And when we observe children at play, we often see enjoyment and delight. Because of this fun aspect, adults sometimes think of play as a form of amusement or fun only, not as something to be taken seriously. However, play is an important childhood activity that helps children master all developmental needs" (Maxim, 1989).

Carlotta Lombroso, a prominent nineteenth-century philosopher of education, wrote in 1896, "Play is for the child an occupation as serious, as important, as study is for the adult; play is his means of development and he needs to play, just as the silkworm needs continually to eat leaves" (source unknown). Even the United Nations, in its 1948 declaration of the rights of children, identified play as a basic right of children.

 Journal 4.1: When you think about play, how would you define it? Reminisce about your childhood and describe your play. What were your play activities? What was your favorite? Why do you think that it was important to you? ■

Characteristics of Play

In addition to those thoughts about play, Rubin, Fein, and Vandenberg (1983) and many others in early childhood education have further refined the definition of *play*. Through their observations and studies of play, they determined that an activity can be described as play only if it contains the following essential characteristics.

1. *Play is intrinsically motivated.* Children are naturally drawn to play activities; that is, the desire to play comes from within them. The satisfaction and pleasure they derive from play is self-motivating. When you spend much time with young children, you realize that you don't have to reward them or offer any incentive to get them to play; getting them to stop playing is another matter, however.

2. *Play is freely chosen by the participants.* Often, play beckons children either through interesting materials, adult encouragement, or peer invitation, but it's the child's decision to play. If it is required, then it is not play. Many adults can relate to this quality. When you cook an elaborate meal because you feel like it, it's play, but when you cook because you have to, it's a chore. Similarly, when you work in your garden because you love to putter with plants, it's play, but when you have to weed and water the garden, it's work.

3. *Play must be pleasurable and engaging.* If play isn't pleasurable and engaging, it's unlikely that it will be freely chosen by children. If you observe children at play, those qualities are quite evident and a delight to watch. Play can also be serious and frustrating, even engaging children in fearful and violent activity, but there remains a level of satisfaction. The pleasure and satisfaction attracts children to repeat play activities over and over again.

4. *Play is nonliteral.* The best part of play for many is that it doesn't have to be real. Pretending allows one to change reality and to participate in dreams. At a young age, children begin much of their activity with, "Let's pretend. . . ." As their play expands, the pretending allows the children to experience much of the adult world in the safety of fantasy.

5. *Play is actively engaged in by the player.* As Caroline Pratt reminded us, play can be exhausting. When children have played hard, for example, invariably they will sleep well. Some of the activity may be physically engaging, whereas other activity may be mentally engaging. Again, if the play is not intrinsically motivating and pleasurable, children will not engage in it.

6. *Play is process oriented.* The process of play is what invites children. The actual activity is the motivating and sustaining aspect of play. Some play may have products or outcomes, but children are generally unconcerned with them and even forget about them. Much of young children's play is repetitious because they like the process and want to repeat it over and over again.

7. *Play is self-directed.* Play is an opportunity for the child to explore what he can do. It may be a chance to explore what he can do with a new object or with a new friend. Thus, play is a wonderful experience in learning about self. Young children have few opportunities to be in control, so play is their chance to control a situation by either manipulating an object, organizing the activity, or engaging another child.

Children are attracted to play that is intrinsically motivating and pleasurable. Why are these children so engaged in their play activity?

Kostelnik, Soderman, and Whiren (1993) added more dimensions to play by calling it **episodic,** meaning that it changes as it goes along and that shifts occur as children play. They begin with one goal or intent, and as the play develops, the direction changes depending on the play. The dimension of being **meaningful** is also attributed to play because it has the capacity to help children connect and relate their experiences.

Observing the Characteristics of Play

We're going to visit a family with three young children so that you can watch their play activity for the characteristics we have just described. We've been invited to the home of Francis and Akosa and their three boys, Wamalwa (2 years old), Otioli (5 years old), and Chemieti (7 years old). Francis and Akosa are from Kenya. They came to the United States to pursue education and to make their home here. They live in a spacious home in a suburban neighborhood away from the city's hectic pace and traffic. Before watching the boys' play activity, we talk about their family and how their ethnic background may influence the boys' play.

Getting to know the family.   Akosa tells us that she and her family continue to eat their native foods and have a hot meal together each night. Some of the most common foods are ugali, chunks of thick corn meal, and collard greens, which grow in the backyard. Francis shows us the family garden and explains to us that the boys often help him with weeding and watering. "We want the boys to fit in when we take them to Kenya, so we try to maintain important aspects of our life there." The fam-

ily eats with their fingers and uses authentic food names. Francis laughs, "On Friday nights, we have pizza—delivered—and everyone gets to stay up as late as they want." Akosa tells us about how they share their cultural background with the boys: "We tell them stories about our home, like what we did when we were growing up, and about their grandparents. In Kenya, you don't put yourself first. You try to promote the common good by sharing and cooperating. We want the boys to talk about *our* not *mine,* but we have to work at it." She continues, "We don't want our children to be so self-absorbed, so we watch their play activities and their play choices. We haven't bought any video games and we don't watch much TV. When they do ask to watch, we question them with, 'How is it going to help you? What will you learn?' When they do watch TV, they see a lot of negative images of Africans and then we see them appear in their play."

We thank Francis and Akosa for sharing their ideas about raising the boys. Their comments will guide us as we record our observations of the boys at play. It's the kind of information most early childhood educators would want to learn in order to understand the children.

Watching the children.   It's a warm, sunny day and the boys are playing with neighborhood friends, Brittany and Paul, in the front yard. Chemieti, who loves gymnastics, is teaching the other children how to do cartwheels. As they watch, he skillfully performs perfect cartwheels. Soon, there are children's bodies twirling all over the yard. Brittany, age 5, ends up in a kind of somersault when she attempts the cartwheel. Otioli is determined to do cartwheels and he repeats the movements over and over, trying to do as well as his big brother. Chemieti continues to coach him, "Keep your feet up" or "Keep your legs straight," but Otioli isn't coordinated enough. Wamalwa is watching the children and squealing at them. Every so often, he rolls on the grass and then looks to see if anyone is watching his performance. Paul, who is 7 years old, just watches from under a tree. When Otioli asks him to try it, he shakes his head.

Soon, everyone but Chemieti is bored or tired of the cartwheels, and the children turn their attention to the large oak tree in the front yard. Paul, Otioli, and Brittany quickly climb the tree and sit with their legs dangling. Wamalwa stands below the tree and shows us that the children are up there by pointing to them. He has a look that says, "I want to go up there, too." His oldest brother Chemieti comes over and lifts him high enough to

reach a branch. He grabs the branch and swings briefly before he is lifted down. Then Chemieti jumps up and swings himself again with great agility. Before long, the three children up in the tree are pretending to be sentry guards on the lookout for the enemy. We hear:

"You look over that way and yell if you see the enemy."

"I'll look in this direction and give a signal to you if I see anything."

"We can jump down and grab the bad guys if they come by."

Chemieti joins in with, "I'll be the enemy and hide in the bushes and try to sneak up on you." In the meantime, Wamalwa is left out of the play and begins to fuss. Akosa hears him and comes to bring him into the house for a nap. As she settles him into his bed, she puts on a tape of an African children's choir. "He loves that tape. Sometimes he just sits and listens to it for a long time." Once Wamalwa is resting quietly, his mom tells me about his tree climbing: "He just loves to climb trees. I think that he watched his brothers for so long that he became determined to get into a tree. The next thing we knew, we would find him up in the tree. It was frightening, so we took the lower rungs off the tree. We had built a tree house and added rungs to the lower part of the tree. Well, taking off the rungs didn't stop him. One day, he took a little stool and climbed up, and on another day, he took a cooking pot and stood on it to climb up. Once he's up there, he's not real happy. He wants to get down and then to climb up again. If I'm outside with him, he will do it over and over again."

Francis and Akosa's children demonstrated well the characteristics of play that we listed previously. Wamalwa's play—his tree climbing—is especially illustrative of many of those qualities. Wouldn't you love to know what he's thinking each time he figures out a way to climb up that tree? Watching and listening to children like Otioli, Chemieti, and Wamalwa as they play is the best way to learn about play and its value.

The Value of Play

Those outside the early childhood profession who have little understanding of children may be wondering why we place so much emphasis on play. Why devote an entire chapter to play? As early childhood educators, we are often called on to justify scheduling two hours of play in a kindergarten program or encouraging children's play all day in a preschool. As we described earlier, many parents do not understand or appreciate the kind of outcomes that are possible with children's play. Those who have studied children's play and those educators who spend their days observing children at play can describe many rich benefits of play. Look at some of those outcomes that play accomplishes:

- *Children develop a sense of competence.* As children play with materials, they have the opportunity to make things happen or change things; thus, they experience some control over their world. Because they are in control when they play, they generally choose materials and activities for which they have some skills or interest, so they are comfortable. Their play experiences are successful, so their confidence is enhanced.

   At a time in life when they have limited control over their world, it is important for young children to experience situations that they can control. These are essential experiences for the development of self-esteem, autonomy, and responsibility. For example, let's watch 3-year-old Ibrahim as he goes to the shelf where baskets of little figures (a favorite for toddlers) are stored and chooses the basket of dinosaurs. He dumps them out on a table and sits down in front of the pile. One by one, he stands the figures up in a row in front of him. When he finishes, he begins rearranging them into two lines with dinosaurs facing each other. Then he stages little fights between each pair with the result being that one dinosaur is lying on its side after each fight. Ibrahim makes quiet noises as he manipulates the figures to fight with each other. When he finishes the line of fights, he sits back in his chair with a subtle smile on his face.

   If we could get inside of Ibrahim's head, we would probably hear his feelings of power and satisfaction. "I can do it," he may be saying to himself. He continues his play for another 15 minutes, so he obviously likes it and is accomplishing what he set out to do.

- *Children are able to practice skills.* Practice involves the repetition of both physical skills and mental skills. Almost every skill is new when you are a child, so the repetition is actually an enjoyable experience. Each practice can lead to a new or more elaborate skill, so the interest remains high for children. Only when the practice becomes involuntary, required by others, does practice lose its play quality. The best example of play as practice of physical skill is the young child's experience with a tricycle.

   For instance, when Haley first encountered a tricycle out in the play yard, she walked around it a few times before even trying to sit on it. She then got on the tricycle and got off, got on and got off, and continued a few more times. From there, Haley tried to ride the tricycle, and once she felt secure in doing so, she rode and rode and rode. She was able to increase her speed, and eventually she tried to go backwards. Each new skill was practiced.

   In the beginning of her experience with the tricycle, Haley was engaged in a type of practice called **mere practice** (Piaget, 1962). Mere practice is the kind of practice we observe in much of infant play. Other kinds of practice include mental practice, fortuitous combinations, and intentional combinations.

Mental practice is something we all do when we are trying to memorize a new phone number—we say it to ourselves over and over. Mental practice can be a play activity if it's done playfully and for fun. For years, Keeley (we'll learn more about her in Chapter 10) joyfully sang the alphabet song and counted to 100 with great glee. She was accomplishing mental practice in her play. The other two forms of practice are more complex because they build on concepts or skills that children already know, and then add new information or skills, or build new combinations. If those happen by accident, they are called **fortuitous combinations;** if they are planned by the child, they are **intentional combinations.**

Let's look at a couple of examples. Felipe, who is painting at the easel, accidentally discovers that when red and blue paint are mixed, the result is a purple color. He experienced a fortuitous combination, but later he purposefully mixed colors, and experienced intentional combinations. Chemieti, who has always been intrigued with adult conversation, recently memorized a series of jokes he overheard adults telling. He retold the jokes a few times and then added body movements to the lines. When the duck went into the store, for example, Chemieti waddled like a duck, and occasionally he added new lines to the joke. He was engaged in intentional combinations of practice.

Children's play, then, provides practice of the simplest to the most complex skills of sensorimotor and cognitive development.

- *Children are able to develop socially.* Even though young children do not play with peers for a number of years, their early play is often with adults and with materials, and near other children. Without the opportunity to play with others, children would not have the experiences they need to build social concepts and skills. For example, when Otioli plays with his friends, Brittany and Paul, and even with his big brother, he experiences a need to share, to cooperate, to negotiate, to problem solve, and to communicate, and he gradually develops those skills.

- *Children are able to solve problems and make decisions in a safe situation.* That nonliteral quality of play—the freedom to pretend to be or do anything—provides the context for trying out adult roles, solving problems, and making decisions without any real consequences, so it's safe to take risks. Children are comfortable in those situations and can develop the skills needed when they feel safe. It's an opportunity to try out different roles and experience different situations.

- *Children gather and process information.* Through play, children interact with their world and all of its objects, processes, and events. If you watch even the youngest child with an unknown object, you will see first the process of exploration—touching, smelling, tasting, looking, and listening—followed by manipulation of the objects. Play with objects, situations, processes, and other aspects of their world is children's way of gathering information and connecting the new information with what they have previously experienced or already know.

- *Children express emotions, release tension, and explore anxiety-producing situations* (Santrock, 1990). Sometimes through vigorous physical play and sometimes through pretend play, children are able to let adults know what they are feeling. They may not be able to label or tell us about their fear of monsters, but they can show it as they pretend to be ferocious monsters or to run away from the monsters. Children can't tell us that they're frustrated, but they can express it by banging cymbals together or playing a very bossy adult to their dolls. Play allows one to express the full gamut of emotions—joy, pleasure, pain, frustration, anger, and exhilaration. The kind of rough and tumble play that we will talk about later in this chapter is a great form of release for children, as is chasing, shouting, and jumping.

Defending the value of play.   One of your responsibilities as an early childhood educator will probably be to defend the value of play and to communicate how play helps children develop and learn. In addition to the general benefits we just listed, there are specific learning outcomes that children achieve easily through play. Children develop their literacy understandings and skills through play, their mathematical concepts through play, and their science appreciations and processes through play. As you meet the children in this book, notice what is happening when they play. Information about developmental levels of play can guide your observations and enable you to interpret more accurately what you see children doing. Use this chapter to get ready for your professional role by becoming more knowledgeable, appreciative, and articulative about the role of play in children's development and learning.

Journal 4.2: A parent of a 5-year-old comes in to talk to you about his child's learning in your classroom. "When I watch him with his friends in the neighborhood or at home, all they do is play. They play with those little cars and trucks, build things with Legos, and use a lot of cardboard and tape to make garages. I can see that it's kind of creative, but how is he learning?" Practice what you will say to this parent and to others about the value of play.   ■

Play and Development: From Infants to Eight-Year-Olds

Because you will soon be meeting groups of infants, toddlers, preschoolers, and children in kindergarten and primary grades—children in play situations at home and in early childhood education programs—we will describe developmental levels of play and some typical play activities for each of those age groups. Our intent is to get you ready to be a good observer so that you can learn about and understand children's development by watching them.

Infant Play

The kind of play that occurs in the first year of life is full of discovery, repeated practice, and delight at one's own accomplishments. Watching infant play can be one of the most fascinating observational experiences. Until recently, the first month of life was considered a nonplayful time by Piaget and others, but current observations suggest that babies of this age begin using their senses for exploring their environment. That exploration is considered a kind of beginning play.

Exploration and play.   Some experts say that infants explore before they can play, so this is probably a good time to differentiate between *exploration* and *play*. Piaget thought that exploration preceded play in terms of the amount of time spent. **Exploration** was seen as a process to gain information, whereas **play** involved practicing and recombining the information gained through exploration. Play and exploration are highly interrelated and may not be different enough to be separated, but we think that it is important to notice the two kinds of activities when watching children. You can decide for yourself if they are different enough to make a distinction.

For many early childhood educators, the differentiation between exploration and play may help with some decisions about children's activities. We have often seen children who are not interested or ready to participate in a new form of play but who may want to manipulate the materials or playthings for a while, or watch others engage in the activity. They may be exploring and gathering information, and it may be necessary for them to do so before they engage in the play themselves. We adults make decisions about time and schedules for children, and if we appreciate exploration as an important step before play, we may schedule differently. If we observe infants, for example, we will have a real appreciation for the need to explore. Babies can explore visually, imitate facial expressions, and show preferences for faces, patterns, and things that move. Their first months are full of exciting sensorimotor development as they play with their bodies, with objects, and with people.

Primary circular reactions.   From about 1 to 4 months of age, the kind of playful activity seen in infants has been called **primary circular reactions** (Piaget, 1962). Those reactions are simply exercises of reflexes. Infant play continues rather simply—looking and listening. For about the first four months, babies watch faces, movement of objects and people, as well as the movement of their own body parts. They also listen to voices, music, the world around them, and themselves. During that time, they discover, quite accidentally, their ability to cause movement or sounds, if the situation is supportive. Parents or caregivers can set up situations in the baby's crib in such a way that when the baby moves, when a sound is made, or when the baby kicks, a mobile moves or a bell rings. Even during these early months, babies begin to repeat enjoyable activities.

Secondary circular reactions.   Repetitive behaviors that cause effects are categorized as **secondary circular reactions.** This is the time when the baby is able to grasp items—rattles being a favorite. They continue to enjoy simply looking at things but now they begin to explore through manipulation. First, they hold on to the toy; next, they realize they can move it; and finally, they achieve the ultimate—they can feel it with their mouths or taste it. Babies love to put things in their mouths and experience all of the sensations of taste. Manipulation of objects and sometimes people's faces become a favorite form of play for infants.

This is an exciting time for infant play, especially when the baby can hold an object and bang it against something. A large spoon and a pot or just a rattle against the floor provide satisfying play for an infant at this stage. Adults may grow weary of the racket but the infant is completely taken by her ability to create a sound.

Tertiary circular reactions. From ages 8 to 12 months, infants add new skills to their looking, grasping, mouthing, and hitting abilities, referred to as **tertiary circular reactions.** For example, if you watch Luke at this age, he now holds the red plastic ring well, nibbles on it occasionally, then transfers it from one hand to another repeatedly. Sometimes he holds it out in front of him, turns it over and studies it, and puts a finger inside the ring. There doesn't seem to be any end to the things he can do with the ring. Later, Luke may add another item, perhaps a rattle, and eventually bang the rattle against the ring. This is a time when the baby is repeating familiar activities with the ring but trying to change what he does with the ring instead of repeating it in exactly the same way.

When Luke gets a new toy, his dad notices that he touches it with his finger a great deal and looks at the toy from different angles. At this age, Luke is developing an interest in textures and noticing all of the new details of his object. He is also beginning to like to put objects into other objects, so a tub of his family's plastic cookie cutters is a favorite plaything.

Mobility. From ages 6 to 12 months, infants begin to scoot, creep, and crawl until they can navigate all over a house. Some also begin pulling themselves up on chairs or other furniture items and take their first steps. This mobility definitely enhances their play because they can get to items and materials of interest. The fringe on a tablecloth, the legs of a chair, the basket of magazines, and the plant in a pot of dirt become new playthings. You have only to watch an infant squeezing the dirt in his hands or pulling the magazines out of the basket with glee to know that play is going on.

Journal 4.3: Using all of that information about how infants are capable of playing, try to picture an early childhood program for infants. Use the information on exploration; primary, secondary, and tertiary reactions; and mobility of infants. For each, come up with one recommendation for an infant program. ■

As you will find in Chapter 7, quality programs for infants are scarce and yet so important. To add to the recommendations that you developed in Journal 4.3, we add the appropriate and inappropriate practices for supporting infant play from the National Association for the Education of Young Children (NAEYC) in Table 4.1 (Bredekamp & Copple, 1997). Those practices give you a hint of how involved you will be in the play of infants. If you think that infant play is amazing and sometimes exhausting, be prepared to be overwhelmed by the play of toddlers.

■ **TABLE 4.1   Appropriate and Inappropriate Practices Supporting Infant Play**

Appropriate Practices	Inappropriate Practices
The play areas are comfortable; they have pillows, foam-rubber mats, and soft carpeting where babies can lie on their stomachs or backs and be held and read to. A hammock, rocking chair (preferably a glider for safety), overstuffed chair, and big cushions are available for caregivers or parents and infants to relax in together.	The play areas are sterile, designed for easy cleaning, but without the different textures, levels, colors that infants need to stimulate their senses. There is not an area where an adult can sit comfortably with an infant in her arms and read or talk to the baby.
Space is arranged so children can enjoy moments of quiet play by themselves, have ample space to roll over and move freely, and can crawl toward interesting objects. Areas for younger infants are separated from those of crawlers to promote the safe interactions of infants in similar stages of development.	Space is cramped and unsafe for children who are learning how to move their bodies.
Visual displays, such as mobiles, are oriented toward the infant's line of sight and designed so that the interesting sights and effects are clearly visible when the baby is lying on her back. Mobiles are removed when children can grasp them.	Visual displays are not in an infant's line of sight. They are often used as a substitute for appropriate social interaction of infants with adults.
Sturdy cardboard books are placed in book pockets or a sturdy book stand. Books that the adults read to the babies are on a shelf out of reach. Books show children and families of different racial and cultural backgrounds, and people of various ages and abilities.	Books are not available or are made of paper that tears easily. Books do not contain objects familiar or interesting to children.
Toys provided are responsive to the child's actions: a variety of grasping toys that require different types of manipulation; a varied selection of skill-development materials, including nesting and stacking materials, activity boxes, and containers to be filled and emptied; a variety of balls, bells, and rattles.	Toys are battery powered or windup, so the baby just watches. Toys lack a variety of texture, size, and shape.
A variety of safe household items that infants can use as play materials are available, including measuring cups, wooden spoons, nonbreakable bowls, and cardboard boxes.	Household items that help make the infant room more homelike are not available.
Toys are scaled to a size that enables infants to grasp, chew, and manipulate them (clutch balls, rattles, teethers, and soft washable dolls and other play animals.)	Toys are too large to handle or so small that infants could choke on or swallow them.
Mobile infants have an open area where balls, push and pull toys, wagons, and other equipment encourage free movement and testing of large-muscle skills and coordination. Low, climbing structures, ramps, and steps are provided. Structures are well padded and safe for exploration.	Balls and other moving toys are for outdoor use only. Equipment designed for crawling up/down or under/through is not available, or structures are safe only for older, more-mobile children.

(continued)

■ **TABLE 4.1** *(continued)*

Appropriate Practices	Inappropriate Practices
Open shelves within infants' reach contain toys of similar type, spaced so that infants can make choices. Caregivers group materials for related activities on different shelves (e.g., fill-and-empty activities are on a shelf separate from three-piece puzzles or moving/pushing toys).	Toys are dumped in a box or kept out of children's reach, forcing them to depend on adults' selection.
There is ample, accessible storage for extra play materials of a type similar to what is already displayed and for materials with increasing challenge. Caregivers can easily rearrange their space as young infants become mobile. When an infant has explored a toy with his mouth and moved to other things, the toy is picked up for washing and disinfecting and replaced with a similar toy. Everything is nearby, so caregivers do not have to leave the space to replace a toy.	Storage closets are far from the infant space and poorly organized, making it difficult to rotate materials, bring out more complex materials, or add to the variety of activities in the space.
Room temperature can be controlled; vents are clean and provide an even flow of air. Floors are not drafty. Windows provide natural light and fresh air. Caregivers carry infants to the windows to see outside.	The infants' environment suffers from one or more of these deficiencies: the room is either too cold and drafty or too hot; the room has little natural light; and/or the windows are not accessible so that caregivers can hold infants and they are able to look out.
Adults periodically move infants to a different spot (from the floor to an infant seat, from the seat to a stroller, etc.) to give babies differing perspectives and reasonable variety in what they are able to look at and explore.	Babies are confined to cribs, infant seats, playpens, or the floor for long periods indoors.
An outside play space adjacent to the infant area includes sunny and shaded areas. It is enclosed by protective fencing. The ground around climbing structures and in some of the open space is covered with resilient, stable surfacing for safety, making it easy for mobile infants to push wagons and ride-on toys. There are soft areas where young infants can lie on quilts.	Infants rarely go out because there is no adjacent play area, and nearby parks and playgrounds offer no shaded areas or soft surfaces for babies to lie on or crawl about freely.
	Large group size and inadequate staff-child ratios make outdoor play difficult.

Source: Developmentally Appropriate Practice in Early Childhood Programs by S. Bredekamp and C. Copple, (pp. 75–76), 1997, Washington, DC: NAEYC. Copyright 1997 by NAEYC. Reprinted with permission from the National Association for the Education of Young Children.

Toddler Play

As we found when we watched Wamalwa or listened to his mother (in Chapter 3), toddlerhood is an extremely active time. A lot of energy surrounds a toddler—on the part of the toddler as well as on the part of the adult who is both stimulating and supervising him. Wamalwa's climbing was only one of his favorite play activities that required close adult supervision. Another important role of his parents and his older siblings was the provision of toys—objects for play.

Object play.   Unlike the object play of infants, the object play of toddlers involves two or more objects. Remember how Luke began to combine other toys with his favorite ring? Toddlers also use objects appropriately. Luke's red ring fits on a pole for a stacking toy, and as he progressed, he began to use it for stacking. Instead of using blocks simply to empty and fill the box or shelf, toddlers begin stacking them. Instead of mouthing the doll's head, a toddler may cuddle the doll. As toddlers play more and more with objects, their play becomes more sophisticated. A ball that has been bounced for months becomes something for the puppy to eat. This is called the **representational use of objects.** This is the beginning of make-believe or symbolic play.

For Wamalwa, the most appealing play objects are the toys of his brothers. While they build with Legos and blocks, Wamalwa uses them as furniture, guns, and fish. He does not even attempt to play with his older brothers, but he does play nearby quite happily. Most toddlers find the toys used by others most attractive, and this can be a source of frustration among toddler peers, but Wamalwa's brothers are generally kind and understanding.

Motor skills and play.   Toddlerhood is a time of great motor skill development. Their small motor skills develop well and enable them to fit puzzle pieces together, play musical toys, turn the pages in a book, scribble and draw with crayons, mold play-dough into desired shapes, and pour liquids from a small pitcher. Their large motor skills also develop well and enable them to throw a ball, push and pull toys around the house or yard, climb stairs, and run and jump. Think about the skills that Wamalwa used to climb trees. One of his favorite play activities with anyone who will join him is throwing and retrieving a ball. He isn't able to catch the ball yet, but he is deliriously happy running to retrieve it over and over.

Rough and tumble play.   Rough and tumble play occurs during this time, and is a favorite of toddlers as well as adults. Research has documented that infants and young toddlers demonstrate this kind of play independently; research has also shown that very young children see examples of this type of play all around them. Adults initiate rough and tumble play primarily with boys, and the initiation usually comes from fathers (Lamb, 1981). The purpose of rough and tumble play is a puzzle. It's definitely a form of physical exercise, but not to the extent that it is significant source of exercise; it's a kind of play fighting. It doesn't seem to be a practice of any particular skills, but it may contribute to social skills because children have the opportunity to "read" another's actions or facial expressions. In the meantime, it is undoubtedly a favorite of children, both boys and girls.

Many adults do not enjoy or appreciate rough and tumble play, often out of worry that a child will be hurt. This sometimes does occur. When Chemieti and Otioli wrestle

■ **FIGURE 4.1**   Differences between Rough and Tumble Play and Aggression

- Aggression may begin with or be triggered by competition for a toy, equipment, space, or friendship of a peer, but rough and tumble play is not generally related to any competition.
- Aggression is accompanied by serious facial expressions and behavior (frowning, mean talk, sneering, and crying), but rough and tumble play is usually done with smiling, laughter, and playful teasing.
- Aggression is usually between two children, but rough and tumble play can involve many children at a time. Anyone can join in.
- Aggression may result in children going their separate ways, but rough and tumble play usually attracts and keeps children together for other forms of play.
- Aggressive behavior is characterized by children using all their strength to hurt another child, but rough and tumble play is more of a mock fight with no intent to hurt.
- Aggression is accompanied by children's bodies that are taut and full of stress, but in rough and tumble play, children's bodies are relaxed.
- Aggressive behavior is characterized by displeasure, but rough and tumble play is characterized by pleasure and fun.

together, Otioli often runs crying to his parents with an arm twisted or a head bumped. So there's legitimate concern, but that concern turns to frustration when Otioli, after very little comforting, returns just as intensely as before to his wrestling match.

Smith (1989) and Pellegrini and Perlmutter (1988) studied rough and tumble play and identified differences between such play and genuine aggression. Those differences, shown in Figure 4.1, can really help you make decisions about how to respond to rough and tumble play. Knowing some of those differences will remind you to refrain from interfering with children's play fighting or at least may encourage you to observe it more closely.

Sometimes, children's rough and tumble play is a form of drama or pretend play, or at least it begins that way. Playing "bad guys" or "enemies" or "monsters" often turns into rough and tumble play, which isn't surprising, considering both forms of play are developing in children.

Symbolic play.   Early symbolic play is done without words—it is simply using an object to represent another object. The earliest symbolic play is focused on the toddler herself—that is, on her familiar activities such as eating, sleeping, and getting dressed. You can imagine that this is a comfortable starting point for very young children—routines that they know well. This play has been called **autosymbolic play** because chil-

The "rough and tumble" play of these primary grade children began when they were toddlers and continues to be a favorite play activity.

dren represent themselves and are beginning their symbolic play. From there, toddlers begin to use objects to represent other objects. They are able to go beyond themselves and represent the world around them.

As the child advances and begins to use language, her words represent objects or people, a higher level of representation. When Keeley was a toddler, she engaged in intense symbolic play each night as everyone finished dinner. She would place her spoon inside her cloth napkin and it would be her baby. She would go to each person at the table and ask, "Would you like to hold my baby?" Those who chose to hold the baby were expected to do so with care and love, and she would gently hand the "baby" to you. After a while, the spoon in the napkin became other things—a birthday present, a bird, jewelry, and so on.

During toddlerhood, children pretend and involve others in their pretending. Wamalwa often pretends to feed himself and has just recently begun to pretend to feed his mother. He really enjoys that kind of "first me, then you" pretending. When toddlers begin to incorporate others into a sequence of pretending, their pretend play becomes more complex. It is the beginning of a series of increasingly more complex symbolic play. From there, you will see incredible changes as children progress to preschool age, the years from ages 3 to 5, in their abilities to use actions and words to convey nonliteral meanings. Before we progress to preschool years, take a moment to look at some more appropriate and inappropriate practices from NAEYC's recommendations. Table 4.2 on pages 130 and 131 displays those practices for supporting toddler play.

■ **TABLE 4.2   Appropriate and Inappropriate Practices Supporting Toddler Play**

Appropriate Practices	Inappropriate Practices
Adults engage in reciprocal play with toddlers, modeling for children how to play imaginatively, such as playing '"tea party." Caregivers also support toddlers' play so that children stay interested in an object or activity for longer periods of time and their play becomes more complex, moving from simple awareness and exploration of objects to more complicated playlike pretending.	Adults do not play with toddlers because they feel self-conscious or awkward. Caregivers do not understand the importance of supporting children's play, and they control or intrude in the play.
Adults respect toddlers' solitary and parallel play. Caregivers provide several of the same popular toys for children to play with alone or near another child. Caregivers realize that having three or four of the same sought-after toy is more helpful than having one each of many different toys.	Adults do not understand the value of solitary and parallel play and try to force children to play together. Adults arbitrarily expect children to share. Popular toys are not provided in duplicate and are fought over constantly, while other toys are seldom used.
Adults frequently read to toddlers, one individually on a caregiver's lap or in groups of two or three. Caregivers sing with toddlers, do fingerplays, act out simple stories or folktales with children participating actively, or tell stories using a flannel board or magnetic board and allow children to manipulate and place figures on the boards.	Adults impose "grouptime" on toddlers, forcing a large group to listen or watch an activity without providing opportunity for children to participate.
Time schedules are flexible and smooth, dictated more by children's needs than by adults'. There is a relatively predictable sequence to the day to help children feel secure.	Activities are dictated by rigid adherence to time schedules, or the lack of a time schedule makes the day unpredictable.
Adults adapt schedules and activities to meet individual children's needs within the group setting. Recognizing toddlers' need to repeat tasks until they master the steps and skills involved, caregivers allow toddlers to go at their own pace. They have time to assist a child with special needs because the group of toddlers knows what is expected and is engaged.	Adults lose patience with toddlers' desires for repetition. Toddlers must either do things in groups according to the caregivers' plan or follow adult demands that they spend a certain amount of time at an activity. Caregivers have little time for a child with special needs.
Toddlers are given appropriate art materials, such as large crayons, watercolor markers, and large paper. Adults expect toddlers to explore and manipulate art materials and *do not* expect them to produce a finished art product. They use nontoxic materials but avoid using food for art because toddlers are developing self-regulatory skills and must learn to distinguish between food and other objects that are not to be eaten.	Toddlers are "helped" by teachers to produce a product, follow the adult-made model, or color a coloring book or ditto sheet. Because toddlers are likely to put things in their mouths, adults give them edible, often tasty, fingerpaints or playdough.

■ **TABLE 4.2**   *(continued)*

Appropriate Practices	Inappropriate Practices
Children have daily opportunities for exploratory activity, such as water and sand play, painting, and playing with clay or playdough.	Adults do not offer water and sand play, paints, or playdough because they are messy and require supervision. Children's natural enjoyment of water play is frustrated, so children play at sinks whenever they can.
Adults respect toddlers' desires to carry favored objects around with them, to move the objects from one place to another, and to roam around or sit and parallel play with toys and objects.	Adults restrict objects to certain locations and do not tolerate children's hoarding, collecting, or carrying objects about.

Source: Developmentally Appropriate Practice in Early Childhood Programs by S. Bredekamp and C. Copple, (pp. 84–85), 1997, Washington, DC: NAEYC. Copyright 1997 by NAEYC. Reprinted with permission from the National Association for the Education of Young Children.

Preschool Play

The years from ages 3 to 5 are a marvelous time to sit back and watch children represent everything and anything with the greatest of imagination. You begin to get a view of their perspectives of the world, of people, of life, and of who they are. Watching their symbolic play is especially revealing of how they perceive the happenings around them, so we begin to describe preschoolers with a discussion of the changes and capacity of their symbolic play.

Symbolic play.   As they leave toddlerhood, young children continue to represent themselves in their pretend play, but they expand on their representation of and actions upon others (adults and objects). They pretend to comb their own hair, pretend to comb dad's hair, and pretend to comb a doll's hair. That same play begins to get more complex as the child talks for the doll or her dad, or when the child attributes feelings to a stuffed-toy dog or his mom.

Keeley often talked to her pretend baby in the napkin as if the baby had needs or likes. "You like to be rocked, don't you?" she would say. Later, she would talk for the baby: "I want a bottle," she would say in a baby voice. Keeley began to assume other roles and her symbolic play began to reveal much of her life. Her favorite play was in the role of "teacher" and the adults in her family had to sit on the floor to be read to, or to get ready for their naps, or wash their hands for lunch. Her words, tone of voice, and kinds of directions may tell you much about what her day was like.

The kind of symbolic play in which children assume the role of another continues to gain complexity. Children usually begin with familiar roles, that of mother, father, or other relative, then to adults in their lives, such as teacher, doctor, grocery clerk, librarian, or bus driver, to name just a few. The next level of such play is when the child assumes an unfamiliar role, one about which he has little or no information. Even without

> ■ **FIGURE 4.2**   Popular Social Roles of Preschool Pretend Play
>
> - Functional roles related to a job or an action, such as bus drivers drive and babies drink bottles
> - Character roles of occupations, such as teacher, doctor, and store clerk
> - Character roles of stereotyped figures, such as monsters and witches
> - Fictional character roles such as The Big Bad Wolf and Superman or Superwoman
> - Family roles, such as mother, father, brother, and baby

experience, children roleplay astronauts, ballerinas, cowboys, and police officers. Young children of this age also often act out the roles of husband and wife.

During this time, children use objects a great deal but give them human qualities. Keeley could manage two roles—that of herself interacting with her doll and that of the doll expressing her wants. We heard her change voices for each role and it was quite impressive.

Garvey (1977) describes the common or popular types of social roles that preschool children take on in their play. When you look at the roles in Figure 4.2, you probably remember playing some of those yourself and have no doubt seen children playing those roles. In their representation of the roles, each child will contribute her own perceptions of the character or role, and enhance the representation with her own concepts of what is happening in her life. When Otioli plays father, you will probably see traces of the quiet, gentle personality of Francis, and when he plays baby, you will see the glee and curiosity of Wamalwa. That's why children's symbolic play is so fascinating. There is so much to learn by watching.

Journal 4.4: A parent approaches you with concern about her child's "pretend world": "I worry about all the pretending Lisa does. She pretends to have playmates and she plays with them. She pretends to be different characters each night at supper and insists that we go along with her. Is it possible for her to be pretending too much? What benefit could all this pretending have?" Respond to Lisa's mother. ■

You may have some ideas to share with Lisa's mother, but you may also feel that you could use more convincing information. What we have learned from observations of children's play is that we can tell so much about what they understand, what they are thinking, and their concerns and confusions. As we continue, you will learn about other ideas to comfort Lisa's mother.

Communicating understandings.   When you watch preschool children, their interpretation of roles and other forms of pretend play tell you about their understandings. The way they present their understandings is called a **scheme**. Schemes are children's concepts of what is real in terms of objects, actions, and roles. A child may show you her scheme of what a cash register or a scanner is by the way she pretends to use it, or may show you her scheme of what a beach is by the way she pretends to be there. Young children begin with simple schemes, but during preschool years, they combine and carry out different levels of schemes in a sequence, and eventually have multischemes. Watch the children in the following scene and identify the schemes and look for different levels in a sequence.

Eli and Amanda: Schemes

Eli and Amanda are playing "house" (their word) at preschool. Amanda is using a duster to dust the varied furniture items in the dramatic play area. She swishes it over the top of the table and china cabinet, then pauses to appreciate her work. "I'm making the house nice and clean," she tells Eli. "I'm making a stew for us," he responds. He gathers an assortment of plastic vegetables from the refrigerator, pretends to wash them and cut them up, then puts them into a pot. He begins to stir the pot and sniffs it, saying, "Umm, it smells good."

Amanda is pushing a wheel toy and making a vacuum sound all around the area. Later, she appears with a purse over her arm and indicates that she's going to the store. "Do you want anything from the store?' she asks, but Eli shakes his head as he continues to stir. When she returns, Eli tells Amanda that the stew is ready. She sits at the table and waits to be served. Eli brings some dishes to the table and puts the pot in the center. He ladles out the pretend stew into their dishes and begins to eat.

After a minute or so, Amanda says, "I bought some ice cream for us." She goes to the refrigerator, pretends to take something out, and brings them each a dish and spoon. Both children enthusiastically eat their pretend ice cream.

 Journal 4.5: Identify the schemes in the play you just observed. What kind of schemes does Amanda have? How about Eli? What schemes do both children have? ■

The ultimate goal of children's symbolic or pretend play is "to integrate meaning derived from their experience with knowledge and skills from all developmental domains as they create roles or scenarios" (Kostelnik, Soderman, & Whiren, 1993). What that means is that play provides an opportunity for children to pull together previously learned ideas, information, and skills, and connect new ideas, information, and skills into physical, emotional, social and cognitive learning. Figure 4.3 on page 134 shows you the kinds of progress children will make toward that goal as they pretend, taking on roles and creating scenes. Those progressions will continue as children experience kindergarten and primary grades, and their symbolic play will become more complex and exciting. The physical play of preschool-age children changes, too, as they mature, taking on a complexity and seriousness.

Physical play activities. Most preschool children continue to have a great deal of energy and need plenty of physical play activities during their day. Their physical play begins to change, however, as they develop during this time. What began as free and enthusiastic delight with running, jumping, and climbing frequently now has more purpose. Children at this age get a bit serious about their physical play, although rough

■ **FIGURE 4.3** Objectives for Children's Emotional, Physical, Social and Cognitive Learning

As children progress toward the ultimate goal, they will:

1. Mimic in their play behaviors what they have seen or experienced.
2. Use their bodies to represent real or imaginary objects or events.
3. Assign symbolic meaning to real or imaginary objects or events.
4. Take on the role attributes of beings or objects and act out interpretations of those roles.
5. Create play themes.
6. Experiment with a variety of objects, roles (leader, follower, mediator), and characterizations (animal, mother, astronaut, etc.).
7. React to and interact with other children in make-believe situations.
8. Dramatize familiar stories, songs, poems, and past events.
9. Integrate construction into pretend play episodes.

Source: Developmentally Appropriate Programs in Early Childhood Education by M. J. Kostelnik, A. K. Soderman, and A. P. Whiren, © 1993. Reprinted by permission of Prentice-Hall, Inc., Upper Saddle River, NJ.

and tumble play continues with great frequency. This is a time when children begin working on skills—aiming the ball and hitting a target, running fast, jumping high, or performing the perfect cartwheel.

Some of their physical play begins to have rules and organization. Most of the early rules and organization are composed by the children themselves, and you'll hear them come up with rules as they go. Generally, when the situation arises, they make up the necessary rule. Some very simple physical games are played by children during their preschool years. Games such as Tag and Duck, Duck, Goose are simple, energetic, and have minimal rules.

The time between toddlerhood and entry to kindergarten is eventful in children's play. Amazing changes occur as children explore, experiment, and engage in play. The major change related to children's play is the adult attitude toward its legitimacy. When children play in preschool, most adults are delighted and enjoy their play adventures. But when children enter more formal schooling, starting with kindergarten, the acceptance of play becomes limited, and adults begin to have concerns about the amount of time spent in play. The time that children spend in kindergarten and primary grades, their years between ages 5 and 8, is a time when children's play can reach its highest potential to fulfill all aspects of their development. It is a time when play can energize learning, can take symbolic representation to a sophisticated level, and can enhance all school curriculum.

Kindergarten and Primary Grades Play

Family life differences and socioeconomic and cultural backgrounds will have significant influence on children's play at this stage. When general life experiences combine with different levels of maturity, children's play will be marked with huge diversity in terms of pretend themes and content, physical skill and agility, interest and enthusiasm for varied activities, gender differences, and even the children's definitions of play. It is also a time when children are spending their days in environments that don't always support play or that try to present learning activities as play. So, children's perceptions of what is play and what is not play are important for your understanding of their play.

Children's perceptions of play. The research study shown in Box 4.1 (Wing, 1995) is a very meaningful portrait of children's perceptions of play. It is a good starting point

BOX 4.1 ■ Children's Perspectives on Work and Play

A Closer Look

In 1995 to determine what children saw as play, Lisa Wing asked kindergartners, first-graders, and second-graders about their classroom activities. She thought that they could provide important information for teachers, parents, and school policymakers. Children spend the greatest part of their day involved in classroom activities and those activities communicate to children what school is about. Almost immediately in her study, Wing learned that children classified school activities as either work or play. From there, she asked how children made their distinctions, what criteria they used to interpret activities, and what messages they received from adults, peers, and the school environment.

Teachers of the children in the study described their programs as "hands on, with lots of materials, children choosing what to do, free exploration" (Wing, 1995, pp. 225–226) and summed the learning as "a process of playful exploration and discovery" (p. 226). Their classrooms were arranged in learning centers, and children spent the greater part of the day in small group or self-directed activities. Children often made choices about their learning activities and did so in cooperative groups.

"The words *work* and *play* came up repeatedly as children talked about their classroom activities, but in their minds, play was not work" (Wing, 1995, p. 226). Whether an activity was obligatory was the major element to determine the difference between work and play. Teachers' intentions and directions were central to work activities, but children's intentions were central to play. Children used the term *have to* with activities in writing, spelling, math, projects, reading, and calendar. When children talked

about their play activities, the terms *get to* and *can* were used. When children were required to use materials that they typically associated with play—such as blocks, crayons, and sand—in a specific way, those activities became work.

An important insight came from observations about teachers' roles in work and play activities. The researcher noticed that teachers were usually uninvolved in those activities children classified as play, such as painting, block play, sand, and construction activities. Their involvement was quite different in those activities that children called work. Teachers remained close to the children, led them or circulated among them, or assisted and supervised them. Teachers usually gave directions for work activities but seldom for play activities.

Another area of difference for children's differentiation between work and play was seen in their perceptions about the physical and cognitive demands of their activities. Children referred to thinking, concentrating, effort, and neatness with respect to the demands of work. Listen to the children describe the differences between *work* and *play:*

Ted: When you're not using your mind, that's playing. It's a big, big difference. You really try to concentrate really hard when you're working, but not when you're playing (Wing, 1997, p. 234).

Stacey: Well, coloring isn't really playing. It's really working. When it's working, it's something to take your time on and just do your best. The difference is when you take your time and you do your best, it's alled working, and when you just try to do it, do it a little fast and a little taking time it's called playing (Wing, 1997, p. 235).

for your understanding of kindergarten and primary grade children's play in the confines of many of school settings. Bergen (1988) refers to a category of play called "work disguised as play" to describe task-oriented activities that teachers attempt to transform into directed or guided play. Math and spelling games and other learning activities that promote rote learning (learning by repetition) are often presented enthusiastically as enjoyable activities, but Wing's research is a reminder that children know the difference.

Journal 4.6: Put yourself in the role of a primary grade child who has figured out the difference between work and play. Your teacher just gave directions for an activity described as "a fun math game" and it's one in which you end up practicing simple addition facts. What kind of questions might you have about math, about your teacher, and about school and learning? How might you feel about those same areas? ■

The continuum of play and work in Figure 4.4 reflects the ideas children expressed in Wing's interviews about the distinction between the two, and captures their thinking about activities that they could not classify clearly as one or the other. The continuum reflects all of the possibilities between those activities that are clearly work and those that are clearly play.

It is interesting to note in Box 4.1 the differences between the teachers' perceptions of work and play and the children's perceptions of the two. When teachers thought that children had plenty of play activities, children perceived the opposite. It was also noted that during play activities, teachers remained apart from children and clearly did not join in the play. They used that time to finish other projects or work on material preparation or bulletin boards. During work activities, the teachers were very involved, giving directions, supervising, and guiding. Their behavior clearly gave clues to children about which activities were play and which activities were work.

One conclusion you may reach from the study in Box 4.1 is that you will want to become a co-player with children during their work and play. Both Piaget and Vygotsky would support those roles for teachers. If your role is to plan, organize, and encourage children's play, you will probably want to be involved in the play. Later in this chapter, we will talk more about the your adult role in children's play, but for now, it appears that children expect you to be engaged in their play activities.

In addition to children's perceptions of work and play in kindergarten and primary grades, there are changes in their physical play and an upsurge of rough and tumble play. If you spend some time on the playground with first- and second-graders, you will see those changes and the frequency of their rough and tumble play.

Increases in rough and tumble play.   In studies of preschool children's play behaviors, rough and tumble play accounts for 5 percent of their free play, but in early elementary school (kindergarten through third grade), it accounts for up to 17 percent of children's free play. Pellegrini and Boyd (1993) think that the frequency can be explained by the fact that children have moved from preschools where play is valued to an institution where it is not. In many elementary schools, children have little opportunity to engage in self-directed play. When the opportunity does exist, the children are usually on the playground at recess. The researchers note that the playground is a male-preferred setting and many of the play behaviors there are typically male. They also note that as the frequency of fantasy play decreases, rough and tumble play increases.

■ **FIGURE 4.4**   Children's Perceived Work: Play Continuum

PLAY ─── WORK

Nature of the Activity

Free exploration of materials	Activities that are teacher-designed but allow for some discovery or creativity	Teacher-directed and designed activities
Generally involves manipulatives or other objects		Product-oriented
Does not require quiet	Self-selected activities that require concentration or attention to detail	Usually involving pencil and paper
Process-oriented		Sometimes requires quiet
Does not require finishing	Games with rules and academic content	Projects (in kindergarten)
		Must be finished

Child Involvement

Children's intentions central	Teachers' intentions usually central but more choices available to the child	Mental concentration and cognitive activity evident to the child
Usually physically active		Can sometimes interact with peers
Little mental concentration or cognitive activity evident to the child	Can usually interact freely with peers	Usually physically inactive
Can interact freely with peers	Usually fun	Sometimes fun
Always fun		

Teacher Involvement

Few teacher expectations	Generally some teacher evaluation	Teachers' expectations and intentions central
Rarely evaluated by the teacher		Outcomes evaluated by the teacher

Source: "Play Is Not the Work of the Child" by L. A. Wing, 1995, *Early Childhood Research Quarterly,* 10 (2), p. 240. Reprinted by permission of Ablex Publishing Corporation.

Journal 4.7: Think about why researchers have referred to school playgrounds as male-preferred environments. Comment on why you agree or disagree. If you think that this finding is true, how do you think we could begin to change that perspective? ■

On playgrounds, there's a lot of chasing, hitting at, reversing roles from the chaser to the chased or from the police to the enemy, and general playfulness in children's rough and tumble play. When children are socially skilled and liked by their playmates, their play is quite friendly, but if they are rejected or socially immature, their rough and tumble play may become aggressive (Pellegrini, 1988, 1989). Researchers think that these children may not be clear about what rough and tumble play is, that they can't interpret it correctly, that they take it seriously and become aggressive. This information tells you that if you work with kindergarten and early elementary school children, you will need to observe carefully on the playground and be ready to guide and intervene if the play gets serious or dangerous. The same watchfulness is necessary with other kinds of play for these children, because their play has become so complex.

Metacommunication in pretend play.   By ages 5 or 6 through age 8, children's pretend play has the advantage of extensive experiences, a developing sense of humor, and a wide range of understandings. Along with the sophistication of their symbolism, which now extends to words and other written symbols, children engage in what is called **metacommunication.** For example, children are communicating about communicating and these metacommunications are quite complex. When children use them, they are telling their peers what is play and what is not. In fact, children communicate a whole series of messages in their pretend play through metacommunications:

- They set the stage for their play or construct a play frame. ("Let's pretend that we're taking the puppy to the vet.")
- They transform objects and settings. ("This is the puppy [pointing to a pillow] and this is the vet office [pointing to a closet].")
- They extend the play. ("Pretend that our puppy died.")
- They elaborate on character feelings or actions. ("You're very sad about our puppy and you want to buy a new one.")
- They change the role. ("Pretend that I'm in charge of the pet shop now.")
- They end the play or change the sequence. ("Pretend that we're at home and we're going to bed." "I don't want to play anymore.")

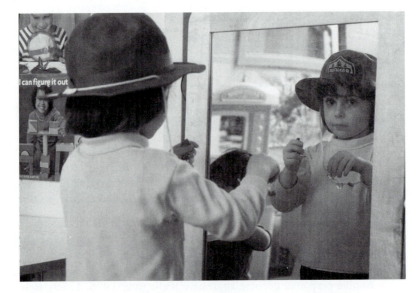

What kind of role might this child be preparing to take and what might she communicate to her peers?

The value of metacommunication is that it communicates the information needed for a pair or small group of children to pretend play together. Metacommunication assures that everyone knows what is happening, what the roles are, what the props represent, and when things change. Like so much of children's pretend play, metacommunication provides good information about children's thinking and social concepts if we will watch and listen. In addition to the metacommunication that occurs in kindergarten and primary grades, there is an increase of problem solving in group pretend play.

Problem solving in group pretend play. As children mature and gain experience, they are able to maintain pretend play in a group for longer periods of time. Those play situations begin to include problems to be solved by the players. Generally, children stay with known and comfortable settings but create stories in them to add excitement, puzzles, and complexity to their play. For instance, they may create a situation of an earthquake happening during a picnic or a mom losing her baby in the grocery store. From their scenarios, they take a consistent series of steps to solve the problem or address the dilemma they created. Here's a sample of a series of steps the children might proceed through in their pretend play:

1. "We're all at the grocery store, okay? And this is the deli, and this is the meat department, and this is the bakery. Jerlean, you're the mom and you lose your baby when you're shopping. I'm the owner of the store and Joey's the cash register guy. Pretend it's real crowded in the store." (setting the stage and describing the problem)

2. "Help, help, I've lost my baby. Somebody help me. Where's the owner?" (identifying the problem)

3. "Here I am, this is my store. We have a big store. This is a very crowded day—lots of people in the store. I don't know how we're going to find your baby. How did you lose him? Let's get the cash register guy to help." (developing of the plot)

4. "I'm the cash register guy and I can talk to people on my microphone. I'll ask all the people to look for your baby. Don't worry, Mrs. Daniels, we will find your baby." (resolving the problem)

5. "Here he is—your baby. He was playing by the cereal boxes. We found him and now everyone is happy. The end." (ending)

As children mature, these problem scenarios become more complicated and extend into unfamiliar settings and plots. This is a time when children need a supportive environment and plenty of time for practice to gain complexity in their play. Often, you will find in a kindergarten or primary grade classroom that some children will be quite skilled at such play. They can play consistently within a theme and they end up coaching and directing the other children (Kostelnik, Soderman, & Whiren, 1993).

The pretend play of children this age is often referred to as *dramatic play*. It is an excellent and comfortable setting in which children can express thoughts and feelings, and work through the uncertainties of worrisome situations such as divorce, job loss, new baby, and so on. Consequently, play supports children's emotional development. The dramatic play of children in kindergarten and primary grades also stimulates language development, with the introduction and clarification of new words and concepts, practice in using language, and opportunity for verbal thinking (Vygotsky, 1962). Much of children's pretend play occurs with literacy activities in settings such as a post office, grocery store, house, train station, or airport. Again, teacher guidance and provision of materials can stimulate both variety and frequency of literacy activities (Morrow, 1990). Those same literacy activities can be part of another form of play for this age group—games with rules.

Games with rules.   This is a time when children have a logical system of thinking and a passion for order, so games with rules are a good fit for this age group. The kinds of games with rules that these children enjoy may be sensorimotor in nature—such as marbles, ball games, tag, hopscotch, jacks, or hide-and-seek—or cognitive in nature—such as checkers, card games, Clue, Monopoly, or other board games. Games with rules introduce new elements into children's play. Up to now, there hasn't been much competition in their play, but games with rules involve competition between two or more players. Additionally, the games are directed by a set of rules that are agreed to in advance by all players and cannot be changed. You might recall that younger children often make rules as they go along or change them in a serendipitous way (when they feel like it). The rules of checkers and Monopoly have been around a long time, so there's not much possibility of change.

> **Journal 4.8:** We have been focusing on the benefits of play all through this chapter. When children begin playing games with rules, there continues to be benefits, but there also may be some disadvantages. Think of a familiar game, such as checkers or Clue, and list the benefits of such a game for children of this age. Then think of the disadvantages of playing the game. ◼

Another development that characterizes children of this age is a concern with fairness. When his family plays games together on Friday nights, Otioli is quick to observe any infractions of the rules, especially on the part of the adults. He is also hard on himself for the least little mistake. His newly developed conscience is especially strict and doesn't tolerate accidents or errors well. The conscience of his older brother, Chemieti, has softened a bit, and he is able to emphasize with others. He will often say to Otioli, "He can't help it. It was an accident" if their friend Paul does something wrong in a game.

This is also a time when children engage in competitive sports, another kind of game with rules. Even with the competitive element, children in kindergarten and primary grades can have a great time out on the soccer field or on a baseball team with their friends, especially if there isn't a great deal of interference by the adults. A friend who coaches soccer with a passion for letting it be the children's game, recalls the casual nature of his team. One child was running down the field next to another child and asked the child if he wanted to come over and spend the night. Seconds later, he ran over to his parent and asked, "Can Andrew spend the night?" in the midst of the game.

Millions of children in the United States participate in organized sports each year, with an average of three to four hours of involvement per week. In other words, sports takes up about 20 percent of the play time of children ages 6 to 8. If we go back to the benefits of play, we'll probably find that organized sports have the potential to achieve some of those benefits. If organized appropriately, children will gain self-esteem and skills of cooperation as well as get good exercise. We've all seen the opposite kind of coaching—the kind that pressures children to win above all else. When you go back to the characteristics of play, you can quickly see that it is no longer play for children on such a team.

Much of the play in kindergarten and primary grades continues through middle childhood, adolescence, and adulthood: games with rules, organized sports, and some fantasy (pretending). But much of the zest and creativity may disappear, due to society's lack of acceptance of play in its true form for children after the age of 8. One aspect of play that does carry on into adulthood very well is the social development that emerges from play. We have not really talked directly about the social aspect of play and the stages that children move through in their play. In order to see the whole picture of children's play, it is important to put that information together with the changes in sensorimotor (physical) and symbolic play that children experience.

Social Development and Play

The social development of children has been studied intensely in the context of play, probably because children's play is the best setting to observe their social development and because play contributes so much to that development. Both perspectives will be important for you to keep in mind as you watch children and plan for their play activities. Let's begin with the value of play for children's social development. The question is: How does play contribute to children's social skills and social understandings? Remember that our goal for children is social competence—that is, the ability to function effectively in society.

Play and Social Competence

To be socially competent, a person needs a number of skills or specific abilities. Sharing, cooperation, perspective taking, conceptions of friendship, interpersonal strategies, and communication skills are just some of the components of social competence (Eisenberg & Harris, 1984; Frost, 1991). Much of the play development we have just described for infants through children in primary grades included social development aspects, but we think that you will need to be even more aware of the exciting possibilities for children when they play.

Sharing and cooperation.   As soon as children begin to play with toys or other materials and are in the company of other children, they have the opportunity to share. Typically, children don't share easily until about age 3, but one of our colleagues (Smith, 1997, personal communication) has videotapes of very young toddlers who respond to another toddler's stress by bringing a toy to him or her. A good early childhood setting should be equipped with enough of each material or toy so that young children do not need to share until they are ready. An example of inappropriate practice for toddlers is "Adults arbitrarily expect children to share. Popular toys are not provided in duplicate and are fought over constantly" (NAEYC, 1997, p. 84). In Chapter 8, you will hear Darren, an early childhood educator of toddlers, talk about a decision not to force sharing and about strategies to help children begin to take turns (which is a kind of sharing).

Sharing and cooperation begin in infancy, when adults and siblings play with babies. When parents play games with babies, infants begin to wait for a turn. There is also the opportunity to develop an awareness of others, which is essential for later co-operation. Although adults initiate games with infants, researchers have noted that once the game begins, babies take on an active role in keeping the game going and are very involved in the game (Ross & Lollis, 1987). As toddlers, children have endless opportunities to share and cooperate, many of which they are not ready for, but nevertheless they begin to see the possibilities and to see examples. Contemporary researchers of children's social play find that 2-year-olds will cooperate when they play with very familiar peers. By the time they are in preschool, they are better able to share and to feel quite good about doing so. You often hear a 4-year-old tell an adult, "I shared with Emily" or "I'm sharing my new Ninja turtle." Sometimes, sharing new toys or favorite items of play is too difficult for children; in fact, some programs even have a policy that children cannot bring in playthings if they aren't able to share them. By kindergarten and primary grades, children are expected to share many materials in school and do so easily.

Perspective taking. **Perspective taking** is kind of like putting yourself in another person's shoes so that you have an understanding or appreciation of that person's thinking and feelings. Rubin and Howe (1986) define it as being able to simultaneously consider one's own thoughts, feelings, and views of the world along with another's (p. 115). When young children begin to pretend play, they begin their development toward perspective taking. When they provide talk about how a doll or stuffed animal is feeling or what the doll wants, they are taking the perspective of another. As they mature and begin to talk for the doll, they continue their development. Later, as they play varying roles, they display their perspective taking of their parents, doctor, teacher, and others in their lives. Within the interactions of dramatic play, children witness and hear other perspectives. In the course of their play, they may challenge those perspectives or accept them to broaden her own perspectives. Rubin (1980) treats us to a delightful interaction between two 4-year-old boys, one of whom is playing the father and one of whom is playing the mother:

Father: "So long, I'll see ya later. It's time to go to work."

Mother: "Hey, wait for me. I gotta go to work too."

Father: "Moms don't work . . . my mom don't work . . . stay here."

Mother: "Well my mom works . . . lots womens work ya know. My mom is a perfessor at the university."

Father: "OK, then, just hurry so we won't be late. Are you sure ya wanna work?" (p. 75)

Some of the sharing we see in young children goes hand in hand with their perspective taking. We hear children say, "Josey is sad, so I gave her my doll." It's the kind of perspective taking and sharing that Smith observed in very young toddlers. Even the youngest of children are surprisingly capable of perspective taking.

Conceptions of friendship. Although conceptions of friendship begin quite early when children are placed in group settings, we cannot be sure of real concepts until later when children are able to display their understanding of what friendship is or what a friend does. Often, a preschool curriculum focuses on friendship as a theme, but for many children it is simply a matter of saying the words associated with friendship rather than a true understanding. By kindergarten and primary grades, children become increasingly interested in establishing quality friendships. According to Hendrick (1990), most children by age 7 find it almost unthinkable not to have a friend. For example, Keeley and her best friend, Dani, can play for hours at a time. They prefer to play with each other over any other choices, and they truly miss each other when one of them is ill or out of town. They share, they cooperate, they take each other's perspective, and they genuinely care about each other. They experience stimulation, assistance, companionship, and affection from their friendship (Parker & Gottman, 1989). Many adults have friendships that began in first grade and have been maintained to adulthood.

Journal 4.9: Instead of a formal curriculum to try to teach children about friendships, we encourage you to use informal approaches whenever an opportunity arises. Can you think of situations when it would be appropriate to teach about friends or friendships? Describe a few of them and consider how you would use the moment to teach about friendship. ■

Interpersonal strategies.   Interpersonal strategies include a wide variety of social approaches that young children are learning and practicing. Some take extensive experience and some come fairly easy. The interpersonal strategies of developing relationships with others and living within our society include:

- *Perceives, interprets, and responds to social situations appropriately.* Young children are often not skilled at judging a situation before responding. When we watched Francis and Akosa's children earlier, we saw the boys' friend, Brittany, ask for permission to have the children come inside her home to play. When Brittany's family said that she couldn't have the boys come in to play because one of them caused problems, Otioli announced it for the entire group in a way that embarrassed everyone concerned. His intentions were good, but he wasn't skilled at responding in a way that was socially acceptable.

- *Establishes contact with others in appropriate ways.* Toddlers make endless errors in their efforts to make contact. They may knock over another child, push a child, grab a toy, or stand nearby without saying a word. We once watched a very shy boy wanting to make contact with a group of children who were building with blocks. After days of watching, he knocked over a very elaborate building and looked surprised when the group became upset with him. After consistent teacher coaching, this child learned appropriate ways to make contact with other children and to request entry into their play.

- *Expresses needs, rights, and emotions appropriately.* It is not surprising to see a toddler bite another child to express a right or an emotion, or to witness a young preschooler throw a tantrum to express a need or an emotion. Even children in kindergarten need practice in naming their needs, rights, or emotions. One of the adult roles needed for children's social development is that of a coach. Young children respond well to the encouragement to "Tell him that you don't like to be bumped" or "Tell us that you feel angry right now." Adults can also model appropriate ways to express needs ("I need everyone to be quiet so that I can read"), rights ("It's my turn to talk"), or emotions ("I am feeling so excited today").

■ *Sustains relationships.* When children are enjoyable to be with, they are able to sustain relationships. A variety of characteristics and skills makes them enjoyable—cooperation, sharing, sense of humor, helpfulness, good judgment, flexibility, and so on. In order to sustain a relationship, a child also has to care about another child or children, so it takes some maturity to sustain a relationship.

■ *Flexes to accommodate others and situations.* Very young children don't flex well. They need routines, a consistent group of peers and adults, and few changes. Being flexible is just too difficult for a toddler or a young preschooler. However, as children become more sociable and have more experiences with peers, they develop the capacity to take another's perspective, to feel empathy for another, and to exhibit a strong sense of fairness. Thus, they can give up a turn, a plaything, a schedule, or a plan. When Wamalwa was injured accidentally by his brother during play, Otioli gave him his treasured Lego model to play with, even though there was a chance that it would be destroyed by the toddler. When Chemieti and Otioli wanted to go down the street to play but their parents asked them to stay home for our visit, they were agreeable about staying.

■ *Negotiates conflicts.* The strategies and examples in Table 4.3 give us a sense of the abilities necessary for children to negotiate conflicts. This is a very complex aspect of developing and maintaining relationships. Some children will have had no experience in negotiation, either because of limited experience with groups of peers or because well-meaning adults solved most of their conflicts. All of the other interpersonal skills we have just described will influence how well a child is able to negotiate conflicts. Again, children will need guidance and coaching of adults to foster the strategies in Table 4.3.

■ **TABLE 4.3 Negotiating Conflicts**

Strategy	Example
Expressing one's own rights, needs, or feelings	"It's my turn to use the stapler."
Listening to and acknowledging others' rights, opinions, and feelings	"Oh, you haven't finished yet."
Suggesting nonviolent solutions to conflict	"How about giving it to me in 2 minutes?"
Explaining the reasons behind the solution suggested	"That way we'll both get to use it before lunch."
Standing up against unreasonable demands	"No, it's not fair if you use it the whole time. I want it, too."
Accepting reasonable disagreement	"OK, I hadn't thought of that."
Compromising on a solution	"I can use tape now, and you can use tape later when I'm using the stapler."

Source: Developmentally Appropriate Programs in Early Childhood Education by M. J. Kostelnik, A. K. Soderman, and A. P. Whiren, © 1993. Reprinted by permission of Prentice-Hall, Inc., Upper Saddle River, NJ.

■ **TABLE 4.4   Examples of Comparisons between Responsive Language and Restrictive Language**

Responsive	Restrictive
We have to pick up all of the blocks today because tonight our carpets are being cleaned.	It doesn't matter why. We just have to clean everything off the floor.
It's choice time and there's room at the easels and at the Lego table. Which would you like?	You haven't painted all week—you need to paint today.
I need your help in getting ready for our field trip. Everyone needs to put on coats and be ready to listen.	We can't go on our field trip until everyone is ready and quiet.
We walk in our classroom so that no one gets hurt.	No running in our classroom.
You really shaped your play-dough into interesting figures. Tell me about them.	You didn't spend much time with the play-dough. Can't you make something?

Communication skills.   Most play situations offer opportunities for speaking and listening. Even if children are playing alone or are not ready to interact with peers, adults can use the situation to ask questions, offer comments, and engage the child in conversation. The way an adult talks with children will send a message about how children are regarded. Children need a stress-free language environment if they are to communicate. Early childhood educators are encouraged to use responsive language when speaking to children. Stone (1993) describes **responsive language** as language that "conveys a positive regard for children, and a respect for and acceptance of their individual ideas and feelings" (p. 13). Responsive language includes giving children reasons for our statements, encouraging children's choices, and making positive comments on children's efforts. Table 4.4 shows a comparison between responsive language and **restrictive language,** language that communicates disrespect and adult control.

Once children begin playing in pairs or groups, they explore vocabulary, expressive conversation, body language, and other forms of communication to interact with each other. Their play provides rich opportunities and support for developing social competence. In addition to observing the multiple benefits of play for children's social development, we know that children progress through levels of play that are indicative of their social development. One of the researchers who intensely studied children's play was Mildred Parten. In the 1930s, she observed and recorded the play of children from ages 2 to 5 and developed a framework of levels of play that continues to be used today when looking at children's social maturity in play.

Parten's Levels of Play

Parten outlined levels of play that started with simple immature social play and increased in social sophistication to a complex level. Those levels or categories of play will be useful for your observations of children's play and for planning curriculum.

Solitary play.   The first level, **solitary play,** is not surprising if you have watched 2-year-olds. For example, Tony is playing with a puzzle in the midst of five other young toddlers, but he does not seem at all aware of them—the puzzle has his full attention. At times, he looks up and observes Annabella playing with play-dough, but he does not interact with her, and, after a brief look, he returns to his own play. This is called **onlooker play** and it occurs during solitary play.

Parallel play.   **Parallel play** is a common form of play in a toddler class and sometimes with young preschoolers. When we visited Ibrahim's class of toddlers (Chapter 8), we often saw four toddlers sitting at a table playing with play-dough. When we watched closely, we could see that each of the four children was playing completely independently, and generally not communicating to each other. That is, they were playing in the same place, with the same materials, but involved in separate and distinct play. That is parallel play. Parten saw parallel play as a transition for children to move from solitary play to more socially interactive play.

Associative play.   **Associative play** is similar to parallel play in that children are focused on separate play activities, but these children interact. They talk, lend materials, share, take turns with common materials, notice each other's play, and are communicative. In Ibrahim's classroom, we often saw associative play when the easels were set up outside on the playground. Two or more children would paint their own creations, but talk about what they're doing, share the red paint, and notice each other's art. We would hear them comment, "I like your painting—it's pretty" or "Oh, that's beautiful" or "You did a good job." Much of what an observer hears will reflect adult comments because children mimic adult comments. At times, it looks like the children are more interested in the social aspects of easel painting than in the painting itself.

Cooperative play.   Parten considered **cooperative play** the highest level of social maturity in play. It is the kind of play in which two or more children engage in a common activity and share a common goal. Sometimes the tasks of the activity are divided among the players and sometimes all of the players are doing the same activity toward the common goal. In Keeley's kindergarten classroom, many hours were spent constructing with blocks. The children's comments reflect their cooperative play: "Let's all get a bunch of blocks and pile them up as high as we can," "Dani, you get the big blocks and put them over here," and "Raul, you get those boards to put across our bridge." Children have watched adults cooperate, have had opportunities to be part of a cooperative venture, and are ready for what a cooperative group can accomplish.

As children gain experience and mature, their cooperative play skills increase. They begin working in small groups, two or three children, and advance to being able to play in groups of five or six. They are also better able to manipulate materials and their environment. They have new skills and competencies, so they are able to contribute to the group goal. Children who have reached this stage are able to elaborate on ideas and to pursue complex plans. They are gradually less dependent on toys and other materials because they can use their imaginations to change the reality of what they are doing or where they are. It is fascinating to watch a group of 5- and 6-year-olds engaged in cooperative pretend play.

Kindergartners: Cooperative pretend play

Their kindergarten teacher, Mr. Hardt, had read them stories of the Pilgrims coming over on the *Mayflower*. The children had intense discussions about the difficult journey and how the children on the ship must have felt. The group made lists of everything they knew about the voyage and researched for more information in the school library. One day, Mr. Hardt suggested that they dramatize the voyage on the *Mayflower*. Eight of the children very enthusiastically volunteered. They went out to the playground where a huge post was to serve as the ship's mast. The children were left on their own to plan their drama. "I have an idea," said Elena, "We can hang sheets from the pole to be sails." The other children got excited with her and continued to come up with other props and a set. From there, the children decided on roles for themselves. Two boys wanted to be the Captain, so they deliberated about another important role for themselves. Alfredo agreed to be the navigator, and Joseph smiled as the Captain. Other children took on the roles of a mother, father, child, and ship workers. Without stopping to plan their script, they began dramatizing the voyage.

> *Joseph:* "Ahoy there, I'm the Captain and I want everyone on the deck. Where is my navigator?"
>
> *Alfredo:* "Here I am, sir. I will get everyone to come on deck."
>
> *Group:* "Good morning, Captain."
>
> *Joseph:* "My navigator tells me that we are going to hit a storm. This could be rough. You might get sick." (Aside to his teacher: "Is it OK if someone gets sick?")
>
> *Alfredo:* "There will be giant waves. Don't be scared."

The scenario continues through the storm and on to a sighting of land. The group finishes excitedly, landing in Plymouth, and is ready to organize to perform for their classmates. Note that Mr. Hardt played a small role in their play but was available for assistance if needed. He would have stepped in if the situation had warranted it, but he observed the children's ability to manage their own drama and arrangements. The adult role in children's play is a critical one, and it's time for you to be thinking of how you will interact with children as they play.

Adult Roles in Children's Play

When you watch children, it may seem that adults do not and should not have any roles in children's play; however, a closer look will tell you that adults have significant roles in the play. Those roles may not be obvious because some of the adult work is a type of preparation for play. That preparation includes providing the setting and materials for play, and setting up the ground rules for a play setting. Other adult roles are obvious. When adults intervene for safety reasons, or to assist a child who doesn't have the skills needed, or to facilitate more complex play, they play significant roles. What's also important when thinking of adult roles is a caution about behaviors that interfere with or stop children's play. If you don't have adequate experience or don't watch children enough, your well-meaning help may have the opposite effect on children's play. As you watch the children and adults in the chapters that follow, you will begin to develop your own role for being involved in children's play. For now, we will talk about some important and supportive roles and caution you about the roles that do not contribute to children's play.

Preparing the Setting for Play

Your decisions about the play setting will depend on the age and development of the children who will use it. It is quite obvious that a play setting for 1-year-olds will be different from a play setting for 6-year-olds. We urge you to study the *Developmentally Appropriate Practice in Early Childhood Programs* (Bredekamp & Copple, 1997) guidelines for how to set up environments for each age group. We begin with a recommendation that is appropriate for all ages—provide for active experiences and for challenge.

Environments for active experiences and challenges.   If the setting is for infants, the room arrangement and the kinds of toys provided will encourage the infants' activities and challenge their newly developing skills. There will be lots of open space for rolling, crawling, and early walking without obstacles, as well as objects that can be grasped, manipulated, and enjoyed. For toddlers, the environment will include puzzles, blocks,

Sand play offers the opportunity for both active enjoyment and learning experiences. Why do you think that sand play is such a favorite?

■ **FIGURE 4.5**   Criteria for Productive Play Activities

1. Investigative play tasks are open-ended. They do not lead students to "the answers."
2. Play tasks call for the generation of ideas, rather than the recall of specific pieces of information.
3. Play activities challenge students' thinking; indeed, they *require* thinking. Higher-order mental challenges are built into each play task.
4. Play activities are "messy." Children are, in fact, playing around. Learning through play is nonlinear, nonsequential (Wasserman, 1989).
5. Play tasks focus on "big ideas"—the important concepts of the curriculum—rather than on trivial details.
6. Each play task provides opportunities for children to grow in their conceptual understanding. When children carry out investigative play, they grow in their ability to understand larger concepts.
7. The children are the players. They are actively involved in learning. They are talking to each other, sharing ideas, speculating, laughing, and getting excited about what they have found. They are not sitting quietly, passively listening to the teacher's thinking.
8. The children are working together, in learning groups. Play is enhanced through cooperative investigations. Cooperation, rather than competitive individual work, is stressed.

Source: Reprinted by permission of the publisher from Wasserman, S. *Serious Players in the Primary Classroom: Empowering the Young Child through Active Learning Experiences* (New York: Teachers College Press, © 1990 by Teachers College, Columbia University. All rights reserved.), p. 27.

balls, and beads to string, as well as providing housekeeping tasks that feel like play to toddlers (washing windows and tables, sweeping the floor, etc.). All of the playthings and activities are designed to challenge the children and to foster a sense of "I can do" (Wasserman, 1990). By the time children are in preschool, they need complex stimulation and changing materials to maintain learning. Many preschool programs arrange materials and equipment in centers to focus children's play. Preschool curricula often follow a project approach, so that children's play integrates all aspects of their development and builds from intense interest in a project.

Supporting productive play.   By kindergarten and primary grades, it takes a skillful adult to provide active learning experiences and challenges. Wasserman (1990) talks about "productive play activities"—activities that promote children's thinking and reasoning, and ultimately learning. Figure 4.5 describes Wasserman's criteria for productive play activities. She urges early childhood educators to adjust these guidelines to children's maturity and experience, to their independence and autonomy, and to their ability to work in groups.

Basic conditions for play.   Bruner (1985a), another researcher of play, says that certain conditions contribute to the "richness and length of play" (p. 604). They are important conditions for you to keep in mind when you set up the environment for play and for deciding on your role. Bruner's conditions include the following:

■ *A playmate.* Anyone who has watched young children at play knows that two children will play longer and engage in more complex play than one child. Many a parent will invite another child over to play because it has such a positive influence on her own child's play and it makes life easier for the parent. When there's more than one child, there is the opportunity to have conversation, to exchange materials, to get feedback on your play, and to negotiate.

■ *Appropriate play materials.* Many of the commercial play materials available today do not sustain children's attention for very long. They appear exotic and complex, but once a child has begun playing with the toy, he finds that the material is not flexible and that it can be used only in singular ways. When we visited Francis and Akosa, they lamented about the attraction of so many toys in the United States and compared those play materials with those of their childhood. "We played with simple materials—with toys that we made ourselves—and they kept us interested so much longer." They expressed regret about many of the boys' toy preferences that offered no challenge and that ended up in the toy box in a short time. They compared those choices with sets of Legos, which were a constant source of challenge as the boys constructed all kinds of things alone or together.

■ *An adult nearby.* The nearby adult is not necessarily involved in the action of play, but is ready to be a buffer, a comforter, or an encourager when needed. Bruner notes that children play longer and with more complexity when an available adult is nearby. Many of us in our parenting have made the same observation and have had our children instruct us in our role. "Stay here in my room," says the child, "I just want you here while Tina and I play."

Key elements of high-quality play. In preparation for play, adults set the stage with time, space, and play materials—three key elements of high-quality play (Ward, 1996). In terms of **time,** children need long stretches of uninterrupted time to sustain different types of play, especially dramatic and constructive play. Those studying play (Johnson, Christie, & Yawkey, 1987) recommend 30- to 50-minute time blocks for free play in preschools and kindergartens in order to allow children the freedom to persist and expand on a play theme. Those observers also note that when children are repeatedly hampered by play periods that are too short, they resort to very simple forms of play.

The second key element is **space.** Children need sufficient space to play effectively. Experts believe that young children need at least 25 to 30 square feet to play well. In addition to the amount of space, the arrangement of space has an impact on children's play. Programs for young children usually avoid large open spaces because those spaces don't encourage high-quality play. In fact, those spaces often encourage running and rough and tumble play. Instead, partitioned spaces encourage focused play, especially dramatic play.

The third key element is **play materials.** Materials must be selected for appropriateness with respect to children's development. An environment with too few materials will not support children's high-quality play, but an environment with too many materials will confuse, distract, and interrupt children's high-quality play. One of the best ways to decide about play materials is to watch children use them and to consider the goals for children. Play materials must provide opportunities to experience and develop toward those goals. For example, if a goal for primary children is literacy, then plenty of literacy materials should be placed in the environment. Those materials will include typewriters, computers, paper of all kinds, a variety of writing utensils, books, games, lap pads, mailboxes, envelopes, and newspapers. If a goal for toddlers is the development of small motor skills, then the play materials should include play-dough, crayons and markers, puzzles, beads, interlocking blocks, and miniature figures.

In time, children can make many choices about their environment and can gather their own play materials. Children as young as age 3 can describe their environmental needs, can suggest ways to rearrange the environment, and are able to propose changes in play materials. In those situations, adults will serve as guides or facilitators.

Children's development advances when they have opportunities to practice newly acquired skills as well as to experience a challenge just beyond their level of present mastery. Your observation of children will be critical in determining what they are ready for, what they need to practice, and what will nudge them with a challenge. If a preschooler enjoys the puzzles currently out on the shelf, and each day appears to be assembling them with increasing ease, then it's probably time to put a few new puzzles out and to make sure that they are just slightly more difficult.

Intervening at the Right Time: Secure Play

Professionals who work with young children worry about inhibiting or disrupting children's play with interventions. There are, however, appropriate times for adult intervention—times when their role is to assist, to challenge, and to question children's play. Beyond safety issues, determining the right time to intervene and how to intervene is a critical decision for early childhood educators. We describe some of the most frequent "right times" and suggest possibilities for your intervention.

Helping children enter ongoing play. Until children develop the skills of making contact with others or of gaining access to a group situation, they may need supportive adults to assist them. Ramsey (1991) encourages adults to help the child who has not been invited to join or who does not know how to make contact with those at play. "Interactions in preschool classrooms are short, so children are constantly having to gain entry into new groups. This process is made more difficult because children who are already engaged with each other tend to protect their interactive space and reject newcomers" (p. 27).

This may be true, depending on how the classroom environment has been set up. Many educators currently work to build a sense of community in classrooms, and in some programs, children take responsibility for each other and take the initiative to help each other. Early childhood educators may nevertheless need to model an entry for the child by encouraging her to say, "I want to play blocks with you" or "I would like to join your game." You may also help the child enter by taking on a new role in the ongoing play by suggesting to her, "Ring the doorbell and announce that the pizza is here."

Another strategy comes form Beatty (1995), who suggests that you encourage the child to begin parallel play next to the group with the hope that the group will eventually let her in. Group or activity entry is a very important social skill and children will need your guidance, encouragement, modeling, and coaching so that they can become skilled.

> Play access struggles with other children are the most critical learning opportunities that young children must deal with. Such conflicts teach profound lessons in getting along with others: how to watch and wait, when to initiate contact, how to learn what is going on in the play, how to blend in with the group, what to say so you won't be rejected, and what to do in case you are rejected. These crucial lessons are repeated over and over as children ebb and flow during free play. (Beatty, 1995, p. 108)

Not only will you be assisting children who need your help in gaining entry to a play group but you will also be teaching crucial social skills when you assist children in those situations.

Addressing unoccupied behavior. In many classrooms and programs, a child will be seen wandering aimlessly or generally unoccupied while all around him are children intensely involved in play. There are several possibilities for a child's unoccupied behavior: boredom, overstimulation, illness, and emotional upset, to name a few. To determine the reason, you will need to have been a good observer so that you know the child well. Using your clues from previous observations, your relationship with the child will assist you in probing the reason for his behavior. If it's boredom, you have some fairly simple approaches easily available. It may be time to bring out some new play materials, adding more interest and challenge to the environment. This is an ideal time to find out what interests the child at home so that you can build on those interests. Be sure to listen to conversations to find out topics of interest that will direct some of your choices of materials.

Sometimes, overstimulation will cause children to wander. Too many choices, too much noise, too many people, or too much activity affects some children with confusion. Find a more secluded part of the room (or make one with partitions) and offer just two or three choices.

If the reason for unoccupied behavior is illness or emotional upset, then you will need to address those issues before the child can play happily. We have often found that when children who are just on the verge of being sick come to the child care center or school, they will wander aimlessly. They're just not themselves, but they don't know what to do about it.

Intervening to add challenge or to stimulate. When you intervene to challenge or stimulate, you run the risk of turning the play into work. So we urge caution here. Here are some examples of when this intervention is warranted:

When children are having difficulty getting along and playing together

When children's play seems repetitious and about to dissolve

When children do not initiate or engage in pretend play (Ward, 1996, p. 22)

You have several possibilities for intervention to address those situations. The first is a good starting point for you when you are developing experience and skill in your role as an early childhood educator.

■ *Parallel play for adults.* We urge you to try parallel play for yourself. Position yourself beside the child and model the play behaviors you are encouraging. Don't try to interact or direct the child's play. This nonthreatening approach is a great way to help children extend their play with new materials and behaviors.

■ *Co-playing for adults.* Another approach is to co-play. Very often, children will invite an adult to co-play with them, and it's a good opportunity to encourage and enrich their play. Children especially like their teachers to join them when they play restaurant, house, or airplane. Once on the scene, the teacher's dialogue can enhance the play. Listen:

Child: Teacher, teacher, come to our house.

Teacher: May I come to visit you today?

Child: Sure, come in and sit down. We're having lunch.

Teacher: Oh, I don't want to interrupt your meal. Maybe I should come back another time.

Child: Oh, no, we want you to come in. You can eat with us.

Teacher: Thanks, I would like that. What are you having for lunch?

Child: Chicken and pizza. Do you want some?

Teacher: Well I'm a vegetarian, so I eat only vegetables. Do you have any?

Child: Oh, sure, I'll fix you some. Honey (directed to second child), can you go to the store and buy some vegetables? (Other child leaves and returns with a brown paper bag.)

Teacher: It smells good in here. How did you cook the chicken?

Child: I just cooked it in the oven, very hot, all night.

Teacher: What kind of vegetables did you get? (addressed to second child).

Child: Carrots and beans. I like those. Do you?

Teacher: Sure, I do like beans and carrots. Did they have any tomatoes and zucchini or eggplant?

Child: I can go get some of those. I'll be right back.

You get the idea. Your conversation begins to add depth and new ideas to the play. Your co-play is nonthreatening because you've established rapport by playing in their setting, one that they have established. In the process, you have the potential to help children persist in their play, to include other children in the play, and to ask higher-level questions to extend the play. Besides that, it's fun.

Deciding to intervene in children's play is a complex decision. Why might this adult be intervening?

Other intervention strategies come from Smilansky (1968), who studied children's pretend play extensively. Her two strategies are more direct but have the potential to stimulate children who are uninvolved or playing rather listlessly.

- *Outside intervention.* With outside intervention, you make suggestions to a child or children from outside the play. You may be sitting nearby and suggest to Julia that she visit the group playing house, or that she schedule an appointment at the beauty shop, or that she apply for a job at the store.

- *Inside intervention.* Inside intervention requires you to put yourself in the middle of the children's play. It's quite intrusive but sometimes necessary. For example, let's say the children are sitting together playing with blocks and not much is happening. There is no interaction and not much construction. You go and sit in the middle, saying, "I think that I'd like to build an airport. Would anyone like to help me?" Hopefully, you will soon have an energetic group busily constructing runways and terminals all around you.

A Playful Attitude

Children watch adults every minute of the day, whether the adults are involved in play or not. What we adults say and do—even what we wear—sends messages about how we feel about play. Our attitude about events in our classrooms or programs sets a tone for the environment.

Our final recommendation about adult roles is for you to be aware of yourself. If you are playful yourself, you send a message about children's play. Perhaps you are thinking, "How do I go about being playful?" Before we answer, we want you to reflect on your personality and your response to little happenings in your life.

Journal 4.10: What characteristics do people use when describing you? When someone is late, how do you react? When it rains and you're without an umbrella or raincoat, how do you respond? What kind of things make you laugh? What do you do for fun? ■

Laughing sends a message.   Our first recommendation for being playful is to find as many opportunities as possible to laugh. When an unexpected event happens in your class or when you're with children, try to find humor in it. It will be especially effective if you can laugh at yourself. Children can learn to do the same if they see significant adults laughing at themselves. Children are learning to tell jokes, so why not consider telling them a simple joke every day? Also, be ready for young children's jokes. They often don't make sense, but children find them hilariously funny.

When children become silly, you will need to determine whether it is an appropriate time to laugh with them, and even be silly yourself, or whether they need a focus or direction. Much will depend on the children's usual play behavior and on the situation (what other children are doing and whether the silliness will disturb the setting). If there is tension or the children are growing weary, then it may be just the right time to unwind with everyone laughing.

You might also consider doing some pretend laughing. Picture this: You are sitting with a group of children and you suggest, "Let's all laugh for one minute." Or you might set the scene—"As you are walking down the street, you see a little red and white dog with a bow on each of his ears and pretzels on his tail and . . ."—and wait for the giggles. Or you might ask each child, in turn, to "laugh like a king," "laugh like a baby," "laugh like a hyena," "laugh like a monster," and so on. Or if it's a noisy day, ask the children to laugh without making any sound.

What we are encouraging here is to communicate that the environment is safe and supportive of play. If children know that you laugh at your mistakes and that you can be silly once in a while (or more often than that), they will be secure in their play.

Join in the play.   At times in this chapter we've urged you to enter children's play for intervention purposes. Now we suggest that you sit and play with children for no reason at all. For example, when a few children are playing with play-dough, sit with them and roll the dough and pat it and make something from it. Or when children are lying on the floor reading books, get down on the floor and read with them. Or when children are painting, get in there and paint, too. You might feel inhibited about finger painting or dancing to music, but you can get used to it well in advance of working with children. Gather a group of your friends who also want to work with young children, and plan a play party. Use the time to experience lots of the play materials and activities that you will later provide for children.

The advantages of joining the play of children are abundant. You send a message about the value of play and about your relationship with them. You also increase their comfort level for interacting with you. While playing with children, you will be able to observe information about their development, and they may tell you about themselves in ways that wouldn't ordinarily happen. They will feel increased security with you. You might also find that you have fun.

In sum, the adult role is a significant one—one of decision making at all times. An early childhood educator can never be on "remote." Constant watching, listening, interacting, and responding are required. Your role in children's play is one that can contribute to and support their learning and development, but you will make frequent decisions about that role.

PRINCIPLES AND INSIGHTS: A Summary and Review

A set of principles of child development and learning inform developmentally appropriate practice for working with children and families from infancy through primary grades. One of those principles clearly states the role and value of play: "Play is an important vehicle for children's social, emotional, and cognitive development, as well as a reflection of their development" (Bredekamp & Copple, 1997, p. 14). Those principles also encompass other important elements for children's development and learning:

- The importance of practice
- The need for different modes of learning
- The need for different ways for children to represent what they know
- The importance of active learning
- The need for direct physical and social knowledge

All of these elements add up to play. It is the one approach that satisfies the principles of development and learning, assuring us that children's growth is furthered and enhanced through play. Therefore, child-initiated, adult-supported play is an essential component of developmentally appropriate practice (Bredekamp & Copple, 1997, p. 14). In the chapters ahead, you will see that children from infancy through primary grades have a need for and greatly benefit from play.

In this chapter, we asked you to begin thinking about play. What does play mean? What is the value of play? What characteristics will you see in children's play? From there, we described the changes in children's play as they mature from infancy to toddlerhood to preschool and to kindergarten and primary grades. Begin watching the children in your life or the children you encounter in the grocery store or at the park so that you become more aware of different levels of play. We put emphasis on children's social development in play so that you would be especially watchful of social changes and growth. Finally, we described your role in children's play. It is a strategic role and one that demands your constant awareness of children and their play.

Children's play will be a rewarding and enjoyable part of your professional life. Be ready to be open to children—their freshness, their creativity, their energy, and their seriousness. Play is truly their business—and they will want your respect, appreciation, and participation.

Becoming an Early Childhood Professional

Your Field Experiences

1. Observe children's play in a variety of settings and record examples of the following:
   a. Characteristics of play
   b. Evidence of the value of play
   c. Parten's levels of play
   d. Adult intervention in play
2. Interview young children of different ages and related adults (parents, family members, teachers, caregivers) about play. Use information from this chapter to formulate your interview questions.

Your Professional Portfolio

1. Record a series of children's play episodes in which there may be a need for adult intervention. Describe your decision about an adult's role in those episodes and give a rationale for what you prescribe.
2. Write a letter to the editor of your local newspaper, advocating better playgrounds for the children of your community. Describe the values of play and the kind of play settings that promote children's development.

Your Professional Library

Books
Bredekamp, S., & Copple, C. (1997). *Developmentally appropriate practice in early childhood programs* (2nd ed.). Washington, DC: NAEYC.

Bronson, M. (1995). *The right stuff for children birth to 8: Selecting play materials to support development.* Washington, DC: NAEYC.

Frost, J. (1991). *Play and playscapes.* Albany, NY: Delmar.

Hirsch, E. S. (Ed.). (1984). *The block book.* Washington, DC: NAEYC.

Paley, V. G. (1990). *The boy who would be helicopter.* Cambridge, MA: Harvard University Press.

Rogers, C., & Sawyer, J. (1988). *Play in the lives of children.* Washington, DC: NAEYC.

Internet Addresses and World Wide Web Sites
www.naeyc.org/naeyc
  Early Years Are Learning Years (Block Play: Building a Child's Mind, 1997)

www.cyfc.umn.edu/Children/naeyc2.html
  Early Years Are Learning Years (Toys: Tools for Learning, 1996)

www.cyfc.umn.edu/Children/naeyc5.html
  Early Years Are Learning Years (Playgrounds: Keeping Outdoor Learning Safe, 1996)

www.wttw.com/wttw_web_pages/productions/10things/10_activities.html
  Activities to Make Learning Fun

chapter

5

Early Childhood Curriculum

THINKING AND PRACTICES

When you finish reading and reflecting on this chapter, you will be able to:

1. Define curriculum and identify its major elements while observing an early childhood program.

2. Describe the philosophy and thinking of major early childhood education curricular approaches and list their intended outcomes for children.

3. Differentiate among programs such as Bank Street, High Scope, Waldorf, and Reggio Emilia.

4. Take a stand in support of one or more particular early childhood curricular approaches or programs as well as take a stand against one or more approaches or programs.

5. Begin to weave several curricular approaches into your future planning for children.

Maybe you've heard the term **curriculum** before or maybe this is your first encounter. If you're currently taking a class in early childhood education, your course syllabus is a form of curriculum. It usually has course goals or objectives, a description of the content, learning activities or an outline of course topics, and information about how your learning will be assessed. So even if you haven't heard the term before, you now have a beginning idea of what curriculum is. We'll begin this chapter with a much broader understanding of curriculum and then look at examples in early childhood education.

What Is Curriculum?

To help you think about curriculum in an expansive way, reflect on how you spend your time on an ordinary day. For example, one of your authors starts her day at 6:00 A.M. with a walk around the downtown area of the city for an hour. It's like a field trip—there are always fresh store windows, new construction, another shop opening, and unusual people watching. The walk is followed by coffee and a quick bath, then breakfast while looking at the local newspaper. Even on the dullest of days, something catches my eye in the news and I learn some new information or hear a story that leaves me thinking all day. Leaving the house for a day at the university includes a look at the calendar to organize for the scheduled events. Most days include a meeting or two, student appointments, and communicating with students, colleagues, and community members by phone or e-mail. Teaching classes fills the late afternoon, and then catching up on paperwork finishes the day. Often, before leaving work, I reflect on the day and assess what was accomplished. I also make a plan for the next day—a "to-do" list. The evening races by—supper, a few phone calls, and reading professional journals or a good novel. Then it's off to sleep at 11:00 P.M. In a sense, that is my daily curriculum—the intent of the day, the activities, the environments, the people with whom I interact, and the assessment of the day's work. Each day, I learn from my friends and family, from the local newspaper, from a discussion at a meeting, from a cookbook, from an e-mail message, from journals or a novel, and from my students. All are sources of ideas, issues, questions, problems, insights, and stimulation. Even on my most ordinary day, the curriculum of my life is rich and full.

Journal 5.1: Pause here and reflect on the curriculum of your life. What kind of ideas or insights do you gain on an ordinary day? Who are the people you learn from? Where do you learn best? What is there about the environment that helps you learn? What keeps you learning? What is the most exciting curriculum your day holds? How much of your typical day is planned and how much emerges or evolves?   ■

After you finish reflecting on your day, see if you can develop a definition of *curriculum*. That will be our starting point as we work together on this chapter's discussion of important ideas about curriculum and significant curricular practices. What are the significant words in your definition? List them in your journal. Now that you have a bit of comfort with the term, we're going to move to an educational context for defining curriculum.

Defining Curriculum

Think of yourself as a teacher. Your definition of curriculum now becomes a kind of teaching plan that emerges from your philosophy about learning. It is influenced by what you know about child development and by your own experiences as a student. When you think about your experiences as a young 4- or 5-year-old student, what do you remember? How would you define curriculum if all you knew were those early educational experiences?

Curriculum plans.   For many teachers, their curriculum or teaching plan usually includes goals and objectives; descriptions of teaching and learning activities; lists of materials, equipment, and resources; schedules, if needed; and assessment strategies. There are year-long curriculum plans, monthly curriculum plans, and daily curriculum plans (see Figure 5.1) as well as written and unwritten curricula (the plural of *curriculum*), commercially developed curricula, and curricula developed by groups of teachers or school districts.

FIGURE 5.1 Weekly Plan from an Elementary Teacher

Sept. | GRADE OR CLASS _____ Post (Robin) | WEEK BEGINNING

Day	Before Sch.	Enter 8:40–9	Arrival (req.) 9–9:30	Whole Group 9:30–10	Recess 10–10:15	Literacy Centers 10:15–11:15	Clean & Inspect 11:15 to 11:25	Lunch 11:30 to 12	Quiet Reading 12–12:30	Share Books 12:20 to 12:30	Math 12:30–1	Learning Centers 1–1:40	Recess 1:50 to 2	Gathering 2:05–2:20
MONDAY 18	Ann Carlson here PSU / New jobs / Zaro's 1st B-day		✓ New jobs / ✓ Calendar / ✓ Zaro's B-day / ✓ Not this Bear	Writing (review use of writers workshop boxes)	10–10:15	10:15–11:15 / finish spelling assess.			Theme tabs Beavers & Squirrels / Ravenbooks otters & Racoons		Discovery time Ask kids rules (review) + Q + Q! / Write down "Math News" (on easel chart?)		←	Read: Buggy Bear or The Garden / take home Zaro ditto!
TUESDAY 19			Calendar / Shoe patter / 8 rules / Read: Bedford Bear	→	Library	Lit Centers 10:45–11:15 / Label room "otter day" / make pick / Diana 10:50–7:10	clean up & inspection 1:40–1:50	→	Ravenbooks otters & Racoons / Theme tabs otters & Racoons	Share Books 12:20 to 12:30	Pattern pages (little brown beans) (first do up real bears again)	Redo Math Assess		Read: Ernest & Celestine discuss care of records
WEDNESDAY 20			Calendar / Dot chart patterns / Read: Breakfast time	Make an award for your bear	P.E.	Literacy Centers 10:30–11:15 (no recess on gym day a.m.) Label room "Squirrel Clan"	Plan here	Cindy here	Magazines to each clan		Discovery time see Mon.	→		Read: Ernest & Celestine / Take home Bear note!
THURSDAY 21	get math books for Ann / ✓ Math paper!	→	Calendar / Dot chart patterns / Read:	Write about your bear (use blank bear ditto)	Music	Lit Centers 10:45–11:15 Meeting Note, Meagan and Matt / Rewriting time expectations	Ann here	→	Textbooks to each clan in color tabs (New—show how to)		Bear Measuring Stations Unifix cubes scale string make booklet	early clean up do Math Assess	ready to go home	Computer 2–2:23 (no recess and leave from comp. back room)
FRIDAY 22	Math paper ✓	→	Calendar / Dot chart patterns / Read: Who will be my friend?	Write about your bear (use blank bear ditto)	Recess 10 to 10:15	Lit Centers 10:15–10:50 Meeting Carilyn, Mario, Jesus ABC cards / Clean time 10:50	Entertainment time 11 to 11:25		Library books Otters & Racoons / Theme tabs Beavers & Squirrels		Math books pp. 1–16	Math Assess	clean & inspect	Outside w/ Bears (Recess & stories)

Source: Robin Lindsley, Primary Teacher, Boise Eliot School, Portland, OR 97227. Reprinted by permission.

161

■ **FIGURE 5.2**   Canby School District: Mathematics

Math Awareness (*Kindergarten*)

Measurement
- Begins to understand differences in length and weight
- Begins to explore measuring using non-standard measurement

Developing Math (*First Grade*)

Measurement
- Explores the concepts of length, weight, money, temperature, and time
- Begins using non-standard measurement
- Begins to make estimates of measurement for length and weight
- Makes predictions using vocabulary: likely, unlikely, and certain

Expanding Math (*Second Grade*)

Measurement
- Uses non-standard and begins to use standard measurement
- Understands the concepts of length, weight, money, time, and temperature
- Makes estimations of measurement for length and weight

Benchmark Level I (*Third Grade*)

Measurement
- Develops understanding of length (U.S. & metric), weight, money, time, temperature, area perimeter, volume, and angle
- Uses non-standard and standard for length, weight, money, time, temperature, area, perimeter, volume, and angle measurement
- Makes and uses estimates to measure length and weight

Source: Canby School District, Canby, OR. Reprinted by permission.

If it's a broad curriculum meant to be used by an entire elementary school, it often has what is called **scope and sequence** (see Figure 5.2). Such curriculum focuses on a set of information or understandings and develops a hierarchy, or a ladder of knowledge, starting with simple concepts for kindergarten and finishing with more abstract and complex ideas for sixth grade. Notice how different the concepts are for grade 1 and grade 3. Some programs or schools will allow you to develop your own curriculum. Either way, you will need to start with what you know and what you believe about children and learning.

The idea of curriculum being a teaching plan is interpreted in many different ways by educators. Some early childhood educators say that you should follow the children's lead for your curriculum. Let's look at another way of defining curriculum to understand that notion of following the lead of the children in your care.

Authentic curriculum.   Another way of thinking about curriculum is what Sobel calls **authentic curriculum**—"the process of movement from the inside out, taking curriculum impulses from the inside of the child and bringing them out into the light of day, into the classroom" (1994, p. 35). Sobel's ideas are much like those of Froebel, the creator of kindergarten, who encouraged us to bring ideas out of children rather than put them in. Listen again to Sobel's words: "Authentic curriculum is what springs forth from the genuine, unmediated individual and developmental fascinations of children and teachers" (p. 33). You won't find this kind of curriculum planned out on paper; it just happens! Hawkins (1973) describes it as "some little accident" that occurs when you are not expecting it, presenting you with the opportunity to encourage a new learning or curiosity. "The bird flies in the window and that's the miracle you needed," says Hawkins (p. 499). Another term for this thinking about curriculum is **emergent curriculum.** When you visit the toddler program in Chapter 7, you will see and hear about this kind of curriculum.

The blend of planned curriculum and spontaneous curriculum is very much like our lives. Even on the most organized or tightly scheduled day, unexpected events are accommodated and often provide the real stimulation and learning of the day. For instance, when your friend calls you to meet for lunch to discuss a problem, your thinking takes off in a new direction. Or when you see an interesting new plant in the park or a striking work of art in a gallery window, your day is enriched.

The two kinds of curricula, planned and spontaneous, can comfortably work together in the way you teach children. You can begin with a well-planned curriculum that expresses your philosophy and matches what you know about child development. Then within that curriculum, you stay flexible to seize the moment when curriculum emerges from the children's interest or curiosity or from an exciting event. Contrast the following examples:

Planned versus spontaneous

Mrs. Mahoney's first-grade children were studying the concept of size and had looked at shoes, houses in the neighborhood, cars, and themselves. They measured items in their classroom and out in the playground. It was an interesting curriculum with lots of real examples. One day, as they were listening to a story about size, a fire drill occurred. Instead of the usual practice, there were fire trucks in the parking lot participating in the drill. When the children returned to their classroom, they could see the trucks outside their classroom window and they talked excitedly about them. Mrs. Mahoney insisted that they return to their circle and finish the story about size. The children did so reluctantly and with little enthusiasm for the concept of size at that moment.

Another group of first-graders were beginning to write about a book they had just read when it began to snow. It was the first snow of the year in a city where it seldom snowed. Needless to say, all of the attention was "out the window" and so Ms. Reeves encouraged the children, "Go and get a good look at the weather." After a few minutes when the excitement eased, she asked the children to think of words to describe the snow. She wrote the ideas on the chalkboard as the children talked about *white, pretty, cold, flakes, wet, dancing, sparkle, shiny,* and *fun,* as they continued to press their noses to the windows. Ms. Reeves then encouraged them to go to their tables and write about the snow. There was little hesitation when children sat down—their ideas seemed to flow onto their papers.

Both Ms. Reeves and Mrs. Mahoney had a curriculum plan. Like many teachers, Mrs. Mahoney felt compelled to finish what she had planned for the children. Being flexible is not easy for many of us, especially after you've spent time planning your objectives and activities. You have probably experienced situations similar to what happened in these first-grade classrooms in your role as an adult learner. One of us was teaching a course about play and its curricular implications when the Gulf War broke out. To have continued with the curriculum plan for the evening class would have been insensitive and frustrating for everyone. The students needed to talk about the war. One had a son stationed overseas and she came to class feeling weepy. Another was teaching kindergarten and wanted to get ideas about how to talk to children about war. Another came into class out of breath, telling us, "This parent stopped me as I was leaving school and she was so thrilled that we were at war. She kept talking about how it was time that we took action and let them know that they can't get away with things." Everyone processed the event in some way that evening. We actually got to the topic of war play for children and had the opportunity to talk about research and philosophy related to children's play with guns and pretend fighting. It was spontaneous and meaningful curriculum connected to the planned curriculum of the course.

Expanding the Definition

By now, you have some beginning ideas of what curriculum is and can be. We think that good teachers start with well-planned curriculum and stay open to authentic curriculum, or "teachable moments." Before exploring ideas about curriculum, we want to add a few more definitions to your picture of curriculum. Some of the more important curricular approaches or aspects of curriculum will be discussed next.

Philosophy of curriculum.   Your **philosophy of curriculum** consists of your beliefs and values related to curriculum. When you have developed such a philosophy, it will be influenced by your beliefs about children and what they need to grow and learn. It will also be influenced by your own experiences as a child—learning from your family, your community, your school situations, and your peers. In Chapter 1, we described the influence of teacher biographies on their teaching. Your philosophy will certainly be influenced by your preparation courses and the materials you read, such as this book. Visits to early childhood programs will affect your philosophy, as will conversations with your peers. If you have children of your own, your parenting role will also influence your philosophy of curriculum.

In the sections ahead, you will encounter the thinking of brilliant early childhood educators who have very distinctive philosophies of curriculum. Their philosophies directed the kind of programs they planned for the children in their care—the type of

materials selected, the manner of environment arranged, the kind of adult/child interactions that occur, the way the day is scheduled, and the variety of activities provided
for the children.

Developmentally appropriate curriculum.   **Developmentally appropriate curriculum**
(or **practices**) is a term for the kind of curriculum that recognizes and appreciates children's levels of development, growth, and interest. It is curriculum that accommodates
a child's physical, emotional, social, and cognitive readiness. Developmentally appropriate curriculum draws in children because it appeals to their natural curiosity, it nur-
tures their spontaneous thinking and doing, and it encourages their creative spirit. In
a program for 2-year-olds, for example, developmentally appropriate curriculum is
seen in the use of low tables that are set up with play-dough, puzzles with three or four
pieces, and lots of water play. Plenty of materials are available, so children don't have
to share and large blocks of time are allotted for free exploration without interruption.
    Developmentally appropriate programs may look very different, but they are char-
acterized by three common principles:

1. They take into account the educator's knowledge of how young children develop
   and learn in the kind of activities and outcomes that are planned for the programs.
2. Children are seen and planned for as individuals, not as groups of 4-year-olds or
   toddlers.
3. Children are treated with respect and understanding—with sensitivity to their
   changing capacities and a "faith in their continuing capacity to change" (Kostelnik, Soderman, & Whiren, 1993, pp. 32–33).

Teachers who have a strong foundation of knowledge of child development and
learning are able to use developmentally appropriate practices (DAP) successfully (Snider
& Fu, 1990). Regardless of the curriculum or the approaches you select, the thinking of
developmentally appropriate practice can frame what you do and how you do it. We will
return to DAP later in this book, but you should also know that developmentally appropriate practices and curriculum are described in a set of guidelines developed by the
National Association for the Education of Young Children (Bredekamp & Copple,
1997). They are an essential to have on hand when making curricular decisions or planning curricular activities. You will find yourself using the NAEYC guidelines so frequently
that the famous green book will be quite worn out when you begin to teach.

Integrated curriculum.   The word *integrated* means interwoven like a braid. **Integrated
curriculum** reflects the natural connections between school and life and promotes a
meaningful and relevant learning context (Nagel, 1996). It promotes holistic learning
and builds on the relationships among science, math, language, the arts, and other curricular subject areas. If the children are exploring math concepts while painting a col-
lage to represent their neighborhood and writing labels for the buildings and streets,
you have integrated curriculum with geometry, literacy, and art. While the children are
constructing their pizza snacks, if you are recording each child's recipe for making pizza

BOX 5.1 ■ The Project Approach

A Closer Look

The project approach, which is being used in classrooms all over the country, is specifically for children ages 4 through 8. During those years, the intellectual development of children progresses rapidly, quite unevenly, and with huge variance among individual children. The project approach accommodates those qualities of development by providing related alternative activities and tasks for a wide range of abilities and experiences. Some of the popularity of the project approach is due to its ease of use in mixed-age settings. Those settings group children of different ages and ability levels, thus making the project approach a good curricular match for the diversity.

What is the project approach? Let's take a look in a classroom in which children are studying architecture. It's a mixed-age classroom in a public school. Children of kindergarten, first grade, and second grade are engaged in building models of homes and other buildings. Some of the children are working in groups, while others are working on individual constructions. Many of them are following a sketch or design that they developed the day before. Some have even used blueprint paper. There is a great deal of labeling being done as the children write the

names of rooms and discuss exteriors such as brick, wood siding, and stucco. Earlier in the week, an architect visited the class and left a display of blueprints and drawings. The children often walk over to the display to study a particular design. After their work session, the children gather with their teacher to discuss their work. They refer to a walk around the neighborhood during which they surveyed and recorded kinds of roofs, types of exteriors, number of stories, and special features. Those charts hang on the wall. Their teacher then shares a book of photographs, showing the work of Frank Lloyd Wright. The children enthusiastically talk about the designs and constructions.

During the month in which the children and their teacher studied architecture, they experienced the important components of the project approach:

Class discussions

Investigations

Field trips

Visiting an expert or having a guest speaker

Real objects or artifacts

Roleplay

and will later read the recipe cards with individual children, you are integrating literacy with a cooking activity, which itself integrates math and science through measurement and combining ingredients to create a new whole (i.e., the pizza).

Thematic curriculum.   As its name implies, **thematic curriculum** is curriculum built around a theme or a project (see Box 5.1). It is an ideal approach to curriculum, especially for young learners, because all of the curricular areas (math, science, literacy, art, music, etc.) can be connected within a theme as the children work on a project. We recently observed a summer curriculum for kindergarten and first-grade children focused on *links* as a theme. During the week of activities, children studied patterns of chain link fences throughout their neighborhood, made paper links, found natural links in the environment, explored ways to link with each in creative movement activities, and made up a song about friendship with the word *links* used repeatedly in the chorus. The *links* theme enabled the teachers and the children to connect science, math, art, music, social skills, and literacy throughout the curriculum.

On different days children have measured rooms, sketched more designs, developed symbols for designs, written descriptions of homes, and pretended to be realtors, architects, and interior designers. Around the room are architectural magazines and books, many blueprints and sketches, photos of homes and buildings, special measurement tools, and a drawing table with special lights.

The topics for project work usually begin with the children's immediate environment and expand outward to information not so closely related to their lives. Many teachers choose topics for their classes; others follow the children's leads for choice of topics or allow topics to emerge from everyday events. There seems to be an endless number of possible topics, but "no particular body of facts or knowledge need be covered through project work" (Katz & Chard, 1989, p. 67).

Project work offers children many choices in their tasks—what work to do, when to work, whom to work with, and where to work. The teacher is primarily a facilitator who provides materials, alternative activities, and logistical arrangements, and who supports information sharing. Project work usually follows a sequence that moves from planning to actual project work to reflection and review.

Planning involves sharing information, describing experiences, and establishing common understandings. During this time, children are encouraged to bring items from home, collect materials, assist with visits and field trip arrangements, and begin their activity plans. The next phase consists of all of the experiences previously described as the main components. This is a time when children are introduced to new information through field trips, guest speakers, books, exhibits, and other forms of study. This is also a time of much drawing, writing, discussion, reading, and investigation. In the final phase, children may display what they have learned through reports, stories or books, displays, projects, plays, and other activities to summarize information. When the children finished their project work on architecture, they invited the class next door to visit their displays and conducted guided tours of their exhibits.

The project approach is an exciting way to organize curriculum. Teachers, children, and parents are enthusiastic about the topics, the depth of learning activities, and the unpredictable possibilities that emerge throughout the study process. The project approach is a truly creative and engaging way to learn.

Chapter Preview

We'll return to these definitions of curriculum later with more examples. We intend to integrate or connect them to other ideas about curriculum, and it will be helpful that you are now somewhat familiar with the terminology. You may encounter these terms as we explore ideas about curriculum from the work and writings of Maria Montessori, Sylvia Ashton-Warner, Caroline Pratt, Constance Kamii and Rheta DeVries, and Carl Bereiter and Siegfried Engelmann, and from programs such as Bank Street, High Scope, Waldorf, and Reggio Emilia. Before moving on to these ideas, take a few moments and go back to Chapter 2. Review the ideas of Froebel, Piaget, and Gardner, for their work is most significant when we talk about curriculum.

Program models: One view of curriculum.   If you had begun your study of early childhood education with your two authors when we were taking classes many years ago, you would have taken a course called Program Models in Early Childhood Education.

You would have studied 8 to 12 different program models, each with their own curriculum and emphasis, and you might have read about a model of parent involvement:

> One of the most widely known models for parent involvement is the Florida Parent Education Program (Gordon, 1968). The Florida model is designed to promote self-improvement among the mothers of children ranging from infancy through primary grades. Maternal self-development or the development of "mothering skills," in other words, is seen as a way to enhance child development. From the period of the child's infancy through age two, trained parent educators make home visits to mothers once a week. Beginning during infancy, the parent educators teach specific mother-infant activities to stimulate cognitive growth during the home visits. Those weekly visits are continued for two and three year olds and are supplemented by a "backyard experience." This experience brings groups of four or five project children together in the home of one of the mothers twice a week for about two hours each time. These sessions include play activities, language activities, and group games. (Evans, 1975, pp. 342–343)

Many of the models of the 1960 and 70s were developed with the intent to study them to learn about how best to teach and care for children and families. Many of them demonstrated good results, but the research conclusions were usually confined to a particular population or setting. As educators have continued to learn more about children and their individual growth and development, and the important role of the family, neighborhood, and society in which those individual children live, the emphasis on models has declined. The incredible diversity of children and their environments makes it inappropriate (and maybe impossible) to adopt a model or to ask you to use one when you begin to educate children. However, you can get some good ideas from observing and reading about models, so we include a few program descriptions in this chapter.

We begin by introducing some early childhood educators whose ideas have influenced curriculum. As a developing early childhood professional, make friends with these great thinkers. Be ready to look at children through their eyes. Later in the chapter, we'll take you to see some programs that have been studied for their curricular strengths. Again, we encourage you to observe the children while listening to the thinking of the adults.

Curriculum ideas: From thinking to practices. A number of great thinkers have spent their lives observing children, creating theories about how children develop and learn, and recommending how best to promote that development and learning. We would be negligent to approach the study of curriculum without looking at these experts' ideas to help you get the "big picture" of what curriculum is and can be. We want to do so with a critical eye, however; that is, we want you to be ready to stop and reflect about each person's ideas. As you read, try to keep your child development information at the forefront and pay attention to your intuition about children and people, in general. We agree with some of the thinking and practices discussed in this chapter, but we also disagree with some of it. We will attempt to present these ideas neutrally because this is a time for you to begin to form opinions, to critique, and to make decisions concerning your beliefs and intentions about work with children. Stop and reflect as you read. Talk about the ideas with your peers. Ask questions in your classes. Be open to many possibilities.

Ideas about Curriculum

Maria Montessori

Maria Montessori is probably the best known of the thinkers we will describe in this chapter. She was the first Italian female physician, and, years ahead of her time, was a feminist and a children's advocate. She became intrigued with the education of young children for various reasons. She did not like the rigidity of Italian public education and she was concerned about the education of children who were mentally retarded or delayed. Montessori abandoned her role in medicine at a time when Italy's economy was precarious, when many families lived in poverty and in facilities without regard to health and safety. As she pondered her concerns about the situation, a reform movement brought about programs of employment for parents. That was the good news. The bad new was that children were left alone for long days.

Montessori's thinking.   The situation of children without care attracted Montessori's attention. Influenced by what she knew as a physician and by her efforts to educate "deficient children," she developed Children's Houses (*Casas dei Bambini*)—schools for children living in the tenement apartments of Rome. Montessori's ideas were reshaped over the years as she worked with both poor and wealthy children, as society changed, and as her ideas were transported to other countries, specifically the United States. To begin to understand her ideas, it's important to look at Montessori's five dominant beliefs:

1. Her method represents a scientific approach to education.
2. The secret of childhood resides in the fact that through their spontaneous activity, children labor to "make themselves into men" [Montessori, 1964].
3. Mental development, similar to physical growth, is the result of a natural, internally regulated force.
4. Liberty is the imperative ingredient that enables education to assist the "unfolding of a child's life" [Montessori, 1964].
5. Order, most especially within the child, but also in the child's environment, is prerequisite to the child becoming an independent, autonomous, and rational individual. (Goffin, 1994, p. 49)

What do these statements mean? Basically, Montessori believed that children could grow and develop very well if left to do so without too many restrictions but with an orderly environment that promoted their efforts at being independent and critical thinkers. Her approach was scientific in that it evolved from studying children and what they could do and in that she prescribed both teaching techniques and materials for her schools.

Journal 5.2: Montessori developed her educational program for children with needs similar to those of many in the United States today. Predict whether you think that her program would work for U.S. children living in poverty with little adult supervision. Accompany your prediction with the reasons supporting your opinion. ■

The attraction between Maria Montessori and children with whom she worked appears to be reciprocal.

Montessori's advice in action.   Montessori urged teachers to conduct naturalistic observations of children in *carefully prepared environments*. This refers to the orderly environments we talked about in Montessori's beliefs—environments planned to promote the children's freedom to take care of their own needs and freedom from dependency on others (the goals described in her beliefs). Teachers in a Montessori program are to observe and direct children's learning, so they are called directresses rather than teachers.

   If you walked into a Montessori program, you would likely see several rooms for different purposes, child-sized furniture and equipment, real dishes and other items, flowers and plants, and well-organized materials with careful storage and labeling. Materials, which are a very important aspect of the curriculum, are generally carefully crafted. They are displayed in open shelves for children's independent use. Many materials, are graded in difficulty; that is, they range from simple to use to very difficult or complex to use. Montessori's materials are often **autotelic,** or self-correcting, so that the child has immediate feedback.

In a Montessori classroom.   Looking back at Montessori's goals for children, it's easy to understand the environment and ultimately the curriculum. As children develop the ability to take care of their own needs, they learn best from firsthand experience. In a

Montessori classroom, they have *practical life experiences* such as gardening, polishing silver, buttoning and zipping, and flower arranging. Directresses make sure that each activity builds a foundation for a more complex and difficult activity or task, because Montessori believed that learning is cumulative. Most of the day is spent in individual tasks or activities, rather than in group activities. Children move freely about the classroom and make their own choices.

Journal 5.3: When we first introduced Montessori and the children for whom she created her program, we asked if you thought that her ideas were appropriate for children in our neighborhoods today. Now that you know more about her thinking, is your prediction the same? If you've changed your opinion, why?

If you are comfortable with Montessori's ideas and want to see them in action, we encourage you to visit a program in your area. There are many Montessori schools and classes in the United States; there are even some Montessori classrooms in public schools. Be aware of the authenticity of the program you observe. Some programs use the Montessori name but are not faithful to her ideas. You can check with the professional associations concerned with implementing Montessori programs. One of them is the American Montessori Society (AMS) founded in 1956. That organization oversees the training of directresses and accreditation of schools in the United States.

From Montessori's advice to watch children in order to know how to teach them, we move to another woman with similar thinking.

Sylvia Ashton-Warner

If asked, Sylvia Ashton-Warner would say that the raw materials of curriculum for children are "patience, caring, listening, intuition, and the elements in nature" (Mamchur, 1983). Like Montessori, her ideas are considered creative and original; unlike Montessori, Ashton-Warner was contemporary. Her ideas originated from over 20 years, most of her adult life, of teaching Maori children and being taught by them.

Ideas about children. To understand Ashton-Warner's ideas about curriculum, it is essential to understand her ideas about children. They are definitely unique. Listen to her words (because we can't possibly capture the meaning without her eloquence) describing the children with whom she worked: "I see the mind of a five year old as a volcano with two vents: destructiveness and creativeness. And I see that to the extent that when we widen the creative channel, we atrophy the destructive one" (1963, p. 33).

With that thinking, it's easy to see why Ashton-Warner would emphasize creative activities and spontaneous expressions of children. Her notion of children also included an emphasis on their aggressiveness. She saw it as an instinct without which many world events would not occur. She labeled children's mental and emotional reactions as aggressive and believed them to be caused by the frustrations of childhood. When Ashton-Warner looked at the school environments of most children, she saw those drives ignored or frustrated even more. She saw children especially discouraged by the written materials used in schools because she observed that children could not relate to the

"Dick and Jane" characters or actions. Using children as a source of curriculum, Ashton-Warner developed innovative approaches and materials, especially in the area of literacy.

Literacy curriculum.   The main idea of Ashton-Warner's approach to literacy is her notion of key vocabulary. **Key vocabulary** are self-chosen words, determined by each child, written on little cards (the 3 × 5 size works well). Ashton-Warner considered key words to be important if they were "one-look" words; that is, the child remembers the word after only one look. As a teacher, she began the day by placing the cards of all the children together on a mat. She described (1963) the children as "making straight for them to find their own, not without quarreling and concentration and satisfaction." Once they found the cards, they would sit with a partner and hear each other's words. In a sense, they teach each other. We observed a teacher using Ashton-Warner's key words approach in a class with 3-, 4-, and 5-year-olds, and each child's words clearly gave us an indication of what was happening in his life. A 4-year-old boy had discovered a small garden snake in his backyard on the previous day, and his words relayed his excitement: *snake, green, grass, tongue, fast,* and *hiding.*

The key words become the focus for writing, reading, and spelling activities. They are important and easy to read if they've been chosen well. *Chosen well* means that the words have real meaning for the children. When the children took their turns going to Ashton-Warner to dictate their words, she found that she often needed to engage them in conversation about their lives before they could come up with meaningful words. Otherwise, the children would just say whatever came to mind simply to take their turn, but the word would be forgotten immediately. The same is true of children's writing experiences. If the story or subject is directed by an adult, it has no value to the children. They may write, but the writing will be an impersonal experience.

Journal 5.4: Can you remember writing about a required topic and experiencing the agony of trying to complete the assignment? Can you think of a writing experience when you were inspired and wrote with passion? Why was it such a rich experience? Suppose you want the children in your care to have the same experience. How would you begin to get them involved in their topics? ■

In addition to the rich literacy activities of her program, Ashton-Warner included regular periods for dance, art, drama, and music. The day's routine even included a designated time for daydreaming. The most impressive quality of Ashton-Warner's approach to education emerges when you read her accounts of her teaching and her children. Whenever something was not working, she immediately took responsibility. For example, when a child came up to her, wanting to go outside instead of doing his work, she thought to herself, "It's my fault that he wants to go outside. Something is wrong with my infant room" (1963).

Although you probably won't find a program in your community that is patterned after Ashton-Warner's curriculum ideas, you will see the same thinking in a classroom in which the teacher is using a **whole language approach** to teach literacy. You will see children's words valued and used as the curriculum for teaching reading and writing. You will probably be able to recognize the whole language curriculum fairly easily. We also encourage you to experience the richness of Ashton-Warner's classroom by reading her book, *Teacher* (1963). Her conversations with children and her reflections about teaching cannot be condensed well into another person's words.

Ashton-Warner developed her ideas about children while working in British schools with Maori children. Our next thinker watched children in New York City in a tiny apartment that became their first play school setting.

Caroline Pratt

Much like Ashton-Warner, Caroline Pratt spent an extensive amount of her time watching children, especially as they played with blocks. From her observations, she developed a belief in children's ability to create and test knowledge about their world through their play. She insisted on calling it their *work* because she saw that children were quite serious about their play. Listen to her passionate expression of ideas about children's work:

> Children have their own meaning for the word play. To them it does not carry the ideas of idleness, purposelessness, relaxation from work as it does to adults. When we began our school, we named it a play school, as a telegraphic way of saying that in our way of teaching, the children learned by playing. It was the children who made us, early in the school's history, delete the word from the school's name. To them it was not a play school but a school, and they were working hard at their schooling.
>
> How hard they work, only we who have watched them really know. They do not waste a precious moment. They are going about their jobs all the time. No father in his office or mother in her home [remember—this was written in 1948] work at such a pace. For a long time I was principally afraid that they would exhaust themselves in this strenuous new kind of school. (1948, p. 9)

Pratt truly modeled the phrase, *learning from children*. She noted that blocks could be used for all kinds of play and testing, so she designed the wooden unit blocks that we have today in many ECE programs. We can credit her with the fact that blocks are a mainstay of programs all over the world.

Pratt's ideas in action.   Pratt's ideas about curriculum can be best understood if you observe the City Country School in New York City—the school she talked about that began with the name *play school*. Children from ages 2 to 8 spend much of their day in work that centers around blocks. On the playgrounds, there are large wooden blocks, boards, and hollow boxes. Children engage in constructive and dramatic play with these materials for hours each day all year long. In the classrooms where the youngest (2 to 4 years) children work, there are multiple shelves of blocks, probably more blocks than you've seen in other programs. In a classroom for 3-year-olds, there are very few accessories— some wooden people, trains, and colorful squares of fabric. At the end of the school year (the month of May) in that same class, we observed intense block building, elaborate structures that extended over about nine feet of floor space. During the play, the teachers spend much of their time observing, recording notes, and "learning from children."

Blocks in curriculum.   Blocks also have a central role in the classroom for 5-year-olds. These children are able to leave their block structures in place all week. There are streets

Think about the value of block play. What kind of learning do you think can occur in block play?

painted on the floor, paths and parks drawn among the buildings, as well as many signs in children's handwriting, labeling streets and most of the structures. The block city emerges as these 5-year-olds visit buildings in their New York City community—sometimes an impromptu trip when a need arises or a planned field trip for the entire class. Every Friday, there is a routine in which the children visit each other's buildings or neighborhoods. The children conduct tours, using the wooden people as guides. When you look closely at activities such as the Friday visits, you get a sense of the integration of curriculum that takes place in the block play (or work) at City Country School. It's impossible not to wonder how many of these children become architects or builders.

Although many parents and children are completely devoted to the City and Country School, and the school's faculty is consistently committed to Caroline Pratt's ideas, it is not a curriculum that everyone appreciates.

Journal 5.5: Reflect from the perspective of a parent who has toured City Country School and listened to a presentation about the philosophy of Caroline Pratt. You decide that City Country School is not for your child. What may be some of your reasons? ■

Pratt was influenced by the thinking of John Dewey, who believed that children are able to direct their own learning if adults provide the structure and opportunities and allow them to learn through real experiences. Our next pair of idea people were influenced by another major theorist of early childhood education: Jean Piaget. Before reading about them, think about Piaget's theories about how children develop and learn.

Constance Kamii and Rheta DeVries

With Piaget's theories as their major focus, Constance Kamii and Rheta DeVries developed many ideas about curriculum. Their ideas have been adopted mostly for preschool programming, but some of their thinking about math, reading, and writing has been extended to public school curriculum for kindergarten and primary grades. Because Piaget's thinking is so prominent in their work, we asked you to reflect on his theories. Review specifically his stages of cognitive development, his description of different types of knowledge, and his concept of constructivism so that you can understand the thinking of Kamii and DeVries. The other theorist whose work influenced their thinking is Kohlberg. His stages of development are illustrated in Figure 5.3 to help you understand the curriculum described here. It is not surprising that Kohlberg's ideas would intersect

■ **FIGURE 5.3**   Kohlberg's Stage Theory of Moral Reasoning

Level 1: Preconventional Moral Reasoning

Judgment is based on personal needs and others' rules.

Stage 1   *Punishment-Obedience Orientation*
Rules are obeyed to avoid punishment. A good or a bad action is determined by its physical consequences.

Stage 2   *Personal Reward Orientation*
Personal needs determine right and wrong. Favors are returned along the lines of "You scratch my back, I'll scratch yours."

Level 2: Conventional Moral Reasoning

Judgment is based on others' approval, family expectations, traditional values, the laws of society, and loyalty to country.

Stage 3   *Good Boy–Nice Girl Orientation*
Good means "nice." It is determined by what pleases, aids, and is approved by others.

Stage 4   *Law and Order Orientation*
Laws are absolute. Authority must be respected and the social order maintained.

Level 3: Postconventional Moral Reasoning

Stage 5   *Social Contract Orientation*
Good is determined by socially agreed-upon standards of individual rights. This is a morality similar to that of the U.S. Constitution.

Stage 6*   *Universal Ethical Principle Orientation*
Good and right are matters of individual conscience and involve abstract concepts of justice, human dignity, and equality.

*In later work, Kohlberg questioned whether Stage 6 exists separately from Stage 5.
Source: "The Claim to Moral Adequacy of a Highest Stage of Moral Judgment" by L. Kohlberg, 1973, *Journal of Philosophy, 70,* pp. 631–632. Adapted by permission.

with Piaget's ideas. If you are feeling confused or uncertain about Piaget and Kohlberg, return to Chapter 3 and spend some time reviewing their thinking.

Outcomes for children.   The work of Kamii and DeVries is quite complex and it keeps changing somewhat as they continue actively to explore curricular ideas and to work with children. Here, we will provide just the general ideas and some applications of their thinking. Let's begin with curriculum for young children, directed by the following goals:

1. The children will be autonomous; that is, they will construct their own learning and develop independent thinking.

2. The children will develop according to the framework of Piaget's stages of cognitive development.

3. The children will develop cooperative relationships, reflecting both social skills and understanding the perspectives of others.

4. The children will develop moral reasoning according to the framework of Kohlberg's stages of development.

When you look at these outcomes, you can deduce that two aspects of curriculum are essential: Children must interact with their social and physical environments, and within children there must be an interaction between their current way of understanding an event or phenomenon and new information about an event or phenomenon. Remember assimilation and accommodation? These two criteria are often described in curriculum language as *hands-on-learning* and *learning by doing,* or, quite simply, as play. Now you're probably feeling a little more comfortable about the ideas of Kamii and DeVries. Use them to help you better understand Piaget and to apply his thinking to work with young children.

Curricular components.   Some basic components of a curriculum directed to the outcomes or goals just listed are the following:

1. Moral reasoning emphasis evolves from a democratic classroom where teachers and children solve problems together, negotiate conflicts, collaborate in rule setting, and take responsibility for classroom life. Group games with rules, as well as discussions about hypothetical dilemmas, will give children opportunities to apply moral reasoning to real-life situation. Observe with us a classroom that uses such a curriculum:

Moral reasoning

A class of 4- and 5-year-olds had a successful cookie sale after a week of excited baking and sign making. "Now it's time to decide how we want to spend our money," Paul reminded the children as they met in their morning circle. He asked the children to make suggestions and listed their ideas on the flip chart. "I want a Barbie house," suggested Aurelia. "I want a remote control car," shouted Ignatio. The list went on. Tessa quietly suggested, "I think that we should give the money to some poor children." Several children nodded. Many suggested, "I think that we should go on a trip with that money." When the list was full, Paul reviewed their ideas. Then he asked, "Would it be OK if we use our money to buy a Barbie house for Aurelia?" His question prompted much animated discussion about why that use of the money wasn't "right." After 20 minutes of discussion, Paul told the children, "I think that we need more time to work on this decision. Think about it some more and tomorrow we'll talk about it again and see if we can decide on one idea with which everyone can agree."

2. Physical-knowledge activities involve children's actions on objects and their observations of the reactions. Their observations will frequently lead to cause-and-effect understandings, to the development of relationships, and to much accommodation and assimilation. Some of the most common activities to provide such experiences for children are water play with float and sink materials, cooking, making and flying kites, mixing paint colors, and weighing and measuring items.

3. Group games will instill in children how to be both collaborative and independent players. With young children, you can begin with very simple games, such as Farmer in the Dell and Duck, Duck, Goose. With primary grade children, more complex games will intrigue them, such as Fruit Basket, Red Rover, and Simon Says.

4. Logico-math activities, especially those embedded in routine situations in which number is a natural issue, will lead to developing skills of logic and organization. Examples include division of materials to the group, keeping class records, recording the weather or the lunch count, and voting for class choices. Logico-math activities are further emphasized in group games.

To implement the ideas of Kamii and DeVries in your work with children, you will need to be an excellent observer of children and have a critical understanding of how each child thinks and understands events. Notice that these qualities keep recurring throughout this book. As you have probably figured out, once you understand children's thinking and understandings, you will be better at connecting what you know about children with the kind of activities you plan and the environment you arrange for children.

Journal 5.6: Stop here for a moment and make a list of 5 to 10 ideas you have about children's thinking and what they understand. You can make your list fit a specific age or you can make a list for children, in general. After you do so, next to each idea you listed, develop a recommendation for an activity or an environment that addresses what you know about children. Let's take one example: We know that young children can't and won't sit for a long period of time (actually, adults don't enjoy sitting for long, either). What would your recommendation be for using that knowledge? Our recommendation for practice that goes with that knowledge is to plan "sitting" for very brief periods and to mix movement into those times as much as possible. A common inappropriate practice is a 20-minute Show and Tell time with the entire class (25 children) sitting in a circle. Many times, the class is split into groups of 5 children so that Show and Tell is shorter and enables each child to be involved. Now it's your turn. Think of 5 to 10 ideas about children and accompanying recommendations. ■

Interactions with children.   You can use your understanding of children to know what questions to ask them, when to be quiet and listen, and when to encourage an answer.

Kamii and DeVries (1978) express concern about the way we adults interact with children and especially caution us against "imposing our ideas and answers" on them because "children will soon learn not to trust their own ability to make sense of their experiences." One of us remembers a year when the arrangement of the classroom didn't feel comfortable, routines weren't running smoothly, and certain areas of the classroom were sometimes very congested. I was hesitant to ask the children, yet I knew that they were the best source of information about the room. To be honest, the other realization was that once the children gave their ideas, it would be important to respect and use their ideas. Otherwise, a lack of trust would certainly occur. We sat together and talked about the feel of the room, and the children certainly agreed that it just wasn't working. Their suggestions primarily focused on the removal of three large circular work tables, and, as a replacement for the work space, using carpet squares for floor sitting. The children, ages 3 to 5, enthusiastically moved the tables to a storage room and rearranged the space with shelves of materials and a case of carpet squares. The days then proceeded more smoothly.

By now, you may be thinking that there's a similar theme to the thinking and curriculum approaches we've been describing for you. You may be wondering if there's any alternative thinking to the theme, so we move next to two thinkers who have different ideas about children and curriculum.

Carl Bereiter and Siegfried Engelmann

Carl Bereiter and Siegfried Engelmann's ideas came from theories of behavioral psychology and the work of Freud, Thorndike, and Watson. (Do you need to return to Chapter 3?) Their thinking was based primarily on stimulus-response theory, which you have likely encountered in your psychology courses. Curriculum designed by Bereiter and Engelmann was not based on child development; instead, it was focused on learning rather than development. Their definition of *learning* will help you to understand how they thought about curriculum. "Learning refers to the change in a subject's behavior to a given situation brought about by repeated experiences in that situation" (Hilgard & Bower, 1975, p. 17). They saw children as recipients of learning, not participants in learning. Today, this viewpoint is called the *banking approach* to learning—one makes regular deposits of information in students, much like one makes deposits of money in a bank.

Catch-up curriculum. Before we go any further, it is important for you to know that Bereiter and Engelmann developed their ideas about curriculum during a time when there was concern about the learning of young children from economically disadvantaged and culturally diverse home environments. At that time, children were mistakenly labeled *culturally deprived* because they didn't have the advantages and the language of their middle-class peers. That thinking was based on the idea that White middle-class culture was the only culture, so that those who didn't experience it were deprived. Today, we call similar children *at risk,* because their home environments and experiences don't match those of their middle-class peers, and most schools are not designed to meet their needs. Many feel that it is the schools and communities that are at risk, because they don't match the needs and experiences of those children.

Bereiter and Engelmann (1966) decided to design curriculum to make sure that those children could catch up, so that they could "emerge from school with the same skills and knowledge as more privileged children" (p. 6). They created an academic curriculum to teach the skills children needed in order to succeed in school.

Teaching with Bereiter and Engelmann.   Bereiter and Engelmann's curricular ideas primarily focused on language, reading, and arithmetic, and began with a preschool model but expanded to current use in kindergarten and primary grades. You may have heard of their programs: Direct Instruction and Distar. Their teaching approach requires that teachers work with small groups of children (5 to 15 in a group), that each subject is taught separately, and that the classroom environment is very businesslike. Much of their curriculum was programmed; that is, teachers were told what to say, how and when to say it, and what children must answer in response. Scripts with directions, structured examples, and sequences of subskills and wordings were supplied. Efficiency was very important—each minute was seen as precious for helping the children catch up. Parents were to work with their children at home, using practice books to reinforce the skills learned in class.

To help you visualize Bereiter and Engelmann's thinking applied to a program for children, listen and observe a teacher using their Distar method with first-grade children:

Distar method

Several children are seated at their desks and working in workbooks. Another group of children is sitting at a long table at the back of the room with headphones on and listening to tapes. The rest of the children are sitting in a semi-circle facing their teacher, David. He is holding a book so that the page with large letters and symbols faces the children. David points to an individual letter on the page and asks one or more children to respond. Sometimes he says, "Everyone, what sound does this make?" The child or children respond immediately by making the sound associated with the letter to which David is pointing. We watch and hear George and Elyssa saying, "Mmmm" when David points to M, but Melaney looks confused and doesn't make a sound. After the children respond, David gives them feedback with, "Wow, you are really with it today!" Within a few minutes, each student in the group has had several turns to respond to the questions. The interactions have been rapid and the entire session has lasted about 12 minutes. At the end, the children practice writing the alphabet sounds they have been working on, and they say the sound out loud each time they write it.

 Journal 5.7: Think about being a child in David's class. What does it feel like for George? For Melaney? ▪

Compare the learning of these children with the learning of children in a Distar classroom.

Summary: Stop and Catch Your Breath

We've been spending a lot of time in people's heads and you may be ready for a break. Maybe the topic of *curriculum* is making you feel overwhelmed with so many ideas and approaches. To help you keep the ideas clear, you might return to each of the professionals and make a list of their general ideas, especially those that feel comfortable with your ideas about children and learning. You might also look for common themes and unique ways of thinking about children and their development. Again, consider those themes in the context of what you believe about children. Spending some time organizing the thinking you have just read about will get you ready for the next section of this chapter. We're going to look at some programs now as a different way to explore ideas. As you read about the programs, stop and reflect on what kind of thinking and decision making is behind what the children and adults doing.

Early Childhood Education Programs

Let's return to New York City, where we met Caroline Pratt. Perhaps it is the dynamic quality of that metropolitan site and the diversity of lives that comprise the richly varied neighborhoods that prompt and promote the creative and courageous thinking and programs we are describing.

Bank Street Approach

At the same time that Caroline Pratt was developing her ideas about curriculum and starting the City Country School, other progressive educators were thinking about the "whole child" and the importance of children to a humane society. Begun as the Bureau of Educational Experiments, the Bank Street approach got its name when the Bureau moved to 69 Bank Street. Later, under the direction of Barbara Biber, the approach was named for its "essential theoretical characteristics" and called the *developmental interaction approach*. The approach was implemented at the Bank Street School for Children, a laboratory and demonstration center for the Bank Street College of Education, with preschool through eighth grades. The school served two important functions. First, it was a research center focused on the study of the application of developmental theory to classrooms. Second, it served as a teacher education center to prepare educators who would plan and implement developmentally appropriate learning environments for children.

The Bank Street tradition.   Over the years, Bank Street has always been thought of as the ideal nursery school program; often, the elementary school aspect is overlooked. If you were to look at any developmentally appropriate preschool, kindergarten, or primary grade classroom in your city or your neighborhood, you would see the teaching strategies, the teacher/child relationship, and the classroom organization and materials of the developmental interaction approach. The qualities of being child centered, experience based, and process oriented appear in the handbooks of many early childhood programs, and they describe the Bank Street program well. A **child-centered** curriculum is one in which the environment, activities, materials, and adult interactions are designed to meet children's interests, needs, and abilities. That may sound familiar by now. **Experience-based curriculum** is one that emphasizes rich, appropriate experiences for children's learning. That, too, may sound familiar by now. **Process-oriented curriculum** focuses on the process rather than the product, so that adults and children will talk about the making rather than what is being made.

The uniqueness of the Bank Street approach is that its advocates insist on the experimental nature of education; that is, instead of a planned curriculum, you teach by continuously studying children and trying out ideas (activities, materials, etc.). The trial-and-error quality of the approach is difficult to imagine for many of us. The approach is such a personal approach—on the part of the teacher and on the part of the child. It depends on the "teacher's knowledge and ability to recognize and skillfully respond to the individuality of each child and his or her interests" (Franklin & Biber, 1977, p. 26). When you think about the diversity among your classmates studying early childhood education, you can imagine the wide variety of responses possible among them, even if they were all responding to the same child. Now, imagine the wide variety of children. Biber (1988) says, "The ideal teacher is aware of the differences in the social codes and styles of interaction among young children from widely different cultural groups" (p. 46). With all those variations possible, Bank Street is truly a personal approach and is intensely dynamic! It can be called individually developmentally appropriate because it doesn't depend on the kind of normative child development stages we described in Chapter 2, but instead on each child's development.

One of us visited Bank Street years ago, and the classroom scene is still vivid because of its rich activities and intense involvement of a large number of children. Somehow, the children had become involved in the study of dyes. It began with one child's curiosity about how his shirt became a certain color and it led to an in-depth project about dyes. The large room contained 3 or 4 adults and over 20 older preschoolers. One group was making dyes from vegetables (beets, carrots, and spinach), plants and other natural materials in one area of the room. Nearby were fabrics and bits of yarn drying from the experiments with dye. Another group was weaving newly dyed strips of cloth. One of the adults was taking dictation from children who were telling stories and sharing bits of information from their library research about dyes. A testing area displayed paper samples and blots of color. Children and adults were pursuing their own interests in varied ways with activities that made sense to them.

Curriculum goals of Bank Street.   Before moving on to another program, it would be beneficial for you to look at the goals of the Bank Street or developmental interaction approach (see Figure 5.4). They don't look vastly different from the goals of other curricular thinking or practices. What is different is that this approach emphasizes that these goals are not end points or outcomes. They are meant to *guide* the work of teachers and the processes of individual children. Ultimately, the developmental interaction approach is concerned with the following (Goffin, 1994, p. 88):

1. *Competence of children.* Their use of knowledge and skills will enable children to live in the environment and with others.

2. *Individuality of children.* Children's autonomy and sense of self-worth are based on knowledge and feelings of their own competence and the views of those around them.

3. *Socialization of children.* Self-regulation of behavior is necessary to participate in forms of society and in relationship with others.

4. *Integration for children.* Connecting disparate experiences and reactions will enable children to possess a "big picture" and appreciate the events of their lives.

■ **FIGURE 5.4**   Program Goals of the Developmental-Interaction Approach

1. Opportunities for children to explore, manipulate, and make an impact on the environment
2. Opportunities for children to expand and extend knowledge of their environment
3. Opportunities for children to cognitively incorporate and order experience in play
4. Opportunities for children to develop impulse control
5. Opportunities for children to cope with and respond to conflict
6. Opportunities for children to develop self-images and feelings of competence
7. Opportunities for children to develop "mutually supporting" interaction patterns

Source: Adapted from "A Developmental-Interaction Approach: Bank Street College of Education" by B. Biber, in *The Preschool In Action: Exploring Early Childhood Programs* (2nd ed.) by M. C. Day & K. Parker (Eds.), 1977, Boston: Allyn and Bacon.

Journal 5.8 When you reflect on the Bank Street program and its practices, consider whether you agree or disagree with its philosophy. Could you work in a program with the goals and intentions of the developmental interaction approach? What would be difficult about working at Bank Street? What would attract you? ■

High Scope Approach

The High Scope approach began as a curriculum model for preschool at the Ypsilanti Perry Preschool and was later extended to curriculum for kindergarten through third grade. The name was meant to communicate high aspirations and a broad scope of interests. David Weikart is the educator responsible for the thinking and organizing of the curriculum ideas of High Scope. Early in the development of the High Scope curriculum, the work of Piaget became influential and the curriculum was renamed the *cognitively oriented curriculum.* Many people continue to call it High Scope, however—even though the name was changed more than 20 years ago.

Emergence of the High Scope curriculum.   When High Scope programs first began, teachers were teaching with very direct methods, often instructing children in motor and perceptual skills. With the influence of Piaget's ideas, they began instructing children in Piagetian tasks because they thought that those tasks would move children to the next stage of cognitive development. As Weikart and his colleagues studied Piaget further, the curriculum was based more on the idea that children are active learners and can construct their own knowledge. Teachers stopped their direct teaching and were free to participate with the children in activities. The preschool curriculum recommends *key experiences* for the children. Those experiences are organized into three categories and within each category are types of learning experiences:

1. *Social and emotional development,* including recognition and solution of problems, understanding routines and expectations, and communicating with others

2. *Movement and physical development,* including block building, climbing, ball throwing and catching, and play with manipulatives

3. *Cognitive development,* including representation, language, classification, seriation, number, space, and time

The key experiences give structure to the curriculum while at the same time maintain a flexibility to accommodate new possibilities. Teachers can use these experiences to organize their planning of activities. They also are linked to how both children and program are assessed. Teachers use them as a framework with which to observe children.

The plan-do-review component.   In addition to the key experiences, another curriculum component is unique to High Scope. It is a sequence called *plan-do-review* and it's used frequently throughout the day. Let's look in a High Scope classroom and see what plan-do-review looks like:

Vanessa: Plan-do-review

It's planning time, and 4-year-old Vanessa approaches her teacher Sylvanna and describes what she is going to do during the outside play period. "I'm going to make a bakery and sell cakes," says Vanessa, pointing to the sandbox. Sylvanna asks, "What kind of cakes?" and adds, "Are you going to sell anything else?" Vanessa talks about chocolate and gingerbread cakes, and cookies and pies. She says that she will put candles in some of them for birthdays. Eagerly, Vanessa heads for the sandbox and a shelf of pails and plastic containers. She begins the "doing" phase of the sequence. After outdoor play, children engage in a recall or review of their activities. Again, their teacher Sylvanna encourages representation of their "doing"—by talking, or drawing, or pantomiming, or writing about their activities. Vanessa draws a shelf of cakes, some with candles, and price tags on each one. She is anxious to show her drawing to the group and to talk about her cakes.

If Vanessa engaged in plan-do-review inside the classroom, she would have a choice of learning centers or work areas, usually a block area, an art area, a quiet area, and a house area. During small group time, the teachers present an activity in which all the children participate—usually in key experiences. This is a time when teachers can observe children, assess their development, and guide their progress. High Scope teachers ask children a lot of questions throughout the day to extend the children's thinking and to promote problem solving and independent thinking.

We have been describing a preschool classroom and curriculum, but if you were to visit a classroom in an elementary setting—kindergarten through third grade—you would still see work areas and key experiences, but they would be related to public school elementary subjects of math, language and literacy, and science. For example, the work areas would include a reading/writing area, a math area, a computer area, an art area, and a construction area. Most teaching would take place in small groups and some cooperative work would be part of the day.

Today, there is a High Scope foundation that sponsors research, curriculum development, professional training for teachers, and public advocacy. As you will learn in Chapter 13, research on High Scope or Ypsilanti Perry Preschool has demonstrated that there are multiple long-term benefits of well-developed early childhood education programs. Through the advocacy of Weikart and his colleagues, policymakers, legislators, and the general public have been convinced of the cost effectiveness and social value of such programs.

Waldorf Approach

The Waldorf approach to education began with one school designed for the children of the workers of the Waldorf-Astoria Cigarette Company and it blossomed into a worldwide educational movement (Uhrmacher, 1993). Basically, Waldorf schools are private, nonsectarian programs with arts-based curriculum. Children learn subjects such as literacy, math, science, and so on through artistic activities.

Waldorf schools apply the thinking of Rudolf Steiner, who developed a system of education in Germany in 1919 as an alternative to traditional education (Foster, 1984). Steiner, like many early childhood educators, believed in educating the whole child, but his interpretation of *whole* included the mind, the heart, and the will. Like so many of the thinkers you've encountered in this chapter, Steiner also believed that curriculum comes from the child. "Education does not give or take but strengthens the forces within each child" (Aeppli, 1986, p. 10). Said differently, you must know children well in order to educate them. Waldorf teachers have two major intentions as they work with children:

1. To develop subject matter through image, rhythm, movement, drawing, painting, poetry, drama, and so on;

2. To involve aesthetics in all that is done throughout the school day (aesthetic conditions) program. (Uhrmacher, 1993, p. 89)

Basic ideas of Rudolf Steiner. Rudolf Steiner's thinking about curriculum was similar to the thinking of John Dewey. Contrary to the thinking of many educators, Steiner pointed out that teachers do not provide experiences for students. You may be startled by that idea, but his thinking was that teachers provide conditions (such as materials, space, schedule, etc.) and then each child has her own experience. So, one way of looking at Steiner's educational system is to examine some of the conditions of his schools (Uhrmacher, 1993, p. 91):

1. *Aesthetic conditions*—those conditions that enhance a child's appreciation of beauty and sensuality

2. *Social conditions*—those conditions that promote or strengthen interactions and relationships between children, and between children and adults

3. *Symbolic conditions*—those conditions such as stories, pictures, rituals, and ceremonies that will teach and influence children indirectly

4. *"Sensitive" conditions*—those conditions that enhance a child's perceptive abilities or a child's "feeling live"

Some of these conditions may sound unusual or be difficult to understand due to a translation of Steiner's ideas into English. However, when we visit a Waldorf classroom, you'll see what those conditions look like in practice.

Visiting a Waldorf School. It would be ideal to spend a whole day in a classroom, but for the sake of brevity, we'll drop in different classes at different times of the day.

Waldorf approach

A first-grade teacher is using images to teach the letters of the alphabet. "The children painted the wild ocean with its towering waves and a vulture flying over them. The waves became *W* and the vulture the *V*." Using these vivid images, the children become acquainted with *W* and *V,* and gradually the pictures fade and only the letters are left. This same teacher then writes children's names on the board for the first time. The symbols associated with the letters have taken on a life for the children. One child offers, "Ooh, Melissa has two nasty old snakes in her name." The teacher adds, "She also has a light and an angel in her name" (Aeppli, 1986, p. 39).

In another class, a third grade, Mr. Stevenson places sunflowers and pumpkins on top of an orange cloth in the center of the room. He asks, "Could we please begin, everyone?" The children who are in the classroom go into the hallway and line up at the door. When the teacher is ready, the children come in one at a time to shake hands and hear, "Good morning Ethan. . . . Good morning Talya. . . ." These greeting are followed by morning circle to recite verses. The students and teacher bend down from the waist, arms stretched toward the ground and say, "The earth is firm beneath my feet." They rise and move their arms above their heads with "The sun shines bright above." They continue with the verse and body movements and re- cite it five more times, using quieter voices each time. When they finish, there is silence for a brief time (Uhrmacher, 1993, pp. 87, 91).

As Ms. Hernandez introduces math thinking or numeracy to young children, she takes a stick and allows the children to see and experience it as a whole. Then the stick is broken into 2, 4, and 8 pieces. "The child observes that by splitting the big 1, the smaller 2, 4, and 8 arise, and that the pieces become smaller the more the stick is broken." An alternative to the stick is to have children work with a large lump of clay and work it into 2, 4, and 8 smaller lumps. After the children have experienced numbers with varied concrete materials, they can begin to count. Counting is done with clapping or foot stamping. We hear, "Clap two times, four times, and eight times." Later, we hear children saying, "I have two eyes, two ears, two arms, two hands, two feet" (Aeppli, 1986, p. 47).

"Local history should gradually awaken the dreaming child to his environment so that he learns to associate with it in a more conscious way. The familiar plants, animals, stones, mountains, rivers, and meadows that are brought to the child's awareness and introduced to his understanding must never be described by the teacher in an abstract way" (Aeppli, 1986, p. 58). The experiences that attend to this thinking include walks and visits to the neighborhood. They involve getting to know the trees intimately—becoming friends with trees and identi- fying with the trees. Children's thinking is heard in comments such as, "You know, I like the pine tree because it rustles, but I like the oak tree even better." We see a child jump up from her seat, hop around the room, and call out, "I am the birch tree and this is how I say hello and wave and greet the children" (Aeppli, 1986, p. 66).

You may want to visit a Waldorf school for yourself to see more of Steiner's think- ing. Before you decide, take a moment to reflect.

Journal 5.9: Think back on Sylvia Ashton-Warner's approach to words and think about Steiner's approach to letters. Is there a contradiction there? Some early childhood educators think that the approach of using images with letters may confuse children. What do you think? ■

The next program we will talk about originated in Italy. This fairly recent discovery for U.S. early childhood educators has prompted many teachers from the United States to visit the Italian community of Reggio Emilia to get ideas. Just in case your passport isn't current, we're going to take you there for a brief visit.

Reggio Emilia Approach

More than 25 years ago, through the efforts of women advocating for children, a law established free education for children ages 3 to 6 (later adding infant/toddler centers) in Italy. The legislated free programs emphasized quality in both education and care. In Reggio Emilia, a small northern town, the programs were literally built by parents with proceeds from the sale of military equipment after the end of World War II. Professor Loris Malaguzzi guided those beginning efforts and continues to provide insightful leadership to the educational program at Reggio Emilia.

Development of the Reggio Emilia approach. With thinking similar to that of the Bank Street approach, the Reggio educators consider their work "an educational experience that consists of practice and careful reflection that is continuously readjusted" (Gandini, 1993, p. 13). Like so many ECE professionals, the Reggio educators have been influenced by the ideas of Dewey, Piaget, Vygotsky, and the latest research in child development. A look at how the Reggio educators describe children will tell you much about their approach. "All children have preparedness, potential, curiosity and interest in constructing their learning, in engaging in social interaction, and in negotiating with everything the environment brings to them" (p. 13). With that image of children, it is not surprising that the Reggio approach studies children as individuals and responds to them appropriately.

Reggio curriculum. Curriculum at Reggio is called *emergent,* meaning that it is not determined beforehand. The educators develop general goals and predict children's responses to activities and projects so that they can prepare the environment. Then the children take over and the curriculum emerges. Much of the curriculum at Reggio takes the form of projects, and those projects may come from children or teachers. Sometimes, an event or a problem may result in a project, such as a study of shoes that occurred when a child came to school with a new pair of shoes. The children were curious about how shoes were made and wanted to investigate the materials of shoes. Projects are actually intensive constructions of knowledge—studies conducted by children guided by adults or with adult resources. Projects can vary in length from a few days to several months. To get a sense of the richness of the Reggio emergent curriculum and the project approach, listen to Carlina Rinaldi, a *pedagogista* (educational advisor) at the school:

Reggio Emilia approach

This project begins at the end of a school year for 4- and 5-year-olds. The teachers talked with the children about remembering their vacation and holiday experiences. The children and parents agreed to take along on their vacations a box with small compartments in which a child could save treasures. "Every fragment, every piece collected would become a memento of an experience imbued with a sense of discovery and emotion" (Edwards, Gandini, & Forman, 1995, p. 108).

In the fall, the teachers began with questions about the holidays, much like teachers do in U.S. schools. They asked, "What did your eyes see?" "What did your ears hear?" One child, Gabriele, shared an experience that prompted an adventure for the children and adults alike. He responded to the teachers' questions about his holiday: "We walked through a narrow long street, called 'the gut,' where one store is next to another and where in the evening it is full of people. There are people who go up, and people who walk down. You cannot see anything, you can only see a crowd of legs, arms, and heads" (p. 109).

The idea of "crowd" caught the teachers' attention and their questions prompted rich meanings from the children. "The teachers immediately apprehended an unusual excitement and potential in the word" (p. 109). Listen to some of the children's thinking about crowds:

Nicola: It is a bunch of people all attached and close to one another.

Luca: There are people who jump on you and push you.

Ivano: It is a bunch of people all bunched up together just like when they go to pay taxes (p. 109).

The concept of *crowd* became the focus of a series of teacher conversations, children's conversations and then an explosion of activity—drawings, walks in the city, more drawings, and paintings. The curriculum truly emerged from Gabriele and the children's responses to his description of a crowd. From there, the children could decide to study *crowds* as a project. Later in the book, you will see toddlers in a classroom where emergent curriculum is in place, and where kindergarten children engaged in the project approach.

Curricular supports at Reggio.   There are several completely unique features of the Reggio Emilia program that deserve description. In addition to teachers and many parent participants, there is a teacher trained in visual arts who is called the *atelierista.* There is also a special space—a studio or workshop—called the *atelier.* Everyone (adults and children) uses the tools and materials of the *atelier.* Another unique feature of the program is the extensive documentation of children's thinking, discussions, work, and progress that is collected and used. The documentation takes the form of photographs, tape recordings, and other records. The Reggio educators value the documentation as a way to understand the children better and a way to assess their own work as educators. At the same time, the process of collecting documentation communicates to children that their work and their efforts are valued.

Some of the Reggio Emilia ideas are finding their way into elementary schools in the United States today. One practice that is becoming common is the teacher and group of students staying together for more than one year. In Reggio, a pair of teachers and a group of children stay together for three years. Although their environment changes as their development progresses, the community of learners stays intact. At Reggio, teachers see themselves as researchers, continually documenting their work with children. Many U.S. elementary teachers conduct *action research* in their classrooms to find answers, to solve problems, and to guide their decision making, just as the Reggio teachers do. Finally, the Reggio approach works with the child in relation to other children, to the family, to the teachers, to the school environment, to the community, and to the wider society—and the interconnections and reciprocity are encouraged and supported. Many programs and schools in the United States have embraced those same important relationships and integrated them into preschool and elementary curriculum.

A Final Curriculum Approach

With all of the ideas swimming around in your head, you are probably saying, "No! No more ideas about curriculum." It is understandable that you are feeling like you don't know where to begin, and that you have so many ideas mixed together that developing curriculum sounds impossible. For that reason, we want to end this chapter with a very straightforward curriculum approach called the *Four Es:* experience, extension, expression, and evaluation. The approach has been used successfully by preservice teachers (like you) and beginning teachers (Van Scoy, 1995). The approach is consistent with child development knowledge and learning theory, and is actually a framework used by many teachers for a long time. Those teachers were working with children in ways that "felt right" to them; that is, they worked intuitively. They didn't know about the Four Es, but if they described their curriculum, it would be the same as the Four Es.

Principles of the Four Es approach.   One of the appeals of this approach is that it pulls together some of the thinking we have described for you. You will recognize some familiar names and ideas. The Four Es model is built on three principles of learning:

1. The younger the children, the more their thinking is tied to concrete, observable experiences (Kamii & DeVries, 1978; Piaget, 1969).

2. Young children construct knowledge through interaction with people and the environment (Ginsberg & Opper, 1969; Kamii, 1989).

3. Although children's thinking is closely tied to observable events, they are also learning the complex notion that one thing can represent another (Piaget & Inhelder, 1969).

■ **FIGURE 5.5**

The Four Es and Their Relationship to One Another

Source: Adapted from "Whole Learning: A Model for Planning" by J. D. Fuqua, April 1991, paper presented at the annual meeting of ACEI, San Diego, CA. Figure from "Trading the Three R's for the Four E's: Transforming Curriculum" by I. J. Van Scoy, 1996, *Childhood Education, 72,* page 20. Reprinted by permission of I. J. Van Scoy and the Association for Childhood Education International, 17904 Georgia Avenue, Suite 215, Olney, MD 20832. Copyright © 1996 by the Association.

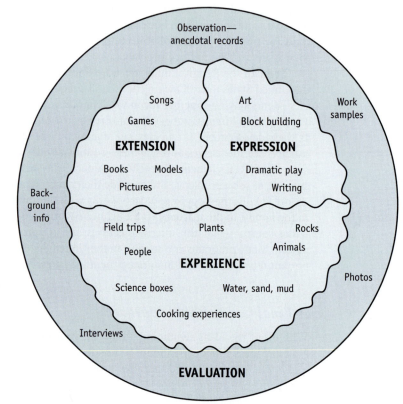

The Four Es at work. Figure 5.5 represents the Four Es. The foundation of the model is *experience.* Keeping in mind the three principles as you develop curriculum will guide you in providing an abundance of firsthand experiences with as many real things as possible. Try to mirror the children's world with attractive and intriguing objects, topics, activities, problems, and people. From their immediate environment, the children can "travel" to novel experiences—visiting an art museum, having a guest from another culture, constructing a rocket ship, and flying a Japanese kite. Even videos, photographs, stories, and roleplaying can provide rich experiences for children.

Extension is a process of building on real experiences with models, language, audiovisuals, and games to extend the children's knowledge and understanding. Once the children have had firsthand experiences, they are motivated and secure in the exploration of symbols. They can then relate the abstractions to the previous concrete experiences. It is important to make connections between those real experiences and the extension activities. For example, after the children have visited a farm, they can extend their experience with a video about a dairy farm or a book about raising chickens.

Expression is similar to extension in that it builds on experiences. The difference is that teachers provide extensions and children provide expression. Expression occurs in the following circumstances:

Children talk about their field trips.

Children engage in dramatic play.

Children build with blocks or other construction materials.

Children develop charts, signs, graphs, and stories.

Children draw, paint, sculpt, or express themselves with visual art media.

Children move their bodies or sign a message.

Expression activities provide information to teachers about what children understand and are able to do. You will need to be a good observer during children's expression in order to know what experiences to provide and how to extend those experiences.

Evaluation surrounds the other three Es in Figure 5.5 because evaluation needs to be part of all classroom activities. Van Scoy (1995) suggests some questions with which to begin your evaluation.

What are the most meaningful areas of study for these children?

What do we know about their lives and their communities?

What are the developmental levels of the children? (p. 22)

From there, you can begin planning experiences. As children engage in these experiences, you will be assessing their responses—their expressions. What you learn from observing them will guide your planning of future experiences and extensions.

Putting It All Together: Weaving the Thinking and Approaches into Your Curriculum

You are probably wondering, "How do I ever begin?" Our response is to go back through the thinking and programs and prioritize. Decide whose ideas and what approaches feel right for your developing philosophy about children and their development. From there, you can begin to try out those applications with children, or at least in your conversations. That's the experience of one of your authors.

Years ago, after studying the thinking of Montessori, Pratt, and Kamii and De-Vries and visiting programs such as Waldorf schools and the Bank Street program, I taught for a year in a demonstration laboratory preschool. The teaching staff was encouraged to experiment with curriculum, and generous supplies and materials were provided. There were no limits on classroom furnishings and equipment. I attempted to incorporate the ideas of many of the thinkers we just introduced. Since I had also observed most of the programs we just described, they, too, also influenced my classroom.

We think that your visit to this classroom will assist you in sorting through all the information presented in this chapter and help you start to develop curriculum. Listen as the planning begins in my thoughts.

Listen to My Thoughts

For the first time in my teaching, I will have 3-, 4-, and 5-year-olds all together in my classroom. I've finally finished graduate school and my head is brimming with ideas to try out. I've always been a bit eclectic in my tastes and my approaches to education, so it feels like the ideal time to put all of these new ideas into a curriculum for my mixed-age classroom. I begin with Piaget and the programs designed by Kamii and DeVries. I want to use Piagetian tasks and have different levels of difficulty within each task to accommodate the differences in my mixed-age class. I also like Montessori's approach, especially the life skills component of her curriculum, because I think that those activities will make sense to children. The aesthetic component of the Waldorf schools appeals to my aesthetic nature and my belief that children will develop well when surrounded by beauty. Sylvia Ashton-Warner's key-word approach makes good sense to me. I read with great enthusiasm of the projects and thematic approaches of the Bank Street classes and have used those curricular approaches with previous groups of children because I observed that children's learning is naturally integrated. I will always appreciate blocks as the most valuable materials for young children, so Caroline Pratt's experiences were compelling. (*Note:* Reggio Emilia was yet unknown to U.S. educators, or I probably would have figured out a way to have an *atelierista*).

And so, I put together a curriculum by blending all of these ideas and welcomed the children one September. It took a few months to get to know the children and their families well and for them to get to know me. We all needed time to get comfortable, to work out routines, and to become a community (Driscoll, 1996, personal communication).

A Day in a Mixed-Age Preschool: Applying the Ideas

It's 8:30 A.M. and the children and parents arrive a few at a time. For those who arrive first, there are several small centers open for their use—usually puzzles, a few trays of play-dough, and some simple games. These are placed close together on the floor so that we can sit in a small group during arrivals—to talk and welcome each other. It's a quiet, relaxed time. While the others arrive, take a look around and get familiar with the room. The space is quite large, almost a square. One wall is all glass and looks out onto the playground. Around the room is basic equipment—a water table, shelves of art materials, manipulatives, dramatic play props, painting easels, many shelves full of blocks, and an adult work space. Three large circular tables can accommodate all 18 of the children. On each table

is a lovely arrangement of bright chrysanthemums and fall leaves. We also see a shelf with an attractive display of gourds, pumpkins, Indian corn, and winter squash on a fabric background.

"Everyone's here—let's begin." Together, adults and children recite several poems. They sound quite adultlike, not cutesy like so many rhymes for children. We hear: "One misty moist morning." Miriam, Christopher, and September use lots of expression as they recite the poems, and their faces display an intense earnestness about the recitation. Each child has a name card on his or her lap. After poetry, the children place the cards in a basket in the center of the circle as they say, "Morgan Hawkins is here," "Tayisha Josephs is here," and so on. When finished, the group counts together the number of cards in the basket and then counts the actual children in the circle. "Sixteen. We have sixteen children here today."

The day's agenda is reviewed and the children talk about their plans for the day. The schedule itself is fairly set, but some of the activities vary from day to day. During this circle time, new activities are described and the day's snack recipe is reviewed. Children have their snacks whenever they feel hungry rather than in a group. Since some preparation is usually involved, the children have learned skills such as spreading with a knife and using measuring spoons.

Small Center Time

Children leave the circle for "small center" time. The small center work takes place at the three large tables, and the materials are placed on a wall of shelves adjacent to the tables. Notice that the tables each have a piece of different-colored tape across the middle of the table. The materials on the shelf are in boxes marked with those same colored tabs. Children choosing the boxes marked with red tabs are soon using the materials at the table with the red tape. These boxes are filled with materials for sorting and classifying (nuts in shells, buttons, screws and bolts, colored shapes, and leaves), matching (fabric squares, textures, and designs), and serration tasks (picture cards, tubes, and colored shapes). Children choosing the boxes marked with blue tabs are soon using the materials at the table with the blue tape. These boxes contain individual children's key words, writing and drawing materials, a typewriter, and clipboards. An adult is at the table to record the children's ideas. Finally, children choosing the boxes marked with yellow tabs are soon using the materials at the table with the yellow tape. Most of the materials in these boxes assist the children in their fine motor skills (tweezers and items to pick up, a nut cracker and nuts, tongs and cotton balls, sewing cards, and commercial materials).

During small center time, the children use colorful cards to record their activities (see Figure 5.6 on page 194). You see Tony color in the square next to the leaves when he finishes sorting the leaves. One of the classroom aides comes over to where he is working and asks, "Why did you put these leaves together, Tony?" "They are all red!" he exclaims. "Is

there any other way to sort these?" the aide asks. Tony pauses and looks at some of the leaves, then says, "I could put all the big ones together and the little ones together." Next to him is Brandy, sorting buttons into sections of an egg carton.

Big Center Time

After about 40 minutes, the children are ready to begin "big center" time. Those who wish to stay with their small center activity are welcome to do so, but most of the children have completed several tasks and have colored in the squares. Big centers include the snack center, wrapping center, science center, math center, reading area, dramatic play area, art area, blocks center, "grown-up" center (the children's name for it), and water play area. Daniel and September go immediately to the snack center. "We're hungry!" says September, and Daniel agrees. They sit down at the small table and review the **rebus recipe** (a recipe composed of symbols and pictures) for making tuna salad to spread on crackers. Daniel spoons two tablespoons of tuna into his bowl, adds a teaspoon of mayonnaise and a teaspoon of pickle relish, and mixes it together. September is cutting up a small stalk of celery and putting the pieces into her bowl. Daniel looks over and says, "I don't like celery." Julianna's mom comes over to the table and joins the children. She comments on Daniel's measuring and September's chopping, and records her observations on a chart hanging near the table. "How does your tuna salad taste, Daniel?" she asks. Daniel smiles broadly and responds, "Delicious." The adult and two children continue to chat about a variety of topics—September's new puppy, the weather, and the day's activities. When Daniel finishes eating, the parent asks him to describe how he made his tuna salad and records his recipe.

Several children are intensely busy at the wrapping center. Tayisha has covered a cereal box with plaid wrapping paper and lots of tape (fortunately, someone donated an entire carton of tape rolls), and is struggling to make a bow. "Ms. Caroline, I need

■ **FIGURE 5.6** Small Center Recording Form

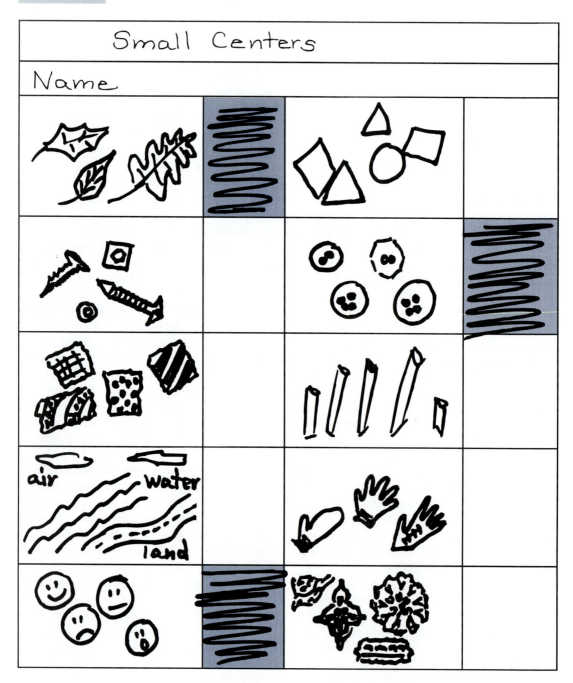

help." Caroline, a student teacher, comes over and asks, "How can I help you?" Tayisha shows her what she has been trying to do and they talk about bow making. Two other children are wrapping boxes and they will later make cards for their "pretend gifts."

Nearby is Will sitting at a table, polishing shoes. He has newspaper spread over the table and he is concentrating with great seriousness on a pair of very large men's shoes. As he generously spreads the black polish, he says to no one in particular, "My dad wears these shoes to parties." His conversation attracts Miriam, who comes over and watches for a while. She reminds Will to remember to "buff shoes really well." (Miriam likes to take care of the class!) Later, 3-year-old Will asks his teacher to write *polish, dad,* and *shoes* on his word cards. Now he is walking around, "reading the cards," saying the words to himself.

At the end of the day, these children will talk about their activities—their work. Will's dad's shoes will prompt a conversation about shoe sizes, and children will predict what could be in Tayisha's package. Some days, the group writes about their experiences, and some weeks the big centers are focused on a project or a thematic focus. For example, when the children became interested in babies, the dramatic play center focused on babies—preparing baby bottles, washing baby clothes, bathing babies, and so on. Books about babies appeared in the library. Even the block center had accessories related to babies.

Both children and adults learn in a classroom where there is respect for differences and a spirit of discovery.

The year was full of surprises, as children polished the insides of shoes and frustrated younger siblings at home were presented with wrapped but empty gift boxes. It was also a year of insight about children as we watched them grow and develop and become a community in our classroom. The year was full of experimentation, and some curriculum ideas weren't right for the children. Those were immediately obvious and abandoned quickly. Other curriculum ideas were embraced enthusiastically by the children. The gift wrap center evolved from Miriam's desire to wrap a birthday gift for her mom and was meant to be a month-long experience, but at the children's insistence, they were still wrapping on the last day of school (seven months later).

Journal 5.10: Observe these classroom activities again by rereading the descriptions and make connections between what the children and adults are doing and the curriculum ideas and programs you encountered in this chapter. ■

Notice how the classroom we described was the result of a blend of teaching experiences, new ideas, philosophy, and signals from the children and their families. It was a learning experience for everyone, especially the teacher. Be assured that you will always be learning. Children vary so much that you will be adjusting constantly, both personally and professionally.

PRINCIPLES AND INSIGHTS: ## A Summary and Review

In sum, we encourage you to "learn from the children" as Caroline Pratt has urged, observe their development, listen to what emerges from their conversations and activities, and be flexible. Be open to that "bird flying in the window" that David Hawkins described so enthusiastically. Experiment, as Bank Street urges teachers to do, and don't be afraid to make mistakes. Heed the lessons of Sylvia Ashton-Warner and have the "patience, caring, listening, and intuition" to be creative and original with your curricular approaches. At the same time, be cautious not to impose your ideas and answers on children, as Kamii and DeVries warned. When you make mistakes, talk about them with the children. Contemplate the lives of the children and provide real-life activities and materials, as Maria Montessori did.

As we encouraged in Chapter 1 and in this chapter, continue being a learner of early childhood education. There are numerous workshops on curriculum, great books to read, and wonderful teachers all around you with ideas as rich as any we've described in this chapter. As you meet the children in the chapters that follow and observe them both at home and in early childhood programs, you will see much more curriculum. You will be anxious to finish your studies and have a classroom of your own so that you can try out some of your ideas as well as the ideas of others. Look forward to that time, for it is a time of discovery and excitement.

Becoming an Early Childhood Professional

Your Field Experiences

1. This is a good time to observe in a variety of classrooms with a focus on curriculum. After watching children and adults, try to summarize the curriculum of the program. If possible, interview the teacher about his or her curriculum. See if you can connect your observations with one of the thinkers or programs we described in this chapter.

2. Review curriculum materials for a school district or preschool program (check an education library) for the following: philosophy, developmentally appropriateness, and interest for children.

Your Professional Portfolio

1. After observing a class (preschool or kindergarten) for a day, develop a one-day plan for yourself. Assume that you are the teacher and use the ideas of this chapter to plan a day for a specific group of children. Along with your plan, describe a rationale for each of the routines or activities you plan.

2. Read one of the books listed in the section that follows and write a critique of the curriculum. Describe your agreement and disagreement with the ideas of the book. In doing so, begin to develop your philosophy of curriculum.

Your Professional Library

The comprehensive nature of this chapter makes it difficult to confine this reading list to just a few books and addresses. If you want to read more, check the references at the end of the book. Don't be put off by the age of some of our recommendations—some of these curriculum books are ageless.

Books and Articles

Ashton-Warner, S. (1963). *Teacher.* New York: Simon & Schuster.

Driscoll, A. (1995). *Cases in early childhood education: Stories of programs and practices.* Boston: Allyn & Bacon.

Edwards, C., Gandini, L., & Forman, G. (1995). *The hundred languages of children: The Reggio Emilia approach to early childhood education.* Norwood, NJ: Ablex.

Goffin, S. (1994). *Curriculum models and early childhood education.* New York: Macmillan.

Hochman, C., Barnet, M., & Weikart, D. (1979). *Young children in action: A manual for preschool educators.* Ypsilanti: MI: High Scope Press.

Nagel, N. (1996). *Learning through real-world problem solving: The power of integrative teaching.* Thousand Oaks, CA: Corwin.

Pratt, C. (1948). *I learn from children.* New York: Harper & Row.

Van Scoy, I. (1995). Trading the three R's for the four E's: Transforming curriculum. *Child Education, 72* (1), 19–23.

Internet Addresses and World Wide Web Sites

www.amshq.org
Montessori Education (J. Chattin-McNichols, Seattle University)

www.bnkst.edu/sfc/SFC.html
Bank Street School for Children & Family Center (R. Jordan, 1997)

ericps.ed.uiuc.edu/eece/pubs/books/reggio.html
Reflections on the Reggio Emilia Approach (L. Katz & B. Cesarone)

www.purchase.edu/children/world/internet.html
Internet Starting Points for Early Childhood Educators

www.bnkst.edu
Bank Street College of Education

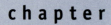

Families and Communities

CONTEXT FOR

UNDERSTANDING CHILDREN

When you finish reading and reflecting on this chapter, you will be able to:

1. Show awareness of and be sensitive to the wide diversity of family structures, organizations, and demographics.

2. Appreciate the contemporary issues faced by families.

3. Articulate reasons for involving families in the education of young children.

4. Describe guidelines for building partnerships with families.

5. Assess communities as contexts for understanding young children and their families.

The door framed in ruffled curtains opens and a man in a suit and tie steps into the kitchen with a sigh, "Honey, I'm home." No answer. He pokes around the kitchen, opens the pot on the stove, and sniffs with a smile just as his wife enters the kitchen. She hugs him warmly and asks, "How was your day, dear?" to which he replies, "Oh, it was so busy, but we met our deadline." He sighs wearily and asks, "Where are the boys?" She tells him that they're up in their rooms finishing their homework and encourages him to go to his favorite chair and put his feet up and read the paper. "Supper will be ready soon," she assures him.

Looking Back at Families

Years ago, this scene depicted a favorite television show, *Ozzie and Harriet* about Ozzie, a husband and father, Harriet, a wife and mother, and their two sons. No matter what incident or theme the weekly series described, the familiar scenes were always there: Ozzie arriving home from work to be greeted by Harriet in her apron in the kitchen; Ozzie sitting in his easy chair with his feet up on an ottoman and reading the paper; and the family sitting around the dinner table talking about their day. If you don't remember these scenes, ask one of the older members of your family to recall the show. Other television shows show similar scenes—*Leave It to Beaver, The Dick Van Dyke Show,* and more. Some of us even remember those scenes in our own homes and in the homes of our friends when we were growing up.

Years later, a favorite television show was *The Brady Bunch,* about a single man and a single woman, each with three children, who got married and joined their families into the "bunch." Mrs. Brady still stayed home and took care of the house and the children, and Mr. Brady went off to work each day in a suit, but somehow the scenes weren't quite like those in *Ozzie and Harriet*. Life began to look a lot more complex, and the mother and father roles weren't so distinct. For many of us, the scenes continued to be comfortable and familiar.

Today, favorite television shows present almost every variation of family and home life that exists in our society: *Roseanne, Married with Children, Ellen, Family Matters, Party of Five,* and others. A few years ago, there was an outcry because the lead character on *Murphy Brown* was unmarried and having a child, but many were drawn by the reality about the situation. In fact, sociologists and historians insist that the *Ozzie and Harriet* family was a myth. In her book, *The Way We Never Were: American Families and the Nostalgia Trap* (1992), Coontz says:

> Through most of American history, families have needed more than one breadwinner; either both parents worked, or the children worked. Not until the 1920's did a bare majority of children come to live in a breadwinner/homemaker family. The "Ozzie and Harriet" model held sway for only 50 years, and at no point—even in the 1950's—did more than 60% of children live in such families for their entire childhood. (p. 5)

Today's Families and "Work Sweet Work"

In a recent article in the *New York Times* magazine (April 1997), Hochschild tells about interviews with 130 adults and about following them through their "typical days" of juggling families and work. Hochschild describes the trend of working parents who work more hours than ever before—men averaging 48.8 hours and women averaging 41.7. When the question of Why? was explored, one would expect the answer to be money, fear of job loss, or advancement reasons. Hochschild's research suggests, however, that for many adults the attractions are emotional and social. In spite of long hours and guilt over leaving their children for long days, the women and men talked about the enjoyment of conversations with colleagues, the satisfaction of their work quality and decision making, and the sense of being valued and appreciated that they experience in their work settings. In contrast, these working adults find home life stressful, complex, and demanding, without much satisfaction. The demands of raising children, the complexity of new family configurations (stepparents and stepchildren), and the stresses of caring for elderly parents feel overwhelming. Work offers escape. In addition, the kind of satisfaction formerly found at home appears to be transferred to work.

Not everyone, not even a majority of families, are making the switch from home to work, but there is evidence that the number of adults making the substitution is growing. With this trend comes increased demands on those who decide to take care of and educate the children. It is important for you to understand the complexity and stresses of family lives if you are going to understand the children. Partnering with families is essential to good early childhood education practices, and those families will vary as widely as their individual children. You will need to have knowledge of their diverse family structures and values, an understanding of their stresses and the complexity of their lives, and an attitude of acceptance toward their diverse life-styles and priorities. At the same time, you will be working to meet their needs and collaborating with them to set common goals related to their children. If all this sounds like a call for "Super-Professional," it is! Children deserve that kind of working relationship between their early childhood educator and their families. This chapter begins to prepare you for that relationship by exploring many of the possible variations in families and communities and describing the issues of today's families.

Families and Communities: Significant Understandings

Today's television shows, even with their diverse portrayals of families, are but a microcosm of the complexity of families in society today. Not only are families organized differently but the roles within families are also vastly different. Families today are characterized by changes from traditional patterns and issues that were never talked about or addressed openly even when they existed. No matter what ECE role you pursue, your interactions with children will need to be sensitive to the complexity and changes in families.

In addition to the individual variation of each family unit, you will also need to consider the community in which children live. Ozzie and Harriet and the Brady Bunch lived in neighborhoods where everyone knew each other and looked out for each other, which was the norm in many communities. Today, such a neighborhood is a rarity! Our communities are vastly different from each other—socioeconomically, geographically, politically, and in the subtleties of relationships, values, communication, and so on. Children will arrive in your classroom, influenced by both their families and their communities, with experiences, values, attitudes, socialization, and motivations.

In a great many situations, early childhood professionals, especially teachers, come from backgrounds that are quite different from the children they teach. It is most unlikely that you will work in the same community in which you live. In Ozzie and Harriet's day, the boys' teachers probably lived a few blocks away. Harriet may have encountered the school principal and his wife in the grocery store on Saturdays. Many teachers today have never seen the neighborhoods in which the children in their classrooms live.

Our experiences in education and related professions have confirmed the importance of families and communities—of knowing them, involving them, and viewing them as partners, resources, and advocates. Project Head Start has provided excellent leadership for many years in how to involve families and communities. Its programs have demonstrated how to integrate the diversity of families and communities in curriculum, how to respect the variation in family life-styles, and how to work in partnership with communities to better serve the needs of children and families. Today, Goals 2000 mandates that families be involved in schools and classrooms to better educate children. That national recognition of the knowledge and attitudes are the focus of this chapter.

In this chapter, we will guide you in your development of understandings and sensitivities regarding the diversity of families and communities, and we will demonstrate the skills you will need to involve and work in partnership with them. We'll begin by looking at the nature and functions of families today. We will explore the contemporary changes in families that may help you understand why the families of today's children may be different from the families you may have experienced. We will look at some of the stresses and issues that families face. Child-rearing differences will help explain some of the variations in children with whom you work, and we'll describe those differences with examples that may be familiar.

A Lens for Viewing Communities

We will look at communities from an **ecological perspective**—that is, from the perspective of the relationship between humans and their environment. That relationship can be psychological, physical, economic, political, and social, and the variation in children and families will be better understood within that relationship. Children develop different strengths, different needs, and different understandings as a result of the ecology of the community in which they live. The relationship between the children and their families and their environment develops in response to all kinds of factors, some of which are discussed next.

Density of the communities.   The feeling of being crowded together is quite real in some communities where many people live in small spaces. Some inner cities are quite dense with either cramped low-income houses packed together or tiny expensive condos stacked on top of each other. Some people prefer such living, paying a great deal to live close to each other and to community services, and some people have no choice. Research has shown that density affects human behavior and emotions. Children in a crowded classroom often misbehave out of frustration with the closeness of others—one of the effects of the density of communities in which children and families live.

Arrangement of the homes.   The arrangement of homes, which is often related to economics, refers to the amount of open space—such as yards, sidewalks, alleyways, paths, parks, and so on—that can be found even in the most dense community. Some U.S. communities are "gated communities," which are clusters of homes (usually expensive) and expansive yards surrounded by fences or walls. Other families live on the border of busy streets with barely a sidewalk intervening. A lack of parks or areas in which to play may influence children's behavior or family needs. There is also a diversity of homes that can be separated into rented versus owned, or expensive versus substandard, or one-family versus multiple-family dwellings. In Ozzie and Harriet's day, everyone had a front porch or a front yard and people spent time there. Today, front yards are disappearing and front porches are at a premium, so chatting with neighbors is much less frequent.

Population characteristics.   So many demographics can characterize a community. One can consider the racial and ethnic characteristics. Portland, Oregon, for example, has well-defined neighborhoods and some of them have been segregated at times. One particular neighborhood was traditionally settled by African Americans for many years.

Today, it is a diverse neighborhood with a rich mix of cultures. Another part of the city has a large population of Asian families, and the effect of this demographic can easily be seen in the businesses, the churches, and the family activities.

Some communities are segregated by age—clusters of elderly people living in close proximity either in formal retirement communities or informally in old neighborhoods. There are also neighborhood areas in which new families with young children congregate. With each of these segregations, there are the advantages of common interests and concerns, but there is also the lack of diversity and the richness it brings to individual and family lives.

Economics.   Economics is definitely a significant demographic and it influences many of the other characteristics of communities. It is the underlying factor in many people's decisions about where and how to live. Economics goes beyond housing prices and neighborhood amenities (streetlights, sidewalks, fountains, flower beds) to quality and kind of businesses, recreational facilities, and even the kinds of churches. One can see its influence in how families spend their time, the pace of life, and the supports available. Wealth does not guarantee that such influence will always be positive for families. Sometimes, the wealthiest family will not have much free time together, and the poorest family will have a strong support system among the other poor families in the neighborhood.

Setting.   One of your authors lives in a condominium arranged in a row with many other condominiums and surrounded mostly by apartment complexes and busy traffic. This dense neighborhood sits on the edge of the bustling downtown but it has a narrow park running through the center. Perhaps one of the families you will encounter might live in a crowded neighborhood with run-down apartments and noisy traffic, bordered by streets of businesses whose windows are covered by boards, and a playground with broken glass, garbage strewn about, and little equipment left for play activities.

Pace of life.   A recent study conducted in major cities around the world found that although people reported being happier in communities with a fast pace, they did not enjoy good health (Levine, 1997). The pace of a community may influence the kind of interactions that occur within it, as well as within the family. A constant fast pace may be a source of stress to some family members, yet stimulate other members.

In sum, community differences will certainly influence the physical and emotional health, the socialization, and the life-styles of the families and children who live in them. Each child and each family, however, will respond uniquely to the environments we described. One child may rebel against the crowded, hectic conditions of a neighborhood, whereas another child may find interest and stimulation in the same conditions. Your task in this chapter is to balance the generalizations about families and communities with a sensitivity to the individual variation you will encounter.

Personal assessment for awareness.   Before beginning, you'll find it helpful to assess your own family and community. It's a comfortable starting point for thinking about the differences and influences of family and community.

■ **FIGURE 6.1**   Framework for Reflection

Family Reflection

1. List the members of your family (with names, ages, and relation to you).
2. What is the educational background of the adults?
3. What is the employment of the adults?
4. Describe the decision-making process of the family.
5. What are the recreational activities of the family when they are together?
6. How are the household chores distributed?
7. Describe the home.
8. What are the family values or priorities?
9. What kind of support do the adults provide to the children?
10. Who and what are the important influences (people, events, etc.)?

Community Reflection

1. Define your community.
2. Describe the demographics of your community (urban/rural, size, socioeconomics, etc.).
3. List your community's resources.
4. What are the common community meeting places?
5. What kind of attention and support are given to children and families?
6. What are the community issues?
7. What are the advantages of your community? The disadvantages of your community?
8. What are the important influences in the community?

Journal 6.1: Reflect on your childhood and analyze your family and community at the time when you were young. We've developed a framework (see Figure 6.1) for you to record your impressions—it will prompt you to think about influences that may not come immediately to the surface. The major ideas in the framework are important concepts of this chapter. When you finish reflecting on your childhood, take a break. After a few days, reflect again. This second time, analyze your current living situation—your family and community today. ■

The framework in Figure 6.1 easily converted to a set of questions to pose to families. Their answers will be one source of information to help you get to know the children and their families. It is possible that families will pause and reflect on their own situations as they answer your questions. As we continue throughout this chapter to talk about families, you may come up with additional questions. While you are reading, think about what kind of information will help you better understand children and families and meet their needs.

As people go through life, they are socialized by everyone and everything they encounter. Socialization begins with one's family and the communities in which one lives. It doesn't stop when one reaches adulthood. People continue to be socialized and to change as a result. Today, as we write this chapter, a list of possibilities has affected who we are. Early this morning, a newspaper story of a 90-year-old who wrote her first book stirred up our enthusiasm and energy to write. A colleague at work has been diagnosed with cancer, and we think about immortality and become philosophical about our lives. Later, we meet with teachers and listen to their experiences with children who face issues that none of us is prepared to address. We pause and question our approaches to teaching. Some of these experiences may be only fleeting influences but others stay with us and affect our thinking and behavior for years. That process, called **socialization,** is a powerful lens through which to observe children. We begin this section on families with descriptions of how families socialize children, because it helps us convince you of the importance of studying families while studying children.

Family Socialization

Family socialization begins a process through which humans learn and develop to be the adult persons they become. Has this happened to you? You have a close friend, Joan, whom you've known for many years, and finally you meet her family and think to yourself, "Now I understand where Joan gets those habits and behaviors from." For some, the effects of family socialization are very evident and long lasting; for others, there is not much obvious effect; and for still others, it looks like there's no relationship at all. If you look closely, you'll see that some adults choose to adopt behaviors and values that are completely opposite those of their families. For those individuals, you might also say, "Now I understand why Allan is that way." The socialization is just as strong, but it has a different effect.

Family socialization occurs through daily interactions between adults and children. What socialization messages might this child be learning?

For some adults, their interactions with family continues in such a close relationship that the family maintains a dominant role in their ongoing socialization. You probably know some friends in that kind of situation. When you used Figure 6.1 to reflect on your family, did you find different influences during your childhood and your current situation?

Effects of family socialization.   In Chapters 2 and 3, we described Erikson's stages of development. Those stages offer another model for understanding socialization. Figure 6.2 shows the socialization influences or agents that have an impact on each stage of development. As people develop the qualities that enable them to be successful members of society, their development is influenced by different socialization agents and a strengthening or weakening of those influences. Erikson's stages explain much about

■ FIGURE 6.2   Erikson's Eight Stages of Psychosocial Development

Stage	Positive	Socializing Agents	Negative
Infancy	Trust	Family	Mistrust
Early Childhood	Autonomy	Family	Shame/Doubt
Play Age	Initiative	Family School (Childcare)	Guilt
School Age	Industry	Family Peers Schools Community	Inferiority
Adolescence	Identity	Family Peers Schools Community	Identity Diffusion
Young Adulthood	Intimacy	Family Peers Community	Isolation
Adulthood	Generativity	Family Peers Community	Self-Absorption
Senescence	Integrity	Family Peers	Despair

Note that an individual's self-concept could be described as being at any point on the horizontal dimension lines, rather than at one extreme or another. The importance of interactions with one's social environment in the development of a self-concept is indicated by the socializing agents that are most significant at various stages.

Source: Excerpt from *Child, Family, Community,* Third Edition by Roberta M. Berns, copyright © 1993 by Holt, Rinehart and Winston, reprinted by permission of the publisher.

how families, friends, school, and community influences a person. Their socialization plays a role in:

- The development of trust
- The development of independence
- The tendency to take initiative
- The sense of competence and ambition
- Decisions about who one is
- Relationships with others
- Decisions about future generations
- Reflections on one's life.

Intentional and unintentional socialization.   Some of the influence of families is intentional and some of it is unintentional, a result of some spontaneous interaction. Watch Keeley and her mom and see if you can pick out the intentional and unintentional socialization.

Keeley: Socialization

Kerry, Keeley's mom, is getting ready for work. She stands in front of the mirror and spends a long time putting on makeup. Keeley is sitting near her on the floor playing, but she mostly watches her mom's makeup routine. Then Kerry fixes her hair, pushing it over her ears a certain way and checking her reflection in the mirror frequently. "It's your turn," she says to Keeley and she begins to brush Keeley's hair. "I want a French braid," Keeley says to her mom in a demanding tone. "Is that the way you ask for things?" her mom asks. Keeley gets quiet and says, "Mom, would you fix my hair in a French braid, please?" Her mom smiles and responds lovingly, and immediately starts forming the braid.

The intentional lesson Kerry was trying to teach Keeley is pretty obvious. But what was Keeley learning without Kerry intending to teach it to her? This may take some discussion and there may be some disagreement among your classmates about the unintentional socialization occurring for Keeley. The important idea is that Kerry is not even thinking about teaching Keeley anything in particular. She is simply going about the process of getting herself ready for work, but socialization is occurring.

Journal 6.2: Continue reflecting on your own family socialization as a way of understanding the influence of families. Can you identify an intentional socialization from your family and an unintentional lesson from your childhood? Many of us learned lessons from our families that our families certainly didn't want us to learn. Reflect on those lessons. What do you remember?

Family Structures, Organizational Patterns, and Functions

Using the language of the U.S. Bureau of the Census, *families* are defined as "two or more related people living in a household." That sounds like a fairly generic definition, but it is a bit confining for today's families. Some families don't live together in a household but they are families, and two people living together don't have to be related but they can still be a family. If you were to survey your peers and list the variations in family structures, you would probably find the following:

Two married adults living together
Two unmarried adults living together
One adult and a child or children
Two married adults and a child or children
Two unmarried adults and a child or children
One adult and one adult child
Two married adults, a child or children, and a parent of one of the adults
Two adults with a child or children from other marriages
One adult with a child or children and a grandchild or grandchildren.

The list goes on, and with every possible variation. Within family structures, you find more complex differences, such as foster parents, gay or lesbian parents, stepchildren, adopted children, and so on.

Organizational patterns.   The possible variation within family structures contributes some information about a child's socialization but from there, the organization of families complicates the socialization process. When we talk about family organization, we are referring to three basic emphases in the way a family handles responsibilities and decision making. Those organizational emphases may be culturally influenced, a family tradition, or a response to societal conditions:

1. **Matriarchal organizations** are those families in which the mother is the primary adult with responsibility for socialization of the children. The mother has the authority to make the family decisions and usually controls the resources for carrying out the responsibilities and decisions.

2. **Patriarchal organizations** are those families in which the father is the primary adult with those same responsibilities, authority, and resources.

3. **Egalitarian organizations** are those families in which the responsibilities, authority, and resources are shared by the adults and the children. It's a family structure in which there is a lot of shared decision making.

Family functions.   In addition to the organizational differences, there are three major functions of families: economic functions, socialization functions, and support functions. Those functions serve both families and society. They are essential for our survival.

Some families carry out the *economic function* with one adult working outside the home to earn an income and the other adult taking care of the home and family. Some carry it out with two adults earning incomes and sharing the home responsibilities.

One of your authors had a grandmother who was widowed and left with 13 children. While Grandma baked bread to sell and took in ironing, the six oldest children worked at odd jobs around the neighborhood to earn money to help support the family. There are families in which one of the children supports the entire family. There are also families in which the family works together raising crops to earn the family income. Those are but a few examples, but already you can appreciate the huge variation in families' economic functions.

The second function is one you have already encountered in this chapter. Another way of thinking of the *socialization function* of the family is through the teaching or lessons learned in the family context. The most basic lessons are related to values and beliefs, but the family is also a major educator of children's knowledge and understandings, skills, and attitudes. In the early days of this country's history, families were the main educators, but today, the function is been shared between home and school. However, some families feel too busy and stressed to deal with the ever extending issues and lessons that children need. On the other hand, some families are hesitant about turning this important function to others. As a future early childhood professional, you will need to check in with families about your curriculum and be aware of the influence of your own attitudes and beliefs on what you teach children.

The third function is about the *emotional and social support* that every human needs. Children who are developing emotional security and social skills need to be surrounded and cared for by nurturing adults. This function is especially important during early childhood, illness, and old age. This nurturance function is augmented for many families by child care providers of all kinds as more and more parents work to fulfill the economic functions.

An additional function of families for the survival of society is the *reproduction function*. The attitude toward this function has changed over the last 30 years and many adults are making the decision not to have children. Some of the pressure for this decision has come from the economics of society, and some from the professional opportunities expanded for women. There also appears to be less pressure placed on those adults who decide not to have children.

Although all families fulfill the basic functions just described, they prioritize them differently. Some families place their economic function as their highest priority, making money to provide for the family as most important. Others, not as concerned about financial matters, make the support or socialization of their children a priority. Many families balance the functions. It's actually quite a complicated balance and is dependent on a wide range of other circumstances. What is important is to realize that families are struggling to handle multiple functions in the midst of multiple challenges. Those challenges faced by today's families will require your study and sensitivity.

Contemporary Challenges Faced by Families

Entire books are devoted to the topic of challenges faced by families. Each time you open a newspaper, there's a human-interest story of a new challenge faced by families in the midst of rapidly changing federal and state policies and programs. These challenges include poverty, homelessness, divorce, single parenting, and stress, to name just a few. We'll begin with stresses on today's families.

Stress on Families

Stress is not a new challenge for families. Life must have been quite stressful for the early pioneer families with the many dangers, the harsh weather and living conditions, and the transition from living in other countries. Today, families, including children, appear to face more stress and to create more stress. The traditional **stressors** (conditions or situations that cause stress) for children include separation anxiety, sibling rivalry, transition to child care or school, peer pressure, and developing independence. For adults, too, the traditional stressors continue—economic pressures, crime, traffic, crowded conditions, and the responsibility of raising a child. The less predictive nature of family life has become a stressor for both adults and children. Even the youngest of children knows of someone whose spouse or parent has left the home. With the doubling of the divorce rate since 1965, both adults and children worry about the possibility or face the feelings of "being abandoned" or the guilt that the divorce is their fault.

Work stress. The work life of most adults has become more complicated and stressful, and with it comes another list of stressors. In some working situations, there is a constant threat of job loss due to technological change and management reorganization. Even for those employees who learn new skills and embrace new technology, there are no guarantees. Samuelson (1996) reminds families that it is the most modern innovative industries that are shedding employees the fastest.

In addition to the insecurities and pressures of today's fast-paced work world, many parents come home to additional pressures and insecurities. At the end of a typical long day, Kerry feels guilty because she is often too tired to play with Keeley. She has barely enough energy to feed her and get her to bed. Sometimes she is not as patient as she would like to be, and that realization is stressful. There's also the stress of taking care of their home in the few hours that are available. There's little chance for a social life— an evening out with a friend, or a late movie once in a while—and that's another source of stress.

Child care stress. The need for child care adds to the stresses of young families. Issues of availability, quality, cost, and scheduling complicate the situation. Even with the best care at an affordable price in a convenient location with a schedule that accommodates one's work life, many families still feel guilty about not spending time with their children. Finding affordable, quality child care is considered one of the biggest problems for families (Coontz, 1997).

In 1993, nearly 10 million children under age 5 required child care while their parent(s) were at work. Those children were cared for the following ways:

- Thirty percent were cared for in organized child care centers.
- Twenty-two percent were cared for by nonrelated caregivers (neighbors, friends, and others).
- Forty-eight percent were cared for by relatives.

In some families, children are cared for by alternating parents working opposing shifts so that one is home while the other is at work. No child care option is ideal. Much center care is of uneven quality, with frequent changes in caregivers. Low-income families, who spend almost a quarter of their total income on child care, cannot afford good-quality centers. Many of the informal home care arrangements are not licensed and may have too many children or unsafe conditions. Even relatives may not be ideal caregivers if they are doing it only to earn money. Many relatives are grandparents, and, as we describe later in this chapter, they are worn out by child care responsibilities. "Tag team" care by two parents is also wearing on the adults' relationship and well-being. In the next chapter, you will meet three families who are struggling with child care issues and experiencing the stresses and discomfort associated with not being completely satisfied and secure with their infant care arrangements. Their stress is common among today's families.

Stress from within.   Some of the stresses in family life originate within the family. The perfectionist adult and the high-achieving child, for example, can bring stress to all of the family members. Many of us have observed the stress in a family when one parent is determined to have a baseball champion or a star pianist in the family. The pressure for straight As will also be felt by all members of the family.

A great deal of stress accompanies the need to be the so-called perfect family—the family that Coontz says never existed. The home that has to be decorated perfectly, and kept spotless and shining, the children who excel at school, the parents who are trim and fit, and the hospitality that would put Martha Stewart to shame—are all sources of stress for all family members. The family who has to be dressed in the latest style, appear publicly as the model happy family, and speak to each other only in friendly positive tones is probably storing a number of stresses to save for a later explosion.

Symptoms of a stressful family.   Curran's (1985, pp. 8–10) symptoms of a stressful family provide a vignette of many of today's families struggling with the pressures of careers, child raising, and living conditions that do not support families. As you read the following list, think of how the symptoms will affect the relationships within a family and think about the unintended socialization the symptoms will pass on to children. The symptoms, which are familiar enough to be worrisome, include the following:

1. Constant sense of tension and urgency; no time to relax
2. Short tempers; sharp words; siblings fighting; misunderstandings
3. Mania to escape (to work, to one's room, to the television)
4. Feelings of frustration over not getting things done
5. Feeling that time is going too quickly and that children are growing up too fast
6. Nagging desire for simpler times
7. Little time for self and spouse
8. Pervasive sense of guilt for not being and doing everything for everyone in your life. (pp. 8–10)

Journal 6.3: Select two or three of the preceding symptoms and reflect on the short-term effects and the long-term effects on children and adults. What will happen to the families if the symptoms persist over a long period of time? ■

When you look at the top 10 family stresses, the symptoms are quite understandable. Curran (1985, pp. 8–10) listed the most prominent family stresses as:

1. Economics
2. Children's behavior
3. Insufficient couple time
4. Lack of shared responsibility in the family
5. Communicating with children
6. Insufficient "me" time
7. Guilt for not accomplishing more
8. Spousal relationship
9. Insufficient family play time
10. Overscheduled family calendar

Although many families take great pride in their ability to juggle demanding careers, a beautiful home, community involvement, and a calendar overflowing with children's dance classes and soccer games, doctor and dentist appointments, adult time for aerobics and golf, birthday parties, dinner parties, volunteering at the schools, and time with grandparents, one wonders about the cost of such a pace. As you watch a group of children, see if you can determine how their home life may look and sound.

Four-year-old adults

Jonathan, Erika, and Manny (all 4 years old) are in the dramatic play center one morning. Jonathan says, "I'll be the dad and you be the mom, Erika." "OK, let's pretend that we're going to brunch," says Erika. Jonathan objects, "No, I will cook." Erika insists, "No, I want to go out." "Too spensive," Jonathan says, "I want to stay home." Erika pouts and says nothing. "OK, you get the baby ready," says Jonathan, pointing to Manny. Manny quickly gets down on the floor and cries like a baby. Erika talks to him softly and brings a jacket to put on him. "Here, baby, we're going out to eat now." "Hurry up, dear," Jonathan says. Erika responds, "I can't do everything—I need help." Jonathan shrugs his shoulders and says, "OK, I'll help with the baby."

As the three children continue to play, they pretend to take the subway and discuss getting off at 45th street. Erika shouts to Darcy across the room, "Wanna be our waitress?" Darcy rushes over to the area, begins pulling out dishes from the cupboard, and says, "We don't have menus." Erika assures her that it's okay, and that she can just tell them what the "specials" are today. Conversations abound concerning cereal, eggs, sausage, orange juice, and bananas. Erika asks, "Do you have waffles today?" Darcy answers that there are two kinds of waffles: blueberry and chocolate. Erika tells Jonathan and Manny that the waffles are low fat and "very healthy." "No fat for me," she said. Jonathan nags, "Hurry. I have a meeting soon."

Can you begin to predict what you would encounter if you were to visit Erika's home? What information have you gathered in your very brief observation?

As we talk about the common issues facing families today, you will get a preview of scenarios played out in children's interactions with each other or with adults. Children portray what they see in the lives around them, playing roles that are significant in the world around them. For many young children, a common happening in their lives or the lives of their friends is divorce.

Divorce and Single Parenting

The stresses of the divorce process and the obstacles facing single-parent families are many and sometimes formidable. The process begins with a negative public image, even though the number of divorced parents and single-parent households is undeniably significant. The general public still regards divorced parents as being defective and views the adults as failures. The term *broken homes* continues to reinforce the negative stereotype associated with single parents and their children.

Economics of divorce.   Divorce often begins with a costly financial and intensely emotional legal process. Even with the ease with which divorces are granted under no-fault divorce laws and the lack of assigning blame, there are significant and immediate consequences for the family. In her book *The Divorce Revolution,* Weitzman (1985) documents that divorce usually reduces the economic position of women and children and improves that of men. In fact, the husband's standard of living improves by 42 percent, whereas the wife's standard of living declines by 73 percent. Men typically earn larger salaries, so they continue to increase their standard of living as time goes on. In addition, when the family's assets are divided, it usually is an equal division between the parents, so the parent who has custody of the children then divides his or her half with the children.

The parent who has custody of the children now faces the functions of a family (economic, socialization, and support) alone. For many of those parents, there is a need to work outside of the home, so that the time available for family functions is diminished. In addition to society's tendency to treat the single parent as deviant or abnormal, their families suffer discrimination when they are held to the same expectations to which two-parent families are held (Howard & Johnson, 1985). In general, single-parent families, particularly those in which the mother does not remarry, remain disadvantaged in economic status, health, and housing conditions.

Effects on children.   Before looking more closely at single-parent families, we need to look at what has been learned about the impact divorce has on children. Many studies have been conducted to learn about the effects of family dissolution. In your future work with young children, you will encounter those whose parents have been divorced for a long time and those whose parents have just finished divorce proceedings. You will probably experience a divorce in progress while working with children and parents. One of your authors worked in a large child care facility for several years and regularly experienced a visit from a parent that started with, "I want you to watch Erin closely for the next few months. Her father and I are getting a divorce and I'm worried about how

BOX 6.1 ■ Lizzy's Story

A Closer Look

The Parent's Story

I expected Lizzy to be very excited about visiting her dad for Thanksgiving. But she seems glum and worried about her visit.

Lizzy's father and I have been separated for several months now, and I guess the changes haven't been easy for my daughter. She and her dad were always close. So when my husband moved out, Lizzy became clingy, whiny, and angry. She asked question after question. "When is Daddy coming back? Are you going to go away too? Did I do something bad?" I was miserable myself at the time, and it took a lot of effort to comfort my little girl.

Lately, things have been much better. Lizzy loves school. She speaks to her father on the phone regularly, and they see each other at least twice a week. Yet Lizzy still gets upset if her dad is just a few minutes late picking her up. I've noticed, too, that she's a little shy and on her best behavior when her dad is around.

Since every moment with her dad seems very precious to her, I was really surprised that she was upset about going to her father's for Thanksgiving. For the last few nights, Lizzy's had bad dreams. She also found her old security blanket and is sucking her thumb again. It's hard to know how to reassure her, especially since I'm a little nervous myself about spending this first holiday away from my child.

The Teacher's Story

When I greeted Lizzy this morning, I noticed that she looked awfully sullen. I made a mental note to be especially alert to her needs.

Later, Lizzy volunteered what was on her mind: "On Thanksgiving, my dad is taking me to the parade and we're going to my aunt's house. In the nighttime, I'm sleeping over at my dad's house—for my first vacation."

I tried to reassure her as best I could. "Sometimes it's hard to do new things," I said, "but I bet you'll have fun, and you'll be able to tell your mom all about it when you get back."

In spite of my pep talk, Lizzy didn't seem particularly reassured.

Dr. Brodkin's Assessment

Young children often grieve over the breakup of their parents' marriage. Among other things, the departure of a parent exaggerates an underlying fear of abandonment. Lizzy is convinced that because Dad left home, Mom might leave too.

Lizzy's concern about spending this first holiday with only one parent is understandable for another reason: Preschoolers in this situation often

it is affecting her." The details varied in each case, but the parents were always genuinely concerned about their children. In most cases, the adult sitting in that office was in need of comfort and support just like her or his child.

The period during and immediately following divorce is often a disruptive one. There are usually changes in the parents' work habits. Many parents have to seek employment for the first time, or have to work more hours, or change jobs. Divorce may precipitate a move to a different home. Research shows that during and after divorce, children often show changes in behavior (Hetherington, 1988, 1989). Young children experience new fears, sadness, anger, and heightened anxiety. They may act out and become aggressive, perhaps taking responsibility for the divorce, thinking that it was something they did or didn't do. For a short time after the divorce, these young children will be on their best behavior, thinking that their change will bring the other parent back. We've often heard parents say with great relief that their child didn't show any effect of the divorce, and then, months later, be amazed when the child displays very comfort themselves by denying that their parents' separation is permanent. However, Thanksgiving spent alone with Dad and Dad's side of the family will dash Lizzy's hopes for the family to be reunited.

What Can the Teacher Do?

The support of this caring teacher is very important to Lizzy right now. The teacher's pep talk was very valuable, even though the child didn't respond to it.

Preschoolers whose parents are separated often rely on their teachers' constancy and reassurance. Just a few moments spent alone with her teacher and a special cheerful word from her each day will help Lizzy continue to adapt to the changes in her life.

The teacher should continue listening to Lizzy's concerns. Later, when Lizzy is ready, the teacher can introduce her to some new activities she might enjoy. Whatever helps Lizzy to feel worthy of love is worth doing, and chatting with her mom will enable the teacher to find the best way of accomplishing that.

What Can the Parents Do?

Fortunately for Lizzy, her parents are not feuding over her. Her mother respects the child's relationship with her father and may sense that this separate holiday will help Lizzy gradually accept the impending divorce. Of course, Lizzy and her mother will miss each other. Lizzy's mom should acknowledge that and continue to reassure her daughter that she'll be there when Lizzy gets back. She could point out that Lizzy can speak to her on the phone when she's away, just like she speaks to Dad.

Gentle corrections of the child's misconceptions, along with acceptance of her feelings, will bolster Lizzy's self-esteem. In time, Lizzy will realize that the breakup of the marriage is not her fault. And with such understanding parents, one day she is likely to see that she is loved by both her mom and her dad—and that she will never lose either one of them.

Resources on Divorce

How to Help Your Child Overcome Your Divorce by Elissa P. Benedek, M.D., and Catherine F. Brown. Washington, D.C.: American Psychiatric Press, Inc., 1995.

How to Win as a Stepfamily by Emily B. Visher, Ph.D. & John S. Visher, M.D.; 2nd edition, New York: Brunner-Mazel, 1982.

contradictory behavior or becomes aggressive and miserable. Lizzy's story (see Box 6.1) illustrates a common occurrence for children whose parents are separated or divorced. It is very likely that you will meet Lizzy in your future role as an early childhood educator, so her story and the perspectives of her parent and teacher are important to hear.

Some studies have found children of divorce to be more dependent, demanding, unaffectionate, and disobedient in behavior than children from intact families (Hetheringron, Cox, & Cox, 1976). The children in the studies feared abandonment, harm, and loss of love. So much of children's responses depend on the way the parents handle the divorce. Custody battles take a huge toll on the children, and those parents who continue their divorce battles over time will usually raise children with more problems than those who maintain a good relationship.

Depending on the availability of the two parents, children are often without the live-in father role model. Some experts see a serious long-range effect of divorce as the removal of marriage models. They express concern about children growing up without

■ **FIGURE 6.3**   Adjustment Tasks Faced by Children of Divorce

1. Acknowledgment of the reality of the marriage break-up. Many children cannot face the fact that their parents have split and that they are not living together anymore. They hold on to the hope that everything will get fixed eventually.
2. Detach from any parental conflict and focus on usual pursuits. Most children have their own agenda of interest and needs and under ordinary circumstances focus on themselves and their friends. For a time they will focus on the divorce, their parents, and any conflict that is occurring, rather than their own pursuits.
3. Adapt to the loss. For a while children will be absorbed with their sense of loss. Many experience feelings of rejection and disappointment, and will need time to get over those feelings.
4. Resolve anger and self-blame. Children need to get over their self-blame and blaming their parents, and come to terms with the situation without the aspect of blame. They also need to express and let go of the anger they feel toward their parents and the situation.
5. Accept the permanence of divorce. For a long time children hold on to the hope that their parents will get back together. It is an important task for them to accept the idea that their parents will never be together again.
6. Achieve realistic hopes about human relationships. This may take a lifetime and lots of experience, but it is contingent upon completion of the other tasks.

Source: Table from *Child, Family, Community,* Third Edition by Roberta M. Berns, copyright © 1993 by Holt, Rinehart and Winston, reproduced by permission of the publisher.

realistic expectations of relationships and future mates as a result. Simons and Associates (1996), however, offer a different look at families of divorce. In some situations, the extended family of the single parent may provide attention and assistance to the family. Often, a close support of friends becomes an extended family. One of your authors was a single parent with four young children. Several of the older couples in our neighborhood became "grandma" and "grandpa" to the children and provided generous support to them.

Journal 6.4: From whom or what do you think children acquire their expectations of relationships? If they don't have models in their families, what other sources do they have? Reflect on the potential for those influences. ■

All in all, children face significant adjustment even in the most amiable of divorces. Berns (1993) summarized the extensive research of Wallerstein and Kelly (1980) into a set of important tasks that children must master before they can truly adjust to the divorce of their parents (see Figure 6.3). Without the accomplishment of the those tasks, children continue to face the problems often seen in the families of divorce. From there, the effects of divorce on children are mediated by the kind of family configurations in which they live.

Family configurations after divorce.   Divorce has led to several configurations of families: single-parent mothers, single-parent fathers, joint custody arrangements, and the emergence of stepparents. These configurations are not exclusive, just the most common. A brief look at each of these and how they might influence children will extend your understandings of families and your ability to address family differences. Table 6.1 provides a profile of the kind of family organizations in which children live, as well as information about the employment, economics, parent educational levels, health and

■ TABLE 6.1 A Profile of America's Children (March 1996)

Percent of Children under 18	Total	White	Black	American Indian	Asian Americans	Hispanic
Living with both parents	71.6%	78.0%	38.7%	57.1%	84.0%	67.2%
Living with only a father	3.4	3.3	3.9	6.0	3.1	3.2
Living with only a mother	24.2	17.9	56.9	36.5	12.5	28.6
Living with grandparents only	2.0	1.4	5.4	3.5	0.9	2.4
Who are foster children	0.6	0.5	1.3	1.1	0.2	0.7
With a grandparent in the home	8.0	6.1	15.7	11.9	13.4	10.2
Received some child support in 1995	12.5	12.4	14.4	15.6	4.7	7.9
Parents own their home	56.9	63.4	28.2	35.9	50.3	33.4
Family had earnings in 1995	92.1	94.7	80.7	85.5	88.8	86.4
At least one parent at work	84.1	88.5	64.9	73.5	79.7	75.4
A parent unemployed	6.5	5.8	9.4	12.9	6.0	10.5
Whose mother works	59.6	61.1	53.7	54.1	55.9	43.3
Father works, mother at thome	20.4	23.2	7.7	12.4	20.4	27.4
A parent completed college	27.7	30.0	13.2	15.2	45.2	8.1
Neither parent is a HS graduate	14.7	12.6	23.9	23.4	16.2	43.9
Child is not a citizen	3.4	2.8	1.9	1.2	21.3	12.1
Living below poverty	20.5	16.0	41.3	41.4	19.2	39.5
Living above poverty and below 4 times poverty	56.8	58.8	49.4	48.4	51.3	53.9
Living over 4 times poverty	22.6	25.2	9.3	10.1	29.4	6.6
Living in central city	24.7	19.1	48.1	27.5	38.1	40.0
Covered by private health insurance	66.1	71.0	43.9	44.6	67.2	38.3
Covered by employer-provided health insurance	61.6	66.0	41.6	42.9	61.3	36.7
Covered by Medicaid	23.2	18.3	45.4	51.8	21.9	37.4
Covered by any health insurance	86.2	86.6	84.7	86.3	86.0	73.2
Without health insurance	13.8	13.4	15.3	13.7	14.0	26.8
Family received food stamps in 1995	18.1	13.5	40.3	33.2	14.8	31.6
Family received SSI benefits in 1995	4.2	2.8	9.5	5.1	8.9	4.8
Family received AFDC/General Assistance in 1995	12.6	8.7	30.5	24.6	12.9	21.5

nutritional support, and benefits to children of each of the major ethnic groups in the United States. It gives you a current preview of the home situations you can expect for the children with whom you will work.

Single-parent mothers are the most frequent configurations after divorce. The latest predictions are that at least 50 percent of all children born today will spend some part of their childhood living in single-parent families, generally headed by women (Bianchi, 1990). In many female-headed families, poverty or reduced income results from divorce. Women typically earn less than men, so the family economics are seriously affected when the mother is awarded custody of the children. The resulting poverty can be associated with more than half of the disadvantages of single-parent families. Persistent poverty during the first five years of life leaves children with an IQ deficit of more than nine points, regardless of family structure (Coontz, 1992).

The absence of a father may also contribute to the development of children. For years after a divorce, boys may have trouble concentrating and may interact aggressively with their mothers, teachers, and other boys (Hetherington, Cox, & Cox, 1985). Girls are also influenced by the father's absence, displaying one of two possible patterns. The first pattern is behavior characterized by passiveness, withdrawal, and shyness with males; the other pattern is aggressiveness, overt activity, and flirtatiousness with males (Hetherington, 1972).

Many variables determine what happens to both boys and girls: their age when the father leaves, the quality of the mother/father relationship before the divorce, the length of the father's absence, the availability of other male models, and the emotional state of the mother during and after the divorce (Wallerstein & Kelly, 1980). So much is dependent on the role of the nonresidential father and how he interacts with children. The effects of divorce and single parents are influenced by a wide range of complex factors, so we urge you to use caution in generalizing about what happens to children.

It is interesting to note that current studies have documented that mothers in divorced families spend more time on homework projects with their children than do married women working. It has also been noted that single parents (mothers or fathers) are more likely to praise good grades and are more likely to get upset and angry when their children receive bad grades. Recent studies documented a noteworthy pattern: Single parents spend more time talking with their children than do married parents (Dornbusch & Gray, 1988; Morrison, 1995; Richards & Schmiedge, 1993).

Single-parent fathers are a second configuration. As you can see from Table 6.1 only 3.4 percent of all children live with a single-parent father. Consequently, little has been written about them and few research studies have been conducted. Until recently, it was an automatic decision that children would live with their mother, but now the courts are taking into consideration the actual needs of the children and specific situations, so fathers are beginning to get custody.

When fathers do get custody of children, much of the child raising is done by others—caregivers, grandparents, other relatives, and friends—more so than with single-parent mothers. Thus, children with single-parent fathers do usually have contact with female role models. Research has also shown that children living with a single-parent father have more contact with their mothers than children living with a single-parent mother have with their fathers.

Single parents often struggle to balance employment, housework, and child rearing. It's often difficult to maintain children's needs as a priority.

Single-parent fathers appear to have more of a struggle balancing employment, housework, and child rearing. Society doesn't prepare boys for those roles very well, so assuming domestic tasks and parenting are often more difficult for men than women. Support groups for men have sprung up to assist with the isolation men have felt in those roles. Operation Fatherhood (begun in 1992) was designed for noncustodial fathers, but it provides parenting groups and outings for fathers and children. One of the positive outcomes for fathers involved in the program is "discussions with their peers (other single-parent fathers) around parenting issues" (Ijames-Bryant, 1997).

Joint custody is a third configuration that may respond to the needs of children while providing a solution to the dilemma of deciding which parent should have custody of the children. Joint custody divides decision making and physical custody between two parents and has resulted in what is being called the *binuclear family.* In general, children do not feel abandoned, for they are part of two homes and two family groups. The real advantage of joint custody is the necessity for both parents to put aside their differences and focus on the children, if this arrangement is to succeed. Joint custody requires real cooperation and communication to work well. There are issues of scheduling, agreement on decisions, consistency of discipline, and, for some children, the stress of continual separation and reattachment. This configuration is too new to know the long range effects of this arrangement.

 Journal 6.5: Put yourself in the place of a 6-year-old child whose parents are getting a divorce. The parents decide on joint custody and work hard to make it a smooth

and healthy relationship. What messages do their efforts communicate to you, as a 6-year-old? Contrast those messages with those you might perceive if your parents are bitterly arguing and one of them wins the custody battle and the other is granted visiting rights. ■

Families with stepparents are a fourth configuration. With approximately 1.5 million adults remarrying each year, and most of them with children, there are many stepparents to be considered when we look at the whole picture of children's families. The biggest issue for stepparents is the lack of legal rights. Many stepparents share in the parenting and support of children but have no rights.

The new family that forms when two adults with children from other marriages get together is called a *blended family*. In many cases, the remarriage process is almost as traumatic to the family as divorce. The adjustments that go with forming a blended family are significant:

New roles and relationships

New rules and values

Less family cohesion

Newly defined family communication

Loyalty dilemmas for children

Competition for attention

Hostility toward the new parent and new siblings

In the first few years of the remarriage, every decision is a complex process with new relationships and roles. Those first few years are difficult and require understanding, patience, consistent communication, and positive working processes. Groups such as the Stepfamily Association can be helpful to blended families. If a child in your preschool or kindergarten is in a newly blended family, you may want to stay in close contact with the family, knowing that a huge transition is taking place.

A final configuration that has followed divorce is that of grandparents as parents The *new nuclear family,* or *skipped generational parenting,* is becoming a prominent alternative family structure that continues to increase at a rapid pace. Over three million children live in households where their grandparents are present, and, according to the 1994 Census, in more than one-third of the homes, grandparents are the sole caregivers of the children (Nelson, 1997). Although grandparents as parents is not a completely new phenomenon, the contributing factors for such family structures today are different from the past. The major causes are teen pregnancy, high divorce rates, domestic violence, incarceration of parents, substance abuse, and AIDS. The rise in skipped generational parenting is prevalent in all ethnic and socioeconomic groups, but a large percentage (46 percent) of all children being raised exclusively by grandparents are African American. Many of those grandparents (61 percent) live on fixed incomes, so the issues of poverty, health care, and sometimes homelessness add challenges to the already challenging task of raising grandchildren.

Although most grandparents are quite experienced in child raising, becoming a parent again brings on a sudden life-style change for most grandparents. Many of the children turned over to their care are emotionally and/or physically impaired. The older adults are often impaired themselves, so the parenting role and related responsibilities are doubly challenging. An additional stress in the relationship comes from guilt and a need to come to terms with the situation that is keeping the children's natural parents from handling their own child-rearing responsibilities. Many of the grandparents blame themselves for the situation in which their son or daughter becomes a drug addict, or abuses a child, or needs to work long hours due to financial difficulties associated with divorce.

As an early childhood educator, it will be important for you to develop new understandings and sensitivities with respect to this family structure. Some of you may have been raised by grandparents, and you will have some good insights about what issues are faced by this new nuclear family. For those of you who were not raised by grandparents, it is important for you to reflect on this issue.

Journal 6.6: It's the end of the day in your preschool program or first-grade class and one of the children in your care, Tomas, is being picked up by grandparents who are his sole caregivers. In addition to the sensitivities you would have for parents, in general, at the end of the day, what would you keep in mind as you greet Tomas's grandparents? ■

The configurations that we have described may follow divorce or they may result from choices made by adults to embrace alternative parenting and family configurations. What is important for your professional role is your awareness of these configurations. That awareness, accompanied by frequent and sensitive communication, will support your capacity to respond to the diversity of young children and their families

Poverty

Since 1985, the richest 5 percent of U.S. families have received a larger share of the nation's income than the poorest 40 percent. A look at the data in Figure 6.4 on page 222 shows that the changing economy, with all its good news for some families, has not been kind to children or families with children. Some of the direct effects of the current economy on that group are the following:

1. The median income of families with children has not kept up with inflation. The difference between families with and without children represents a growing generational divide. Young workers in their child-bearing years are suffering most of the brunt of economic losses.

2. It takes two earners to support children. Millions of families have been forced to send a second parent into the work force to compensate for the lower wages now earned by one worker. Even with those two parents working, declining wages have meant that family incomes don't keep up with the cost of living.

3. Child care expenses and other work-related costs reduce the new lower incomes even further.

4. Job-related benefits are shrinking. Fewer and fewer employers are providing essential fringe benefits.

■ **FIGURE 6.4**   National Statistics on Wealth and Poverty

- Between 1983 and 1989, incomes of the richest 1% of Americans—some 800,000 households—grew more than 87%. With approximately $5.7 trillion in net worth, the top 1% was worth more than the total bottom 90% (84 million households, with a combined net worth of about $4.8 trillion). (Meisler, 1992),
- Each year since 1986 has broken a postwar record for the gap between rich and poor. The median income of young families (families with parents 30 years or younger) plunged by one-third between 1973 and 1990, despite the fact that many families sent a second wage earner into the workforce (Children's Defense Fund, 1995).
- Between 1987 and 1992, the number of poor children under six grew from 5 to 6 million, and the poverty rate for children under six reached 26%. 40% of children in young families are poor (Children's Defense Fund, 1995). More than one-third—2.8 million—of the nation's three and four-year-old children were from low-income families in 1990, a growth of 17% since 1980 (GAO, March 1995).
- A majority of poor children under age six have parents who work, full-time or part-time. A full-time wage earner in a family of four earning minimum wage would generate income worth 52% of the poverty line. With the Earned Income Credit, the family's income would reach only 66% of the poverty line (National Center for Children in Poverty, 1995).
- Between 1969 and 1989, the number of young white men earning less than the poverty figure for a family of four rose from 1 in 10 to almost 1 in 4. For African-American men, the comparable figure rose from 26% to 37%; for Hispanics, from 25% to 40% (Schneider & Houston, 1993).
- Aid to Families with Dependent Children (AFDC) accounted for only 1% of all federal expenditures and has been declining in proportion to other spending. Between 1975 and 1990, welfare benefits declined 35% (Schram, 1991).
- There is an inverse relationship between welfare spending and "dependent" poverty. Dependent poverty, or the inability to get out of poverty without relying on government expenditures, *decreased* when expenditures grew (Schram, 1991). When families are helped with child care, health care, and work-related expenses, they are far more likely to find and keep jobs.
- Affordable housing for low-income families is increasingly difficult to find. There are two applicants for each subsidized housing unit, with further cuts proposed by the legislature. Over half of poor families spent more than half their income on housing (Children's Defense Fund, 1995).

Source: Working Respectfully with Families: A Practical Guide for Educators and Human Service Workers, by C. Connard, R. Novick, and H. Nissani, 1996, Portland, OR: Northwest Regional Educational Laboratory. Reprinted by permission.

Effects on children.   For children of all ages, poverty has some devastating effects. Poor children are two times more likely than nonpoor children to have stunted growth, iron deficiency, and severe asthma. A government study in 1996 showed that poverty placed children at greater risk of dying before their first birthdays than did a mother's smoking during pregnancy. Another study conducted by the U.S. Department of Education found that for every year a child spends in poverty, there is the chance that the child will fall behind grade level by age 18. In the 1994 book *Wasting America's Future,* the Children's Defense Fund estimates that every year of child poverty at current levels will cost the nation at least $36 billion in lost future productivity alone, because poor children will be less educated and less effective workers.

For parents struggling to raise a child, poverty adds extensive stress to the family. McLoyd (1990) states that economic hardship experienced by lower-class families is associated with anxiety, depression, and irritability. With those qualities may come a tendency on the part of parents to be punitive, inconsistent, authoritarian, and generally nonsupportive of their children. The strain of poverty may also promote the use of disciplinary approaches that take less time and effort than approaches such as reasoning and negotiating. Spanking and forms of physical punishment are quick; they may relieve frustration and they don't demand much thinking in the midst of multiple worries and stress.

Effects on parents.   Families in poverty, when parents are working, are influenced by the kind of occupations in which the parents work. Kohn (1977) has found that lower-class parents look at their children's behavior with a focus on its immediate consequences and its external characteristics, whereas middle-class parents explore their children's motives and the attitudes expressed by their behavior. Kohn interpreted these differences as connected to the characteristics associated with the level of occupation. Bronfenbrenner and Crouter (1982) concur that parents' workplaces affect their perceptions of life and the way they interact with family members. Consequently, their parenting styles reflect aspects of their work life. Again, as you watch children play, you will see indications of these influences in their conversations, roleplaying, interactions, vocabulary, and perspectives.

It is possible that parents from higher socioeconomic statuses—parents with enough money to be comfortable while raising their families—are more likely to show more warmth and affection, talk to their children more, be more democratic, be receptive to their children's opinions, and stress creativity, independence, curiosity, ambition, and self-control. When you put yourself in the shoes of parents from lower socioeconomic statuses—parents without enough money to be comfortable while raising their families, with constant worries about how to feed, clothe, and shelter their children—you can begin to understand why their behavior might differ significantly from the behavior of parents from higher socioeconomic statuses.

Poverty and housing.   The information on poverty previously described looks even more bleak when reviewed in the context of housing costs. While the incomes of families with children have declined, rent increases have exceeded inflation and much low-income housing has been lost to decay, gentrification, and urban development. The National Low-Income Housing Coalition reported in 1996 that a full-time minimum-wage income is now inadequate to afford moderate-cost, moderate-quality housing in every one of the 404 metropolitan areas that were studied (Bernstine, 1997). At the same time, the federal government is cutting back on housing assistance for low- and moderate-income families, slashing its support for both public housing and assisted housing. In cities where housing assistance is available, waiting periods for housing averages 19 months for public housing and 31 months for housing certificates. Some of this information on housing costs helps explain the prominence of another challenge to families—homelessness.

Homelessness

Each family's experience of being homeless is different. Much depends on why they are homeless—loss of job, substance abuse, psychiatric disability, divorce, recent immigration, illness, runaway situations, or poverty. That experience is also filtered through a range of temporary homes—a safe and clean family shelter, a welfare hotel/motel, a large crowded gymnasium-type shelter, the family car, or a make-shift tent along the highway. The information on the costs and lack of housing described in the previous section has been cited most frequently as a major cause of homelessness. Much about the experience also depends on what kind of services are available to the family from federal, state, and local sources.

The McKinney Act, passed in 1987 and amended in 1988, defines a *homeless person* as "an individual who lacks a fixed, regular, and adequate nighttime residence, or has as a primary nighttime residence that is a publicly operated shelter, an institution providing temporary shelter, or a public or private place not designed for the accommodation of human beings." The McKinney Act provides the states with funds to assist homeless people, including funds to schools in an effort to be sure that homeless children have an education.

The composition of homeless families (now one-third of all homeless people) includes the full range of kinds of families. Every possible family structure is present, from two-parent families with an unemployed breadwinner to a single mom who is fleeing with her children from domestic violence. Homelessness puts families, and especially young children, in environments that often feel chaotic and disorganized. There is little of the security and comfort that young children need for their healthy development. Childhood is a time when young children are working toward a sense of self, autonomy, and trust in their world, and it's difficult to do so in some of the shelter situations or in a daily move from place to place.

The problem of homeless young children has become so significant that two trends have occurred: Research has focused on these children to determine the effects of homelessness, and early childhood programs (schools and child care centers) have been developed to meet the needs of these children (McCall, 1990). The research is important because of its implications for policymakers, educators, and service providers. You will get some idea of what these young children need by looking at the studies that have been done.

Research on homeless young children.   In general, research has documented widespread developmental delays and emotional disturbances in young children who are homeless (Bassuk & Rosenberg, 1990; Grant, 1990). Studies of the effects of homelessness have documented poor health status, higher-than-expected developmental delays, and emotional and behavioral problems exhibited by the children (Molnar, Rath, & Klein, 1990; Rafferty & Shinn, 1991). Educators and caregivers report short attention span, withdrawal, aggression, speech delays, sleep disorders, difficulty in organizing behavior, regressive behaviors, awkward motor behavior, and immature social skills (Klein, Bittle, & Molnar, 1993). Many of these behaviors can interfere with a child's healthy development and self-esteem.

Some researchers, however, interpret quite differently what the studies show. They see the behaviors as coping mechanisms, or "highly developed inner strengths" (Douglass, 1996). Douglass and colleagues intensely studied individual young children in an urban family shelter with an on-site early childhood education program. The researchers saw deficiencies in coping strategies, or ways of managing and mediating stressful events. We are going to look at one of the children in that early childhood program to see what the researchers noticed.

Keisha

Four-year-old Keisha lived in the shelter for one year and attended the ECE program during that time. During her first four weeks in the program, she showed almost no attention span or ability to focus on a task or activity. Her standard greeting to others was a rude "shut up" or "get away from me." She was aggressive, she bit others, and she spit. According to her mother, these behaviors began shortly after the family lost their apartment and became homeless. An assessment of Keisha during this initial period found her to be angry, defensive, unable to form meaningful or supportive relationships with peers or adults, unable to focus on a task, aggressive with her peers, and lacking in verbal skills.

By her fifth week in the shelter and the ECE program, Keisha had begun to settle in. She began to smile, to speak, and to carry on elaborate conversations with both children and adults. She tentatively developed friendships, reaching out to children and teachers. She sought attention from teachers by using positive behaviors, rather than by negative behaviors. She seemed to magically transform into a loving, warm, happy child who dived into projects and activities with depth, understanding, a readiness to learn, and enthusiasm. Feeling safe, loved, "at home," and adjusted to her new home and school, Keisha was able to leave behind her reactions to the stress of moving and to continue meeting the developmental challenges and milestones of a typical four year old (Douglass, 1996, pp. 747–748).

Considerations of homeless young children.   If in the future you were to work with a homeless family, what could you expect? Even the simplest of registration forms and other kinds of data are problematic for homeless families. They have no permanent address or telephone number, nor do they generally have records on the children. Basic essentials such as clothing and food may also be issues for the homeless families.

In working with the child of a homeless family, you may need to address issues of cleanliness and health. Children may be tired, hungry, or ill. In spite of homeless families' best efforts, there may not be adequate facilities to care for their children. If the children have been homeless for a long period, a room full of play materials may be overwhelming to them. You will need to provide extensive support to the child and to the family.

Journal 6.7: If you were caring for a homeless child and needed to know more about the issues of homeless families, where would you turn for information? If you had the opportunity to interview the family, what questions would you ask? What kind of sensitivities would you have in your interactions with the family? ■

A major issue for homeless families is health. Their living conditions are not very supportive of good health habits, and they seldom have health care benefits. It is one more source of stress in their lives and the lives of many families.

Health

The dilemma surrounding health insurance and benefits for families is much like that of housing costs and availability. The Children's Defense Fund 1997 Yearbook describes the situation for children and families: "The erosion of private, employer-based insurance coverage for American children of working parents is threatening their chances of getting a healthy start in life . . . As a result, the number of uninsured children has risen from 8.2 million in 1987 to 9.8 million in 1995" (p. 21). Many of those children have one or more working parents but the parents' incomes are too high to qualify for Medicaid, and their jobs don't provide employer-paid insurance coverage for their families. Seldom can they afford the high cost of premiums for family health insurance coverage.

Lack of health coverage: Effects on children and families.   The human costs of children's and families' lack of health coverage are fairly predictable. Those families are more likely to report poorer health, and see doctors less often, and more likely to be without preventive care. A decision these families frequently face is whether to spend their money on prescriptions or food. Most children in these families have ear infections and asthma that go untreated, miss school more often due to illness and seldom have regular checkups. These same children often were born to women who did not have prenatal care.

Good news about children's health.   The good news with respect to children's health is that many states have taken the initiative to fund programs that support the families who need health coverage and services. For example, New York funded a Child Health Plus program that helps working families buy private health insurance for children. Massachusetts has passed legislation to extend health coverage to at least 125,000 of the state's 160,000 previously uninsured children.

The other good news can be seen in Figure 6.5 with improved immunization rates. Congress and the states have expanded efforts toward this end, and the efforts have paid off: The rate of common children's diseases has decreased significantly and in 1996 were the lowest ever reported. There is, however, an alarming number of children who have died (roughly 1,000 each year) and who have been diagnosed (roughly 30,000 since 1981) with AIDS and HIV infection. This is another health battle to be waged with respect to young children.

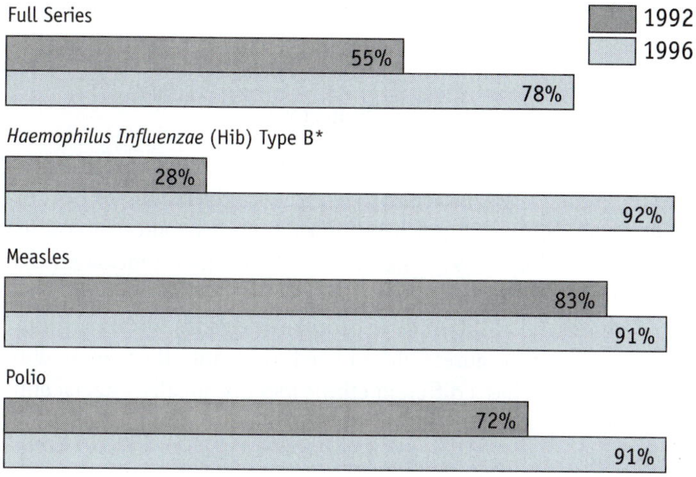

Full Series

■ **FIGURE 6.5**

Percentage of U.S. Toddlers Receiving Immunization, 1992 versus 1996

*Major cause of bacterial meningitis. Hib disease was not reported officially until 1991.

Interracial Marriages and Biracial Children

Children of mixed parentage account for a growing population in early childhood programs. The National Center for Health Statistics (NCHS) reported 620,000 births of children with one Black and one White parent in 1990 and predicted a continuing increase. The NCHS suggested that the reported numbers were probably low compared to actual births. A similar pattern is seen for marriages between other races and for the birth of children with other dual heritages. Much like divorce, the stress related to interracial marriages comes from society's disapproval of the unions of two people of different races. The stress for children comes from a kind of ambiguous ethnicity or conflicts about their dual ethnic identity.

Socialization of biracial children.   What typically happens to **biracial and bicultural children** is that they are socialized much more in one culture than the other. "The child of dual heritage is not likely to have equal exposure to both of her cultural heritages" (Morrison & Rogers, 1996, p. 30). At the same time, the biracial child is aware of the values, perceptions, and typical behaviors of the two cultural systems. Very early in these children's lives, they become aware of being different. Whether it be in child care or preschool, or in the community, the biracial child may experience the social pressure that is often directed to someone who is different.

When parents are asked about the racial or cultural identity of their biracial child, their responses vary significantly. Those responses indicate their uncertainty about the dual heritage or their discouragement with societal pressure. Morrison and Rogers (1996) describe the four different responses that Black and White parents give when asked about their child's ethnic identity:

1. Some parents believe that their child of Black and White parentage will be considered Black by society, so they simply identify their child as Black.

2. A few parents take the approach that the child is a human being and eliminate the decision between Black and White.

3. Some parents can't respond to the question because they are undecided about their child's identification.

4. Many parents are teaching their children to accept both cultural backgrounds and will state clearly that their children are Black and White. (p. 32)

The variation in parents' responses is one indication of the stress that is experienced by families of dual races or cultures. Biracial children experience the feeling of not "fitting in" anywhere during their childhood and it becomes a serious source of conflict for many biracial adolescents (Gibbs, 1989). One of those socialization messages that we talked about earlier in this chapter comes from society and it tells children that everyone belongs in a group. From there, children develop their identities within a group. The situation is further complicated because children need to identify themselves with their parents, and each of the parents has a different ethnic identity. Ideally, biracial children need to identify with both of their parents, but society and the parents themselves don't support such development.

Maintaining languages and cultures.   In Chapter 8, you will meet Ibrahim, his brother Mohammed, and the boys' parents, Faridah and Amr. They talk about the difficulties of keeping both parent languages available to their children and describe their awareness of Ibrahim and Mohammed becoming part of the dominant White culture. Faridah tells us that the common language of the two adults is English because neither of them speaks the other's language. "When we talk with the boys, however, we each use our own language, so that they are becoming fluent in both languages—Malay and Arabic." We realized as we listened to Mohammed's excellent English that the boys are trilingual. Faridah moves smoothly from speaking with us in English to speaking with her sons in Malay, and Amr did the same.

When we ask Faridah about how she and Amr work to keep the two cultures part of their family and the boys' heritage, she describes her role as one of acquainting the boys with foods and home traditions from her country. "The way we furnish our home also reflects our cultures," she states as she describes the lack of items hanging on the walls. She laments that her husband has many books and materials from his country to use with the boys because his friends send packages to him regularly, and that most of her materials have been translated into English. "What we have most in common is our religion," Faridah tells us. That common culture is their Muslim religion, and it influences their eating habits, their social life, and their support network, which is primarily composed of friends who attend the same mosque.

When you get to know parents like Faridah and Amr, you realize the complexity of raising biracial or, in their case, tricultural children. During our conversation, we realized the importance of the information they were sharing for the early childhood educators who work with their children.

Summary of Contemporary Challenges

You may be wondering how you can use this information if you are a teacher or a caregiver. After reading about divorce and poverty, you may be also be feeling overwhelmed by the enormity of family issues. Before talking about how to work in partnership with families, we think that it's important to reflect on those issues, to talk about how you are feeling, and to plan to use some of those new awarenesses.

Journal 6.8: How will your new awareness of the health status of children or the housing of their families influence what you do with children in a classroom? Think about two or three new understandings you have about the issues faced by today's families, and reflect about their impact on your future professional role. We would like you to reflect first on the possibilities and later to discuss the potential use of the information with your peers in class, with your instructor, and with any of the early childhood educators you know. ■

Family Involvement in Early Childhood Education

Before reading this chapter, you may not have thought much about families and the role they will play in your future work in early childhood education. We have all been very focused on the children and their development and their play up to this point, so it's not surprising that parents and families have not been a major consideration. Stop and think about your own experience as a learner and about how your family was involved in your education.

New Thinking about Family Involvement

How many of you remember your parents going to conferences or to Open House nights? How many of you remember your parent serving as a driver or chaperone for field trips or other events? Those are fairly common experiences. As you will read in the next part of this chapter, educators now think much more holistically about family involvement. There's compelling information from research about the importance of that involvement, and there are both state and national policies recognizing and recommending that involvement. As you read about the children in Chapters 7 through 11, you will see their families involved in their early childhood programs and classes in a wide variety of ways. Before you observe those involvement strategies and approaches, let's talk about why family involvement is important and how to develop a philosophy about family involvement.

When families are involved, there is a communication to children about the value of their families. Sometimes, that value may not be what is intended. When Keeley's mom, Kerry, assists in the computer lab at her school, Keeley may think that the school believes that her mom is smart and that Keeley's teacher appreciates her mom. However, if Keeley only observes her teacher communicating with her mom to talk about Keeley's problems in class, there is another message. If the only request for help is to bake a cake for the school fair, there is yet another message.

All children want to feel pride in their families, and that pride will probably influence how the child feels about herself. Extensive research, much of it very current, shows that families are critical to children's success. We think that the findings of some of those studies are an important foundation to your philosophy about family involvement and to your decisions about the role families will play in your future work.

Research on Family Involvement

In 1981, when *The Evidence Grows* (Henderson, 1981) was published (a first report on parent involvement), there were only 35 studies. It was a time when it was not generally recognized that involving parents (not families) would influence children's success. The studies were conducted in a climate when few professionals realized the importance of involving families. In 1987, when *The Evidence Continues to Grow* (Henderson, 1987) was released, the number of studies increased and so did the awareness of the importance of families. No longer was the vocabulary limited to parent involvement. Researchers such as Coleman and Hoffer (1987) looked at the relationships between families and schools. Parent involvement was viewed as one indication of the relationship but a "critical factor to the child's success in school" (p. 52). Although Coleman and Hoffer's work was conducted in high schools, it is important for all educators, because their research supports a more holistic vision of the family and the community and the critical importance of involvement beyond parents.

New emphasis.   In the latest edition of the report, *The Family Is Critical to Student Achievement: A New Generation of Evidence* (1996), there are 66 studies, and the range of involvement goes far beyond parent involvement to family/school partnerships, community-based programs, and family literacy programs, and to topics such as changes in family structure and status and the contributions of families to children's general development. One important change is the emphasis on families, consistent with the focus of this chapter. Henderson and Berla (1996) describe their reasons for the term *family* rather than *parents:* "In many communities, children are raised by adults who are not their parents, or by older siblings. For many, this provides an extended support system and those who are responsible for the children and who function effectively as their family deserve recognition" (p. x).

A look at the summary of the findings will give you a sense of the specific recommendations that emerged from those 66 studies. The authors are quite enthusiastic: "The evidence is now beyond dispute: When schools and families work together, children have a much better chance for success, not just in school, but throughout life" (Henderson & Berla, 1996, p. 1). What's also exciting about the findings is that the impact of family involvement in children's education goes beyond children's success. There are benefits for everyone. Let's look briefly at those outcomes.

Benefits for children as students.   The benefits for children may look like they are too broad for your thinking about young children because they generalize across a wide age span (ECE to high school). If you keep in mind that the patterns for success begin in early childhood, then the benefits have much relevance for work with young children. Those benefits of family involvement include:

- Higher grades and test scores
- Better attendance and more homework done
- Fewer placements in special education
- More positive attitudes and behavior
- Greater enrollment in postsecondary education

These benefits are very much in parallel with the kind of results reported for high-quality early childhood programs such as Head Start and the Perry Preschool Project (Schweinhart, Barnes, & Weikart, 1993). Although few studies have followed young children to adulthood, those that have done so have similar findings. When you look at the benefits of family involvement, there are definitely habits and values that you will want to encourage from the first encounter a child has with any type of educational program. It is so important for young children to like school, be it preschool or child care or kindergarten, so that those positive attitudes begin early. You can nurture a pattern of lifelong learning in early childhood education by encouraging curiosity and exploration. If you think about those kind of benefits, you can't possibly ignore the family. The development of attitudes, values, and lifelong habits calls for a partnership between you, the early childhood educator, and the families of your children. What about the families? What happens to them when they are involved with schools or programs?

Benefits for families.   The benefits to families are encouraging, and especially critical when you think about the difficult issues that today's families face while raising children. The major benefit to families is that they experience an increase of confidence in themselves and in their child's educational program. Because they feel valued by the educators working with their children, they see themselves as more capable of assisting those educators, but, even more importantly, they see themselves as more capable of helping their children at home. That kind of confidence is bound to increase the levels of involvement of families in children's education, and ultimately children's success in school.

One of the additional benefits that often accompanies family involvement is the increase in the number of parents who, themselves, pursue additional education. Head Start has consistently demonstrated this benefit. Although it has not been well documented, there are countless stories of parents and other family members who have experienced success as family participants in the Head Start programs. From there, many of those family members progress to workshops and training sessions, and again experience success. Once they complete this step, postsecondary education (community colleges and universities) doesn't look so daunting. In our travels to Head Start centers around the country, many an early childhood educator talks about how she or he started as a parent volunteer or a member of the advisory board. Those stories are definitely enough to encourage our work toward family involvement. But how about our programs and schools? What kind of benefits can we expect from family involvement?

Benefits for schools and communities.   The kind of benefits that schools gain include improved teacher morale and higher ratings of teachers by parents. It follows that if teachers are feeling valued and there is a culture of energy and positive thinking, children will be affected and learning will be enhanced. Other benefits include the kind of assistance and support families can provide to programs. Sometimes, it's an extra pair of hands; sometimes, it's resources from a parent's hobby, career, experiences, or travels. That support and help again influence the quality of educational opportunities that are offered to children. Ultimately, those schools have students with higher achievement, and everyone feels good about that kind of benefit. It makes sense that those schools would also have better reputations in the community. Most communities care about the education of the children who live in them. Those schools that produce high achievement will naturally be valued and supported by community members.

The research on family involvement leaves little doubt about the importance and the benefits of families' participation in children's education. Early childhood educators have traditionally encouraged parent involvement, so the transition may not be so difficult to involve families. Understanding families and communities is the starting point, and the goal of this chapter. From that understanding, it will be important to develop a philosophy about families. One of the basic tenets of successful family involvement approaches is that families are seen as the child's first teacher and are valued for their support and caring of their children. Think of families as learning environments for the children you meet.

Families as Learning Environments

As you continue to develop your philosophy for working with families, we suggest that you consider the findings of studies that looked at families with high-achieving students and those with low-achieving students. When you think about how much time children spend with their families, a consideration of how that time is used is critical. As you get to know the families of the children with whom you work, an important question to ask is: How does your family spend time together? Rather than ask about how much time families spend together, which may be threatening to already stressed parents, a question about family activities will be comfortable and will give you a picture of the child's home life.

Research on everyday family activities.   Studies (Henderson & Berla, 1996; Moles, 1992) of families whose children experience success in school found the following aspects in their home life:

- A daily family routine that includes a sharing of household chores, consistent bedtimes and times to get up, meals together, and quiet places and time for study or reading
- Monitoring of children's activities, including TV watching, neighborhood play, and arrangements for child care, especially care before and after school
- Modeling the value of learning, self-discipline, and hard work through family conversations and adult modeling and demonstrations that success comes from working hard, studying, and using the library
- Setting high but reasonable expectations for achievement with goals that are appropriate for the children's age and development, as well as recognition of talents and achievements
- Encouraging children's efforts and progress in school, including a relationship with teachers and other staff, communication about the importance of education, and provision of support and interest in schoolwork

- Reading, writing, and discussions among family members so that literacy, in all its forms, is part of the daily family interactions
- Using community resources for family needs, including sports and recreational opportunities, instruction and entertainment related to the arts, inclusion of other role models and mentors, and access to libraries and museums

When parents interact with their children, such as spending time together in activities on the weekend or socializing together at mealtimes, they can significantly influence the learning of their children. Knowing how difficult it is for many contemporary families to have that kind of time together adds a challenge to our multiple roles as early childhood educators. As family advocates and educators, we need to share the research information. As child advocates and educators, we want to support the family's efforts and be sensitive to the diversity of their situations. The research confirms the critical role of families in the growth and development of children, which says to us that we need to do all we can to learn about families and to work in partnership with them. The new generation of evidence about the family's importance will remind us over and over that we need to understand today's families—their stresses, their organizations, their issues, and their strengths. The more we can support families in their roles in children's lives, the better the lives of children will be.

Community context for families.   We have tried to show and highlight the ethnic, cultural, and socioeconomic diversity of the national community in which children live, and the diversity of family structures and organizations from which children come to early childhood education programs. For children to develop and learn optimally, you will need to understand and be able to respond to children's diverse developmental, cultural, linguistic, and educational needs. That understanding and ability to respond will require your knowledge and acceptance of children's diverse family units with a broad range of values, experiences, socialization, and environments. In their recommendations for working with families, the NAEYC guidelines urge us to "actively involve parents and families in the early learning program and settings," and to "recognize that parents and families must rely on caregivers and educators to honor and support their children in the cultural values and norms of the home" (1996b).

Much of what we have said about families can be applied to communities. There is a growing awareness that communities contribute significantly to children's growth and development. The complexity of society demands the involvement of all the individuals and organizations that can possibly have an impact on one's life. In a later chapter, you will meet Angela Russo and all of the community members who influence her life and that of her mom, Marie. She is an example of the importance of understanding the context in which families live if you are to understand the children and families. That understanding is a first step to the goal of building partnerships with families.

Building Partnerships with Families

The NAEYC guidelines for developmentally appropriate practice (Bredekamp & Copple, 1997) are a good beginning for your thinking about building partnerships with

Authentic involvement of families in program decisions may require many discussions and preparation.

families. The guidelines talk about programs in which "professionals and parents work together to achieve shared goals for children."

Developmentally appropriate practice: Involving families.   The NAEYC guidelines recommend the following:

1. Reciprocal relationships between teachers and families require mutual respect, cooperation, shared responsibility, and negotiation of conflicts toward achievement of shared goals.

This guideline means that there must be some opportunities for cooperation, shared responsibility, and negotiation. Some of the basic parent conferences or Open Houses don't really provide those opportunities. Even the development of mutual trust requires enough interaction to get to know the families and to make sincere efforts to understand each perspective. One early childhood program scheduled evening sessions called Family Story Time, in which family members and educators sat in comfortably small circles and shared family stories—sometimes funny stories, sometimes sad stories, and sometimes stories of unique family traditions. Although the Family Story Time sessions were slow starting, in time, family members and educators bonded through their stories and became much more comfortable with each other. Bruner (1990) confirmed the use of stories to help people understand each other's cultures and to build relationships. When you meet the children and families in Chapters 7 through 11, you will observe and hear about other approaches to build trust and to prepare for cooperation and shared responsibility. One very important reminder here is that you can't very well negotiate with families if you haven't developed a relationship first. Negotiation is not a healthy starting point for partnerships.

■ **FIGURE 6.6**   Basic Tenets of Successful Programs

- The first and most basic tenet is that parents are their children's first teachers and have a lifelong influence on their children's values, attitudes, and aspirations.
- Children's educational success requires congruence between the values that are taught at school and the values expressed in the home.
- Most parents, regardless of their level of education, economic status, or cultural background, care deeply about their children's education and can provide substantial support if given specific opportunities and knowledge.
- Schools must take the lead in eliminating, or at least reducing, traditional barriers to parental involvement

Source: Working Respectfully with Families: A Practical Guide for Educators and Human Service Workers by C. Connard, R. Novick, and H. Nissani, 1996, Portland, OR: Northwest Regional Educational Laboratory. Reprinted by permission.

2. Early childhood educators work in collaborative partnerships with families, establishing and maintaining regular, frequent two-way communication with children's parents.

Partnerships don't happen if the only communication is during parent conferences and an Open House, and yet that has been the traditional approach to communication. Much of the communication has been one way, from the educator to the parent. Following this guideline begins with an attitude of respect for families. The tenets of successful family involvement programs in Figure 6.6 offer a foundation the communication of partnerships.

3. Parents are welcome in the program and participate in the decisions about their children's care and education. Parents observe, participate, and serve in decision-making roles in the program.

Many programs have successfully involved families in making significant decisions. Head Start has parents and other family members serve on hiring committees, curriculum committees, and a range of policy committees. This kind of involvement means that educators have to assure families that they have a real voice in the decisions, not just token representation on committees without real impact on decisions. Authentic involvement also may require preparation. One of your authors worked with a program in which parents were involved in major hiring and curricular decisions, and I quickly learned that parents needed a great deal of information and discussion before they could actively engage in important decisions. Their preparation empowered them to be decision makers.

4. Early childhood educators acknowledge parents' choices and goals for children and respond with sensitivity and respect to parents' preferences and concerns without abdicating professional responsibility to children.

One of the most common situations in which parents' preferences present a dilemma for early childhood educators is related to children's naps. For a variety of reasons, parents will ask the teachers or caregivers to "not let Emily sleep too long at naptime" or to "wake Eli after one hour of nap." The difficulty arises when Emily or Eli is then grouchy, tired, or listless for the rest of the day or appears to need more sleep and even asks to sleep some more. Many early childhood educators have had intense negotiations with parents or family members over this issue, usually with a balance between parent needs and child needs.

Darren, the educator in the toddler program in Chapter 8, talks about the goals of many parents of toddlers: "So often, they want their toddler to be able to share." He tells us about the conversations with parents in which he describes the needs of toddlers to become independent and to establish identity, and his assurance to parents that their children will eventually be able to share but that it will probably take all year. "I talk a lot about not insisting on sharing or forcing children to do so," says Darren, and he describes for parents the possible outcomes of forced sharing. Darren really models the guideline of respecting parents while keeping the integrity of his responsibility to children.

5. Teachers and parents share their knowledge of the child and understanding of children's development and learning as part of day-to-day communication and planned conferences. Teachers support families in ways that maximally promote family decision making capabilities and competence.

Recently, one of your authors asked a group of families and teachers to make two lists. The first list consisted of all the kinds of information that families could contribute to programs or schools to help make a child's experience successful. With no hesitation, families and teachers came up with the following examples:

Interests	Kinds of playthings
Fears	Responses to stress
Play activities	Difficulties
Eating habits	Health
Family experiences	Family reading patterns
(travel, recreation, etc.)	Home guidance/disciplines
Previous educational or	TV watching habits
child care experiences	Influence of extended family

Their lists continued to fill several large sheets of chart paper. The group sat back and studied their lists and sighed, then responded to a second question. What kinds of information can teachers provide to families to help them understand their child's experiences outside of the home? Again, the hesitation was brief, and the following are some of their examples:

Interactions with peers	Memory
Strengths and limitations	Persistence at tasks
Favorite activities	Leadership/follower roles
Responses to success and failure	Contributions to the group

The outcome of this list-making activity was a wonderfully mutual appreciation for the wealth of information available when there is two-way communication about children. That very comprehensive picture of children is essential to the ability of teachers and caregivers and families to work together to understand children and to support their development.

6. To ensure more accurate and complete information, the program involves families in assessing and planning for individual children.

Many programs are using a variety of strategies to involve families in both assessment and planning processes. Elementary schools have initiated goal-setting conferences for teachers, parents, and children, and are experimenting with children-led teacher/family conferences. Parents are often asked to contribute to and comment on children's work in portfolios. Darren (in Chapter 8) works with parents during his first home visit to set goals for the year for children, and later refers to those goals when he meets with parents for conferences. When communication is consistent and comfortable, families feel secure about suggesting curriculum topics or activities for their children.

7. The program links families with a range of services, based on identified resources, priorities, and concerns.

Although this guideline expands the responsibilities of the early childhood educator, the challenges for today's families and children that we have described in this chapter remind us that educational programs cannot exist in isolation of other services for families. The kind of programs that truly meet family needs have libraries of resources (parenting books and magazines), information about community services, knowledge of and networks with health agencies, and economic support. An exceptional program in Gainesville, Florida, has what they call *one-stop shopping* for families—a facility with preschool and child care programs, library extensions, parenting classes, adult education courses, a medical clinic, and a social service center (Driscoll, 1996). The program communicates sensitivity to the stresses of family lives and challenges of supporting family needs.

8. Teachers, parents, programs, social service and health agencies, and consultants who may have educational responsibility for the child at different times should, with family participation, share developmental information about children as they pass from one level or program to another.

Information sharing takes different forms, depending on the programs involved, the purpose of the information sharing, and the kinds of responsibilities participants have for the child. One very important reminder for such sharing is the need for clear language. Educators are known for using a great deal of jargon in their work, and studies have shown that parents especially are put off by such talk (Buskin, 1975). One of your authors is currently working with kindergarten and primary grade teachers from six schools in a district to develop a common recording form so that children and families will be assured that children's information can be shared consistently when they move and change schools or when they change grade levels. It's the kind of communication that we need to develop between preschool and child care programs and elementary

Information sharing between educators and families takes different forms. Many families appreciate informal conversations that take place in the classroom.

schools so that as children begin kindergarten, their new teachers have profiles of their initial early childhood education experiences.

The impression with which you may be left after considering the guidelines for developmentally appropriate practice is that family involvement and partnerships are hard work. Yes, it does take an attitude of respect for families, planning for consistent two-way communication, negotiation between family preferences and developmental decisions, and ongoing attention to the relationship with families. With all of the effort needed to build and maintain partnerships, you may be asking: Why?

Journal 6.9: We think that you can come up with some good answers. Why spend the time and energy to build relationships with families? Why involve families in decisions? Why work toward regular two-way communication? ■

To add further complexity to family involvement, let's return to the ecological perspective we proposed when we began this chapter. Today, when we build partnerships, we need to consider both families and communities.

Linking Families, Communities, and Early Childhood Programs

In her work to promote family involvement, Epstein (1992) has posed three important attributes to successful family involvement. The attributes are appropriate, even when, they are extended to include communities. Remember the basic tenets of Figure 6.6 for successful family involvement programs. From there, the list proceeds to Epstein's attributes:

1. Effective partnership practices are developmental. The interests and needs of families are in flux as their children grow and develop, so relationships must accommodate the changes. Healthy partnerships also grow, develop, and require nurturance for development, just as children and families do.

2. Effective partnership practices must be responsive to both common and unique family needs. This attributes rests on one of the main ideas of this chapter: the diversity of families and communities. There is no "one size fits all" for partnerships between families and communities.

3. Children must be key participants (Heleen, 1992, p. 6). Whatever direction partnerships take and whatever activities are planned, the focus must be on children. Goals for children are the heart of successful partnerships.

As part of her work with the Center on Families, Communities, Schools, and Children's Learning, Epstein has categorized the major types of activities that are found in successful involvement programs. Figure 6.7 on page 240 displays those categories and sample activities. Some of them are traditional; in fact, your own parents probably engaged in some of the activities. Some of the activities are innovative and will require significant changes in the way educators work with families and communities. Figure 6.8 on page 241 describes the challenges and redefinitions of the categories if educators truly want to work collaboratively with families and communities.

You will need to spend some time studying the challenges and redefinitions of the categories if you intend to truly respect and work in partnership with all families and communities. Return to the figures as you meet families in the chapters ahead. Here are a few additional sensitivities for your future work with today's diverse families and communities:

1. Assess your language when addressing families. If the notes or letters sent home begin with "Dear Parents," you are eliminating a number of family members from involvement.

2. Check your scheduling of activities to be sure that you accommodate the diversity of families' schedules. Some can attend daytime events; others can attend only evening events.

3. Be sure that communication is sent in languages that reflect the demographics of the families and community. Provide an interpreter for events so that all families can understand the messages.

Those are some basic starting points. Remember that this is a *developing* process—don't become overwhelmed by the enormity of possibilities for family and community partnerships. You won't be alone in your efforts. Early childhood programs have traditionally been oriented to parent involvement, and current efforts are expanding the concept to families and communities.

TYPE 1	TYPE 2	TYPE 3	TYPE 4	TYPE 5	TYPE 6
Parenting	**Communicating**	**Volunteering**	**Learning at Home**	**Decision Making**	**Collaborating with Community**
Help all families establish home environments to support children as students.	Design effective forms of school-to-home and home-to-school communications about school programs and children's progress.	Recruit and organize parent help and support.	Provide information and ideas to families about how to help students at home with homework and other curriculum-related activities, decisions, and planning.	Include parents in school decisions, developing parent leaders and representatives.	Identify and integrate resources and services from the community to strengthen school programs, family practices, and student learning and development.
Sample Practices	**Sample Practices**	**Sample Practices**	**Sample Practices**	**Sample Practices**	**Sample Practices**
Suggestions for home conditions that support learning at each grade level.	Conferences with every parent at least once a year, with follow-ups as needed.	School and classroom volunteer program to help teachers, administrators, students, and other parents.	Information for families on skills required for students in all subjects at each grade.	Active PTA/PTO or other parent organizations, advisory councils, or committees (e.g., curriculum, safety personnel) for parent leadership and participation.	Information for students and families on community health, cultural, recreational, social support, and other programs or services.
Workshops, videotapes, computerized phone messages on parenting and child rearing at each age and level.	Language translators to assist families as needed.	Parent room or family center for volunteer work, meetings, resources for families.	Information on homework policies and how to monitor and discuss schoolwork at home.	Independent advocacy groups to lobby and work for school reform and improvements.	Information on community activities that link to learning skills and talents, including summer programs for students.
Parent education and other courses or training for parents (e.g., GED, college credit, family literacy).	Weekly or monthly folders of student work sent home for review and comments.	Annual postcard survey to identify all available talents, times, and locations of volunteers.	Information an how to assist students to improve skills on various class and school assessments.	District level councils, and committees for family and community involvement.	Service integration through partnerships involving school, civic, counseling, cultural, health, recreation and other agencies and organizations, and businesses.
Family support programs to assist families with health, nutrition, and other services.	Parent/student pickup of report card, with conferences on improving grades.	Class parent, telephone tree, or other structures to provide all families with needed information.	Regular schedule of homework that requires students to discuss and interact with families on what they are learning in class.	Information on school or local elections for school representatives.	Service to the community by students, families, and schools (e.g., recycling, art, music, drama, and other activities for seniors or others).
Home visits at transition points to pre-school, elementary, middle, and high school. Neighborhood meetings to help families understand schools and to help schools understand families.	Regular schedule of useful notices, memos, phone calls, newsletters, and other communications.	Parent patrols or other activities to aid safety and operation of school programs.	Calendars with activities for parents and students at home.	Networks to link all families with parent representatives.	Participation of alumni in school programs for students.
	Clear information on choosing schools or courses, programs, and activities within schools.		Family math, science, and reading activities at school.		
	Clear information on all school policies, programs, reforms, and transitions.		Summer learning packets or activities.		
			Family participation in setting student goals each year and in planning for college or work.		

Source: "School/Family/Community Partnerships: Caring for the Children We Share" by J. L. Epstein, May 1995, *Phi Delta Kappan*, pp. 701–712. Reprinted by permission.

TYPE 1	TYPE 2	TYPE 3	TYPE 4	TYPE 5	TYPE 6
Parenting	**Communicating**	**Volunteering**	**Learning at Home**	**Decision Making**	**Collaborating with Community**
Challenges	**Challenges**	**Challenges**	**Challenges**	**Challenges**	**Challenges**
Provide information to *all* families who want it or who need it, not just to the few who can attend workshops or meetings at the school building.	Review the readability, clarity, form, and frequency of all memos. notices, and other print and nonprint communications.	Recruit volunteers widely so that *all* families know that their time and talents are welcome.	Design and organize a regular schedule of interactive homework (e.g., weekly or bimonthly) that gives *students* responsibility for discussing important things they are learning and helps families stay aware of the content of their children's classwork.	Include parent leaders from all racial, ethnic, socioeconomic, and other groups in the school.	Solve turf problems of responsibilities, funds, staff, and locations for collaborative activities.
Enable families to share information with schools about culture, background, children's talents and needs.	Consider parents who do not speak English well, do not read well, or need large type.	Make flexible schedules for volunteers, assemblies, and events to enable parents who work to participate.		Offer training to enable leaders to serve as representatives of other families, with input from and return of information to all parents.	Inform families of community programs for students, such as mentoring, tutoring, business partnerships.
Make sure that all information for and from families is clear, usable and linked to children's success in school.	Review the quality of major communications (newsletters, report cards. conference schedules, and so on).	Organize volunteer work: provide training: match time and talent with school, teacher, and student needs, and recognize efforts so that participants are productive.	Coordinate family-linked homework activities, if students have several teachers.	Include students (alone with parent) in decision-making groups.	Assure equity of opportunities for students and families to participate in community programs or to obtain services.
	Establish clear two-way channels for communications from home to school and from school to home.		Involve families and their children in all important curriculum-related decisions.		Match community contributions with school goals; integrate child and family services with education.
Redefinitions	**Redefinitions**	**Redefinitions**	**Redefinitions**	**Redefinitions**	**Redefinitions**
"Workshop" to mean more than a *meeting* about a topic held at the school building at a particular time. "Workshop" may also mean making information about a topic available in a variety of forms that can be viewed, heard, or read anywhere, anytime, in varied forms.	"Communications about school programs and student progress" to mean two-way, three-way, and many-way channels of communication that connect schools, families, students, and the community.	"Volunteer" to mean anyone who supports school goals and children's learning, or development in any way, it any place, and at any time—not just during the school day and at the school building	"Homework" to mean not only work done alone, but also interactive activities shared with others at home or in the community, linking, schoolwork to real life. "Help" at home to mean encouraging, listening, reacting, praising, guiding, monitoring, and discussing—not "teaching" school subjects.	"Decision making" to mean a process of partnership, of shared views and actions toward shared goals, not just a power struggle between conflicting ideas. Parent "leader" to mean a real representative, with opportunities and support to hear from and communicate with other families.	"Community" to mean not only the neighborhoods where students' homes and schools are located but also any neighborhoods that influence their learning and development. "Community" rated not only by low or high social or economic qualities, but by strengths and talents to support students, families, and schools. "Community" means all who are interested in and affected by the quality of education, not just those with children in schools.

Source: "School/Family/Community Partnerships: Caring for the Children We Share" by J. L. Epstein, May 1995, *Phi Delta Kappan,* pp. 701–712. Reprinted by permission.

PRINCIPLES AND INSIGHTS: A Summary and Review

This chapter has been packed with facts and figures, as well as guidelines, suggestions, and examples to illustrate the diversity of families and communities. As you meet the children and families in the chapters that follow, you will be even more aware of that diversity and what it means for you as an early childhood educator. Our best advice is to notice those differences in your everyday life. Observe families in grocery stores, in libraries, in restaurants, on buses and trains, and as you walk through your town or city. Begin to take note of family structures and organizations. Be aware of how families socialize children—the messages that are communicated. Listen to the issues and challenges faced by families.

As you prepare to be an early childhood educator, get to know your community better. Perhaps you could assemble a scrapbook or album about your community. This is called *advancework* (Frieberg & Driscoll, 1996). It's what a company does when there is a move planned and employees will be transferred to a different community. The company sends in an advance person to study the new community. Put yourself in that role. Here are some possibilities for your advancework:

- Interview some parents and business owners in the community.
- Take photos of key facilities.
- Walk through major neighborhoods.
- Take an inventory of recreational facilities.
- Visit the Chamber of Commerce.
- Read local newspapers.
- Scan local bulletin boards (often found in grocery stores).
- Check on adult education programs.
- Inventory the child care and early childhood programs.
- Check the library use by families.
- Attend a city council meeting or a school board meeting.
- Inventory the churches of the community.
- Observe families as they use community facilities.

That's just a beginning! As you study your community and its families, you will extend that list to all kinds of interesting and informative aspects of the place where you live. As you do so, be open to the richness of the diversity of today's families and communities. There are some Ozzie and Harriet families left, and there's also Keeley and her single mom, Kerry; Faridah and Amr and their sons Ibrahim and Mohammed; Felipe and his mom and grandmother; and there's a whole village helping Marie Russo raise her daughter Angela. Celebrate their differences as you join us to meet and observe the children and families.

Becoming an Early Childhood Professional

Your Field Experiences

1. Visit one or more community agencies that provide services to families in your community. Gather information and evaluate the services from the perspective of a family with young children.

2. Interview several families about their involvement in schools or programs for their children. Try to have a range of programs represented, such as a public school kindergarten and primary grade, a private preschool, a child care center, a Head Start program, and an employer sponsored program. Use the chapter contents to help you develop your interview questions.

Your Professional Portfolio

1. The advancework we described in the chapter summary is an ideal entry for your portfolio Be sure to describe the importance of each of the contents of your advancework for understanding children and families.

2. Volunteer to assist with a family event in your community or at a agency that provides services to families. Document that participation and keep a journal of your insights and concerns.

Your Professional Library

Books and Articles

Coontz, S. (1992). *The way we never were: American families and the nostalgic trap.* New York: Basic Books.

Coontz, S. (1997). *The way we really are: Coming to terms with America's changing families.* New York: Basic Books.

Diffily, D., & Morrisson, K. (Eds.). (1996). *Family-friendly communication for early childhood programs.* Washington, DC: NAEYC.

Epstein, J. L. (1995). *School and family partnerships.* Baltimore: Center on Families, Communities, Schools and Children's Learning, Johns Hopkins University.

Espinosa, L. (1995). *Hispanic parent involvement in early childhood programs.* ERIC EDO-PS 95–3.

Henderson, A. T., & Berla, N. (1996). *The family is critical to student achievement.* Washington, DC: Center for Law and Education.

Lee, F. Y. (1995). Asian parents as partners. *Young Children, 50* (3), 4–9.

Stone, J. (1987). *Teacher-parent relationships.* Washington, DC: NAEYC.

World Wide Web Addresses and Internet Sites

www.medaccess.com/h_child/
   Healthy Children, 1996, MedAccess Corporation

www.latinolink.com/opinion/spec0602.html
   Latino Children Wonder about Their Future, 1997, LatinoLink Enterprises, Inc.

www.sprc.org/
   Single Parent Resource Center, 1997

www.acf.dhhs.gov/
   Administration for Children and Families, Dept. of Health and Human Services, 1997

bs.yahoo.com/Society_and_Culture/Families/Parenting/Single_Parents/
   Single Parents—Organizations and Resources, 1997

Infant Care Programs

and Practices

LUKE'S STORY

When you finish reading and reflecting on this chapter, you will be able to:

1. Discuss the 10 principles of infant care giving.

2. Describe care giving and play as curriculum with infants.

3. Define the role of the primary caregiver in an infant care setting.

4. Explain the rationale for individualized curriculum in infant care programs.

5. Recognize the benefits of employer-sponsored child care.

Over half of infants under 12 months of age are currently in the care of someone other than their parents (National Institute of Child Health and Human Development, 1997). Who is caring for these infants? What options are available for infant care? As you think about these questions, consider the dilemmas and anxiety that many parents face as they begin their search for infant care. You will be briefly introduced to three families who are experiencing stress and concerns about infant care, and then you will meet a family who feels secure and involved in their child care situation.

Finding Good Infant Care

Child care for infants is such a juggling act—trying to find the right balance and the optimal place for an infant during the important first year of life.

Mei-Ling: Grandparent as caregiver

Mei-Ling has been worried for the past few months. It is difficult for her to feel right about her decision. Vivian, her infant daughter, is only four weeks old, and Mei-Ling finds herself constantly worrying about her plans for Vivian's care. During her pregnancy, Mei-Ling began searching for infant care options, knowing she would return to work when her baby was eight weeks old. After many discussions with her husband and friends, she began visiting recommended child care centers. Those visits were discouraging—she could not see herself putting Vivian in these settings. It seemed that several centers operated with an assembly-line format. Certain infants were placed in cribs at established times; at the same time, other infants were placed in a row of six high chairs and being fed. Mei-Ling was distressed with the thought of leaving Vivian in a setting that did not appear to meet the individual needs of infants.

After discussing her observations, Mei-Ling and Jeff made a decision to ask Jeff's mother if she would be willing to care for Vivian for her first year. Jeff's mother, Grace, had previously offered to care for her granddaughter, so it seemed the best option for all involved. Mei-Ling and Jeff wanted Vivian to be loved and safe while they are at work, and they knew that Grace would attend to Vivian's needs.

Three months later, Mei-Ling and Jeff have new concerns—not so much about Vivian, but about taking time and energy away from Grace's normal routine. When they pick up Vivian in the evening, it appears that Grace is often exhausted from her day. She isn't able to meet friends for outings, as she did in the past. Now, Mei-Ling and Jeff feel guilty about taking up her time, yet they want to keep Vivian with a family member until she is one year old. Grace has agreed to continue, but Mei-Ling can't help but wonder if she should try to come up with a different plan or perhaps work four longer days so Grace could have one weekday off.

Brynna: Family home care

Brynna, a single mother, questioned friends about child care arrangements when she decided to return to work when Carl, her son, was four months old. While talking with friends, she found out that a neighbor, Summer, cares for toddlers in her home. Brynna decides to go to Summer's apartment to discuss the possibility of Carl being cared for by Summer. Carl is younger than the toddlers Summer takes care of along with her own daughter. Summer agrees to include Carl in her home care program, but she wants Brynna to understand that, with four toddlers in her care, she won't have much time to play with Carl.

Brynna feels a family home care situation is the best option for her. Summer is a creative, high-energy woman, and having Carl in a home nearby will help with commuting time. Sometimes it seems that Summer's home is messy or in need of cleaning, but that is a compromise Brynna will make to find nearby care for Carl. Right now, Brynna hopes that this arrangement will work for Carl and Summer. It's not the same as staying home with Carl, but Brynna knows she needs to return to work to keep her position in the company.

Neil and Karen: Child care center

Neil and Karen work at a company that assembles parts for large trucks. Near their plant is a child care center. Neil drops by to visit and finds the infant and toddler room to be a busy place. He notices on the daily schedule that there are activities scheduled for the mornings, but mostly free choice for toddlers and caring for infants in the afternoon. The infants appear clean and have a lot to watch with the toddler activity going on around them. There is an opening for an infant right now, so Neil decides to enroll Katy, their five-month-old daughter, in this day care center. The center has a sliding scale for monthly costs, which means that their income level qualifies them for a discount on the monthly cost of infant care. Neil and Karen are pleased about the costs but feel a little insecure about the center and the large number of infants and toddlers in one room. Their friends reassure them and remind them that they are lucky to have found affordable care for Katy.

Selecting Child Care

You have just read about three different options for families with infants. Each family had similar struggles and worries when looking for quality infant care. A study conducted by the National Institute of Child Health and Human Development (NICHD) (1997) shows that child care does not harm children's development, as long as that child care is of high quality (see Box 7.1).

How do parents determine if an infant care program is of high quality? Although there are specific indicators that help determine the quality of a program, parents must

---

A Closer Look

BOX 7.1 ■ What Are the Results of the NICHD Study of Mother/Child Interactions and Cognitive Outcomes Associated with Early Child Care?

The National Institute of Child Health and Human Development (NICHD) investigated the impact of child care on two different domains: mother/child interactions and cognitive and language development in the first three years of life. A frequent, yet difficult, question to answer regarding child care is the effect of child care on infants' and toddlers' development. To answer this question, over 1,360 children participated in the study conducted at 10 different sites.

Assessments included observations of mother/child interactions, observations of the child's child care environment, observations of the child in his or her home, and standardized measures of the child's cognitive and language development. Children were assessed at the ages of 6, 15, 24, and 36 months.

Study results found that although family, maternal, and child characteristics contributed greatly to social and cognitive development, early child care provided small, yet significant, influences on the qualities of mother/child interaction and on children's cognitive and language development. For example, more hours of child care related to less sensitive interactions between a mother and her child during the child's first three years of life. At the same time, it was found that more hours of child care was not related to the child's cognitive or language development (NICHD, 1997).

It was also found that the quality of child care affected a child's cognitive and language development. The increased positive child care situations with rich language stimulation related to children's higher performance on language and cognitive tests. Perhaps a warm, engaging child care situation stimulated children in their language development. More positive care giving in the child care situation also related to more positive involvement and more sensitivity between mothers with their children.

Although family, maternal, and child characteristics are attributed with a larger proportion of the total variance in findings of the study, results did show contributions made by child care to a child's cognitive and language development and in mother/child interactions. These results emphasize the importance of *quality* child care, as well as help answer the question of what impact early child care has on child development and mother/child interactions.

take the time to observe, watch caregiver and infant interactions, and interview the director or responsible adult about the program, his or her qualifications, and references. Ultimately, the parent is responsible for making the final decision about the infant care program.

With the lack of quality care and the lack of infant programs, in general, many parents feel they have to compromise their standards. As a nation, the difficult issue of ensuring that all families have access to quality child care during this critical period of development—the first year of life—has not been resolved. In contrast to these three families faced with compromises in finding ideal infant care, you will now meet a family that feels they have the best possible infant care for their son, Luke, and visit his infant care program.

Visiting the Infant Care Program

Winding through the large complex of red brick buildings of Mentor Graphics, you look around for the Child Development Center (CDC). There it is! You don't need a sign to tell you this brightly colored building is the Child Development Center. You have heard about the reputation of Mentor Graphics Infant Care Program and have read that for the past five years, Mentor Graphics was named one of the "100 Best Companies to Work For" by *Working Mother Magazine*.

Entering the building, you are met by Sue, coordinator of the infant care program. Sue greets you warmly. "We are glad to have you visit us today. Why don't we go directly to the Infant Suite, and then meet later to discuss the infant care program and any questions you might have."

Your First Impression

As you walk inside the door of the Infant Suite, you see two infants on the floor with a caregiver. She is talking with them, sharing her thoughts about their movements and interactions. "You seem to be enjoying the sunshine coming in the window, Amil." He responds to her talk by kicking his legs and moving his arms. She continues, "Look at how you can reach the mirror, Emory." Emory smiles and continues to stretch her arms toward the mirror. There seems to be ongoing interaction between the infants and their caregiver, and you sense a special connection between them.

In a small room adjacent to the large area is a changing room, where an infant and her caregiver are cheerfully engaged in a diaper change. On the wall above this area is an organization system holding a tub labeled with the name of each infant, containing diapers, supplies, and extra clothes. A caregiver and infant are in the changing room, where you listen to their conversation. "Now we are going to put on the clean diaper," says Caryl, the caregiver, in an encouraging and inviting tone. The infant seems familiar with the routine and reaches to feel the clean diaper. They seem to be in partnership in the process of changing the diaper. This is not a task *done to* the child, but rather a **care-giving activity** accomplished *with* the child. Each step was explained and shared out loud. As they finish up and Caryl washes her hands, she says, "Marta, now we are finished and will go back to the floor where you were visiting with Emory."

You follow Caryl and Marta to the floor area, noticing that this room is like an apartment or small home. There is a kitchen off to the right side with a refrigerator, microwave, stove, and dishwasher. On the other side of the room is a living room area, with pillows and pads on the floor and a couch separating this area from the rest of the room. The sleeping area has a door and is similar to a separate bedroom. There are also several other sleeping areas or nooks for infants within the large room, with mats for infants. Each door in this room

Each infant has her or his own storage bin for clothing and diaper supplies in the changing room.

has a window near the bottom, so when infants are crawling they can look through these windows, either into the toddler room or outside. The light airy atmosphere is inviting. It is easy to appreciate the windows and the connection with the outdoors. The entire backyard is landscaped with grass and trees. The whole area, both inside and outside, seems comforting and comfortable.

Journal 7.1: Why do you think a homelike setting was chosen for the infant care program? ▪

You also sense a calm atmosphere in this setting, with caregivers very attentive and tuned in to the infants. Sandy, one of the caregivers, is feeding Oliver a bottle while sitting on the couch. She talks softly to him, "You look like you're enjoying this bottle and this time to rest," while he snuggles close to her. He has her full attention while he is being held and fed. You again observe that the caregivers have special relationships with the infants and seem to be tuned in to their needs and personalities.

Near the back of the room you notice Caryl coming out of the separate sleeping room. As you walk over to the room, you see a chart on the wall, with the names of the infants and times recorded near the names. You ask Caryl about the chart. She explains that caregivers check infants while they are sleeping every 10 minutes or so. They then record the activity and position of the infant on the chart next to the time of the "sleeping room check." You peek in the window and see there are three infants in cribs in the room. There are eight cribs in the room. Caryl also tells you that each child has her or his own crib and has an individual routine for help getting to sleep. Some infants like to be left in the crib with a soft pat on the back; others like to have their caregiver talk or sing to them for a few minutes; and still others relax with a back rub.

Arrival Routine and the Morning

The door to the hall opens and Ingrid arrives with her mother, Sharon. Sharon checks in at the door by signing in and bringing the **Daily Log** up to date (see Figure 7.1 on page 250). After filling in the log, Sharon brings Ingrid into the room. Caryl, Ingrid's caregiver, greets them with, "I knew it was about time for Ingrid to arrive. I am so glad to see you. We have lots of great things planned, including outdoor time today." Ingrid's face lights up and she smiles as Caryl talks with her. Sharon changes Ingrid's diaper and checks the diaper and clothing supplies in her storage tub. They then come back into the main room, "Let's put your lunch and snacks in Ingrid's space in the refrigerator." Ingrid is 11 months old and beginning to walk. She heads over to the table where several toddlers are finishing up their morning snack. Sharon walks over with her, sharing, "Honey, I have two meetings to plan for and a big one to go to today," as she says good-bye to Ingrid. Ingrid doesn't respond, so Sharon gently touches her shoulder saying, "I am leaving for my work now and will be back later for you. Have fun with your good friends today." Caryl goes over to the table and sits near Ingrid, placing some cereal in her bowl as she responds to Sharon, "We'll see you later."

■ **FIGURE 7.1**   Daily Log

Infant Room Notes

Name _____Luke_____   Date _____12/17_____

My Child woke up at _____5:30_____
My Child last ate at _____6:45_____

Have you given your child any medication today?

   Y (N)

   What kind _____

Anticipated time of pick-up: _____5:30_____

Is there any other information about your child that would be helpful to us?

_____

_____

Feedings:

Time	Food/amount	Liquids
9:05	cereal / ½ banana	
9:35		4 oz bottle
11:40	cereal	milk in cup
2:15	cracker	2 oz apple juice
4:30		5 oz bottle

Diapers:

9:15	12:45	3:15 (B.M.)	
10:40	2:10	4:15	(5:00)

Naps:

_____9:45_____ to _____10:35_____   _____ to _____   _____12:55_____ to _____2:05_____

Anecdotal Notes:

Luke was very snuggly today. He also used a lot of chewies to help his teeth.

Source: Mentor Graphics Child Development Center. Reprinted by permission.

You notice that each time a parent and infant arrive, the parent changes the baby's diaper and then spends some time with the infant before leaving for work. Being curious about this interchange, you check with Caryl. Caryl explains that each family develops a **Good-Bye Plan** that they follow when they bring their child to infant care. The staff feels that it is important for each family to develop a comfortable routine, similar to a bedtime ritual. This might include looking around the room while visiting with their infant, diapering the infant into a "center" diaper, or simply sitting with the child for a few minutes. The infant care Good-bye Plan follows one developed by NAEYC (see Figure 7.2). Each family creates their own routine and shares this with the staff. Some families have

■ **FIGURE 7.2**   Good-Bye Plan

Saying "Good-bye" is a very hard thing to do for both parents and children. Children may scream, cry, or cling when you attempt to leave. This behavior is called separation anxiety and it is a normal part of growing up. It is important to acknowledge that it is not easy for parents to leave their child with someone else for long periods of time. Separation evokes strong feelings in us all—guilt, sadness, anger.

There are some things than can help make the process a little easier for parents and children. We ask parents to establish a written arrival plan for their child. These routines, like bedtime stories, add predictability and are comforting. Elements of an arrival plan include such things as consistency, giving your child your full and focused attention during brief play time, simple caregiving routines like changing a diaper, and always saying good-bye. We ask that parents always tell their children "good-bye" before they go. This enables the child to play freely without worrying when the parent might disappear and also forms the very basis of their ability to trust you.

It is our hope that parents and teachers be supportive of one another in this good-bye process. We can do this by consistently following a departure plan and working together on this ongoing process of saying "good-bye."

Child's name: *Luke*
Date: *September*

Approximate length of time I can spend with my child each day:
5-10 mins., plus occasionally come by during lunch hour

The routine I plan to follow:
Bring Luke to Infant room.
Drop Luke off after a smooch and a few minutes of play.
Arrive between 8:15 & 8:45.

What things can the teachers do to support your plan?
Notice Luke's mood when I leave and remind him I will
be back after his afternoon snack.

Source: Mentor Graphics Child Development Center. Reprinted by permission. Adapted from *So Many Goodbyes,* 1990, Washington DC: NAEYC.

more time at the end of the workday or come for a visit during the day, which allows them to make a connection with their infant and their infant's caregiver in the setting of the care center.

Now that you have had a chance to become familiar with the setting in the Infant Suite, it's time to meet Luke.

Meeting Luke

Over by the sleeping room is a window that is only about one foot from the floor and goes up about three feet. There is Luke! He is watching the toddlers outside in the play yard. Luke taps on the window. Kristine, his caregiver, walks over to him and sits down next to him. She says, "Oh, look, there's your brother, Isaac. We will go visit him in his room later today." Kristine turns to you and explains, "We take the infants to the other rooms, especially to visit siblings. We want them to interact with other children, feel at home, and spend time with family members. It's an important part of our day."

Luke has a smile for anyone who comes near him. He is nine months old and recently learned to stand by pulling himself up on furniture or windowsills. When Kristine notices that he's no longer looking out the window, she asks, "Would you like to hear a story?" She carries him over to a sitting area and pulls several small books from a shelf. Luke taps one about ducks and Kristine starts reading to him. She makes duck noises and Luke nods his head with her quack sounds, making small grunt sounds of his own. It appears that this is a familiar story and routine to him. He smiles each time she quacks.

When they finish the story, they notice Emory has crawled over to visit. She looks at the mobile hanging near the window. Next to the mobile is a display with photographs of Luke and his family. You look around this part of the room and see similar displays, all at floor level. A sheet of Plexiglas covers a 3' × 4' display of family photographs—another homelike touch! Kristine, Luke, and Emory look at the photographs of Luke's family. Kristine points out, "Look, here's Luke and his brother all wet and soapy in the bathtub." The infants are

looking at the photographs and seem to enjoy her story about Luke's family.

Just then, Emory reaches out and bumps Luke with her head. Luke is startled and begins to cry. Kristine pats Luke on the back, telling him, "I know that surprised you and hurt. Emory, it is important to be careful with people. If you want to play with Luke, you must be gentle." Kristine provided attention to both infants while responding to Emory's behavior. Kristine tells you, "We need to interrupt situations that could cause injury and give immediate feedback to both infants. It's my role to provide **guidance.** Emory might want extra attention or might be hungry, but she also needs to respect Luke's personal space. I have to make a quick decision about stopping any physical harm." After this interaction, Luke appears calm again and crawls toward the climbing stairs.

If you were observing in a classroom with older children, Kristine's interactions with Luke and Emory in this situation might be viewed as classroom management. With young infants, a primary goal is for each infant to learn to respect himself and others. Setting clear boundaries about appropriate behavior and building on positive interactions helps infants learn to interact with others in a supportive, healthy environment.

Emory's caregiver, Caryl, comes over to pick Emory up for a bottle and diaper change. "Hello there, Emory. I think you're feeling a bit hungry. Am I right?" Kristine tells you, "You've probably noticed that we always give individual attention during bottle feeding and diapering. We continually talk with our infants and engage them in whatever we are doing with them. It is important for them to feel safe and respected."

Lunchtime. Luke begins to make whining noises and Kristine asks him if he is getting hungry. By now, it's late morning. She brings him over to the table and helps him sit in one of the special wooden chairs made for the infants ready to support themselves in a sitting position. She helps him into the chair and allows him to make as many of the movements himself without her help. "Look, here's a bib with Luke's name on it," she tells Luke as she puts the bib on him. Then Kristine looks in the refrigerator on the shelf marked with Luke's name. "Your father brought a rice and squash lunch for you." Kristine tells you, "Since the infants are on an individual plan, their families provide meals until they are 1 year old and then they can choose to eat the center meals or continue with food from home. This way, we make sure each infant has the food the family wishes him to eat at this young age."

During lunch, Luke and Kristine engage in a conversation about his meal. She asks him, "Do you want more squash or banana?" He picks up a piece of banana and she says to him, "Oh, so you are hungry for banana." They continue their conversation. Luke notices what other children are eating and points at the applesauce that Emory is eating. Kristine asks him, "Do you want some of your pears?" He looks at her and opens his mouth, waiting for the spoonful of pears. The infants who are able to pick up small pieces of food are busy feeding themselves, with attempts at eating with a spoon also occurring. No one seems to worry about spilled food or messy faces—it's all part of learning how to feed yourself! The atmosphere is pleasant, similar to a family dinner together, with conversation and encouraging words.

Afternoon nap.　Luke prefers to sleep for short periods of time, and one of his nap times is right after lunch. He typically has three short naps (about one hour long) during his day at the center. His after-lunch routine includes a diaper change, drinking a small bottle while cradled by Kristine, and falling asleep soon after being placed in his crib. When he wakes up, he is ready for more exploring. Kristine says, "If he hasn't had enough sleep, he'll be grouchy, which is not like Luke. When this happens, we place him back in his crib to sleep some more. He most often wakes up ready to play again."

Luke's favorite activities.　Figuring out Luke's favorite activities is difficult. He seems to enjoy exploring everything in the room. Now that he is pulling himself up, he looks for furniture to stand near so he can pull himself upright. Kristine tells you, "Luke never seems bored. He loves to play

with everything he finds." Right now, Luke likes to touch faces and hair. He will play with most any toy he finds. Perhaps he does have a favorite, though. One of Luke's favorite activities is outdoor time. He notices when the stroller is brought into the room and the caregivers begin getting children ready for outdoor time.

Outside play.　Each day, caregivers take the children outside. Parents bring warm coats, hats, and mittens for their children during the cooler parts of the year. Strollers are available at the center for the infants. Kristine tells you, "The world outdoors is an important part of children's development and learning. We want them to experience and enjoy the outside air, sounds, and smells."

Looking out the window, you notice a low fence between the infant and toddler play yards and the yards where the older children play. You also notice that there are no typical playground structures, such as swings or slides, but there are trees, grass, toys to bring outside, and two covered play areas. Kristine says, "I enjoy time outside each day myself. Since this is early winter, many days are rainy or damp, so we take the infants outside in strollers or buggies. Luke enjoys these buggy rides. During the drier days last fall, Luke spent time exploring the play yard. He liked to pull the grass and grab handfuls of grass." Kristine continues, "I find it relaxing to spend time visiting with the infants outside. There is a lot to see when you slow down and look around from an infant's perspective." You've already noticed that Luke will often crawl over to the window to look out on the play yard. He does seem to find the out of doors interesting.

 Journal 7.2: Why might outdoor time be an important part of a day for infants?　■

Visiting brother.　Several times a week, Kristine and Luke go down the hall to the preschool room to visit Isaac. She tells you, "Sometimes Luke just watches Isaac play and other times Isaac will come over and sit near Luke and tell him about the other kids and what they've been doing." Isaac greets Luke when they arrive, saying, "Luke is here! Look,

Luke, I made this little snake today. When it's dry, I can take it home." Luke responds by smiling and pointing to the snake. After 15 minutes of visiting, Kristine says, "Good-bye, Isaac. We're headed back for Luke's nap." Isaac comes over and hugs his brother, then rushes off to play with large blocks. Both brothers seem to enjoy the visit.

Dad picks up Luke.   Luke wakes up from his last nap around 5:00 and is rested and ready to greet Dad. George arrives around 5:45. Several parents have already arrived to pick up their infants, so Luke senses it must be about time for his Dad to arrive. When George comes in the door, he walks over to the rug area where Luke is holding a play telephone. "So, are you calling Dad to come pick you up?" asks George. Luke smiles his special smile. George picks up Luke and carries him over to Kristine. "Well, how was today?" Kristine is filling out Luke's Daily Log for George to take home with him. "Luke had a busy day, with three naps and time to go outside and ride around in the buggy and look for birds. We also went to visit Isaac."

Both Luke and George look forward to their time together. Parents and families are an important component of the infant care program.

Kristine asks if George has noticed Luke being fussy or pulling his ear the past day or so at home. She tells him, "Today, I noticed Luke touching his right ear several times, so I wondered if he might be getting another ear infection." George thanks her for the observation and says, "Julie and I will watch and let you know if we notice anything tonight or in the morning with his ear." With Luke still in his arm, George checks the Daily Log, picks up Luke's dirty clothes and food containers, and heads for the door. "Thanks, Kristine. We'll see you tomorrow." And off they go.

What an interesting day! Infants are absorbing so much while also needing warmth and interactions with a caring adult. Luke and Kristine seem so comfortable with each other. Kristine recognizes Luke's individuality and works hard at creating a day that best meets his developmental needs and his style of interacting with his environment. Luke's day at infant care is certainly a symbol of the investment that his father's company is making through their support of employer-sponsored infant care program.

A Conversation with Luke's Dad

A visit has been arranged with Luke's father, who works at Mentor Graphics and is usually the parent who brings Luke to the center and picks him up in the evening. You will enjoy meeting George, who is enthusiastic about the Child Development Center and the philosophy of the center. Both of his children spend their days during the week at the center and have been doing so since they were several months old.

George arrives in the early afternoon. He begins the conversation by stating, "The Child Development Center here at Mentor Graphics allows our family to feel guilt free about working. It's provided peace of mind for us." George is an accountant with Mentor Graphics and Julie is an engineer at a nearby firm.

Benefits of an Employer-Sponsored Child Development Center

When George and Julie were married, they became curious about the on-site, **employer-sponsored child care program.** George had no idea of the actual benefit that the Child Development Center provided until his children were born and enrolled in the center. He now recognizes the stance that management has taken in sponsoring the center and the benefits provided through employer-sponsored child care. In fact, when George recruits new employees with young children, he discusses the important benefit of the employer-sponsored Child Development Center at Mentor Graphics. George feels that the CDC affects loyalty and employee commitment to the company. He definitely sees the CDC as a "world-class" child care program and promotes the center as a recruiting tool and important employee benefit.

Impact of the Infant Care Program on Family Life

When asked about the effect of the infant care program on family life, George responds, "I feel our children are the most needy in their first 12 months of life, and without the quality of this program, I am not sure we both would have continued working. We would have had to consider a different style of caring for our infants or a different life-style."

George also talks about the impact the program philosophy has made on his family life. He feels that he has learned a great deal about parenting from the caregivers at the center. Many of their approaches to infant care have been adopted by George and Julie in their own home. For example, George says, "Both of our children have learned to entertain themselves as floor babies. They don't expect to be put in swings or bouncy chairs. They seem to be quite content moving around the floor and looking around." You certainly noticed this when observing Luke. He was often engaged in exploring his environment.

Communication between Families and the Center

Luke's family finds that **communication** is essential between families and caregivers. The infant care center has established several different formats for communication and actively invites frequent input and feedback from families. Some of the formats for communication include conferences, which are scheduled on a regular basis and as needed, e-mail (there are computers in each of the center's rooms and all employees have access to e-mail), voice mail or phone calls, portfolios developed by each caregiver, drop-in visits by parents, and the Daily Log. Kristine and Luke send George or Julie e-mail messages several times a week. Sometimes Kristine might write about something Luke

Luke is sending an e-mail message to Dad—in code?

is doing, and often Luke will tap the computer keys and add his own message. George appreciates the connections and feels part of Luke's day.

Daily Log.   When George "signs in" Luke in the morning, he fills out information about Luke's wake-up time, meals, diaper changes, and other facets of his morning. Kristine reads the log and continues to complete the log as the day goes on. At the end of the day, Kristine adds a brief note about a highlight of the day or a concern she wants to discuss with George. Often, the end of the day can become quite busy and the Daily Log helps Kristine and George note information about Luke that they want to share. George finds that he looks over the Daily Log during the evenings when Luke seems to be fussy or tired. He can then check when Luke last slept, how long his naps were, or if he might be hungry. Kristine also writes down times when she thinks Luke might be getting a cold or feeling ill. Then George and Julie keep a close watch for similar symptoms in the evening and the next morning. The log serves as a communication tool for everyone who interacts with Luke and it keeps information flowing to help Luke's transition from home to the center and back home again.

Portfolios.   Kristine developed a **portfolio** for each of the three children for whom she is the primary caregiver. George shared how impressed he was with Luke's portfolio. He felt that Kristine captured the last five months of Luke's development and growth through the photographs and journal entries she entered in the portfolio. Kristine adds to the portfolio over the two-year period that she is caregiver with each child, and then presents it to the family at the final conference.

■ **FIGURE 7.3**   Portfolio Entry

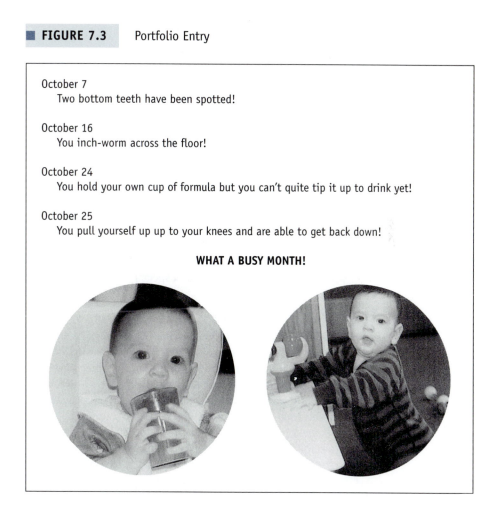

October 7
    Two bottom teeth have been spotted!

October 16
    You inch-worm across the floor!

October 24
    You hold your own cup of formula but you can't quite tip it up to drink yet!

October 25
    You pull yourself up up to your knees and are able to get back down!

WHAT A BUSY MONTH!

Source: Mentor Graphics Child Development Center. Reprinted by permission.

Final Thoughts

George summed up his thoughts about employer-sponsored child care by expressing, "The center seems to make the company more family friendly. It feels like the company is taking care of things in our life that are important. And, of course, it helps to have your child in the 'Ivy League' of child care programs." The program and the company yield stability and a strong commitment to the importance of children and families. As you end your visit with George, he reminds you, "I look forward to your visit at our home next week with Kristine and our family. But be forewarned—it's likely to be a whirlwind with our two young children!"

George provided valuable insights into infant care from a parent's perspective. He also shared thoughts about working for an employer that sponsors an excellent child development center and what that means to employees.

Visiting Luke's Home with Kristine

Kristine will be taking you to Luke's home as she makes a visit to the family. She was also the primary caregiver for Isaac, Luke's older brother, and has been to their home several times. Driving through the newly developed area, you see Luke's home, which has many windows. Maybe that's why he enjoys standing at windows at the center. He has already learned that he can see a lot of action by looking outdoors.

Luke's Home

George and Julie greet you at the door, along with Luke and Isaac. You go into the family room, where the coffee table is immediately put to use, as Luke pulls himself up to be part of the group. Outside the window you notice the backyard has several plastic cars, a "short" basketball hoop, and some riding toys. Julie tells you, "When we're home on weekends, we enjoy having neighborhood children visit and play in the yard. We like having lots of children come over here to play." This reminds you of your conversation with George. The family places a special priority on the children.

A Typical Evening

Kristine thinks it might be helpful to you to hear about a "typical" family evening. Julie and George groan, and George says, "Well, as soon as we arrive home, we seem to be on fast forward. I bring home the boys and Julie starts dinner. We try to eat by 6:30 and spend dinnertime talking about our days. We encourage the boys to share their days. Having the Daily Log from the infant center helps us talk about Luke's day and include him in the conversation." Julie continues, "By 7:30, we start the bedtime routine with baths. The boys bathe together, so one of us sits with them in the bathroom. They have lots of floating toys for the tub and this is a "wind-down" time for us. Next is storytime. We all pile onto the bed and read one or two stories. By then, Isaac and Luke are ready to sleep."

George again brings up the Daily Log from the infant center. "We know at what time and how long Luke's naps were for the day, so we can pretty much predict his bedtime from that." After the boys are asleep, George and Julie have time to visit with each other and get ready for the next day. George tells Kristine, "Knowing you will be there for Luke is important to us. The infant center makes it possible for us to feel positive about where Luke is each day while we're at work."

Thanking the family for the visit and saying good-bye, you turn to Kristine and also thank her for inviting you along for the visit. Kristine replies, "Visiting the family at home is how I learn more about their routines and it also helps the child feel more comfortable with me, knowing that I have been to their home."

Visiting with Sue, the Infant Care Coordinator

Some of your first questions are about the employer-sponsored Child Development Center, program philosophy, and curriculum. You wonder about the program and employer-sponsored child care. Sue, the infant care program coordinator, responds to your first question about employer-sponsored child care by describing Mentor Graphics Corporation's involvement in developing and implementing the Child Development Center.

Mentor Graphics Corporation-Sponsored Child Care

Mentor Graphics Corporation is known as a "leading manufacturer of software used by semi-conductor and circuit board designers" (Crockett, 1997, p. C1). In the late 1980s, the corporation made a decision to build a new campus to serve as corporate headquarters. At this time, the company's Facilities Department surveyed employees about desired facilities at the new site. Many employees requested on-site day care. The Human Resources Division formed a committee to study the feasibility and options of developing on-site day care. The committee explored different child care options and eventually made the decision to go forward with the development of a quality, on-site Child Development Center to serve the children of its employees. The program at the Child Development Center would also be congruent with company beliefs—stressing the importance of education for its employees and the community, and if it is worth doing, it is worth doing right.

Consequently, the Mentor Graphics Child Development Center is a model early childhood and family support program. The center has three main purposes: to facilitate the development of young children and their families; to enhance the ability of employee-parents at Mentor Graphics to be productive by supporting them in their work/family roles; and to make a contribution to the community by providing a high-quality model of care and education for young children. The center serves 95 children each day in the 12,000-square-foot building located at corporate headquarters.

Now that you have a basic understanding of the role of the corporation in supporting this child care program, you are probably interested in learning more about the infant program itself.

Philosophy of Care

Sue suggests a good overview and starting place for you might be with the *Mentor Graphics Parent Handbook* that the center developed. In the Philosophy of Care section, you read:

> Parents are respected as the most important people in a child's life. . . .Goals for infants and toddlers in our care include: respecting each child as a unique and special person; attending to each child's physical and psychological needs; fostering and developing a relationship with a caregiver the child can trust; providing a safe, healthy and developmentally appropriate environment; creating opportunities to interact with other infants and toddlers; and supporting each child in their exploration and use of all their senses. (Mentor Graphics Child Development Center, 1996, p. 15)

As you continue to read the *Handbook,* you notice the program goals are clearly designed to create an environment that promotes the development of a healthy and curious child. Sue shares that the philosophy of care was developed over a period of time by a group of caregivers, teachers, and parents. Everyone read pertinent articles and discussed their vision for the Child Development Center, which was translated into a philosophy of care.

Infant Care Program

The infant care program includes children from age 6 weeks to approximately 18 months of age. Sue explains, "In the infant care program, each child has a different routine and caregivers are very aware of **individual routines.** We establish the day for each child based on her particular needs, interests, and personality. The program is developed around the child, which is why we consider it to be an **individual program."** This means that feeding, sleeping, play, diapering, and other activities are developed around the needs and developmental levels of each infant. In contrast, due to inadequate staffing or lack of knowledge about infant development, some centers feed all infants at the same time or put them down for naps at the same time. (Remember the places that Mei-Ling visited?) Another feature in the Mentor Graphics infant program is that each caregiver (infant specialist) is assigned three infants and develops daily programs around the needs and desires of each infant in her care.

The caregiver remains the **primary caregiver** for the infant throughout the infant's program. Caregivers start out with infants when they enter the program at 6 weeks of age (or older) and continue with them through the toddler program, until they are close to 3 years old and enter the preschool program.

   Journal 7.3: Why would the center have a caregiver work with the same child for a two- to three-year period? What might be some benefits of this arrangement? Can you think of some disadvantages? ▪

Kristine, Luke's caregiver, expressed the importance of the individual schedule when she shared her thoughts about working with three infants as a primary caregiver. "Being responsible for the primary care for three infants ensures that no child gets lost in the shuffle. We learn each infant's schedule, personality, and preferences and are able to respond to them as individuals." The role of primary caregiver with infants is one that requires knowledge, skills, and dedication to the development and uniqueness of each child. Although each caregiver is the primary caregiver for three infants, we also attend to each other's infants when the need arises. Remember when Luke visited his brother? Caryl then assumed care for the other two infants until Kristine returned. The quality of infant care is indeed dependent on the quality of the staff, as you have heard from parents, educators, and researchers. Also, quality infant programs embrace curriculum that is developmentally appropriate for the needs of each infant.

Curriculum of infant program.   Sue is clear that the two major components of the infant curriculum are **care giving** and **play.** When a caregiver is providing care for an

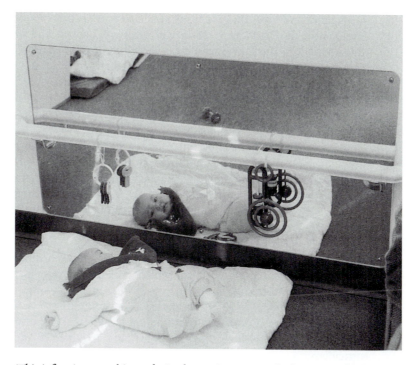

This infant is engaged in exploring her environment. Which senses might she be using?

infant, her attention is focused fully on that infant. She explains, "Care-giving interactions provide for social, language, and self-help skills. Each time an infant is fed or diapered, we talk with her and tell her what we are doing. We want the infant to feel respected and part of the caregiver interaction."

The second component Sue mentioned was play, and she shares, "The importance of play cannot be emphasized enough. You'll notice we don't have bouncy chairs or playpens or any mechanical infant devices. We want infants to feel empowered in their own environment. Our infants spend a lot of time each day on the floor. They learn to roll over, move their necks and heads, reach for objects with their hands, and scoot around when they are developmentally ready."

While you observed the program, you rarely saw infants being "entertained." Much of the time, infants are busy on the floor with toys, engaging with other infants (closely monitored by a caregiver), interacting with a caregiver, or having their caregiving needs met. So this is what is meant by play! The infants actually "learn about themselves, other people and the world around them" (Mentor Graphics Child Development Center, 1996) by interacting within a safe and comfortable environment.

The curriculum in the infant care program at Mentor Graphics is consistent with **developmentally appropriate practice** for infants. Activities, toys and other objects, interactions, and program guidelines are created using the knowledge base of child development during infancy along with strengths, needs, and interests of specific children and families. **Development** is viewed as a continual process, with each child reaching milestones at various ages. For example, most children learn to walk without assistance between the ages of 9 and 17 months. Understanding that there is a wide range of time when children accomplish certain developmental skills helps caregivers provide different activities and learn to have different expectations for individual children.

Many early childhood educators consider Magda Gerber's contributions to be the most influential on infant care philosophy and practice. Gerber worked with infants in Hungary at Loczy, an institution for children from birth to age 3. In her subsequent work with caregivers of infants, Gerber emphasized an infant's need for respect, individualized care giving, and a connection with a constant person (1979). These needs should be reflected in the everyday curriculum and practices with infants. Gerber's teachings are apparent in Mentor Graphics Infant Care Program.

As you observed in Luke's infant care, activities and schedules were planned for the infants on an individual basis, which promotes developmentally appropriate practices. Remember Luke's desire to pull himself up on objects so he could be standing? Kristine made sure that Luke had opportunities to be near stable objects so he could use his muscles and coordination to pull himself upright. She was aware of his developmental level and of appropriate activities to incorporate into his curriculum.

 Emily is an 11-month-old infant at the center. Her curriculum is planned to meet her special needs, as her physical development is delayed. She receives special education services from Ryka, a physical therapist. Ryka works with Emily from 2:00 to 3:00 on Wednesdays and Fridays. Most of the time is spent increasing Emily's muscle strength, so she can sustain a sitting position for longer time periods. Emily is now able to sit without support for several minutes. After this amount of time, she usually leans over and falls down. Ryka also meets with Emily's family and caregiver to discuss activities they can be working on with Emily. Emily participates in most of the same activities as the other infants, but planned attention and efforts are given to assist Emily in her physical development. Planning developmentally appropriate curriculum also requires knowledge and respect of the child's family and culture.

Respect for infants and their families.   Sue continues, "Another important belief of our program is respect for the child and family. While you observed, did you notice how caregivers interacted with parents and how the center welcomes input from the family about their child?" This is all part of the Child Development Center's philosophy in action. The **open communication** and request for individual family and child information and preferences allow the caregivers to create that individualized program for each infant. Input provided by the family is an important component in the development of each individual plan. Parents are also welcome at the center at any time. The caregivers want to provide the best care they can and do so in a way that supports the family's preferences."

Each infant has individual food containers with food prepared and brought from home.

When you observed Luke's lunchtime, you saw each infant eating food provided by his parents. Sue notes, "We have learned that our families' cultures are often expressed in their food and food preparation. Several of our children continue bringing food from home so that their family's preferences continue throughout their time in the Child Development Center." For example, Marta often has beans and rice with her lunch, following a custom of her family. This would not be a common dish served on a regular basis. Knowing the family preference enables the caregivers to respect the family culture.

"Learning about the infant program before the child enters is important to the continuity of our program philosophy and characteristics such as our curriculum and our belief about respecting infants." Sue has developed a procedure to help orient "new" families.

New families. Before enrolling an infant in the center, parents meet with Sue at the center for an hour-long orientation and discussion of the center's philosophy and activities. Parents then arrange to visit the center. Three weeks after their visit, they make a final decision about enrolling their infant in the care center. After this time, the primary caregiver makes a home visit, with the purpose of easing the transition from home to the center for the infant and family. Following the home visit, the family writes a letter to the caregiver about their infant's typical schedule, routine, and particular needs

■ **FIGURE 7.4**   Letter from Family

Date: January 2

To: Caryl and Infant Room Care Givers:

We'd like to introduce our daughter, Ingrid. Born on September 12, she is a pretty little girl with lots of hair—that is usually what people comment on first when meeting her. Ingrid lives with her Mom and Dad, and big brother James (18 months her senior). Mom is looking forward to visiting Ingrid at lunchtime, when time permits, sometime between noon and 1 p.m. Ingrid will spend Monday–Friday from 8:00 a.m. to 5:30 p.m. in the CDC. Mom will normally do drop off and pick up.

Ingrid generally has a happy and laid-back personality when she is not bored or hungry or tired or in need of a new diaper. Ingrid will let you know when she needs service by crying. In time, you'll be able to guess what she needs by the time of day in her schedule or, when you really get to know her, by the type of cry. Ingrid will reflect your mood—if you have a happy smile, Ingrid will be happy to give you one in return. If you are stressed or hurried, Ingrid will become anxious as well.

Ingrid loves to be talked to as well as talk herself. She can babble on and on about whatever. Her Mom and Dad "talk" with her to encourage vocalization. Mom and Dad also read and sing to Ingrid. It has a great calming effect. Ingrid LOVES music, musical mobiles, toys, and singing. She has a musical bear in her crib that you can pull to help calm her to sleep. Please bring music to Ingrid each and every day if you can. You don't have to have a good voice (as Mom knows) to sing to Ingrid—she loves to watch facial expressions—the more animated, the more she likes it.

Ingrid has been used to one-on-one care with Mommy at home. Full-time group care will be new for her. If you cannot attend to her needs immediately when she sends out her usual distress signal (a cry), please respond to her verbally to let her know she has been heard and you are on the way. Mom and Dad have been using this technique at home successfully. Especially when big brother James is around.

Ingrid loves motion. She will be a big fan of stroller rides, both indoors and outdoors. There should be a pink fuzzy suit in her day bag for outdoor rides. Let us know when you have a hard time getting her into it. It fits her right now. Ingrid also loves to be held and cuddled. When all her obvious needs are met and she is still in distress, she is calmed by being held and walked. We offer her a pacifier at these times as well but she is finding her thumb more now.

Ingrid is a very sweet girl and learning to give lots of smiles. She's starting to coo and really interact. I find that when she is overstimulated and ready to stop eye to eye contact, she really looks away and sometimes starts to fuss a bit. She gives pretty clear messages.

Let's see, I guess there's not much else. I look forward to getting to know all of you better. Please don't hesitate to ask questions or let me know if there is something else you need.

Thank you,

Bonnie & Erik

Source: Mentor Graphics Child Development Center. Reprinted by permission.

and comforts (see Figure 7.4). The letter informs the caregivers about any specific wishes of the family. Sue wants her families to feel welcome at the center and to spend time with their infant at the center. She finds this connection helps both parents and infants understand the role of the center in their lives.

Once the parents decide to enroll their child in the infant program, they set up a **"starting schedule"** with Sue. Each schedule varies according to the infant's needs and acclimation to the infant center. Infants might begin coming to the center for several mornings a week, then gradually move to full days once the infant seems comfortable with her caregiver and the surroundings.

Sue shares, "Often, I spend more time helping the parent adjust to the center and being separated from their child. We try to learn the best routine or schedule for each infant, based on individual needs and personalities. But sometimes it is harder for the parent. They feel torn about leaving their infant in child care." Sue has found several books that are helpful for parents to read. She also introduces families to each other. Often it helps "new" parents to talk with other families who have made this transition. It seems that establishing a planned routine helps both the infant and the parent in their separation each morning.

Commitment to a quality program.   As you may have noted through your conversation with Sue, there is a strong commitment to a **quality program** shown by the corporation, CDC staff, and families. The staff understands the role of the primary caregiver and how important this person is to the infant and to the infant's family. Frequent communication, parent education, visits and conferences at the center, and a sharing of the goals of the Child Development Center lead to a common vision for child care. Families, staff, and management work together to create an employer-sponsored child care program that is viewed as a program that supports the growth and development of healthy children, healthy employees, and healthy families.

Now that you have visited the Mentor Graphics Infant Care Program and have had an introduction to the philosophy and curriculum of its infant care program, let's take a closer look at infant care programs, in general.

A Closer Look at Infant Care Programs

Infancy is a special time when caregivers and parents have the opportunity to nourish a child while he is most dependent on adults to meet his needs. Infants need adults to feed, clothe, clean, and care for them. They also need a safe, stimulating environment in which to grow. Currently, there is a rapidly increasing need for good infant care. Unfortunately, there is a greater lack of adequate care for infants and toddlers than for any other age group (Cost, Quality, and Child Outcomes Study Team, 1995).

Children might begin child care as early as 6 weeks of age. Infant care programs differ on the age that they accept infants and also on the age for transition to the toddler program. Some programs make the change to toddler programs near 12 months of age, when many infants begin walking. Other programs continue the child in the infant program until they reach 18 to 24 months, adjusting the curriculum for young infants (2 to 10 months) and older infants (11 to 24 months). As more and more mothers of infants return to work, families are faced with the dilemma of finding the right care for their infant. Let's take a look at the basic needs of infants, a general overview or description of quality infant care programs, and current issues and trends relevant to infant care.

BOX 7.2 ■ What Are Current Findings on Brain Development during Infancy?

The human brain begins forming while still in the womb. In early infancy and through the first three years of life, brain connections develop in response to stimulation (Newberger, 1997). At birth, an infant brain has approximately 100 billion neurons. These neurons form over 50 trillion connections, known as *synapses*. In the first months of life, the brain connections continue to grow rapidly. This means that the experiences an infant encounters will have an impact on the growth of her brain. Contrary to prior beliefs, infants do not enter the world with a fully formed brain. The brain is still growing and receiving connections in response to interactions and stimulation from the infant's environment.

The infant's environment exerts a tremendous impact on how the circuits or wiring of the brain are formed (Newberger, 1997). Children who have opportunities for warm interactions and stimulating experiences will tend to strengthen the synapses (connections) in the brain. In contrast, children with little stimulation have fewer synapses developed, and, if not used, will wither during this critical growth period. Children with negative experiences have more difficulty with learning and in developing healthy emotional responses in general (Newberger, 1997).

These recent findings hold great importance for early childhood educators, particularly those who work with the youngest children. Rich interactive environments, both at home and in infant care programs, will help children develop their mental and emotional capacities to their fullest potential. Developmentally appropriate activities are essential to the promotion of healthy growth in infants. Interacting with an infant by playing games such as peek-aboo or hide-and-seek, talking about ordinary objects in the grocery store, and going on walks in the woods or neighborhood are activities that affect an infant's development (Jabs, 1996). Just as most parents and early childhood educators have long believed, positive and stimulating experiences in infancy do create a foundation that continues to affect learning throughout the child's life.

Programs and Infant Needs

All infants have similar needs in the first months of life. They share a **common need** for "good health and safety; warm, loving relationships with their primary caregivers; and care that is responsive to their individual differences" (Lally et al., 1995). Infant care programs that recognize the importance of close relationships to an infant's development address this need by designating one primary caregiver for each infant.

Recent research on **brain growth** during the first years of life helps caregivers recognize the importance of talking with infants, encouraging movement and social interactions, and providing stimulating curriculum throughout the day (see Box 7.2).

Role of the primary caregiver. The primary caregiver learns the unique needs, moods, characteristics, and biological rhythms of an infant in her care. An infant caregiver must be nurturing and possess **keen observational skills** (Honig, 1985, p. 40). These observational skills are necessary to know when and how to respond effectively with an infant. Infants have different responses to stimuli, such as light, noise, activities, or smell. Some infants delight in loud music, whereas others cry and prefer quieter music. It takes time to learn to observe and honor preferences while also trying to balance the need for stimulation and a variety of experiences in the curriculum. Since infants are not talking and expressing their thoughts through verbal language, the caregiver learns to watch their faces and body language. Does the infant tighten her fists and start taking shallow breaths? This might mean she wants out of a situation. Does a gentle rub on the back produce a small smile and relaxed posture? Back rubs might be an effective way to help this infant relax.

It is the role of the primary caregiver to recognize the specific signals that an infant is sending. When Luke was making little whining sounds late in the morning, Kristine recognized he was communicating his desire for food. He was hungry and ready to eat lunch. She was in tune with Luke's signals and able to respond to his needs. Luke was learning that he had the ability to influence his environment and receive food when he was hungry. This interaction helps build security in the infant's life through the realization that his signals or communications lead to a response from a person he trusts —his primary caregiver.

Beyond recognizing Luke's needs, Kristine involves him in each **care-giving interaction.** A care-giving interaction takes place each time the caregiver connects, communicates, responds, or relates with an infant. Gonzalez-Mena and Eyer (1997) emphasize the importance of developing a relationship between a caregiver and an infant, and have outlined 10 principles of care giving, as shown in Figure 7.5.

 Involving infants and toddlers in things that concern them is the first principle of care giving described by Gonzalez-Mena and Eyer (1997). In their work, they have found it important to engage and involve infants in the "ordinary" events of the day, such as diapering, feeding, and playing. Keeping the infant's attention and describing

■ **FIGURE 7.5**   Principles of Care Giving

Principle 1:	Involve infants and toddlers in things that concern them.
Principle 2:	Invest in quality time.
Principle 3:	Learn each child's unique ways of communicating and teach them yours.
Principle 4:	Invest in time and energy to build a total person.
Principle 5:	Respect infants and toddlers as worthy people.
Principle 6:	Be honest about your feelings.
Principle 7:	Model the behavior you want to teach.
Principle 8:	Recognize problems as learning opportunities and let infants and toddlers try to solve their own.
Principle 9:	Build security by teaching trust.
Principle 10:	Be concerned about the quality of development in each stage.

Source: Adapted from *Infants, Toddlers, and Caregivers* (4th ed.) (pp. 9–23) by J. Gonzalez-Mena and D. Eyer, 1997, Mountain View, CA: Mayfield.

the actions includes the child in "what is being done to her" and makes her a partner in activities that concern her.

This intense involvement can also be characterized as quality time, which is the second principle of care giving. Remember when Luke was eating lunch and Kristine carried on a conversation with him? She was fully engaged in his activity and gave him her attention. It is an expectation of the infant care program at Mentor Graphics that caregivers help each other when they are aware that one caregiver is engaged in quality time with an infant and another child in their care needs attention. The contrast to this would be a situation where a caregiver was feeding three infants lined up in front of her in infant seats.

When you first met Luke, he was standing at the window and watching his brother outside in the play yard. He was banging on the window and intent on watching Isaac. Kristine talked to Luke about his brother and told him that they would visit Isaac later in the day. She recognized his banging on the window and his attentiveness to watching Isaac at play. She also verbalized descriptions of Luke's actions. This interaction is an example of the third principle: learning a child's individual communication patterns and teaching him your communication style. Kristine shared her thoughts with Luke, "We will go visit Isaac this afternoon after lunch. You'll like that, won't you? I feel ready for a visit myself."

 Journal 7.4: Why did Kristine share her thoughts with Luke? What might be some reasons for talking with an infant? ■

Throughout the day, there are numerous opportunities to engage infants in learning about their environment, which contributes to their development. During outside play, Kristine described the environment around Luke. She told him, "If we listen carefully, we can hear the birds that you like to hear. And look, you are pulling the green grass. Doesn't it feel slippery today?" She purposely communicates about everyday events and activities and pays attention to experiences that foster Luke's social, emotional, physical, and intellectual development. While playing on the grass, Luke was using fine motor skills, learning the names of objects, sharing a social time, and having his emotional needs met. All developmental areas were engaged. These discussions are based on the fourth principle of caregiving: expending the time and energy to assist an infant in his development.

If Luke wakes up from his nap a bit early and seems grumpy, Kristine talks to him and says, "You seem to be feeling grumpy and need a bit more sleep. Let's take you back to your crib and let you get the rest you need." Using her observational skills and her knowledge of Luke's unique signals, she communicates to him what she sees, what Luke will be doing next, and where she is taking him. This is far different from picking up an infant and carrying him back to the crib without talking to him. The difference is called *respect* for the infant, which is the fifth principle of care giving.

Respect for an infant also means allowing the infant to work things our for herself. For example, 10-month-old Emory was attempting to crawl toward a soft ball on the carpet. She seemed to go backwards with her efforts and began to fuss. Instead of rescuing her immediately, Caryl, her caregiver, waited to see if Emory would be able to change her direction and head toward the ball. Caryl then talked soothingly to Emory, "Look where the ball is Emory. You are close." Emory laid down her head and was quiet for a moment. She then rolled over and reached out with her arm and touched the ball. Instead of interrupting the learning at the first sign of frustration, Caryl respected the infant's learning and encouraged her to keep trying.

 Journal 7.5: *Liking* infants is different from *respecting* infants. Describe a basic difference between these two actions or beliefs. ■

The sixth principle recommends that caregivers recognize their own feelings and be honest about feelings. It is also important to learn to express feelings in a safe and healthy manner.

Modeling behavior you want infants to learn is the seventh principle, which is related to expressing feelings in a healthy format. Young children learn a great deal from their observations. When an infant sees a caregiver respond in a comforting way to a child who is crying, the infant begins to learn to connect comforting from a caregiver as an empathetic behavior.

The next principle is viewing problems as learning situations and allowing infants to attempt to solve their own problems when feasible. Remember Bruner's and Vygotsky's discussion about scaffolding, where the adult provides the structure or assistance to enable the child to accomplish a task or activity? This principle builds on this concept. It is tempting to "rescue" an infant and hurry and move a toy into his grasping range. On the other hand, if you want the child to develop the motor skills to reach the toy, allowing him to make attempts to do so is helping him learn to solve his own problem.

Being dependable so an infant learns to trust in a secure environment is the ninth principle. The Good-Bye Plan at Mentor Graphics highlights this principle. The adult is asked to let his infant know that he is leaving and have an established routine so the child begins to trust that his parent will return. This is vastly different from sneaking out of the room while the child is involved in an activity and later notices he is abandoned.

The tenth principle is providing for each stage of infant development. Knowledge of child development is critical to this stage, as is awareness of the infant's individual development in the various developmental domains. Appreciating the infant's current level of development and allowing time for the infant to explore and grow in this area is showing respect and encouragement for what the infant can do.

Did you notice that Kristine, Luke's caregiver, follows these 10 principles in her work with infants? She has developed a close, respectful relationship with each of the three infants in her care.

Characteristics of an infant care program.   The day in infant care is constructed around care giving and care-giving routines. A typical infant care program would ensure there was a **safe, clean environment** for the care-giving activities of diapering, eating, sleeping, and playing. In the Mentor Graphics Infant Care Program, you saw a designated area for each of these activities. Supplies are stored so caregivers can access them easily, yet the items are out of reach of older infants who are mobile. Caregivers wash their

Luke has learned to go up the stairs but is cautious about going back down.

hands frequently throughout the day and always after diaper changes and before meals and bottle times.

Toys and other objects for play are placed in spots that infants can reach, whether on a low bookshelf or on the floor. Since infants learn much from **sensory interactions,** a variety of tactile, visual, and motor experiences should be available. Within the infant play room, various textures should be available for infant touching. For example, a rough texture from a Berber-type rug contrasts with a spongy texture from foam rubber balls. Infants need opportunities to touch, crawl on, and walk on many surfaces. Different textures within their environment provides for a variety of touch sensations.

Toys and furniture should provide for a variety of uses and be selected for durability, ease of cleaning, and interest to infants. Homemade toys can create as much or more interest than expensive toys. Kristine shared, "The clear plastic pop bottle half-filled with oil, colored water, and large buttons is a favorite of some of our infants. They can hold on to the bottle, bump it to make it roll, or grab it and shake it. Just make sure to check the tape around the lid often during the day!" Some toys are left in the closed cupboard and then exchanged with other toys periodically. Sue explains, "Too many toys are overstimulating. It's better to have a few available at a time and rotate them every week or so."

In the play area, Luke enjoys the climbing ramp, which has three stair steps enclosed in a wooden structure. He likes to climb and crawl on this, as he attempts to reach the top step. Another favorite object is a long mirror placed low on the wall. An infant can lay on the pad in front of the mirror and watch himself. This provides **visual and motor stimulation,** as older infants attempt to touch the mirror when they recognize body parts such as their faces. Infants also respond to **auditory stimuli.** A tape of music or a caregiver singing a song provides an enjoyable experience. Some caregivers like to play quiet music to calm an infant or rhythmic music when the infant is alert and playful. Singing can be reassuring and soothing to an infant, as he listens to melodies and familiar words (Honig, 1995) sung by his caregiver. A variety of objects such as soft balls, wooden blocks, rolling bottles, and larger play structures encourage the infant to explore and learn within an interesting environment.

Just as a variety of objects within the infant care room create interest, so do a variety of surfaces. Different tactile surfaces, which might include smooth, hard surfaces (perhaps a tile floor) and soft surfaces (such as a pad where the infant lies when she watches herself in the mirror) provide variety. The quiet area might have dim lights, whereas the kitchen is bright. These **differences in the infant's environment** provide a range of texture, size, brightness, and color that stimulates sensory experiences.

Journal 7.6: Infants respond to interesting, inviting environments. In order to learn more about an infant's environment, you would need to sit or lay on the floor and look around you. Find a comfortable spot on the floor to lay on and look around. What are two things you notice from this observation point that you did not pay much attention to before? ■

Goals for Infant Care Programs

The **primary goal** of quality infant care programs is to provide a healthy, safe, and caring environment. Within this environment, another goal is the development of an appropriate individual program for each infant, based on the caregiver's knowledge of infant development, her observations of the infant, and input from the infant's family.

While parents are at work, they want to know that their infant is safe, secure, and being cared for by someone who understands infant development and is committed to a special relationship with their infant. A program goal that focuses on nurturing a respectful relationship between an infant and her caregiver would meet these parental expectations, along with viewing families as the primary caregivers in the infant's life. **Program goals** are reflected in the curriculum of an infant care program.

Curriculum

Curriculum, or the schedule of activities and events, varies greatly among ages and developmental levels of young children. Infants have needs that are very different from the needs of preschool age children, and would be frustrated in an atmosphere where they were expected to eat, sleep, play, and be diapered on a group schedule. Infant care programs create **individual plans** around the needs, family wishes, and personality of each child. Care giving, play, and quiet time compose the curriculum in infant care.

Curriculum and different developmental areas. Each day, an infant is learning and growing. As discussed earlier, an infant does not need to be directly taught specific skills. Infants learn when they are in a safe, secure atmosphere, with multiple opportunities to interact with others and with their environment. Growth is occurring in each of the developmental domains. **Developmental milestones,** as seen in Table 7.1 on pages 272 and 273, provide a guideline of when infants acquire certain behaviors or skills.

	Interest in Others	Self-Awareness	Motor Milestones and Eye-Hand Skills
The early months (birth through 8 months)	■ Newborns prefer the human face and human sound. Within the first two weeks, they recognize and prefer the sight, smell, and sound of the principal caregiver. ■ Social smile and mutual gazing is evidence of early social interaction. The infant can initiate and terminate the interactions. ■ Anticipates being lifted or fed and moves body to participate. ■ Sees adults as objects of interest and novelty. Seeks out adults for play. Stretches arms to be taken.	■ Sucks fingers or hand fortuitously. ■ Observes own hands. ■ Raises hands as if to protect self when object comes close to face. ■ Looks to the place on body where being touched. ■ Reaches for and grasps toys. ■ Clasps hands together and fingers them. ■ Tries to cause things to happen. ■ Begins to distinguish friends from strangers. Shows preference for being held by familiar people.	■ The young infant uses many complex reflexes: searches for something to suck; holds on when falling; turns head to avoid obstruction of breathing; avoids brightness, strong smells, and pain. ■ Puts hand or object in mouth. ■ Begins reaching towards interesting objects. ■ Grasps, releases, regrasps, and releases object again. ■ Lifts head. Holds head up. Sits up without support. Rolls over. Transfers and manipulates objects with hands. Crawls.
Crawlers and walkers (8 to 18 months)	■ Exhibits anxious behavior around unfamiliar adults. ■ Enjoys exploring objects with another as the basis for establishing relationships. ■ Gets others to do things for child's pleasure (wind-up toys, read books, get dolls). ■ Shows considerable interest in peers. ■ Demonstrates intense attention to adult language.	■ Knows own name. ■ Smiles or plays with self in mirror. ■ Uses large and small muscles to explore confidently when a sense of security is offered by presence of caregiver. Frequently checks for caregivers presence. ■ Has heightened awareness of opportunities to make things happen, yet limited awareness of responsibility for own actions. ■ Indicates strong sense of self through assertiveness. Directs action of others (e.g., "Sit there!"). ■ Identifies one or more body parts. ■ Begins to use *me, you, I*.	■ Sits well in chairs. ■ Pulls self up, stands holding furniture. ■ Walks when led. Walks alone. ■ Throws objects. ■ Climbs stairs. ■ Uses marker on paper. ■ Stoops, trots, walks backward a few steps.

Note: This list is not intended to be exhaustive. Many of the behaviors indicated here will happen earlier or later for individual infants. The chart suggests an approximate time when a behavior might appear, but it should not be rigidly interpreted. Often, but not always, the behaviors appear in the order in which they emerge. Particularly for younger infants, the behaviors listed in one domain overlap considerably with several other developmental domains. Some behaviors are placed under more than one category to emphasize this interrelationship.

Language Development/ Communication	Physical, Spatial, and Temporal Awareness	Purposeful Action and Use of Tools	Expression of Feelings
■ Cries to signal pain or distress. ■ Smiles or vocalizes to initiate social contact. ■ Responds to human voices. Gazes at faces. ■ Uses vocal and nonvocal communication to express interest and to exert influence. ■ Babbles using all types of sounds. Engages in private conversations when alone. ■ Combines babbles. Understands names of familiar people and objects. Laughs. Listens to conversations.	■ Comforts self by sucking thumb or finding pacifier. ■ Follows a slowly moving object with eyes. ■ Reaches and grasps toys. ■ Looks for dropped toy. ■ Identifies objects from various viewpoints. Finds a toy hidden under a blanket when placed there while watching.	■ Observes own hands. ■ Grasps rattle when hand and rattle are both in view. ■ Hits or kicks an object to make a pleasing sight or sound continue. ■ Tries to resume a knee ride by bouncing to get adult started again.	■ Expresses discomfort and comfort/pleasure unambiguously. ■ Responds with more animation and pleasure to primary caregiver than to others. ■ Can usually be comforted by familiar adult when distressed. ■ Smiles and activates the obvious pleasure in response to social stimulation. Very interested in people. Shows displeasure at loss of social contact. ■ Laughs aloud (belly laugh). ■ Shows displeasure of disappointment at loss of toy. ■ Expresses several clearly differentiated emotions: pleasure, anger, anxiety or fear, sadness, joy, excitement, disappointment, exuberance. ■ Reacts to strangers with soberness or anxiety.
■ Understands many more words than can say. Looks toward 20 or more objects when named. ■ Creates long, babbled sentences. ■ Shakes head no. Says two or three clear words. ■ Looks at picture books with interest, points to objects. ■ Uses vocal signals other than crying to gain assistance. ■ Begins to use *me, you, I.*	■ Tries to build with blocks. ■ If toy is hidden under one of three cloths while child watches, looks under the right cloth for the toy. ■ Persists in a search for a desired toy even when toy is hidden under a distracting object, such as pillows. ■ When chasing a ball that has rolled under the sofa and out the other side, will make a detour around sofa to get ball. ■ Pushes foot into shoe, arm into sleeve.	■ When a toy winds down, continues the activity manually. ■ Uses a stick as a tool to obtain a toy. ■ When music box winds down, searches for the key to wind it up again. ■ Brings a stool to use for reaching for something. ■ Pushes away someone or something not wanted. ■ Creeps or walks to get something or to avoid unpleasantness. ■ Pushes foot into shoe, arm into sleeve. ■ Feeds self finger food (bits of fruit, crackers). ■ Partially feeds self with fingers or spoon. ■ Handles cup well with minimal spilling. ■ Handles spoon well for self-feeding.	■ Actively shows affection for familiar person: hugs, smiles at, runs toward, leans against, and so forth. ■ Shows anxiety at separation from primary caregiver. ■ Shows anger focused on people or objects. ■ Expresses negative feelings. ■ Shows pride and pleasure in new accomplishments. ■ Shows intense feelings for parents. ■ Continues to show pleasure in mastery. ■ Asserts self, indicating strong sense of self.

Source: Reprinted with permission from *Caring for Infants and Toddlers in Groups: Developmentally Appropriate Practice,* ZERO TO THREE: National Center for Infants, Toddlers, and Families, 1995. Reprinted by permission.

This guideline assists caretakers in creating curriculum to meet the needs of infants in their care. Kristine finds it helpful to refer to these milestones when she plans activities. The guidelines help her assess whether the curriculum is appropriate for an infant's development, as well as provide a check to be sure that she has planned for each of the **different developmental areas.**

Very young infants begin to recognize the sight and smell of their primary caregiver within a few weeks of birth. By several months of age, the infant will imitate facial expressions such as opening her mouth wide or smiling. When she reaches 1 year of age, she tends to be quite interested in her peers. These are representations of **social interactions** (interest in others) that start at birth. Curriculum planning for the social domain would include a warm relationship with the primary caregiver along with opportunities for exploring and interacting with peers.

If you observe a young infant, from 2 to 4 months old, you might notice the infant sucking his fingers or gazing at his hands. He is beginning to learn to distinguish himself from the rest of his environment. As he grows in **self-awareness,** he begins to respond to his name and identify his body parts. Infant caregivers plan many activities that help infants identify themselves. You might observe games with infants, such as "Where is Manuel?" Manuel will hide behind an object and peek out and respond, "Manuel here." Infants from 6 to 18 months old enjoy games of naming and touching their body parts. Emory will respond to "Where is your nose?" by touching her nose. The next step for older infants would be for the caregiver to ask, "Where is my nose?" They are now ready to distinguish between their own selves and another person as they grow in self-awareness.

Infants learn a great deal from being touched and touching objects. A young infant finds that moving her arms can expand her immediate environment as she reaches for and touches things around her. As she grows older and her motor and physical skills expand, she is able to sit in chairs, walk, and build with blocks. Assessment of an infant's **physical development** provides direction for curriculum planning. The infant care environment must also be assessed for safety reasons. As an infant becomes mobile, her environment must reflect her range of accessibility. For example, wall sockets should be covered with safety plugs, cords should be placed out of reach, cupboards should contain "safe" items only, and large objects that could be pulled over or dropped should be moved out of the way. These safety precautions allow the infant to move more freely within her environment, building her motor and physical skills as she learns to roll over, crawl, sit up, walk, and climb.

The environment of the infant becomes more interesting as the infant learns to use tools and or movement. For instance, a 2-month-old might discover that jiggling in his crib causes a mobile to move slightly. As he grows older, he is able to make more **purposeful movements** to reach particular results. Scott found that he could push a stool over to the counter and climb on the stool to see and reach what was placed on the counter. He was able to use tools and movements to accomplish his goals. When an infant has developed eye-hand coordination and small muscle coordination to the point where he can grasp a spoon and begin to control arm movement, he is ready to learn to use a spoon (a tool). Eating applesauce or other semi-solid foods is great practice for learning to coordinate a spoon. Gradually, the infant learns that the tool (spoon) allows him to eat faster and to end up with more food in his mouth. Be prepared with bibs, cloths, and plenty of trial and error learning!

BOX 7.3 ■ When Does Language Development Begin?

Language is a complex, specialized skill, which develops in the child spontaneously, without conscious effort or formal instruction, is deployed without awareness of its underlying logic, is qualitatively the same in every individual, and is distinct from more general abilities to process information or behave intelligently. (Pinker, 1994, p. 18)

The development of language in infants occurs on approximately the same time line across different cultures. Newborns are sensitive to nuances in language and begin to discriminate the speech sounds that are part of the language spoken in their environments. By the time an infant reaches 3 months of age, she has already focused on the speech sounds she hears, including the patterns of accents, syllables, rhythms, and intonations of language. Jusczyk (1997) has reviewed research conducted on language development and found that these studies indicate that infants have the capacity or ability to "discriminate many different kinds of speech contrasts" (p. 56).

Kuhl (1992) has found that infants' brains create auditory maps of the phonemes (small units of sound) that they hear. By 6 months of age, English-speaking infants have developed a different auditory map in their brain than infants in Swedish-speaking homes. Familiar sounds (phonemes) now form the infant's spoken language. When a child reaches 12 months of age, her auditory map is formed. As peo-

ple age, it becomes increasingly difficult to learn new sounds that are unfamiliar. This, in part, explains why adults have more difficulty learning a foreign language than young children. The young infant's brain is considered more "plastic" and able to respond to and imitate sounds.

Studies have also shown that there is a clear relationship between the amount of parent speech the child hears and the child's vocabulary growth (Huttenlocher et al., 1991). Infants seem to build the foundation of their language development during the early months of life. The more sounds a child hears, the larger her vocabulary. The sounds of words builds up neural circuitry for learning more words and new sounds (Begley, 1996). By 1 year of age, most children are connecting words with meaning, knowing that *puppy* refers to their dog, *ice cream* is something good to eat, and *bottle* holds something to drink.

The implications of these findings of language development support what many early childhood educators have long practiced—talking with an infant is important to her development. Babbling and cooing as forms of communication encourage adult interaction and shape language development. During the early months of life, auditory connections are formed in the brain and they affect language development, vocabulary, and use of language for the child's entire life.

Infants learn through language (**cognitive and language development**) as they make sounds, listen, and respond to others (see Box 7.3). Communication starts on the first day of life. An infant learns to distinguish familiar voices and to discriminate between happy and not as happy sounds at a young age. By the time he is a year old, he begins to babble and combine babbles to create his own words. He also begins to look at objects that are named out loud. For instance, when Amil hears someone say "ball," he looks toward the ball storage basket and often will start crawling in that direction. He connects the word with an object. His curriculum includes making frequent conversations, listening to books read to him, playing games that name objects, and hearing responses from his caregiver to his use of language. Infants are continually developing language during this period of their lives.

Responding to sounds and use of language also affects an infant's **emotional development.** He learns what creates or causes pleasure or displeasure and how to obtain comfort. Infants also learn how to express feelings. Remember when Luke knocked on the window while his brother was playing outside? He had learned that this gesture would catch someone's attention and he might be able to interact with his brother. A major curriculum goal includes responding to an infant's feelings. This response helps him feel more secure and understand that he is empowered to interact with and have an impact on his own environment.

Journal 7.7: In Chapter 3, in the discussion of child development and developmental theories, you read about the different developmental domain: cognitive, social, emotional, and physical. Describe a play situation for an infant where these developmental areas might be incorporated into one activity. ■

Care giving as curriculum. Since care-giving routines are designed for an individual infant, the curriculum or daily schedule of activities differ for each child. Luke prefers three short naps each day, whereas Emory has a morning and afternoon nap. Emory arrives earlier in the morning than Luke and leaves by 4:00 P.M. Her **individual plan** is adjusted to meet her needs. For instance, Emory occasionally takes longer morning naps and then decreases the length of her afternoon nap. Her caregiver, Caryl, pays attention to changes in her routine and notes changes on her Daily Log. Diapering and eating times are also accommodated on each individual schedule. Caregivers learn when their infants need snacks, or seem to want early or late lunches. Of course, such schedules are adjusted daily to meet infant needs.

Looking back at the role of a caregiver and the 10 principles of care giving that Gonzalez-Mena and Eyer developed, can you see the curriculum for infants embedded within these principles? The exchange between the caregiver and the infant during lunch becomes a learning situation for the infant. Kristine talks about bananas with Luke, naming the fruit as she talks about his action of picking up a banana. She asks, "Would you like another piece of this yellow banana?" The language she uses is rich and descriptive, and her tone is calm and conversational.

Kristine also gives Luke her full attention as she communicates with him. When she is feeding Luke his bottle, Kristine often sits on the couch in the living room area. She talks quietly with Luke, talking about his family, their day together, or planned activities. **Care-giving interactions** are opportunities to enhance the healthy development of infants. Kristine continually involves Luke in each care-giving activity. She is not doing something *to* him, but *with* him. This philosophy of care giving empowers Luke to become an active participant in his care, learning about himself and his world in the process.

Journal 7.8: Describe an interaction between Kristine and Luke that represents the philosophy that caregiving is curriculum. What might Luke be learning in this interaction? ■

Play as part of the infant care program curriculum. **Play** is an integral component of curriculum in early childhood programs, including infant care programs. When you observed the Mentor Graphics Infant Care Program, you saw that infants did not require

Meagan notices a lot going on around her from a safe viewpoint.

highly stimulating toys, bouncy chairs, or other apparatus to learn. They do need a close relationship with a nurturing, observant caregiver. Infants learn best when they feel safe and trust the person caring for them. They also learn through interacting with objects in their environment. An infant might pick up a block and try to place it in his other hand. During this action, he is learning to transfer an object using eye-hand coordination and small muscle control. Doing these actions *for* the child does not help his growth and development. He must have the opportunity to physically go through these motions at his own speed and for as long as he is satisfied and interested in the learning. When an infant learns on his own, he is adding to "his emerging sense of positive self-esteem and love of learning" (Greenberg, 1993, p. 108).

The environment or setting of the play area affects the learning that takes place through infant play. Infants need a protected place, free from older children running through the area, dropping toys, or otherwise placing the infant in danger. Infants who are not yet walking are safest on the floor or carpet, where they can begin to learn to roll over, creep, crawl, and pull up on nearby furniture. When the infant play area is safe and free of obstacles, adults have more time to spend observing or interacting with infants, assuming a less directive role in the infant's play.

Quiet time.   Infants also need **quiet time** during the day. With several other infants and caregivers in one setting, naturally, there is a lot of activity and stimulation. Quiet time provides an opportunity for an infant to regroup. Some infants wake up from their naps and seem to be thinking while laying in their cribs until a caregiver arrives. This might be their quiet time. Other infants might like to spend some time in a quiet part of the care center, where they might relax and look around for a few minutes. Again, this is an individual need. Some infants like several quiet breaks each day, whereas others seem to be able to find their own quiet time within the day.

Care giving, play, and quiet time form the curriculum in an infant care program. The curriculum also reflects the philosophy and goals of the program. In Luke's infant care program, each caregiver worked with three infants and their families. Kristine learned the priorities and needs of her three families and planned curriculum accordingly. She also developed close, nurturing relationships with each infant. These relationships reflect the philosophy of the Mentor Graphics Child Development Center and were evident when analyzing the curriculum of the infant care program. Curriculum for any program must be based on developmentally appropriate practices and on the philosophy and goals of the program. Appropriate curriculum for infants "should be built into the infant's every experience" (Gerber, 1981, p. 84).

Curriculum development and curriculum implementation are responsibilities of each caregiver. Now let's explore the different roles of staff who work in infant care programs and their preparation or education.

Infant Care Programs and Staff

Programs for infants require a special type of teacher or caregiver. Knowledge of infant development, interest in working closely with families, and understanding the importance of nurturing while providing opportunities for exploration are essential requirements for the position of infant caregiver. Let's look at some of the different positions that might be available in an infant care program, along with the training or education needed for each position.

Infant care program director or coordinator. Depending on the size of the program, there is a **program director or coordinator** who is responsible for administrative duties. That individual might also be a caregiver part of the day. The director is responsible for program budget, facilities, communicating with parents and the community, supervising staff, enrolling children, meeting codes established by state and local agencies, and preserving continuity of the program philosophy and curriculum. Although requirements vary, most programs require that the director has a bachelor's or master's degree in early childhood education, some coursework in program administration, and three or more years of care giving or teaching in a similar program. The program director sets the tone for the program and is the liaison between parents, caregivers, and the community.

Infant caregiver. Since the **caregiver** is directly responsible for a small group of infants, she must have a solid understanding of infant development and be able to translate this knowledge into appropriate care-giving and play experiences. She must also have the "ability to work with infants warmly, calmly, and in an unhurried way" (Gordon, 1988, p. 47). Most programs expect their caregivers to have an associate degree with coursework in child development or early childhood education, along with experience working with infants.

Infant caregiver assistant.   The **caregiver assistant** is also responsible for a small group of infants. A characteristic of quality caregiver assistants is continued interest in learning about infant care and early childhood education. Most assistants have completed high school and several courses or workshops in child development. A program director would be more likely to hire candidates who had prior experience in early childhood education and a commitment to reading and learning more about infancy and child development.

One of the best ways that a center can ensure that their staff keeps current with the best practices in infant care is to encourage caregivers to attend workshops or courses in early childhood education, specifically those focused on infant care. All staff should participate in professional development in order to continue to build their knowledge base in infant care practices.

Professional Development

Many centers find that **continuing education** plays a key role in keeping staff knowledgeable of infant care practices. Continuing education provides opportunities for staff to improve and expand their knowledge base. At the same time, this continuing education or **professional development** also assists staff to reflect on and shape their program philosophy as they consider curriculum and activities appropriate for infants.

Examples of professional development activities include participating in workshops, courses, a planned degree program, or professional conferences on early childhood education. In addition to outside resources, on-site staff may hold expertise in a specific area and might share this expertise with the rest of the staff. Some infant care programs find that setting aside one afternoon a month to work together on professional development greatly improves their shared knowledge.

Early childhood educators recognize that the knowledge in their field is expanding rapidly. Continuing education is required to keep up with the latest research findings. For example, the prior discussion on brain research with infants translates into the need to provide rich, stimulating experiences for all infants. Attending workshops or courses that help caregivers plan curriculum for their infants based on new knowledge in brain research will affect the learning environment of the infants.

As recent as 10 years ago, there was little knowledge about working with drug-affected infants. It is important to learn about the best practices to help these infants, as the number of drug-affected infants has increased significantly. Caregivers can acquire a repertoire of ways to comfort and help drug-affected infants develop, as infants respond differently to their prenatal exposure to drugs. Alcohol- and drug-affected infants may exhibit a variety of behavioral and cognitive symptoms (Edelstein, 1995). Participating in courses or workshops about caring for drug-affected infants is another example of professional development.

Many caregivers assess their own professional knowledge base and seek continuing education to expand their learning. Some centers choose an annual theme for professional development, such as working with families or language development, and offer to pay for workshops and programs that support these themes. Providing funds for continued education is one of the most cost-effective ways that a center can ensure continual professional growth of their staff.

Having discussed infant care programs, curriculum of these programs, and the staff preparation and roles of infant programs, let's turn to some current issues and trends in infant care. These issues are in the midst of much debate and discussion. As you read this section, think about your personal stance or views on these issues.

Current Issues and Trends in Infant Care Programs

Role of Family

In the past 20 years, there has been increased "interest on the role of the family in the care and education of young children" (Powell, 1989, p. 1). A family, after all, does have extensive knowledge about their infant. Partnerships between infant caregivers and families "build bridges for children between their worlds of home and child care, helping them feel safe, secure, and happy in both places" (Dombro, 1995, p. 22).

Journal 7.9: What were some communication formats that George and Kristine used to bridge the worlds of home and child care for Luke? Briefly describe two different formats you might select to use. ■

Parents are experts about their child's particular needs, dislikes, and preferences. Caregivers have worked with different infants over a period of time and have gained a perspective of child development that can help the family "understand their child in terms of a broad spectrum of development" (Dombro, 1995, p. 23). Caregivers can also assist parents in parenting skills and can offer support to parents, which leads to a better environment for the infant (Miller, 1995).

As more is learned from research conducted by those who study infant care programs, more support is given to actively **involving families** in infant care. Parents are the infant's most important people (Dombro, 1995) and their involvement in infant care enables them to see and share what the infant experiences on a daily basis. Families that have a Daily Log to refer to, along with a brief chat with the caregiver, feel that they were part of the infant's day and are aware of events that occur in their child's life. Communication between caregivers and families supports continuity in the infant's life through the sharing of information and ideas.

Curriculum Issues and Infant Care Programs

The issue of curriculum resurfaces with the push to increase academics in early childhood programs. It seems that curriculum for each age group is sometimes being pushed to the next lowest age group, creating the "hurried child" (Elkind, 1981). Although the model of individual programs for infants is accepted as the "best" model, financial concerns may overrule this priority, creating programs more group oriented and increasing the ratio of children to caregiver.

Courtney is busily exploring different perspectives from her cube. This corner of the room has a padded mat to ensure safety for infants.

You may have seen advertisements for reading programs for infants, or programs that expectant mothers can purchase that will supposedly raise their child's IQ while still in the womb. In contrast, Elkind (1981) has an important message about infancy. He feels that this is the time when children develop their basic concepts about the world and "form their most critical attachments and social orientations" (p. 100). This learning and development takes "time and effort and cannot be rushed" (p. 100). Infants who feel safe and secure are ready to explore their world and learn through these explorations. The curriculum should fit the child, rather than the infant fit an established curriculum or expectations beyond his developmental level.

Should Companies Sponsor or Support Infant Care Programs?

Each morning, George arrives at work with his two sons. His first stop is the Child Development Center. Then off George goes to his job, knowing that his children are nearby and in an optimal child care environment. His employer, Mentor Graphics Corporation, is dedicated to providing benefits to employees that help them in the workplace, whether this means professional development opportunities, an on-site gym and trails for exercising, or sponsoring a quality child care program.

Ralph Larson, Chair of Johnson and Johnson, states, "By recognizing and supporting the child care responsibilities of our employees, we are investing in our future" (Neugebauer, 1991b, p. 5). Some employers contract with a child care center, but other options include creating an employer-owned and operated child care center, or providing financial assistance for participation in a nearby child care center. Perhaps the most pressing issue is not availability of child care, but availability of high-quality child care. More corporate executives are becoming aware of the need for high-quality child care and the devastating results of poor child care on both the infant and the parent. With this knowledge, companies are stepping in to fill the large gaps between what is available and what is needed in child care, especially for infants.

Starting Points: Meeting the Needs of Our Youngest Children (Carnegie Task Force, 1994) reports the findings and recommendations of a group of experts who examined the issue of the need for quality child care. The co-chairs of this task force, Eleanor Maccoby and Julius Richmond, found that there is a growing awareness of the **"quiet crisis"** in the lives of many young children, which affects their lives and the future of our nation. One of the areas targeted for improvement is substandard child care. According to *Starting Points,* corporations can play a role in changing the current status of young children by creating more family-friendly workplaces that include on-site or nearby child care along with options for flexible work schedules (Russell, 1994).

Today, there is more interest on the part of the employee and the employer in child care as an option within employee benefits. But Employees are not the only ones who benefit when their children are in a high-quality, nearby child care program. As Earl Hess, President of Lancaster Laboratories shares, "Initially the decision to set up child care came from the heart. But now we know it makes good business sense, too. The center helps us recruit in a tight labor market, keep valued employees, and increase job satisfaction" (Neugebauer, 1991b, p. 5). Indeed, there are many benefactors from employer-sponsored child care.

Journal 7.10: When you visited with George, Luke's dad, he mentioned several advantages to having Luke in an infant care center at his work site. What would you select as an important reason for employer-sponsored infant care and why? ■

Social Issues and Policies in Infant Care

Major social issues directly related to infant care programs include the growing number of mothers of infants entering the work force, an increased recognition of the need for quality programs for infants, and equal access to quality programs for all families. In Chapter 12, you will read about social influences on early childhood, so the discussion in this section will briefly focus on issues pertinent to infant care. You have been reading about the importance of quality care for infants and factors that contribute to a high-quality infant care program. How does a family find a program that meets their needs and expectations? This is a dilemma faced by many parents as they search for good programs for their infants.

Over half of all infants in the United States are in some type of infant care, whether the program is in a family home, a relative's home, or an infant care center. The number of infants expected to need infant care continues to increase. This trend translates into a considerable need for infant care programs. Throughout this chapter, you have read about the importance of the relationship between an infant and his primary caregiver, and how critical this bond is in creating a rich environment for the infant. The establishment of standards and government funding for infant programs are ways that society can influence the quality and availability of programs. Needs for infant programs vary in the staffing ratio and in the type of structure and setting for the infant. These needs must be addressed in the standards that are developed and reflected in the design of quality infant care programs.

Development during infancy affects a child for the rest of his life. All children in infant care should have access to quality infant care. This is the responsibility of the community, both in terms of the local community and the broader community of the nation. Legislature, funding, and establishment of standards that promote both quality infant care programs and access to infant care programs address social issues and the development of policy affecting infant care.

PRINCIPLES AND INSIGHTS: A Summary and Review

The more one learns about infant care, the more one comes to understand the importance of a quality care program for children of this age. Infant caregivers are important professionals who contribute greatly to the well-being and growth of infants and to the needs of young families. As you continue in your early childhood studies, you will undoubtedly be asked for recommendations of high-quality infant programs. Knowledge gained from this chapter will help you answer this questions as you apply your knowledge to local programs.

In discussions with others about infant care programs, you will likely bring up the critical role of the infant caregiver. The interaction or relationship between the infant and the caregiver forms the foundation of an individually designed program for each infant, based on her needs and those of her family. Besides the individual design of each infant's program, the caregiver also looks to developmentally appropriate activities and experiences for infants. Understanding infant development and application of infant development into curriculum is a key responsibility of each caregiver. Curriculum for infants is a combination of care giving and play, based on each infant's individual needs.

Another point you are likely to share is the family's role in infant care programs and the partnership between families and the caregivers. Frequent communication between the family and caregiver help each of them do a better job. You have learned several formats for communication from Luke's caregiver and you have seen how these worked with his family and Kristine. Caregivers learn much from each family about working with their infant, and families learn more about this special developmental period from the caregiver.

We have asked you to think about the larger issue of availability of infant care programs. Luke was participating in his father's employer-sponsored child care program. This is one approach to the growing need for child care programs. As more parents with young children enter the work force, the demand for infant care programs increases greatly. Who will care for these children and how will the quality of these programs be assured? Later in this book, you will read about becoming an advocate for young children, which is essential to the development of quality early childhood programs.

Infancy is a time of enormous learning and development. Special people are needed to provide interactions that stimulate and create safe, nurturing environments for infants, whether these people are parents or caregivers. Remember Mei-Ling and Jeff, Brynna, and Neil and Karen? They are the parents of the infants you met in the beginning of this chapter. Think how they might have felt if they had located infant care with a caregiver whose primary role was to create an individualized infant care program for their infant. Think how they might have felt if they were able to find a caregiver to build this program on the current knowledge base in infant development and developmentally appropriate practices. Although the infant care they found was adequate, did it meet your criteria for a high-quality infant care program? Our hope is that all families have access to state-of-the-art infant care, whether it be with relatives, child care centers, or family home care.

Becoming an Early Childhood Professional

Your Field Experiences

1. Make arrangements to visit an infant program, whether it's in a family home setting or a child care center. What types of activities are caregivers and infants involved in during the day? Would you characterize the curriculum as individualized to each infant's needs and developmental level? Why or why not?

2. Call a physical therapist in your area who works with infants and their families. During your interview with the therapist, find out how the therapist determines if a child has physical development delays. What are some physical therapy activities specific to infancy?

1. Expand on Journal Entry 7.5. How does a caregiver show respect for an infant? Do you think an infant knows if she is respected? Put your thoughts about this topic in your portfolio.

Your Professional Portfolio

2. Pretend you are the parent of an infant and develop a Good-Bye Plan for your family. What might be a good routine when you leave your infant in the care of someone else? When finished, share your plan with someone else in your class and place it in your portfolio.

Your Professional Library

Books

Brazelton, T. B. (1992). *Touchpoints: Your child's emotional and behavioral development.* Reading, MA: Addison-Wesley.

Gerber, M. (Ed.). (1979). *Resources for infant educators: A manual for parents and professionals.* Los Angeles: Resources for Infant Educators.

Griffin, A. (1993). *Preventing preventable harm to babies: Promoting health and safety in child care.* Arlington, VA: Zero to Three.

Lally, R. J., & Steward, J. (1990). *Infant/toddler caregiving: A guide to setting up environments.* Sacramento: California State Department of Education.

Mangione, P. L. (Ed.). (1995). *Infant/toddler caregiving: A guide to culturally sensitive care.* Sacramento: California State Department of Education.

Surbeck, E., & Kelley, M. (Eds.). (1990). *Personalizing care with infants, toddlers, and families.* Wheaton, MD: Association for Childhood International.

Internet Addresses and World Wide Web Sites

http://www.zerotothree.org
  Zero to Three (current information and research on many aspects of infant and toddler development)

http://www.exnet.iastate.edu/pages/nncc/child.Dev/grow.infant.html
  Growing Together: Infant Development

http://www.kidsource.com/kidsource/content/infant_care.html
  Infant Child Care

http://odshp.osophs.dhhs.gov/pubs/HP2000/14mom2.htm
  Healthy People 2000: Maternal and Infant Health

http://www.aap.org/
  American Academy of Pediatrics (Information on infants' and young children's health, safety, and other related topics)

http://www.iamyourchild.org/
  I Am Your Child (brain research and how it affects infant's lives)

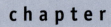

Toddler Care

IBRAHIM'S STORY

When you finish reading and reflecting on this chapter, you will be able to:

1. Describe the concept of *emergent curriculum* and why it is appropriate for toddlers.

2. Assess the appropriateness of materials and equipment, activities, environments, and adult interactions for toddlers.

3. Plan appropriate activities or select materials for toddler play.

4. Develop awareness of bias and stereotypes in yourself and others.

5. Interpret a toddler's needs, interests, and interactions.

In Chapter 2, we promised that you would never get bored around a toddler, and here's a chance to prove it. Gather your energy and concentration! You are about to join four other adults and a room full of toddlers. The location is a toddler program at a university laboratory school.

Visiting the Helen Gordon Child Development Center

The expression *the calm before the storm* needs to be reversed to describe the situation into which we are entering. It's truly "the storm before the calm" and anyone who has been around a toddler or a group of toddlers when they are tired knows what we mean.

Meeting Ibrahim and His Peers

It's 12:35 P.M., and at first glance it looks like bedlam in this room full of toddlers. Amidst the noise and movement, however, everyone seems comfortable and engrossed in their routines. There's soft music playing in the background. At one rectangular table, Harry eats two peanut butter sand-

wiches, one in each hand. He's completely focused on the sandwiches, and stops only to pour himself a glass of juice. When he finishes, another toddler, Ibrahim, reaches for the pitcher and spills the small amount of remaining juice. He becomes upset, but is quickly assured by Cindy, one of the adults, that it is not a problem: "It's OK, Ibrahim. You can wipe it up." She hands him a sponge, but he continues to fuss. Cindy, realizing that he is upset about his shirt sleeve being wet, responds with, "Let's go get another shirt out of your cubbie, and we'll hang this one up so that it can dry while you're resting." Ibrahim takes her hand and looks more relaxed about the situation.

At the table in a nearby chair is Ruth, repeating whenever an adult is near, "More watermelon." Occasionally, one of the early childhood teachers reminds her that there isn't any more, but Ruth is

287

determined. Haley, with her wide face and blunt cut bangs of auburn hair, is walking round with her pacifier in her mouth, dragging her blanket, and whining a little to herself. In an adjacent room leading to the bathroom, two children struggle to remove their slacks and underwear. One of them, Andy, shouts, "I need my diaper, Darren," and he is assured from across the room by Darren, "I'll be right there to help you." Several toddlers are placing their plates in the tub of water and suds, and some are settling onto cots that have been placed around the two rooms that make up the toddler area. Everyone appears to have a routine and there's plenty of adult support.

Suddenly, Rikku cries out and Jennifer tries to comfort him, asking, "What's wrong?" He sobs loudly that his blanket is gone, and she takes his hand, saying softly, "Let's go and look for it together." They look around the room and in all of the cubbies. In a nearby room, Alex is sound asleep. He went to sleep as soon as he and his friends came in from the play yard. "Alex was too tired to eat," Jennifer tells Rikku as they walk by the sleeping child. "Me, too," sniffs Rikku.

With his blanket found and under his arm, Rikku heads for one of the cots. Jennifer tells him and Anita, who is already resting on the next cot, "I'll get you two some books to read while you relax." She returns and sits between the children. "Which book would you like me to read?" she asks.

Anita points to the animal book and Rikku says, "Me, too." She begins to read softly to the two children. On the other side of the room, Heather is rubbing the backs of children who are just starting to rest. The room is beginning to quiet, but we still hear Ruth asking for more watermelon and from the bathroom there's one last request for a diaper.

Meeting Individual Needs

Assured that most of the children are starting to sleep, Jennifer goes to Ruth and sits next to her at the table. "You really liked that watermelon, didn't you?" she asks Ruth. With the beginning of a whine, Ruth talks about wanting more. Jennifer explains again that there isn't any more watermelon, "But I have an idea for you," she gently tells Ruth. "Before you go to sleep, let's write a note to your dad and ask him to buy you some watermelon at the store after work today. Then you can have some for supper. Would you like that?" Ruth nods, and Jennifer brings a piece of paper to her and they begin to write the note.

We see that Darren is wrapping up a lunch for Alex so that when he wakes up, he will be able to eat. The other early childhood teachers are still rubbing backs or reading softly, and soon most of the toddlers are asleep. Ruth is feeling better and ready to rest, too. Jennifer takes her hand and walks to Ruth's cot with her.

We're at the Helen Gordon Child Development Center, a university lab school in the heart of the city. We stopped here in Chapter 1, as we acquainted you with the range of options in the early childhood profession. The Center is 23 years old, is nationally accredited, and is a pride of the university and the community. The center staff works hard to attract a diverse group of children and to hire a diverse staff. The program has featured an antibias curriculum for about five years and the staff continues to study and assess their practices to assure that children are not learning bias in their classrooms as they learn about their world. You will see evidence of their commitment to antibias curriculum as we spend time with the toddlers. Many parents are very involved in the Helen Gordon Center. The staff values their participation and pursues it in varied ways. We will talk to some of the staff and get to know one set of parents later, but for now, it's back to the toddler room.

Remember that your observations of children are intended to help you learn about their development and the characteristics of their age. Your observations of the interactions between adults and children will provide models for you of good practices in terms of curriculum, guidance and discipline, materials and equipment, and parent involvement. Look around the room, listen to the conversations, and watch the children and adults for ideas about how to work with toddlers.

Meeting the Needs of Toddlers

If you had been here in the toddler room at 8:40 A.M., you would have seen the children arrive with their parents. Darren and Jennifer are the early childhood educators in this toddler program and they're both working in an area near the door. As children come in, they stop and greet each child and adult. We hear: "What a bright yellow jacket you are wearing today, Haley! How are you feeling?" "Rikku, you and your dad look like you got a good rest last night." "Good morning, Ibrahim. Good morning, Faridah. How are you this morning?"

A little more sleep. One of the children, Bryanna, arrived exhausted. "She just didn't sleep well. I could barely get her up, but I have to get to class," sighed her mom. "Bryanna, would you like to rest a little more?" Darren asks. She nods her head wearily and walks to a little adjoining room with two cots. "I sleepy" she says, with a little whine in her voice. Within minutes, she is sound asleep. Some of the toddlers are clinging to parents and others have forsaken their parents and are happily engaged in play. Audrey and Melissa are already sitting at a table with play-dough and accessories, and other children are climbing in and out of a wooden structure.

A quick breakfast. Ruth arrives with her dad, carrying a tiny paper bag. "Ruthie is going to eat her breakfast for a few minutes," her dad tells the two early childhood educators. "It was a hectic morning at home, so we went to the bakery on our way. Ruthie, tell them what you picked out, honey," her dad asks. Ruth opens the little bag and pulls out a croissant. She looks at her dad and says sadly, "I for-

Ruth and her dad spend time together before he leaves her at the center. How does this help Ruth make the transition into her day away from home?

get." He hugs her and says. "That's OK. It's a croissant." He pulls a bagel out of his bag and Ruth shouts, "Bagel." "Yes, a bagel is dad's favorite," her dad responds. They eat together until Ruth appears to be satisfied and ready to play.

Curriculum and Guidance with Toddlers

Soon, there are 16 children present. Two early childhood student teachers, Heather and Cindy, have arrived, making the ratio 4 children to 1 adult. We watch and note that children do not have to do much waiting for attention or for assistance. The adults move about, making themselves available to facilitate problem solving or to guide behavior whenever necessary. When Kim and Dion squabble over a favorite toy, Darren approaches them. "Kim, I know that you want that camera, but Dion had it first. While you wait, would you like to help me check the play yard to see if everything is in order?" Kim appears happy to join Darren. Once outside, Kim notices a puddle and crouches down to touch the water. Darren immediately walks over to her and watches. Kim proceeds to pat the water and watch the ripples. Darren waits and then says, "You're making ripples. When you pat the water, you're making ripples." We hear Kim say softly to herself, "Ripples . . . ripples . . . ripples."

Beginning literacy.   On the other side of the room, Cindy, one of the student teachers, is reading *The Very Hungry Caterpillar* to two children who are sitting near her legs and listening quietly. Another child stands next to her, rubbing her hair. "Let's read it together," suggests Cindy. The children obviously know the story, because they join in the familiar phrases. As Cindy reads each phrase of the book, the toddlers finish each page with, "But he was still hungry." As we listen, we can feel the children's excitement as they continue filling in the words. They are experiencing reading and there's a thrill that accompanies their sense of accomplishment. We hear Cindy affirm their efforts with, "You really know how to read *The Very Hungry Caterpillar!*"

Essential limits.   While they were reading, Rikku climbed up the adjacent bookshelf and now he looks like he's about to jump. Cindy turns to him, saying, "You can sit up there, and you can climb up and down, but you can't jump." Rikku sits and watches the children's activities in the nearby house center. Cindy remains on the floor near him and waits. "Would you read me a story?" Rikku asks. "Sure," Cindy answers. "Come and

pick out a book that you would like to hear." He climbs down from the shelf and looks at the book selection.

Diversity in the environment.   As Rikku studies the book possibilities, we move near him and observe the choices for toddlers. We see that there is a variety of books with fairly simple text and lots of excellent illustrations or photos. We also see different cultures represented in the book selections, such as

> *A Is for Aloha* by S. Feeney (University of Hawaii Press, 1985)
>
> *Hello Amigos* by T. Brown (Henry Holt & Co., 1986)
>
> *Do I Have a Daddy?* by J. W. Lindsay (Morning Glory Press, 1982)
>
> *Rehema's Journey* by B. A. Margolis (Scholastic Inc., 1990)
>
> *All the Colors We Are* by K. Kissinger (Redleaf Press, 1994)

As we walk through the room, we note the various posters and artwork hanging on the walls. There's a Persian Alphabet Tree and a colorful poster of a preschool classroom with the title El Espuerzo Bien Vale la Pena Lleva a Tus Hijos a Vacunar. We also see a measuring chart with photos of children from four different cultures. Pictures of families decorate all the walls, and we review them to see what kinds of families are represented: an African American couple, a Hispanic dad and baby, two Anglo girls, an African American mom holding a briefcase and hugging her son, and a Chinese toddler with two adults. The diversity represented in this toddler environment makes us want to learn more about the antibias curriculum emphasis of this center.

In the small adjoining playroom, we see large graphs drawn on chart paper: one is titled Our Eye Colors and the other is called Our Hair Colors. There are also collections of photos of the children on field trips. In both rooms, we notice that there are labels on items in the room—clock, window, door, books, and so on.

In the bathroom is a shelf full of boxes of disposable diapers. Each box is labeled with a child's name. There are two small sinks and toilets close to the floor, all with the label *sink* or *toilet*. We notice a large box of extra clothes and bottles of sunscreen on the shelf. There's also posters urging children to wash their hands.

Safety with toddlers.   As we look across the room, we see that Ibrahim has put a pail on his head and is pretending to be a monster. He tries to walk around but bumps into shelves and the wall and almost knocks himself over. Jennifer is watching and decides that Ibrahim is going to get hurt. She stops him by putting her arms around his waist and says, "Listen to my words, please. I don't want you to get hurt, and when you can't see where you are going, you could get hurt. You've been bumping into things and I'd like you to wear the pail in a way that lets you see." Ibrahim looks at her, takes off the pail and places it on a shelf, and runs off to the table where he left his helicopter. He brings it back, saying, "It go round and round." "Yes, it spins," says Jennifer. "No, it go round and round." He continues to turn the wheels, making the propeller spin. "Have you been on a helicopter?" asks Jennifer. Ibrahim just looks at her, offering no answer. "Have you been on an airplane?" she asks. "Yes," he says, "I go with my father." He goes and gets an airplane off the shelf and shows Jennifer that it doesn't have a propeller. He sits down at the table and plays with the helicopter, but he becomes distracted by the group of children at the other side of the room who are doing a finger-play. We hear:

"Rolly Polly up up up. Rolly Polly up up up.
Rolly Polly out out out. Rolly Polly out out out.
Rolly Polly clap clap clap. Rolly Polly clap clap clap.
Rolly Polly roll to your lap."

Participation from a distance.   Ibrahim stays at his table but he begins to do the motions to the finger-play and his mouth is moving with the words.

Another toddler sits across from him and we notice that he, too, is mouthing the words. When the group finishes the finger-play, Ibrahim goes back to his helicopter, saying, "Round and round." During this time, several children have gone outside with Bob, another educator. When we watch them, it's obvious that the large wheel toys are their favorites—doll carriages, wagons, a pretend lawnmower, and several very sturdy tricycles.

Toddler persistence.   Ibrahim has gone outside, and soon we see him opening the door and trying to bring a rolling cart into the classroom. Bob stops Ibrahim and says, "The cart stays outside." Ibrahim continues to push it through the doorway, as if he didn't hear. Bob repeats, "It stays outside." As Ibrahim continues to push it in, Bob takes the handle from Ibrahim's hands and turns it around, saying, "It needs to stay outside and I'm going to push it out." Ibrahim shows no response and runs outside to join a group of children.

If we had been watching these toddlers in September or October, soon after they began coming to this program, several of the incidents like the one between Ibrahim and Bob may have resulted in a temper tantrum, or with Ibrahim protesting loudly, "No," or holding tightly to the cart and refusing to let go. As 2-year-olds, many of these children were asserting themselves and doing so at every opportunity. It's May, however, and most of these children have celebrated their third birthday and have begun to develop some social maturity. The tenacity and the "nos" remain, along with an occasional temper tantrum, but, in general, these children are exhibiting a willingness to conform to the expectations of others.

Taking turns.   Throughout the morning, individual children have been painting at the easels set up along the wall. Now, the easels are empty, and we hear Darren going around the room, asking children, "Would you like a turn at the easel?" Most of the children are very involved in another activity, but Melissa nods her head to indicate that she would like a turn. Haley is watching and shouts,

"Me, too. My turn at the easel." Darren walks with the girls over to the easels and they begin to paint. He tells us, "We keep a list each day of the activities for which children have to wait for a turn." He adds, "We don't like to have children waiting, but with activities like painting at the easels, we can't manage more than these three easels at a time. In the beginning of the year, it was hard for the children to wait. They would hang around the easels because they weren't certain that they would really get a turn. But now, they go off to other activities; they know that we keep a list so that we remember to find them and offer a turn. We also assure them with information such as 'Ned is having a turn, and you will follow him.' "

Finger painting is an important activity for toddlers. What aspects of development are addressed by this painting activity?

Reviewing Our Observations

Soon, the group will be getting ready for lunch and Ruth will want her watermelon. We're going to stop and reflect for a few minutes about what you have seen in the toddler classroom. Remember: Your observations are a source of information about the children and their programs. We think that you can come up with sound ideas about early childhood programs for toddlers from even a brief morning of observations.

Journal 8.1: What characteristics of toddlers' development became apparent as you watched their play and interactions with people and objects? Consider their motor development, their social development, their emotional development, and their language. What are they able to do? ■

Journal 8.2: What kind of guidance strategies did you see as you watched the early childhood educators handle problems or situations that could turn into problems? For example, recall when Ruth insisted on more watermelon, or when Kim and Dion were struggling over a camera, or when there was the potential for Ibrahim to hurt himself. ■

Accommodating toddler development and using appropriate guidance strategies are the heart of a good program for toddlers. Attending to the developmental characteristics of toddlers is first and foremost in terms of programming for them. Because they are active explorers developing autonomy, the kind of guidance strategies adults use with toddlers will determine whether they develop a sense of doubt and shame or a sense of autonomy. The curriculum is not a package, as you must have noticed. It appears to originate from the children, from the interactions with each other, the adults, the materials and equipment, and the environment. Darren and Jennifer call their curriculum **emergent curriculum**—curriculum that emerges from the children. Jones and Nimmo (1994) call emergent curriculum "a planning process that takes place among a particular group of people" (p. 1) and confirm that it isn't a plan or a product. We will explore that idea of curriculum in our conversations with Darren and Jennifer and the guidance that accompanies their way of working with the toddlers.

Toddler Development: Responding with Curriculum and Guidance

We hope that your observations of toddlers prompted your awareness of what toddlers are like and what their needs and interests are. Before we start, let's go back to our definition of *toddlers* from Chapter 2. We said that toddlerhood begins when a child starts walking and talking, somewhere around 12 months. Toddlerhood has been called a transition between infancy and childhood. Some educators think in terms of young toddlers, ranging from 12 months to 24 months, and older toddlers, ranging from 24 months to 36 months. Darren and Jennifer are really experts when it comes to toddler development and their ideas about curriculum and guidance will further your understanding of toddlers, in general.

Conversations with Darren and Jennifer

Darren arrives in plaid shorts, a T-shirt, and tennis shoes, a little breathless from his run from the kitchen. "I had to bake the children's cookies while they're resting," he tells us. He is the head teacher of the toddler room and he describes his responsibility as one of "keeping the room flowing so that all children have the opportunity to take advantage of all the materials/activities." He says that the most difficult part of his role is delegating to other staff and "helping them to see the big picture behind decisions." Jennifer arrives and is also dressed casually in slacks and a T-shirt. She is a mother of a young child (3 years old) herself and she feels that her role is ideal for blending career and parenting. Both Darren and Jennifer have degrees in early childhood education and have worked at the Center for several years.

Talking about curriculum.   We ask about the curriculum in the toddler program, and Jennifer immediately uses the term *emergent curriculum*. She expands with, "We build off of the children's interests or curiosities and develop materials and activities." Darren adds, "We spend a great deal of our time getting to know each child's strengths, interests, and experiences so that we can plan from the child." (Remember that the idea of curriculum originating with children was pioneered by early educators Maria Montessori and Friedrich Froebel. Both educators were avid observers of children and used their observational information to design play materials and activities [Spodek & Saracho, 1994b].)

Recalling the busy quality of the toddler room and the many interactions between adults and children, we ask about how these two educators maintain their information about the children. "We keep written notes about our observations of the children's interests, especially our conversations with individual children," Jennifer responds. Darren jumps in, "Bugs, caterpillars, worms, birds, animals, flowers—they're really into nature, the world around them."

From there, the two educators describe their efforts to integrate basic concepts of math, science, language, and other curricular areas. "It's pretty easy," Darren says, "Most of their interests lend themselves easily to such concepts as colors, counting, size, and vocabulary." Darren describes a recent interest in trucks and the ease with which they were able to focus all kinds of activities around trucks. He sheepishly admits, "Occasionally, some of the curriculum comes from us. I wanted to plant a garden, so I asked if any of the children would like to help me get a garden ready." Not surprisingly, the children were quite enthused about the garden and all of the related activities. Jones and Nimmo's (1994, p. 127) sources of emergent curriculum confirm using children's interests and teachers' interests as sources. Other sources include things in the physical environment, people in the social environment, curriculum resource materials, serendipity (that is, unexpected events), the daily tasks of living together, and values of the school, community, families, and cultures. If we were to observe for months, we would probably see all of those sources reflected in Darren and Jennifer's emergent curriculum.

Jennifer tells us that they repeat activities that they know the toddlers enjoy. Toddlers like repetition, so it makes sense. She says, "For example, they have consistent interest in play-dough—it's a security for them. They know it's there and they can always go to it."

Talking about guidance.   Although we observed numerous guidance strategies when we visited their classroom, guidance is such a prominent part of their work with toddlers that we wanted to discuss it further with Darren and Jennifer. "We try not to step in unless someone's having a really hard time or is affecting the other children." They describe their efforts to model language for the toddlers, knowing that many of their inappropriate behaviors come from the inability to express what they want or their lack of social skills. "When Rikku hurts Ibrahim, we encourage Ibrahim to tell Rikku how it feels," explains Darren, "And we encourage Rikku to talk about what he was trying to say or do when he hurt Ibrahim." The other response made by the educators is to look at the environment and remove something or change it to be sure that it supports the children's development. They talk about wanting to be certain that they are not contributing to the child's inappropriate behavior.

When all else fails, their final response in certain situations is to remove children from the group for a brief time period. That removal is often necessary for children to "settle down" and regain their composure. "We mostly talk with them about whatever happened and try to get them to talk about it," adds Jennifer.

It's almost impossible to separate those elements of programs for toddlers—development, guidance, and curriculum. In fact, another major source of emergent curriculum are the developmental tasks of the children. Toddlers are exploring every moment, and their exploration demands boundaries to keep them safe and to teach the rules of life. You will find that when we talk about an aspect of toddler motor development, we immediately connect that development with curriculum—an activity or kind of equipment that is appropriate to promote that aspect of development—and at the same time we remind you of the guidance needed for that development.

Observing Ibrahim in His Family Context

As we described them earlier, toddlers are active explorers. All of a sudden, they have the skills and the capacity to try out so many things. Their fine motor and gross motor abilities allow them to pursue all kinds of activities. At the same time, they're working very hard at becoming independent. "Toddlers are concerned about who they are and who is in charge" (Bredekamp & Copple, 1997). This is a time of "me do it" yet it is also a time when lots of security, comforting, and limits are needed from the adults in their lives. Many of the new adventures for toddlers are related to human interactions and to interactions with the world around them. A major part of the toddlers' world is their families. It is important to consider the context of family when observing children, so we visited Ibrahim's family in order to better understand his development and his activities at the center.

Visiting Ibrahim at home.   Ibrahim and his parents, Faridah and Amr, and his brother, Muhammed, live in a small apartment on campus. Their home is simply furnished and absent of much decoration. Faridah explains, "We can't put figures on the walls due to religious beliefs—besides, I prefer this spartan look." There is one mirror and children's drawings on the door. Each parent has a computer, one in the living room and one in the dining room. The boys have a closet for their belongings and some shelves for books, paper, and crayons.

The family is preparing to move because Faridah has taken a teaching position at a university in Malaysia. Faridah speaks Malay and Amr speaks Arabic. He teaches Arabic to adults and children, and consults with small businesses. English is the common language for the two parents.

The family has a flexible schedule in order to spend time with the boys. After Faridah, Muhammed, and Ibrahim leave the Center each day, they go home for supper. Some nights she eats with the boys, and on other nights, Amr eats with the boys. "We sit on the floor around a piece of oilcloth to catch the crumbs," Faridah describes for us when we ask about their family meals. The family observes some dietary rules of their Muslim religion and prays five times daily.

Muhammed described the boys' favorite activity as one of jumping and flying around the living room. He tells us, "Sometimes we put stickers all over us like feathers, but we never fly from the window—only from the couch." Faridah describes the boys' use of the couch pillows for dramatic play: "One day, they were pretending to be frogs, and they told me that the pillows were lilypads." The boys also play with large Legos, guns, and cars. Both parents read to the boys each night. Muhammed interrupts to tell us, "Our father reads usually one book when he puts us to bed." He says, "This one or this one and we have to pick." He continues with, "Our mom reads one or two or three books."

Our home visit to Ibrahim's family really helps us interpret his behavior at the Center. A look at the physical, social, emotional, and cognitive aspects of toddler development in the context of individual families will help you understand what we observed in Ibrahim's classroom and will give you the skills to predict what will happen in his class on other days or when he is at home with his family.

Physical Development: Curriculum and Guidance

Physical development includes extensive and expanding motor abilities, nutritional issues and eating habits, and highly individualized needs for sleep and rest. The changing quality of toddlers' physical development directs major components of an early childhood program—schedule, environment, number of adults, activities, and materials and equipment.

Motor development.   Toddlers (approximately 2 years and older) not only like to roll and jump and climb and run but they also are fairly good at those motor skills. They take great pride in pushing and pulling wheel toys and can steer well. The outdoor play space at the Helen Gordon Center has a variety of wheel toys as well as structures for climbing and jumping. Toddlers are not especially skilled at watching for others when jumping or steering, so they need constant supervision and occasional reminders to be careful of other children. We heard Jennifer frequently say, "When you get ready to jump, look around the ground to see if anyone else is there, so you are a careful jumper." A few of the children have begun to hang from the parallel bars, but they like to have Darren and Jennifer next to them. "It's scary," says Rikku, but his face is full of delight with his new skill.

Throwing and retrieving (sometimes catching) objects is a never-ending favorite activity for toddlers. A box near the door to the outdoor play space is full of all kinds of items to throw—basketballs, foam balls, rubber balls, bean bags, and plastic darts. Again, toddlers need reminders about appropriate places to throw balls and about being careful of others. Various receptacles for throwing balls and bean bags are both inside and outside. Boxes and baskets and even an old tire give toddlers places to aim for with their new throwing skills. Most toddlers have learned to stand on one foot, and you will observe them experimenting with that skill as they watch other children playing. Toddlers have also become quite skilled at walking on tiptoes. "Sometimes when we walk to the library or the grocery story, it takes a long time," describes Jennifer. She adds, "They're always experimenting with new ways to move, so we have to give ourselves plenty of time to get places, rather than rush them."

By age 2½, they have good hand and finger coordination and enjoy playing with small objects and manipulating their small parts. The play-dough trays and accessories are out on a table almost everyday in the toddler room, and there's a huge collection of plastic figures—zoo and farm animals, dinosaurs, cars and trucks, airplanes and helicopters, and people. They are also quite possessive of the figures, so there's potential for conflict. "It's one of the reasons why we have so many bins and pails of figures," Darren explains. If you were to watch the toddlers over a period of time, you would see that they enjoy putting many items in their mouths, so early childhood educators need to be watchful of these materials. Those situations offer an opportunity to teach toddlers about safety issues.

 Journal 8.3: Put yourself in the role of an adult who is talking with a toddler about putting toys or other small items in her mouth, ear, or nose, as toddlers are apt to do.

How would you talk to a child of age 2 or 3 about the dangers of her behavior? What would you do if the child continues to put small items in her mouth, nose, or ear?   ■

Their fine motor control also encourages toddlers to draw, paint, and enjoy other creative activities. The large colored markers are their favorite, but they also use crayons, colored chalk, tempera paint with brushes, finger paint, and blunt scissors. Early in the year, most of their drawing with markers and crayons was of scribble quality, but now many toddlers are making deliberate strokes, circles, and figures. They are frequently intrigued with drawing on themselves, on walls, or on unintended surfaces, so again, you will need to provide guidance for their artistic tendencies.

The finger-plays like "Rolly Polly" that we heard the toddlers chanting when Ibrahim decided to participate from a distance are another favorite activity to develop the small muscles of the hands as well as coordination. Finger-plays are a good example of activities that integrate many aspects of development simultaneously. In Figure 8.1, Diffily and Morrison (1996) offer their description and use of finger-plays for the development of communication with parents. It is an example of the kind of in-

■ **FIGURE 8.1**   Finger-Plays and Action Songs

Rhymes and movements for the hands and fingers, some of which date back almost 2,000 years, are still used in early childhood classrooms, as well as the more modern action songs that involve the whole body.

As children learn fingerplays and action songs, they learn the names of body parts, numbers, and shapes. They also learn other concepts and skills, including

- manual dexterity and muscle control;
- sense of rhythm of speech and music;
- new vocabulary;
- ability to follow directions;
- grasp of order and sequence;
- increased attention spans; and
- listening skills.

Fingerplays and action songs are a fun way to learn. They are a great way to pass a few minutes of transition time—while you are waiting in the car, in line at the grocery store, before or after dinner.

Children love repeating familiar rhymes, so come back to the same songs often enough that your child can learn the words of the rhyme and the movements that accompany the words.

Perhaps you remember a fingerplay from your childhood that you can share with us. If you would like to learn more fingerplays or action songs that are hits with kids of your child's age, just ask us—we'll be happy to share some great ones.

Source: Family-Friendly Communication for Early Children Programs by D. Diffily and K. Morrison (p. 48), 1996, Washington, DC: NAEYC. Copyright 1996 by NAEYC. Reprinted with permission from the National Association for the Education of Young Children.

Toddlers are not especially skilled at steering their toys, but their attempts are intense and a source of pride.

formation that the educators at the Center often send home to help parents understand the value of simple activities and to share some of the curriculum for use at home.

Speaking of tiny items, toddlers are able to thread beads and can enjoy the activity for brief time periods. If you watch toddlers in an activity such as threading beads, you will notice intense concentration and will also notice that most toddlers can't sustain the concentration for long periods. So, bead work is usually a brief activity, and, depending on bead size, one that probably should have close supervision.

Many of the materials and the kinds of equipment needed to stimulate and support toddlers' motor development will require close supervision. Environments for toddlers will also require careful maintenance to keep them safe in the midst of the children's very active play. Figure 8.2 displays a basic safety checklist that you could use to set up a classroom for toddlers. It can also be used for daily checking of the condition of equipment and materials.

Need for rest and sleep.   Toddlers have a great amount of energy, but most of them also require a significant amount of rest and sleep. As you observed in the toddler classroom, they can't keep going when they get tired—they just have to sleep. The sounds in the classroom just before naps reminded us of their need for sleep—whining, crying, demands for diapers, pacifiers in mouth—they seemed to be quite aware of their need and ready to give in to their exhaustion. Similar to the flexibility accommodating toddler appetites was the flexibility accommodating toddler fatigue levels. Remember how Bryanna went right to sleep as soon as she arrived in the toddler room one morning?

FIGURE 8.2   Classroom Safety Checklist

Art Area
___ Scissors use supervised
___ Water spills cleaned up
___ Hazardous materials eliminated (sprays, solvents, glazes, permanent markers)

Block-Building Area
___ Building space adequate
___ Blocks free from splinters
___ Construction height within limits
___ Toy accessories free from sharp edges, broken parts

Book Area
___ Floor area covered
___ Heating vents, pipes covered
___ Rocking chairs away from children on floor

Computer Area
___ Electric cords, plugs out of children's reach
___ Location away from water
___ Children seated with computer on low table or stand

Cooking Area
___ Cooking appliances in compliance with local safety codes
___ Electric appliances, microwave ovens controlled by adult
___ Sharp implement use supervised by adult
___ Number of children in area limited

Dramatic Play Area
___ Clothes hooks away from eye level
___ Plastic dishes, cutlery unbroken
___ Play jewelry, earrings, beads unbroken
___ Dolls, toys with no small removable parts (e.g., buttons)

Large Motor Area
___ Climbing, sliding equipment cushioned
___ Wheeled vehicle use controlled
___ Safety rules established and enforced by adult

Manipulative Area
___ Tiny beads, counters eliminated
___ Sharp or pointed objects eliminated
___ Objects with splinters, peeling paint, broken parts discarded

Music Area
___ Cords on record players, radios, tape recorders out of reach
___ Equipment using small batteries eliminated

Sand/Water Area
___ Sand or water spills cleaned up
___ Broken, rusty, or sharp-edged toys removed
___ Glass implements eliminated
___ Safety goggles used at sand table

Science/Math Area
___ Aquarium and incubator wires out of reach
___ Houseplants nonpoisonous

Woodworking Area
___ Adult-size tools supervised
___ Safety goggles used
___ Safety rules established and enforced by adult
___ Number of children limited

General Room Conditions
___ Floor covering smooth, unbroken, and untorn
___ Traffic patterns between areas clear
___ Heaters, pipes, vents covered and sectioned off
___ Electric cords, wires, plugs out of children's reach
___ Electric outlets covered
___ Smoke detectors in appropriate locations
___ Fire extinguishers accessible
___ Peeling paint removed, refinished
___ Broken furniture, toys removed, repaired
___ Sharp corners of room dividers padded
___ Emergency procedures, phone numbers, clearly posted

Bathroom
___ Sinks, toilets child-size
___ Stands, stools sturdy
___ Slippery floors cleaned up
___ Cleaning and disinfecting materials locked up
___ First-aid kit out of children's reach; accessible to adults

Stairs/Exits
___ Exits clearly labeled
___ Stair steps smooth, unbroken, of nonskid material
___ Carpeting, mats smooth, untorn, not slippery
___ Stair railings reachable by children
___ Two exits in every classroom
___ Stairs well lighted

Outdoor Playground
___ Playground enclosed with fence
___ Debris, broken glass removed
___ Cushioning under climbers, slides
___ Large equipment anchored in ground
___ Swings of safe material (belts, tires)
___ Young-child-size equipment used
___ Railings around high platforms, on steps
___ Sharp edges, missing or loose parts, splinters on equipment corrected
___ Adequate supervision when in use

Source: Skills for Preschool Teachers, 5th ed. by J. J. Beatty, © 1996. Reprinted by permission of Prentice-Hall, Inc., Upper Saddle River, NJ.

Toddlers are often exhausted from their exploration, successes, curiosity, and creativity.

She hadn't slept well the night before, so it was important to respond to her fatigue. Remember when Alex couldn't even make it to lunch because he was so tired from his morning of play? These two children needed long sleep periods, whereas other children in the room may take very brief naps and be ready to play again. What we aren't able to observe is the bedtimes and times of waking for all of the children. That kind of information would be helpful to the teachers and caregivers who respond to the children during the day. Some of the variation in children's need for sleep and rest is due to individual development and some is due to family scheduling. Notice that not only were the adults at the Helen Gordon Center flexible about the toddlers' need for sleep but there was also a small area out of the traffic where one or two toddlers could rest undisturbed. Both scheduling and the environment responded to the toddlers' individual variations in their rest and sleep patterns.

Eating and nutrition.   The eating habits of toddlers vary significantly from one to another, but also for individual toddlers from one day to the next. Jennifer noted that Harry was eating twice as much as anyone else for about a week now, but a month ago, he would barely eat anything. Most toddlers eat small amounts and need frequent snacks to support their energetic routines during the day. At the Helen Gordon Center, there is a morning snack, lunch, and an afternoon snack. Fruit or crackers are also available for those times when toddlers get hungry between snacks and lunch.

Toddlers' food preferences vary so much that meal planning for them is a challenge. Some of their preferences are influenced by their families and meals at home, but much of what looks like food preferences is a part of their development of who they are. You will see some toddlers ready to try anything as a kind of adventure, and then brag about it to all who will listen. You will also see some toddlers hesitant to try anything that looks different or that they haven't tried before. If you observe in the toddler room for a couple of weeks at the Helen Gordon Center, you will see a fairly basic menu with occasional seasonal additions such as watermelon. If you were to observe for several months, you would probably get bored with the lunch menu. The same foods are repeated over and over. Actually, the research on young children's food acceptance patterns has demonstrated that repeated exposures to specific foods increase children's acceptance of them (Sullivan & Birch, 1990; Birch, Johnson, & Fisher, 1995). The research also recommends getting children to taste new food with encouragement but not manipulation.

If we had observed the toddlers at the beginning of their lunchtime, we would have heard Haley announce, "I'm going to try these" (holding up her carrot sticks). Jennifer responded with, "Now you will know if you like carrots." Other children at the table chimed in that they did or did not like carrots. In the meantime, Haley took a generous bite, chewed briefly, then walked over to the bin where plates are scraped and spit out the carrots. She did so rather nonchalantly and no one seemed to pay attention; however, during the meal, several children copied her method of getting rid of food. It looked like they were trying out something new. Haley tried the carrot but decided that she didn't like it. No one made a fuss about her trying it or about her rejecting it. That feeling of acceptance and respect for her likes and dislikes will encourage Haley to try to learn to like many new foods. Beyond attention to minimum meal components and nutrient requirements, some tips for menu planning are helpful for all early childhood programs but especially useful for toddlers' meals. Figure 8.3 provides those basic tips.

Journal 8.4: Do you recall your childhood and how you learned to try new foods? What kind of approaches were used to get you to eat? Do you see any effect of your early eating experiences in your eating patterns today? Describe. ■

■ **FIGURE 8.3**   Tips for Menu Planning

- Offer a variety of colors, textures, temperatures, and flavors that encourage children to eat more and to try new foods. *Examples:* raw vegetables, applesauce, macaroni and cheese

- Prepare foods so that they retain natural flavors, aromas, and nutrients. Children may like raw fruits and vegetables better than cooked ones. *Examples:* raw broccoli, cauliflower, yams, green beans (especially with a dip)

- Serve children what they generally prefer—plain, identifiable foods. Casseroles and other combined foods are not typically appealing to children. *Examples:* potatoes and chicken bits, hamburger patties and noodles, ham slice and rice

- Offer choices to help ensure that children eat from each of the meal components. *Examples:* carrot and celery sticks, apple and pear slices

Toddlers are refining their abilities for feeding themselves (Poulton & Sexton, 1995/96) and are especially interested in serving themselves and pouring their own drinks. Spills are frequent and are generally not an issue for the children or adults. Did you notice that the adults barely responded to Ibrahim's spilled milk? Even the process of wiping up a spill is a motor activity and a move toward independence for the toddler. If you were to observe the toddler class for an extended time period, you would see that mealtimes offer very important learning opportunities for every aspect of development for toddlers.

When you look at the big picture of toddler physical development, you can see that they have developed both fine and large motor skills, so your program will provide a variety of opportunities, space, and equipment for them to use those skills. When you watch toddlers, you also see that their appetites and sleep habits are very much in flux, so your program will need to provide the flexibility and space arrangements to meet those needs. Bredekamp and Copple (1997) recommend the following practices for that flexibility:

- Time schedules are flexible and smooth, dictated more by children's needs than by adults'. There is a relatively predictable sequence to the day to help children feel secure. (p. 84)

- Adults respect children's schedules with regard to eating and sleeping. Toddlers are provided snacks more frequently and in smaller portions than older children. For example, two morning snacks are offered at earlier hours than the usual snack time for preschoolers. Liquids are provided frequently. Children's food preferences are respected. (p. 85)

Throughout our description of the physical development of toddlers and appropriate curriculum and guidance, the key words are *active* and *flexibility*. Toddlers are on the move and we must be constantly alert to keep them safe while supporting their need and drive to explore physically. That flexibility required of us means that toddlers won't have to conform their physical needs to our scheduling needs. What we saw in Darren and Jennifer's room and have discussed in the pages you just completed is *individually appropriate practice*. Bryanna's needs were met, and Rikku's needs were met, and the two children are quite different. You will note the same individuality with respect to social development, described in the next section.

Social Development: Curriculum and Guidance

Here are some familiar scenes in the toddler room at the Helen Gordon Center:

Haley comes up to Ruth and puts her arms around her and hugs tightly. Ruth objects and squeals, "No!" On another day, when Haley hugs her, Ruth may hug back, and the two girls will stand there for a time hugging and giggling.

Ibrahim is playing with the plastic dinosaurs and Rikku sits at the table next to him and watches. Without a word being said, Ibrahim hands one of the dinosaurs to Rikku, and the two of them play side by side.

Ned is playing with the plastic dinosaurs and Rikku sits at the table next to him and watches. Almost immediately, Ned scoops the dinosaurs into a little pile in front of him, and turns slightly away from Rikku.

At the play-dough table, Melissa and Ned are sitting next to each other. Each child is intensely working with play-dough, molding it with their hands, and only occasionally looking at the other child. There is no conversation. On other days, Ned may hand Melissa a piece of dough.

What we see in these scenarios is that toddlers are beginning to develop social maturity as they show affection for others, share occasionally, communicate with peers, and begin to play cooperatively. "Social contact among two-year-olds is brief and fleeting," but three-year-olds "seek out social interaction and want to be part of a group" (Hughes, 1991). People are more important to these toddlers than they were a year ago, and their increasing social skills have much to say to their early childhood educators about appropriate curriculum and guidance.

Sharing.   The ability to share is emerging in the toddler room, but it's difficult for Ned some days and easy for Ibrahim some days. That ability to share applies to toys, friends, the adults in the room, and attention. Depending on how they're feeling, toddlers can even take pleasure in sharing, but much depends on their levels of security and their experiences with sharing (Wittmer, 1996).

As in so many aspects of the toddler program, the adults are key to the development of sharing. First, they, along with each child's family members, are models of sharing. In the toddler room, we often hear Darren say, "I'd love to share my crayons with you. Let's color together" or "Would anyone like to share the play-dough with me?" The guidance used by the adults will also teach sharing. Although it's not always possible and not consistently a good idea, it is appropriate at times to encourage sharing. For example, when Ned pulls all of the animals toward him to shut out Rikku and keep him from taking one of the toys, Cindy notices that Rikku is just sitting and so she might urge Ned with, "It looks like Rikku would like to play with you," followed by, "Would you share a few animals with him?" Depending on the kind of day Ned is having, how he is feeling, and what kind of experiences he has had with sharing, he may say, "Sure" or "No" with great emphasis. As Hughes (1991) reminds us, "Toddlers enjoy being near other children, but they are still limited in their ability to share and to cooperate."

When we talked with Darren, he told us that many of the toddlers' parents wanted them to learn to share. "It's taken all year for most of the children to share some of the time. We think that forced sharing interferes with security, so we don't insist—we just encourage." So much of the toddlers' sharing is related to their simultaneous development of autonomy and identity that they must retain some control of that behavior. As they become more social, people matter more than objects and it becomes easier to give up that truck, or doll, or dinosaur.

Journal 8.5: Sharing is apparently quite important to parents and to educators. Reflect on why parents emphasize sharing to such an extent. Write a note to a parent who inquires about his toddler child's progress toward being able to share and explain why it's taking a long time to develop. ■

The importance of others.   Sharing is but one aspect of the social development of a toddler. Other social milestones (Bredekamp & Copple, 1997) include:

- Shows increased awareness of being seen and evaluated by others
- Sees others as a barrier to immediate gratification
- Begins to realize that others have rights and privileges
- Gains greater enjoyment from peer play and joint exploration
- Begins to see benefits of cooperation
- Identifies self with children of same age and sex
- Is more aware of the feelings of others
- Exhibits more impulse control and self-regulation in relation to others
- Enjoys small group activities (Bredekamp & Copple, 1997, p. 70)

Those milestones are not exhaustive and should probably all contain the word *sometimes*. They are written with attention to the changes from infancy, so when the milestone is "exhibits more impulse control," we are talking about them in comparison to their impulse control during infancy. Toddlers are changing so rapidly—progressing and regressing—that the milestones have a tentative quality. Look at those milestones again. Because they are about social development, they require other people.

Zeavin (1997) says that the critical factor in programs for toddlers is the *human environment*—other toddlers who are experiencing similar social development and adults who understand that development and respond to their "trial and error" with sensitivity and guidance. Every issue for toddlers is a relationship issue. Throughout their day, they express their relationships with materials, with adults, with peers, and with themselves.

Early childhood educators who work with toddlers are very loved by them—verbally and physically. Toddlers are fascinated with their caregiver adults and other adults in their lives. This is a time when they begin to project to their own future, to being in adult roles. Consequently, toddlers are very good at "being the teacher"—Darren may hear himself in the script as Rikku plays him, or as Haley plays Jennifer. Not only are they trying out adult roles but toddlers also use pretend play to expand their social understandings.

Social understandings.   One of the favorite activities of toddlers that develops social understandings and extends their interactions with others and their world is dramatic play. The toddler room at the Helen Gordon Center has extensive materials and equipment for pretend play—for example:

Dolls of all sizes and colors	Dishes, pots and pans, and plastic food
Child-size furniture	Blankets
Telephones	Suitcases
Dress-up clothes (shoes, purses, jackets, long skirts, and hats)	Broom and dustpan

Notice how basic these materials are and how many ways children play with them. Toddlers do not need extensive accessories for their pretend play.

 Journal 8.6: Be creative. Use your imagination and add five more items to the list of items for pretend play. Keep in mind simplicity and safety. ■

We did notice a large number of dolls in the toddler room—realistic dolls, dolls of different colors, large dolls, durable dolls and more—all unclothed and most looking like they had been bathed many times. Some early childhood educators see toddlerhood as the beginning of true doll play. The children give more meaning and characteristics to the doll, and the doll takes on more complex roles in pretend play. One day in the toddler room, Ruth had two of the dolls propped in chairs, one on each side of her. She had named them and they were her "babies." She had a dish and utensil in front of each and was encouraging them to "eat your supper all up." Ruth's mom would probably hear herself in that role—her expressions, her tone of voice, and her mannerisms.

Toddlers also begin to use materials to represent objects or props for their pretend play. One morning, Ned brought a tube of Chapstick to school and it became his "bone" as he played dog for part of the morning. Sometimes the large wheel toys became a bus or train for pretend play on the playground, or a bucket of sand became soup or a grocery item. Toddlers have begun to use their immediate world at preschool and at home to explore and make sense of their lives. Pretending with an adult is especially appealing to toddlers. Research has shown that 2- and 3-year-olds will sustain their pretend play much longer with an adult roleplaying with them than when they are pretending alone (Haight & Miller, 1993). Ned often says to one of the adults at the center, "Pretend I'm your dog" and they do. It's a pretend situation that he repeats almost daily, so it's comfortable for him. Research also shows that pretending with adults leads to pretending with peers. Pretending with a mom or an uncle provides practice and vocabulary, so that a child can get ready for playing and pretending with others.

Early cooperation.   In a few years, the toddlers we observed will be able to engage in cooperative play and participate in games with rules, but for now, most children play alone. Occasionally, you will see scenes like the one that follows:

Rikku

Rikku has a drum and stick and begins marching in the open space in the toddler room. He marches around the tables and weaves around the room. Ibrahim watches briefly, then goes to the basket of instruments, takes a drum and stick, and follows Rikku. Haley looks up from her play with dolls, hurries to the basket, gets another drum and stick, and joins in the march. The marching pace has picked up and the three children are quite tickled with themselves and their small parade. Ned goes over to the basket and gets out a xylophone and sits at the table and plays it, watching the three marchers as he does so. Rikku speeds up his marching and the other two follow. When he slows down, they do, too. When he yells, "Stop," the others get quiet and stop their movement. He marches again and they follow.

Zeavin (1997) calls this "gleeful and exuberantly contagious" play that indicates the beginning of cooperation and even early stages of a game with rules. Haley and Ibrahim were cooperating with Rikku in his marching game, and Ned followed to a lesser degree. We've seen similar scenes on the playground with the wheel toys in which one child establishes a kind of routine, and one or more toddlers will follow. Because toddlers are usually isolated or engaged in parallel play, the incidents of cooperation are fairly limited. Most social interactions by toddlers are with adults. Their teachers and caregivers are the focal point of their conversations, their interactions, and even much of their pretend play.

When Darren and Jennifer talk about the rewards of working with toddlers, they both describe social development. If you were able to observe their toddlers throughout the year, you would be as impressed as they are. Children accomplish incredible growth toward very complex social understandings and skills during toddlerhood. The curriculum and guidance provided in the toddler room supports that growth by providing and guiding countless interactions each day. Many of those same interactions nurture emotional development, which is described in the next section.

Emotional Development: Curriculum and Guidance

Toddlers are making rapid advances in the area of emotional development, and it is a time for very sensitive support and guidance from adults. A major focus of development is identity formation accompanied by emotional thinking and ideas, and the ability to express feelings. Observing toddlers at play will provide extensive information about their emotional development. From there, guidance strategies will play a prominent role in nurturing the development.

Identity formation.   Toddlers are working hard to develop a sense of self. Much of their resistance to adult limits, or their "no" responses to requests, are attempts to establish themselves as individuals. When you watch them, you see other signs of this development; for example, they talk about themselves, assign characteristics to themselves, and evaluate themselves. As toddlers explore their room at the Helen Gordon Center, we see them work hard to master a variety of tasks, such as assembling puzzles, forming the play-dough into a specific shape, or arranging the animals in a line. Most of these efforts are accompanied by an acknowledgment of "I can do it" to themselves or to a caregiver or teacher. These toddlers are feeling some power and establishing themselves as capable of doing things.

As children go about their business of play in the toddler room, everything going on about them is contributing to their sense of self. The conversations in the room, the actions and interactions of adults and other children, and the materials and activities are all incorporated into lessons that toddlers integrate into their developing identity formation. Lally (1995) suggests that some of these lessons can include:

- What to fear
- Which of one's behaviors are seen as appropriate
- How one's messages are received and acted upon
- How successful one is at getting one's needs met by others
- What emotions and intensity level of emotions one can safely display
- How interesting one is (p. 61)

Journal 8.7: Go back to the first part of this chapter, when we spent the morning in the toddler room. Watch Rikku, Ruth, or Ibrahim again and then think about the lessons they are learning about who they are. What ideas are they getting from their interactions? What messages are being communicated for their identity formation? ■

The importance of both curriculum and guidance is that they are sending key messages to the children. Toddlers are learning that they are capable, that they are respected, and that they are enjoyable. They are learning that they have choices and that others like to be with them. The next time you see an adult and a child in a grocery store, observe them to determine what messages are being communicated to the child about himself. Do the same as you watch children and adults on the bus, or at the library, or walking down the street. Those messages contribute significantly to the child's overall emotional development and specifically to her identity formation. Equally important are the opportunities for toddlers to try out all kinds of roles and to experiment with their own potential. Toddlers need to build a sense of themselves from their own efforts.

Emotional thinking and ideas.   Greenspan (1995), who describes stages of emotional development, sees toddlers experiencing stages of emotional ideas at about age 18 months and emotional thinking at about age 30 months. Around 18 to 24 months, toddlers create images in their minds and begin to play those images out with make believe or pretend play. This is the beginning of their ability to put labels on their feelings through gestures or words. Some toddlers are quite expressive and play out aggression, violence, separation, anger, and fears. This is where the adult role is critical. Toddlers need acceptance of what they express, and guidance in their expression. When Haley makes monster sounds and faces, says "I scare you," and gets louder and more fierce in her gestures, your response will teach her about the feelings and ideas she is expressing. Sometimes, the tendency is to ignore or to humor such play, or even to stop it because of feelings of discomfort. Instead, when Haley hears, "It really is scary to see a monster, isn't it?" she will probably expand on her feelings or she will process something that's been bothering her. We may hear "I don't like monsters" or "There's a monster in my bedroom" or "My brother makes monsters and he chases me." Toddlers' imaginations can create fears and their explorations of the world can contribute new concerns. This is an important time for them to express those fears and to know that they will receive support, assurance, and sometimes clarification.

Journal 8.8: Can you remember some of the fears of your childhood? If not, think about children you know and the fears they have. Reflect on the origin of those fears. Where are they coming from? Think about the different ways an adult could respond to childhood fears. ■

Since toddlers do not have the language to express many of the feelings they have, they need other outlets for their emotions. Music and movement activities are excellent for expressing feelings. Toddlers really like upbeat rhythms and respond naturally through simple movement (Wittmer, 1996). Darren and Jennifer often have this kind of music playing in their classroom in the mornings. Painting to music is a favorite activity. A recording of *Fantasia* or the *Grand Canyon Suite* will provide stimulating background for painting. The toddlers also enjoy percussion instruments, as you observed earlier, and they do a lot of experimenting with different sounds. Toddlers can also get overstimulated by some kinds of music, however, so it's important to provide a variety of rhythms. Remember that during lunch and preparation for naps, there was soft music playing in the toddler room. Toddlers do well with music to calm them at different times of day.

Establishing independence.   Early in the year, as Darren and Jennifer reminded us, the toddlers were asserting their independence by being stubborn or rigid and sometimes negative. "No" was heard throughout the room. Many of their activities were repeated over and over and usually in the exact same way. Any adult who has read and reread a favorite story to a child knows that you don't dare skip a page or change a word, or you will hear vehement complaints. Recently, one of your authors read a book to her granddaughter and was told, "You didn't finish! You forgot to say who wrote it."

Young toddlers often object to routines and requests simply on principle. If you ask them to go outside, they will want to stay in. If you ask them to stay in, they will want to go outside. They are often expressing their developing need for autonomy. Older toddlers continue their expression but in much more enjoyable ways. They want to show what they created or what they can do. As Hughes (1991) describes it, "There is a joy in accomplishment and an interest in showing off one's creations and talents" (p. 75). Ibrahim often approaches Jennifer with, "Teacher, I made a building" or "Look at my snake."

This period of accomplishment is a time when early childhood educators and caregivers may feel compelled to lavish praise on the toddlers: "What a great job you did!" "That's a beautiful painting!" "I like the way you cleaned up all the animals." Recently, however, early childhood educators have begun to examine those responses and the idea of frequently praising children's accomplishments. Marshall (1995) says, "If we look closely at our children taking a new step or seeing their progress or success at a task, their facial expressions will tell us that they are pleased even before we have a chance to spout a word of praise" (p. 27).

Children need encouragement and acknowledgment of their accomplishments (Hitz & Driscoll, 1988) rather than adult approval. At the same time, the adults can help the children begin to evaluate themselves. Instead of praise, toddlers will hear, "You painted a colorful picture. Tell me about it" or "You have picked up all the animals. What do you think of the job you've done?" As children develop their abilities, they need to express their feelings about those abilities. Rather than establishing the need for adult praise or rewards, it is an important time to acknowledge and support their efforts while helping them develop independence from adult evaluation. Figure 8.4 provides examples of encouraging responses.

The emotional development of toddlers is also complex and not always visible. It takes consistent observations and good listening to maintain awareness of toddlers emotional needs. Again, the curriculum and kind of guidance approaches with which you respond to them will promote their emotional health, just as you promote their physical and social health. You will see in the section that follows that cognitive development requires the same kind of respectful and nurturing response that is needed during emotional development.

■ **FIGURE 8.4**   Examples of Encouragement

Setting 1
Carmen helped set the table for snack.

Encouraging Statements
  Thank you for helping us set the table.
  You put a spoon by every bowl.

Setting 2
Tommy helped to pick up the blocks in the block corner.

Encouraging Statements
  You picked up many more blocks than you have ever picked up before.
  When you help us pick up the blocks we all get finished much sooner.

Setting 3
Jaci listened intently during storytime.

Encouraging Statements
  I could tell by the look on your face that you really enjoyed listening to the story today.
  I noticed that you listened very carefully to the story.

Setting 4
Denise played with Jimmy at the sand table. They experimented with funnels for more than 20 minutes.

Encouraging Statements
  You and Jimmy played together for a long time at the sand table.
  You were able to share with Jimmy at the sand table today.

Setting 5
Marc needed help with a project and Ben helped him.

Encouraging Statements
  It looks like Marc really appreciates the way you helped him with his work.
  Thank you for helping Marc.
  You noticed that Marc was having a problem and you gave him some help with his project.

Setting 6
Sue seldom talks in the group but today she told a short story about Halloween.

Encouraging Statements
  That was a very scary story you told.
  When you told that story I could just picture ghosts in our classroom. It gave me goosebumps.

Setting 7
Daniel just finished a painting. He comes to you, the teacher, and says, "Look at my painting, isn't it beautiful!"

Encouraging Statements
  You look happy about your painting.
  Look at all the colors you used.

Setting 8
Michele completed an assignment all by herself.

Encouraging Statements
  It must feel good to you to be finished. You must be very pleased that you were able to do that all by yourself.

Setting 9
Matthew says, "Look how fast I can run!"

Encouraging Statements
  You are running much faster than you used to run.
  You must feel excited when you run that fast.

Source: "Praise or Encouragement? New Insights into Praise Implications for Early Childhood Teachers" by R. Hitz and A. Driscoll, 1988, *Young Children, 43*(5), p. 12. Washington, DC: NAEYC. Copyright 1988 by NAEYC. Reprinted with permission from the National Association for the Education of Young Children.

Cognitive Development: Curriculum and Guidance

The lives of toddlers are full of exploration, questioning, discovery, and determination to understand events, objects, and words. This is a time of exciting new mental activity. Toddlers are fascinated by language. Remember Haley repeating "Dinosaur" to herself, and Kim saying "Ripple" over and over? Toddlers are discovering the power of words and they use them for every possible function. Along with their language development is the beginning of literacy development. The period from ages 16 to 36 months are full of new awarenesses: perceptual, temporal, and spatial. Sensory materials continue to be very important to toddlers and they use a great number of tools. They are interested in the effects of their behaviors on the world around them. Once again, all of these developments have many implications for curriculum and guidance in a toddler program.

Exploration and discovery.   The kinds of materials and the arrangement of the environment will certainly determine the depth of toddlers' exploration and discovery. Guidance strategies will communicate how much freedom they will have to conduct their study of the world. If materials can be used in only one way, then the potential to explore will be limited. In some classes, you will hear that the dolls must stay in the house center. In Jennifer and Darren's class, the dolls are taken all over the room, they are bathed, they are transported in wagons, and they sit in chairs to hear stories. Remember when Rikku was not discouraged from climbing? This gave him the opportunity to experience the classroom from another height. Educators of toddlers have the challenge once again of balancing safety and stimulation, and every situation may be different, just as each child is unique.

In the process of exploring, children discover that objects are different colors, different sizes and shapes, and different textures. Equipment and materials such as water tables, play-dough, fingerprint, sand and dirt, and fabric encourage those discoveries. Those endless collections of plastic figures (animals, cars, and so on) and blocks encourage discoveries daily. Most child development experts describe toddlers' ability to go from simple stacking of blocks to elaborate and interesting structures that represent their world (a garage, the zoo, a bridge, and so on).

Although the toddler room at the Helen Gordon Center was well equipped with blocks, we saw little use of blocks during our observations. We decided to ask Jennifer about this. She commented, "They don't use them unless you sit down with them and encourage with something like 'Let's build a garage.' " This is a bit strange, because we can't ever remember an early childhood program in which the blocks were not used extensively. In fact, our observations of the Town and Country School in New York City considered blocks the major focus of their curriculum for 3-year-olds (Driscoll, 1995). Jennifer expressed the same puzzlement we were feeling. We begin to question this issue together.

One possibility for the lack of block play is the location of the blocks. This may be a good time to look at the floor plan of Darren and Jennifer's room for toddlers (see Figure 8.5). Our observations told us that most of the activity took place in the large main room and the outdoor area. Children had the freedom to go outside at any time and they did so. Most of our observations of children in the smaller room consisted of one-on-one interactions with adults and saying good-bye to parents and family members. This may be an example of the environment sending a message about specific materials (the blocks).

Journal 8.9:   Children take messages from materials and the environment. What message(s) might the toddlers at the Helen Gordon Center be getting about play with blocks? If you were Jennifer or Darren, and you believed that block play was important, but

FIGURE 8.5   Floor Plan of the Toddler Rooms

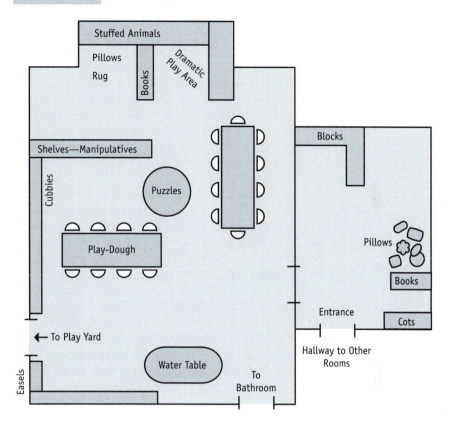

your children didn't seem attracted to the blocks, what would you do? Think of a number of possibilities for this situation. ■

As you can see from this section, the environment is very much a curriculum for toddlers who are exploring and discovering their world. The materials and equipment that Darren and Jennifer provide throughout their room motivate and encourage those activities. The way the room is arranged continues to nurture the toddlers' desire to explore, yet keeps them safe from themselves and others. It's a "balancing act" of providing limits that don't inhibit exploration while keeping this lively age group safe.

Perceptual awareness.   Toddlers show much interest in the attributes of objects. They enjoy matching a group of similar objects and even sequencing items in order of size. Their discovery of shapes, colors, sizes, and textures now leads to sorting and grouping. Remember Piaget's classification and seriation skills discussed in Chapter 3? All those plastic figures that end up everywhere are essential materials for the sorting and classifying that toddlers are learning. Many commercially developed materials with shape, color, and size differences are enjoyed over and over by toddlers who sort and resort them. Teacher-made materials and items from home are ideal for children to sort. Some of the simplest materials engage children in these new awarenesses: leaves in the summer and fall, cloth scraps, large shells and rocks, and so on.

Can you add to the list? The possibilities are endless. Toddlers will develop patterns with these items, and will enjoy creating their own matching games: texture matching games, color matching games, and the like. You will hear them begin to count as they manipulate their plastic figures or other items. They will also display a beginning understanding of quantity. You will hear Haley ask, "How big?" or "How little?" Her understanding of quantity is not systematic but it is beginning. When you plan and use items for perceptual awareness, remember that close supervision will be important.

Toddlers are also attracted to puzzles with four to eight pieces. When you watch the children, you will begin to notice that they are starting to work out problems mentally, rather than always using trial and error. Toddlers talk to themselves a great deal because there is so much going on in their heads. Piaget called this talk "egocentric speech" and Vygotsky called it "inner speech." The research on the connection between thought and language refers to the talk as "private speech" (Berk, 1992) and has demonstrated that children who talk to themselves have higher rates of social participation and are more socially competent than children who do less talking to themselves (Berk, 1984, 1985).

As children manipulate objects—sorting and classifying them as big and small, or hard and soft, or dark and light—they are extending their vocabulary at the same time. Their language development and communication skills are expanding as rapidly as their discoveries and awarenesses, and with the expansion comes the beginning of literacy.

Language and literacy.   Everything in the toddler environment and every encounter with another child or an adult is an opportunity for toddlers to develop their language and communication skills. Young toddlers put together two-word sentences, which we heard during our observations in the toddler room. As they gain new experiences and maturity, their sentences get longer and more complex. Most 3-year olds speak in compound sentences and use adjectives and adverbs well. Listen to some of Ibrahim's talk as he interacts with his mom, Faridah, and Jennifer:

Faridah: Good morning, Jennifer. Ibrahim has something exciting to tell you.

Jennifer: Good morning, Faridah and Ibrahim. I'm anxious to hear your news.

Ibrahim: Yesterday we see "Hercules."

Jennifer: Wow! Tell me about it.

Ibrahim: It was scarey and lots of swords. Me and Muhammed play Hercules.

Ibrahim's speech is well developed. It's obvious that there is much conversation at home and lots of opportunities for language development. Some of the other toddlers are speaking more simply with two-word sentences such as, "Me sleepy" or "I swinging," whereas others, such as Ibrahim, speak in sentences.

This is a time for *approximations,* which are children's attempts at adult or conventional language. They are listening to adults all the time, so it's not surprising that they would attempt to sound like them. When Haley says "I goed there," she is approximating adult talk. This is also a time for *overextensions,* which are young children's use of a word for similar but different objects, situations, or categories. When Ned learned the word *plant,* he called everything with leaves a plant—trees, bushes, artificial flower arrangements, and so on. This is a time for *creative vocabulary,* as well. When Rikku doesn't have a word for what he wants to say, he creates one. A common example of creative vocabulary is the word *cooker* to refer to the person who cooks.

Toddlers learn how to ask questions, and the adults who work with them can tell you that this new skill is used constantly. From 18 months to 3 years of age, toddlers are developing vocabulary, using every experience, every object, and every conversation they hear. They learn vocabulary quite rapidly by a process called *fast mapping* (Carey, 1978). Fast mapping is used when young children relate a new word to a concept they already have, and they remember it after only one encounter with that word. With fast mapping, children are learning an average of nine words a day. It's not surprising that by age 3, they may have a speaking vocabulary that reaches 200 words, and by age 6, they have acquired approximately 14,000 words.

As they are rapidly developing language, toddlers are also beginning to develop literacy. Toddlers are very interested in print. They frequently ask, "What does this say?" When they see adults writing, they are curious about the content. Some toddlers recognize familiar words such as *stop, McDonalds,* and *Exit.* They see words and expressions all around them, so it is not surprising that they are interested and that they begin to "read." They also begin to write. You will occasionally see a toddler with a pencil or crayon and paper "writing note my mom." In spite of her stress, Ruth sat and watched as Jennifer wrote a note to Ruth's dad. She felt satisfied that the note (which Jennifer read aloud to her) would help her get more watermelon.

Studies of early readers and their families reveal some interesting insights about children's early literacy. The behaviors displayed by parents that seemed to facilitate early reading in children are actually appropriate for early childhood programs. They can be translated into basic guidelines for a classroom for young children, and are quite relevant for toddler programs. These include (Durkin, 1996; Wells, 1981):

- Adults read to children on a consistent and regular basis.
- Adults provide children with access to a wide range of print materials.
- Adults read and interact with print.
- Adults respond to children's questions about print.
- Adults make writing and drawing tools and paper available to children.

Journal 8.10: If you were setting up a room for toddlers, what other kind of print materials could you provide besides books? What other kind of writing and drawing tools? ▪

BOX 8.1 ■ Language Development of Bilingual Children: Insights for Teachers and Caregivers

A Closer Look

Based on research in bilingualism and multiculturalism, Berk (1996b) offers some important insights for understanding the language development of bilingual children:

- Children who do not yet speak English may be very quiet. Their lack of verbalization should not be interpreted as a lack of cognitive ability.
- A second language is acquired with the same differences in rates and strategies that a first language is acquired.
- Oral language in the first language will not be affected because the child is learning a new language.
- The patterns of second language acquisition parallel those of first language acquisition. (pp. 248–249)

Based on those insights, we suggest that you observe bilingual children carefully so that you are aware of the complexity of their language development. Talk with their families about language use at home so that you know what home experiences are contributing to their language development in one or both of the languages. From there, structure the environment and activities in ways that provide opportunities to support the development of one or both languages. Find time to interact with the child on a one-to-one basis and converse about familiar topics—a pet, a favorite toy, and so on. It's also effective to encourage the bilingual child's play with a peer who has well-developed language skills.

Second language acquisition. In the toddler room at the Helen Gordon Center, several children are learning two languages at the same time. They are referred to as *simultaneous bilingual*—their dual language development began at birth. Ibrahim is becoming trilingual. His mother speaks Malay, his father speaks Arabic, and he is learning English at the preschool. Many young children are growing up in homes in which other languages are spoken and are attending programs in which English is spoken. Box 8.1 shares some insights from research and suggestions for supporting the language development of bilingual children.

Professionals who work with young children will be experiencing an increasing number of bilingual learners in the coming years. It will be important for you to understand more about language development as you continue your professional preparation, so that you can respond to the complexity of children's language development and to the possibilities of second language learning.

Summary and Additional Insights

One conclusion you may have reached after observing in the toddler room and then thinking about curriculum is that materials and equipment (toys) are really a major part of the curriculum. They promote all aspects of development—physical, social, emotional, and cognitive. Toddlers interact with materials and equipment (play materials) from morning until night, as they explore, develop new language, experiment with relationships, and communicate feelings. The match between their play materials and toddler development is essential for feelings of success, interest and curiosity, and exploration and creativity.

Tables 8.1 and 8.2 give an overview of play materials for young toddlers and older toddlers. If we had observed in Darren and Jennifer's room early in the year, we might

Social and Fantasy Play Materials	Exploration and Mastery Play Materials

Mirrors
Well-secured wall mirrors (rounded edges, unbreakable)
Full-length (upright), unbreakable mirror, firmly mounted or in nontippable stand
Hand mirrors (light, sturdy, unbreakable)

Dolls
Soft-bodied or washable rubber/vinyl baby dolls
Simple accessories for caregiving: bottle, blanket
Simple doll clothes—need not be detachable (lightweight; painted, stitched, or molded hair and features; no moving eyes or articulated limbs; sized to fit easily in child's arms: 6 or 8–13 inches)

(from about 18 months)
Small peg people (not swallowable)

Role-Play Materials
Play telephone
Simple housekeeping and work-role equipment
Simple doll equipment—bed, baby carriage (sturdy and large enough to hold child)

Puppets
Puppets operated by adult

(from about 18 months)
Small hand puppets, sized to fit child's hand

Stuffed Toys/Play Animals
Washable, soft animals (simple in design, with bright colors, contrasting features that are painted, stitched, or molded)
Soft rubber or vinyl animals (6–8 inches)—a few for exploring and beginning pretend play

Play Scenes
(from about 18 months)
Small people/animal figures, with simple supporting materials (vehicle, barn) to make familiar scenes

Transportation Toys
Simple, lightweight vehicles (6–8 inches, with large wheels or rollers. lightweight; rounded/molded appearance, may make noise when pushed)
First train—1–2 cars, no tracks, simple or no coupling system

(from about 18 months)
More detailed vehicles—can have a few simple, sturdy moving parts (doors or hoods that open)
Trains with simple coupling system (wood link, large blunt hook, magnet)

Grasping Toys
(toddlers are losing interest in the small, hand-held manipulables enjoyed by infants)

Sand/Water Play Materials
Simple floating objects, easily grasped in one hand
Small shovel and pail

(from about 18 months)
Nesting materials useful for pouring
Funnels, colanders
Water activity centers
Small sand tools (container with shovel or scoop; rake with blunt teeth

Construction Materials
Light blocks (soft cloth, rubber, rounded plastic, or wood cubes for grasping and stacking, 2–4 inches on a side)—15–25 pieces

(from about 18 months)
Unit blocks (suggested by some experts and teachers)—20–40 pieces
Large plastic bricks (2–4 inches, press-together type)

Puzzles
Simple prepuzzles or form boards, 2–3 pieces, in familiar shapes

(from about 18 months)
3–5-piece fit-in puzzles (knobs make them easier to use but must be very firmly attached)

Dressing, Lacing, Stringing Materials
Large, colored beads (fewer than 10)
(from about 18 months)
Lacing cubes or board with thick, blunt spindle

Specific Skill-Development Materials
Pop-up boxes (easy operation)
Simple activity boxes/cubes (with doors, lids, switches)
Nesting cups (with round shapes, few pieces)
Simple stacking materials—no order necessary

(from about 18 months)
Activity boxes with more complex mechanisms (turning knob or dial or simple key)
Simple lock boxes
Nesting materials of more complex shapes (square)
Objects in closed containers that may be opened (by simple screwing action)
4–5-piece stacking materials
Cylinder blocks
Pegboards (with a few large pegs)
Simple matching and lotto materials

Books
Cloth, plastic, or cardboard picture books
Simple picture and rhyme books with repetition for lap reading
(from about 18 months)
Touch-me or tactile books

(continued)

■ **TABLE 8.1** *(continued)*

Music, Art, and Movement Play Materials	Gross Motor Play Materials
Art and Craft Materials Few large, nontoxic crayons Large paper taped to surface **Musical Instruments** Rhythm instruments for shaking—bells, rattles *(from about 18 months)* Rhythm instruments for banging—cymbals, drums **Audiovisual Materials** Adult-operated players and records, tapes, CDs, etc., with simple repeating rhythms, rhymes, and songs *(from about 14 months)* Music to "dance" (bounce) to *(from about 18 months)* Simple "point to" and finger-play games and songs	**Push and Pull Toys** Push toys with rods (rods with large handles on ends) Toys to push along the floor—simple cars, animals on large wheels or rollers For steady walkers, pull toys on short strings (broad based to tip less easily) *(from about 18 months)* Simple doll carriages and wagons (low, open, big enough for child to get into) Push/pull toys filled with multiple objects **Balls and Sports Equipment** Soft, lightweight balls, especially those with interesting audio or visual effects (noises, unpredictable movement) Larger balls, including beach ball size *(from about 18 months)* Balls for beginning throwing and kicking **Ride-On Equipment** Stable ride-ons propelled by pushing with feet (no pedals; no steering mechanism; four or more wheels spaced wide apart for stability; child's feet flat on floor when seated) Ride-ons with storage bins *(from about 18 months)* Bouncing or rocking ride-ons (with confined rocking arc and gentle bounce for toddlers; child's feet touch floor when seated) **Outdoor and Gym Equipment** Low, soft or padded climbing platforms Tunnels for crawling through Swings (pushed and monitored by adult), with seats curved or body shaped, front closing, and made of energy-absorbing materials *(from about 18 months)* Low toddler stairs with handrail

Note: Although the four categories provide a useful classification, play materials can typically be used in more than one way and could be listed under more than one of the categories.

Source: The Right Stuff: Selecting Play Materials to Support Development by M. B. Bronson (pp. 60–61), 1995, Washington, DC: NAEYC. Copyright 1995 by NAEYC. Reprinted with permission from the National Association for the Education of Young Children.

have seen more of the play materials listed in Table 8.1. Some centers do not have the budget to have a vast array of play materials like we've seen in our observations. The Helen Gordon Center is a university laboratory school, so it has support for maintaining the latest equipment and materials. We'll discuss other elements of the uniqueness of a laboratory school or program next.

■ TABLE 8.2   Overview of Play Materials for Older Toddlers: Two Years Old

Social and Fantasy Play Materials	Exploration and Mastery Play Materials
Mirrors	**Sand/Water Play Materials**

Mirrors

Full-length unbreakable mirror firmly mounted or in nontippable stand

Hand mirrors (light, sturdy, unbreakable)

Dolls

Soft-bodied or washable rubber/vinyl baby dolls (12–15 inches)

Simple accessories for caretaking-feeding, diapering, and sleeping

Simple, removable doll clothes (closed by Velcro, large hook and loop, or snap; 12–15 inches)

Small peg or other people figures (not swallowable) for fantasy scenes

Role-Play Materials

Dress-up materials

Housekeeping equipment—stove, refrigerator, ironing board and iron, telephone, pots and pans, cleaning equipment

Simple doll equipments, baby carriage (sturdy and large enough to hold child)

Puppets

Small hand puppets sized to fit child's hand (that represent familiar human and animal figures and community diversity)

Stuffed Toys/Play Animals

Soft rubber, wood, or vinyl animals (6–8 inches) for exploration and pretend play

Mother and baby animals

Play Scenes

Small people/animal figures, with simple supporting materials (vehicle, barn) or unit blocks to make familiar scenes

Transportation Toys

Small cars and vehicles to use with unit blocks (4–5 inches; sturdy wood or plastic)

Larger vehicles for pushing and fantasy play

Large wood trucks to ride on

Trains with simple coupling system and no tracks (for use with unit blocks)

Sand/Water Play Materials

People, animals, vehicles for fantasy play in sand/water

Nesting materials useful for pouring

Funnels, colanders, sprinklers, sand/water mills

Small sand tools—container with shovel or scoop; rake with blunt teeth

Construction Materials

Wooden unit blocks (50–60 pieces)—no need for specialized forms (arches, curves)

Large plastic bricks (2–4 inches; press-together)

Large nuts and bolts

Puzzles

(from about 24 months)

4–5-piece fit-in puzzles

(from about 30 months)

6–12-piece fit-in puzzles (knobs make them easier to use but must be firmly attached)

Pattern-Making Materials

Pegboards with large pegs

Color cubes

Magnetic boards with forms

Dressing, Lacing, Stringing Materials

Large beads for stringing

Cards or wooden shoe for lacing

Dressing frames and materials

Specific Skill-Development Materials

5–10 pieces to nest/stack

One turn screw-on (barrel) nesting

Simple lock boxes

Hidden-object pop-up boxes (with lids, doors, dials, switches, knobs)

Safe pounding/hammering toys

Cylinder blocks

Shape sorters with common shapes

Simple matching and lotto materials

Color/picture dominoes

Feel bag/box, smell jars

Books

Sturdy books with heavy paper or cardboard pages (short, simple stories or rhymes with repetition and familiar subjects; simple, clear pictures and colors)

Tactile/touch-me, pop-up, hidden-picture, and dressing books

(continued)

■ **TABLE 8.2** *(continued)*

Music, Art, and Movement Play Materials	Gross Motor Play Materials
Art and Craft Materials Large, nontoxic crayons Large, nontoxic markers Adjustable easel Large, blunt paintbrushes Nontoxic paint and fingerpaint Large paper for drawing, painting, fingerpaints Colored construction paper Easy-to-use, blunt-ended scissors Chalkboard and large chalk **Musical Instruments** Rhythm instruments operated by shaking (bells, rattles) or banging (cymbals, drums) and more complex instruments (tambourine, sand blocks, triangle, rhythm sticks) **Audiovisual Materials** Adult-oriented players and records, tapes, CDs, etc. Music with repeating rhythms—for rhythm instruments Music to "dance" (bounce) to Simple point-to and finger-play games and songs Short films and videos of familiar objects and activities	**Push and Pull Toys** Simple doll carriages and wagons (low, open, big enough for child to get inside) Push toys that look like adult equipment (vacuum cleaner, lawn mower, shopping cart) **Balls and Sports Equipment** Balls of all shapes and sizes, especially 10–12-inch balls for kicking and throwing **Ride-On Equipment** Stable ride-ons propelled by pushing with feet (steering devices but no pedals; wheels spaced wide apart for stability; child's feet flat on floor when seated) Bouncing or rocking ride-ons (with confined rocking arc and gentle bounce for toddlers; child's feet touch floor. when seated) *(as child nears age 3)* Small tricycles (with 10-inch wheels) **Outdoor and Gym Equipment** Tunnels Swings with seats curved or body shaped and made of energy-absorbing materials Low climbing structures and slides, with soft material underneath

Note: Although the four categories provide a useful classification, play materials can typically be used in more than one way and could be listed under more than one of the categories.

Source: The Right Stuff: Selecting Play Materials to Support Development by M. B. Bronson (pp. 76–77), 1995, Washington, DC: NAEYC. Copyright 1995 by NAEYC. Reprinted with permission from the National Association for the Education of Young Children.

The Helen Gordon Child Development Center: A University Laboratory School

As you learned in Chapter 1, laboratory nursery schools or preschools have been an important institution in early childhood education for many years. They have a long and rich history and have provided leadership models to the early childhood education profession since the early 1900s.

The Role of Laboratory Schools

The early laboratory schools were sites of teacher training and research, much like the Helen Gordon Center is today. The research focus has helped maintain the role of lab school programs in times of shrinking resources on campuses nationwide (McBride &

Lee, 1995). Early in their history, lab schools were the site of research that manipulated the environment or activities to study various aspects of children's development. Today, you will find much more naturalistic research being conducted—that is, observational studies of children as they work and play together in the usual settings.

The use of the Helen Gordon Center for both research and professional preparation has had an impact on the quality of the program. As you observed in the toddler room, college students such as Cindy and Heather practice by working with the children, under the guidance of the early childhood educators. Administration and staff are constantly assessing the practices at the Center in order to model the best practices. Because the staff interacts with teachers-in-training, who question early childhood practices, the staff consistently reflects on their decisions. Consequently, the staff at the lab schools are thoughtful and clear about their reasons for why they interact with children the way they do. Our conversations with Darren and Jennifer demonstrated their commitments to children's development as the first consideration for what they do. Those conversations also illustrated the high level of professionalism found in the staff of the center. We have a few questions left, so let's have one last discussion with Darren and Jennifer.

A Conversation about Assessment with Darren and Jennifer

We've learned a lot about curriculum and guidance from our observations and previous conversations with these two early childhood educators, but we have some questions about assessment. With their emphasis on knowing the children in order to make decisions so that curriculum emerges from them, we're curious about how Darren and Jennifer learn about and keep track of all the toddlers. Darren describes their initial information gathering with a family history form (see Figure 8.6 on page 320): "We encourage families to provide as much detail as they are comfortable with and explain how the information will help us plan for their children." He tells us that during the home visits "we don't have any agenda. We try to follow the child's lead, play with the child, and visit with the parent. Primarily, we want them to be comfortable with us before they come to the center." The home visit information is usually extensive and the recordings begin the process of information gathering for each child. Darren adds emphatically, "We learn so much in the home visits."

Once children enter the toddler program, Darren and Jennifer keep anecdotal records on each child. "By the first parent conference, I usually have at least 60 anecdotal notes on each child, and can put together a profile—my picture of the child—for the parents and family members." Darren describes a process for assessment that begins with the home visit: "During our first home visit, we work with the parents and other family members to develop goals for their child. From there, I have those goals in mind as I observe the child and keep notes. Sometimes, I develop a checklist based on specific goals or an aspect of development, and I often keep frequency counts on each child's play choices. There are so many adults in the room that it's easy to gather information on each child. At intervals during the year, I am able to provide a kind of narrative report card with that profile of each child."

■ **FIGURE 8.6**   Helen Gordon Child Development Center: Child History Form

We would like to find out about your child before she/he enters the program. The information provided to us on this form will assist with your child's transition to the program and allow us to provide the best possible care for your child and support for your family. Thank you for taking the time to fill out this form.

Name/Nickname _____ Birth date _____ Sex _____

Who are the important people in your child's life? _____

_____

_____

What are your child's special interests? _____

_____

_____

What should we know about her/his personal habits (eating, sleeping, toilet, dressing)?

_____

_____

What are your child's fears or dislikes (e.g., people, places, activities, or routines)? _____

_____

_____

Have there been any changes in your child's life recently that might impact her/his

adjustment to this program (a birth, death, separation, etc.)? _____

_____

_____

Has your child had previous experience with child care? What kind? How many hours?

How did she/he adjust? _____

_____

_____

Has your child experienced any recent developmental milestones (physical, cognitive, or

emotional struggles or accomplishments, such as toilet training, language)?_____

_____

_____

■ **FIGURE 8.6**　　*(continued)*

What language does your child speak at home? _____

_____

What can you tell us about your family culture, values, traditions, or routines that will

better enable us to build connections for your child between home and school and help

her/him to feel comfortable in this program? _____

_____

_____

_____

_____

How does your child express emotions (joy, tension, anger, fear, etc.)?_____

_____

_____

Does your child have any dietary restrictions or health considerations that we should be

aware of? _____

_____

_____

What are your expectations for your child this year at HGCDC?

_____

_____

_____

_____

In what way can we provide extra support to you in your relationship with your child?

_____

_____

_____

Source: Helen Gordon Child Development Center staff. Reprinted by permission.

■ **FIGURE 8.7**   Suggestions for Classroom Observations

1. Begin by recording the date, time, location, and activity that is occurring. Note the length of observation.
2. Focus the observation as much as possible on what the child or children are doing and saying. (Record quotes whenever possible.)
3. Develop a shorthand or abbreviation system for efficient recording (for example, initials for children, *T* for table, *Bl* for blocks, *PD* for play-dough, etc.).
4. Consider occasional use of a floor plan to record a child's use of the environment by tracking with symbols or arrows where he or she spends time.
5. Make note of unusual circumstances (for example, child's health, weather, changes in routine, etc.).
6. Be sensitive to issues of confidentiality by maintaining records in secure cabinets.
7. Include a variety of settings (group times, outdoor play, center time, etc.), times of day, and other variations in your observations to obtain an authentic profile.
8. As much as possible, hold your judgments while recording an observation. When finished, read your notes and then add your impressions or an evaluation of what you observed. Another possibility is to wait until you have a series of observations before making judgments.
9. For ideal observations, ask another adult to be in charge of supervising the children, so that you can observe without distractions. You may even want to let children know that you cannot be interrupted for a particular time frame.

It's clear when talking to Darren and Jennifer that observation is key to assessment of young children, especially active and changing toddlers. Figure 8.7 provides some beginning guidelines for observations. It's also clear that there must be a commitment to be consistent in recording what the toddlers are doing and saying in order to develop a holistic and authentic picture of each child. Those pictures of children are important for the kind of planning that Darren and Jennifer do and for communicating with parents about children's progress.

Journal 8.11: In addition to the way Darren and Jennifer observe children for both assessment purposes and for curriculum planning purposes, what would be the advantages of their observations for a parent? ■

Our conversations with Darren and Jennifer have given you a snapshot of the thinking and experience you will encounter at the Helen Gordon Center and in laboratory schools in general. Antibias thinking and curriculum is a kind of expertise for which the entire staff is known and it is an important topic for you to explore before you leave the center. We scheduled time with the director of the center in the hope that her insight will help you understand and begin to develop awareness of bias in yourself.

Antibias Curriculum

Ellie Nolan is the director of the Helen Gordon Child Development Center and we meet with her to learn about how the staff began their study and their efforts to assure an antibias curriculum for the center. Ellie describes the early work originating from her own interest in multicultural education during her graduate studies. She is passionate about the staff's commitment. "We began questioning how well we were representing cultures, race, and values in our curriculum, how race and culture issues influence interactions between children, between children and teachers, between teachers and teachers, and between parents and the center." From there, the center moved to a self-assessment focused on antibias curriculum. Their work was inspired and guided by NAEYC's *Anti-Bias Curriculum: Tools for Empowering Young Children* (Derman-Sparks, 1989).

Goals for children.   Antibias curriculum "enables children to comfortably explore the differences and similarities that make up our individual and group identities, and to develop skills for identifying and countering the hurtful impact of bias on themselves and their peers" (Derman-Sparks, 1992, p. 3). When teachers who have embraced anti-bias curriculum were asked to discuss their goals for children, their responses included phrases such as "to become tolerant, understanding, and compassionate," "to be able to make judgments about what's fair and what's not," "to sort out what they have the power to change and what they can't do anything about," and "to become effective thinkers and problem solvers, not accepters of dogma" (pp. 2–3).

Those educators who have explored antibias curriculum have discovered that they were not just embracing new methods, but that their thinking also had to change. As the educators at the Helen Gordon Center discovered, the process takes time and it demands ongoing attention. We asked Ellie Nolan about the beginnings.

"We started very simply by assessing our environment and our materials for varied kinds of bias." Ellie describes careful assessment of books, posters, dolls, songs, and music for cultural values. "If everything in the environment is about White people, what does that tell children?" The staff went beyond race and considered diversity of family structures and family traditions. Gender stereotypes became an additional focus as the staff examined their classroom resources. The criteria for the selection of books and materials in Figure 8.8 will give you an idea of the kinds of questions and thinking you need to use when you have your own classroom. Although the criteria were designed for books and toys, they can be used to help you examine the many sources of messages for children.

■ **FIGURE 8.8**	Criteria for the Selection of Books and Materials: Look for the Messages in Children's Books

---

Evaluate the Characters

Yes	No	
❐	❐	Do the characters in the story have personalities like real people?
❐	❐	Do they seem authentic in the way they act and react?
❐	❐	Do they speak in a style and language that fits their situation?
❐	❐	Are they real people with strengths and weaknesses rather than stereotypes?
❐	❐	Are characters allowed to learn and grow?
❐	❐	Is their lifestyle represented fairly and respectfully?

(continued)

■ **FIGURE 8.8** *(continued)*

Evaluate the Situation
- ☐ ☐ Do the characters have power over their own lives?
- ☐ ☐ Do they resolve their own problems and reap their own rewards?
- ☐ ☐ Are human qualities emphasized?

Evaluate the Illustrations
- ☐ ☐ Do the illustrations respectfully depict ethnic, age, cultural, economic, ability, and sexual differences? (Illustrations can be humorous, but they must fit the context of the story line and be consistent in portrayal.)
- ☐ ☐ Do the illustrations and the text work well together to communicate the story?
- ☐ ☐ Is the style of illustration appropriate to the story?

Evaluate the Messages
- ☐ ☐ Do the messages conveyed, both directly and indirectly, respectfully and accurately portray the human condition?
- ☐ ☐ Are there hidden messages that are demeaning in any way or that reinforce stereotypes?

Evaluate the Author/Illustrator's Credibility
- ☐ ☐ Does the author/illustrator's background and training prepare her or him to present this story? (Do not disregard, but do consider carefully, stories about women written by men, stories about people with handicaps written by people without handicaps, and stories about one ethnic group written by another.)

Consider Your Selections as a Whole
It is not possible for any one book to portray all that we want to say to children, so it is important to look at your whole library:
- ☐ ☐ Are there stories about the contemporary life of a given ethnic group, as well as tales and legends?
- ☐ ☐ Do the cultures represented in your library at least cover (and, optimally, extend well beyond) those cultures represented by the families in your program?
- ☐ ☐ Are there books in which the disability or racial or economic difference is just part of the context for a story about people's lives, as well as books that focus on that particular difference?

Look for the Messages in Materials and Equipment
Yes No
- ☐ ☐ Does this toy stereotype people by sex. race, age, family situation, physical skills, or intellectual skills?
- ☐ ☐ Does the selection of materials as a whole represent the diversity of humankind?
- ☐ ☐ How long will this toy hold a child's interest?
- ☐ ☐ Can the toy be adapted or used in different ways to change with different interests and ages of children?

■ **FIGURE 8.8**   *(continued)*

❏ ❏ Can the toy be combined with other play materials to extend its possibilities?

❏ ❏ Is the toy safe, sturdy, and appealing?

❏ ❏ Does the packaging of the toy reflect diversity? (If not, throw it away or use it for discussion, and write to the manufacturer.)

❏ ❏ Is the way in which children play with these materials consistent with your program's philosophy and goals?

Source: "What Are We Really Saying to Children? Criteria for the Selection of Books and Materials" by B. Neugebauer from *Alike and Different: Exploring Our Humanity with Young Children* by B. Neugebauer (Ed.) (pp. 160–162), 1992, Washington, DC: NAEYC. Copyright 1992 by NAEYC. Reprinted with permission from the National Association for the Education of Young Children.

Those messages come "through our words and actions and silences" and you need to be vigilant about checking that the messages are what you intend for children to hear and learn (Neugebauer, 1992).

Journal 8.12: Review the criteria given in Figure 8.8. Which of the questions caused you to pause? Why? Did any of them surprise you? Why? Select a toy or a book and use the criteria to assess it. Keep the criteria in mind as you watch television, browse through a magazine, or notice advertising. ■

You might think that bias is not relevant for work with toddlers, but research shows that by age 2, children have begun to develop their own gender and racial identities (Honig, 1983) and are influenced by the stereotypes and prejudices around them (Derman-Sparks, 1992). You only have to listen to young children to know that bias is already part of their thinking and attitudes. You might see very young African American children reject their own skin color as "dirty" or "not pretty" or 3-year-old girls put themselves in the role of making dinner while the boys go off to work. The goal of antibias curriculum is for children "to become tolerant, understanding, and compassionate by the time they are five" (Derman-Sparks, 1992, p. 3). That goal is integral to the goals of effective early childhood education programs, but it takes concerted effort and study on the part of the educators to truly achieve that goal.

Antibias thinking.   Returning to our discussion with Ellie, we ask about what followed the review of materials and assessment of the environment. "We wanted antibias thinking to become part of our thinking, we wanted to be proactive about bias, and we wanted to be truly different in our practices, not just look different." At this point, she used the term "questioned our assumptions," and we asked for an example. She laughs a bit uncomfortably and describes an example with which many of us with a history in early childhood education could identify: "Well, we had always been concerned with children getting to the center at a specific time each morning because we began routines and activities at 9:00 A.M. We disliked having children miss the opening exercises. We used very strong language in our parent handbook about being on time: Children *must* arrive at 9:00 A.M. We were judgmental of those tardy families. Some of our thoughts included: They must not value education or That parent is irresponsible. I know that in classrooms when a family was late, there were looks directed to them and attitudes directed to them. We even went so far as to say that parents had to get permission to bring children in late."

Ellie continues, "Well, when we began examining our assumptions, we stopped short. This whole issue of time being so important is a White cultural value. It doesn't have the same meaning for other cultures. We were communicating that other cultural values didn't count—were not good. We were reinforcing stereotypes about other cultures always being late. We went back to our handbook and softened the wording. We wanted to acknowledge the importance of family's individual schedules and time priorities." Ellie shares a section of the parent handbook to illustrate the changes in wording that resulted from their realization:

> Teachers need a stable, consistent group of children and block of time to successfully meet their curriculum goals. Therefore, we suggest that your child be here by 9:00 A.M. Children who arrive late often have a difficult time adjusting to the day or separating from their parent(s) as they are not familiar with the day's plans. Children need time to greet friends and "settle in." We recognize that it is impossible not to be late once in a while! If you are going to be late, please make arrangements with the teachers in advance, and if that is not possible, call the Center so that they know when to expect your child. It may be that the class is going on a field trip or has made other special plans that you will need to know about. (Helen Gordon Child Development Center, p. 11)

Ongoing professional development. Ellie acknowledges that the time example is but one in a long series of realizations. The staff begins each year with an intense awareness workshop that covers activities such as the following:

- Book groups in which all staff read a book about cultural awareness and antibias work and then have discussion sessions
- A reflection session at weekly staff meetings, often beginning with each individual staff member's own experiences and extending to awarenesses
- Annual workshops with experts in diversity training, antibias curriculum, and related topics
- Book analysis projects, ongoing examinations of children's literature for subtle bias, stereotypes, and so on
- An Antibias Curriculum Open House for staff and families
- An aggressive recruitment and hiring process to maintain diversity in staff

Ellie describes the varied cultures and races represented in their staffing and adds, "We also have variation in terms of socioeconomic groups." We ask about the diversity of children and families, wondering if that, too, is the result of "aggressive recruitment." Ellie tells us that at one time the center did consciously admit children and families with racial and socioeconomic criteria, but their current practice focuses only on a ratio of students, faculty, and general community. Yet, there is diversity among the children! "We attract diverse families now," Ellie explains, "because of what we stand for, because of what we value." She adds, "Families talk to each other, they share their impressions and their experiences with other families, so we attract families that want this kind of environment for their children." An example is a message in the gay and lesbian community that the center is a "safe place for all families." Recommendations and opinions given among families is a strong force for recruiting diverse families and children.

The diversity of children, families, and staff at the Helen Gordon Center is definitely an attraction for those families who choose the program for their young children, but there are other program qualities that families list when describing the reasons for their choice. Many of the families value their involvement in the center. Ellie and the staff make family involvement a high priority right alongside antibias curriculum. It's part of their thinking about how to provide the best environment for the children who walk through the doors each day. The center's family involvement approach is another model for you as a future teacher and caregiver.

Family Involvement

As you can tell from listening to Ellie, as well as Darren and Jennifer, families of the children at the Helen Gordon Center are very important and their involvement is a critical component of the center. Like the antibias curriculum, it's not so much the strategies of involving the families as it is the thinking of the staff and administration that makes a difference. High levels of family involvement begin with respect and trust, and those messages are communicated directly and, more importantly, subtly through so many means.

Daily interactions with families. Ellie says, "There aren't necessarily formal mechanisms for family involvement, but we think about the families in all of the decisions we make." She describes the center's staffing as being at a level that allows for daily quality interactions with parents or family members. Remember Darren and Jennifer's conversations with the toddlers' parents as the children arrived? There wasn't that rushed feeling experienced at some centers when children are "dropped off" or gently pushed into the room by a fleeting adult. Many parents barely get a "Good-bye, have a nice day," because teachers or caregivers are busy taking care of a group of children. There's enough staff in the toddler room that either Darren or Jennifer or both can take the time to discuss Bryanna's lack of sleep or listen to Faridah and Ibrahim's news.

Limited time for communication was listed as the most common barrier to parent involvement (Swap, 1987). Those time limits are true for both educators and family members. "Most often, parents and teachers interpret the other's lack of availability as a signal of their lack of concern for the child" (p. 8). Staff at the center have found a mutually convenient time for consistent availability that seems to work for both ed-

■ **FIGURE 8.9**

Example of Parent Bulletin Board:
Encouraging Input to Playground
Redesign

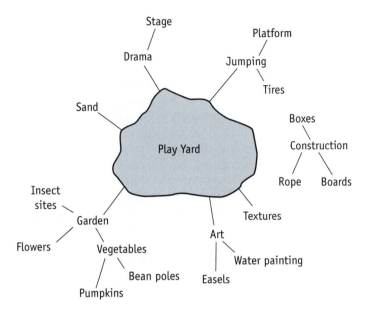

ucators and families. Those morning conversations are important, and when combined with home visits and several conferences, they can contribute to a relationship of trust and respect.

Remember how Ruth's dad came in and had breakfast with her before leaving for the day? It was obvious that it was not an unusual occurrence. Ellie tells us, "Many parents or family members come in and have lunch with their children on a regular basis." She explains, "Some of that is the ease of our location—middle of the campus and middle of downtown." She adds that it is greatly encouraged. Family members hear the message all the time: We need you, your presence is valued, come in and read a story, go with us on a field trip. "Those are pretty traditional, but they're comfortable and both adults and children are happy."

Giving families a voice.   Besides home visits, parent conferences, and newsletters from each class to keep families informed about curriculum, there's also a Parent Advisory Board, which is a formal structure to involve parents in the decisions and policies of the center. "The board provides feedback to the Center and advises on such matters as budget, and the board acts as an advocacy group on behalf of the Center when necessary" (Helen Gordon Child Development Center, p. 10). Ellie tells us, "When we anticipate major changes, especially those that influence all of the children, we try to involve all of the families, not just those on the advisory board." She describes a recent bulletin board that was designed to encourage and stimulate family contributions to plans for restructuring the playground area. Figure 8.9 shows the "web" of thinking about playgrounds that appeared on the bulletin board after the following note went home to parents and family members:

We are planing to make some changes in our playground and we need your ideas. In the lobby you will find a bulletin board labeled "Playground Ideas." Think back to when you were a child. . . . What kind of games, activities, and materials did you use for playing outside? What do you feel would be important for your child to experience here at the Center?

We are using a brainstorming method called "webbing," which is one of the ways we plan curriculum and build on the ideas of children and teachers. Our web theme is outdoor play, and the bulletin board displays the beginning of the web. Please contribute to the web with your ideas—new ones or ones that build or connect to another. We will also have a notebook available for you to share pictures of play yards that you have seen or for additional comments you want to share. The webbing process will continue through March 7th.

Thank you for your time and interest. More information will be coming your way soon.

The strategy of involving families communicates a value for families' ideas and input that goes beyond most involvement approaches. Family members have a voice in what happens at the center. Involvement empowers parents; they consider themselves as partners with staff in the education of their children. We scheduled some time with Ibrahim's parents to ask how they feel about their son's experiences at the center. We're especially interested in their ideas because Ibrahim is one of the many biracial children at the center, and we wonder about the impact of the center's curriculum on his development. Talking with his parents will also give us more insights about toddlers and their needs.

A conversation with Faridah and Amr.   Faridah and Amr's first interaction with the staff of the Helen Gordon Center occurred when Mohammed attended the program. Faridah described her fears and insecurities: "It was difficult—he was my first child. I was not familiar with child care—had never used a program—and the media examples of what can happen were frightening." Amr commented that he was surprised at the level of accommodation they received from the staff. Mohammed had unusual eating habits and required a special diet, and the staff worked with the family so that he could be comfortable. "They reported so carefully to us about his daily activities—always so much information about his interests, his mood, his feelings," he added.

Faridah admitted, "I learned a lot from watching in the classrooms and from parent conferences." She continued, "I began seeing different parts of my children, and my parenting skills have changed since the boys came here." She laughed when she told us about how her friends noticed Mohammed's maturity and his language development and that they decided to send their children to school, too. Amr summarized the effects of the boys' experience: "They taught my children to make choices (not what I would have thought of doing in my culture) and they've become independent."

Our conversation with Faridah and Amr added to our understanding of their family and of Ibrahim's development. It also provided insight into parents' perceptions and appreciations of the center's approach to involving families.

PRINCIPLES AND INSIGHTS: A Summary and Review

Remember how we promised that you would not get bored spending time with toddlers? The same is true for those families and early childhood professionals who surround toddlers. There is an energy and vitality to their conversations and interactions. Perhaps you are now thinking about toddlers and feeling attracted to working with them. Maybe you are thinking that toddlers are not for you. Regardless of your decision, it will be important to understand their development as part of your knowledge base of human development and child development. We urge you to extend your observational experience from this chapter by spending time in other classes for toddlers. Listen to educators like Darren and Jennifer. Meet with parents like Faridah and Amr to understand toddlers and, more importantly, to see them in the context of their families and their culture.

As part of your professional development, you have observed a university laboratory school in this chapter and have been introduced to antibias curriculum. As you continue your studies and other professional experiences, we urge you to expand your awareness of and sensitivity to bias by reading more about the topic, by attending workshops about antibias curriculum and teaching approaches, and by discussing the topic with educators who are committed to the concept.

Becoming an Early Childhood Professional

Your Field Experiences

1. Using the observation guide in Figure 8.7, practice conducting observations of toddlers in settings in which they are the only child (at home with a parent), in a small group, and in a larger group setting. Work to include observations of physical, social, emotional, and cognitive development, and notice the influence of the presence or absence of other children.

2. If possible, observe toddlers in two different programs. Watch them in a program that uses an *emergent curriculum* approach and flexible scheduling like you read about in this chapter. Try to find a contrasting program in which toddlers follow a strict schedule and a preplanned curriculum with themes and fewer choices of activities. After observing and recording what you see, compare the children's behavior.

Your Professional Portfolio

1. Your observational data will be a good entry in your portfolio, but be sure to accompany the recordings with a summary and reflection on what you learned about toddlers and the effect of their settings, curriculum, and adult interactions.

2. Develop a floor plan for a developmentally appropriate program for toddlers. You might want to consult *Developmentally Appropriate Practice in Early Childhood Education Programs* (Bredekamp & Copple, 1997).

Your Professional Library

Books

Concerned Educators Allied for a Safe Environment.
(1997). *Wampanoag Project: An anti-bias curriculum
for early childhood classrooms.* Cambridge, MA:
Boston CEASE Network.

Cryer, D., & Harms, T. (1988). *Active learning for twos.*
Reading, MA: Addison-Wesley.

Greenberg, P. (1991). *Character development: Encouraging self-esteem and self-discipline in infants, toddlers, and
two year olds.* Washington, DC: NAEYC.

Jones, E., & Nimmo, J. (1994). *Emergent curriculum.*
Washington, DC: NAEYC.

Miller, K. (1988). *More things to do with toddlers and
twos.* Mt. Ranier, MD: Gryphon House.

Neugebauer, B. (1992). *Alike and different: Exploring
our humanity with young children.* Washington, DC:
NAEYC.

Swap, S. (1987). *Enhancing parent involvement in schools.*
New York: Teachers College Press.

Teaching Tolerance Project. (1997). *Starting small.*
Montgomery, AL: Teaching Tolerance Project,
Southern Poverty Law Center.

Internet Addresses and World Wide Web Sites

www.exnet.iastate.edu/pages/nncc/Child.Dev/intel.dev.
todd.html
Intellectual Development of Toddlers (M. Lopes, 1994)

www.exnet.iastate.edu/pages/famil..ncc/Diversity/
dc31_celebrate.divers.html
Celebrating Diversity: Resisting Bias (W. Horikoshi, 1993)

www.cortland.edu/www/libwww/tmc/anti-bias_curr.htmix
*Anti-Bias Curriculum Evaluation (SUNY Cortland
Library, 1995)*

Head Start

FELIPE'S STORY

When you finish reading and reflecting on this chapter, you will be able to:

1. Outline different curricular activities planned for a preschool setting.

2. Describe the history of and need for Head Start programs.

3. Summarize the role of families in Head Start programs.

4. List and justify several changes needed in Head Start programs.

5. Describe strategies to support cultural and linguistic diversity with young children.

In 1965, Head Start began as a federally funded comprehensive preschool program designed to break the cycle of intergenerational poverty. Initially, Head Start consisted of summer programs, focused on preparing 5-year-olds to succeed in kindergarten. The program has gone through numerous changes over the years, yet it continues to assist young children and their families gain access to education, health care, and social services. Now, let's join Felipe as he begins his morning at Washington County Head Start.

Washington County Head Start

It's 8:15 in the morning and the Head Start mini-buses are just arriving. About 8 to 10 children and several adults step out of each bus. With the morning rain, everyone hurries into the Community Action Building and heads for different classrooms. The children, 3 and 4 years old, hang up their coats and go to the sinks to wash their hands in the common area. Susana, the teacher in Felipe's classroom, greets her 20 students (all 4 year olds) as they enter the room.

Breakfast

The children quickly find a place to sit at the tables, which are already set with dishes and food. Each morning, they begin their day with breakfast. "Estan bueno comer con amigos (It's so nice to eat with friends)," the children say together before eating. Food is served family style, with children passing bowls of cereal, pouring milk, and helping themselves to bananas. Susana, Rita (the teaching assistant), and Rosa (a parent volunteer) sit with the children and join in the morning conversation. "Bananas taste good," says Madalena. "Whoops," announces Isabella as she spills her milk. She quickly picks up the dishcloth and cleans up her milk. The conversation and eating continues. You observe that many children are speaking Spanish, with some English words mixed in their sentences.

As the children finish breakfast, they carry their dishes to the dish-washing area, where a parent volunteer helps them. Estella scrapes her leftovers into one tub, leaves her silverware in the soaking pail,

Valentin begins breakfast by sharing the fruit basket. The children enjoy making their own decisions about their food.

and rinses her plate. She shows you how to clean your dishes, "Put your glass over here and leave the banana peels in the garbage."

Raul leaves his dishes on the table as he heads for the blocks. Susana walks over to Raul and quietly reminds him, "Remember, we clean up our own dishes. Then you play." Raul heads back to the table and picks up his bowl, spoon, and cup. "Now I play," he announces. Susana tells you, "We prefer gentle reminders to provide **guidance.** It is like 'reading' the environment, always keeping an eye on what is going on and being ready to step in to help the children choose an appropriate action." You admit it didn't seem punishing, merely helpful, when she provided direction to assist Raul.

Outside Play

After the children clear their spots at the tables they put on coats for outside play. There are two outside times each morning. Today, they have a choice of playing a game called Red Light, Green Light, playing with balls, or choosing other activities. Pepe and Ramon eagerly climb the climbing structure, which looks like a fort with ladders and slides. Part of the outside area is covered, so children play here without getting wet. Everywhere you look, you see children moving around, some individually and others playing together. You are reminded of the physical development of 4-year-olds and their need for activities that involve the use of large muscles. With the space and equipment outside, these children are developing coordination and balance through the games and activities, promoting the use of their large muscles. Rita, Jessica, and Eduardo are drawing enormous pictures with sidewalk chalk. "Look at the giant man I made," exclaims Jessica. Indeed, it is huge—at least eight feet tall. Rosa is with Felipe and Estella, who are playing some type of tag game, running and skipping along the edge of the play area. "Try to catch me," teases Felipe as he darts around the corner.

Thinking about Susana's comment about reading or scanning the environment, you watch Rita and Rosa and, indeed, although they are both involved with activities with children, they do scan the entire play area continually. Just as Ramon starts to jump from the perch of the fort, Rosa walks over and asks him, "How are you supposed to get down from the fort, Ramon?" Ramon looks at her and moves off of the perch and then starts to climb down the ladder. So, this is why people say teachers have eyes in the back of their heads. These teachers seem to process what is going on around them and make good predictions about what might happen next. They also know when to step in to help the children problem solve. For example, after Rosa asked Ramon how to get down from the fort, she waited until he moved away from the perch and toward the ladder. She seemed to know that prompting with a brief question was enough to change Ramon's activity and that it was not necessary for her to help Ramon down the ladder.

After 15 minutes outside, Rita calls to the children, "Time to go inside. Think about what you might like to do today during choice time."

Journal 9.1: Children ride the bus, arrive at school, eat breakfast, and then go outside to play. What might be a benefit of scheduling outside time this early in the morning? ∎

Choice Time

Today, children are busy with puzzles, books, blocks, the dramatic play and kitchen area, or working at a gardening table with plastic plants and real garden tools such as trowels and gardening gloves. There are many choices in the classroom for free play. Eduardo shows you how to plant. "Put on your gloves first. See, this is the dirt. Put that in the pot and then put a flower in to grow. And here is the water." Susana tells you that sometimes this is a sand table or a water table, but right now, it's the gardening table. The activities planned for this week revolve around the theme of spring, and the gardening table fits right in with this theme.

You notice that besides the gardening area, there are several different centers set up around the room: a reading center, mail center, puzzle table, and a blocks and transportation center. A **center** (also called *learning center, activity center,* or *interest center*) is an area with materials that support active learning and typically include activities planned around children's interests, individual and small group learning, and developmentally appropriate learning. Near the rug in the front of the room is the reading center, with large pillows, a couch, and a cart with books (some written in Spanish and some in English). On one of the tables are several puzzles, with Isabella and Josue working with these. "Look, I found the piece to fit here!" At another table, Rita has placed a typewriter, paper, envelopes, stamps, pencils, and crayons. Three children are talking about mailing their letters, "We better get our letters ready before the mail goes out." In the back of the room are two different areas. In the one area with clothes for dramatic play and a small kitchen with real pots and pans, Miguel, Esteban, and Floranna are "making a huge cake for everybody." The other area has blocks, cars, trucks, and traffic signs. Felipe, Eduardo, Berenise, and Deanna are building a town. "Let's make this the store and the school goes here. Put the stop sign near the school, OK?" It looks like choice time really offers lots of choices for the children. In most any preschool setting, you would find a free-play or choice time similar to the one you are observing.

The New Community Action Organization Building

Carolyne, the program coordinator, comes to the door of the classroom. She asks you, "Would you like to talk about our program while the children are involved in choice time? We would have about 20 minutes before their next activity." Sounds great—you have observed just enough to have even more questions than when you first arrived this morning.

Community Action Organization

Walking down the hallway toward Carolyne's office, you wonder, "Is this a new building?" "Yes, it's two years old. We are housed within the Community Action Organization Building," replies Carolyne. "We had a 10-year building drive to raise the funds for this building. This was truly a collaborative effort, with block grants, fund raising, and donations from local businesses and donors supporting the Community Action Building." Other Community Action programs are housed in the adjacent wing of the building. The programs range from social services, emergency housing assistance, to skills training for adults. Head Start is viewed as a branch of these resources, as children and families receive education and social services to support family needs.

Overview of Washington County Head Start Program

Carolyne suggests that she start with a brief overview of their Head Start program. "We are a countywide program, with about 350 children and their families. Our overall purpose is to increase the social competence of children from low-income families by providing 'developmentally appropriate education and care for children, involve and support their parents, and offer early childhood services that meet family needs'" (Washington County Community Action Organization, 1996). At each of the centers, staff includes a center coordinator, one teacher/home visitor per class, and one or more assistant teachers. In addition, consulting staff include mental health consultants, early childhood special education consultants, and family workers. "We work together toward our goal of increasing social competence of our children, and we meet frequently to accomplish this goal."

In order to enroll in Head Start, families must meet certain criteria, as the program is established to provide services for children and families with low-income levels. Figure 9.1 describes the ser-

■ **FIGURE 9.1**   Washington County Head Start: Community Action Organization

To Enroll:
- Call office nearest your home. Make an appointment to visit the office for intake.
  Office hours are Monday–Friday, 8:30 a.m.–5 p.m.
- Prepare to bring the following:
  Income information
  Immunization record
  Birth certificate (child must be 3 or 4 by September 1 of the school year)
  Information about your child's disability, if he or she has one
- There are ten Head Start Centers in Washington County serving 346 children.
- Head Start has limited enrollment; children are enrolled as space becomes available.
- Children are enrolled in the site nearest their home that offers the services they need.
- Enrollment opportunities for children with disabilities are available.

Options:
- Head Start preschool (no cost to income-eligible families)
- Paid preschool and full child care, before and after school care, available in Gaston only

Head Start Services:
- Quality preschool, focus on constructive play, cultural diversity, personal safety/abuse prevention, social skills
- Individualized education plan and ongoing assessment for every child
- Comprehensive screening including vision, hearing, nutrition, height/weight, developmental, speech/language, assessment of physical and dental exams
- Social services—family worker available to assess family needs, follow up as indicated
- In-home visits by teacher support parent as educator and home as learning environment
- Transportation provided by Head Start in some areas
- Parent involvement opportunities include Policy Council, parent committees, classroom volunteering, employment, and training

Source: Community Action Organization Head Start. Reprinted by permission.

vices provided by this particular Head Start program. Families who qualify (that is, who are below a certain income level) are able to participate in the program without any fees. In this center, Carolyne explains, "We reserve approximately 10 percent of our program enrollment for children with special needs. Unfortunately, only about one-third of children who qualify are able to attend Head Start. We do not have enough funding to provide services for the other two-thirds of eligible children." Hopefully, this situation will change as more legislators support approval of an increased budget for Head Start funding. One of the national education goals is to ensure that all children begin school ready to learn. Certainly, Head Start programs are one way to help children from low-income families be prepared for school.

Hispanic Population of Children in Washington County Head Start

Many children in Washington County's Head Start Program are of Hispanic descent. In fact, in Felipe's classroom, all 20 children are Hispanic. The teachers acknowledge and celebrate the different cultures of the children and include many activities to promote cultural awareness and appreciation.

According to a Head Start program information report, the largest number of culturally and linguistically diverse children enrolled in Head Start across the nation are Spanish speaking, with many other language groups represented in increasing numbers (Head Start Bureau, 1995). All the teachers at this Washington County Head Start Center speak Spanish and English, which reflects the importance of communicating and learning in a child's and family's first language. When you visit Felipe's classroom and later meet with Susana, Felipe's teacher, she will share her thoughts about bilingual and bicultural education.

Role of Families in Head Start

Families are an integral component of Head Start. Family involvement includes volunteer work in classrooms or the school, serving as a representative on the Policy Council (each classroom elects one parent representative), or participating in parenting classes. There is a **Family Services Staff** at the center that provides social services through a coordinated model. This model identifies and supports the strengths, needs, and interests of each family through accessing social services (such as medical services or housing programs), providing educational training, or linking parents with employment programs.

Home visits.   In addition to support through social services, Head Start teachers visit each family in their home a minimum of five times each year. These home visits are seen as "the most effective way to produce changes in the child's long-term dispositions toward learning. The parent who understands the school program and who sees the child as a learner is better equipped to advocate for the child. Home visits also enable us to reach out to the parent . . . so we can build parent self-esteem and help families reach their goals" (Washington County Community Action Organization, 1996). Later, Susana will share the format and themes of the home visits with you.

Parent/teacher conferences.   Teachers also hold two parent/teacher conferences during the school year to focus on goals for each child and to provide support needed for the child to reach these goals. Teachers make phone calls home and send frequent notes to keep in contact with families. Carolyne finds, "All of these different communication formats are essential to involving families in Head Start." Another way families are involved is through adult education. A classroom for adult education is located in the Washington County Community Action Building.

Adult education program.   Passing classrooms as you walk back down the hall toward Felipe's classroom, Carolyne points out the five classrooms in this section of the building. Four of them house Head Start classes and one is for an adult education program. "Each morning, parents of Head Start children who are interested in pursuing a G. E. D. (Graduate Equivalency Diploma), job training, or improving their English language competency spend time in this classroom. Tutors and volunteers assist parents in achieving educational goals." Carolyne continues, "Parents are welcome to ride the school bus, volunteer in the classroom, attend adult education classes, and share meals with their children." Helping parents improve their education is a goal of Head Start. "It's important to meet both the child's and parent's educational needs. Their learning is woven together. For example, many children are being introduced to the English language in their Head Start classrooms. At the same time, their mother and/or father might be learning English in the adult literacy program. They can share and practice their new language skills together at home." You glance in the adult education classroom and see several people at computers, two small groups in conversation, and several individuals filling out forms. This does seem to be a logical place for an adult education program, right next door to their child's classroom.

Journal 9.2: How might educational opportunities for parents at the Head Start Center relate to their child's learning? ■

With this brief introduction to Washington County's Head Start Program, you head back to the classroom, eager to observe Felipe, his classmates, and Susana in action. Curious about the curriculum and the bilingual nature of this classroom, you enter the room just as the children begin circle time.

Felipe's Morning

Circle Time

Circle time follows breakfast, outside play, and choice time. Susana turns to José and says, "It's your turn to ring the bell." José rushes over to the counter, picks up the bell, and rings it, saying, "Time to go to circle!" The children clean up the areas where they have been playing, with parent volunteers and teacher assistants helping them. Susana is seated on the large rug near the front of the classroom. Children begin to join her there. Rita, the teacher assistant, is helping Manuel put puzzles away. Each time Rita looks away, Manuel dumps the puzzle out again. Rita notices what Manuel is doing and provides guidance by saying, "This time we will put the pieces in, leave them in, and then go to the rug." Together, they finish the puzzle and walk over to the circle.

When the children are settled at the circle, Susana puts a tape in the tape player. The music starts and Susana begins singing, "We all go around walking together." The children stand up and start walking around the circle, joining in the song. The first verse is in English, the second verse in Spanish. During the second verse, the children change direction and walk the other way. Julio and Isauro hold hands with Rita, as they walk along. Julio has some difficulty with his balance, so Rita is nearby to provide support as needed. "Not too much," she says, "Only enough to make it safe for him." Julio has motor challenges, sometimes bumping into objects or falling down. Susana referred him for further testing and diagnosis, as she wanted him to receive support services to help him in his development. She shares, "I'm glad he's in our class. He has such a cheerful attitude. I want him to have the support he needs to help him with his physical coordination and development."

As the song ends, the children stop walking. Several children bump into each other, which causes some giggles. Susana requests, "Sit down, please, and let's think about today's weather and our job chart." You've noticed that she starts many of the activities with a brief overview about the activity. This must help the children focus on what is going to happen next and know what Susana expects of them. Felipe points to the job chart, "Today, I want to check for the bus." Susana holds up cards with names and asks Rosina to pick five cards. "These are today's workers: Marcos, Gerardo, Francisco, Julio, and Jenesis." The five children come up to the pocket chart and each places his or her name card into a pocket with a picture of a job on the outside. Two children will wash tables after lunch, one child will inform Susana when the bus arrives, and Julio and Jenesis will each choose a book for story time. Felipe laments, "I wanted a job, teacher." Susana reminds him, "You had a job yesterday and we have to take turns. But you can ring the bell for outside play today." That brings a smile to Felipe's face.

Project Time

Susana asks the children about today's weather. "It's rainy today. We need coats," says Ariel. "You are so right," responds Rosa, the parent volunteer. Looking at the calendar, Susana places a raindrop on March 12. "Two more days and then we have a long vacation. See these days? We do not have school for one, two, three, four, five, six, seven, eight, nine days." Spring vacation is arriving soon. Susana points to March 11. "That was yesterday. Do you remember something we did together yesterday?" Manuel remembers, "The funny clown came to see us. She painted our faces, too." This brings up a lot of conversation about the clown and face designs. Susana replies, "Right, the clown came here yesterday. And, this is today on our calendar, and here is tomorrow."

Rita turns to you and explains, "Susana introduces the calendar to the 4-year-olds during the early spring months. She wants the children to talk about today, yesterday, and tomorrow as they begin to gain an understanding of time and events." Using the calendar is a way for teachers to help children gain a visual connection to days and events. There is some controversy regarding the use of calendars with young children and whether the idea of time is too abstract for children before kindergarten age.

Journal 9.3: Do you think it is appropriate for 4-year-olds to talk about today, tomorrow, and yesterday? What do you think about the controversy surrounding the use of month-long calendars with young children? ■

"Now, let's think about our 'Getting Ready for Spring' project," suggests Susana. "Remember, we have been dressing the dolls the past few days. What did we want them to wear to be ready for spring weather?" Teresa smiles, "I put boots on the little boy and made an umbrella for him." Rita holds up the doll wearing a raincoat, boots, and holding an umbrella made from fabric and a pipe cleaner. "Look at him. He's ready for the weather now," shares Rita. Felipe says, "Just like today—rain, rain, rain." Susana holds up a handful of pipe cleaners and a basket of fabric. "Today, when you go to one of the centers, you may choose to make a rainy-day picture with umbrellas, or paint a picture about any other ideas you have about rainy spring days, or make rainy-day things."

Rita has already prepared paint and placed brushes at two of the tables. The third table has scissors, glue, fabric pieces, pipe cleaners, and construction paper on it. "You may choose to paint first and then add decorations, or make decorations first and then paint the picture," says Rita. The children go to the tables, picking up paint smocks placed over the back of chairs. Rita and Susana help the children get started. Rita also turns on the tape player, so they can sing along with rainy-day songs.

During these different activities, children make choices about their projects. Some children use paints, others use construction paper or fabric. Isuaro finds the glue stick and is gluing clouds all over his paper. At another table, Marcos and Berenise are making lots of colorful boots. At the painting easels, Jessica is painting large circles. She says, "These are suns trying to come out today."

At the construction table, Rosa, the parent volunteer, is helping children cut out fabric for umbrellas. Felipe wants to "make lots and lots of raindrops." He likes to add extra details to his pictures, and he's excited about the idea of shiny raindrops. Felipe finds some aluminum foil for his rain drops. "Wow, everyone will see my rain now!" Next to him, Madalena is cutting out little boots. She wants to make "a whole page of boots so kids can keep their feet dry." Sounds like a good idea, as you notice rain is still falling outside.

Trying to scan the entire classroom, you see an adult with each of the three groups of children at

The painting easels are a popular spot in this classroom. What do you notice about the paint supplies, materials, and related equipment?

the different activity tables or centers. The children have choices about their projects, with adult supervision and assistance nearby. The activities or choices are designed to be developmentally appropriate for 4-year-olds, including large pieces of paper for paintings, glue sticks instead of large bottles of glue (it's difficult for 4-year-olds to control the amount of glue on their project), fabric already cut in small pieces, and paints in stable containers to reduce spills.

While the children work on activities, the adults are engaged in conversation with the children about their creative work without directing their work. You hear Lucero exclaim, "Oh, look at the raindrops. They keep moving down your page." Ruben explains, "Sí, I want a rainy, rainy picture." They both seem pleased with Ruben's work.

Susana explains to you, "I integrated art, music, and science into our Spring Project theme. I think it helps the children understand the season better when they connect with lots of different subjects and real occurrences in their life. So talk-ing about weather in relation to what to wear in this season is important for them to learn."

The children work at the centers on their projects for about 40 minutes. At this point, Rita and Susana remind the children, "Clean your hands first, then take off your paint smocks. We will let your paintings dry while you are outside playing." After washing their hands, the children head for the coat racks, pull on their coats, and go out to play.

Outside Play

During this second outside play, Susana brings out three pairs of boots and a tub of water. Several children pull on a boot, put their foot in the colored water, and make a footprint on the playground. "Look," exclaims Susana, "Your foot is really big." Estella and Roberto begin measuring their boot prints and try to decide who has the biggest boot. After a few more minutes spent measuring boot prints, Felipe asks, "Teacher, is it time for me to ring the bell yet?" "Sure," says Rita. Felipe reaches for the bell and reminds everyone, "Time to wash your hands for lunch."

Lunch Time

Again, the children start their meal by saying, "Estan bueno comer con amigos." Conversations are about rainy-day pictures, boot prints, and plans for their afternoon. Ruben remembers, "Today, we are going to my friend's house and see his new kittens." That starts a string of stories about cats and kittens. You hear Susana asking Teresa, "What is your favorite fruit?" Several conversations are about the food the children are eating. You think of the Head Start Parent Handbook you saw in Carolyne's office and recall that nutrition was included in the program goals. This leads you to assume that is a reason the children and adults are discussing food and food groups. Rita is sitting near Felipe and Marcos as they discuss pizza. Felipe says, "Next to ice cream, pizza is my favorite." Rita asks him, "What is on top of pizza?" He says, "Ketchup and cheese." "Close," says Rita. "This red sauce is made out of tomatoes, just like ketchup." "Well, I like tomatoes," agrees Felipe.

Soon, the meal is ending. Children follow the same routine as they did at breakfast, bringing dishes to the cleaning cart, scraping food into a bin, and sorting dishes, glasses, and silverware into appropriate soaking containers. They then head for a story on the rug before going home. Rosa, the parent volunteer, reads the story in Spanish, chosen by Julio. Just as she finishes, Marcos looks out the door and announces, "I see buses!" Susana walks toward the door with the children. They begin singing, "Adios amigos, es hora a parte (Good-bye my friends, it's time to go)." Susana, Rita, and Rosa help with coats and walk with them to the door. "See you mañana, and remember to tell your family about your rainy-day painting and boot prints."

Susana turns to you and says, "I need to make a quick phone call to Jessica's mother. Then let's meet in the classroom for a visit about our program." You help Rita hang up the rainy-day paintings. Several of the children added umbrellas or boots from different fabrics or papers. The paintings are all different and quite colorful.

A Visit with Susana

Susana's Philosophy of Teaching

You ask Susana to tell you how she came to work at Head Start. She responds, "My college work was in psychology and I began working in a child care center following graduation. After a year at that center, I heard about an opening in Head Start. I started five years ago as an assistant teacher and two years ago was promoted to lead teacher."

Knowing that a teacher with five years of experience has a rationale or a philosophy for what happens in her classroom, you ask Susana about her philosophy of teaching. She tells you, "In my classroom, my major goal is to help children become the best that they can. By this, I want children to learn social skills and learn how to solve problems in getting along with each other as well as academic skills to help them in their development. I also spend part of each school day working with families. I teach from 8:30 to 12:00 and then spend from 12:30 to 4:00 meeting with parents, talking on the phone with families, or planning for or going on a home visit, along with my curriculum planning. So my philosophy of teaching also includes working with families to help them support their child's learning."

When you observed the children in Felipe's classroom, you saw that choice time activities were designed to allow for student-centered learning. You ask Susana why she plans for choice or free-play time for the children each day. She explains. "We have a 45-minute block planned each day for free-play or choice time. Although there may be a theme connected with a project we are working on, we want children to choose their activities and friends to play with. Children learn so much from play. At 4 years of age, they are ready to spend time negotiating activities and making choices. Did you notice the children working with the typewriter?" she asks. "Some of them are typing their names with the typewriter. They are learning to use a keyboard and to put letters together. The children who select this activity are successful, whether they type their name or make up pretend words. They can finish the activity with a stamped letter, perhaps draw a picture on it, and we send it to their home or friend's home. All of this is developmentally appropriate for this age child. It also fits with my philosophy of teaching—structuring or planning activities that have an **expected outcome or objective,** such

What might these girls be talking about in this gardening activity?

as learning about letters and about the mail system, yet is open ended enough to allow children from differing ability levels to be successful learners. The children have freedom to choose which activities they want to be involved in during this free-play period."

Another aspect of Susana's philosophy is revealed when reviewing her **written plans.** When you look at her planning book, you see that she has a system to check if each of the developmental areas (cognitive, social, emotional, and physical) are incorporated in activities throughout the day. Remember the children working in the gardening table? They were talking about what plants need to grow (cognitive development), planning their garden together (social development), expressing satisfaction and delight with their planting skills (emotional development), and using small muscles and eye-hand coordination skills (physical development) to place the dirt in the pot with garden scoops. This was a developmentally appropriate activity for 4-year-old children, as it incorporated activities at their level as well as extended the skills and knowledge they were learning in class.

Journal 9.4: Thinking back to the gardening activity, you remember Susana standing near the gardening table talking with Jessica. She noticed Pepe starting to sprinkle dirt in Jessica's pot and tossing dirt around the table. Gerardo complained about the dirt being thrown at the table. If you were Susana, what might you do to guide this interaction? ■

As Susana translates her philosophy of education into practice, she thinks about the children's learning needs and goals. In order to develop these goals, a screening assessment is conducted in the early part of the school year that helps her develop appropriate learning goals.

Screening

During the fall, each new student entering Head Start is administered the Early Screening Inventory (ESI). The ESI is an individual **developmental screening assessment** designed for use with children from 3 to 6 years of age. The ESI takes 15 to 20 minutes to administer and is composed of 25 items that are scored from 0 to 3 points, according to the child's response. The purpose of the ESI is to provide staff and family with information about the child's functioning in three major developmental areas:

1. *Visual-Motor.* Includes a Draw-a-Person task and items that examine fine-motor control, eye-hand coordination, and ability to remember visual sequences and to reproduce two and three dimensional visual tasks

2. *Language and cognition.* Includes items that examine language comprehension and verbal expression, and ability to reason, count, and remember auditory sequences

3. *Gross motor/Body awareness.* Includes items that evaluate a child's large muscle coordination, balance, ability to hop, skip, and imitate body positions from verbal cues. (C. Westlake, personal communication, July 3, 1997)

The ESI is administered in the child's primary language. As in most developmental screening assessments, different developmental areas are broken into observable tasks, which the child performs during the individual assessment session. Tasks are sequenced on a developmental continuum and linked to an age at which a child should typically be able to perform the task. The results of the assessment show significant developmental delays or areas where children are more advanced.

Children are not "screened out" of the program; rather, the purpose of the screening is to develop individual educational plans for the child, based on her current level of development. When Julio was screened, it was found that he had developmental motor delays. The result of the screening led to a referral for further testing and diagnosis, in the process of securing special education services to support and assist Julio in his development. Some 10 percent of the enrollment in Head Start Programs is designated for children with special needs. These children are included in their classroom with their peers, with special education services coming to the program.

Susana explains, "Since screening is administered early in the school year, I can discuss the strengths and needs of each child with his or her parents. We then work together to develop each child's educational plan to reflect goals drawn from this assessment."

You ask Susana about the controversy regarding the use of screening inventories. You've heard that some educators feel that screening children leads to categorizing them and looking at their weaknesses more than at each child as a whole. Susana tells you, "We think of the screening inventory as a piece of information about each child. The screening helps us see if there are areas we should focus on to help the child learn. And if the child knows more than was shown on the inventory, we are quite pleased and move to other areas in his or her education plan." Her comments help you see that in this Head Start program, the screening inventory is used for information purposes and not as the sole representation of what a child knows or can do.

Now that you have learned more about the educational philosophy that Susana works from, let's look at the curriculum in her classroom, which is grounded in her philosophy of teaching.

Curriculum

 When asked about curriculum, Susana shares, "My curriculum comes mainly from the learning needs of my students and my knowledge of developmentally appropriate learning activities for 4-year-olds. Also, many of the major ideas for projects and themes come from ideas shared by the teachers in our center. We plan together in the beginning of the year and then make many changes according to the children's learning needs and interests that emerge during the year. We also look at individual education plans for each child and make sure this is incorporated in our day-to-day curriculum. And, of course, since all of my children are Hispanic and speak Spanish, we work with a bilingual and bicultural curriculum." These areas of curriculum will be explored in this section.

Shared planning time.   At this Head Start center, teachers have a **shared planning time** on Mondays. They plan several large projects for the month and make more specific plans for the week. Susana finds she gets lots of great ideas from other teachers. "It seems we each have special interests or talents and share these with each other. One of the teachers is an artist and we really appreciate her ideas about painting and drawing."

An example of shared planning is evident in the current project theme of spring. One teacher owns a nursery and brings in seeds and soil for other teachers to use in their classrooms. She also donated gardening tools. The children will take a field trip to the nursery soon. Working together has brought expertise and additional resources into the classrooms and benefited both teachers and children. Susana reflects, "When I first started here, I had no experience in curriculum planning. I relish the ideas and the sharing among the teachers here and have learned a lot about curriculum and teaching from working together."

Education plan.   Each child in the Washington County Head Start Program has an individualized **education plan** that was developed between the family and the teacher. During an early fall visit, the teacher makes a home visit to each child's family with the goal to develop the education plan for the school year (see Figure 9.2). Parents discuss what they would like their child to learn that year in Head Start with Susana. She listens to their thoughts and their goals for the child and discusses different strategies for accomplishing these goals. Susana explains, "For each goal, we develop a home strategy and a school strategy so we work together toward the same goal." At the end of the home visit, Susana leaves a copy of the goals and strategies developed in the visit with the family. Each child has two to five goals for the year, which then translate into classroom curriculum.

For example, Manuel's parents expressed concerned about his language development. "Manuel mostly uses two- or three-word phrases when he talks with us," they explain. "It seems like his brother was using more words when he was age 4." Susana assures them that Manuel's language is within the normal range of development for his age, but she agrees that focusing on this would be a good idea, especially through spontaneous play and conversational activities. Manuel's family and Susana developed a goal in this area that would encourage Manuel to use 4- and 5-word phrases and respond back to him with full sentences. Each day, Susana plans time for Manuel to spend in an activity that encourages conversation, such as sharing about the calendar or events at home. She records his progress each week and shares this with Manuel's family (see Figure 9.3 on page 346).

■ **FIGURE 9.2**   The Education Plan

The Teacher and Parent will develop an Individualized Education Plan for each child in the program. The Plan will describe educational goals for the child based on family goals as well as the results of comprehensive screening and assessment. It will form the basis for individualized educational activities throughout the year. The child's progress will be tracked and goals adjusted as circumstances change or goals are achieved.

For children starting in September or October, the Plan must be complete and in the child's file before the Winter break. For children starting after October, the Plan must be complete within 6 weeks of the child's first attendance. If this is the child's second year in the program, a new Education Plan should be written based on this year's Assessments.

One week prior to Ed Plan home visit send home Parent IEP Questionnaire **to be filled out by parent. Be sure to have extra copies at the conference for parents who forgot. Just looking at the questions ahead of time helps get the parents thinking, even if they don't write anything down.**

Children who were three on September 1st should have the Education Plan for Three Year Olds; children who were four on September 1st should have the Education Plan for Fours.

Assessment Tools to Take to the Education Plan Conference

Refer to Screenings and Assessments to identify the child's Strengths and Goals (Needs).
- Early Screening Inventory
- Health and Developmental Assessment
- Classroom and home visit observations
- Home Visit Plan and Record
- Oregon Assessment

Parent Involvement

As you review the IEP Questionnaire, invite parents to discuss what they hope their child will learn at Head Start. Be aware that parents have probably been conveying their goals all along, but in different words. (Example: "He has nobody to play with" is a way of saying, "I hope my child will make friends at Head Start.") The teacher can reflect the goals s/he believes the parent has been communicating rather than asking the intimidating question, "What are your goals?"

Writing and Goals

"What do we want the child to learn by the end of this school year?" Your goals for the child will relate mostly to the child's functioning in an educational environment. The family goals will be broader, looking at the child's functioning at home, in the neighborhood, and at school. Both are valuable.

Source: Community Action Organization Head Start. Reprinted by permission.

■ **FIGURE 9.3**

Note Home to Manuel's Family

> Dear Inez and Ramon:
>
> Several times this week Manuel spoke in four or five word phrases! He was very interested in our gardening table. When I worked near him, I asked him to tell me about planting. He said, "Put lots of dirt here." You might want to talk about planting with him. He has some great ideas.
>
> See you at our home visit next Thursday.
>
> Susana

His mother is also encouraging longer phrases and sentences in her interactions with Manuel. By learning what each family considers important for their child's learning, Susana finds, "I am able to plan curriculum that incorporates these individual education plans in our time at school."

Individual educational plans assist students with special needs to receive appropriate education and services through Head Start. In Susana's classroom, three children were identified as having special needs as a result of the developmental screening in September. Julio is now participating in physical therapy to improve his motor skill development. The physical therapist comes to the classroom and works with Julio one morning each week and them meets once a month with Susana to discuss Julio's progress and ways to integrate physical therapy in his classroom activities. The speech and language therapist meets with two children in the classroom on a weekly basis. Her recommendations for the children are included in their individual education plans, so the families and Susana work together to meet the child's needs. The early childhood special education specialist is a consultant who works with the specialists and with teachers and families to develop and monitor individual family service plans (IFSP). These plans are developed to assist the child in improving in specific areas that were identified as needing special attention. In most cases, the goals in the IFSP are also included in the child's individual education plan.

 Bilingual curriculum. Throughout the morning, Susana most often speaks in Spanish for instructional purposes and other times in English during conversations with the children. Most of her students' first language is Spanish. Susana's intent in using Spanish for instruction is to ensure that the children's learning is comprehensible, which requires use of the child's primary language. **Bilingual education** is interpreted differently by many educators. We will refer to bilingual education as the presentation of curriculum in two languages—the home or primary language of the child for acquisition of new knowledge and English for learning the dominant language. In this model of bilingual education, the teacher consciously organizes instruction so that the primary language is used as a tool for learning. The purpose of using the second-language, English, is to promote second language development. Susana has had her own experiences with learning a new language and culture as a child. She tells us, "I came to America from Peru when I was 14 years old. I did not know English and wanted to make new friends. I was so lonely. It is very important to me to find a way to honor the language the child speaks and also to help that child learn English so he or she can be successful in school. And for the children who primarily speak English, I think it's important for them to learn Spanish. Most of them have relatives who speak Spanish only. If these children learn Spanish, they can communicate with their grandparents and learn more about their heritage and culture. One language or culture should not be discarded for another. Both should be honored."

Journal 9.5: Susana shared some struggles she experienced with learning English and living in a new culture. How might these experiences affect her belief about bilingualism and biculturalism in her classroom?

Susana's comments about bilingualism and biculturalism are similar to those made by the NAEYC in its position statement on linguistic and cultural diversity and by other prominent educators (Garcia, 1994, 1997) and sociologists. Garcia (1997) encourages early childhood educators to view cultural and linguistic diversity as a strength and a resource that children and their families bring to the school. Susana acknowledges and celebrates the cultural diversity of her students, while providing the educational experiences necessary to help prepare them for their future schooling.

One of Susana's professional development goals is to learn more about language development for children coming from a monolingual home. She wants to help Spanish-speaking parents understand the importance of communicating in the language in which they are strongest at home. She wants the children to have rich conversations with their family, which Susana feels occur more often when families use the language in which they are most familiar.

To meet her goal of increased competence in bilingual education, Susana feels, "I need to take some courses and workshops about bilingual education in early childhood and supporting families to retain their primary language and culture. I have much to learn about current research and findings about best practices to support linguistic and cultural diversity." You appreciate Susana's interest in continuing her learning in this area and you know her students and their families will benefit from her drive to learn more. Later in this chapter, you will read an in-depth discussion about supporting linguistic and cultural diversity.

Families are such an important component of Head Start, as you will experience when going to Felipe's home with Susana.

Home visits.   Susana visits each family at their home five times a year. Every visit has a focus, as well as time to talk about the child's progress and any questions or concerns the family might raise. Home visits support the connection between home and school

■ **FIGURE 9.4**   Education Home Visits and Parent-Teacher Conferences

---

**Washington County Head Start
POLICY**

Teacher home visits are the most effective way to produce changes in the child's long-term disposition toward learning. The parent who understands the school program and who sees the child as a learner is better equipped to advocate for the child, to seek out growthful experiences for the child, and to make sure the child gets to school. Home visits also enable us to reach out to the parent in a personal and supportive way, so we can build parent self-esteem and help families reach their goals.

Home Visits

Each enrolled family will be visited in their home by the lead teacher within two weeks of the child's first attendance. Families remaining in the program more than 3 months will have a second home visit. Families participating for more than 5 months will have a third home visit.

Home visits must be scheduled by the teacher two to seven days in advance of the visit. The Center Coordinator must be informed in advance of the home visit schedule of the teacher. The teacher uses the Parent Participation Record form to record the date, time, and content of the home visit. The parent initials this record.

Home visits cannot be conducted with daytime caregivers in lieu of parents. Caregivers may be included in home visits if the parent desires. It is acceptable to conduct home visits with another adult relative who lives with the child provided the parent who enrolled the child agrees.

Parent-Teacher Conferences

The teacher will meet with the parent(s) to review the child's status, needs, progress, and goals twice during the program year. Conferences are held at the center unless the parent needs to meet somewhere else (place of employment, home).

For children who enroll before Thanksgiving, the fall conference will be held before the Winter Holiday. For children enrolling later, the first conference will be held within 45 days of first attendance. The Individual Education Plan will be completed and approved by the parent at this conference. For children receiving Early Childhood Special Education services, the teacher should participate in the IFSP meeting in lieu of writing a separate Individual Education Plan. The teacher should assess the parent's need for support in preparing for the IFSP and serve as the parent's advocate.

The final conference is held upon withdrawal from the program or in May. The child's progress on Education Plan goals is reviewed and the parent and teacher write the Transition Plan, looking forward to the child's next educational placement.

Source: Community Action Organization Head Start. Reprinted by permission.

and improve communication. Figure 9.4 shows an overview of the home visits and parent/teacher conferences.

Prior to the visit, Susana calls the family to schedule a time to meet and to share the primary reason for the visit. "I want them to have time to think about the topic so we can share ideas during the discussion," she explains. The five topics for this year include:

- Orientation to the program, including completing any paperwork or forms
- Developing the educational plan
- Educational projects (includes projects that support the child's educational plan)
- Poster project (All about Me)
- Transition to kindergarten plan (reviews what the child has learned and goals to work on over the summer; the plan is sent to the kindergarten program)

Since you and Susana have a 3:00 appointment with Felipe's family, it's time to leave. Today, the focus is making a poster about Felipe.

A Home Visit with Felipe's Family

This is Susana's fourth visit of the year to Felipe's home. Susana has sent home a note to remind Felipe's family about materials they might want to have ready for the poster—perhaps photographs and ideas about favorite foods, friends, or places. Susana brings a basket of ribbons, glue, scissors, and fabric scraps for decorating the poster.

Felipe's Family and Home

You drive with Susana and arrive at the apartment complex where Felipe lives with his mother, brother Antonio, and grandmother. Susana tells you, "Our conversation will be in Spanish if the grandmother is home. If she is not there, we will converse in English. Felipe's mother is fluent in both English and Spanish. I always talk with each family the first time I meet them and ask if we should talk in Spanish or English. It is most important that we are able to have a good discussion in the strongest language of the family." Felipe and Antonio are waiting outside the door. "Hello. We are up here," calls Felipe. You wave and walk upstairs with Susana. Felipe's mother, Anna, is standing at the door. "Welcome and come inside, please," greets Anna. Anna shares, "My mother is at church, making handmade projects for the upcoming church bazaar. She said to tell you hello and hopes to be here for our next home visit."

Poster project.   After greetings are exchanged and Anna serves coffee, Susana starts unpacking her basket of materials. "Well, everyone, I hope you will enjoy this project as much as I do," shares Susana. She pulls out a questionnaire to get the conversation about Felipe started. "Let's talk about Felipe's favorite things, and then he can make some pictures and glue them on the poster." Felipe says, "I like Street Sharks and dinosaurs. Can I start making them for the poster?" "Yes, go ahead and start drawing," responds Susana. "What about favorite foods?" "Oh, ice cream, always more ice cream." Susana writes Felipe's name at the top of the poster and leaves room for a photograph. She then writes *Favorite Food: Ice Cream* below his name. Felipe says, "Here are the Street

Sharks." Susana writes *Favorite Toy: Street Sharks* on the poster. Susana asks Felipe if he and Antonio would like to make some ice-cream cones with the construction paper. "Sure, we can make different colors," replies Felipe.

They then look at the photographs that Anna has on the table. Anna tells about Felipe when he was a toddler. "See him riding his truck with Antonio? He always loved to be moving around." Felipe chooses that photograph to put on his poster, "Oh, I want the one with the truck and Antonio." Antonio asks, "Can I glue this on?" Felipe helps him use the glue stick and says, "You did a good job, Antonio." After adding his favorite color (red) and his favorite friend (Miguel), the poster is finished. Susana tells the family, "Doesn't this look wonderful? We will bring this to school for a few days to share with the class. Felipe, you can tell your friends at school about the pictures on your poster. Then you will bring this home to keep."

Anna's job.   With the poster project finished, Felipe and Antonio leave the table to play with their Street Sharks. Susana asks Anna to tell you about her job at Pine Hill Elementary School. "I am a teacher's assistant working with younger children and helping them with their reading and English. In first grade, many of the children learn to read in Spanish. Over half of the children speak Spanish as their first language. As they get older, more of their instruction and assignments are in English. I feel fortunate to be able to use my Spanish to help the children. School is important and they must learn as much as they can. Felipe will start kindergarten there next year. I am very proud of him." Anna has worked at the school for two years. She was divorced from Felipe's father several years ago. His father is involved in Felipe's Head Start program and assisted on the last field trip. Anna adds, "I want the best possible for my two sons. We will work hard together to help them do well in school."

Anna's hopes for her sons.   Anna's work at the elementary school provides her with a larger view of the complexity of bilingualism and biculturalism. Being raised in a country different from where one's parents were raised and learning a new language different from the home language has both benefits and challenges for families. Anna shares her belief about preserving the family's Hispanic heritage: "Felipe was born here, but my parents are from Mexico. My mother lives with us and helps a lot with the boys. She does not speak much English, so it is good for Felipe and Antonio to talk with her in Spanish. I try to have them teach her some English, too. She helps me cook meals and watches the boys if I have errands or appointments. Sometimes I cook American-type food, while other times we have tortillas, beans, and rice. I want the boys to learn about both cultures and languages."

Susana compliments Anna on her thoughtfulness in continuing the boys' culture. "It's important for them to learn about their heritage and customs in Mexico. You are doing a wonderful job teaching them about Hispanic ways while also preparing them for school."

Anna serves on the Policy Council at Head Start. She shares, "I learn a lot about schools at work that I can share with other parents. At Head Start, the parents work together with the teachers. I think it is important for parents to learn to be involved in their children's school. When we learn this at Head Start, then we can continue our involvement when our children start kindergarten in the public schools. Many Hispanic parents feel that they cannot go to school because their English is not good enough or that they do not know enough to ask questions. At Head Start, we learn that we do have good questions and that our children learn better when we know what is going on at school."

You think about the long-term impact made by involving parents during the preschool years, and realize that Anna has shared some insightful knowledge. All parents need to feel welcome at schools, and learning this through Head Start involvement helps parents continue to interact with their children's schools.

Journal 9.6: If you were the teacher in a program with children and their families speaking languages other than English, how might you encourage parents to become involved in their child's education and related activities? ■

Saying good-bye.   Susana notes the time. The visit was scheduled for one hour. First, Susana tells Felipe, "You have been working very hard in school—I want to share that with you and your family. And also to let everyone know how helpful you are with the other children in the class. I know you always try to help others work out problems. I do appreciate that." Then Susana thanks Anna, "We appreciate your time with us this afternoon and your work on the Policy Council. You have a lot of important knowledge and insights to share with parents." Anna calls the boys over, "Let's say good-bye to teacher Susana and her guest." Felipe says, "Thank you for helping me make the pictures, teacher Susana." Antonio adds, "When I get bigger, can we make one for me, too?" Susana assures Antonio, "Yes, when you are 4 we will make your poster!"

Susana reminds Anna, "Our next home visit is in five weeks and we will talk about Felipe's transition to kindergarten. Please think of any questions you have and we can talk about those. Also, remember you can call me any afternoon." Anna shares, "I have been thinking about kindergarten, so I'm glad that's our next topic. Thank you, Susana." You also thank Felipe, Anna, and Antonio for the enjoyable and informative visit.

With this introduction to Felipe and his family's experience with Head Start, let's take a closer look at Head Start and other preschool programs.

What Is Head Start?

History of Head Start

Head Start was designed in 1965 as a comprehensive program to help children from low-income families gain access to educational, social, and health services prior to entering kindergarten. It was viewed as a transition program to prepare children to be successful

■ **FIGURE 9.5** Project Head Start Memo

EXECUTIVE OFICE OF THE PRESIDENT
WASHINGTON, D.C. 20506

OFFICE OF ECONOMIC
OPPORTUNITY

February 12, 1965

MEMORANDUM

TO: All CAP Staff

FROM: Jule Sugarman

SUBJECT: Project Head-Start

OEO will be announcing this weekend the initiation of Project Head-Start. This program is focused on providing federal assistance to communities for the establishment of child development programs during this coming summer. These programs will involve health, social services and educational activities for children who are to enter school in the fall. Tentatively, it is planned to finance these programs under Section 207 although there is a possibility that at least some of them will be financed under Section 205. Fiscal Year 1965 funds will be used. The summer program will no doubt lead to increased community interest in similar programs beginning in September.

A special staff is being assembled in Washington to handle Project Head-Start. It will be headed by Dr. Julius Richmond who is currently Dean of the Medical School at the State Medical College of New York (Syracuse). Ben Tryck is Administrative Officer for the group and should be the point of liaison for CAP personnel. Mrs. Lyndon Johnson will be honorary chairman of the national committee supporting the program.

Mr. Shriver is sending letters to community leaders throughout the nation which will call their attention to Project Head-Start. His letter will include a registration card which can be returned to OEO indicating that the community is interested.

Source: "Before the Beginning: A Participant's View" by P. Greenberg, 1990, *Young Children, 45* (6), p. 41. Washington, DC: NAEYC. Copyright 1990 by NAEYC. Reprinted with permission from the National Association for the Education of Young Children.

in their initial public school experience. In the memo shown in Figure 9.5, you can capture some of the excitement and energy behind the beginning of Head Start.

During the 1960s there was a heightened awareness of the effects of children living in poverty on their later education and life success. As a nation, there was concern about these young children, which prompted development of a program to help break the cycle of failure. Head Start was part of the War on Poverty. Because the recipients were young children, it was supported by many legislators, including President Lyndon B. Johnson and much of the general public. Sargent Shriver was a chief supporter of Head Start, viewing it as an opportunity to support the victims of poverty—young children (Greenberg, 1990).

Shriver had been discussing programs for young children with experts in the fields of medicine, child development, psychology, and education. Several of these experts—including Robert Cooke, Urie Bronfenbrenner, and Ed Zigler—later became involved in Head Start and were influential in program development and design. Richard Boone, director of the Office of Economic Opportunity, made the suggestion that Shriver consider adding medical screening, nutrition components, and hiring of paraprofessionals (primarily parents of Head Start children) for one-fourth of the staff (Zigler & Muenchow, 1992). The next steps included establishing a planning committee to lay the foundation for the first summer program.

In the summer of 1965, Head Start was launched as a national program under the direction of Dr. Julius Richmond, a pediatrician, and Jule Sugarman. Nearly half a million children enrolled in Head Start that first summer, receiving educational programs, medical and dental attention, social services, and nutritious meals. The program soon evolved into a nine-month program, continuing an emphasis on education, social services, and family involvement. Through the history and evolution of Head Start, there have been many program changes while much of the original philosophy behind the program has stayed in place. Head Start is considered the "nation's most successful educational and social experiment" (Zigler & Muenchow, 1992, p. 244).

 Journal 9.7: Why do you think Head Start is considered to be such a successful program? ▪

Program Goals

Although changes have occurred in Head Start over the past 30 years, many of the current program goals are similar to those you would have seen in the early years of the program. The overall goal of Head Start is to provide comprehensive services to improve the education, social, and health of disadvantaged children (Currie & Thomas, 1994) so that these children will begin school ready to succeed.

In each state and community, Head Start looks slightly different. Some programs find their community health or social services offer adequate resource for their families, and see the role of Head Start as helping families access existing services. Programs are also allowed flexibility within the structure of federal guidelines, which enables local communities to develop programs to reflect their needs.

At the same time, there has been discussion lamenting the uneven quality among programs. In 1993 and 1994, the Advisory Committee on Head Start Quality and Expansion reviewed the Head Start program and made recommendations for improvement and expansion (Advisory Committee on Head Start Quality and Expansion, 1994). Their recommendations for Head Start in the twenty-first century included:

- Ensure quality through increased staff training, improvements in management, program standards, and better facilities.
- Adjust program services to meet the changing needs of families.
- Create new partnerships at community, state, and federal levels to meet the needs of families, communities, and state and national policy.

Meeting these recommendations means evaluating current programs and practices to assure that children and families are receiving the level of quality in services necessary to prepare children for success in school.

To meet the major program goals, assessment of activities and accomplishments within the areas of education, social services, and family involvement is required to determine if goals have been met. The next section looks at each of these areas and discusses how these components support the child and family.

 Education. As you saw in Felipe's classroom, the school day includes activities to support learning in each developmental area. With the knowledge base in early childhood education increasing, so does the commitment to developmentally appropriate curriculum in Head Start programs. Curriculum is planned to meet the current needs of 3- and 4-year-old children and to help children be successful in kindergarten and school in general. The curriculum includes lessons and activities that promote cognitive, social, emotional, and physical development. The goals from each child's individual education plan influence the curriculum. Attention in the curriculum is also given to the cultural background of the families in the program and of the larger community.

The curriculum schedule that Susana developed includes many activities that encourage active play and social interactions. During the morning, children are involved in large group activities (circle time) and in small groups (choice and project time). She also alternates activities that are teacher directed with activities that allow for more individual choice. Most 4-year-olds are beginning to be able to stay with an interesting

A parent volunteer works with four children as they cut and glue during choice time.

■ **FIGURE 9.6**   Family Services

Head Start believes that supporting a family's development also supports the child's development. Every center has staff who work with parents at home and in the center to solve problems and utilize resources identified through a family strengths assessment and plan. The program is using two models this year:

- The coordinated model which has a Family Service Specialist providing social services as assigned to approximately 60 families in one or two sites.

- The integrated model in which the Center Coordinator and Lead Teacher teach the class cooperatively and each provides social services and home visits to about 10 families.

Family Services Staff Can Help by:

Identifying strengths, needs, and interests.
Finding resources and services.
Working with parents in times of crisis.
Advocating with Welfare, Housing, Food Stamps and other agencies.
Providing assistance to parents seeking a GED, education or training.
Linking parents with employment programs.

Getting Ready for Head Start: Family Strengths Assessment

What are the strengths and challenges your family is facing today?
Do you feel safe and secure in your home?
Do you have access to health care for yourself and children?
Do you have enough food each month?

Source: Community Action Organization Head Start. Reprinted by permission.

project for an extended time period, so Susana plans some longer time blocks (45 minutes) for projects. Not only does this allow children to explore and create projects but it also helps them stay focused on an activity, which is a skill they will need when they enter kindergarten the following year. Many of the activities that you saw in Felipe's class would be found in other preschool programs for 3- and 4-year-old children, as well.

Social services.   Head Start programs are an important resource for many low-income families. Although families may have accessed different social services prior to their child's enrollment in Head Start, often this is the first time that these services are coordinated, with assistance available to help strengthen the entire family. Figure 9.6 discusses some of the family services available at Felipe's Head Start program.

Through support of the entire family and their needs, the child is more likely to experience a healthier home environment, leading to improved learning. For example, in times of monetary crisis, Head Start staffs are able to refer parents to the appropriate agency to access Food Stamps, thus ensuring that the family in need is able to obtain food.

Medical and dental screenings and follow-up services are also provided through Head Start. Prior to enrollment, a child must have a physical examination and be current with immunizations. If parents are unable to pay for these services, Head Start will assist them in obtaining medical services, and, in some programs, Head Start will pay for necessary medical care.

Another social service provided focuses on nutrition. A nutrition assessment is conducted with each family. Children and their families receive nutritional counseling during the year, with specific outcomes established for each family based on the nutritional assessment. Children also eat two meals during their day at Head Start, which are planned to meet the federal guidelines for nutritional requirements.

Family involvement. Each Head Start program offers various opportunities for family involvement. As you learned earlier, Felipe's mother, Anna, serves on the Policy Council, which works with Head Start administration to make program decisions. Other parent options include volunteering in or preparing materials for the classroom, attending parenting classes, helping on field trips or projects, and assisting in fund-raising activities or special events. In many programs, family events are planned throughout the year to encourage interactions between families and to offer opportunities for families to get to know each other.

Besides these activities, parents are involved in the program through their role in developing their child's education plan, and by participating in parent/teacher conferences and home visits. Family involvement is clearly a priority in all Head Start programs.

Head Start programs and preschool programs serve children of the same age—3- and 4-year-olds. Head Start was selected for this chapter in this book for several reasons. Head Start is far more comprehensive than most preschool programs. Few preschools have the funding to support parental involvement and social services in the capacity that Head Start does. Highlighting Head Start in this chapter enables you to observe a broad, comprehensive program for children of preschool age. The curriculum of many preschool programs is similar to Felipe's program. Thus, you are gaining knowledge about appropriate programs for 3- and 4-year-olds while also learning about support services for children and their families associated with Head Start. A look at preschool programs and at some general commonalties between preschool and Head Start will help describe a variety of programs available for this age group.

Preschool Programs

Preschools were called *nursery schools* in the early 1900s. Rachel and Margaret McMillan are considered to be pioneers in education for young children. These sisters were concerned about the health and development of children in England and consequently established a "nurture school" in the slums of London in 1911. The program in these schools included preventive health care (bathing, dressing in clean clothes, nutritious meals, and rest) and outdoor play. The goal of these activities was to nurture the child and to address the needs of children living in poverty. Some of these same goals are seen in Head Start programs today.

The beginning of preschool. In the United States, Abigail Eliot began the nursery school movement in 1922. Eliot had worked in England with the McMillan sisters as they developed the first nursery schools. Many of the early nursery schools in the United States were connected to colleges or universities and were viewed as a rich setting for teacher preparation and research. Eliot emphasized the need for a program to be established at nursery schools, with activities planned each day as part of this program. A major interest of Eliot's was the involvement of parents in their child's education. Her background was in social work and she viewed the relationship between parents and children as an important component of nursery school programs. Many people attribute the focus on parental involvement in early childhood to this emphasis initiated by Abigail Eliot.

In the 1930s, during the Depression, a large number of public school teachers found themselves out of work. Under the Works Project Administration (WPA), unemployed teachers were hired to work in nursery schools. Because of government funding for these unemployed teachers, the number of nursery schools increased significantly. As the Depression ended and World War II began, federal funding was no longer available for the WPA nursery schools. Child care programs were developed during World War II for the children of mothers working in war-related industry through the Lanham Act.

At the end of the war, government funding for child care programs stopped. Program support now came from tuition fees paid by families. In the early 1950s, parent-cooperative nursery schools began to spring up around the country. Cooperative nursery schools provided child care and education at reasonable costs, with parents involved in the school administration and the day-to-day running of the school. Because many of the nursery schools required tuition or time commitments from parents, nursery school education was primarily available for children from middle-class families. With this change, less emphasis was given to health care and the school day was shortened, often with 3-year-olds attending a program two mornings a week and 4-year-olds attending nursery school three mornings each week. Parent-cooperative preschools are still in existence today, as you saw when you visited the preschool with the theorists in Chapter 3.

Preschools of today. Parents looking for a preschool for their child have many different options available. Preschool programs are now part of the day at most child care centers and home care centers. The preschool portion of the day might be a half-day or full-day program. Parent-cooperative preschools are often half-day programs, several days per week, although some are on a full-day schedule. Another type of preschool program is connected to universities. These programs, which are often called *laboratory schools,* serve as a site for research and the study of child development and education. Some churches provide preschool programs, as well, with financial support subsidized by the church.

As you can see, there are many options for parents to examine as they make choices about a preschool program for their child. Parents would want to observe at the preschool and discuss program goals, schedules, priorities, and family involvement with the program director and caregivers before making a decision about enrolling their child. The curriculum and day-to-day activities differ widely at these preschools. Some schools focus on art, music, and movement, while others may have a strong academic focus. Other preschools emphasize social development. Parents find they need to become informed about early childhood education to make a good decision about a preschool for their child. Also, as you have learned, another important preschool option is Head Start, serving children from low-income families.

 Similarities and differences between Head Start and other preschool programs. It is difficult to make specific comparisons between Head Start and all other preschool programs. Head Start programs around the country differ from each other, as do preschool programs. There are several commonalties that most programs for 3- and 4-year-olds share, however. Most all Head Start and preschool programs include art, music, and movement activities. Young children enjoy expressing themselves through these forms of art. Play is another common aspect, as play provides for many enjoyable learning experiences appropriate for this age group. Listening to stories read by adults is another favorite activity of children this age.

The emphasis on beginning academics varies widely between preschools. Most preschools leave these skills for later years, although a few schools do begin teaching the alphabet and printing letters and numbers. As Head Start and preschool programs move toward a developmentally appropriate curriculum, there is increased emphasis on creating a balance in cognitive, language, social, and emotional development, with free-play and project-based learning as important parts of the curriculum.

As mentioned earlier, some of the greatest differences between preschools and Head Start are found in the role of support for families and access to social and health services. Head Start is highly regarded for its comprehensive program, which attends to social, educational, and family services in order to support the development of the whole child. Some preschools have parent activities or classes; few have access to adult education programs for parents of preschoolers similar to those at Head Start. The same is true of social services. In Felipe's Head Start program, social services are located in the adjacent wing to his classroom building, and adult education programs are two classrooms away from his class. Although some preschools have lists of community resources and local agencies, they typically have less connection to social services as those found in Head Start programs.

Research conducted on Head Start programs has provided a wealth of knowledge and information about best practices in early childhood education. Two critical learnings gained from Head Start experiences are the importance of involving parents in the child's education and the need for the preschool curriculum to address individual education plans. Incorporating these two program components as goals of any preschool program strengthen the overall program, regardless of the family income level. The knowledge gained from studying Head Start programs has been disseminated to early childhood educators, which has led to benefits in other programs, young children, and their families. With over 30 years of successful Head Start programs and an extensive research agenda, more has been learned about early childhood education, child development, family involvement in early childhood education programs, and the importance of qualified staff working with young children. These research findings are pertinent to all early childhood settings.

A priority in Head Start is the recognition of the importance of qualified and prepared staff. Although there are federal guidelines for staff qualifications, some centers may adapt these requirements to meet their local needs, such as competence in the home language of many children in the program.

Staff Preparation

Staffing patterns vary from center to center, based on the number of children enrolled, specific needs of the center and/or community, and state or local requirements. Head Start is credited with establishing the Child Development Associate (CDA) credential, which is required of at least one of the adults working in a Head Start classroom. Many CDA staff members are parents of children in the programs. The establishment of the CDA was in response to the need for qualified child care workers. In Chapter 12 you will find an in-depth discussion of CDA requirements.

As you read through the following descriptions of the different staff positions required at Felipe's center (Oregon Department of Education, 1995) think of the connections between the positions and the goals of Head Start in educational, social, and family services. Except for the position of teacher assistant, all staff are required to hold a baccalaureate (bachelor's) degree in their field of expertise.

Program director. The program director assumes responsibility for administration of the program. She has training or experience in administration and is responsible for administrative decisions. For example, when a staff position is open, the program director would work with an advisory group to conduct interviews and make a decision about hiring new staff. If the program director is an early childhood specialist, she would also assume the role of directing the educational component of the program.

Education service coordinator. The education service coordinator oversees the educational program. He works with teachers to assure that a developmentally appropriate curriculum is in place for all children. Another role is to monitor the individual education plans. This position requires a degree in early childhood education or child development as well as at least three years of full-time teaching young children. An advanced degree in early childhood education or child development may be substituted in lieu of the teaching experience requirement.

Health services coordinator. A person in this position would have a degree in public health education, nursing, or a related health field. She is responsible for monitoring the medical, dental, and nutritional records of the children. She also assists families in locating affordable health care.

Social services coordinator.   This position requires a degree in social work, psychology, or a related field and three years of experience in social services (or an advanced degree in the field of social services). His role includes assisting families when they need help in securing housing, Food Stamps, clothing, parent education, or crisis intervention.

Family advocate.   The family advocate facilitates communication between families and the center. She makes sure parent voices are heard in program decisions. Her background includes a degree in social work, psychology, or a related field.

Disabilities services coordinator.   This coordinator works with children with special needs in the program. These children are included in the regular classrooms, with special adaptations or assistance as determined in their individual family services plan. The disability services coordinator also works with families and the early childhood special education specialist to ensure that the family understands and carries out activities described in the individual family services plan. A person in this position would have a degree in education or a related field with extensive coursework in special education and early childhood education.

Teacher.   Since you spent time talking with and observing Susana, you are aware of her professional responsibilities. She plans and carries out the curriculum, makes home visits, conducts parent/teacher conferences, and records the progress and development of the children. Teachers are required to hold a degree in early childhood education or child development, or have extensive experience or training that qualifies them for the position of teacher.

Teacher Assistant.   Teacher assistants work under the direct supervision of the teacher and have a high school diploma or equivalent, experience working with young children, and some training in early childhood. The teacher assistant works closely with the teacher, children, and families. Rita is familiar with Susana's curriculum and her guidance procedures and follows these in her interactions with the children.

Other support positions might include a transportation supervisor, a facilities supervisor (these two positions might be part of the program director's role in some centers), food preparers, secretaries, volunteer coordinator, and bus drivers. In many centers, parents are hired in paraprofessional roles. Consultants are available to work with staff, children, and families on a part-time basis and might include family workers, mental health consultants, and early childhood education specialists.

Although there are many success stories from the past 30 years of Head Start, times have changed and new challenges have entered the picture. These issues and concerns are the subject of debate at the local, state, and national levels.

Current Issues and Trends in Head Start Programs

The Silver Ribbon Panel is a committee "of leaders with expertise in Head Start, other early childhood programs, health services, policy, and business" (Lombardi, 1990). This group studied Head Start programs and made recommendations for improvement. Edward Zigler and Susan Muenchow (1992) also examined current Head Start practices and programs and made additional recommendations based on their findings and those of the Silver Ribbon Panel. Many of their recommendations reflect current issues and trends in Head Start, as discussed in this section.

Improving staff salaries and benefits.   Both groups agreed that investments must be made to ensure the quality of effective comprehensive services continue for children and families. Funding should be increased to improve salaries and benefits for staff. Teachers in Head Start make considerably less money than teachers in public schools. Some counties and states are recognizing this inequity and are contributing funds to Head Start beyond the required matching requirements. Quality programs require quality staff, and improving salaries for staff in Head Start is an issue that requires attention.

Addressing issues of quality among programs.   With local influence exerted in each Head Start program, there is a wide range of quality across programs. There are over 1,300 Head Start sites, with quality ranging from excellent to poor (Zigler, Styfco, & Gilman, 1993). Currently, there is a push to expand programs to ensure access for all children qualified to enter Head Start. Before expansion, quality issues must be addressed.

Quality issues arise in each of the main service areas, but the largest threat to quality is found in staffing (Zigler, Styfco, & Gilman, 1993). As you have read in previous chapters, the quality of a center or program is directly related to the quality of the staff. Improvements are needed in staff salaries and benefits to retain qualified personnel. The requirement of the CDA credential for staff should be supported by salary increases. Many of the quality issues in Head Start relate to financial needs to improve staff compensation and services to children and families. Cuts in the federal food program and health services relate to the quality of services the child and family receive in Head Start. Financial support must be in place to ensure that all children and families involved in Head Start participate in a program of high quality.

Improving facilities.   Many Head Start programs are located in churches, synagogues, public school buildings, or community buildings. Most often, the programs are renting or borrowing space, and may end up having to move if the owners need the space for other programs. Obtaining permanent space that is appropriate for Head Start programs reaffirms that "Head Start is no longer a temporary program, and it should be housed in permanent quarters" (Zigler & Muenchow, 1992).

The children and families in the Washington County Head Start Program are fortunate. As part of the Community Action Organization, they participated in the 10-year building fund raising and consequently were able to move into permanent classrooms and space specifically designed for their program. Funding for permanent buildings is necessary for Head Start to acquire and maintain facilities.

Meeting current needs of families.   Juggling a half-day program and half-day child care with a full-time job is difficult for families. In fact, the most frequently cited need stated by Head Start families responding to the Silver Ribbon Panel survey was the need for full-day programs. It is ironic that the efforts to assist parents with job training might not result in employment if parents are caught with the decision to keep their child in Head Start (a half-day program) and remain unemployed because they cannot afford child care for the other half of the day. Supporting families means listening to their needs. If a critical need is for a full-day program to accommodate the changing needs of the family, this suggestion should be carefully reviewed. Several Head Start programs have been successful in coordinating with community-sponsored child care programs and facilitating the connection between Head Start and the child care. Efforts such as these could be explored as an option to help those families in need of full-day programs for their children.

Additional recommendations from the Silver Ribbon Panel. Several additional recommendations made by the Silver Ribbon Panel include improvement of the education component to ensure that the curriculum is developmentally appropriate and culturally responsive, increased family support, enhancement of parent involvement, and increased funding for continued education for staff and technical assistance. Both Zigler and Muenchow (1992) and the Silver Ribbon Panel urge the development of programs to serve infants and toddlers.

Extending the Head Start model to infants and toddlers. When you read about infant development and infant care programs in an earlier chapter, you were presented with current research about infant brain growth and the need for stimulation in the early years, particularly from birth to age 3. If children from low-income families do not begin an early childhood education until age 3, many opportunities for stimulation and learning may have been lost.

For many parents of Head Start children, this is their introduction to parenting education and formal education to support their child's developmental growth. Parents form their parenting skills and behaviors in the early months of their child's life. Involvement with other parents and Head Start teachers during the infant years would assist parents in their development of good parenting skills.

Another consideration is access to social services. Infants and toddlers certainly require good nutrition and medical services to thrive as they develop. Waiting until they reach 3 years of age and are eligible to enter Head Start seems to ignore knowledge of children's needs for healthy development. Adapting and expanding the Head Start model of multiple support and resource systems for families to meet the needs of infants and toddlers would provide great benefits for a healthy start in life.

Journal 9.8: If you were asked to provide a rationale for developing an infant program based on the Head Start model, what components would you find essential to transfer to the new program? ■

Another issue or concern is the segregation of children in Head Start programs from the general population of 3- and 4-year-old children.

Segregation. In 1965, the beginning era of Head Start, there were few early childhood programs for 3- and 4-year-olds. This is no longer true. Head Start programs have provided a standard for many of the current early childhood programs that analyzed the Head Start curriculum and emphasis on the development of the whole child.

Now that there are more early childhood education options available for children from low-income families, a critical question that Bowman (1993) raises is: "Should these children from poor families be segregated from other children in early childhood programs?" In other words, should Head Start be maintained as a separate program solely for children from low-income families or children with special needs? Would it be better for these children to support their involvement in established programs available to all children?

To address these questions, one weighs the value of the integration of education, social services, and family support that forms the foundation of Head Start. Many programs may provide the educational component, but social services would need to be accessed in separate locations and systems, most often through the county. More and more early childhood programs are including parent education, but the needs of low-income parents may be beyond what is available in a typical preschool parenting class. Obviously, these are complicated and complex questions without easy answers. Research on the effectiveness on child development and preparedness for school drawn from various models of Head Start and other early childhood programs might help us uncover portions of the answer.

Research and evaluation of Head Start programs.   Early research focused on evaluating the effects of Head Start on children and their learning. In light of the drive to end the War on Poverty, there was an eagerness to predict that Head Start would significantly affect a child's development. The early research looked for intellectual gains, as measured by IQ increases. After conflicting findings and concern that intelligence was a narrow measure of gains from participating in Head Start Programs, the research agenda shifted to a more qualitative or holistic view of Head Start's benefits (Zigler, Styfco, & Gilman, 1993).

Looking at gains from this broader perspective, researchers have found that children who had been in Head Start programs experienced higher rates of immunization, improved overall health, better nutrition, and better social and economic characteristics (McKey et al., 1985). This research agenda was more closely aligned with the program goals.

Much has been learned from Head Start programs about early childhood education practices, child development, and the success of combining education, social services, and family involvement in one program. Further research is needed to help us understand the impact of Head Start on the whole family. A research agenda that focuses on many of the issues just discussed would yield information about best practices and substantiate continuation of program components or the need for change. For example, the questions raised about segregation of Head Start children might be researched through integration of other children into Head Start programs. Evaluating the success of children and their families would help answer the question about different program models.

Demonstration projects, where successful programs disseminate information about their program, would help other programs that are struggling with quality issues.

Observing developmentally appropriate practices in a classroom of children is a format that would assist other teachers in learning about curriculum and instruction. There is much to learn through research on different components of Head Start and their impact on children and their families. Dissemination of these findings will help Head Start programs and other early childhood programs make improvements based on research findings.

Collaboration between Head Start and other agencies.   Felipe and his family are fortunate. Their Head Start program is located in the County Community Action building and program. Connections between social services are available at the same site. Other Head Start programs might be located in a church or an extra room in a housing project, with no close link to the community agencies. As resources become limited, collaboration and connections become more essential. Linkages between public school programs, other early childhood programs, and the business community yield more comprehensive services for children and families.

In some states, state collaboration grants and projects have been launched to promote connections between Head Start and other programs assisting low-income families with young children. Because of their experience and successful track record in providing comprehensive services to children and families, Head Start staff can provide leadership in these collaborative ventures. Some programs have been successful in integrating families into the larger community and bringing community resources to the program to better serve children and their families (Replogle, 1994). Replogle recommends strengthening connections between Head Start and community agencies, schools, and family needs. Through these partnerships, services become available that support long-term changes for low-income families and their children, both in Head Start and in the larger community.

Another large issue or trend in Head Start, as well as in other programs nationwide, is the need to develop responsive environments to support the rapidly increasing number of culturally and linguistically diverse children and families.

Supporting Cultural and Linguistic Diversity

The term **linguistically and culturally diverse** is used by educators to identify children from homes where English is not used as the primary language (Garcia, 1991). In the broader picture, children and their families may be considered linguistically or culturally diverse although they speak English. For example, a child might be a third-generation member of a family speaking English, yet "maintain the dominant accent of their heritage language" (NAEYC, 1996a, p. 7), or cultural values, beliefs, or customs. As the number of young children that are culturally and linguistically diverse increase, early childhood educators are attempting to meet the challenge of providing programs to meet the needs of these children and their families.

Cultural Diversity of Young Children

The demographics of the population making up the United States is rapidly changing. Children in early childhood programs today represent different cultural and linguistic backgrounds than the children of 10 years ago and the children you will be working with

■ **TABLE 9.1 Percentage Change in the Population of Children Aged 5 to 17, by Race/Ethnicity**

	PERCENTAGE CHANGE	
RACE/ETHNICITY	1993 to 2000	2000 to 2020
White		
Aged 5–13	2.9	−11.2
Aged 14–17	10.1	−10.3
Black		
Aged 5–13	12.9	15.4
Aged 14–17	11.5	20.0
Hispanic		
Aged 5–13	29.8	47.0
Aged 14–17	23.6	60.6
Other		
Aged 5–13	32.5	67.2
Aged 14–17	45.1	73.3

Source: U.S. Department of Education, National Center for Education Statistics, *Youth Indicators 1996,* Indicator 2.

in the future. Waggoner (1994) finds that almost 10 million of the 45 million school-age children in the United States come from homes in which languages other than English are the primary language. Predictions of the number of children from culturally and linguistically diverse homes is expected to increase through the next two decades. Early in the twenty-first century, the number of nonwhite and Hispanic children will increase and the percentage of White children enrolled in schools will decrease, as shown in Table 9.1.

In fact, in some states and many large cities, the percentage of minority children have represented the majority of students in the public schools since the mid-1990s. This is called the *minority majority*. These changing demographics present important data to early childhood educators, who are attempting to learn what is involved in becoming responsive educators for children from diverse cultures. Let's look at teaching strategies and practices, as well as basic understandings, that support culturally and linguistically diverse children.

Creating an Environment Responsive to Diverse Children

In the past, the quickest route to success for immigrants arriving in the United States was to learn basic English and fit in with the dominant culture. High levels of English were not needed to earn a living. This is no longer the dominant view in education.

Development of language is closely connected to cognitive development. Learning in the first language helps a young child gain knowledge (NAEYC, 1996a) more than attempting to learn the same knowledge in a language in which the child has little comprehension. NAEYC's recommendations for early childhood education for cultural and linguistic diversity include the following:

- Recognize that all children are cognitively, linguistically, and emotionally connected to the language and culture of their home.
- Acknowledge that children can demonstrate their knowledge and capabilities in many ways.
- Understand that without comprehensible input, second-language learning can be difficult.

These recommendations help create a learning environment that supports continued growth in the child's first language as she learns English, while also supporting and honoring the language and culture in her home (see Box 9.1).

 Bilingualism.   Learning a new language (English) while continuing to develop the home language (also called the *first* or *primary* language) is referred to as **bilingualism.** When Susana presents new information, she speaks in Spanish to assist children in gaining new knowledge in their home language. She wants the children to learn new concepts in their primary language, rather than learning new language and new concepts at the same time. Susana's active encouragement of families to continue speaking Spanish with their young children supports the cognitive development of the children. The

---

A Closer Look

BOX 9.1 ■ What Are Some Instructional Strategies Used by Culturally Responsive Educators?

The literature in teacher education has examined different teaching practices that contribute to student learning. These educational practices are often termed *effective instructional or teaching strategies* (Brophy & Good, 1986). Many of these strategies are also effective for learners in culturally and linguistically diverse classrooms. Villegas (1991) adds to the list of effective teaching strategies by emphasizing that effectiveness in these settings is "defined primarily by the ability to create meaningful classroom activities that take into account students' background experiences" (p. 18). The students' background experiences reflect their cultural experiences. Acknowledgment and incorporation of these experiences into the child's curriculum and instruction in the classroom helps students bridge the cultural gap between home and school. Villegas (1991) and Tikunoff (1985) have noted several practices demonstrated by culturally responsive educators.

Instructional Practices of Culturally Responsive Teachers

1. Hold high expectations for students.
2. Achieve and maintain high levels of student involvement in learning tasks.
3. Have a strong sense of self-efficacy.
4. Create meaningful classroom activities built on students' home cultural experiences.

Susana is reading in Spanish, the first language of these three children.

continued use of the primary language at home also facilitates the family's ability to communicate with each other.

 Journal 9.9: Describe an activity that might be done at home with a 4-year-old child to reinforce learning in the first or home language. ■

The continued presence of both languages in this Head Start classroom promotes learning in the primary language and retention of the primary language while learning a second language. Susana's teaching follows recommendations made by Krashen (1996):

1. Comprehensible input is provided in English, as long as students understand the subject matter (often music, art, or physical education) when it is presented in English (the second language).

2. New subject matter is taught in primary or first language, without translation.

3. Literacy development is presented in the first language.

All written material in Felipe's classroom is displayed in Spanish and in English. For example, the job chart is written in Spanish, with English "subtitles" listed below each job. It has been found that literacy developed in the first language later transfers to the second language (Krashen, 1992), and students progress more quickly in learning to read when they do not make continual translations to understand written material.

Children share their thoughts about the story, recognizing their ideas are valued by Carolyne.

Wong Fillmore (1991) discusses additional problems caused by early assimilation into English, which often forces the loss of the home language in children under the age of 5. When children lose their home language as they learn English, they may lose their means to communicate with their parents. If parents are not speaking the same language as their child, a major disruption in the family can result from the loss of this critical link of communication between parents and child. Parents can no longer talk to their child about values, beliefs, and understandings that transmit the family culture from parent to child. Paying attention to the possibility of disrupting the family unit reinforces the model of bilingualism that helps the child retain and grow in her home language as she learns English.

It becomes more complicated when several different home or first languages are spoken by children in the classroom and the teacher does not speak these languages. Recommendations for a multilingual situation include:

- Learn to speak several words in each of the children's home language.
- Group children who speak the same language together at least once each day to help them continue language development.
- Arrange for an interpreter to assist in parent conferences and home visits.
- Include books, music, and games representative of each child's cultural heritage in the classroom.

In addition to these recommendations, educators who incorporate project-based learning (such as the projects around the theme of spring in Felipe's classroom) and cooperative learning (students working together in small groups) are building an environment that supports cultural and linguistic diversity. Children have opportunities to work together, share ideas, talk with each other, and learn to cooperate with others.

Valuing cultural diversity.   Creating a learning environment responsive to cultural and linguistic diversity is an important goal and challenge for each early childhood professional. Preserving and continuing the child's first or home language and culture while learning English and the "school culture" supports an environment that honors and respects each child and family as well as helps the child develop to his fullest potential. Garcia (1997) challenges early childhood educators to:

> care about and be an advocate for our linguistically and culturally diverse children and families by nurturing, celebrating, and challenging them. They do not need our pity or remorse for what they do not have; they, like any individual and family, require our respect and the use of what they bring as a resource. (p. 13)

PRINCIPLES AND INSIGHTS: A Summary and Review

Learning about Head Start is also learning about the recent history of the support of young children and their families in the United States. Your visit to Felipe's Head Start program highlighted Head Start's focus on children and families. When you arrived, you saw children and several parents arriving on the bus together. The children went to their classrooms, while the parents headed for the adult education classroom or volunteered at the center. Through education, social services, and other family services, the child and family are supported in their development.

Your morning in Head Start proved to be a busy one. Children were involved in projects, interactions, and activities that encouraged their learning in each developmental area. Felipe and the other children in Susana's class worked on several different activities related to the topic of spring, through art, music, listening to stories, expressing ideas, and connecting clothing and weather to spring. You observed many activities you might see in other preschool programs.

Felipe's mother, Anna, serves on the Policy Council. His father often goes on field trips with the class. All parents participate in home visits and parent/teacher conferences, along with establishing educational goals for their child. Families are an integral component of Head Start, with the belief that helping the family is helping the child.

Susana is aware of the challenges of working with children speaking languages other than English. One of her priorities in teaching is to help parents understand the importance of bilingualism and biculturalism. Susana discusses the importance of maintaining the child's home language with families. She also follows specific recommendations for creating a responsive environment for culturally and linguistically diverse children, communicating her respect for and appreciation of the richness children bring to the classroom.

■ **FIGURE 9.7**

Washington County Head
Start Mission Statement
Source: Community Action
Organization Head Start.
Reprinted by permission.

> Our Mission:
>
> We will provide developmentally appropriate
> education and care for
>
> # children,
>
> involve and support
>
> # parents,
>
> and offer early childhood services that meet
>
> # family needs.

After more than 30 years of existence, changes are needed in Head Start, just as in any program. Some of these changes include increasing staff salaries, making curricular changes that reflect developmentally appropriate practices and responsiveness to cultural and linguistic diversity, acknowledging and adapting to current needs of families (full-day programs, increased family support, and enhanced family involvement), ensuring quality in all programs, and providing programs for infants and toddlers. Collaboration between agencies fosters sharing of limited resources and helps families gain access to needed resources. Research and evaluation of existing programs provide data to make improvements that promote successful early childhood practices.

Over the past three decades, millions of children and their families have benefited from involvement in Head Start. By observing Felipe in his Head Start program and meeting with his family and teacher, you had the opportunity to see why this program is considered the nation's greatest educational experiment (Zigler & Muenchow, 1992). The mission of Washington County Head Start (Figure 9.7) does, indeed, provide a framework for the holistic emphasis of education, social services, and family involvement woven together to create a head start for children.

Becoming an Early Childhood Professional

Your Field Experiences

1. Make arrangements to visit a Head Start or preschool program in your area. While observing, listen to interactions between the children. What are several topics of conversation that are of interest to children of this age?

2. While visiting a preschool or Head Start program or through a phone interview, discuss the role of families in the program. What options are available for family involvement? What sense do you have about the actual involvement of families in this program?

Your Professional Portfolio

1. After observing a preschool, draw a diagram of the setting. What types of activities occur in different areas of the room? How is the space designed to encourage children to take initiative in projects and activities (e.g., sinks and faucets at a child's level for independent use). Label the areas, furniture, and fixtures in the room and place the diagram in your portfolio.

2. In Felipe's program, you observed his involvement in a project about springtime. If you were teaching 4-year-olds, what project might you like to incorporate into the curriculum? Develop your project idea in an outline form, including some major themes and resources you would want to make available for the children.

Your Professional Library

Books

Advisory Committee on Head Start Quality and Expansion. (1994). *Creating a 21st century Head Start, Final report.* Washington, DC: Author.

Bradburn, E. (1989). *Margaret McMillan: Portrait of a pioneer.* New York: Routledge.

Cole, R. W. (Ed.). (1995). *Educating everybody's children: Diverse teaching strategies for diverse learners.* Alexandria, VA: Association for Supervision and Curriculum Development.

Dodge, D., & Colker, L. (1992). *The creative curriculum for early childhood.* Washington, DC: Teaching Strategies.

Hecht, M. L., Collier, M. J., & Riberan, S. A. (1993). *African American communication.* Newbury Park, CA: Sage.

Wasik, B. H., Bryant, D., & Lyons, C. (1990). *Home visiting: Procedures for helping families.* Newbury Park, CA: Sage.

Internet Addresses and World Wide Web Sites

www.kidscampaignsorg/Whoseside/Parenting/Publibrary/preschool.html
Preschool Programs: How Your Public Library Can Help Kids

www.k12.ca.us/child/headstar.htm
Head Start Home Page

www.nauticom.net/www/cokids/
Early Childhood Educator's and Family Web Corner

www.nhsa.org
National Head Start Association

www.earlychildhood.com/articles/artbiacq.html
Bilingual Acquisition in Preschool Children

www.pan.ci.seattle.waus/seattle/dnhs/youth/headstrt/what.htm
What Is Head Start?

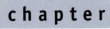

chapter

Kindergarten

KEELEY'S STORY

When you finish reading and reflecting on this chapter, you will be able to:

1. Describe the curriculum in a kindergarten program, including your stance on increased pressure for academics.

2. Summarize a philosophy of classroom management for kindergarten-age children.

3. Justify the use of technology with young children.

4. Discuss the content of and need for after-school care programs.

5. Identify developmentally appropriate activities for kindergarten-age children.

Keeley and her mother, Kerry, live in a rented house that needs paint and some repair but is brightened with plants and flowers, a birdhouse, and decorations made by Keeley. Keeley is waiting on the porch for you. She opens the front door and joins you as you enter the living room. Kerry welcomes you and shows you a project the two of them have been working on recently. On the kitchen table are some clay figures waiting to dry. Keeley is anxious to show you around the house, so you begin her tour.

Visiting Keeley

The rooms in Keeley and Kerry's home are comfortably furnished with lots of evidence of Keeley's activities. In the living room is a little table and chairs that are Keeley-size. In the kitchen is an easel with paints. A large dollhouse stands in the dining room. It's definitely their home and Keeley shares some of the housekeeping chores. "I empty the little trash cans," she tells you proudly. "And I set the table, "she adds. Kerry and Keeley plan menus for the week each Sunday, and often bake and cook items for lunchboxes and dinners.

In spite of working long hours at her job, Kerry spends a large amount of quality time with Keeley. They read for hours, have tea parties, dress up, and plant a garden together. Every year, Keeley plants sunflower seeds and cares for the plants for months. Needless to say, everyone who comes to visit has to see the sunflowers. Kerry tells the story of their first sunflower garden: "The plants had grown to a height of 4 feet—they towered above Keeley and she loved them. Every day she would water them. One morning, we saw that someone had cut most of the sunflowers down. Keeley was devastated.

We both cried and then made plans to paint a giant sign to put in the garden. The sign read 'ME AND MY MOMMY LOVE THESE SUNFLOWERS. PLEASE DON'T TAKE ANYMORE. KEELEY.' "

Kerry has dedicated herself to raising Keeley. She faces many struggles as a single parent but is always mindful of providing a wonderful, rich home and childhood for Keeley.

Starting Kindergarten

When it came time for kindergarten, Kerry sought advice from the early childhood staff at the university lab school that Keeley attended for almost three years. They recommended a neighborhood public elementary school, Eliot School, which has a high level of parent involvement and a focus on the arts. Kerry and Keeley visited the school and the kindergarten classrooms and both felt enthusiastic about what they observed. "It felt right—we both knew it was the place for Keeley," says Kerry. They also found a good after-school program and looked forward to kindergarten.

By September and the start of kindergarten, Keeley could read a number of her books and frequently wrote notes to others as well as phrases on her artwork. She approached Eliot School with great enthusiasm. Kerry tells of seeing her, "I could have cried. There she was, skipping down the walk on the first day—she was so eager to start kindergarten." Like many parents at Keeley's school, Kerry volunteers two days each month. She takes these afternoons off from her job and works at night to make up the hours. She is determined to be involved in Keeley's school. "I want her to be successful in school—she is so smart."

In kindergarten, Keeley has made new friends easily, is invited to other children's homes, and loves to invite others to her home. Her best friend Daniella often spends the night, and Daniella's mom has become good friends with Kerry. Both girls go to the after-school program at Eliot School. When Kerry or Oma (Keeley's grandmother) pick Keeley up at 5:30 P.M., they often find her listening to a story with a small group of friends, or playing a game, or drawing with markers. She is content, hungry, and ready to be with her family. She signs herself out, and once again, skips out to the car.

Learning about Keeley, her prior school experiences, and her family helps you understand why Kerry selected the kindergarten program she did for Keeley. Kerry knew that another school nearby was noted for a strong academic program. When she visited this school, she observed children sitting in rows at their desks and spending long blocks of time on worksheets. It was often quiet in the classroom, which seemed odd to Kerry after her experiences with the busy atmosphere in Keeley's preschool.

Although Kerry wanted Keeley to learn all she could, she also sensed that the learning atmosphere affected how a kindergarten child experienced learning. Kerry discussed learning environments with her family and with the preschool teachers and felt more confident that Eliot School's kindergarten was the right choice for Keeley. The kindergarten teachers were committed to providing a curriculum based on the learning needs of 5-year-olds within a developmentally appropriate curriculum. In fact, on the day that Keeley and Kerry visited Eliot's kindergarten, they observed the children in water play with bubbles, building structures with blocks, and engaged in different choice activities.

Soon you will have the opportunity to observe this kindergarten and meet the school principal and teacher. As you visit, think about the difference between a classroom where children are expected to work with a lot of time spent sitting at their desk in quiet concentration and a classroom where children are moving about, talking, exploring, and engaged in active learning.

The History of Kindergarten

Kindergarten is placed in a unique position within the schooling system. Children entering kindergarten typically have had preschool experience and will move to more formal schooling the year following kindergarten. This places kindergarten in between preschool and the primary grades. Is it the bridge between preschool and first grade? Should kindergarten be more like preschool or more like the primary grades? Or can kindergarten be a special educational experience that helps young children learn social and beginning academic skills?

Kerry found herself facing these questions as she selected a kindergarten program for Keeley. When she visited the kindergarten at Eliot School, she saw centers of activities around the classroom. Children were painting, reading, working on computers, building with blocks, and making snacks. Jim, the teacher, had a schedule on the board, and there seemed to be an easy flow to the daily routine. In the second kindergarten program Kerry visited, the children were also busy, but they all were working at their desks in workbooks. Children were writing letters of the alphabet and drawing pictures of objects that began with that alphabet letter. Kerry noticed that there were painting easels in the room, a reading corner with books at a table, and blocks on a rug in the back of the room. She learned that these activities were available after children finished their work. Kerry thought, "It seems like the activities that children this age should be involved in are only available after a child finishes work. This seems strange, because the real work and learning is with the painting, blocks, and books." Kerry did, indeed, encounter the controversy of defining what makes a good kindergarten.

From the earliest beginnings of public kindergarten, these questions and controversies have been discussed and debated by early childhood educators, parents, and the general public. Keeley's teacher, Jim, addresses some of these questions as he describes the kindergarten program and his philosophy of appropriate curriculum for 5-year-olds. You will meet him soon.

The examination of kindergarten and the purpose of kindergarten is part of the larger educational reform movement. The curriculum and the goals of a particular kindergarten reflect the views of those who make decisions about the purpose of kindergarten. Many kindergarten teachers find that part of their job is to explain to parents and other educators the rationale for their curriculum. As others learn more about the importance of the kindergarten year, greater acceptance is found for this special time of learning for young children.

■ **TABLE 10.1**   **Developmental Highlights in 5- and 6-Year-Old Children**

Cognitive	Social	Emotional	Physical
Beginning organization patterns *Example:* Patterning (such as the calendar patterns)	Playing/interacting with a group of children for increasing time periods *Example:* Planning for and playing a game during a 15- to 20-minute time period	Expressing feelings in words *Example:* Telling another child "I was sad when you were sick"	Refining use of large muscles *Example:* Running, hopping, beginning to skip, and throwing and catching a ball
Connecting symbols to representations *Example:* The numeral 3 refers to an amount of 3 objects	Having a "special" friend, although these may change suddenly and/or frequently *Example:* Sharing a computer program each day with one friend, then tiring of the program and shifting to another special friend interested in building blocks	Learning to interpret emotional expressions of others *Example:* Consoling a friend who feels sad or upset	Using small muscles *Example:* Painting, drawing, cutting with scissors, and printing letters/numerals

The term **kindergarten** is derived from the German translation meaning *children's garden.* Visualizing a children's garden brings to mind many bright colors and a cheerful environment. What do you visualize when you think of a children's garden? We'll explore a kindergarten where the teacher has developed a program that is considered developmentally appropriate for 5- and 6-year-olds. **Developmentally appropriate curriculum** is built around knowledge of child development and learning in conjunction with knowledge of individual children's variations, needs, and interests (Bredekamp & Copple, 1997). Table 10.1 lists developmental highlights of kindergarten-age children, while recognizing that each child progresses at her own rate. You will be observing examples of each developmental highlight in Keeley's kindergarten.

The program you are about to visit includes many components that support and nourish growing children, similar to the care of a special garden. In Keeley's kindergarten, you will see children engaged in a wide variety of play activities while at the same time gaining knowledge and skills expected of them when they enter first grade in the coming fall. You will also notice a strong focus on technology in this classroom. The children are computer literate and spend time each day accessing the Internet and checking features on their World Wide Web site. You might wonder, Is it appropriate for children this young to spend time on the computers? This question is also a focus of much discussion and some controversy. Keep the question about technology in mind as you observe the children and teacher in the kindergarten at Eliot School.

Kindergarten at Eliot School

Driving up to Eliot School, you notice that the school is located in a residential/business area. Although there are houses and trees lining many of the nearby streets, the school is a block away from a busy intersection with several businesses. Eliot School is located in a 40-year-old brick building two stories high. Currently, 542 students are attending the school in kindergarten through fifth grade. Approximately half of the school population resides in the school boundaries; the other half of the students applied to enroll in the school because of the emphasis on fine arts. This school is part of a large city school district and designated as the Arts Magnet School. You will learn more about the fine arts program when you meet the principal.

After checking in at the office, you pick up your name badge, identifying you as a visitor. The principal greets you and invites you into her office.

Visiting the Principal

Pam Bradley has been principal at Eliot School for six years. She tells you, "I feel fortunate to be working with such an active volunteer group of parents and community members. Last year, they helped with performances, art projects, working with students in reading, and numerous other activities. This is impressive, considering the large number of working families in our school." Most of the volunteers are parents, but others are artists from the community.

Eliot School's Magnet Arts Program.   You ask Pam about the arts program as a context for the kindergarten program. She is delighted to talk about this topic. "Right now, we have three full-time and one half-time art specialists at Eliot School. These specialists represent dance, drama, visual arts, and music, which supports our focus as an arts **magnet school.** Half of our students are from the local neighborhood and the other half come from around the entire school district." She continues, "Children from kindergarten through fifth grade participate

in each of these arts. The schedule is set up to allow students to participate in two of these art programs each semester. This is in addition to their regular curriculum." Sounds like a busy schedule, but one that certainly offers rich learning opportunities!

The purpose of your visit is to learn about the kindergarten program and the context of kindergarten within the larger school setting. You are curious about gathering more information about kindergarten in the district and at Eliot School.

Kindergarten curriculum.   Kindergarten programs reflect differences in philosophies and practice. When you asked Pam how the kindergarten curriculum is established at each school in this district, she responds, "Most of our school curriculum is guided by state standards and the curriculum set by the Department of Education. Within this framework, kindergarten teachers develop programs to meet the needs of our students."

Pam confides, "I think there is much more pressure to include academics in kindergarten now than there was 5 to 10 years ago." Her advice to you is to educate parents about the importance of providing appropriate education for young children, which includes play and exploratory activities. "Let parents know that play and learning can be synonymous in a rich early childhood environment. This helps them understand the rationale of our kindergarten curriculum." This education process is part of Pam's job as well as part of the kindergarten teacher's job.

Hiring future kindergarten teachers.   The teacher is ultimately responsible for the learning and activities in her classroom. You ask Pam what she looks for when she hires a kindergarten teacher. Her response to your question about qualities of a good kindergarten teacher is enlightening: "I look for someone who genuinely enjoys children and has the flexibility to work with a large number of parent volunteers and specialists. Whoever teaches in this school must be a collegial worker and willing to collaborate with others. I also want someone with current training and understanding of early childhood and with the ability to articulate their philosophy of kindergarten. We believe in developmentally appropriate activities and learning for this age child, and we want our kindergarten teachers to take a leadership role in promoting developmentally appropriate learning." Pam's description of a kindergarten teacher emphasizes the importance of understanding the decisions a teacher will make about the activities and learning in a classroom, along with the ability to explain a personal philosophy of kindergarten and kindergarten curriculum.

Journal 10.1: When you read the description of the "future" kindergarten teacher, what qualities do you have that match the ones described by Pam? If you are interested in teaching kindergarten, what might you do to continue to develop other characteristics or qualities of a kindergarten teacher as described by Pam? ■

A First Look at Kindergarten

Leaving the office, the secretary points you toward the kindergarten classrooms. The children are arriving for the morning with a buzz of excitement. You listen to their conversations and learn that last night's snowfall is the topic of most of their talk. One girl exclaims, "We stayed up late and made a huge snowball last night. We rolled it over and over until it was huge." The children are dressed in warm coats, with scarves, mittens, boots, and hats. It takes a bit of time for everyone to hang up all this winter clothing, but you notice several children helping each other with buckles, buttons, and untying scarves and hats. You overhear, "Wow, I looked like a snowman with all that stuff on me!" The first snow of the winter is certainly greeted with enthusiasm by these children!

Starting the day. After hanging up their coats, each child walks over to a sheet of paper placed on a desk near the door. You ask 5-year-old Macy what everyone is writing on the paper and she tells you, "We write our name on the paper next to

These three girls are interested in the mouse and her new babies. In what ways are they showing respect for the needs of the mother mouse?

the line that has our name on it. Then Jim knows who is here today. See, this is my name—Macy." After signing in, the children head toward any center, station, or activity of their choice. There is Keeley! She has a huge purple scarf wrapped around her neck and head, and exclaims, "My mom gave me her scarf today." After she signs in, she goes to look at the mice in a glass terrarium. The mother mouse had several babies two days ago, and the children are watching her care for the babies. They are quiet and whisper as they watch, reminding each other, "Remember to use our eyes and our quiet voice near the new babies."

During the 10 minutes that children are involved in their activities, you notice that Jim, the teacher, greets each child. He has wandered to most of the activity areas and interacted with each child. When Jim stops at the mouse terrarium, Keeley tells him, "Mom and I went out in the snow and made a big snow-lady last night. She has my scarf on her neck." Jim says, "I am sure she is one fancy snow-lady. You and your mom make great projects."

Jim walks by and tells you, "You're in for a busy morning. After the first snowstorm, the children are excited to talk about the snow angels, forts, and people they have made at home." Jim lets you know that during calendar and weather time, the children will be discussing this topic. He also informs you that other exciting events are planned for today—a folktale told by a haiku artist and a performance by the kindergartners for Grandparents' and Other Special Friends' Day. This will be an interesting morning to observe!

Later, you learn from Jim that he starts the morning with time for the children to greet each other, share news, and get settled into the new day. He finds this important to the children's **social development.** They are learning to get along with a group of children as well as play with a "special friend." Starting the morning this way helps children make the transition from home to school and allows for social interactions.

Morning opening time. You watch the children gather on the rug in front of their calendar. They talk about the date and day of the week. Meredith places an orange leaf on the November 19 space on the calendar. She has followed a pattern on the calendar, with two brown leaves followed by two orange leaves. She leads the class in reading the color pattern, "Brown, brown, orange, orange." Next, Hawthorne checks the thermometer. He has some difficulty reading the numbers, so Becky, the intern teacher in the classroom this year, helps him. Together, they decide that it is 41 degrees outside. Tyson also looks out the window. He sees a cloud outside and says, "We have a cloudy day, so I will put this cloud on our weather board."

The children then burst into talk about the snow on the ground and what they did in the snow. Brandy and Maria made a fort together with older brothers and sisters. They described the fort as "really, really huge, as big as our house. Today, we will finish making windows when we get home." Hawthorne shared, "My dad and I made

snow angels by laying in the snow. But then I rolled over and my angel got flatter." When they finished sharing their snow experiences, the children picked up their weather journals and recorded the date and daily weather, and colored a picture to represent today's weather. Keeley's weather picture showed her snow-lady. When she finished drawing, she called Becky over to write *snow-lady* in her journal.

Haiku art. As they placed their journals back into the weather journal box, the haiku artist arrived. She is part of the Community–Eliot School Partnership, which is composed of artists who share their work with the children at this school. Today, she tells a Japanese folktale. She describes a mountain that is thought to have magical powers. The children are enchanted with the tale and listen intently. When she finishes the tale, the children move back to their tables with boxes of chalk and crayons. Jim brings paper to each table and the children illustrate the magical mountain they heard described in the folktale. There is a quiet hum of conversation as the children work on their drawings. Some of the children are talking about their drawings, while others quietly concentrate on their art.

As they finish their work, they join a circle on the floor near the side of the room and discuss their drawings with the other children and Jim. Becky collects the drawings and assures the students she will be hanging them on the bulletin board after school this afternoon. She tells them, "Be sure to come and look at your drawings tomorrow and see all the different illustrations for the folktale."

Performance for Grandparents' and Special Friends' Day. Just then, Becky looks at the clock and reminds the class that this is Grandparents' and Special Friends' Day and it is time to go to the auditorium. The class has been practicing a dance for the presentation. The children helped with the choreography and are ready to go! As they take off their shoes and prepare to head for the stage, Isaac decides he is too nervous to dance. Becky talks to him about all of his practice time and what a great dancer he is, but he refuses to go on stage. Hearing this exchange, Isaac's friend Bradley says, "I feel worried, too, and won't dance." Becky helps the rest of the children start their performance, while Isaac and Bradley sit with her. As the music and dancing begin, Isaac starts crying. "I really did want to dance with the kids." Becky places her arm on his shoulder and he settles in to watch the dance. At the end of their dance, the children grab their shoes and head back to the classroom.

Journal 10.2: Before the performance, Becky suggested to Isaac that he might want to go up on the stage for the dance. After his third refusal, she suggested he sit in the audience and watch. What might have happened if she insisted he dance? What might Isaac learn from making his own choice?   ■

Becky was aware of the **emotional developmental level** typical of most kindergarten-age children. Children are beginning to express their feelings through words (verbally). It is important for adults to recognize a child's feelings and respond to his needs. This does not mean that the child always "gets his way" but it does mean that the child receives a reply or feedback. Knowing that some children are fearful of performing in front of others, Becky recognized Isaac's emotions and let him make his own choice. She responded in a developmentally appropriate way to his emotional needs.

Now that the children are back in the classroom, they are preparing for the arrival of their guests.

Showing off the classroom. Along come the grandparents and special friends, just in time to help buckle and tie shoes! Jim and Becky welcome everyone as they serve apple juice with chocolate chip cookies. The children show their grandparents and friends their work around the room. Tyson brings his father over to the mice. "Look, dad, see all the babies in here. We can watch them change. This one has hair on it now!"

Many of the children are clustered around the computer center, which has eight computers. Keeley is showing her grandmother how to access the Internet. She exclaims, "See, Oma, here is our web site. It has my sunflower on it. Remember when I cut it down to take to school?" Jim has made it simple for the children to find certain programs or sites by using "bookmarks" that the children locate with symbols.

On their web site, the kindergarten class has a photograph of a sunflower head taken with a special camera that displays photographs on computers. Hawthorne says, "We asked people to guess the number of sunflower seeds in our sunflower head. There are a lot of seeds." Replies are coming in from all around the world. Meanwhile, the kindergarten students have counted the seeds by counting and placing them in little cups with 10 seeds in each cup. The older students at the school will be coming in to help the kindergartners chart the total number of seeds before they respond to the people who sent in estimates.

Jim and Becky are now walking around the room, thanking everyone for their part in making a good morning. The children begin getting ready for lunch. There's Keeley with her grandmother, who is encouraging her to pull her boots on. Once she has her boots on, they look for her mittens. Keeley wants to make sure she has her cold weather clothes together for recess. You can't help but think that it was a good thing there were guests here today to help the children with coats, boots, mittens, and hats. Maybe the snowy day and the Grandparents' and Special Friends' Day worked well together, after all.

As the classroom empties, Jim and Becky ask if you would like to come back in a week or so and observe a more typical day. Jim says, "This morning has been very interesting, but it might be helpful to see more of the "regular" curriculum in action." He adds, "We never have a typical day, but that's what makes teaching kindergarten so interesting." Jim's outlook on teaching is very engaging, so you look forward to another visit.

A Full Day at Kindergarten

Today, you arrive with the children at 8:30. You watch them sign in and check the mice and their babies. Wow! Now there are six babies in the terrarium. Eli and Paul head straight for the Legos. They start building race cars and spaceships. Eli states, "I want all the wheels at the Lego table. I'm going to build a dune buggy." A group of children settle in at the computers. Though one child is using the keyboard, at least three others are at the computer, discussing the game or graphics. Keeley is with another group at the computers, checking their web site. This the last day for their sunflower seed guessing contest. Keeley wonders, "Will anyone get the right number? There are so many seeds in our sunflower!" The fourth-graders are coming to the kindergarten class tomorrow to help count the cups of sunflower seeds that were counted into groups of 10.

Jim uses a combination of drawings and words to list the daily schedule.

Calendar time. At 8:50, Jim calls the children over to the rug facing their calendar. It is a new month today. Maria looks at the new calendar and exclaims, "Look at the icicles that we get to use for our calendar. Some icicles are short and fat and others are long and skinny." The children are already thinking of patterns. Jim asks Maria if she wants to put up the first icicle. She chooses a short fat icicle. "I am thinking about an ABBB pattern, then I can see a short icicle and then 3 long ones. That will make a good pattern." They talk about other possible patterns for the coming month.

Next is a discussion about today's weather. Pedro goes to the window and tells the class, "Oh, guess what? It's cloudy again." The parent volunteer helps Pedro read the thermometer and he reports, "It is 43 degrees outside." The children then pick up their weather journals and draw the daily weather. Jim reminds them, "Use lots of colors in your pictures." Also near the calendar is the schedule for today. You glance at this to see what will be going on today.

The Gingerbread Man *(9:05–9:40).* When the children finish their weather journals, they gather on the rug for a story. Today, Jim reads *The Gingerbread Man*. Throughout the story, he asks the children to predict what might happen next. Some of the children are familiar with the story and seem to wait for the next sentence. When the old woman gets ready to open the oven, Hawthorne says, "Oh, I think the Gingerbread Man might be able to run away now that he is finished baking." Jim responds, "What makes you think he can run?" The children enjoy coming up with reasons to support their predictions. You notice that there aren't any "right" or "wrong" answers—just interesting predictions.

Jim also asks some children to pretend they are one of the characters and repeat the lines from the story. They certainly enjoy this story. When the story ends, Jim asks them to think of each of the characters in this story, starting with the first person they met. They name a character and then describe the character to Jim so he can draw it on the board. When he draws the Gingerbread Man, Eli said, "Make sure he has buttons on his tummy."

When they remember the wolf, Keeley wants Jim to make huge teeth. After they list all the characters, Jim gives them a large piece of paper folded into eight sections. They are to draw one character in each section.

Back at their tables, they visit with each other while drawing their pictures. "My old man has a mustache," says Marietta. "And my old man has a funny hat," replies Marie. A parent volunteer and Jim walk around the tables of children, asking questions about the story and commenting on the pictures. Jim tells Keeley, "Look at all the different colors you are using! This wolf is so scary." Keeley answers, "Yep, I wanted it to look like I painted a picture of the scary wolf." Jim asks her if she might like to paint later today during choice time and she enthusiastically answers, "Yes!"

When the pictures are finished, Jim asks the children to tell a short story about their pictures to their neighbor and then listen to their neighbor's short story. Each child has a special embellishment that gives the story a different twist. Pedro shows the Gingerbread Man running to school and turning into a boy who loves to build with blocks. Jeremiah says, "Re tons." Pedro turns to him and looks at his picture. "Oh, yeah! I see red buttons on your gingerbread man." Jeremiah had just finished working with Mariko, the speech and language specialist. Mariko comes into the kindergarten room and works with Jeremiah and Sheila three times a week for 30 minutes. With Jeremiah, the goal is to help him improve his language and pronunciation, as his language is developmentally similar to that of a 3- or 4-year-old child. Most of the children now understand Jeremiah's language, as demonstrated by Pedro's response. Jim makes sure that Jeremiah has many opportunities during the day to speak with him and the children. Mariko suggested that communication within the context of activities in the classroom would contribute to Jeremiah's learning. Since Jeremiah is involved in speech and language activities within the classroom, Mariko tailors the activities to correspond to the curriculum in the classroom. Jim is also able to note what Mariko is working on with Jeremiah and

Sheila and incorporate these sounds, words, and phrases into his communication with the children.

The children finish sharing their creative pictures and stories. Jim tells the children to share their pictures and stories at home with their families that evening. He announces, "Your stories are better than television. I bet your families will enjoy these!"

For the activities Jim planned around the story of *The Gingerbread Man,* he purposely included the use of language and sequencing of events in the story. He knows that kindergarten children rely on language to connect the story events and characters. By encouraging the children to talk with each other and share their stories, he is incorporating developmentally appropriate learning in the realm of cognitive development for 5-year-old children. He is also aware of the language needs of the two children receiving special education services from Mariko, and includes these goals into the lesson through the story sharing on an individual level.

After a long work session developing the story characters and telling stories, it's time for a break. The children are going to eat a snack and then have some free-time.

Snack time.   It's now 9:40, time for snack. Most of the children brought a snack from home, although Jim put out a box of crackers for anyone who was hungry. Jim sits down with Marietta, Pedro, and Keeley as he eats his apple. As the children finish their snacks, they move to different play areas and centers. Jim lets them know that they have 15 minutes until 10:00, when they leave for their P. E. (physical education) time.

Physical education (10:00–10:30).   Right next door to the kindergarten class is a large multipurpose room. In the morning, this room is used for physical education classes; during lunch, it becomes a cafeteria; and when school ends, it's the room for the after-school care program. Sabrina, the physical education teacher, is waiting outside the door for the kindergartners. They soon find their "spots" to sit on, which are numbers painted on the floor throughout the room. While waiting for each child to find his or her own number, Sabrina notices Hawthorne sliding onto his number from a run. She quietly asks him to come over to her and then asks him if he remembers how to find his number. He nods and walks to his number and sits down.

Sabrina begins talking about the first part of their class today. The children will be skipping, jogging, hopping, and walking on the large circle painted around the perimeter of the room. They get up and begin moving around. Sabrina tells you, "We start with the same type of activity to warm up and also to let them move around some before we move into our major activity of the day. This helps them get some wiggles out and then they are more ready to follow instructions for the game or activity."

When their movement time ends, the children go back to their numbered spots and wait for the next activity. Sabrina tells them that today they are using the parachute. "Yea," says Keeley. "I love to see the colors and dance around with the big parachute." There is a lot of agreement with that comment. Sabrina asks the children if they remember how to hold the parachute and Pedro reminds the class, "Fold the outside over, one, two, three, and then hold on tight." "Right," agrees Sabrina. "Then we will walk around the circle, carrying the parachute. We will make it go up and down."

The children gather around the parachute and fold over the edges and hang on. They then make the parachute go up. Cheri says, "When you pull really hard, the parachute gets straight and then it won't go up. I think we should pull out and then raise our arms when we want the parachute to go up." "Yep," says Pedro, "When our arms go up, it will go up, too." They continue with the parachute activity for another 10 minutes. Sabrina asks them what they would like to do for the last 5 minutes of class. They decide to get out the large foam balls and play catch or roll the balls to hit the wall on the far side of the room.

By then, it's time to go back to the classroom. Sabrina asks them, "How do you make a parachute

It takes group collaboration and the ability to follow instructions to make the parachute move up and down.

go up?" Marie responds, "Make your arms go up high, but we all have to do it together." "You are so right," says Sabrina, "and during our next class, we will put some little ping pong balls on the parachute and see what we can make them do."

The activities the children were involved in during P. E. relate to the physical development of motor skills for most children of 5 and 6 years of age. Catching and throwing balls, skipping, and combining the use of large and small muscles are part of the activities Sabrina plans for the kindergarten children. When playing with the parachute, their large and small muscles are in use as they pull the parachute with their fingers and lift it up with the arms. This is an example of a developmentally appropriate activity for children of kindergarten age.

Choice activities (10:30–11:10). "Yes, yes, yes!" Keeley sees that the paint supplies are in place at the easels. "I have been wanting to paint all day." Jim asks the children to name the different choices available today. Hawthorne looks around the classroom and says, "We can go to the Legos, the building blocks, the dramatic play corner, the painting corner, the computers, or the science table." "And also the reading corner," adds Paul. Keeley remembers, "Oh, we take our name card over to the place we want to go, and then take it with us if we change. But if the spaces are filled, we find another place to go." Jim nods and then gives a brief introduction to the different activities. Two parent helpers are here for the choice time and they are helping the children get set up.

Journal 10.3: Jim asked the children to identify the choices that were available for choice time today. Why would he ask the children instead of describing the choices himself? ■

Before any activity begins, Jim ensures that the children have directions and **clear expectations,** whether he states these or has a child or children explain the steps or process of the next activity. Jim shares part of his classroom management plan: "When everyone is clear on the expectations, there is less confusion and need for me to interrupt and get children back on task. I guess this is preventative classroom management, by planning ahead."

Of course, Keeley heads right for the painting corner. She places her name card in the pocket and finds a paint apron. Examining the colors and brushes that are out, she decides, "Today I will paint a dancing snow-lady to send to my Aunt Kelly. I'm going to be an artist like her when I grow up." She begins to paint, visiting with the other children at the easels. The 40 minutes pass quickly. Some children stay at their first choice activity the entire time, while others make several moves.

Over at the blocks, Marietta and Bradley are making a tall tower. "I like to see if we can make it as high as we are," shares Marietta. "Watch out for the blue blocks, though, they can make it tip too much," offers Bradley. Just then, Cheri walks over and stands very close to the tower. Sensing there might be a negative interaction about to occur, Jim provides **guidance** and encourages Cheri, "Let's find some blocks to help place on the tower. What about this red one?" Cheri then picks up a large block and asks Marietta, "Will this one work?" All three children cooperate and share blocks, continuing to encourage each other "to make it taller and taller."

Jim seems to keep track of who is at which activity and helps some of the children who appear minimally interested in their current activity. Sometimes he asks them questions about their plans and other times he makes suggestions or talks about what he sees them doing. One parent is helping at the block center, while another parent helps with the paints and hangs up finished pictures to dry.

Jim is now over at the computer station, clearly one of his favorite activities. He is demonstrating a new science program to a group of four students. This interactive science activity is on a CD-ROM. Jim tells you, "The intent of the program is to help young children express their categorization and classification strategies, along with sharpening their observation skills." On the computer screen, you see three fish and two trees in random order. The children are to use the mouse to identify which objects seem to go together by clicking on the similar objects. The computer then talks to them, "You show the two trees go together. Tell your partner why you decided the trees are together." The children giggle and then talk to each other about their reasons for grouping the trees. This activity continues, with different objects and increasingly difficult categorizations. Jim tells you, "I have been asked to preview different software, and the only way it makes sense to me to find out if it is any good is to have the children use the programs. Some of my personal rules for selecting good software are that it must interest the children, not contain any violence, and really teach them something that they might not experience otherwise. So far, this program seems to be somewhat useful."

The children work together on the activity. Maria tells Keeley, "Look, I can put these trees here and then move the fish over there and then they look like each other." "But what if we put all the big trees and big fish together and then the little trees and little fish are here?" asks Keeley. "I like groups of bigs and littles." They continue discussing their categorization or classification strategies, thinking up lots of possibilities and moving the objects into groups. The program also allows them to correct errors or move ahead to more difficult strategies, so it appears that learning is paced for individual learning levels.

This reminds you of an earlier question: How would technology look in a developmentally appropriate curriculum? You note that the children are engaged and able to navigate through the programs. They can also make choices and move to more advanced levels quickly. You see lots of interaction. Jim will share more tips and thoughts about technology in his classroom when you have a chance to visit with him later.

Clean up.   The next few minutes are spent cleaning up the classroom, putting supplies and materials away, and then washing hands in the classroom sink. Occasionally, you hear Becky or Jim remind someone that he needs to help clean an area where he had been playing. You can tell that the children must be hungry. They finish cleaning and hand washing rather quickly.

Lunch and recess (11:20–12:00).   The cafeteria is across the hall from the kindergarten classroom, and the smell of pizza has been drifting through the room for the last few minutes. You notice that you are also hungry and looking forward to your lunch. The children find their lunch tickets in their name pockets (decorated by each child with designs and stickers) and head for the cafeteria. This is a time that Jim gets a break. He tells you, "After lunch, the teacher on duty dismisses the students for recess, on the playground outside the cafeteria door." So that's why they all wear their coats to lunch!

Quiet time (12:00–12:20).   When the children enter their classroom after the noon recess, the lights are off and a tape of classical music is playing softly. Jim and Becky greet the children as they enter, and invite them to find their quiet time place. Pedro and Eli go over to the rug and lay down, as do several other children. Keeley and Marie each find a book and sit at a table together. They whisper quietly as they share their books. Some of the

children fall asleep after a few minutes, while most of the others are involved in a quiet activity. Cheri begins to talk loudly to a child near her. Jim walks over to her and reminds her that this is the time for everyone to rest quietly. He asks her if she would like to find another quiet activity. She then goes over to the mouse terrarium and sits quietly on the floor, watching the mice.

Journal 10.4: Why do you think Jim asked Cheri if she would like to find another quiet time activity instead of asking her to be quiet? ■

When quiet time ends, Becky turns the lights on. In a whisper, she asks the children to go sit on the rug. "While you are sitting on the rug, close your eyes and picture our mice in the terrarium." You wonder what this visualization is leading to.

Graphing (12:20–1:00).   Before the next activity, Jim tells you, "You will notice one of the ways I try to ensure that the curriculum is **relevant and meaningful** for these 5- and 6-year-olds." The graphing activity the children work on today is about something with which they are familiar—the mice in their classroom terrarium. Jim has a tub of small toy figures that represent the seven mice in the terrarium. He asks the children to think of what is different and what is the same about the mice. As they talk, children come to the tub and pick up one or more mice figures and tell something that they noticed about the mice or group of mice. They also walk over to the terrarium and check for characteristics that they could use for grouping or categorization.

After 10 minutes of discussion, Jim asks the children to think of how they might make up a group of mice. Pedro says, "Let's see how many baby mice there are." The children check in the terrarium and count the babies. They decide they see six baby mice. So Jim asks Marie to find six baby mice figures. She counts the six mice. Jim then places one of the mice figures on the graph paper and asks Keeley to decide where the next baby mice figure should go. She places it above the first one and then places three more mice on the paper. "Look, we have five baby mice on our paper." "Yes," says Jim, "Do we need more to show how many are in our terrarium?" "I want to count now," says Eli. "Now it's six!" "Wow," responds Jim, "You ended up with six mice on our graph paper." "And that's the same as in our mice house," says Marie.

Throughout this activity, the children were comparing the number of mice figures to the actual mice in their terrarium. They were using **language** that described the size of the mice, the color of the mice, and the number of mice. The focus of the graphing activity was mathematics, but the children were also developing **vocabulary** and an understanding of terminology used in mathematics.

After the group made a graph together, Jim explains that they are now going to make their own graphs at their tables with mice figures. The children may use the mice figures on the graph paper to tell a story about mice. Kerry, Keeley's mother, is helping in the classroom during this activity. Jim, Becky, and Kerry work with different groups of children and record their stories about the mice. Watching Kerry, it is apparent that she has spent time in this classroom. She knows all of the children's names and seems comfortable interacting with them as she records their mice stories. At Isaac's table, the children decide to make two groups according to the color of the mice. There are two white mice and five gray mice. Kerry asks them, "What would you like your story to say?" Isaac takes the lead and responds, "We know that five of our mice are gray and the other two are white." The children nod in agreement as Kerry writes their story on a large sheet of paper. She then leaves the paper on the table so the children can illustrate their story or graph. "I'll be back to see your illustrations and then we can share your story." She then goes to another table of children and talks with them about their graph.

Once all of the graph stories are recorded, the children come together on the rug and share their stories. Becky clips them to the chart rack as they discuss different ways to group their mice. Jim suggests that they think of what they might want to group and graph next, maybe bringing a collection of something from home. This sets the children off to discussing their ideas.

Journal 10.5: How was the graphing activity related to the children's prior experiences or relevant knowledge? Why is it developmentally appropriate for these children to spend time working with grouping, classifying, and graphing with mice figures? ■

Jim reminds the children that today they are working on their pottery puppets in art class. He walks down the hall with the children and watches as they enter the studio.

Studio art (1:00–1:35). During the past two weeks, the kindergartners have been making clay puppets. The art teacher has three parent helpers today, who help students find their supplies and their own projects. Some of the children are ready to paint their puppets, while others are still working on the final shaping of the puppet. You peek in for a minute and notice conversation going on about the puppets. The studio is set up with low tables, so children are able to stand as they work on their projects. The parent helpers and the teacher each work with a small group of children.

Thinking this might be a good time to visit with Jim, you leave the art room and go back to the classroom. Jim is getting ready for project time in the classroom, and you help him prepare materials for project time. The children have studio art and then recess, and since there's a lot to learn from Jim, you appreciate the time he spends with you.

Project time (1:50–2:25). **Project time** is planned for three afternoons each week. The projects tend to be long term, lasting from two to three weeks. Jim and Becky work with the children to develop projects that are of high interest, often finding that projects change direction once the children become involved in their work. Following the model of projects developed by Katz & Chard (1989), a project in this kindergarten is an "in-depth study of a particular topic" (p. 2). Children are involved in the development of the project, and as the project progresses, children "interact with people, objects, and the environment in ways that have personal meaning to them" (Katz & Chard, 1989, p. 3). The project approach refers to a way of teaching and learning that emphasizes the child's active participation in meaningful activities. With the model of project learning, children's intellectual and social development is stimulated as they learn through their involvement in an interesting project.

Remember our conversation about **integrated curriculum** and projects that include **multiple curricular areas?** This is what happens during project time in this kindergarten. New ideas and directions emerge once the project gets started, drawing from different areas of the curriculum as needed for exploration and solving the problem (Nagel, 1996). Jim explains to you, "It's important to allow for changes based on what the children are learning and where their interests lie. When we studied plants, student interest was very high in the sunflower heads that Keeley brought to class. We went with their interests and ended up with a web page highlighting our largest sunflower head and a contest to guess how many seeds were in the head. Throughout the plant project, the children were involved in art (when they painted and drew plants), math (when they counted plants, measured plants that they were growing, and grouped seeds by tens), literature (when they listened to stories about plants), and science (when they learned more about the life cycle of plants). Being aware of their interests helps me keep the projects flowing in a child-centered direction."

Right now the children are considering how to solve the problem of homeless dogs and cats that live in the school neighborhood. The problem came about through a discussion that several children were having about a dog they had seen for several days outside the school. Marietta and Bradley worried about a brown dog that they had seen on their walk to school. Marietta speculated, "I don't think he has a home. He looks so sad, except when he sees us coming." Bradley thought,

"Where does he go at night and what does he eat? I bet he gets so hungry." Becky and Jim overheard the conversation and decided this would be a good topic for their next class project.

Becky will begin her full-time student teaching soon and is responsible for this unit of study. She began the project by reading newspaper stories about homelessness and animals and asking the children what they think this means. Becky wanted to make sure that the unit began with the current knowledge level of each child, so she spent time discussing this topic with small groups and individual children. Based on their input, she then planned activities.

Each project incorporates community involvement and is linked to the children's neighborhood in some way. When they were involved in the plant project, the children grew flowers from seeds in decorated milk cartons and then brought these to a nearby assisted-care center. In their current project, they have already visited the local veterinarian, who talked about the problem of homeless animals and about the care of animals. The children are also making comparisons between human needs and animal needs, seeing that both humans and animals need food, water, shelter, and medical care. "I think we should try to help other people know that they need to take care of their pets," shares Hawthorne. "We can paint posters and hang them in the stores near here," suggests Keeley. Several students agree this is a great idea and are ready to start the posters. Jim, Becky, and parent volunteers will help with the writing on the posters, but each child will make his own poster with a message to people in his neighborhood. Becky finds that the link to the community is so important. "I notice that the children feel that they have something to offer to others when they learn in these projects. This is a powerful message for me to remember."

Today is the first day the class works on their posters. Some children are using paint, others opt for chalk or crayons. Several children are working together and drawing different parts of their pictures. Another group is cutting out magazine pictures for

Norma is thinking intently about her drawing for the poster.

their posters. Jim, Becky, and the parent volunteer circulate around the room to record the child's message on the poster. Next week, they will go on a walk around the school and ask local stores and businesses if they can put a poster up in their business.

Becky was concerned that this problem might cause anxiety or concern for the children, but she now feels assured. "The children are committed to finding a way to help these animals and to try to help others learn that they should take good care of their animals." Looking at the posters, you realize that the topic matters to the children and that they do want to help the animals. You see messages such as "Please take care of your cat," "Every dog and puppy needs a good home," and "Keep your animal safe." This is an important issue that these children have chosen to help solve for their community.

Assessment of student learning with portfolios. As in most kindergarten learning, **assessment** of projects occurs on a continuous basis. With young

children, it is important to look at their learning and development over a period of time. A **portfolio,** or a collection of important documents, of each child's work is kept throughout projects. During the first days of the project, Becky and Jim talk to each child individually and record the child's observations about the topic. This is helpful as a beginning point for the current knowledge level of the child and it also helps guide the direction of the project. Drawings, activities, and photographs of the children involved in the activities are added to the portfolio. At the end of the project, a photograph of the child's culminating activity (such as the animal poster or the flower planted in the milk carton) is placed in the portfolio. Jim and Becky make notes on much of the portfolio content, describing progress, learning of new skills, understandings that the child demonstrated, and specific interests the child had with the project. A final addition is the child's review of what they learned during the project, which is a summary dictated to the teacher or parent volunteer and added to the portfolio.

Comparing the beginning discussion of a topic to the final summary several weeks later provides insights into each child's learning throughout the unit or project. For instance, in the plant project, Marie began by saying, "Plants are green and are in the dirt." At the end of the project, she talked about seeds, light, water, and growing, along with other terms that indicated a growth in language and knowledge of plants. The portfolio also provides a visual documentation of the activities and involvement of each child in learning. Kerry looks forward to seeing the portfolios, as she find it keeps her informed of the curriculum and Keeley's activities in kindergarten. She has saved all of the portfolios that Keeley has brought home this year.

Journal 10.6: Have you ever developed a portfolio? Perhaps you saved some papers you have written for school over a period of time or your art projects from elementary school. What can you learn by looking over this documentation of your learning and progression? Why might parents of young children enjoy viewing their child's portfolio? ■

Closing circle (2:25–2:45). When the project areas have been cleaned up and the projects stored for the next work session, the children gather on the rug again. There is about 15 minutes left to talk about their day and their plans for tomorrow. Jim asks Eli to sit in the "leader's chair" and help with the discussion. Eli eagerly sits in the chair and asks the children to close their eyes and think of their special times they had today. Keeley has her arm up high. "I loved painting. My mom and Aunt Kelly will really like my dancing snow-lady picture. This was a super day for me." Several other

children add their thoughts of the day, as do Jim and Becky. Becky talks about plans for tomorrow. Then it is time to find coats (again), boots, hats, and papers to take home. Some of the children will be going next door to after-school care, while others will head for home or other child care arrangement. About one-third of the class does attend the after-school care program here at Eliot School, where you will visit later.

Saying good-bye to the children and the teachers, you start down the hall yourself. Looking back, you see Keeley as she goes into the after-school care room. She is carrying her dancing snow-lady picture very carefully and telling her friend that she is going to mail it to Aunt Kelly in New York!

Learning from Jim

Jim has been teaching for 15 years. All but one year have been at the kindergarten level. He began college in the midwest at a large university, majoring in elementary education. "I always wanted to be a teacher, so I knew this would be my major even before I began college," he says. During college, he moved to the West Coast and completed his degree in education. His student teaching took place in a first-and second-grade blended classroom. After graduation, his first job was at the kindergarten level. Although his college work focused on elementary-age children, he says, "I was interested in the kindergarten position, and was eager to teach at this level. During the past 15 years, I have taken many courses and attended workshops about early childhood education. I knew I needed to continue my own education."

Jim's Interest in Technology

Once Jim started teaching, he saw the need to become more versed in education for young children, and has continued to learn more each year. Another interest has been **technology** and early childhood education, which he has pursued for the past seven years. He finds, "Technology is an amazing tool in the classroom. My students are learning incredible things as they search the Internet, use software programs, or create presentations with the digital camera and computer." Jim is regarded as a leader in technology education and has been active in helping other teachers gain knowledge and experience with the use of technology. Technology is truly an integral part of his classroom, as you saw when you visited for the day.

Jim states, "I'm picky about the software in our classroom. Most of the programs I prefer are open ended and allow children to be in control of the actions. I want them to find out things on the computer that they can't learn through hands-on experiences."

The Eliot School Home Page is being investigated by this young child.

Jim searches for developmentally appropriate software that is "open ended and exploratory" (Haugland & Wright, 1997).

Jim also selects programs that allow for discovery and repetition. "I watch the children go back to programs that they had used earlier and see how they repeat and review prior learning. Most of these programs are very patient and allow children to select choices and return to previous sites." Jim also recognizes the need for hands-on experiences. "I would never substitute a software program for playing with blocks. The tactile and spatial senses need to developed through three dimensional play. Yet the computer serves as a wonderful communication tool." When you ask Jim for an example, he tells you, "For Valentine's Day, the class list was on the computer. Five-year-olds would have a difficult time writing our 26 names for valentines. But with the computer, they can print the names, then cut and glue or tape the names on valentines." The children learn how to navigate on the computer and the computer becomes a tool that helps them in their learning.

 ## Jim's Philosophy of Classroom Management

"You might have noticed how we work together in our classroom. My **classroom management plan** includes helping children learn to become a community and negotiate problems," shares Jim. When he begins an activity, Jim explains the steps or asks a child to explain the process, in order to ensure clear expectations of the process and children's behavior throughout the process. "We have situations each day where we need to discuss behavior and remind ourselves of our class rules. In the fall, we decided what we needed for rules to make our classroom work for us, and we look back to our rules when needed." Students are expected to talk over problems and go to adults when they need help solving a problem. For instance, when Brandy and Chantel both wanted to use a new bottle of glue, they had to negotiate whether to take turns, find another bottle of glue, or use tape or paste instead. They ended up sharing the glue and sitting at the same table. Becky noticed the situation early enough and stayed nearby in case the girls needed an adult to help in their negotiation. This time, they figured out what to do and continued their work. After several months in the classroom, Jim finds, "With practice, they are learning to express their feelings and work things out. It takes continual practice and reminders, but I think it is worth the effort."

Jim also finds his role to be one of **facilitator of learning** in the classroom. Offering children choices in their learning and listening to their interests places him in the role of a facilitator. He says, "I much prefer to be in there with the kids. The role of a direct instructor is not for me. It just doesn't fit with my picture of kindergarten." He sees kindergarten as a time of transition for most children. "I want them to be excited about school and learning. Kindergarten is that special year. My program is flexible and takes kids from where they are. Remember Keeley's interest in sunflowers? We were able to expand that and really explore sunflowers." As you observed, the kindergarten program is an active, hands-on experience. It was also based on student interests and it provided a solid foundation for future learning. After thanking Jim for sharing his students and his classroom today, you realize you have much to think about in terms of kindergarten programs. It truly is a special year of learning, and Keeley's attitudes toward school and learning have certainly helped you recognize the impact of a developmentally appropriate program.

After-School Care Program

As the kindergarten children left school, Jim pointed out where the class was headed after school. About eight children walked home, where a parent, older sibling, or neighbor will care for them. There were several parents waiting outside the school in cars, ready to take their child home or to a family home care situation. Bradley, Marietta, and Paul got on a yellow van to go to a for-profit child care center, which is part of a large national chain. Jim related, "Unfortunately, a few children will be heading home alone and wait until a parent or older sibling arrives." These **latch-key children,** so called because they often carry a key to their homes, lack the supervision and care that they need at this young age. One of the reasons Eliot School made an arrangement with an after-school care program is to meet the needs of families who may not be able to afford other care for their child. The program at Eliot School offers financial assistance to families needing a reduced rate. Keeley, Pedro, Brandy, Macy, and Hawthorne join the other children in the after-school care program at Eliot School, Fremont Hills Child Care. This program is run by a nonprofit agency. Many of the elementary schools in this city and nearby suburban districts offer after-school programs run by this child care company.

Fremont Hills After-School Program

At Eliot School, 75 children attend the after-school program. Parents may register their child on a full-time or part-time basis. Fremont Hills programs are built on the philosophy that providing a secure and warm environment promotes the self-esteem of children and supports the family. **After-school care** refers to programs in family day care homes, centers, or schools that provide supervision and activities for young children after school. The programs differ from those during the school day, with a more relaxed schedule and pacing for after school. As soon as Kerry learned that Keeley was accepted at Eliot School, she visited the after-school care program and made arrangements for Keeley to attend four afternoons a week. One afternoon a week Keeley goes to a friend's home. Kerry knew that the staff at the after-school care program received training and staff development before the program began as well as throughout the school year. She wanted Keeley in a setting where she was comfortable and where Keeley could make choices about her late afternoon activities (see Box 10.1).

Curriculum in the after-school care program.   A monthly curriculum plan is developed by the teachers at each site, with teachers from all of the Fremont Hills Centers sharing and exchanging ideas through a monthly newsletter. There is a monthly theme with activities related to this theme. During February, children at Eliot School were involved in creating a monthly calendar of events and activities around the theme of tall tales. Activities included writing and illustrating stories, acting out plays, and making puppets for the tall tales.

It's now time to visit the after-school care program. Let's see what Keeley is doing now!

BOX 10.1 ■ What Are Some Issues of After-School Care?

A Closer Look

Two major issues of after-school care are quality of the programs and availability of care for school-age children. The Cost, Quality, and Child Outcomes Study Team (1995) defines *quality child care* "as that which is most likely to support children's positive development" (p. 1). Findings from this study indicate that quality of child care is related to the staff-to-child ratio, the education of the staff, and the prior experience of the administrator(s). In high-quality programs, more staff are available to interact frequently with children, changing the environment to an enriching learning setting. Parents should be provided with indicators of quality child care, as they are responsible for making child care decisions. At the same time, standards for high-quality child care must be enforced in each state to help eliminate poor-quality child care.

With the increasing number of parents working outside of the home comes a growing need for child care. Availability of affordable after-school care remains a constant worry for parents. Families do not want to leave a young child at home alone after school, but with financial considerations, after-school care may be too costly. The Children's Defense Fund (1997) found that schools in low-income areas were less likely to offer programs for children before and after school. In 1993, only one-third of the schools in low-income neighborhoods offered extended-day programs (before and after school) and enrichment programs. Increasing the number of after-school care programs that provide financial assistance for families will enable more young children to access the care they need.

Keeley's After-School Care

As you enter the room that serves as the after-school care room, you notice bins of tissue paper and construction paper on the tables. Several children are talking about the different colors and what they need for the next stage of puppetry. Chantel sees the black strips of paper and announces, "This is perfect for the straight hair on my mother puppet." She is making a mother puppet for the story *Jack and the Beanstalk.* Jon is looking for green paper, as he is working on a giant with Keeley. They talk about "huge green boots, because he has the biggest feet you ever did see."

Miss Teresa, the caregiver, had read the story several times to the group of children and they were now telling parts of the story to each other as they explained the role of the puppet. You wish you would be here next week to see the puppet show. These children, from kindergarten through third grade, work together in a productive and fun way. Miss Teresa and the other caregivers are sitting with groups of children and making their own puppets. The plays will have lots of colorful characters.

Over in the corner is a book cart and several tape players with headsets. One of the caregivers is sitting on the floor with four children. Some are listening to him read, while others are listening to tapes on the headset. After observing the busy day at kindergarten, you understand that sometimes children need a quiet place to relax and unwind, and may choose this type of activity to balance their day. Choices are important, and honoring differences in needs for stimulation and quiet time is essential for young children.

You ask Keeley what she will be doing after she finishes her giant puppet this afternoon. Keeley tells you, "Well, we just ate our snack, then we had project time. Next it will be outdoor time and we can choose games or just play if we want. After that, we come inside and have games. Today, I will ask if we can play Hokey-Pokey because I like to sing that song. And then we have choosing time until we go home. I don't know what I will choose yet, but I want to play with Pedro, so I will see what he wants to do today." Looking over at the schedule on the wall, you note that Keeley accurately described the entire afternoon. She is certainly familiar with the daily schedule, and seems to be looking forward to her choices for the afternoon.

Family Involvement in the Program

Several parents appear at the door, reading the notices on the bulletin board as they enter. You wander over to this area and also read the notices. There is an announcement about plans for activities during winter vacation in two weeks, as well as an invitation to families to join in the monthly staff development activity concerning outside games and activities.

Chantel sees her dad, "Oh, Dad, come here and see my mother puppet." He walks over and she shares the new additions to her puppet, "Look at all the hair she has now. Tomorrow I want to finish her face and then make a dress for her. Can you come to our puppet show next week?" Miss Teresa has planned several different times for the puppet shows, so that families could attend. She explains, "It's important for the families to be involved in after-school care, also. We are definitely not a babysitting service, but a place where children continue to learn at their own paces and developmental levels. See the differences in the puppets? We try to incorporate projects where many different ages and developmental levels of children can work together and be successful. When they leave after-school care each evening, we want them to think about their afternoon and feel that they were engaged in interesting activities. We try to check in with families each day and have notices on the board of upcoming events. Families also receive a monthly newsletter and we hold bimonthly meetings to encourage family involvement in program planning."

Watching parents arrive to pick up their children, you think about the afternoon and the interactions between the caregivers and children and between the families and caregivers. The philosophy of Fremont Hills is apparent in the way the staff includes families and children in developing and implementing the program. You watched Keeley and her friends make choices throughout the afternoon, occasionally with guidance from Miss Teresa or other caregivers. The staff noticed if children were tired or hungry and responded to those needs. Jon spent an hour sitting with books on the large pillows, quietly looking at the books and resting. His need for quiet time was honored, as caregivers did not force him to join a game. Miss Teresa also told his father that Jon seemed tired today and wondered if he might be getting sick. His dad thanked her for noticing and said they would try to get him to bed early tonight. You also noticed that caregivers tried to check in with families to share something about their child as they left for the evening.

As you think back over the after-school program you have just visited, you realize how fortunate Keeley and her friends are to be in a safe and enriching program after they finish school each day. Keeley can make choices about how she spends her afternoon, just as she might at home. She also has a caring adult to talk with and her friends to play with. Kerry fully appreciates the quality of the program, as well as the reduced cost of the program based on her salary. She says, "It is such a welcome relief knowing that Keeley is at Fremont Hills after school. I don't worry about her and I also know she will enjoy her afternoon."

A Closer Look at Kindergarten

What Is Kindergarten?

Nearly all children in the United States—98 percent—attend kindergarten prior to first grade (Zill et al., 1995). Although kindergartens have been in existence for 150 years, it is difficult to define precisely the kindergarten of today. Most kindergartens provide experiences in art, music, and children's literature, while also planning time for play and for activities that promote physical and motor development.

How the children experience these activities reflects the philosophy of the kindergarten program. In some programs, children might choose their own activities and spend much of their time socializing and in play. In other programs, the teacher may **direct** more of the learning, planning activities that all children are expected to complete, perhaps incorporating beginning reading skills into the program. In the kindergarten that you observed, Jim planned many **free choice** activities throughout each day. He believes that children learn most from participating in a few structured activities, such as the calendar and weather discussion each morning, and then moving to activities of their own choice. Some days, the children's activities have a theme, such as friends. When there is a theme, it is woven throughout their day, including art, singing, dance, literacy, science, and play time.

Schools basically define their own kindergarten programs. This definition may vary according to current pressures or beliefs within the district and from national organizations representing early childhood education. There might even be two kindergarten teachers working in the same school with different programs. Do you recall the two very different kindergarten programs that Kerry visited prior to selecting Eliot School

BOX 10.2 ■ What Was the Beginning of Kindergarten?

A Closer Look

In the early part of the nineteenth century in Germany, Friedrich Froebel developed the first kindergarten program, centered on the religious philosophy of nature, God, and humanity. Froebel believed that God was of central importance and that each individual has a specific role or purpose to accomplish. He felt that young children need a rich learning environment provided by teachers who understand how to implement the Froebelian philosophy with children from age 3 to 6. Certain types of play and materials were essential to this learning environment. Learning rhymes with hand or body actions is an example of Froebel's approach to kindergarten.

Froebel established training programs for future kindergarten teachers. Teachers learned how to incorporate the tools of learning in kindergarten, called the "gifts," which were the first educational materials developed for young children. These gifts were materials that reflected forms found in nature, such as squares, circles, triangles, or cylinders. Through play with these materials, children would come to understand relationships in nature.

During the mid-1850s, German immigration to the United States brought many young women with kindergarten training to this country. In 1856, Margarethe Schurz taught her children and those of her relatives in her home in Watertown, Wisconsin. This became the first kindergarten established in the United States.

Froebel's influence is still in place in U.S. kindergartens today. When you observe an environment where children are nourished and cared for, and provided with learning activities that include blocks, plants, pets, and finger-plays, you are seeing the influence of Friedrich Froebel, the father of kindergarten.

for Keeley? Differences and contrasts between programs such as these make it difficult to provide a specific definition of kindergarten.

Kindergartens began in the 1850s as learning experiences for children from age 3 to 6. They evolved into programs in the public schools for children prior to the year they enter first grade, although kindergartens are also found in private schools, churches, and child care centers. Today's kindergartens have retained some of the components or features from the earliest programs, as you will notice in Box 10.2, which describes the beginning of kindergarten.

Journal 10.7: When reading about Froebel's kindergarten programs in Box 10.2, what do you notice that has been carried from his time period into Keeley's kindergarten class? ■

Increased pressure for academics. During the past 20 years, there has been renewed interest and debate about the role of kindergarten in the educational system. Remember Pam, the principal at Keeley's school, discussing the pressure for increased academics in her district's kindergarten? This push toward more academics in kindergarten is being felt in all parts of the nation. Pam's response was to hire teachers who understood and articulated the importance of a developmentally appropriate program, and who also could educate parents about the best learning environment for young children. Some early childhood educators, such as Pam, reconfirm their interest and support of kindergarten programs that reflect children's developmental levels, whereas other educators push for an increased emphasis on academics and preparation for first grade. The controversy continues.

Are programs from each of these two stances mutually exclusive? Or could developmentally appropriate learning also include academic learning or preparation for some 5- and 6-year-olds? Take the opportunity to consider these questions as you read about and observe kindergartens, watching especially how children respond to different curricula. Drawing from your reading, your experiences with younger and older children, and your personal philosophy of early childhood education will help you develop your position in this current debate. Later in this chapter, you will return to this issue, but first, let's take a closer look at kindergarten programs.

Kindergarten programs.   When attempting to define kindergarten, the **content of the program** must first be analyzed. *What* is taught must be separated from *how* it is taught to help you clearly see the content of the program (Spodek, 1988). Understanding the developmental stages of children at this age will help you realize how children learn best in kindergarten and what they are capable of learning. Beliefs about the best learning environment for 5- and 6-year-olds should guide educators to develop programs that view the young child as an active learner, curious about her world, and ready to explore and discover (McLean, Haas, & Butler, 1994). These beliefs were certainly important to Kerry as she thought about the type of kindergarten program she wanted for Keeley.

Program formats vary widely. Some children attend an all-day kindergarten, others attend a half-day kindergarten, and still others attend full days every other day (alternate-days program). In some schools, enrichment kindergartens are offered for part of a day in addition to the regular kindergarten program.

More important than the format of the program is the *content* of each program. Programs should be based on reasonable expectations for children and for the **range of children's developmental levels** in the classroom (Peck, McCaig, & Sapp, 1988). In Keeley's classroom, you saw children at varying developmental levels, yet Jim had designed the curriculum to allow for learning at different levels. Many of the activities involved hands-on learning and could be completed in small groups or individually. Children had choices throughout the day, including the choice of an activity or whether to work with others or individually. When Marie needed help remembering the characters in *The Gingerbread Man,* she looked at the large chart that Jim had made and asked Keeley about the characters. Some of the children printed the names of the characters, while others spent their time drawing the different characters. Each child completed the assignment at his own level. This is typical of the activities in that classroom. There is room for the large range of developmental levels and activities that promote ways for all children to be successful learners.

Perhaps one of the largest influences on the curriculum of a kindergarten comes from the larger society. Think of kindergarten as a small circle and society as a larger circle surrounding kindergarten. The larger circle (society) does have an impact on kindergartens.

Societal influence.   Many different factors influence the content of the kindergarten program. Each society determines what it feels is important for children at this age to

Norma shares her thoughts about the characters in The Gingerbread Man *as she draws and visits.*

know (Spodek, 1988). The content of the kindergarten program is also highly influenced by the expectations of society at the local and national levels. Children learn about the American way of life through children's literature, songs, interactions with other children and with adults, and comments from adults regarding these social interactions (Spodek, 1988). For example, listening to folktales and discussing traditions and customs of "long ago" weave part of the American culture into the kindergarten program.

 Journal 10.8: Recall some of the folktales that were read to you as a young child. Select one of your favorite tales and describe a social factor portrayed in the story. ■

As an early childhood educator, you will want to be able to articulate the content of your program as well as be able to explain why you include certain content. Knowing why you incorporate certain activities and topics in your classroom helps you recognize the societal influence on your program content.

Kindergarten Curriculum

 The traditional curriculum of a **developmentally appropriate kindergarten program** is grounded in child development theory and research (Peck, McCaig, & Sapp, 1988). The child's learning occurs throughout the entire day, with play as the primary learning activity. Children learn from doing and being involved in real experiences, whether they are composing a song with a friend or busily finger painting with all 10 fingers. At 5 and 6 years of age, children generally want to learn and are eager to gain new knowledge and explore new places.

When Hawthorne plans his morning snack and fixes apple slices with peanut butter, he is also developing his fine motor skills as he spreads the peanut butter. His language and cognitive abilities are engaged when he explains to a friend that they will soon be eating fruit with protein for snack. He starts talking about fruit and different fruits he has eaten. His ability to sort and label demonstrates his **classification strategy,** which is important to cognitive development.

His teacher made sure that Hawthorne had a choice for snack and also was expected to take an active role in preparing his food. A teacher's assistant was working with the children in the kitchen area and encouraged their conversation throughout their snack preparation. Hawthorne was learning through this purposeful activity—one that he chose. This is very different from a scenario where a child might practice spreading "play clay" on a play apple or being asked questions about a snack already prepared for her. **Meaningful activities** help children feel that their work is important, and eating the delicious apple snack is a great way to end the important activity of meal preparation.

Curriculum content.   All areas of child development should be included within the kindergarten curriculum. Attention to including activities that foster the development of intellectual, social, emotional, and physical development will be part of the curriculum planning process.

> **Journal 10.9:** When Hawthorne was making his snack, in which developmental areas was he engaged? Give a brief example of each developmental area you noted and the related activity. ■

Overemphasis on one area, such as intellectual development, leads to a stilted curriculum, which does not meet the needs of 5-year-old children. Spending all day on one area of development, such as physical activity, would create an imbalance in the curriculum. Children who are 5 and 6 years old are growing in each of these areas and need the stimulation and learning from engaging across all of the developmental areas.

Remember when Keeley was painting in her kindergarten classroom? She put a tape on the tape player and was singing, moving to the music, visiting with a friend, and painting at the same time. Her curriculum included activities planned by the teacher and activities chosen by herself in all of the developmental areas. A **developmentally appropriate curriculum** purposely includes experiences throughout each of the developmental areas and at the developmental levels that match the range of a particular age group of children. In following examples of appropriate practice outlined in *Developmentally Appropriate Practice in Early Childhood Programs* (Bredekamp & Copple, 1997), Jim attempted to create a "learning environment that fosters children's initiative, active exploration of materials, and sustained engagement with other children, adults, and activities" (p. 125).

Throughout your second visit to Jim's kindergarten class, you saw a typical kindergarten day. Children were involved in learning in many different curricular areas, as well as in the various developmental domains. Jim plans his curriculum loosely for the school year, and then organizes his plans month by month. He makes sure he has planned projects that will integrate math, science, literacy, health, and social studies. Many of the activities or experiences are planned with "real" examples, such as the mother and baby mice terrarium or the plant unit. Jim believes the children learn far more when the activities are meaningful and relevant, which often leads to integrated learning experiences.

When Keeley showed her grandmother the class's World Wide Web site and the sunflower project the students had put on the Web, you observed how these different subject areas blended to create an **integrated curriculum.** The students used math to count the seeds and group them into cups representing 10 seeds. Their science came into play when they found the sunflower head molding. This led to a discussion on decomposing and discussions about garbage. The children used literacy skills to read the responses and record them in their sunflower data books. They also listened to stories about sunflowers. Several of the children painted pictures and dictated short stories about sunflowers and made a sunflower book for the school library. When studying the use of sunflowers, the children were interested to learn that sunflower seeds in the grocery store were once seeds in a sunflower plant.

The content of the program and the way the children experience the program make up the curriculum. For example, several kindergarten classes might study plants during the year. Think about how Jim approached this unit. He listened to the children and learned of their prior knowledge and interests in plants. He then designed activities to build on their current knowledge levels. He also left flexibility for emergent activities, or activities that seemed to grow out of a teachable moment. An example of this occurred when Keeley brought several sunflower heads in from her garden. Jim had not thought about sunflowers when he began the project on plants, but this eventually became a major focus of the project. Because he was aware of the children's interests, he was able to create a project and curriculum that moved in the direction of their interests. This is also called **learner-centered curriculum**—curriculum that is determined by children's needs and interests.

When you become a teacher, you will find ways to weave some of your interests and expertise into the curriculum. This helps you share your interests with the children in your care. Of course, since Jim is highly interested in computers and technology, this is a daily part of his kindergarten program. Keep in mind some of the examples of computer learning that occurred in Keeley's kindergarten as we further explore technology in the kindergarten curriculum.

 Technology and curriculum.   Young children can use technology in a variety of ways. Some are beneficial to learning, while others might be considered a waste of time or even harmful to a child's development. Children see the use of computers on a daily

BOX 10.3 ■ What Is the Place of Technology in Early Childhood Education?

A Closer Look

The NAEYC Position Statement: Technology and Young Children—Ages Three through Eight (1996) regarding technology and young children emphasizes that "professional judgment by the teacher is required to determine if a specific use of technology is age appropriate, individually appropriate, and culturally appropriate" (p. 11). This means a teacher has to evaluate software and other technology and decide if those tools create the best learning situation for the children.

Although it is accepted that the use of computers is part of the elementary and secondary school curriculum, it remains a question to many whether there is a place for computers in kindergarten. You obviously saw one answer to this question when you observed in Jim's classroom. The children used the computer as a learning tool on a daily basis, accessing information and sharing resources and ideas with other children around the world. Richard Riley, U.S. Secretary of Education, believes that today's students still need to learn the basics in education, but they also need to learn how to utilize learning opportunities on the Internet (U.S. Department of Education, 1996).

How do you decide if computer usage is helpful or harmful? Ultimately, the teacher is responsible for evaluating appropriate uses and potential benefits of technology in his or her program, as well as how to integrate the technology into the learning environment (NAEYC, 1996a). Shade (1996) suggests looking for the following terms when evaluating software:

  Active learning
  Possible experimentation
  Child uses independently
  Operate from picture menu

These terms often describe software that is more likely to be open ended and allow for child input. More comprehensive checklists for evaluating software are available to help teachers select appropriate programs for their students.

In a kindergarten setting, computers and multimedia technology do not take the place of hands-on experiences in traditional early childhood programs. Playing at sand tables, painting, drawing, working with clay, exploring bubbles, building with blocks, and reading books are best experienced with the "real" material—that is, the actual object.

Think about mixing soap and water to make a bubble mixture and then twirling the bubble ring through the mixture until you are ready to blow a bubble. Then you pick up the bubble ring (leaving some drips down the front of your shirt) and you blow carefully until you have a large, colorful bubble. This is an experience that is hard to duplicate on a software program. The three-dimensional aspect and the senses of smell, texture, and visual pleasure come from the actual experience. A computer might duplicate the color and allow a child to draw the bubble, but the exposure to the actual experience will help the child create meaning from the computer program after the actual experience itself.

Teachers will be faced with many decisions about the appropriate use of technology in their classrooms. By viewing technology and computers as powerful tools that help children achieve their potential (Bredekamp & Rosegrant, 1994), teachers may be receptive to the numerous learning opportunities technology offers young children.

basis. Whether they are at a bank, grocery store, gas station, or library, computers are generally part of the operation of most enterprises today (see Box 10.3).

Perhaps the best uses for computers with young children come from the connections made with other children in the classroom on learning games on the computer or connections made over the network. Keeley is quite interested in her kindergarten's

World Wide Web page and checks daily for responses to the question about how many sunflower seeds are in the class sunflower. This is an example of extending the classroom experience to a wider audience, yet keeping the use of technology in a meaningful context. Keeley could also find out more information about sunflowers through the encyclopedia programs on the computer as well as artwork about sunflowers. The use of technology is integrated into her regular learning environment and is one option to support her learning (NAEYC, 1996a).

Jim has worked with several parents in reviewing and selecting software for the class computers. He is concerned about the number of children's software programs that focus on violent activity, even within an educational game. He finds that some software encourages interactions and collaboration and this appeals to him, as he builds a community with his students. Technology is another tool in his classroom, serving as an inviting way to learn more with and from others.

Now that you have read about the kindergarten curriculum, let's look at the preparation of people who implement the curriculum—the kindergarten staff. The current trend is a move toward a national level certification, but at this time, each state has different preparation requirements.

Preparation of Kindergarten Staff

Kindergarten teachers complete different types of preparation programs according to specific program requirements for licensure or certification established by each state. In some states, preparation for kindergarten certification for teachers is placed within a university's elementary education program. This structure means that a teacher preparing to teach kindergarten completes coursework focused on teaching children who range in age from 5 through 12 years or older. Other states have specific early childhood certification or licensure requirements, with the early grades seen as a separate preparation program. In the early 1990s, 12 states did not offer early childhood education certification. Certification requirements are changing rapidly. If you are interested in teaching kindergarten, contact someone in the certification office at your closest university or your state's Department of Education for current requirements in your state.

Journal 10.10: If you are planning to be a kindergarten teacher, would you prefer to "learn to teach" with students who were preparing for kindergarten through eighth-grade teaching, or would you rather work with other students interested in early childhood education only? What might be benefits of each type of preparation program? ■

Jim's preparation for teaching kindergarten. Keeley's teacher, Jim, completed an elementary education program. When he started teaching kindergarten, he enrolled in workshops and continuing education courses within his school district. He recognized the special needs of kindergarten-age students. He also observed different kindergarten programs. From his teaching experience, his observations, and his coursework, he decided that he wanted to acquire the skills and knowledge needed to create an interactive and developmentally appropriate learning environment. He states, "There is more to kindergarten than 'watering down' the academic requirements expected in many first through third grades. I have observed several public and private kindergartens and have always been impressed with a focus on child-directed learning, free play, and project-based learning. I knew this was the type of program I wanted to develop."

Remember our brief discussion on integrated curriculum (the project time in Keeley's kindergarten) in Chapter 5? Jim knew that these projects were the right approach for his curriculum. "In fact, the projects are actually the foundation for my entire kindergarten program," he says. Think back to the discussions about the plant projects and homeless cats and dogs near the school. These were projects that were important to the students and mattered to their local community. Jim shares, "The projects help students recognize that their learning is meaningful and connected to the real world." This curriculum interest of Jim's led to his taking more workshops and courses in curriculum integration.

Some kindergarten teachers have had experience with preschool teaching prior to entering a teacher preparation program. Their experiences might become part of their certification program in early childhood, with their work experience with families and young children recognized as practicum experience. Some early childhood professionals make changes in the age level of children with which they work. Although many states do not require certification to teach preschool children, almost all states require kindergarten teachers to have a teaching certificate. Professional organizations are pushing states to recognize the specialization of early childhood philosophy and child development and to separate early childhood education programs and certificates from elementary education.

Teacher assistants.   Teacher assistants are typically called *classified personnel* in school districts. The kindergarten teacher assistant may or may not have preparation in early childhood education. Many school districts offer workshops or other education opportunities for teacher assistants, which supports the professional growth and development of these important personnel.

The need for qualified staff.   Quality teaching staff is essential to a quality kindergarten program. Keeley is fortunate that Jim has participated in workshops and courses that focused on the development and learning of 5- and 6-year-olds. Her class is not a mini-first grade. Keeley is engaged in an active learning environment that encourages the growth and learning of each child within a developmentally appropriate curriculum.

In the NAEYC's list of indicators for quality early childhood programs, the caliber and competence of the staff are considered to be important indicators of the quality of an early childhood program. The education, training, and experience of the staff is reflected throughout each hour of each day. You see this in how the staff works with children, what activities are planned in the curriculum by the staff, and the staff's communication with parents, families, and colleagues. The preparation of early childhood professionals translates directly into the quality of early childhood programs. Good training programs and experiences are necessary to support effective early childhood programs.

Teacher preparation and teacher certification are definitely current issues in early childhood education. Let's examine some other important issues, as well as current trends surrounding kindergarten programs.

Current Issues and Trends Surrounding Kindergarten

As you read articles about kindergartens written over the past several years, you will notice the appearance of several dominant issues or themes. Educators and parents seem to wonder about the curriculum of kindergarten and how to determine if a child is ready for kindergarten. Actually, these two issues are closely connected. If the curriculum becomes increasingly academic, with expectations for great deal of time spent on worksheets each day, one will find fewer 5-year-old children "ready" for this type of kindergarten. When the kindergarten curriculum truly focuses on the developmental levels and needs of 5- and 6-year-old children, then the issue of being "ready" for kindergarten changes substantially.

Academics and kindergarten.   Here, we'll take a closer look at the question of academics within the kindergarten curriculum. Shepard and Smith (1988) believe that there has been an increasing emphasis on academics in kindergarten over the past 20 years. More kindergartens are including formal reading instruction in their programs. Many school administrators and parents want kindergartners to acquire academic knowledge. Shepard and Smith (1988) refer to this demand for academics in kindergarten as the "escalation of curriculum." Curriculum that was formerly taught in first grade is now expected in some kindergartens. Is this the right age for children to be learning formal academic skills?

Spodek (1988) looks at the kindergarten experience through the lens of society and what each society demands of children at specific ages. He suggests that developmentally oriented programs can also support "cultural knowledge and the foundations of academic scholarship" (p. 203). How can this happen? We often hear that the different emphases within these programs are at opposite ends and would not allow for a connection between child-centered learning and academics. Spodek (1988) cautions teachers and parents that they "should not be misled by the false dichotomy between socializing kindergartens and academic kindergartens" (p. 210). What would a kindergarten where academic learning occurs within a developmentally appropriate environment look like?

Spodek's suggestions are in alignment with those made by NAEYC (Bredekamp & Copple, 1997) for constructing an appropriate curriculum. According to Bredekamp and Copple, curriculum content should reflect social or cultural values,

There is a feeling of accomplishment when creating a moving vehicle.

parental input, and "consideration of age and experience of the learners" (p. 20). Kindergarten curriculum focused on learning rote skills and memorization is considered narrow and inappropriate for most 5-year-olds. Rather, a curriculum that promotes successful learning in a challenging and active learning environment while also providing for growth in each of the developmental areas could be labeled developmentally appropriate. Kindergarten curriculum should also include activities that encourage creativity, curiosity, play, and building of self-esteem and interest (Freeman, 1990).

Thinking of the developmental domains discussed in Chapter 3, you will recall discussions about cognitive, physical, emotional, and social growth. Learning within each of these areas would be incorporated in a developmentally appropriate curriculum, with balance sought among the domains. A strong focus on academics would skew this balance and provide fewer experiences in other developmental areas.

Perhaps this is one of the more important roles of a kindergarten—that of creating a **curriculum balance** among the developmental areas and looking for ways to blend activities to create a holistic program. For example, socialization can take place in many different settings. Academics does not mean always sitting at a desk and working on a worksheet alone. Children are learning when they explore their environment, draw pictures of their observations, and share these interpretations with others. Keeley learned new classification skills when she was grouping the mice figures. This activity was different from completing a worksheet about mice. She was able to tell her own story about her classification process and the rationale for her work.

When the kindergarten program is clear about the content of its curriculum and the *why, what,* and *how* of teaching and learning, there is room to begin academic foundations within a creative, active learning environment. While Keeley and her classmates studied sunflowers, they were engaged in singing, painting, listening to stories, writing their own stories, and counting sunflower seeds. These are all beginning academic skills, yet they were woven into a project that was interesting to this group of children. Children are so curious at this age and truly want to learn. The key is to watch and learn from each child and to help all children expand their knowledge within a supportive, balanced learning environment.

Journal 10.11: What made the sunflower project developmentally appropriate for this group of kindergarten children? What might make it developmentally inappropriate? ◼

The answer to the issue of increased academics within the kindergarten has not been reached yet. You will provide insights and input into this discussion as you learn more about early childhood education and visit kindergarten classrooms. Remembering the importance of developmentally appropriate curriculum provides a context for this issue. Perhaps as the debate continues, Spodek's suggestions will be revisited. Combining a child-centered developmental philosophy that supports the foundations of academic skills and knowledge when appropriate might be one answer to this issue.

An issue closely related to the curriculum of kindergarten is readiness for kindergarten. How is it determined when a child is ready for kindergarten? Does a child have to demonstrate specific knowledge to be ready for kindergarten? These questions are part of the kindergarten debate taking place right now. Different states have different mandates or requirements for entrance to kindergarten. What is the answer to these questions? Or are there any "right" answers?

Readiness for kindergarten.   Being ready for kindergarten brings many assumptions into the picture. Is the child supposed to be ready for kindergarten or is the school supposed to have a kindergarten program that is ready for the child? You can see how framing this issue shapes the question. Some states are pushing back the entrance age for kindergarten to turning age 5 in the fall or even in the summer in order to enroll in kindergarten. Other states are requiring children to take placement or screening tests to determine readiness.

NAEYC strongly opposes the use of testing to determine eligibility or readiness for kindergarten. The NAEYC Position Statement on School Readiness (1990) says there are no reliable tests to determine if a child is ready for kindergarten. The statement proposes that "the only legal and ethically defensible criterion for determining school entry is whether the child has reached the legal chronological age of school entry" (p. 22). Peck, McCaig, and Sapp (1988) caution that children with the most need for kindergarten may actually be the ones denied entry when using tests to determine readiness.

BOX 10.4 ■ What Is the Ready School?

A Closer Look

Kagan (1994) uses the phrase "ready school" to describe a school where the responsibilities for children are shared across the community. She proposes several strategies to make schools and communities ready for children. In following Kagan's strategies, families would be involved as active partners and decision makers with community programs that support early childhood education. Shifting the focus to making schools ready for children helps you see the importance of preparing schools for the diversity among children and their families. *Readying schools* means making them accessible and supportive of learning for each child in every community. Thus, the readiness debate shifts from readying or testing the child to ensuring the school program is committed to working with families and the community in developing the optimal learning environment.

These children then lose a year of early childhood education that is important to their development (see Box 10.4).

 Journal 10.12: What do you think is the main difference between checking to see if a child is ready for kindergarten or if a school is ready for a child? ■

While the debate about readiness for kindergarten continues, a connected issue, length of the school day, is also a topic of intense discussion. Some educators feel that extending the school day will improve the learning of kindergarten-age children, but others contend that the content of the program is the factor that most affects the learning.

Length of school day.   Perhaps the two most pressing reasons for extending the school day for kindergartners are the need for child care and the previous experiences in preschool for the majority of these children. With rising numbers of parents in the work force, young children are increasingly in need of child care. Over half of all mothers return to work within a year of their child's birth (Carnegie Task Force on Meeting the Needs of Young Children, 1994). If a kindergarten is a half-day program, children are often bused to other centers for after-school care programs. With this approach to kindergarten and child care, children experience discontinuity in their day.

Children who have already spent full days in preschool and care centers are often ready for a full-day experience in kindergarten. Instead of increasing the amount of time spent on academics, children could expand their half-day learning experiences throughout the day, having time to explore all of the centers in the room and choose more activities in their play. In Keeley's kindergarten, the full day allowed for more time in project-based learning and more time to participate in the art program at the school. There definitely was not a shift to increased academics, but a shift to a balanced day of learning appropriate for this age child.

When a school district reviews its policy regarding the amount of time allocated for kindergarten, it is imperative that these discussions include the importance of program options for young children and their families. Several researchers have studied the effect of attending a full-day versus half-day kindergarten on academic achievement and social behavior and found no significant differences between either schedule (Gullo & Clements, 1984). Including after-school care at the same school or providing a full-day kindergarten option acknowledges the life-style of many families of today. Perhaps the decision about full-day or half-day kindergarten schedules is best left as a choice for families. Kerry had decided that Keeley was ready for a full-day kindergarten program because she had spent several years in preschool on a full-day basis. Kerry appreciated the option of selecting a program that met Keeley's needs and her own as a single parent who works full time.

When there are program options, the family and early childhood educator would work together to decide which schedule works best for this particular child's needs (Peck, McCaig, & Sapp, 1988). Providing quality programs and options for schedules based on a child's and family's needs, in both kindergarten and child care, should be a consideration when school districts and school boards review their kindergarten programs.

PRINCIPLES AND INSIGHTS: A Summary and Review

After reading about kindergarten and the different types of programs offered at the kindergarten level, you are now more aware of the changes and pressures that early childhood educators are facing. When examining the debate about the goals for kindergarten, it is helpful to keep in mind that the purpose of the kindergarten year is to promote the learning and development of each child (Peck, McCaig, & Sapp, 1988). Pushing children through escalated academics in kindergarten will not be beneficial to their overall development. The more the curriculum is rushed, the more children are sorted and short changed.

When you think about an effective kindergarten program, you know that it is important that the program philosophy be developed around the needs of a particular community. The families and culture of the community must be an integral part of early childhood programs. Effective kindergarten programs are built around *readying the school* for the children and including developmentally appropriate curriculum based on these children's developmental levels, learning needs, and interests.

Technology provided for enhanced learning opportunities for Keeley and her classmates. They enjoyed communicating with people around the world as well as accessing resources for projects. Jim found Internet and web sites that allowed children to tap into current information as they developed questions or needs for answers and information.

Keeley's kindergarten year provided her with rich, diverse experiences in each of the developmental areas. By the end of the year, she was drawing pictures and writing short stories with invented spelling. She could count by 10s to 100 and was eager to learn more about addition. Along with her classmates, she was an active participant in art and drama activities. She was pleased with her work and looking forward to spending time with her friends at school, both in the classroom and at after-school day care. Keeley is a curious learner with many questions and multiple interests. She also is confident about her work and her contributions to her class. What better way to spend this very important year in her life?

Becoming an Early Childhood Professional

Your Field Experiences

1. Visit a kindergarten with the purpose of exploring developmental highlights of this age child. Looking at Table 10.1, take notice of the developmental highlights in the four developmental domains. While at the kindergarten, look for examples of activities in each developmental area. Describe the children's behavior that characterizes each developmental area.

2. Visit two different after-school care programs. What similarities and differences did you notice? What type of free choices do children have and what type of structures or schedules are in place? Are there after-school care options available in your community for families with limited incomes?

Your Professional Portfolio

1. Visit a nearby elementary school and talk with the media specialist about software for young children. How does she make decisions about software purchases for her school? How do children access these programs? What guidelines does the school have for access to the Internet? Record your findings in a short paper for your portfolio.

2. Describe two activities that you consider to be developmentally appropriate for a 5- or 6-year-old child. Why are these activities developmentally appropriate? How did you make this determination?

Your Professional Library

Books

Goffin, S. G., & Stealing, D. (Eds.). (1992). *Changing kindergartens: Four success stories.* Washington, DC: NAEYC.

Peck, J., McCaig, G., & Sapp, M. (1988). *Kindergarten policies: What is best for children?* Washington, DC: NAEYC.

Shores, E. F. (1992). *Explorers' classrooms: Good practice for kindergarten and primary grades.* Little Rock, AR: Southern Association on Children Under Six.

Spodek, B. (Ed.). (1986). *Today's kindergarten: Exploring its knowledge base, extending its curriculum.* New York: Teachers College Press.

Walmsley, B. B., Camp, A. M., & Walmsley, S. A. (1992). *Teaching kindergarten: A developmentally appropriate approach.* Portsmouth, NH: Heinemann.

Wright, J. L., & Shade, D. D. (1994). *Young children: Active learners in a technological age.* Washington, DC: NAEYC.

Internet Addresses and World Wide Web Sites
ericps.ed.uiuc.edu/ecce/pubs/digests/1993/koste193.html
  ERIC Digest: Developmentally Appropriate Programs

www.superkids.com/
  SuperKids Educational Software Review

www.brighthorizons.com/curriculum.html
  Curriculum and Assessment in Kindergarten

www.otan.dni.us/webfarm/transitions/keys/html
  Easing the Transitions from Preschool to Kindergarten

encps.ed.uiuc.edu/readyweb/s4c/sreb-gsr/staffdev.html
  Getting Schools Ready for Children: The Other Side of the Readiness Goal

www.nauticom.net/www/cokids/dapQnA.html
  Answers to Commonly Asked Questions Concerning Developmentally Appropriate Practice

The Primary Grades

JODIE'S STORY OF

SPECIAL EDUCATION

When you finish reading and reflecting on this chapter, you will be able to:

1. Define *inclusion.*

2. Outline the curriculum for a day in a primary classroom.

3. Describe the role of an early childhood education specialist.

4. Summarize the legislation affecting the education of children with special needs.

5. Describe instructional strategies and curriculum modifications that support learning for children with special needs.

You are about to meet Jodie, her family, and several of her classmates and teachers. She is a delightful 7-year-old with light brown hair, brown eyes, a frequent smile, and the wonderful ability to make a positive impact on others. In fact, as you become acquainted with Jodie, you will clearly see that her primary interest lies in interacting with those around her. She was diagnosed with **Down syndrome** at birth, a chromosomal abnormality that affects her intellectual capability and her physical health but most definitely does not limit her ability to care about people.

Visiting Jodie at Home

Jodie lives in a neighborhood selected by her parents because of the local school district's strong reputation. They learned that this school district is committed to including children with disabilities in their neighborhood schools to the fullest extent possible. Including children in classrooms with their peers matches Jodie's parents' belief regarding the "unconditional acceptance of the uniqueness of each child" (Sugawara, 1996).

As you turn down Jodie's street, you see bicycles in several driveways, basketball hoops above garage doors, and children playing across the way in the park. It looks like Jodie's parents were not alone in their choice of neighborhoods. You begin to knock on the door when Jodie and her mother, Lynn, open the door to welcome you.

Jodie asks, "Could I please hang up your coat?" She then runs over to her mother and whispers to her. After this interchange, she comes back with, "Do you want coffee or tea?" You decide on coffee. Jodie carries a basket of cookies over to the coffee table while her mother brings the coffee.

Jodie begins talking about school and enthusiastically tells you about her teacher and her friends at school. "My favorite time is reading, but I like painting and recess,

411

too." Jodie points to the refrigerator. "Look at my rainbow painting and my school pa-pers. These are mine and these are Tracy's and these are made by my brother, Kurt." It is obvious that Jodie is pleased with her accomplishments and those of her siblings.

Jodie's Tour

Lynn turns to Jodie, saying, "OK, now it's time for you to show our guest your room." Jodie starts in the family room, where you notice photographs on the wall. Jodie points out, "That's my grandma, my sister, my mom and dad, and my brother." You then head upstairs.

Jodie stops before her door and says, "You are going to see my pretty pink room with lots of things in it." She opens the door and points to her walls, "See—I have wall-paper with pink flowers." On her dresser is a collection of dolls. As she shows you her favorite, she explains, "This is Anna. She sleeps in my bed and goes in the car with me." It looks like Anna is well loved. On the bookshelf are many books and tapes, along with a cassette player. Jodie says, "I like to play tapes with songs and stories when I go to bed." She adds, "I had to help Mom clean my room after school." "Right," says Lynn, "You like it clean, but you don't like to clean it." Off to the side, Lynn tells us, "Jodie has a tendency to pretend she can't do something in order to enlist the help of some-one else, but I am usually on to her scheme and work with her to finish tasks."

Ending Your Visit

You head downstairs just as the rest of the family comes home. Jerry is home from work early and all three children greet him enthusiastically. Tracy and Kurt were dropped off from soccer practice. Jerry says hello as he finishes hugs for everyone in the family. All at once, everyone is talking. Jerry tells us laughingly, "Seems like you visited us on a typical afternoon!"

You head out the door, thanking the family for their hospitality. You now have a bet-ter understanding of Jodie after visiting her family and home. Lynn invites you back for another conversation about Jodie's early childhood, perhaps during the day when every-one is at school. You take her up on the offer and make a date for two weeks from now.

Walking back to the car, you think how fortunate Jodie is to have such a warm, caring family. She is fully accepted as a family member, with responsibilities and ex-pectations like those of the other children. You look forward to your return visit, and to a visit with Jodie, her classmates, teacher, and principal at school next week.

 Journal 11.1: What did you learn about Jodie from the home visit that might be help-ful to you as her teacher? ■

Forest Hills School

Driving up the lane toward Forest Hills School, you notice the striking architecture of the school building. The front of the school has an angled atrium surrounding the front door. Playing fields are on the north and west sides of the school, along with two large playground areas.

Entering the office, you are greeted cheerfully by the school secretary. As you sign in on the daily visitor sheet, she gives you a name badge to wear in the building. Right next to the visitor sign-in is a clipboard for parent volunteers to log their volunteer work hours. At a glance, it looks like there are many active parent volunteers at this school.

While waiting to meet the principal, you see three kindergarten-age children enter the office. One boy announces, "We came to show our special work. We wrote some of our names and here is a picture of us." The office staff exclaims over their work and the children proudly walk back to their classroom. What a pleasant introduction to the atmosphere at Forest Hills Elementary School.

Meeting the Principal

The principal, Carol, invites you into her office. Over coffee, she begins a conversation about the school. Carol knows you are interested in how her staff works with children who have special needs. She says, "You'll learn a lot from visiting Jodie in her classroom. Her teacher, Paula, has done an exceptional job at making all of the children feel part of the class."

Inclusion at Forest Hills School.   Before we talk about **inclusion,** Carol wants to discuss the general teaching philosophy of the staff and their school improvement focus. She begins, "A district goal is to implement classroom practices that ensure all children will learn. To us, this means including children with special needs in their neighborhood schools with their neighborhood friends to the fullest extent possible for each child." (Box 11.1 presents a definition of *inclusion* according to a national professional organization, which is similar to the practice at Forest Hills.) Carol shares, "Marty is our

BOX 11.1 ■ What Is Inclusion?

A Closer Look

Inclusion, as a value, supports the right of all children, regardless of their diverse abilities, to participate actively in natural settings within their communities. A natural setting is one in which the child would spend time had he or she not had a disability. Such settings include but are not limited to home and family, play groups, child care, nursery schools, Head Start programs, kindergartens, and neighborhood school classrooms. (Division for Early Childhood, 1993)

Sometimes inclusion is referred to as *inclusive education* or *inclusionary practices.* An *inclusive school* can be defined as "a place where everyone belongs, is accepted, supports, and is supported . . . in the course of having his or her educational needs met" (Stainback & Stainback, 1992, p. 3). The inclusion movement has raised great controversy among educators and parents. Proponents view full inclusion as the best way to educate every child, both academically

and socially. Inclusion provides for more interaction and contact between children with special needs and children without disabilities. As they will be interacting with each other as adults, it makes sense to lessen boundaries and isolation during their school years. Opponents of inclusion raise concerns about the lack of training in special education for general educators and concerns about the time taken away from students in the regular classroom to meet the needs of children with special needs.

The debate continues as the inclusion movement expands. Collaborative teaching, where general and special education teachers team teach or work together, is one model that blends the expertise of both teachers and strengthens the educational practices for all children. General educators need to be included in the debate surrounding inclusion. It is they who are the teachers of children with special needs in the inclusive school and who will determine the success of inclusion.

resource teacher and a special educator. She works closely with the teachers and supports their learning and work with our children with special needs. Marty's expertise in collaborating is what makes inclusion work in our school."

Forest Hills School and students. The discussion turns to the school building. There are 28 classrooms, two gymnasiums, a music room, a staff room, several small conference rooms, a media center, and a lunchroom. Currently, there are 553 students enrolled at Forest Hills, with 24 teachers and 9 support staff. Carol explains, "The area around the school has been under continuous development for the past several years, with the construction of several housing subdivisions."

Most of the children attending Forest Hills are from middle-income families, with 18 percent of the students receiving free or reduced lunches. Carol tells you, "Families are active partners in their children's education and are frequently seen here at school, whether as regular volunteers, special presenters, or visiting their child for lunch. The parent club raised almost $4,000 last year, and we used these funds for classroom materials, playground equipment, field trips, and other special projects." You remember the list in the office and think volunteer support must really help teachers and students.

Multiage classes. You ask about the classroom arrangements and Carol explains that approximately half of the classrooms are multiage classrooms that include children from two or three grade levels, such as a first and second grade; the other half are single-grade classrooms. Jodie is in a first/second-grade multiage classroom. According to Carol, some advantages of the multiage classroom include:

- Learning with the same teacher for two or more years reduces the changes that occur with learning new routines and expectations each fall.
- Working with students who have a wide range of maturity and abilities can facilitate cooperative group learning.
- The group of students that remains with the teacher can assist the new group of students as they enter the multiage class.
- The teacher's knowledge of the child and family increases during the extended time period of two years with the same teacher.
- The teacher's knowledge of and assessment of the child's learning has greater continuity.

 Journal 11.2: Why might Jodie's parents and the principal decide that a multiage classroom would be an appropriate educational setting for Jodie? ■

Resource teacher. Forest Hills also has a resource room, with one full-time and one part-time resource teacher working with classroom teachers to support the learning of children identified with special needs. Marty, the full-time resource teacher, also works with some children on an individual basis. Jodie spends most of her day in her regular classroom setting, but she meets with Marty three times each week to work on beginning reading and writing acquisition skills. The resource teacher consults with Paula

(Jodie's classroom teacher) on a weekly basis to discuss Paula's curriculum plans for the coming week and modifications that might help Jodie in her learning with the group. Carol suggests, "Let's go down the hall now and visit Jodie in her classroom." After your observation, you will be able to meet with Paula after school and discuss her successes and challenges in including Jodie in her classroom.

Walking down the hall you see bulletin boards with children's artwork and writing projects. Right past the media center is a pod of four rooms that share a common center. There are groups of two or three children clustered at computers in the common space. Carol tells you, "These children are editing stories and discussing changes they want on their rough drafts. Most of our teachers use a writing process similar to this in their classrooms."

Jodie's Classroom

On the right-hand side of the pod of four classrooms, you see Jodie's classroom. As you enter, you notice paintings hanging on the walls, groups of desks clustered around the room, a large bookcase filled with children's books, and a colorful assortment of blocks, tiles, and wooden cubes in tubs on the back counter near the sinks.

Math time. All 25 children are seated on the floor facing the calendar on the wall. They are discussing today's date. Courtney describes the pattern she found with the pumpkins marking the days of the month to date on the October calendar. She says, "I found an ABBA pattern. See, there is one big pumpkin first, then two little pumpkins, and today we can put a big pumpkin on October 4, then we'll have ABBA for the pattern." Paula, the teacher asks, "So if we go big, little, little, big pumpkins, we have an ABBA pattern?" Courtney nods, as do several other students. "Wait," say Jordan. "I think it could be ABBB if we put up another little pumpkin for October 4, right?" Paula turns to the class, "What do you think?" "Let's put a little pumpkin up and see if this can be ABBB." The students look excited when they discover there is more than one pattern. Paula asks them to go to their desks and find different combinations of patterns and equations to make with the number 4, reminding them, "If you need help, check with one of your neighbors."

Jodie, who is walking with Tonya, tells her, "Let's color some big and little pumpkins, OK?" The two girls gather some wooden tiles, crayons, and paper, and begin making pumpkins. After a few minutes, Tonya is repeating the ABBA pattern, whereas Jodie has several small pumpkins on her picture. Jordan reaches across the desk and points to Jodie's pumpkins, saying, "Hey, Jodie, if you make a big pumpkin here you will have an ABBB pattern on your picture." Jodie looks at his paper and then starts making a huge pumpkin in front of her three little pumpkins.

Paula walks over to the table and asks each child to tell her about the pumpkin pattern. Jordan is eager to say, "ABBB. I like to make lots of little pumpkins." Paula asks Jodie to read her pattern. Jodie looks at her page and says, "Big, little, little, little." "Yes," responds Paula, "And what about if you use As and Bs to name your pumpkins?" "Oh, ABBB, right?" asks Jodie. "Yup," says Jordan. "Look, I can make my pattern with colored tiles. See? Yellow, red, red, red is the same as ABBB!" Paula responds enthusiastically, "Jordan, you found several ways to show your patterns." Paula moves to the next table, telling Jordan, Tonya, and Jodie, "You three are working great together, and you certainly have some colorful pumpkins."

Journal 11.3: Describe how collaborative group work helped these students in their work with patterning. ■

Paula is adapting the curriculum to meet the learning needs of a diverse group of students. The common element, calendar math with patterns and combinations of numbers that make 4, met the learning needs of the large range of abilities in mathematics. Paula moved from the current knowledge of each child and provided manipulatives, visual activities, written symbols, and rhythmic patterns about the number 4 on the calendar. These activities allowed for the use of multiple intelligences and concrete experiences in the learning process. Paula also asked individual children questions that led them into their zone of proximal development, challenging them to stretch their thinking. She then made sure each child had a partner to work with as they discovered new ways to express the number 4.

For example, in the pumpkin activity, Paula asked Jodie about her pattern. With help from Paula and Jordan, Jodie was able to name her pattern. Other children were using subtraction to find four pumpkins, for instance, you might have noticed Natasha subtracting 6 pumpkins from 10 pumpkins and drawing this equation. Several students were finding all of the different addition combinations for the number 4, such as $2 + 2$, $0 + 4$, and $3 + 1$. During the same time with similar activities, children were working at different levels, yet all were engaged in learning mathematics. As you continue to observe in Jodie's first/second-grade multiage classroom, watch for different ways Paula shapes or modifies the curriculum to meet children's learning needs during the day.

Today's schedule.   The daily schedule is written on the chalkboard and you see that the class had book time from 8:30 to 8:45. During this time, each child chose a book to read to a partner or to himself. At 8:45, the children gathered on the rug for sharing time until 9:00. You arrived in the classroom at 9:35, when the students were involved in calendar math. Paula had just asked the students to share their work at their table. You check the schedule on the board to see what is planned next.

Today's Schedule

8:30–8:45	Book Time
8:45–9:00	Sharing
9:00–9:45	Math/Calendar
9:45–10:30	Writer's Workshop
10:30–10:45	Recess
10:45–11:30	Reading
11:30–12:15	Lunch/Recess
12:15–12:45	Library
12:45–1:30	Projects
1:30–2:00	Music
2:00–2:30	Choice
2:30	Good-bye!

One of the students, Natasha, strikes a note on the xylophone. She waits for the class to be quiet, then reminds them to look at the clock and the schedule on the board. "Now it is time for writer's workshop!" announces Natasha. The children go to the rug and sit facing a child's chair.

Writer's workshop.   Holding a red file folder, Sam takes a seat in the author's chair. He pulls out his story and begins reading his story about bugs coming to his backyard from another planet. The bugs are strange colors and move backwards. He has many colorful illustrations to go with his story. When he finishes, he asks his classmates if they have any questions. Tonya wonders why the bugs move backwards. Sam replies, "Where they come from, everything goes backwards, so they do, too." "Oh," says Tonya, "Now I get it." Jodie tells Sam, "You made pretty pictures." "Thanks," says Sam.

After a few more questions about Sam's story, Paula suggests that it is time to work at their desks on their own stories. Each child pulls a file folder from the writing center tub and gets to work. Some children are editing stories, some are developing topics, and others are drawing pictures to get ideas for story topics. The writing center is on the side counter and has a supply of paper, pencils, crayons, tape, staplers, and colored paper for covers. Paula is circulating around the room and helping individual children. After 10 minutes, some of the children begin working with a partner, reading their story out loud and asking for feedback on their writing. This is part of the peer edit/review process. At the end of writer's workshop, several children share the work they completed that morning with the rest of the class. As the children leave for recess, they place their writing folder in the tub, grabbing coats and playground balls on the way.

You also take a quick break and then head back to the classroom to watch Jodie during reading. Paula informs you that this is one of the days that Marty, the **resource teacher** from special education, comes to the classroom to work with Jodie. Marty is licensed in special education and works with children according to their learning needs on a regular schedule. Part of her job is also to meet with classroom teachers to discuss curriculum and modifications or accommodations that can be made to help children be successful in learning.

Reading with the resource teacher.   Marty is carrying a stack of books and an envelope with several cards with one word written on each card. Marty and Jodie move to the side of the room, where they sit at a small table. Jodie looks at the cards and says, "I remember my words we wrote. I picked *bug* and *grass*." Marty opens the envelope and lays out four cards on the table. Jodie quickly picks up *bug* and then spends some time looking at the other words. "It has squiggly marks at the end that go 'ssss,' so here it is." She picks up a card with the word *grass* and moves that card to the side of the table. After reading the other two cards, Marty and Jodie spend some time developing two new word cards, with words that Jodie chooses. Jodie draws a picture on the back of each card to represent the word.

Journal 11.4: In this reading activity, what were some ways that Marty structures the lesson to allow Jodie to incorporate her own interests? What might be another way to incorporate a child's interest in an activity such as this? ■

The aroma of freshly baked rolls drifts in from the lunchroom. The children mention lunch as they quickly move back to their tables, wash their hands, find lunch tickets or lunch boxes, and head down the hall to the lunchroom. You follow behind, just as ready for your lunch, which you will eat in the staff lunch room. Saying good-bye to the children, you tell them you'll see them back in the classroom after library time. You spend lunchtime visiting with the staff and talking about schools, teaching, and the news of the day.

Insect project.   When you enter the classroom after the children return from the library, you are greeted by Sam. He eagerly tells you, "We are learning about bugs from our yards and we collected some in jars with holes in the lid. Come see my bug." You go look at his bug and admire a large grasshopper with some sticks and grass in the jar. The children are working in small groups, using magnifying glasses and drawing their insect on a piece of paper attached to their clipboards. They are taking turns using descriptive words to talk about their insect.

You wander over to Jodie's group and listen to the children. One boy says, "Look at how many legs are on our insect." The children check this out and try to count the legs. They then add legs to their drawing. It is Jodie's turn to describe something and she says, "I don't know more about the bug." The girl next to her says to Jodie, "What color is the bug, Jodie?" This prompts Jodie to say, "Green, green—the bug is green!" So now the group colors their insect, drawing with green crayons. They then walk over to the insect posters on the wall and see if they can find the picture and name of their insect. The group looks at all of the posters and decides that their insect is a beetle, so they write *beetle* on their papers. Jodie has some difficulty with writing the entire word. She finishes a *b* and puts her pencil down. One of the boys asks her, "Want me to write more of the word?" She replies, "No, I have 'nough."

The children then place their clipboards on their desks and move over to the circle rug, where Paula is reading a story about insects. Jodie sits down and listens intently to the story. Paula asks several questions about insects and prompts the children to describe what they see in the book's pictures before she reads the story. Jodie doesn't volunteer any information until they reach the grasshopper page, then she exclaims, "It's green!" Sam says, "You're right." Paula finishes the story and the children talk some more about the insects in their jars. It is almost time for music, so Paula announces, "Time to head back to your desks to clean up and get ready to go to the music room." As the children head down the hall, Natasha comes over to Jodie and holds her hand, saying, "I get to walk with you today," as they head toward the music room.

A few minutes with the teacher. You spend a few minutes talking with Paula while the children are in music. She says, "I really want the children to learn from each other, so much of the work in the classroom is structured in a **cooperative learning format,** with small groups of children working together toward a shared learning goal. For example, during math time, those who have figured out the concept or skill they are working on will often explain the concepts using manipulative materials and then have other children show another way to solve a problem." Paula attended a workshop on cooperative learning and discovered strategies to use small groups to maximize individual learning and that of the other group members (Johnson, Johnson, & Holubec, 1994). She found it important to check in with the small groups to assess their understanding and knowledge level and to keep track of individual learning on a chart she carries around on her clipboard.

Since there is such a wide range of abilities and knowledge levels in this multiage class, Paula combines whole group instruction with cooperative learning groups and individual sessions with each student throughout a typical week. "I think I can reach the individual learner's needs best with this arrangement." You ask how this structure works for students like Jodie, and Paula shows you a blank copy of the chart (see Figure 11.1) she uses to record her observations of individual children's work.

FIGURE 11.1   Class Observation Record

Class Observation Record		
Student Name	Activity/Skill	Observation Comments

■ FIGURE 11.2 Anecdotal Observation

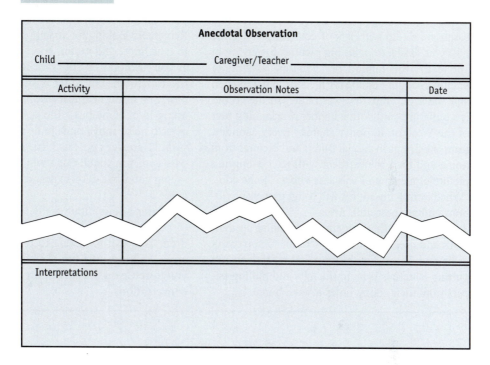

Jodie has been working on numeracy skills and has already moved through addition and subtraction of numbers up to 4 since school started last month. This means that Jodie is able to think of combinations of numbers that total 4. Some children are working on subtraction skills with two-digit numbers. According to Paula, "This charting system provides a clear record of the children's current learning and what skills or concepts they will be working on next."

Paula has noticed a change in her observation skills since Jodie arrived in the classroom. "I used to watch and later think about the child and her learning. I now use an anecdotal record to keep track of my observations. It seems that documenting is more accurate and helpful in making changes in curriculum or learning goals." Figure 11.2 displays an example of an anecdotal record form.

It's now time for the children to return to the classroom. Let's resume our observations.

Touring with Jodie and Tonya. As the children enter, Paula reminds Jodie, "You get to pick someone in the classroom to go with you to show our visitor around the classroom while the rest of the class finishes maps of their neighborhoods." School will be ending in 30 minutes, so you are eager to begin a classroom tour with Jodie and Tonya. You start in the back of the room, looking at the interesting variety of insects in jars. Next, Jodie and Tonya take you to the math center. Tonya says, "See our tubs of tiles, blocks, rods, and rulers. We can use these any time we are working. It's choice time right now and these kids are working on neighborhood drawings. Some of us are working together to make drawings and maps about our own neighborhoods and what is in them."

The next stop is the art corner, where two easels are set up with jars of colorful paint. Jodie tells you, "I like to paint big pictures for my mom and dad." You remind her you saw a rainbow painting hanging on the refrigerator in her kitchen and she says, "Yup, that was mine." In the corner is a bulletin board with a banner proclaiming Star of the Week on it. Tonya shares, "Every Monday, someone brings in special things and pictures from home and then shares them with us. I brought a picture of me when I was a newborn." Jodie adds, "When I bring my stuff, I will bring gymnastic ribbons and my best doll, Anna."

You notice that students are packing up their work and preparing to leave school, so you thank Jodie and Tonya for the great tour. Students are putting materials back in the tubs and pulling papers from their cubby holes to take home.

End of the school day.   It's time to leave school! The bustle at the end of the day is similar to what you experienced in your elementary schooldays. Remember looking for an important piece of paper to take home and saying good-bye to the teacher as you rush out the door? Most students have left the classroom, but Jodie is still looking for her coat. She seems near tears as she says, "Oh, no. I'm going to miss my bus." Tonya sees her and comes over to help. Tonya finds Jodie's coat by the lunch pails. "Here, let's go, fast." They yell "Bye" as they pass you. You watch out a window and see Paula saying good-bye to them near the school bus. They made it!

After a few minutes, the school seems quiet in contrast to the exit of several hundred children. You wait for Paula to return from the bus area. Walking into the classroom, Paula invites you to settle on the sofa in the reading area for a conversation.

Learning from Paula

Paula begins by telling you, "Having Jodie in our class is good for all of us. Her involvement and participation in the classroom is going smoothly now. At first, she wanted my attention a lot, but now she seems familiar with our routine. I talked with the kindergarten teacher and paired Jodie with two favorite friends from last year to help her feel comfortable in the class. Because much of our classroom instruction is in small groups or individual sessions, Jodie progresses at her own level and interacts with other students." From your brief observation today, you agree with Paula. It did seem that the children worked together cooperatively, helping each other on many different activities.

Developing learning goals for Jodie.   Paula and Jodie's parents had a conference early in the school year to set learning goals for Jodie. An area of importance to Jodie's family and to Paula is learning appropriate social skills. They feel that Jodie's academic areas will progress at a steady rate, but it is very important to Lynn and Jerry that Jodie gets along with others and learns socially acceptable behaviors. She enjoys interacting with others but she has a tendency to become the "baby" in a group, and her parents are concerned with the long-term effects of this role. They realize that as she matures, she needs to become more independent. Paula agrees and looks for ways to help Jodie assume leadership roles in the classroom. For the past month, Jodie has been responsible for taking notes to the office and delivering messages to the office staff. She has enjoyed this responsibility and has been a great messenger.

Journal 11.5: Describe what Jodie might gain from her role as office messenger. ■

Other goals for Jodie include beginning literacy and numeracy skills and improving her verbal communication. Do you see a connection between Jodie's messenger position and the goal of verbal communication? This is one example of how Paula builds real-life contexts for Jodie's learning, such as assuming the role of messenger. Paula says, "Some of these ideas are mine; others come from Marty, the resource teacher. Marty meets with me on a weekly basis and we look at upcoming lessons and projects and find ways to ensure Jodie is fully included and challenged in her learning. Marty often brings books and materials for me to use with Jodie and the other students." The frequent contact with a special educator brings curriculum and instruction support for Jodie and for Paula, as well as assists Paula in assessing Jodie's learning and planning future learning needs. Including Jodie in the multiage classroom—relying on support from Marty and curriculum changes made by Paula—creates a positive learning for environment for Jodie in her neighborhood school. Paula also notes that her awareness of guidance strategies has increased since she began working with Jodie and gaining ideas from Marty.

Providing guidance in the classroom. Paula explains, "One thing I have learned is to be explicit in my instructions, whether talking about curriculum or behavior expectations. This really helps Jodie and the other students and it prevents possible classroom disruptions. It is amazing to see the difference when students start to work on their own if they have had clear directions." Paula also breaks tasks into small steps so a task is more manageable. "With Jodie, I find that giving her several small steps for a task is better than telling her the entire task at once. She is more successful when she is expected to complete a few steps at a time."

Another important aspect that provides guidance for students is maintaining consistency and routines in the classroom. Paula noticed that creating routines "not only helped Jodie navigate through the school day, but also helped several other students who began to thrive once they learned the routine and structure of the day. This doesn't mean we do the same thing the same way all day, but, for example, we do line up for lunch and recess in the same spot and use the same procedure. We also talk about our schedule, activities, and expectations for behavior, such as quiet time or talking time, and build these discussions into our daily routine." Paula's remarks about consistency and routines point out ways teachers can create a framework of structure for the classroom. This framework or foundation communicates expectations and provides clear guidance for students sharing space, time, and activities in a classroom.

Paula has created a positive atmosphere in the classroom. Students share successful accomplishments and comment favorably about each other's work. She has also planned classroom procedures to eliminate "down time" or time spent waiting for the next activity. When students finish work, they know they can choose to go to the back counter for a center activity or go to the couch area to read or play a quiet game. Again, Paula has made these expectations for choices clear to the children, thereby providing guidance for their behavior in the classroom.

Referring students for special education services.   Within Forest Hills Elementary Schools 66 of the 553 students have been identified as needing special education. These students were referred to the District's Special Education Department and receive support and services at Forest Hills.

You might be wondering how a child is chosen to receive special education services. The **identification and placement process** begins with a referral. Referrals for obtaining special education services for a child might come from a teacher, a parent, or a prereferral team of teachers, school administrator, and specialists (a multidisciplinary team). Once a referral reaches the special education department, parental consent for evaluating the child is obtained. The next step includes an evaluation of the child's current levels of functioning in areas where delays are suspected. The evaluation might be completed by the school psychologist or a team of specialists and is followed with a conference with the parents and the multidisciplinary team. The outcome of this conference is to determine if the child is eligible for special education services. If so, an individual educational program (IEP) meeting is then scheduled to determine the best learning environment for the child and to secure appropriate special education support and resources. Jodie was already receiving special education services prior to entering the school district, so her evaluation paperwork was transferred to the school district before she enrolled at Forest Hills School.

Looking Back at Your School Visit

Leaving the school, your thoughts turn to the active learning and the positive learning atmosphere you just observed. Paula created a learning environment that encourages children to be engaged in active learning activities. Remember their work with pumpkin patterns and exploring insects from their backyards? The students worked in small groups and shared knowledge and ideas. When a child needed help, he was just as likely to ask another student as go to Paula for assistance.

Paula's frequent communication with Marty, Lynn, and Jerry was evident in her learning goals for Jodie. The work of the teachers, Jodie's parents, and the school staff contributed to a classroom and school where Jodie *is* included. You observed Jodie participating with her classmates as they explored math, studied insects, went to music, and left school at the end of the day. It is obvious why Jodie's parents chose to live in this neighborhood. The teachers and principal work together to create a learning environment that supports and encourages the learning of all students.

Following your day-long observation of Jodie at school, you look forward to your upcoming visit with Jodie's parents.

Visiting with Jodie's Parents

Two weeks later, you visit at Jodie's house with Lynn and Jerry, this time while Jodie is at school. Jodie's mother, Lynn, opens the conversation: "For me, it is important to share our family story and early childhood experiences with Jodie. I want others to come to know Jodie and understand that Jodie is a member of our family and she also happens to have challenges. I had a normal pregnancy and was shocked when the doctor told us that our baby was born with Down syndrome. We knew very little about Down syndrome and had no idea what to expect for our daughter. Maybe some of what we have experienced and learned will be helpful to people thinking of working with young children." Lynn then started sharing about Jodie's infancy and childhood.

Jodie's Infant Years

When Jodie was a few weeks old, Lynn received a phone call from a woman, Sue, also a mother of a Down syndrome child. While at the hospital, a nurse had asked Lynn and Jerry if they would be interested in connecting with another family with a Down syndrome child.

Support from other families.   Sue invited Lynn and Jerry to join a support group of parents to learn more from these parents who have children with similar developmental delays. She suggested, "Their stories might be helpful to you as you hear how families coped with problems and experiences that your family might encounter." Sue also offered to visit Lynn. "She prepared me for the roller coaster of emotions associated with learning your child has Down syndrome." Lynn adds, "This was the first of many visits with Sue, who has become a close friend." Jerry then offers, "Both Lynn and I had a lot of difficulty accepting the fact that our child would have limitations and was not the perfect baby we had dreamed of for many months. We were physically and emotionally exhausted with the efforts and energy needed to care for an infant. Added to that was the stress of trying to learn about Down syndrome and what it meant for our daughter. I had recently completed law school and was beginning my career in a law firm. I was working long hours, often into the late evening. Fortunately, Lynn's mother lived nearby and visited several times a week, helping Lynn with caring for Jodie, bringing groceries, and supporting her during this time. We are really grateful for her support." Lynn agrees that she doesn't know how she would have made it without the frequent help from her mother and the support group.

Infancy and early intervention specialists.   Lynn and Jerry learned about early intervention services from other members of the parent support group. They contacted their local Family Services office and Jodie began participating in **early intervention services** when she was only a few months old. Until she was 2 years old, Jodie was visited weekly by an early intervention specialist who worked with her and her parents on developmental skills.

Jerry remembers those early sessions with the early intervention specialist and recalls, "We had so many questions. It was helpful to know that there would be another session coming up and a time and place to get some answers to our questions." The specialist also used each session as a time to catch up on new skills Jodie was learning and any special challenges Jodie or the family were having. During the early months (until Jodie was 1 year old), many of these sessions were spent encouraging Jodie to reach for objects, drop objects, roll over, sit with support, and learn to balance herself in an upright position.

Through direct teaching, practice, and lots of encouragement, Jodie was able to accomplish most of the large motor skills of a 2-year-old at only a slightly delayed time frame. Fine motor skills, such as using a spoon, seemed more difficult for Jodie, and took much practice. Jerry recalls, "Tracy, who is a year younger, was also learning many of the same skills at the same time, so both girls would mirror each other. It seemed that the interaction with her sister encouraged Jodie to keep trying until she mastered a skill. We were discouraged sometimes, but the interaction with the early intervention specialist helped us see the progress that Jodie was making and gave us a plan and ways to help Jodie."

Toddler Time

At age 2, Jodie started attending a community play group one morning a week. This provided her with a time to be with other children and to learn in a setting other than her home. The early intervention specialist continued to visit the home twice a month. She also met with the person coordinating the play group, assisting her in modifying activities so Jodie would be included and successful with her peers.

Modifying play group activities.   Lynn recalls, "Jodie loved music, singing, and moving to music with the other 2-year-olds." During play group, Jodie would sing a word or two in each song. She was encouraged to clap with the music. The other children were learning entire verses in songs, while Jodie was expected to learn one or two words. This was an example of modifying the activities to meet Jodie's learning needs. Lynn says, "Jodie seemed to enjoy her morning at the community play group and made progress with her language development." Unfortunately, it was not always as easy to make modifications in public situations.

What would be some possible benefits Jodie might gain by participating in a community play group with other children?

Reactions from the public. When Jodie was 2 years old, the family became aware that others were looking at them. Lynn and Jerry talked about the obvious stares they received when they were at restaurants, stores, or events with Jodie. Jerry explains, "Some people look at us with pity or sympathy in their eyes; others walk far around us to avoid our family; and others come up to us and tell us how sorry they are about our little girl." These interchanges have been awkward for Lynn and Jerry, especially as Jodie began to understand what strangers were saying. Lynn decided to be proactive and tell strangers who approach them, "We are a happy, active family." She believes it is important to take the initiative and send a clear message to people about Jodie.

Lynn and Jerry acknowledge that people often do not know what it is like to have a child with special needs. "Often, others don't realize that this child brings many gifts to our family. One of the reasons we pursue Jodie's education at our neighborhood school is to help others around Jodie accept her and appreciate her for who she is." They feel that once other children spend time with Jodie, the focus is less on what she can't do and more on what she can do with them.

 Journal 11.6: The experiences that Jodie's family shared have implications for a classroom teacher and the children in the class. If you were Jodie's teacher and you were planning a field trip to a grocery store, how might you handle stares and comments from strangers? ■

The Three's Class

When Jodie turned 3 years old, she started preschool. She received early childhood special education services, which were now integrated into her day at the preschool. Her early childhood special education specialist worked with the preschool teacher and with Jodie's parents to develop an **individualized family services plan (IFSP).** As an important aside, it is interesting to note that the use of an IFSP, or an individual educational plan (IEP), with children age 3 through 6 varies from state to state. In the state where Jodie lives, the IFSP continues until the child begins kindergarten in the public school setting. When the child begins kindergarten, the local school district is then responsible for providing special education services and uses an IEP. In most other states, an IEP is implemented at age 3.

Individualized family services plan. The IFSP outlined goals that the family, teacher, and specialist felt were important to focus on during the year. Several goals included communication skills, such as responding when asked a question and using full sentences when talking with others. Jodie made progress with her goals, supported by her parents' work with her at home and her teacher, Karla, at preschool.

An IFSP reflects the individual learning goals of a child, based on her current level of functioning and learning considered important by the family, early childhood special educator, and other specialists involved on the team. The IFSP also includes a description of early intervention services needed to help the child obtain the goals and a time line for evaluating progress. Figure 11.3 on pages 426 to 429 provides an example of an IFSP.

FIGURE 11.3 Individual Family Services Plan (IFSP) (Portion of an Example)

Child _Carmen Martinez_   Birthdate _6-5-95_

Parent(s)/Guardian _Mr. & Mrs. Martinez_   Home Phone _321-8712_   Work Phone _321-0050_

Address _527 Main Street, Westin, Oregon_

Service Coordinator _Janice Lacey_   Resident School District _Mountain_

Date Eligibility
Established _11-18-97_
IFSP Meeting Date _11-20-97_
Projected Dates For:
6 Month Review _____
Annual Review _11-20-98_

_Indicate the amount of time (or the activities) each week the child is with typically developing children when addressing IFSP goals and objectives _____

Service/Method	How Often	Where	Who Will Do This	Who Will Pay	Start Date	Stop Date
Communication Skill training 1-1	2x wk 30 mins each	Home	Early childhood Special educator	Early childhood special ed. program	11-25-97	11-25-98
Communication consultation to family and early childhood special educator	1x month 60 mins	Home	Speech therapist	Early childhood special ed. program	11-25-97	11-25-98
Other Services: Respite care (Babysitting)			Mom & service coordinator will work on this	No cost — service coord. will initiate		

Form 581-5150E-X (Revised 2/95) page 1

IFSP Team Page

List the IFSP team members who have contributed to the development of this IFSP. Indicate after each name who was present or not present at the IFSP meeting.

	Present	Not Present
Margaret Smith		
Subcontractor Representative/Role	☑	☐
Mrs. Martinez		
School District Representative	☐	☐
Janice Lacey		
Parent(s)	☑	☐
Service Coordinator	☐	☑
Parent(s)	☐	☐
Other/Role	☐	☐
Janice Lacey		
EI/ECSE Provider/Role	☑	☐
Other/Role	☐	☐
Jane Johnson		
Evaluator (Required for EI and the initial IFSP for ECSE)	☑	☐
Other/Role	☐	☐

Parent Consent for Early Intervention Services (*For children birth to three*)

I have participated in the development of this IFSP and understand the content. My signature indicates written informed consent to the services in this plan. I understand that my consent for services may be withdrawn at any time.

Mrs. Martinez   11-20-97

Signature _____   Date _____

Parent Participation in IFSP Meeting for Early Childhood Special Education (*For children three to five*)

My signature indicates that I have participated in the development of this IFSP.

_____   _____

Signature   Date

Dates this IFSP was revised with a meeting: ___/___/___ ; ___/___/___ ; ___/___/___ ; ___/___/___ ;

Note: Parents must indicate their approval for changes made to EI IFSPs by initialing and dating the changes. For ECSE, parents indicate their participation in IFSP changes by initialing and dating the changes.

Form 581-5150E-X (Revised 2/95) page 2

(continued)

FIGURE 11.3 (continued)

Carmen 's Current Developmental Information

Summary as of November 20, 1997

Child's Strengths and Interests: Carmen loves music, likes to explore and snuggle with her parents. Likes books.

Sources of information and dates in developing this IFSP:
Parent report 10/31/97
Assessment, Evaluation and Programming Systems (AEPs) 10/28/97
Generic Skills Inventory 10/28/97
Hearing Screening: Passed 11/12/97

Health Status: Healthy—Doctor report 11/97

Vision Screening: Passed 11/12/97

Present Levels of Development

Can Do	*Needs to Learn	Can Do	*Needs to Learn
Cognitive: Pretend plays with toys Enjoys books Knows body parts Adaptive: Will use fingers to eat Will drink out of tippercup Participates in dressing + undressing Social or Emotional: Plays with toys Interested in other children Sometimes takes turns	Use spoon Eat off of plate	Physical: Run Play Use toys in backyard (climbing toys) Communication: Follows directions Understands "no" Request by reaching Beginning use of gestures Follows some verbal directions Uses 2 one words: "dad" "pop"	Work on fine motor skills—in functional manner—to play with toys Dependent on gesturing Expand prelanguage Use words

*Note: For each development area under Needs to Learn, there must be corresponding goals and objectives

Form 581-5150E-X (Revised 2/95) page 3

Child Goals and Objectives

Child _Carmen Martinez_   Area(s) _Communication_   Date _11-20-97_

What we want to happen (Long Term Goal) _Carmen will spontaneously use words to express her needs and interests ten times daily._

Who will work on it (Service) _Family & early childhood special educator_   Who will keep track of progress? _Early childhood special educator_

What the Child Will Learn (Short Term Objectives and Criteria)	Evaluation Procedures and Schedule	Six Month Review Date and Data	Annual Review Date and Data
1. Carmen will indicate her needs by pointing to a photo or picture and imitate the word represented on 5 times during snack or play time.	Parent Report 1x week Staff observation during snack (1x week (language sample)		
2. Carmen will indicate her needs by pointing to a photo or picture and saying the word represented spontaneously on 5 times during snack or play time.	"same"		
3. Carmen will purposefully call her mom (mama) 2x day.	" "		
4. Carmen will wave "hi" and "bye, bye" & say words spontaneously 1x each day.	" "		

Form 581-5150E-X (Revised 2/95) page 4

Note: Missing in this IFSP are the Family Outcomes page and the Modifications/Transition page.

Being part of the group.   There were 12 children in Jodie's class, with one other child receiving early childhood special education services for language development. Jodie often invited other children to come home with her for lunch and to play. "We were relieved that Jodie was 'part' of the group," say Lynn and Jerry, "But then we would feel guilty for being relieved. There's that roller coaster again. Parenting a child with special needs can be overwhelming. You want your child to have as full a life as possible, yet you aren't sure what is possible."

The Four's Class

At 4 years of age, Jodie remained at the same preschool and moved into the "Four's Class" with her group of friends. She attended school each weekday morning. An **early childhood special educator** visited the school weekly to meet with Karla, the teacher. She also participated in bimonthly meetings with Lynn, Jerry, and Karla. Box 11.2 highlights the role of an early childhood special education specialist.

During late winter, Lynn raised concerns about the coming school year, wondering, "Should Jodie remain at preschool another year?" Lynn and Jerry talked about Jodie's progress and thought about what she needed to be ready for public school kindergarten. The focus of her IFSP continued with language development, with a goal of expanded sentences or phrases, and a second goal centered on fine motor skills. Jodie was beginning to grasp a crayon or paintbrush, making large slashes of color on her paper.

By the spring of her Four's Class, most of the children were drawing symbols or primitive objects representing objects or images, while Jodie was still learning to grasp the crayon or paintbrush and move it around on the paper. Karla, Lynn, Jerry, and the early childhood special educator met to discuss Lynn and Jerry's concerns about Jodie's transition to kindergarten. Jerry said, "I was reluctant to move Jodie into a large elementary school for kindergarten until she acquired more communication skills." The team of specialists discussed with Lynn and Jerry the benefits of Jodie learning from her chronological age peers. This discussion helped Lynn and Jerry understand the reasons for keeping Jodie with children her age to help her social and communication skills. During the meeting, the team agreed that the most appropriate placement for Jodie would be in kindergarten.

Lynn, Jerry, Karla, and the early childhood special educator also decided that Jodie should be involved with summer activities. Jerry suggested gymnastics, in which Jodie showed interest. She had recently watched the summer Olympic Games and was intrigued with the floor exercises and the low balance beam. Her involvement in gymnastics held potential for work on communication skills in another setting. Jerry recalls, "I met with the gymnastics coach to discuss different ways Jodie might be encouraged to talk with other children." It was important for Jodie to continue her language development and Jerry and Lynn wanted the coach to be aware of this goal.

Moving to Kindergarten

By the end of the Four's Class school year, Jerry, Lynn, and Jodie were looking forward to Jodie's transition to elementary school for her kindergarten experience. The early childhood special educator arranged a **transition meeting** with a special educator from the school district, the family, and Karla. The purpose of the transition meeting was to discuss Jodie's current levels of functioning and the support and resources she would need to be

BOX 11.2 ■ What Is the Role of an Early Childhood Special Educator?

A Closer Look

Staff who provide developmental and educational services for children from birth to age 5 and their families are referred to as *early childhood special educators*. The role of the early childhood special educator varies across states and programs. The following is a general description of services provided by a professional who implements or coordinates the implementation of services for young children (birth to age 5) with disabilities. In your state or local program, a person providing these services may be referred to as *an early interventionist, a case manager, a service coordinator, or a family interventionist*.

The early childhood special educator meets the family and child as soon as the child is referred to the program, perhaps by a pediatrician, caregiver, or social worker. One of the early childhood special educator's first jobs with the family is to assist the family through the evaluation process and to link the family with other community resources. If the child is eligible for services as a child with a disability, the early childhood special educator organizes a meeting to plan services for the child and family. This is called the *individualized family service plan (IFSP)*. The early childhood special educator is the lead person of the child's team to whom the family directs their questions and or concerns. This means that he or she is responsible for finding answers to the family's concerns about the child's development education and/or other services that may be available for the family.

Another responsibility of the early childhood special educator is to provide developmental or educational services to the child. These services are provided in supportive environments where the child usually spends his or her day. Very young or medically vulnerable children typically receive services at home. Children 3 and 4 years of age may receive services at home, preschool, or day care. Service delivery methods vary from program to program, depending on the needs of the child and family.

The early childhood special educator typically teaches others (parents, day care providers, teachers, etc.) in the child's setting ways to teach the child new skills and to encourage the child's development. For example, the early childhood special educator may work with a child's mother to teach the child how to hold a spoon and scoop from a bowl. Another example is an early childhood special educator who works with a preschool teacher on techniques for promoting language skills from a 4-year-old with language delays.

Early childhood special educators also may provide services by directly teaching a child new skills. This usually occurs when the childhood special educator sees a child two or more times a week. What, how, and who teaches the child is determined by the child's team at the child's IFSP meeting. The IFSP is reviewed every six months, and changes may be made at that time based on the child's progress. The early childhood special educator plays an essential role in monitoring the child's development and learning, working with the family, and ensuring the child has access to community resources and support services.

Source: Nancy Johnson-Dorn, Education Program Specialist, Oregon Department of Education. Reprinted by permission.

---

successful as she moved into the kindergarten setting. At the end of the meeting, it was suggested that the parents and Jodie call the school and visit the kindergarten before school was out for the summer. The three of them did go to Forest Hills Elementary School, met the principal and met Janis, the kindergarten teacher that the principal had determined would be Jodie's teacher. The early childhood special educator was also at the school meeting. Jerry and Lynn remember, "Having someone we knew at the meeting made us feel much more comfortable. We knew she would advocate for Jodie's inclusion in the school."

 The principal, Carol, talked with Jerry and Lynn about the goals of the kindergarten teachers, who place emphasis on social development through learning to work with others and on a developmentally appropriate curriculum. There were several other children with special needs also entering kindergarten that fall. For example, several children would be entering kindergarten in September with English as their second language. Carol felt that placing no more than two or three children with special needs in each class would help the teacher develop activities and lessons that would allow them to reach these children on an individual level.

One teacher, Janis, had worked with several children with special needs. Carol suggested, "With her experience, I feel Janis would be an excellent teacher for Jodie." Carol took Lynn, Jerry, and Jodie to the kindergarten area to observe the classes. Jerry says, "I really enjoyed watching the children and having a brief chat with Janis. She came over to say hello to Jodie and see if she wanted to look at the gerbils. Jodie thought they were kind of smelly." On their way back to the office, Lynn and Jerry agreed that Janis seemed to be a good choice for Jodie's kindergarten teacher. Lynn recalls, "It was helpful to visit the school and classroom and meet the teacher in the spring. I was less anxious about Jodie's transition to elementary school after our visit."

Kindergarten year was challenging for Jodie. It was an adjustment to be in a class of 24 students, along with so much movement and noise going on around her. Jodie enjoyed music and art and loved listening to stories. Her educational goals again focused on communication skills, fine motor skills, and beginning numeracy and literacy development. She also had to work on not being the center of attention and sharing toys and materials with other students.

During the winter, Jodie had several colds and was home for a week three different times. Jerry thought, "Jodie's language skills, particularly her sentence length, seemed to decrease when she was home for long periods of time. I think her interaction with other children was an important factor in her development of language." Lynn and Jerry met with the kindergarten teacher and Marty, the special educator at the school, every two to three months throughout the school year. Janis was open to their concerns and opinions and incorporated their ideas into Jodie's individual learning goals. Kindergarten was an important year for Jodie. Lynn says, "Jodie matured and learned many new skills in getting along with others during her kindergarten experience. We all felt she was ready for first grade."

First Grade

At the end of the kindergarten year, another meeting was held with the special education resource teacher, Janis, Jerry, and Lynn. They met to discuss goals for Jodie's first-grade school year. After discussion of the various classroom settings, and on the suggestion of the team of specialists, it was agreed that the multiage classroom would be an ideal setting for Jodie. Much of the day in these classrooms was spent in small group learning time or with the teacher in individual sessions. Students also stayed with the teacher for two years. Lynn says, "The benefit of being with the same teacher and group of students for two years would help Jodie, who is reluctant to make large changes and feels more comfortable with a familiar teacher or adult." At the recommendation of the specialist team, Jerry and Lynn also made plans for Jodie to attend a summer camp program and another summer of gymnastics.

At this point of the conversation, you were up to date on events in Jodie's life and her schooling. Thanking Jerry and Lynn for sharing so much of their story, you express admiration of their warm supportive family and their advocacy for Jodie.

Reflecting on Your Visits

Jodie shares many characteristics similar with other 7-year-olds, while also displaying academic and fine motor skills of a child one to two years younger than her chronological age. Remember her interests in painting and storytelling? Many other 7-year-olds would also say that these are favorite activities. When you visited Jodie at her home, you found her to be an active member of her family. She is included in the busy family schedule, as well as participating in activities of her own choice, such as gymnastics, just like other 7-year-olds.

Jodie looks forward to going to school each day and to being with her teacher and classmates. Although Jodie is not working at the same level academically as other children in her classroom, her work is challenging to her and she is showing progress in many areas. She is included in her neighborhood school, where she has been accepted as a member of her early childhood community (Sugawara, 1996). Her current teacher, Paula, attributes Jodie's success in school to her earlier school experiences, her parents' support and encouragement, and her friendly nature that draws others to her. Her best friend, Tonya, enjoys playing with Jodie at school and at their houses after school. This friendship really supports Jodie's development.

Jodie's early childhood experiences have supported and shaped her development and growth and have been enhanced by teachers, specialists, friends, and her family. You realize that she has many challenges ahead, but from your visits, you see Jodie as an eager, active member of her family, school, and community.

In the next section of this chapter, you will look at special education legislation, services, and programs. Keep in mind the different programs and services that Jodie and her family were involved with as you learn what prompted the development and continuation of early childhood special education services.

Special Education for Young Children

What Is Special Education?

As you read about Jodie, you may have wondered about the source of services she receives. The array of services and support for young children with special needs and for their families has increased significantly in both quantity and quality in the past 20 years. Legislation now provides funding for programs and mandates services to meet the needs of children from birth through age 21. These programs for children with special needs are typically called *special education programs*.

When discussing **special education,** the focus is on programs that meet the special learning needs of children. As the learning needs of each child vary, so does special education. For one child, inclusion on a full-time basis in a regular preschool, along with weekly sessions with a physical therapist for large muscle motor development (hopping, jumping, and running), would be special education. In the same preschool, another child might be attending the preschool for two hours a week and spending the rest of his time in a special education classroom for children with hearing impairments. In such a special education classroom, the emphasis is on assisting children learn sign language and

speechreading (understanding spoken language by watching the speaker's face). Yet another type of special education program would be in a hospital, where a child with chronic health problems receives special education services appropriate to her developmental level and learning needs. Recognizing that the educational and related services support the individual learning needs of the child helps you understand that special education is developed around the specific needs of a child rather than around a set curriculum or program.

Who Are the Children Receiving Special Education?

Children with special needs include children with disabilities or developmental delays whose learning and development will be compromised if they do not receive special and expert attention in their early education (Wolery & Wilbers, 1994). When describing children with special needs, a distinction has been made in discussing their disability by using the term *children* first and then adding the disability, such as *children with visual impairments.* This terminology reminds us to focus on the child as a child who happens to have a disability or developmental delay.

Categories of children with disabilities. In the *Eighteenth Annual Report to Congress on the Implementation of IDEA* (U.S. Department of Education, Office of Special Education Programs, 1996), 12 categories of children with disabilities was used by the federal government. Table 11.1 shows the percentage of students ages 6 through 21 who received special education services during the 1994–95 school year in each of these categories.

Prior to entering kindergarten, most of the children who have been identified as having special needs are those with more severe or obvious disabilities, such as physi-

■ TABLE 11.1 Number and Percentage of Students Ages 6 to 21 Receiving Special Education by Disability (1994–95)

Disability	Total	Percent of Total
Specific learning disabilities	2,513,977	51.1
Speech or language impairments	1,023,655	20.8
Mental retardation	570,855	11.6
Serious emotional disturbance	428,168	8.7
Multiple disabilities	89,646	1.8
Hearing impairments	65,568	1.3
Orthopedic impairments	60,604	1.2
Other health impairments	106,509	2.2
Visual impairments	24,877	0.5
Autism	22,780	0.5
Deaf-blindness	1,331	0.02
Traumatic brain injury	7,188	0.1
All disabilities	4,915,168	100.0

Source: U.S. Department of Education, 1996, *Eighteenth Annual Report to Congress on the Implementation of the Individuals with Disabilities Education Act,* p. 7.

cal impairments, mental retardation, or emotional disturbances. Specific learning disabilities are often not diagnosed until a child enters school and it becomes evident that she needs special assistance to achieve her potential. In the 1995 school year, 12 percent of the total student population were children with disabilities who received special education in the public schools (U.S. Department of Education, Office of Special Education Programs Rehabilitative Services, 1996). The percentage of younger children receiving special education services is lower than for school-age children for several reasons. As you read the following story about Jackson, consider why it is often difficult to identify some children with special needs prior to kindergarten.

Jackson: A child with attention-deficit disorder

Jackson is a 5-year-old in the kindergarten class next to Jodie's classroom. If you had a chance to observe in his kindergarten while you were at the school, you would have noticed the children building a city with milk cartons. Several centers are set up around Jackson's classroom, with parent volunteers helping the children decorate their milk cartons and construct buildings, trees, cars, and people for their city. You would have seen Jackson at the back center: He picks up the scissors and loudly says, "Now cut the paper." Jackson then makes several quick cuts in the paper, drops the paper and scissors, and hurries over to another center, where he grabs a glue bottle and starts squeezing glue on the table. Saul, the kindergarten teacher, approaches Jackson and quietly tells him, "It's time to go over to the couch and take a few deep breaths. Let's talk about your plans for building your store for the city."

Saul takes Jackson's hand as they walk together to the couch. Once seated, Saul asks Jackson, "What are your plans for making your store?" Jackson replies, "I want a big store." "So, how will you make it and what supplies do you need?" After a few minutes of conversation, Saul asks Jackson, "What are your next two steps?" Jackson thinks about this and says, "First, I will get my milk carton and then I will cut paper to glue on it for the store." "Great, then come find me and we will do the next two steps together, OK?" Jackson nods and goes back to the first center where he picks up scissors and paper and begins cutting, at a much slower pace than last time.

Jackson has recently been identified as having **attention-deficit disorder (ADD),** which is characterized by a "persistent pattern of inattention and/or hyperactivity-impulsivity" than is typically seen in children at a similar level of development (American Psychiatric Association, 1994, p. 78). Attention-deficit disorder or attention-deficit/hyperactivity disorder (ADHD) is not currently recognized or supported by special education services as a disability category unless the child's behavior difficulty negatively affects academic performance. Saul decided to implement an individual educational program for Jackson based on his prior experiences in working with children with special needs. Saul found that breaking activities into smaller segments helps Jackson be more successful in his learning, along with asking him to verbalize his plans to Saul. You listened to the conversation between Jackson and Saul, where Jackson was thinking through his next two steps in an activity. At that time, Saul might decide Jackson is ready for a "quiet break" with the headphones and some calming music or to continue with the building activity. Saul is trying to teach Jackson to self-monitor his behavior and decisions and to be successful with each small step.

Sometimes one-on-one attention helps a child make the transition to a positive activity.

When Jackson was in preschool, his teacher thought he had a short attention span and that he was a "talkative" child. At that time, however, and with that age group, his behavior did not seem vastly different from the norm. Jackson attended preschool three mornings a week for two hours at a time. There was a lot of activity going on, as well as outdoor play, which he frequently enjoyed. When Jackson entered kindergarten, Saul noticed that he often made impulsive comments, darted around the classroom, and seemed to have difficulty staying with a project for more than a few minutes. Saul began charting Jackson's "time on an activity" and soon found that he was staying with one activity for 2 to 3 minutes and then moving to another area. The other children were spending 10 to 20 minutes at centers before they seemed ready to move to another activity. Saul asked the school psychologist to observe Jackson.

The psychologist noted that Jackson was forgetful in routine activities, blurted out comments frequently during discussions, had difficulty moving through a sequenced activity, and was easily distracted by other activities in the classroom. With this information, the school psychologist and Saul met with Jackson's father (his parents are divorced and his mother lives in another state). At this meeting, a decision was made to begin a program both at school and at home to help Jackson create his own structure in his activities to help him be more successful. In the past two months, both Saul and Jackson's father agree that Jackson is responding to the program, as he is now able to spend 5 to 10 minutes on an activity before moving to something else.

When you think about child development and children of preschool age, you realize that many of Jackson's behaviors appeared similar to and within the range of other preschoolers. When he entered kindergarten and it was apparent he was not able to attend to one activity for an extended time, Jackson's learning needs became more obvious. It has been estimated that in most classrooms, there will be from one to three children who have behaviors typically associated with ADD or ADHD. Teachers and caregivers will want to know how to recognize the behaviors of children with ADD or ADHD, such as inattention, hyperactivity, or impulsivity that seems to be beyond that of the norm for this developmental level. If it is determined that a child does have ADD or ADHD, the teacher and family would develop strategies to help these children have positive learning experiences in the classroom and at home, similar to the program Saul and Jackson's father implemented to help Jackson.

Uniqueness of each child.   Jackson and Jodie serve as a good reminder that children with special needs are very different from each other. It is a misnomer to assume all children with special needs should be treated the same way or have the same program. Jodie is working on increasing her sentence length, whereas Jackson is working on not talking out as often in the classroom. Their programs are different and are developed to meet their individual learning needs. Just as all children differ from each other, so do children with special needs.

Children who are gifted and talented.   Another group of children who have special learning needs are children who are gifted and talented. Approximately 5 percent of the school-age population is recognized as gifted and talented (Clark, 1992). Special education for these children is not required by federal law, although many individual states have legislation requiring educational experiences that meet learning needs of gifted and talented children. Box 11.3 provides an overview of educational practices for gifted and talented children.

BOX 11.3 ■ What Are Some Educational Approaches for Children Who Are Gifted and Talented?

A Closer Look

How is it determined if a child is talented and gifted? A current definition of *talented children* was outlined in the government report *National Excellence: A Case for Developing America's Talent* (U. S. Department of Education, 1993). According to this definition, children with exceptional talent "exhibit high performance capability in intellectual, creative, and/or artistic areas, possess an unusual leadership capacity, or excel in specific academic fields (p. 26). Students who are talented are often identified through IQ tests or from results on a standard achievement test. More recently, a combination of test scores as well as input from teachers and parents are used to identify children with exceptional talent.

Three common educational approaches for working with talented children are ability grouping, ac-

celeration, and enrichment (Heward, 1996). With *ability grouping,* children with similar high levels of talent are grouped together for advanced courses, special classes, or enrichment activities. At the elementary school level, this might consist of a pull-out program, with children identified as talented meeting together two or three times a week for special classes. *Acceleration* is used to move a child through the curriculum at a faster pace, with options such as moving ahead a grade or more in school, testing out of courses, or earning college credit through advanced placement tests. *Enrichment* provides for more depth in learning, allowing children who are talented to explore learning outside the typical curriculum. These three educational approaches facilitate the development of a child with talented and gifted abilities, providing a rich and stimulating learning environment.

Now that you have looked at what special education is and who is served by special education, let's examine how special education has evolved over the past several decades. Some of the earliest programs for young children with special needs were implemented when the Handicapped Children's Early Education Assistance Act was enacted in 1968. Legislation at the federal government level has had a tremendous impact on the implementation and funding for special education programs and services across our nation. This legislation affects the kind of services Jodie and her family receive.

Public Law 94-142: Education for All Handicapped Children Act

In 1975, **P.L. 94-142 (Education for All Handicapped Children Act)** was signed by President Gerald Ford. This law established that every child with a handicap is entitled to a free appropriate public education (FAPE), and that this education will take place in the least restrictive environment (LRE) for that child. Remember when Jodie was entering the public school district? The philosophy of her school district was to think of special education programs on a continuum, with placement in a regular classroom in the child's neighborhood school as the first choice of a least restrictive environment. P.L. 94-142 assumed a preference for teaching the child in a regular educational environment to the extent possible, using resources to support the child within the setting that is least restrictive (Safford, 1989). Figure 11.4 displays a continuum of educational settings from least restrictive (regular class) to most restrictive (homebound/hospital).

■ **FIGURE 11.4**   Continuum of Educational Environments for Students with Disabilities

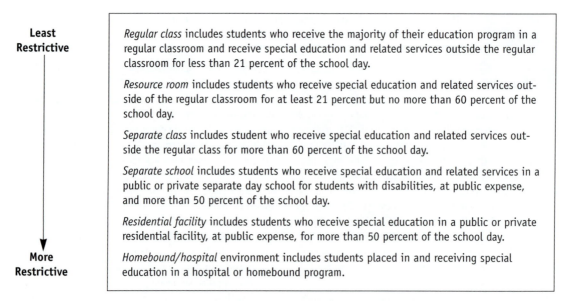

Least Restrictive

Regular class includes students who receive the majority of their education program in a regular classroom and receive special education and related services outside the regular classroom for less than 21 percent of the school day.

Resource room includes students who receive special education and related services outside of the regular classroom for at least 21 percent but no more than 60 percent of the school day.

Separate class includes student who receive special education and related services outside the regular class for more than 60 percent of the school day.

Separate school includes students who receive special education and related services in a public or private separate day school for students with disabilities, at public expense, and more than 50 percent of the school day.

Residential facility includes students who receive special education in a public or private residential facility, at public expense, for more than 50 percent of the school day.

Homebound/hospital environment includes students placed in and receiving special education in a hospital or homebound program.

More Restrictive

Source: U.S. Department of Education, 1996, *Eighteenth Annual Report to Congress on the Implementation of the Individuals with Disabilities Education Act,* p. 69.

Individualized education program.   P.L. 94-142 also required that an individualized education program is designed for each child, with parents participating on the planning
team. The law directed educators to create an IEP for each child and use the IEP to make
educational decisions regarding what is taught to the child and where the child is taught
on an individual basis. An educational plan must be developed for each child by the
teacher or a teacher and several specialists and with parental input. The IEP includes
current level of educational functioning, annual learning goals, short-term instructional
goals, evaluation criteria to determine when goals are met, educational services and support required to reach the goals, and instructional and service provision schedule. The
IEP must be reviewed at least once each year, with the child's parent or guardian con-
senting to the IEP. Formats of IEPs differ between school districts and states. Changes
have been made to IEP requirements over the years, with Figure 11.5 on pages 440 to
443 reflecting an IEP based on reauthorization and amendments implemented in 1997.

P.L. 94-142 also directed federal funding to states and local education agencies for
the education of children and young adults requiring special education between the ages
of 3 to 21 (McCollum & Maude, 1993). Prior to P.L. 94-142, many children with special needs were denied an education. Their options included institutionalization, private schools for handicapped children with handicaps, special schools or special
classrooms, or exclusion to any schooling. Each of these options led to segregation of
children with special needs from the general population. Although P.L. 94-142 opened
the door to education within the regular school setting for school-age children, it did
not specifically include services for younger children. Each state had the option to decide if it would offer programs for children from ages 3 to 5. This option left many young
children unserved.

Another area important to early childhood education is the focus on family-centered programs. P.L. 94-142 did include parents in the IEP planning meetings, but the
parents' role was often minimal. The jargon of special education can be confusing and
intimidating, leaving parents with varying levels of success in providing direction and
input in their child's learning program. If you are feeling some of the same frustration
in trying to understand the various terms and practices of special education, you can well
imagine what parents might experience.

 Journal 11.7: Do you remember any children with special needs at your elementary school? What type of program was available for children with special needs at your
school? ■

Categorizing or labeling disabilities.   P.L. 94-142 also required that a child fit within
a specific category of eligibility, such as severe emotional disorder or communication
disorder, in order to obtain services. This requirement introduces some problems. First,
diagnostic procedures and the use of measurement methods with an infant or young
child to determine eligibility is not as reliable or valid as with a school-age child
(Meisels, 1989). Second, there is a cultural and social affect that occurs from labeling
a child. Again, as you recognize and appreciate the positive changes made in education
for school-age children with special needs, you see that there are several areas of the law
that need modification.

Individualized Education Program

740

FULL LEGAL NAME		BIRTHDATE	STUDENT NUMBER	OFFICE USE ONLY
John Aaron Wright		8/3/90	38291-1923	

SCHOOL NAME	SCHOOL NUMBER	SEX	GRADE	
Elm Creek Elementary	*53729*	M	1	

Meeting Date: *3/15/97*	Consider Extended School Year: ☒ Yes ☐ No	Transition Services: ☐ Yes ☒ No

MEETING PARTICIPANTS

Marion Wright	*Lori Sterling*	*Shannon Ruiz*
PARENT/GUARDIAN SIGNATURE	STUDENT'S TEACHER	CASE COORDINATOR

I participated in the meeting to develop this individualized education plan, and I have received a statement of my legal rights as the parent of a student with a disability.

Jeff Ruben, Resource Teacher
DISTRICT REPRESENTATIVE/TITLE

OTHER/TITLE

STUDENT, WHEN APPROPRIATE

OTHER/TITLE

Services	Start/End Dates	Service Description
Specially Designed Instruction		
Specially Designed Instruction (SDI)-- reading and written language	3/21/97–3/20/98	120 minutes/week of direct instruction in strategies for reading and written language in a small group setting
Related Services		
None at this time		
Supplementary Services		
Classroom modifications	3/21/97–3/20/98	Modifications to classroom assignments

PROGRAM DESCRIPTION

Type of physical education program required: ☒ Regular P.E.   ☐ Adapted P.E.   ☐ Requirement Met

Percent of time **NOT** in regular education programs: 15 % of school day.

Explanation of the extent, if any, to which the child will **NOT** participate with nondisabled children in regular classes or activities.

Academic support provided in the resource room to support reading, written language, and math.

■ FIGURE 11.5   *(continued)*

Individualized Education Program
Goals and Objectives

741

FULL LEGAL NAME	BIRTHDATE	STUDENT NUMBER	DATE	
John Aaron Wright	8/3/90	38291-1923	*3/15/97*	Page _1_ of _2_ pages

Present Level of Performance (Evaluation, evaluator, and date), including:
a. How the child's disability affects the child's involvement and progress in the general curriculum; and
b. For pre-school children (as appropriate), how the disability affects the child's participation in appropriate activities.

Woodcock Johnson, Revised (WJ-R); Test of Early Reading Ability-2 (TERA-2); Resource Teacher, 1/97. On the WJ-R John earned a Broad Reading Standard Score of 75. He identified letters and early words - to, in. On the comprehension section of the test he correctly responded to 1 item. On the TERA-2 he was able to identify some words when paired with illustrations although had difficulty when more than 2 words were put together. John does not appear to see himself as a reader yet, although the spark is there. He asks questions for clarification and is showing interest in the reading process.

Annual Goals	Short-Term Objectives	Evaluation Procedure		
		Eval Method	*Eval Criteria*	*Eval Sched*
READING 1. John will read a late 1st-level story with 75% comprehension.	a. Given instruction, John will use effective strategies to decode or make a meaningful substitution for an unknown word.	Reading miscue samples	50% of the time with a text at his reading level	Monthly
	b. John will read a text at his instructional level with 60% of the sentences maintaining the meaning of the text.	Informal reading miscues	60%	Monthly
2. John will read and retell a text or passage.		Informal reading samples	80% accuracy in 8 out of 10 trials	Trimester
	a. John will read a text at his reading level and retell the events in order.	Teacher data and observation	80% accuracy in 8 out of 10 trials	Twice monthly
	b. John will read a story or part of a story and summarize what he has just read accurately.	Teacher data	8 out of 10 trials	Monthly
	c. John will retell a late Level 1 story including: plot, theme, characters, events.	Reading Miscue Inventory	Earning 50/100 possible points	Trimester

(continued)

■ **FIGURE 11.5** *(continued)*

Individualized Education Program
Goals and Objectives

741

FULL LEGAL NAME	BIRTHDATE	STUDENT NUMBER	DATE	
John Aaron Wright	8/3/90	38291-1923	*3/15/97*	Page _2_ of _2_ pages

Present Level of Performance (Evaluation, evaluator, and date), including:
a. How the child's disability affects the child's involvement and progress in the general curriculum; and
b. For pre-school children (as appropriate), how the disability affects the child's participation in appropriate activities.

Woodcock Johnson, Revised (WJ-R); Test of Early Written Language-2 (TEWL-2); Resource Teacher; 3/97. On the WJ-R John earned a Standard Score (SS) of 93 in Written Language and on the TEWL-2 he earned a SS of 90 on the Basic subtest. He had difficulty remembering all of the alphabet letters to write; most writing is prephonetic although he is getting initial sounds into the writing. He is looking at the models around him for the letters and words that he is wanting to write.

Annual Goals	Short-Term Objectives	Evaluation Procedure		
		Eval Method	*Eval Criteria*	*Eval Sched*
3. John will produce a writing piece that conveys meaning and that another individual is able to read independently.		Writing samples	8 out of 10 trials	Trimester
	a. John will produce a written piece with a minimum of 20 words that are phonetically spelled that he is able to read back accurately the following day.	Writing samples	8 out of 10 trials	Monthly
	b. John will edit and revise his writing piece with an adult for mechanics and meaning.	Edited writing sample	80% accuracy in 2 out of 5 trials	Monthly
	c. John will complete 8 out of 10 writing pieces to a final product.	Completed writing pieces	8 out of 10 completed writing pieces	Trimester

■ **FIGURE 11.5**   *(continued)*

Individualized Education Program **Supplementary Aids and Services**				**742**

FULL LEGAL NAME	BIRTHDATE	STUDENT NUMBER	DATE	
John Aaron Wright	8/3/90	38291-1923	6/7/97	Page ___1___ of ___1___ pages

Supplementary Aids and Services	**Specific description of adaptions and/or modifications necessary to benefit from participation in the educational program**
Classroom Modifications	a. Assignments may be presented in other than written format. b. Directions may be given more than once. c. Standardized test questions may be read aloud to John. d. Answers to standardized tests may be dictated.

Public Law 99-457: Support for Early Childhood Intervention

In 1986, President Ronald Reagan signed P.L. 99-457, an amendment to P.L. 94-142. P.L. 99-457 extended federal funding to serving children with disabilities from birth to age 5, while also eliminating the need for specific categories or labels of disability. This law made special education services mandatory for children from ages 3 to 5. It established a new part of the law, Part H, which covers services from birth to age 3. This amendment also allowed states to add a new category, that of **developmentally delayed,** which is broad enough to encompass many different areas of need. Lazarus (1992) defines the developmental delay of a child under the age of 5 as a delay in mental, social, emotional, or physical development when compared to the norm for a specific chronological age. This term opened up the identification and labeling process by connoting a more general delay of development rather than a specific deficit, handicap, or disability.

Depending on available services within her particular community, Jodie most likely would not have worked with an early intervention specialist as an infant and toddler if she had been born prior to 1986. She benefited from the legislature that provided funding for early intervention services to young children and their families from birth.

State-level responsibility.   By 1991–92, educational programs for children ages 3 to 21 became the responsibility of each state's department of education within the special education system (McCollum & Maude, 1993). For children from birth through age 3, it was not mandatory for the state to provide services, but funding was available for services and programs for children with special needs at this age, and for their families. Services for children from birth to age 3 are often provided by a state agency such as the Health Department or Mental Health Division. Each state differs in the housing and responsibility for early special education services for infants with special needs and their families.

Jodie and her family received support and services from the time she was 3 months old. Lynn and Jerry were partners in developing and assessing the individual family services plan (IFSP) and had input in the developmental goals established for Jodie. They also were involved in parent education, both in small groups and in individual settings. The parent education helped them with Jodie as she developed throughout her childhood. Lynn and Jerry learned many different techniques and methods to encourage Jodie at home along with ways to stimulate her and involve her in as many typical activities as possible.

Interagency collaboration.   One of the important strands of P.L. 94-457—for Part H, which affects children from birth through age 3—is an emphasis placed on interagency collaboration. **Interagency collaboration** is the coordination of services from several different agencies; it helps families access services and reduce the fragmentation between programs. Although services might have been available prior to this law, there was minimal connection between agencies or services. Collaboration between agencies "is the glue that holds early childhood programs together, making them inclusive communities for the benefit of children and their families" (Sugawara, 1996). Prior to P.L. 94-457, parents had to learn how to access different agencies to find programs for their child and for the family. For example, an education program for infants might be run by the local university, whereas family services were available through the state's social services. When the child was ready to move to a toddler program, the parent then had to locate this program, and yet another agency might then be responsible for parent education.

Support for families.   Another strength found in P.L. 94-457 for Part H (children from birth through age 3) is the importance given to families of young children with special needs. The intent of P.L. 94-457 is to recognize the central role families play in the development of young children. Young children spend a majority of their time with their families. Supporting families of young children with special needs can lead to improved learning environments for children during crucial developmental periods of their lives. Lynn confirms this: "The services and resources we accessed during Jodie's early years were invaluable. I am sure that Jodie would not have reached her same level of development and learned so many essential skills before entering school." The early intervention specialist provided comprehensive services and coordination of resources for Jodie. Lynn and Jerry were active partners in decisions about Jodie and her education: "We were able to make informed decisions from the knowledge gained in parent edu-

cation classes, workshops, and individual sessions." Jodie and her entire family benefited from enactment of P.L. 99-457, which is the true intent of this legislature.

Journal 11.8: Briefly discuss an important benefit that Jodie and her family gained
from P.L. 99-457. ■

Individuals with Disabilities Education Act (IDEA)

In 1991, the **Individuals with Disabilities Education Act (IDEA)** replaced the Education of the Handicapped Act (P.L. 94-142 and P.L. 99-457). IDEA states that children with disabilities are entitled to a free appropriate public education and that each
child's education will be planned and monitored with an individualized education program or an individualized family service plan (IFSP). Section 612 of IDEA states:

> to the maximum extent appropriate, children with disabilities, including children in pub-
> lic or private institutions or other care facilities, are educated with children, who are not
> disabled, and that special classes, separate schooling, or other removal of children with
> disabilities from the regular educational environment occurs only when the nature or
> severity of the disability is such that education in regular classes with the use of supple-
> mentary aids and services cannot be achieved satisfactorily. (Individual with Disabilities
> Education Act, 1990)

When IDEA replaced prior legislature, the age range mandated in P.L. 94-142 (6
through 21 years) and in P.L. 99-457 (3 through age 6) was combined to promote the
involvement of the family and to offer a wide range of services and specialists to support the child in a least restrictive environment. IDEA also changed the language of the
law, focusing more on the individual with disabilities rather than on handicapped children. This new terminology focuses attention to the individual, not to the label or condition. Categories of eligibility for special education services are included in IDEA.

To early childhood professionals, IDEA means that more children with special
needs are now eligible for programs, with services and resources available to support
the child, family, and teacher in providing education for the child. The requirement of
appropriate services to support the child in her learning through IDEA brings early
childhood professionals into a team of specialists working together in planning, implementing, and assessing a child's learning. The child with special needs is granted
access to the programs, but there is also the requirement of **support services** accompanying the child. These support services, such as occupational therapy or speech therapy, are critical to the child's development and to her success in a least restrictive setting.

When Jodie required the help of an occupational therapist to develop programs to
help her with eating skills and fine motor development, the occupational therapist went
to Jodie's preschool and provided the services at that site. She communicated with Karla
(Jodie's preschool teacher), the speech/language therapist, the early intervention specialist, and Lynn and Jerry. Together, this team of specialists designed an educational
plan for Jodie and shared her learning and her challenges. This is an example of a **multidisciplinary** or **transdisciplinary team**—that is, a group of specialists working together across areas of expertise.

What structural changes that support physical accessibility do you see in this photograph?

American Disabilities Act (ADA)

The **American Disabilities Act (ADA)** ensures that all people with disabilities have equal rights in employment, public services, and public accommodations. ADA is a federal civil rights law that has been in effect since 1992. Young children with special needs have a right to participate in child care centers, preschool programs, or family child care homes, as these are considered public accommodations. Physical and other types of barriers must be removed to enable these children to participate fully in programs.

In early childhood education, most professionals already focus on meeting the needs of each individual child and his family, making this law an extension of existing practice. Changes may be needed in admission policies, employment practices, physical accessibility, or accommodations to meet the needs of children, staff, or families with disabilities. Reasonable changes or program modifications generally will meet the child, staff member, or family member's special need.

 Journal 11.9: Have you seen the effect of ADA in your community? Describe one or two changes you have noticed. ■

Importance of These Laws

Each of these laws has considerably shaped programs for young children with special needs. It is essential for you to be knowledgeable of the laws and to have an understanding of the support and services they provide for young children. You will also want to follow the laws and their intent in your program. Jodie's parents learned about their rights and about available programs through their parent support group and from the early intervention specialist who helped coordinate services for Jodie.

As an early childhood professional, you will want to provide the best learning environment possible. It is reassuring to know that you will have the help of specialists when working with children with special needs. Now, let's take a closer look at early childhood special education.

Early Childhood Special Education

In the previous section, the focus was on legislation that has affected special education services for all children with special needs from birth through age 21. Now, you will examine programs, settings, and services that are the outcome of this legislation.

What Is Early Childhood Special Education?

The term *early childhood special education* describes a multitude of services and programs for young children and their families. A child might be attending a day care center, involved in a toddler class at a preschool, receiving home visits, or enrolled in a public school kindergarten program. *Special education* refers to the services the child receives and the goal and content of the teaching (Safford, 1989), not the physical setting of the child's placement. With the successful integration of many children with special needs in regular settings, most children are involved in learning for some or all of the time in a regular classroom setting. When you visited Jodie at her school, you saw her learning about insects with other children. You also learned that she worked with Marty, the resource teacher, several times a week. The support from Marty to Jodie and to Paula, her teacher, was important in helping Jodie learn within the regular classroom setting.

The focus of special education is on developing a program or plan to meet the individual needs of the child, with changes made to the curriculum to meet the need of the learner. One important element of curriculum content and design for children with special needs is age appropriateness (Brown et al., 1979). When you design curriculum for a child with special needs, you want to take into consideration the age of the child and the usefulness of the activity in everyday life. Does this remind you of Jodie's assignment as the messenger to the school office? She was learning skills and acquiring knowledge that was applicable to school and to settings outside of school.

Early Childhood Special Education Services and Settings

With these descriptions of special education in mind, you can see that a child with special needs might be attending any of the early childhood settings described throughout this book. An infant might be in her own home, a home care center, or an employer-sponsored infant care program; a toddler might go to a play group or be in child care; 3- and 4-year-olds might be in a preschool setting, a child care center, or a home care center. No matter what the setting, the caregiver or teacher will likely need to learn some general adaptation strategies to help a child with special needs succeed.

Instructional strategies.   Good instructional strategies, guidance, curriculum modifications or adaptations, and modifying the classroom and/or schedule are practices that work together to create a successful inclusion program. *Cooperative learning* (sometimes called *collaborative learning, peer teaching,* or *group projects*) is another instructional strategy that has proven successful in inclusive classrooms. Students teach each other and assume responsibility for the learning of others. Cooperative learning captures the affective and social aspect of learning, along with academic learning. In cooperative learning, students communicate with each other and become members of a group working toward the common goal of accomplishing a task or gaining knowledge. Many teachers find it useful to take workshops or courses on cooperative learning to help them understand how to teach the process of group work and create a community of learners.

Direct instruction is an instructional strategy that assists children in learning specific information or knowledge, often basic skills in reading or mathematics, or life skills. The format of direct teaching typically includes small group or individual sessions, a high level of feedback and interaction, and a concentrated focus on specific skills. With young children, a caregiver might provide direct instruction to a child with special learning needs within the mainstream or regular setting (Safford, 1989). For example, a 2-year-old with physical challenges might have difficulty using a spoon without spilling the contents. While the other children are involved in various activities, the child care provider might help the child practice using a spoon for a favorite snack of pudding. This extra time and practice helps the child learn the skill as she works toward gaining the fine motor coordination needed to master the spoon. In this situation, the adult provides direct instruction, focuses on a specific skill, and gives frequent feedback to the child, helping her learn a useful life skill.

A comprehensive program that assists teachers in making modifications to support the learning of children with special needs in inclusive settings is the Adaptive Learning Environments Model (ALEM) (Wang & Zollers, 1990). ALEM provides direct instruction in a structured program, which includes both social and academic skills. Whatever program is used or adaptations made, the goal should be to promote learning based on knowledge and skills identified in a child's individual education program.

 Curriculum modifications or adaptations.   In Jodie's classroom, Marty, the resource teacher, assisted Paula in making curriculum modifications to match Jodie's learning needs. When you observed Jodie working on her number facts, you saw that she was making combinations of objects to find a total of 4. Other children were involved in double-digit addition and subtraction. Paula had modified the curriculum so Jodie could be successful in learning the numeracy skills that she needed before moving to higher-level skills. Because Jodie's individual education program specified the skills she was working on in mathematics, it was fairly simple to modify the curriculum to meet her needs.

Curriculum adaptations often reflect an accommodation of the amount of the curriculum a child with special needs is expected to learn. When Jodie's class was studying insects, Jodie was expected to learn the colors of her insect and what her insect liked to eat. Other children were learning about the life cycle of insects and the body parts of insects. Jodie was participating in the same curriculum at the same time, but with different expectations for the amount of knowledge she was to learn.

Since many general education teachers have not had coursework in special education, frameworks for learning to plan for inclusion have been developed. The SMART model (Winter, 1997) is an acronym for **S**elect curriculum and approaches, **M**atch instruction to the child, **A**dapt when necessary, **R**elevant skills are targeted, and **T**est to inform instruction. These five steps were designed to help teachers plan and modify instruction to meet the learning needs of individual children.

Other modifications to a program are time and schedule changes. Some children with special needs may need to have a schedule that allows for frequent breaks or time to choose low-key activities balanced with intensive learning time. Time modifications might also include lengthening the time for practicing a skill and preparing home activity packets to allow the child to continue an activity at his own pace after school. Most of the modification or adaptation techniques discussed in this chapter are helpful to other children, as well. Learning to implement these strategies helps teachers and caregivers become more aware of the individual learning needs of all children.

Program options or settings. Program options also provide a format to meet the diverse learning needs of children with special needs. Many different options are available and these can be combined or altered to meet individual needs. For example, a child could attend a second program concurrent with his early childhood program. The specialized program might provide therapy or specific resources at the same center or at another site (Safford, 1989). A young child who is developmentally delayed in her speech or language would spend time with a speech/language therapist on a regular basis. The speech/language therapist would also collaborate with the preschool teacher to find ways that both might incorporate similar activities to help the child with her language development. Remember when Jodie's IFSP goals included expanding her sentence length beyond two-word responses? In this situation, the preschool teacher and assistants, parents, and speech/language therapist met to discuss this goal and how to help Jodie increase her vocabulary and sentence length. The collaboration of all who work with Jodie helped create a coherent approach to Jodie's language development.

When children are working with several specialists and professionals, regular communication between specialists and parents is essential to help everyone keep abreast of the child's progress. Lynn found these meetings very helpful: "I always felt involved in the decision making and was able to talk about what I saw Jodie doing at home." The attitude or tone of these collaborations or partnerships is often established by the early childhood specialist and her willingness to actively include all parties in the planning and assessing of a child's learning and development.

Journal 11.10: What might be some benefits gained by people representing different programs and agencies if they work together to assess Jodie's needs and develop plans to guide her learning?

Special Education in the Public Schools

Once Jodie entered the public school system in her kindergarten year, her education and services were provided by the local education agency. States differ on the age when local school districts begin providing special education services. Most start providing services through the school districts at age 3. The school district receives federal funding for special education, which is allocated according to the number of special education students enrolled in the district. This funding formula again brings up the problem of labeling children and requiring children to fit into a specific category of need so that the district will receive funding. Often, a child may be functioning below grade level in some subject areas and need special services to support her learning. Unless her disability meets eligibility criteria and she needs special education in order to benefit from the education program, she may not be eligible for services.

Special education programs at the district level follow procedures and requirements monitored by the state department of education. If a district is not large enough to require full-time services of an occupational therapist, physical therapist, psychologist, speech therapist, or other specialist, it might contract with the county or several other districts to share a specialist. By law, school districts are required to provide the necessary services to each child identified with special needs as prescribed in the child's individual educational program (IEP). School districts must also provide necessary medical support to assist children with medical conditions to participate as fully as possible in their local school district.

The focus of education gradually shifts from the family unit to the child as the child moves through the school years, although many school districts continue parent education programs and parents often form support groups through formal associations, such as the ARC (previously called the Association of Retarded Citizens), or on an informal level. Children with more severe disabilities typically spend time in some type of career preparation or life skills program to prepare them for adulthood. The goal for these young adults is to learn skills needed to become as independent as possible when they leave school. Many of the skills learned in early childhood lay the foundation for adult skills. Learning to get along with others, follow directions, accept responsibility for one's own actions, share with others, and similar social skills are as important to a 30-year-old as to a 5-year-old. The social goals for Jodie as a 4-year-old would be modified to be developmentally and age appropriate, but they would still focus on her learning to participate as a contributing and active member of society.

Role of Families in Early Childhood Special Education

As discussed in several sections of this book, families are an integral part of early childhood education. This is especially true in special education, because these families may need specific assistance in learning how best to help their child. Often, the role of the early childhood professional is to share day-to-day experiences of the child's interactions and activities at his setting, much like the communication you might have with all of your students' families. Many parents of children with special needs have a strong need to hear good news about their child, and your feedback is so important to them. A simple note or a quick chat at the door can help the family learn that their child has a unique place in your program. Jerry appreciated the notes home about Jodie's progress at preschool. He remembers, "After one particularly hard day at work, I arrived home to find a note from the preschool teacher describing Jodie's creative storytelling with her classmates. This was the first time Jodie had told stories at school and we were so glad to hear that her language was growing. That note made my day and my week!"

A family-centered approach to early childhood education and to early special education have similar rationales. Finding out the priorities of the family helps in developing an individualized learning program for the child. For instance, if Jodie's family is interested in having Jodie increase her vocabulary, the early intervention specialist, speech/language therapist, and early childhood professional would work with her family to identify specific goals for Jodie. These goals might include providing frequent and interesting opportunities for Jodie to communicate with other children and her family. When a family is more concerned with a child learning certain skills, it makes sense to help focus learning activities in this direction and all work together in providing activities that help the child accomplish these skills.

In order to know which areas are of interest to the family, an early childhood provider might spend time during a conference discussing areas that the family is concentrating on at home and successes and challenges they have faced. For a child with learning difficulties, it certainly seems appropriate to have people working together to make her learning more connected in the home and at her early childhood setting. The learning goals come from the partnership of the family and the specialists. This active partnership empowers the family as they work with their child and notice their child's new accomplishments. The partnership you help develop with this family may not differ much from those with other families. You will find that communicating the experiences, successes, and challenges that occur throughout a day helps you build on what the family is doing and enables the family to make connections with the activities in your setting.

Families and teachers work together to communicate about a child's progress.

Jodie's family is economically and educationally advantaged, with Jerry and Lynn being college graduates, and they have the support of an extended family. Many families of children with disabilities are not as fortunate. Jerry and Lynn expressed many trials and tribulations they experienced when learning how to find the best services for Jodie in her early years. Remember their gratitude for the support from Lynn's mother and from the families in their parent support group? This support was an essential resource in their understanding of Jodie's disability and their search to find services for Jodie.

Journal 11.11: Imagine the many challenges that a single parent, perhaps a teen mother, would face as the mother of a child with Down syndrome. As a teacher, what community resources might you suggest to the family to help support them in their unique challenges? ■

Rationale for Early Intervention for Children with Special Needs

At some point in your career, you might be asked why there is a need for early intervention programs for children with special needs. It is important for you to be able to explain the rationale for such programs. Many programs for young children have included children with special learning needs prior to legislation and mandates. Young children are typically in learning situations that allow them to grow and develop at their individual pace, which contributes to a nurturing setting for children with special needs. The early childhood profession views each child as an individual with appreciation for the diversity children bring with them to the setting. This approach to learning is congruent with the stance of special educators, who see individualized learning programs as the key to helping each child reach his potential.

Early intervention and its influence on later life.   Early intervention for a child with special learning needs can make a significant difference throughout the child's life (Safford, 1989). During the 1960s and the War on Poverty, one outcome was to provide early childhood programs for children living in poverty. The belief was that reaching children and their families while the children were young could make positive influences on their academic and social development. Results from a preschool project that followed children into early adulthood, the Perry Preschool Project, found that early intervention during preschool years had impacts in multiple areas, including higher academic performance, lower teenage pregnancy rate, higher enrollment at higher education levels, and higher high school graduation rate (Schweinhart & Weikart, 1985). The researchers also concluded that early intervention was a sound cost-effective program. Preschool intervention led to later cost savings that would have occurred if these children had not participated in preschool. For example, when the group was followed into adulthood, it was found that only 18 percent of the Perry Preschool group was on welfare, compared to 32 percent of the control group (made up of a similar population who had not attended the Perry Preschool.) This difference is reflected in savings with reduced costs of welfare for society. (The Perry Preschool Study will be discussed further in Chapter 12, when we examine the economics of early childhood programs.)

Another important longitudinal study, the Consortium of Longitudinal Studies, was conducted by Lazar and Darlington (1982) and investigated the graduates of 12 early intervention projects. The children in the early intervention programs were compared to children who did not receive early intervention services. The results show that these early intervention programs led to a reduction in the number of children who were later placed in special education classes or retained at the same grade level for a second year. The children who participated in early intervention scored higher on math and reading achievement tests. The researchers concluded that participation in early intervention programs leads to an overall reduction in special education services and remedial education, which leads to lower costs for educational programs. For early childhood professionals and special educators, the sense that early intervention significantly affects later learning and success is evident in the data and findings presented in these studies.

Early intervention and prevention. Safford (1989) raises a critical question about preventing labeling of children and their consequent placement in special education programs. If children at risk of failing in school are involved in good early intervention programs, will their chances for success in school increase? Thus, early intervention and prevention become interwoven. Prevention and intervention work together around the same goal of helping each child reach his potential in his intellectual, physical, emotional, and social development. The longitudinal studies support the long-term gains made by children who received early intervention services, both in personal growth and gains and in financial savings to society. Clearly, early childhood special education plays a critical role in helping children and their families learn and grow together.

 Journal 11.12: What argument or rationale would you develop to the question, Why is it necessary to provide early intervention for children with special needs? ■

PRINCIPLES AND INSIGHTS: **A Summary and Review**

You began this chapter by taking a quick visit to Jodie's home. Teachers and caregivers who have not worked with children with special needs often feel unqualified or uncertain about their expertise in special education. By meeting Jodie at her home, we hoped to dispel some of these feelings by sharing how Jodie is much like other children in her needs, interests, and support from her family.

At Forest Hills School, you observed Jodie in her multiage first/second-grade classroom. Children were involved in math activities and exploring the world of insects. You saw how Paula, the teacher, included Jodie in the class activities and wove Jodie's learning goals into the everyday curriculum of this classroom. Paula also shared successful guidance or classroom management strategies, such as stating clear expectations and breaking large tasks into small steps. Marty, the resource teacher, was available as a support for Jodie and Paula. Marty provided direct instruction with Jodie and assisted Paula in making curriculum modifications, based on goals established in Jodie's IEP.

The early intervention childhood specialist made home visits and involved Lynn and Jerry throughout the years she worked with Jodie. Struggles and challenges were discussed and plans were developed to help Jodie succeed. In a preschool program, you might typically notice when a child progresses in language development and begins talking in full sentences. With Jodie, progress was noted when she began moving from one-word responses to two-word phrases. Each small step was acknowledged, with future plans or learning goals built on her successful experiences and activities.

Take a few minutes to review your journal entries from this chapter while thinking about the impact of legislation on the programs and services that Jodie and her family have experienced. You will likely recognize that through legislative decisions, special education provided support, resources, and an educational program for Jodie and her family. Each of the programs she was involved in built on her strengths and her prior accomplishments, and focused on specific goals.

Jodie's parents were partners in planning their child's programs and decisions about her learning. Jodie was often involved with several different specialists, who collaborated to define individual learning activities and situations to help her meet learning goals established by her family and specialists.

Jodie also had input in her planning. Adults working with her learned to acknowledge her frustration and alter activities or step back and let Jodie determine what she planned to do next. Jodie has certain likes and dislikes, as do all children, and her early childhood specialists designed experiences that allowed her to make choices and develop her own interests. Seeing each and every child as an individual, with unique dispositions and developmental patterns, enables you to reach the children you work with and create an optimal learning environment.

Working with children with special needs will most likely be part of your future. Approximately 12 percent of the school-age population of children are eligible for special education services. From this chapter, you now know that specialists will be available to assist and support you, the child, and his family. You also know about the importance of including children with special needs and supporting their growth and development in early childhood programs, as both an intervention and a prevention practice. This knowledge, along with your introduction to Jodie and her experiences, may reduce the anxiety many professionals experience when they have not yet worked with children with special needs. Hopefully, you will have the opportunity to help children such as Jodie become active, eager learners in your early childhood program.

Becoming an Early Childhood Professional

Your Field Experiences

1. Observe a child with special needs in an early childhood setting in your community. Ask the caregiver or teacher about a goal that has been identified in the child's IFSP or IEP. What activities or support to meet this goal did you observe? How is the child's family involved in meeting this goal?

2. Using Figure 11.4, identify the name and location of one local program for each of the six different settings. Set up an observation at one of the programs to find out more about the children and the program. Here are some questions you might ask: Why is this the most appropriate education environment for these children? What is included in the education program? Share your thoughts about your observation with other students in your class.

Your Professional Portfolio

1. Anecdotal records or notes include a description of the setting, activity, and people involved, along with the observed behaviors (McLean, Bailey, & Wolery, 1996). An *anecdotal record* is a brief written entry that factually describes a specific scene or incident. Using Figure 11.2, observe a young child interacting with other children, playing with a toy, or practicing a skill. After your observation, assume you have recorded several similar scenes. Do your observation notes reflect what you observed? What interpretations would you make about this child's learning or development? Keep a copy of your completed anecdotal record in your portfolio.

2. Interview a special education teacher or teacher assistant. Why did she choose this career? What education or training is required for his position? Ask her to describe a "typical" workday. What part of his job sounds the most rewarding to you? Summarize the interview findings and your thoughts about these findings in a short paper for your portfolio.

Your Professional Library

Books

Chandler, P. (1994). *A place for me: Including children with special needs in early care and education settings.* Washington, DC: NAEYC.

Cook, R., Tessier, A., & Klein, M. (1992). *Adapting early childhood curricula for children with special needs* (3rd ed.). New York: Macmillan.

Neugebauer, B. (Ed.). (1992). *Alike and different: Exploring our humanity with young children* (rev. ed.). Washington, DC: NAEYC.

Putnam, J. (Ed.). (1993). *Cooperative learning and strategies for inclusion: Celebrating diversity in the classroom.* Baltimore, MD: Paul H. Brookes.

Smarte, L., & McLane, K. (1994). *How to find answers to your special education questions* (rev. ed.). Reston, VA: Council for Exceptional Children.

Wolery, M., & Wilbers, J. (Eds.). (1994). *Including children with special needs in early childhood programs.* Washington, DC: NAEYC.

Internet Addresses and World Wide Web Sites

www.cec.sped.org/cec.htm
   ERIC Clearinghouse on Disabilities and Gifted Education

www.weac.org/resource/june96/speced.htm
   Special Education Inclusion Issues Series

oilpatch.prn.bc.ca/SpecialServices/strategies.html
   Inclusion of Students with Special Needs, Peace River North: Classroom Strategies

zinnia.umfacad.maine.edu/cgibin/about/public/ecs/ 856980278/answers
   Welcome to the Early Childhood Special Education Discussion Group

www.nas.nasa.gov/HPCC/K12/EDRC23.html
   The Gifted Education Center of the National Capitol Area Public Access Network

k12.ed.special
   Newsgroup that discusses special education topics

The Changing World
of Early Childhood

When you finish reading and reflecting on this chapter, you will be able to:

1. Summarize political influences on early childhood programs.

2. Appreciate the economic impacts on early childhood.

3. Discuss the social forces that influence early childhood.

4. Clarify and define your role as an advocate for early childhood.

5. Define, in your own words, *early childhood professional*.

Nothing is more important to our shared future than the well-being of our children. . . . Just as it takes a village to raise a child, it takes children to raise up a village to become all it should be. The village we build with them in mind will be a better place for us all" (Clinton, 1996). As you read this chapter and prepare to work with young children, you are learning and making decisions that will change your life as well as the lives of children. In the book *It Takes a Village and Other Lessons Children Teach Us,* Hillary Clinton (1996) reminds us that the way we raise our children influences their future as well as our own future and the quality of our lives.

As individuals and professionals, the economic, political, and social decisions you make individually and collectively about the care of and programs for young children demonstrate your commitment to young children. These decisions and actions are determined by members of a modern-day village, composed of people both near and far who share the raising of children. Years ago, villages were much simpler; one could easily recognize most of the members of one's village. Villages of today are much more complex; one probably will not know—or even see all the members who help raise one's children. Come meet Angela and some of the people helping to raise her.

Angela's Village

Angela Russo is 4 years old and lives in Brooklyn, New York. At first glance, it appears that her village is quite small. Her mother, Marie, is a single parent working from 8:30 to 5:00 each day in a nearby law office. Living close by (each only several bus stops from Angela's apartment) are two sets of grandparents, Edward and Betty Deluiso, and Frank and Anna Russo. In the apartment upstairs live Mr. and Mrs. Ponzi, who occasionally watch Angela when her mother works late or goes out for an evening. Emily

Weiss, who cares for four young children in her home, one of whom is Angela, lives three blocks away. And finally, one of Angela's favorite stops, is the corner bakery, where Mrs. Gianolla lets Angela pick out a biscottini (an Italian cookie) when she and her mom stop in to buy a loaf of bread.

Four blocks away is the public library, where Jerome Washington is the children's librarian. He knows that stories about cats are Angela's favorite books. She checks out at least one "cat" book each week when she comes to the library. Jerome often puts aside a new book about cats, saving it for Angela.

Recently, Cindy Kim was at Angela's apartment building to inspect the building for evidence of lead. Cindy is a county health inspector who has been trained in detecting levels of lead in buildings. Her report could have an impact on Angela's health.

Last week, Angela visited the local public health clinic for her latest immunization, administered by Jessica Pederson. Jessica reviewed Angela's medical record and discussed the benefit of fluoride treatments with Angela and her mother.

Kent Larson is Marie Russo's employer. He has been reviewing employee benefit packages that provide child care benefits by deducting monthly amounts targeted for such benefits. The new plan would allow employees to chose from different options for child care.

All of the people you have just met make many decisions that have a direct impact on Angela. These are local people who are part of the village raising Angela. Angela's well-being is constantly influenced by decisions made at state, regional, and federal levels.

Politics, social forces, and economics influence the types of programs available for young children, the number of social services available for young children and their families, and the quality of these programs. The priority for the care of children is reflected in the support designated for early childhood programs and for families. Although politics, economics, and societal issues are often intertwined, each area will be examined separately, with a look at their affects on early childhood programs. You will also look at what these influences mean to the professional in early childhood education and the growing expectations and responsibilities of these professionals. Angela's life is influenced by political, economic, and social decisions, and yours is, too. Thus, it is advantageous for you to be knowledgeable of these powerful forces.

Politics and Early Childhood Programs

The influence of politics on the education system of the United States has a long history. When discussing **political influence,** we are referring to the role of government (national, state, and local levels) as it affects early childhood programs and the support and funding that comes from the government. Private kindergarten programs in the United States began as early as 1860, later followed by nursery school programs for younger children. During the 1930s and the period of the Great Depression, the government sponsored nearly 3,000 child care programs to provide work for unemployed women as child care workers. When World War II began, the labor of most women was essential to war-related employment, so child care was again supported by the government. Once the war ended in 1945, women generally returned to their work at home and government support for child care was terminated.

Politics and Early Childhood Education in the 1960s

During the 1960s, the rapidly increasing number of children raised in poverty became unacceptable. Social consciousness was high and, as a nation, there was concern about the effects of poverty on young children. It was determined that early education programs were a major factor leading to later success in school and throughout life. Remember the Bereiter-Englemann program discussed in Chapter 5? This was a program of the 1960s, with a goal of preparing economically disadvantaged young children to succeed in school.

The concern and regard for equality in the nation led to the passage of the Economic Opportunity Act during the Lyndon B. Johnson administration. One of the major purposes of this act was to declare a "war on poverty" by disrupting the pattern of **intergenerational poverty.** This meant it was necessary to find a way to assist families at or below the poverty level to prevent the children from becoming adults who repeat the same cycle with limited opportunities. Programs and support would be provided by the federal government for children and families at or below the poverty level.

Head Start Programs

Through the Office of Economic Opportunity, Project Head Start was implemented in 1965 and continues today. A group of scientists and policymakers reviewed the research on early intervention and determined that educational failure of low-income children could be averted through their participation in a specially designed program (Caldwell, 1992). With government funding, eligible children and their families may participate in a comprehensive education, social, health, and nutrition program under Project Head Start. Families are recognized as an integral part of making lasting changes in the life of the child (Gage & Workman, 1994).

It is thought that providing enriching experiences early in a child's life for both the child and her family can help the child succeed in school and in later life, thus breaking the cycle of poverty. Now, we are rediscovering, as in the 1960s, that child and family poverty are intolerable and that Head Start is a solution to address the war on poverty (Greenberg, 1990).

Over 13 million children from low-income families have received Head Start services in the past 30-plus years (Hendrick, 1996). Unfortunately, only about one of three children eligible to participate in Head Start do so, due to lack of funding (Children's Defense Fund, 1997).

Several children who live in Angela's apartment building attend Head Start. (If Marie Russo earned less money, it's possible that Angela could attend a Head Start program in her Brooklyn neighborhood, as well.) By advocating for more funding to support Head Start programs and increasing accessibility to the program, legislators and Head Start advocates have become members of the village raising the children in Angela's neighborhood.

Other Government Programs

Other government-supported programs and/or legislation that affects young children include the Personal Responsibility and Work Opportunity Reconciliation Act of 1996 (welform reform), Child and Adult Food Care Program, Child Care and Development

Block Grant Act, Social Services Block Grants (Title XX programs), Public Law 89–750 (migrant education), Elementary and Secondary Education Act (Title I programs), and other legislation, including child care tax credits. Each of these government programs fund different types of activities related to young children and their developing needs. Let's take a brief look at each of these programs before moving to a current political force in education—the Goals 2000 agenda.

Welfare reform and early childhood. In 1996, Congress enacted sweeping changes in the welfare system. The intent of the Personal Responsibility and Work Opportunity Reconciliation Act of 1996 is to move people from welfare to work (Gnezda, 1996). The new law created a program called Temporary Assistance for Needy Families (TANF). Each state receives a block grant for TANF. The state is responsible for establishing criteria for granting aid to needy families, which is submitted to the federal government as a written plan. One major change noted in this program is found in guaranteed assistance. Even if a family meets the state criteria for needing assistance, they are no longer assured of obtaining food stamps, cash, job training or other assistance they need. **Entitlement,** the assurance that a person receives the assistance he or she qualifies for, is no longer part of the welfare system. If a state runs low on TANF funds, the state may place families on waiting lists, reduce assistance to all families, or turn families away.

Two federal requirements must be included in each state's plan: a five-year limit on receiving TANF during a lifetime and a requirement that parents must work within two years of receiving cash assistance. These two requirements are the maximum time periods, and states have the discretion to shorten either time period. States may choose to include a work exemption for parents with children under the age of 1.

The work requirement dramatically increases the need for child care, which is already difficult to obtain, both in terms of adequacy and affordability. Rapid growth and expansion of child care must be carefully monitored. All children should have access to child care that meets the needs of both the child and the family. This child care should also foster child development and learning and meet professional standards (NAEYC, 1997b). The National Association for the Education of Young Children developed a position statement on state implementation of welfare reform, urging early childhood advocates to become involved with state legislators, organizations, and other officials in developing high standards for child care programs. At the same time, attention needs to be given to expanding the number of qualified providers and ensuring adequate assistance for families so they can afford high-quality child care programs (NAEYC, 1997b). Under TANF, there are no guarantees that families with young children will receive assistance with child care (Children's Defense Fund, 1997), although welfare reform did include nearly $1 billion in funding for child care subsidies. These funds assist low-income women with children in obtaining child care as they enter the work force (Clifford, 1997).

Legal immigrants have also been cut from many social services under the welfare reform enacted in 1997. In most cases, these people are no longer eligible for federal programs such as food stamps, child care, Medicaid, or TANF.

These drastic changes in welfare create dramatic results for families with young children who need welfare assistance. There is much concern that more children will be forced into poverty by this new law, and that numerous problems associated with lack of food, medical care, housing, and other basic needs will become more prevalent. At the same time, welfare reform offers an opportunity for early childhood advocates to work at their state level to create access to high-quality child care programs for all young children and families.

Child and Adult Care Food Program. Funding for food at child care centers is available through the Child and Adult Care Food Program (CACFP) sponsored by the U.S. Department of Agriculture (USDA). This program provides money and food to child care centers and homes. The intent of this program in regard to children is to improve the nutrition for children ages 12 and under. Emily Weiss, Angela's caregiver, is eligible to receive supplemental funding for purchasing nutritious food for the children she cares for in her home. CACFP also provides training and support for family child care providers.

As part of the welfare reform in 1996, major changes were made to restructure the CACFP. Food reimbursement rates are now established according to family income levels within the area where the child care provider resides or the family income levels of the providers. Child care providers who do not meet these requirements may apply for reduced funding, although there is concern that the amount of funding may be too low for these providers to continue with the program. CACFP also provides training and support networks, and some child care providers may lose these connections due to the revised guidelines (Gnezda, 1996).

Child Care and Development Block Grant Act. In 1990, the Child Care and Development Block Grant Act was passed as a comprehensive bill supporting child care. Although developed by the federal government, the funds are distributed to the states, with each state responsible for overseeing its program. This bill allows parents to receive assistance through the use of child care certificates that purchase child care. Additional components of the bill include expansion of Head Start to include full-day and year-long programs, and before- and after-school care programs.

Title XX. Some day care centers, family home centers, and schools receive federal or state support through the Social Services Block Grants (SSBG), also known as Title XX. Title XX was passed by Congress in 1974 and has been the largest contributor of federal support directed to state-operated child care (Children's Defense Fund, 1991). Most of the funding supports child care for single mothers who would otherwise not be able to afford child care costs associated with working.

Aid for children in migrant families. Through P.L. 89–750, children of migrant workers are eligible for programs that recognize the needs of children who move often and need special support and programs to complete their schooling. To ensure participation of children, many of these programs for young children begin in the early morning hours, since the field workers may begin their day by 4:00 or 5:00 A.M. Migrant programs address learning at the early childhood, elementary, and secondary school levels. They have also developed systems to track students from location to location to facilitate the continuity of their schooling.

For example, the Rodriguez family moves each year from California in the late spring to Washington, where they prune fruit trees and work in the orchards until late October. They then move back to California to work in the fields from November until late spring. The Rodriguez family returns to work at the same farms and fields, so their children are able to attend the same school each year. Each school keeps track of the child's progress and sends this information to other schools when the family moves. This communication helps the teachers in planning for the children's learning and in building continuity into their schooling.

Title I programs. In 1965, legislation was passed to provide Title I funds to improve education for economically disadvantaged children. This was the Elementary and Secondary Education Act (ESEA). The ESEA provides funding for **compensatory education,** which is education that compensates or seeks to help children from disadvantaged homes improve their school performance. Changes in funding and services provided through Title I (known as Chapter I from 1981 to 1995) have occurred since 1965, although the major intent of helping children improve academically remains in place. Title I services are educational resources that target children functioning below their expected grade level and assist them in improving their basic skills, primarily in reading, language, and mathematics.

Title I programs vary among school districts, although many districts are attempting to move from a **pull-out model** (when a Title I teacher or assistant pulls a child from the classroom to work in another setting) to a model where the Title I teacher or assistant provides services within the child's classroom. A Title I teacher might be responsible for diagnosing and developing programs for individual children or for developing schoolwide programs that improve academic achievement. This federal program reaches approximately 5 million children annually, helping them succeed within their regular school program.

Other government-sponsored support. Additional government support sources include employer-supported (or sponsored) child care, which allows employers tax breaks for providing child care for their employees. Remember hearing earlier in this chapter about Kent Larson, Marie Russo's employer? He is selecting a new employee benefit plan that will provide support for child care benefits.

Another source of government involvement is found in the child care services provided by governmental agencies for the children of their employees. Also, earned income tax credits (EITC) are available for low-income families. The tax credit reduces the amount of tax that some of these families owe the government, whereas other families might receive a refund after deducting their earned income tax credit.

With this introduction to many federal programs that affect early childhood education, let's now explore policies that focus directly on education.

Goals 2000. A current political agenda that directly influences education from birth through adulthood is Goals 2000. During the Educational Summit in 1989, President George Bush met with governors from around the nation and proposed six goals to improve the U.S. educational system by the year 2000. The goals were adopted in 1990 and titled *America 2000*. In 1994, two more goals were added to the original six goals, which became law under the passage of Goals 2000: Educate America Act, signed by President William Clinton. A major function of Goals 2000 is to identify national standards for student learning and for evaluation of schools (Earley, 1994) and to encourage both state and local agencies to work together to develop comprehensive plans that lead to educational improvement. The National Education Goals state that by the year 2000:

1. All children in America will start school ready to learn.

2. The high school graduation rate will increase to at least 90 percent.

3. All students will leave Grades 4, 8, and 12 having demonstrated competency over challenging subject matter including English, mathematics, science, foreign languages, civics and government, economics, arts, history, and geography, and every school in America will ensure that all students learn to use their minds well, so they may be prepared for responsible citizenship, further learning, and productive employment in our Nation's modern economy.

4. The Nation's teaching force will have access to programs for the continued improvement of their professional skills and the opportunity to acquire the knowledge and skills needed to instruct and prepare all American students for the next century.

5. United States students will be first in the world in mathematics and science achievement.

6. Every adult American will be literate and will possess the knowledge and skills necessary to compete in a global economy and exercise the rights and responsibilities of citizenship.

7. Every school in the United States will be free of drugs, violence, and the unauthorized presence of firearms and alcohol and will offer a disciplined environment conducive to learning.

8. Every school will promote partnerships that will increase parental involvement and participation in promoting the social, emotional, and academic growth of children. (National Education Goals Panel, 1995)

These goals are far reaching, much beyond the notion one might hold of schooling. Progress has been made in academic performance in mathematics and science, although insufficient gains have been realized in reading performance and in narrowing the gap in performance between White and minority students (Goals 2000, 1996). Involvement of entire communities in supporting education from the prenatal period to adulthood is required to meet these goals and make significant progress in improving education for our nation's children by the year 2000. Goals 2000 makes a very strong case for the *village* concept (introduced in this chapter).

As Americans become more concerned about the quality of the educational system, politicians have joined the debates about education and have provided policies and guidelines for improving education. In order for these goals to be met, local and state agencies must be prepared to analyze their current educational programs and make changes necessary for alignment with the national goals. In this example of the relationship between politics and education, take notice of the large influence legislation has on shaping the primary goals for the education of this country's children. When you vote for a certain legislator, you are also voting for her or his opinions about plans for early childhood programs. You can see why it is important to be an informed voter and make wise decisions, which come back to you in the form of political and economic support for programs.

Journal 12.1: Find out who among your state representatives and legislators are working for improvements in education, child care, and other children's issues. Record your findings and share your thoughts on current proposed bills with your colleagues in class. ■

Government regulation and early childhood program standards. Specific program standards are developed and monitored by government agencies. There is an expectation that early childhood programs meet standards, whether these are child care centers, home care providers, preschool settings, or the early grades of elementary school. Standards might be in areas of health (e.g., requirement of a food handler's permit for cooking), safety (e.g., no open wiring), or program quality assurances (e.g., the number of children per adult). These expectations are monitored by governmental agencies and are created to ensure the safety and well-being of young children. When thinking about working as a child care provider, you might assume that politics have little to do with your role as a professional in early childhood education. In reality, however, you might be surprised at the amount of involvement your local, state, and national government has in the area of early childhood programs. For example, in most cases, state and local licenses are required to run a home care program, with approval granted after on-site visits document that criteria have been met or exceeded.

Angela's child care provider, Emily, has been visited by an early childhood specialist from the State Office for Services to Children and Families and has received approval for her setting. The early childhood specialist reviewed Emily's daily plans for the children's activities, examined the areas where the children played and rested during the day, and watched Emily interact with the children in her care. She then discussed her observations with Emily, with a written report shared with Emily and filed at the state office. Emily also received approval for her nutrition program and has exceeded the federal guidelines in providing healthy meals and snacks. You can see how a state agency monitors important guidelines for child care providers. This helps ensure that Angela receives quality child care while her mother is at work.

Journal 12.2: What are the requirements in your state (and, for some, city) for becoming a child care provider? Do you feel these standards are set high enough to ensure quality settings for children? Why or why not? ■

Changes in government policy. As we enter the twenty-first century, the locus of policy making and implementation of programs for young children is moving more toward state and local levels. Both fiscal and program responsibilities are being assumed by states and the local communities (Knitzer & Page, 1996). As decision-making processes move to the local level, families and child care providers will have a stronger voice in important decisions about their programs. Early childhood professionals will be working closer with other professionals in their "village." Although it takes more time and effort to work in collaboration with multiple agencies and professionals, the end result can be a program that better meets the needs of the local community and its children. Collaborations actually combine resources to strengthen all of the common or related programs and their effects on children and families.

Summary: Politics and Early Childhood Programs

Looking back over the different governmental programs and agendas that support young children helps you recognize the role of federal funding and the government's influence on early childhood programs. Becoming an informed advocate for young children requires analyzing governmental policy and funding, along with supporting legislators who promote funding in the best interests of young children.

As you think about the social and economic factors affecting early childhood programs, it's easy to see how political influences reflect the social and economic climate of a specific time. More mothers with young children are now in the work force and in need of quality child care. The necessity for quality child care—prompted by political, social, and economic matters—creates an increase in the regulation and licensing involved in child care centers, whether at homes or other facilities. Welfare reform has created a high demand for more child care.

Angela is fortunate to be cared for by Emily while Marie is at work. Emily has met the requirements of the state agency for her child care program. This helps assure Marie that Emily is not only a warm, caring adult but she also has specialized knowledge about young children and has created a safe learning environment for children. Angela's care and future education is influenced by today's political and economic climate. We'll now examine the larger picture of economics and its impact on early childhood education.

Economics and Early Childhood Education

Many of the programs for young children you read about earlier in this chapter were supported by the government and closely linked to economic factors of a specific time period. **Economics** can be thought of as the development and management affecting the overall financial climate in a country.

Economics and Availability of Early Childhood Programs

Remember reading about the need to find child care while women worked in war-related employment during World War II? The economic needs of the United States became the reason for quick development of child care centers while mothers were busy working at shipyards and factories during the war.

Following World War II, preschool and kindergarten programs were primarily attended by middle-class children throughout the 1950s to 1970s. (The major exception was Project Head Start, which originally was a summer program from 1965 to 1972.) The predominant belief during this era was that young children needed to be home with their mothers during the day, and that those who could afford half-day nursery schools or kindergartens might choose to send their child to those programs. Thus, the economics of the day influenced what was available and who could access early childhood programs.

Economy, Early Childhood Programs, and Future Work Force

The economy of the United States is linked to the quality of child care in terms of the potential productivity of these future workers. The early experiences of a child affect his ability to become "a productive adult who contributes to building the nation's economy" (Edelman, 1989). Today, the young family's earning power has declined with inflation, including the low annual income of many teen mothers and single mothers. At the same time, availability of financially supported child care can make the difference between a family receiving welfare checks or being part of the work force. Marie wants to keep her job at the law office, and employee benefits for child care help Marie afford the child care she wants for Angela.

For the child living in poverty, participation in programs such as Head Start help with enrichment, social growth, and developmental learning before the child enrolls in school. It costs far less to invest in quality child care programs for young children than to pay for other programs for older youths and adults who were not successful in school or life. (See the Perry Preschool Project discussion later in this chapter.)

Early childhood experiences set the stage for later life, with high-quality early childhood services likely to create a more skilled labor force (Culkin, Helburn, & Morris, 1990). The nation's future economy is dependent on skilled, productive workers. Financial support of early childhood programs is a beginning in the development of those workers. When Marie picks up Angela at Emily's home, she is usually greeted by a happy, energetic child ready to show Marie what she "learned" that day at Emily's house. Emily's knowledge of early childhood development and her ability to translate this into appropriate and fun activities for the children in her care is evident. Emily is certainly contributing to the healthy growth and development of Angela and other young children, and ultimately to the country's future economy.

Changes in the Work Force

By the late 1970s and through the 1990s, the number of mothers of young children working outside their home steadily increased. According to the U.S. Bureau of the Census (1997) in 1996, nearly 63 percent of mothers with children under age 6 were in the work force. Marie is included in those statistics. In 1996, 76 percent of mothers with children ages 6 to 13 were employed outside the home either full time or part time. Reasons for working vary from purely economic factors to a need of the mother to seek challenges outside of the home, or a combination of several factors. Many households find that the income of the mother is required, either as the sole support in a single-parent home or to balance the family budget. Whatever the reason, it is clear that the need for a variety of options of quality child care for young children is increasing rapidly. Child care programs such as the one Emily has developed must be available.

Journal 12.3: Thinking of a neighborhood that you lived in while growing up, did most of the mothers work at home or at an outside job? What about during your parents' childhoods? What were typical child care arrangements in these two time periods? ■

Employer- or company-based child care programs are increasing, as is the policy for paid leave for parents of newborn children. In the 1990s, the **Family Leave Act** was implemented. This law provides the option of unpaid leave from work to attend to family needs, which might include spending time with a newborn or an aging parent, or taking care of a family medical emergency. This is a welcome support for families, especially considering the frequent conflict that occurs between balancing work and families. Studies are underway to investigate the benefits of allowing working parents to spend time with their newborns and to develop flexible work schedules that support more time with their families. A flexible work schedule or reduced work week would be a welcome option for many young families, allowing parents to spend time with their children and not be penalized in their workplace.

Not all costs can be determined by dollars alone. Supporting families and the time they spend with their children may become part of what attracts employees to a company and ensures their loyalty and long-term employment. More importantly, these options influence the long-term economic health of society. During Angela's first year, Marie worked at the law office four days each week, giving her more time to spend with Angela. Marie also is able to bring some work home during the week and leave the office earlier when either she or Angela have doctor appointments or other needs during the workday. The flexibility of her work schedule is important to Marie as she raises Angela.

Economics and Salaries of Early Child Care Providers

Equally important to consider when thinking about the economic impact on early childhood programs is the salary you, as an early childhood professional, will receive. In 1990, the average annual salary of early childhood teachers working in a center was $11,500 (U.S. Department of Education, 1991). This salary is close to the poverty level for a family of four and less than half of the average salary of a beginning-level public school teacher. Real earnings by child care teachers have declined by nearly 25 percent since the mid-1970s (Kisker et al., 1991). In U.S. society, a person's salary is a symbol of the worth or value placed on that person's work (Bloom, 1993). No wonder many early childhood professionals feel undervalued for their important contributions. Early childhood care providers have been subsidizing programs by contributing their time and expertise for salaries that are far below the value of their services.

The impact that low wages has on the morale and long-term commitment of those who care for young children must be considered. **Turnover** in teaching staff between 1991 and 1992 was 26 percent, that is, over one-fourth of the early childhood staff left their positions during this one-year time period. This turnover rate is close to three times the annual turnover rate reported by all U.S. companies, which is 9.6 percent (Whitebook, Phillips, & Howes, 1993). The high turnover rate of early childhood staff affects the continuity and quality of the care the children receive, creating difficulties for young children and their families as they adjust to a new child care provider and changes in their program.

Unfortunately, it is becoming harder to recruit talented people into the field of early childhood education just at the time when there is a rapid and steadily increasing demand for more early childhood professionals. Attention must be given to increasing the salaries and benefits for qualified staff, as well as giving more recognition to the important role they play in the healthy development of young children.

BOX 12.1 ■ Findings from the Perry Preschool Study

A Closer Look

The Perry Preschool Study examined the economic effects of a quality preschool and looked at the **longitudinal** (long-term) effects. A primary author of this study, Lawrence Schweinhart, states, "More than other educational innovations, high-quality programs for young children living in poverty have demonstrated the promise of lasting benefits and return on investment" (1994, p. 1).

Children selected for this study lived in the attendance area of the Perry Elementary School in Ypsilanti, Michigan. The families in this neighborhood were primarily of low income and of African American descent. Researchers identified preschool-age children in this attendance area and determined socioeconomic levels on the basis of the level of employment, parents' education level, and the ratio of rooms in the home to number of persons living in the home. Children were then given the Stanford-Binet Intelligence Test. Children with scores between 60 and 90 (100 represents an average intelligence score) became part of this study.

The researchers used a random method to assign children to the preschool group or to the group that would not attend preschool. This random assign-

ment process helps make this study credible, as teachers, parents, or researchers did not influence which children would become preschool or nonpreschool participants. In fact, a toss of a coin was used to determine the assignment to the preschool or nonpreschool group, resulting in 58 children being assigned to the preschool group and 65 children assigned to the nonpreschool group. The backgrounds of the children in each group were significantly similar, leading to accurate comparisons between effects that can be attributed to participation in the preschool program.

The curriculum of the preschool program focused on intellectual and social development with preschool in session five days a week for 2½ hours each morning. In addition, teachers made home visits with the mother and child each week. Both groups of children were tested and interviewed at regular intervals, with researchers unaware of whether the child they were interviewing was part of the preschool or nonpreschool group.

The primary sources of data for the Perry Preschool Study were interviews when the child reached age 19, information from the elementary and secondary schools the child attended, police and court

Journal 12.4: Why are you attracted to working in early childhood education? What kind of support and resources will sustain your interest in this profession? ■

Economic Benefits of Early Childhood Education

Let's discuss an informative study that examined early childhood education in terms of economic value. The Perry Preschool Study (see Box 12.1) followed 123 children born between 1958 and 1962 into their early adulthood (Schweinhart et al., 1985).

A later study, the High/Scope study, was conducted by many of the researchers involved in the earlier Perry Preschool Project. Their findings in 1993 supported the earlier findings of the Perry Preschool Project. Schweinhart and colleagues (1993) found that participation in a high-quality preschool created a framework for later success as an adult, "significantly alleviating the negative effects of childhood poverty on educational performance, social responsibility, adult economic status, and family formation" (p. 230). This same study also examined the cost of the preschool program and analyzed the actual costs with the benefits gained from preschool attendance. The re-

records, and social service records. The findings were reported in three major areas: schooling success, social responsibility, and socioeconomic success.

Within the category of *school success,* it was found that children who attended preschool continued in school longer, tested higher on functional competence, were less likely to be classified as mentally retarded, and were less likely to spend some of their school years in special education classes. When *social responsibility* was analyzed, it was found that the group of children who attended preschool were less likely to become pregnant as teenagers and less likely to be arrested than those who did not attend preschool. Finally, in *socioeconomic success,* almost twice as many from the group who attended preschool were employed. Nearly half as many of the preschool group received welfare benefits as compared to those who had not attended preschool. These findings support the long-term, critical impact that preschool or early childhood education can have on a person's life. Children in the Perry Preschool Study who attended preschool showed far more indicators of economic, social, and educational success than the group of children with similar backgrounds but without a preschool experience.

The other area the Perry Preschool Study examined was the economic costs of the program in relation to the long-term costs to society in supporting persons on welfare or in the criminal system. The cost analysis found that the money spent on preschool produced a return of 3½ times the initial investment (Schweinhart et al., 1985). This means that the initial investment (paying for the preschool program) led to a reduction of later costs to society—a strong justification for early childhood education as an economic benefit to society.

The authors of the Perry Preschool Project drew two major conclusions from their research. The first conclusion is specifically linked to the study results where the data proved that good preschool programs can help children move beyond the barriers created by poverty. The second conclusion comes from following these two groups of children for 20 years and noting the numerous long-term effects that preschool exerts on the overall quality of one's life. The economic benefits of prevention (through participation in preschool) versus intervention (paying for welfare benefits, criminal costs, or lower-skilled workforce) show the long-term impact of quality early childhood education.

searchers determined that taxpayers received a $7.16 return on each dollar invested in the preschool program.

These longitudinal studies about the lasting benefits of a high-quality preschool program provide you with useful research and findings. You might be asked to explain to others the rationale for and benefits of good early childhood programs available for all children. Your response might include that benefits are found both in economic factors and in overall quality-of-life issues.

Journal 12.5: You are talking with several acquaintances when one person mentions that preschool seems like a fun—but nonessential—experience. What might you say, drawing on your knowledge of the Perry Preschool Project? ■

Summary: Economics and Early Childhood Education

Economics greatly affects early childhood programs. With increasing numbers of mothers entering the work force, the need for quality child care programs is essential not only to children but also to parents and society (Culkin, Helburn, & Morris, 1990). A healthy economy requires skilled and educated workers. The ability to learn and demonstrate the skills of a productive worker begin to be formed at an early age, hopefully with the guidance and support of a caring family and child care specialists.

We have looked at the support from Marie's employer for child care benefits and a flexible work schedule, the support from Emily in her planning and encouraging activities that lead to productive workers, and the support from programs that help young children become successful learners. These critical mainstays lead to a stronger economy for all of us.

Society and Early Childhood

Each society takes a different stance regarding the importance and value of supporting and educating its young children. In the United States, educational reform has become a priority, as voiced by society. People are worried about the quality of education U.S. children are receiving at all grade levels. This concern with improving education in America reflects a current interest of society. The term **society** refers to a group of people who have common interests with shared institutions and a common culture that generalizes to the larger population.

Society and Educational Reform

In 1983, *A Nation at Risk,* a report about the state of U.S. schools, was published. Do you remember hearing about it? This report immediately raised great concerns about schooling and how schools were preparing the country's future leaders. Subsequent reports repeated the theme that children were not receiving the education they needed to be ready for the twenty-first century. In response to the findings and recommendations from these reports, President George Bush held an educational summit with the governors to discuss education. The outcome of this summit was the presentation of Education 2000, which established six goals for educational reform.

In 1994, two goals were added to the original six goals and the document was renamed Goals 2000. In an earlier section of this chapter, you read about Goals 2000 when we discussed political influences in education. Of particular interest to early childhood professionals are the goals that refer directly to the early childhood years and to families. The first goal states that by the year 2000:

All children in America will start school ready to learn.

The three objectives of this goal are especially relevant for you to think about as you prepare to work with young children:

a. All children will have access to high-quality and developmentally appropriate preschool programs that help prepare children for school.

b. Every parent in America will be a child's first teacher and devote time each day to helping such parent's preschool child learn, and parents will have access to the training and support they need.

c. Children will receive the nutrition, physical activity experiences, and health care needed to arrive at school with healthy minds and bodies, and to maintain the mental alertness necessary to be prepared to learn, and the number of low birth-weight babies will be significantly reduced through enhanced prenatal health systems. (National Education Goals Panel, 1995)

Thinking back to the political and economic issues discussed in the earlier sections of this chapter helps you see the close relationship between political, economic, and social factors that affect early childhood education. Look again at the three objectives of the goal that states all children will start school ready to learn. Realistically, these objectives will be met only if policies are in place with adequate funding to ensure that all children and families can participate in programs that support the development of young children.

An example of a program that attends to this goal and its objectives is Project Head Start. As you know from Chapter 9, Head Start is a comprehensive approach to early childhood education with political, economic, and social support. The program also includes access to medical and social services, nutrition, learning experiences for the child and family, and parent involvement and education. Head Start addresses each of the objectives noted in the goal of that ensuring that all children start school ready to learn. Unfortunately, not all children are eligible for Head Start, and not all eligible children are able to enroll in Head Start due to enrollment limits caused by funding constraints. To truly meet this educational goal of ensuring all children are ready to start school, increased financial support must back up the political, social, and economic rhetoric.

The Committee of Economic Development's (1991) report estimated that as many as 40 percent of the children in the United States begin school at risk of failing due to societal problems, such as poverty, substance abuse, family instability, or racial discrimination (Olson, 1991). Knowing that it is very difficult for children to "catch up" once they enter school, solutions to this situation are urgently needed. Recommendations in *The Unfinished Agenda* include shaping polices and programs for young children to strengthen the family and help parents in their role of "first and primary teacher" (Olson, 1991).

Now, let's focus on families. Many of the programs you've been reading about in this chapter focus on both the young child and the family. Obviously, families exert a large influence on early childhood programs and practices.

Society and Families

Families make up the small, nuclear unit within society. The family of today varies greatly from the family of only one generation ago. Currently, children live in families that might look like one or more of the following:

- Blended families (parents remarrying and creating new family units)
- Single-parent households
- One parent working and one parent at home with the child or children
- Grandparents raising their grandchildren
- Teen parents
- Dual-career families (both parents working outside the home)
- Extended families (several families or generations living in a home)

A young child enjoys reading with her grandmother.

Today, only a minority of children live in a family structure with a father at work and a mother at home with the children. The changing family structure finds nearly 50 percent of marriages end in divorce, with predictions that 4 of 10 children born in the 1990s will spend part of their growing years in a single-parent home (Osborn, 1991). The family is the unit that provides care and primary responsibility for the parent/child relationship. Some changes in family structure are not always in the best interests or welfare of children and families (Bruce, 1995).

Marie (Angela's mother) visited with a parent educator from the Family Services office in Brooklyn. After her divorce, she wanted some assistance in helping Angela adjust to their new family arrangement. Marie was able to talk to the family services counselor several times and gain some insights into ways to help Angela as well as herself. Family Services provided another dimension to the composition of Angela's "village."

Journal 12.6: You are reading a story to the 2- and 3-year-old children in your care. The story continually portrays a family with a mother and father living together in the same household. Several of your children live with one parent and two of the children live with their grandparents. What might you do to help them feel included in this story?   ■

As you look over the list of family structures, you will notice that in many of these situations the child will need child care services in order for the parent (or parents) to work. Again, do you see the close links between political, economic, and social impacts on child care? With the changing economic structure, many families face increased stress and pressures. When early childhood care programs become more family focused and view strengthening the family as an integral part of their curricula, staff work to support and educate families. The Family Strengths Model, for example, helps family members focus on achieving individual goals as they work with staff members to promote the healthy growth and development of the child within their family structure (Gage & Workman, 1994).

As the work force includes more working mothers, the need for more child care options increases. One solution that is popular with parents is employer-supported child care, as discussed in Chapter 7. Another option that helps parents of young children is a flexible work schedule that permits one or both parents to work at home part of the week. Other flexible schedules might allow for part-time work, working longer hours for three or four days instead of five days a week, working several days a week at home with a computer connection to the office, or working every other week. These trends of support for child care and for flexible work schedules by the workplace reflect society's valuing of children. Hopefully, the trends are indicative of future possibilities for supporting children and families.

Marie found support from her neighbors, Mr. and Mrs. Ponzi, who are willing to help when Marie has to work later than usual. Mr. Ponzi walks over to Emily's house and picks up Angela and brings her to their home for dinner. Marie's employer, Kent Larson, is aware of Marie's need to leave work on time to pick up Angela. He asks Marie to work late only on rare occasions when they must finish a project. Marie appreciates his sensitivity to her situation and to her commitment to Angela. Here, again, you can see the Ponzis and Kent Larson as "villagers" helping to raise Angela. Marie's situation is not uncommon—parents all over this country find themselves balancing the demands of work and family.

Society and Children in Need

As discussed earlier, more than one in four children of preschool age is growing up in poverty. This situation creates a large population of children who may have nutritional, learning, language, or emotional deficiencies. Imagine how difficult it would be for a 3-year-old child who is hungry and living in a stressful environment to learn to sing songs or to skip, hop, or jump. The family may be most concerned with having enough food for that day or securing employment, leaving little time and energy to create stimulating experiences for the 3-year-old. Unfortunately, there is a connection between poverty and school failure. Children who begin their school years behind other students have difficulty making up for lost time and often find school to be a discouraging and negative experience. This is how the cycle of poverty continues from generation to generation.

It is important for early childhood professionals to recognize the diversity of family structures and to find ways to support children and families in need. Divorce, long-term illness in the family, death, parent's loss of a job, remarriage, or a new baby can be stressful for children as well as adults. Children need the support and comfort from their child care situation as they adjust to changes in their home living situations. When the child care provider or teacher knows that a family is going through a difficult time or major changes, she can help parents seek support services and work with the child as he reacts to the changes in his family situation. The child may become moody, act less mature than is typical, or express his unhappiness through aggressive behavior. At this time, he needs a sensitive adult to help him through a stressful period.

A teacher or caregiver can provide much needed support and assistance during a time of need, such as helping the family understand that talking about the situation with the child (in terms the child comprehends) provides factual information for him. When a crisis occurs, children sense something is wrong, and when they are excluded from conversations, they may think the situation is worse than it is and feel left out of family concerns. Let's look at a scene from a preschool as an example.

Jermaine's grandmother is ill with cancer and was recently told by her doctor that she has approximately one to two months to live. Of course, the family is upset and talks frequently on the phone to other family members about grandmother's condition. Jermaine, who is 3 years old, hears some of these conversations and knows that his parents are visiting his grandmother often in the hospital. By sharing that his grandmother is very sick and will die soon, Jermaine has an opportunity to make some drawings for his grandmother, talk with her on the phone, make a special visit, and ask questions about dying. Jermaine's parents let him take the lead in asking questions as they talk over problems with him at his level of understanding and inquiry.

At the same time, Jermaine's parents have shared this information with his preschool teacher, Scott. Scott set up a hospital center in the classroom, with a stethoscope, surgical gowns and masks, a chair, and bed. He wants to provide an opportunity for Jermaine and other children to act out their feelings and to experience the hospital setting and procedures. He plans to stay close to this area when Jermaine begins playing, to assist in the play acting and to answer any questions that Jermaine might ask. This type of play setting is also helpful for children who might be entering the hospital or who have family members that are hospitalized.

Scott also will read some children's books about dying to the preschoolers. He knows that young children often assume guilt when a crisis occurs, whether it is death, divorce, family illness, or other crises. By reading books to the class, he can open up a discussion about how bad things sometimes happen, and that these bad things are not the child's fault.

In the classroom, Scott will expect Jermaine to follow his regular routine, but he knows there may need to be allowances made to allow Jermaine to express his feelings in a safe and familiar environment. Scott has suggested to Jermaine's parents that they describe the hospital room and the grandmother's appearance before Jermaine's visit. This will help him when he enters the hospital for his special visit with his grandmother.

Most of these suggestions also apply to other situations, whether they are happy changes or unhappy events. Sharing about the upcoming birth of a sibling and preparing for the baby keeps the child part of an important family event. Coping with their parents' divorce is very difficult for young children. Strategies that Scott used in Jermaine's situation are transferable to a divorce situation also. Play opportunities, absolving the child from guilt about the divorce, talking about separation, and hearing stories about other families and divorce all assist the child as he navigates through a crisis.

As a teacher or caregiver, you will have many times when one or more children in your setting are facing a major crisis or change. Most often, your role is one of support to the family as you provide opportunities for the child to face the difficult situation or change in a stable, caring environment.

Other children in need include those who need special education as part of their education program. It is estimated that 12 percent of the children in the United States between the ages of 3 and 21 receive special education services (U.S. Department of Education, 1996b). The first choice for services for these children is to be included in regular programs with other children and receive additional assistance as needed. As you know from reading Chapter 11, federal funding is available for programs for children with special needs that support their growth and development.

For instance, Shantell, a 2-year-old child at a nearby child care center, has difficulty with large muscle motor development and requires the services of a physical therapist as part of her overall educational program. She recently learned to walk but is unstable and learning how to coordinate her steps. The physical therapist might work with the staff at the center to develop a therapy program that fits the routine at Shantell's child care site. The therapist would also assist the staff in developing activities to help Shantell practice her walking skills. This arrangement would include Shantell in activities at Shantell's site and assurance that she will receive the special services appropriate to her needs.

As an early childhood professional, your attention will be drawn to children in need. The need might be related to the family's economic situation, other family situations, or the child's specific learning needs. Whether the need is temporary or ongoing, it must be addressed to help both the child and family. Let's now turn to other situations that will require your immediate attention and response.

Society and Child Abuse

A critical concern of early childhood professionals is encountering a major societal problem—the occurrence of child abuse. The following descriptions of child abuse and neglect were derived from a Children's Services Division and the State Office for Services to Children and Families publication (1995). **Child abuse** is a form of mistreatment of a child, and it might occur in the form of physical, emotional, or sexual abuse. Any physical injury to a child, other than an accident, is considered **physical abuse.** Possible physical indicators include bruises and welts, burns, lacerations, or fractures. **Emotional abuse** is harm to a child's ability to think or have feelings. Emotional or mental abuse may take the form of extreme negative language or inhumane treatment of the child, such as ridicule, threats, confinement, or torture. **Sexual abuse** includes incidents of sexual contact. **Child neglect** is when a child's basic needs are not met through negligence or maltreatment of the child. A neglected child may lack food, appropriate clothing, hygiene, medical care, or supervision by a responsible adult.

Children who suffer child abuse may take years to recover from the abuse, often carrying the pain and emotional bruises through their entire lives. Unfortunately, the incidence of child abuse and neglect continues to increase significantly, with 3.1 million children reported abused or neglected in the United States in 1994, according to the National Committee to Prevent Child Abuse (Children's Defense Fund, 1996). Again, we see is a connection between economics and social problems, as much of the increase in child abuse and neglect is attributed to economic stresses in families and to drug use (Children's Defense Fund, 1994a).

Of the 3.1 million reported cases of child abuse, 1 million were substantiated. The National Center on Child Abuse and Neglect found that among the 1 million children who were victims of *substantiated maltreatment* in 1994, 53 percent were neglected, 26 percent physically abused, 14 percent sexually abused, 5 percent emotionally abused, and 3 percent medically neglected (U.S. Department of Health and Human Services, 1996). (Because some states report more than one type of abuse per victim, the total is higher than 100 percent.)

One of these children who was reported as a victim was 6-year-old Taylor. He entered kindergarten reluctantly, seeming fearful of joining in any boisterous activity, such as playground games or group activities in the gym. His teacher thought perhaps he was quiet by nature and observed him, while also encouraging him to participate in activities where he seemed to be most comfortable. In October, Taylor was absent for several days. When he returned to school, his clothes were dirty and he was unwashed. He stayed near the door most of the morning. When his teacher talked with him about missing him while he was gone, Taylor told her he had been naughty and had to stay home. More conversations revealed that Taylor was punished frequently and made to sit in a chair for long periods of time. If he was "loud" at home, he was told that he was a bad person and left to sit in a chair in his room for hours at a time.

Taylor's teacher began writing down the information and discussed these conversations with her school principal. Within a few weeks, she felt she had enough indicators of neglect to report her findings. Later, the teacher and principal learned that Taylor's mother was battling alcohol and drug problems and spent most of her afternoons sleeping. Taylor's teacher was knowledgeable about child abuse or neglect indicators, was alert to possible signs, involved the appropriate authorities, and collected information to document her observations. She was advocating for a child's right to a healthy environment and took the responsible steps to help both Taylor and his family.

What can you do about child abuse and neglect? Child care centers and early childhood programs that meet national accreditation standards with licensed or certified staff are seen as part of the solution to ensuring that children are cared for by professionals who provide safe environments. As a child care professional, you will often be the first person to see signs of abuse and neglect. In each state, if you suspect that a child is being abused or neglected, you are legally required to report this information to the appropriate authorities. **Indicators of child abuse** are listed in Figure 12.1.

As a caregiver or teacher of young children, you carry the responsibility to report signs or symptoms of child abuse and to help the child and family during this crisis. As an early childhood professional, you will be in a position to detect signs of child abuse or neglect and advocate for any child you suspect has been abused. The effects of child abuse and neglect affect a child's learning and development. For professional, ethical, and moral reasons, teachers and caregivers are in a position to commit to the well-being of children and families. Awareness of signs and indicators of child abuse is an important step in recognizing a child in need and in assisting the child and family in gaining help.

■ FIGURE 12.1   Observational Chart of Child Behavior and Indicators of Abuse

Parent's Name _____

Child's Name _____

Date _____ Observer's Signature _____

Child:

_____ receives a lot of spankings at home

_____ complains that his/her parent is always angry

_____ comes to school early and finds reasons to stay after school as long as possible

_____ role-plays abusive parents in class or dramatizes abusive situations with puppets and toys or in artwork

_____ abuses younger children

_____ is frequently absent from school, many times with no explanations

_____ wears clothing inappropriate to the weather (usually long sleeves and pants to hide bruises)

_____ shows physical evidence of abuse (describe below)

_____ shows aggressive behavior

_____ is self-abusive or expresses suicidal ideas

Comments _____

_____

_____

_____

_____

_____

_____

_____

_____

Source: From *The Compassionate School* by Gertrude Morrow. Copyright © 1987. Reprinted with permission of The Center for Applied Research in Education/Prentice Hall.

Support for the child is essential. The following steps outline suggestions to follow if you suspect child abuse:

1. Believe the child; children rarely lie about sexual abuse.
2. Commend the child for telling you what happened.
3. Convey your support for the child. Children's greatest fear is that they are at fault and responsible for the incident.
4. Temper your own reactions, recognizing that your perspective and acceptance are critical signals to the child.
5. Report the suspected abuse to the child's parent(s), the designated social service agency and/or the police.
6. Find specialized agencies that evaluate sexual abuse victims and a physician with the experience and training to detect and recognize sexual abuse. (U.S. Department of Health and Human Services, 1986)

Although these guidelines are developed for suspected sexual abuse, they also are helpful to early childhood professionals when suspecting physical or emotional abuse of the young child. When you are in frequent contact with young children, you will often be the first person outside the family to note abuse. You have a responsibility to help the child and to help the family end the abuse and engage in the necessary social services to handle this problem.

Society and Health Issues Affecting Young Children

The United States has one of the most advanced health care systems in the world; yet, many people are unable to afford health care or insurance. One of every seven children in the United States were without health insurance in 1994 and 1995 (Children's Defense Fund, 1997). Health care reforms have been proposed by Congress, with some states adopting health care plans that provide coverage to people with low incomes. Hopefully, the trend toward increasing accessibility to health care will enable more people to afford basic care.

In 1993, only 67 percent of 2-year-olds in the United States received appropriate immunization (Children's Defense Fund, 1995), which prevents many serious illnesses. During the mid-1990s, a federal vaccine purchase initiative was implemented that provided free pediatric vaccines for all uninsured, Medicaid-eligible, or Native American children. The initiative made free vaccines available through community health centers. The Childhood Immunization Initiative went into effect in 1994 and represents society's demand for accessible health care for all children. Angela received several of her immunizations through this program at her local public health office. Again, we see evidence of economic, political, and social forces joined together to implement policy that has a great impact on young children.

Society and Homeless Children

When you think of homelessness, you might picture an adult male living on the street, spending days on a park bench next to a shopping cart piled next to his possessions. Today, families with children are the fastest growing group of homeless people, making up 39 percent of the total homeless population, with some cities finding that over 60 percent of the homeless are families with children (Children's Defense Fund, 1995). It is believed that over 100,000 children each night are homeless (Children's Defense Fund, 1997) and that one of four homeless individuals is a child under the age of 18 (Children's Defense Fund, 1995). This problem is made even more acute when many families are turned away from shelters because such shelters are not structured for families.

Children who are homeless tend to experience more severe health, developmental, and nutritional problems than other poor children. Without decent housing, it is difficult for poor families to access essential social services and obtain medical, educational, or nutritional support for the family.

If families continually move around, school attendance or participation of children in child care centers is spotty or nonexistent. It is estimated that up to 50 percent of children who are homeless and of school age do not attend school. Reasons include lack of immunization records, the feeling that they will move again soon, reluctance of the child to adjust to another group of children and teachers, or the lack of transportation to school. In some cities, schools for homeless children have become part of the shelter and social service network. These schools provide clothing, school supplies, and nutritious meals, but, most of all, they welcome children and develop school programs that fit their individual learning needs.

In 1994, Congress reauthorized the Education for Homeless Children Program, which directed local school districts to allow homeless children to attend the school that their parent requests (Children's Defense Fund, 1995). Hopefully, the attention to the needs of homeless families will increase options for children to access social, medical, and educational programs. Let's now turn our attention to another population that also needs societal support and resources.

Society and Teen Parents

During each year of the early 1990s, about 510,000 adolescent girls in the United States gave birth. Throughout this decade, a trend in this country found young women keeping their babies, rather than give them up for adoption, while at the same time opting to remain single. As a result, the proportion of teen births to unmarried teens was over 70 percent in 1992 (Children's Defense Fund, 1995). With young women taking on the responsibility of raising a child, much support is needed to ensure that both the infant and the mother continue their intellectual and healthy development. Across all countries, the unmarried adolescent mother faces grim prospects for the future (Bruce, 1995). Her schooling is often disrupted or ended, which leads to fewer employment opportunities.

Becoming a parent with the support of a spouse is stressful for most young families. There are daily (hourly) challenges dealing with the demands and needs of an infant. Teenage parents typically know less about child development, feel less positive about their role as a parents, and have less effective interactions with their infants (Sommer et al., 1993). Although these data represent statistical findings, there is belief that adolescent parents and their children can flourish when they are supported as they continue

Infants as well as young parents need nurturing to support their growth.

their education. In earlier chapters, you read about the importance of including the family in early childhood programs. With teen parents, this is critical. Teen parents need the opportunity to finish their education, with child care available for their child (preferably on site, so they can visit the child during the day) and to be involved in parent education classes and peer support groups facilitated by trained specialists. The financial and emotional support received by teen parents and their infants at this time may make the difference between the teen being able to finish school, experiencing success, and finding gainful employment to support themselves and their children.

In a situation with teen parents, the child care provider frequently finds herself nurturing both the infant and the teen parent. Teen families need support in their new role as a family unit. This support might include sharing information about child development, infant needs, and parenting skills. Teen families frequently need assistance in learning how to interact with their children. When a caregiver models comforting and nurturing behavior with teens' infants, she is providing one way for teen families to see how others interact with their children in a positive manner.

Teen parents often need help locating resources to support their continuing development and education. Continuing education and the education level of the mother affects the child's development. The child care staff at any center must be sensitive to involving the teen mother and father in the program activities.

In many cities, programs combine all of these needs within a teen parent program—that is, continued education for the teen, parenting education for the teen mother and father, support for adolescent growth, and a quality infant program. In these programs for teen parents and their children, political, economic, and social factors work together to combine resources in one setting, helping teen families access supportive services.

Society and Community Involvement with Young Children

The relationship between the child care setting or school and the community provides great potential with long-lasting impact for both the community and the children. Partnerships among senior citizens, businesses, local agencies, schools, child care centers, and community organizations create a collaboration built on providing the best possible programs for the young children in the community. For instance, the Lion's Club might hold fund-raisers to assist children needing vision care, and a public school might share a visiting nurse with a preschool. Pooling resources builds on restructuring and decreases the need for duplication of services (Washington, Johnson, & McCracken, 1995).

Sharing resources and opening up communication between agencies and organizations can lead to benefits for the entire community. Senior citizens might be interested in volunteering their time to read to young children or to help them cook or make other projects. When actively involved with young children, the senior citizen feels wanted and useful, while the children benefit from learning new skills and having an interested adult spend time with them.

Emily has invited the children's grandparents to visit during the late morning to read to the children or to simply to watch them play with each other. She wants grandparents to feel welcome and to be part of the growing-up period of their young grandchildren. Angela's grandmother stops in each Thursday, often bringing a book to read to the children. Angela looks forward to her visit, as do the other children and Grandmom.

Businesses are often interested in promoting high-quality programs for young children, realizing that these young people are their employees of the future. Businesses also recognize that the quality of the child care these children receive also affects their parents and the parents' ability to focus on their work. If an employee is worried or concerned about adequate child care or about the quality of their child's program, their attention at work is often distracted. Kent Larson understands these concerns and has offered Marie the opportunity to work at home when Angela is sick and unable to go to Emily's house. This is an example where the employer, employee, and young child all benefit from the work arrangement.

One way that businesses address the importance of early childhood programs is through volunteer work. Some businesses have initiated programs where their employees may spend several hours a week volunteering in a school or early child care program. From the standpoint of the businesses, they know they are making a difference in the preparation of their future work force. Employees are able to share and improve their expertise with the children, and the children benefit from specialized knowledge and skills brought to them. For example, two bilingual employees of a company work with a class of 4- and 5-year-olds twice a week, teaching them Spanish words and phrases. The public school plans to implement a Spanish language program in the primary grades and is eager to receive students who have already started their language study.

In 1996, a packet of information titled *America Goes Back to School: Get Involved* was sent to each school in the United States. This nationwide initiative sponsored by the U.S. Department of Education encourages schools, community members, and families to collaborate in making education better in their community. The information in the packet provides examples of activities and roles communities can play as they work to improve education. United Airlines demonstrated their interest in education by showing a video with examples of how employers and citizens can support educational improvements in their local schools to all airline travelers during September 1996 (U.S. Department of Education, 1996a).

In the larger picture, the essence of community (or village) permeates such collaborations. In this fast-paced world, where you might pass hundreds of people on the street and not recognize anyone, these community efforts help you learn about the place where you live and your common values and goals. Strong communities ensure there are safe places for children to play, recreational programs for all children, community centers for senior citizens, libraries with books for all interests, and family activities that form the core of the community. Angela, Marie, the Ponzis, and Mrs. Deluiso have celebrated the last two Fourth of July holidays by watching an annual parade consisting of neighbors, representatives from local businesses, and, of course, police officers and the fire truck. This has become an important event for their village.

Some neighborhoods in urban cities have given themselves a name (e.g., Rose City Neighbors) and hold several special events each year. The families come together and celebrate new additions to families and share common activities and events. They have found a way to create a true community spirit that supports them and their families. The essence of community enlarges the single family unit to that of a strong, caring village, similar to the one that surrounds Angela.

The people in Angela's neighborhood represent many different cultures and ethnic groups. Recognizing and appreciating diversity will be part of your role as an early childhood professional.

Society and Diversity

The world is enlarging at the same time that it is shrinking. No longer is the place where someone lives defined merely as the name of a road or an apartment building. A place of residence might be connected to many other geographic areas via television, telephone, computers, and fax machines. There is continual access to news and information from around the world. A person could just as easily talk with someone in India on an Internet chat line as walk down the hall or across the street to visit with a friend. With the expansion of access to the world and global awareness increasing, the importance of a shared world must be emphasized with young children.

It is the job of the caregiver or teacher of young children to bring a world perspective and world awareness into the curriculum (King, Chipman, & Cruz-Janzen, 1994). The world of many countries, cultures, and races is connected. Emily is aware of the different ethnic backgrounds of the children in her care. Each year, she talks to the families and asks each family to come to her home care and host one celebration connected to their cultural roots. Many of the books on her bookshelf depict children from different cultures and countries. She wants the children to be proud of their heritage and appreciate the diversity in their village.

Demographic trends.   In the early 1990s, children attending school in California depicted a new demographic trend in the United States. A majority of public school children in California and many other states are now from minority groups. Can *minority,* then, be an accurate term? The school-age population in the 50 largest cities in this country represent more children from various cultures and races than from the Caucasian race. This means that children who are non-White can no longer be labeled as *minority children,* when, in fact, they compose the majority of the population in many cities, towns, and rural areas in America. In 1995, 45 percent of the total public elementary and secondary school population was made up of children of color (U.S. Department of Education, 1997).

What does this mean to early childhood programs? Children as young as 2 or 3 years of age notice racial and gender differences and are developing their thoughts about differences among their peers. Early childhood is a wonderful time to celebrate diversity, to share many cultures, and to learn about contributions of a many ethnic and racial groups. A **diversity perspective** means bringing a positive awareness and including differences among children into the curriculum of the young child (King, Chipman, & Cruz-Janzen, 1994). Young children are open and receptive to learning about each other. These are the years when children can learn to appreciate diversity through the cultural activities and awareness that Emily promotes with the children in her care center.

Cultural pluralism.   **Cultural pluralism** refers to studying, respecting, and celebrating the contributions made by people from many cultures. Numerous benefits can be gained from learning about each other's customs, important beliefs, and traditions. Expectations for developmentally appropriate behavior and learning needs to be analyzed on an individual level to take into account the child's home experiences. Young children bring their cultures with them to their schools or centers. Children are learning through the lens of the culture they have already acquired. Acknowledging this culture and building on it affirms that this individual child is important, as is her family and her culture. Respect for diversity includes spending time learning about each child's background and family culture and then using the children's interests and experiences to develop activities (Morrison, 1995).

At the same time, the teacher or caregiver must also examine his own cultural background and be prepared to share his traditions and beliefs with the children. When educating culturally diverse children, caregivers or "teachers must be sensitive to the similarities and differences between themselves and their students and their families" (Bowman, 1994, p. 224). Emily's roots are from Israel, and she shares stories, clothing, food, and customs from her country with the children. She actively encourages the children and families to share their cultures with the group of children. She is committed to developing a social system with the children and their families (Bowman, 1994).

It is also helpful to look at your curriculum and materials as you determine whether you offer authentic situations to learn about cultures. Do you include many books and stories about children from different cultures? Are the children in these books portrayed accurately? What about your expectations for the children? Do you attempt to get to know each child on an individual level and base program decisions (including expectations for learning) on the child's interests and developmental level? All of these questions probe at the important issue of developing a developmentally appropriate curriculum around the knowledge and beliefs that the children in your care bring with them. It is important to incorporate materials and activities that show respect and interest in each child's cultural background. It is also important to review your materials for possible bias.

Emily enjoys learning about the many countries and cultures of her children as the families bring their customs to her home and to the children in her care. She finds she is also a learner when she invites families to share their traditions, celebrations, and cultures with the children. Often, grandparents, relatives, and friends will participate in events with the children, sharing their customs.

Sensitivity to a child's learning is critical to cultural pluralism. You will want the children in your care to feel positive about the diversity of cultures, find worth in all people, and believe that each person has something special to share with the group. Believing in the importance and worth of each child and her contribution to the larger group models the perspective that you hope to teach as you embrace cultural pluralism.

Bilingual education.   Providing second language instruction to children whose first language is not English is a controversial issue. As you recall from the discussion on bilingual education in Chapter 9, one perspective supports instruction in the native or home language, as this allows the child to progress academically yet retain primary language. A differing view suggests that the sooner the child learns English, the sooner she will become part of the classroom learning environment. Unfortunately, children who are taught in English only at an early age often forget their primary language and may experience difficulty with grasping concepts and understanding new ideas in an unfamiliar language.

Again, going back to the core belief that the learning of each child should be developmentally appropriate, accounting for her prior knowledge and her culture, you are better able to make sound decisions about bilingual instruction. Bilingual models that present concepts in the dominant language and then in English have been shown to be successful (Garcia & August, 1988). These programs value the child's first language while helping the child become proficient in English.

Angela has always spoken English, but Grandma and Grandpa Russo have been teaching her Italian phrases, which she loves to hear. The grandparents speak Italian most of the time, having learned English as adults. They want Angela to learn Italian so she can communicate with them as well as learn the language of her heritage.

Journal 12.7: You have a new child entering your group of 2-year-olds next week. The child is Vietnamese and has been in the United States since birth. How do you prepare for this child? What is some important information you want to gather before the child starts school? What are some resources for you in this area? ■

With regard to cultural diversity within a pluralistic society, you have the ability to influence how the young children in your care think about people from races or cultures different from their own. Modeling appreciation and awareness of diversity is essential to teaching young children to value diversity throughout their lives. The early childhood staff should also reflect the cultural composition of the children and families. Respect for cultures is shown in many forms, as modeled by Emily in her welcoming of families to share their traditions and her invitation to grandparents to become part of her program. In early childhood programs, frequent communication with families and the hiring of qualified staff that represent children of the community is essential to creating a village that values each member.

Summary of Political, Economic, and Social Influences on Early Childhood

Current trends in support for early childhood programs find political, economic, and social forces working together to promote and ensure continuity of services for young children. Upon entering the twenty-first century, the federal government is allocating some of its power and funding responsibilities to state and local levels. At the local level, you will find that programs are more likely to reflect community (or village) priorities of the local region. The federal funding has shifted from direct services to indirect assistance (Garwood et al., 1989).

Accountability for programs and for the learning of children who attend programs is important for renewed funding of government-supported programs. Changes in society, economic status of the nation, and the political agenda bring changes in the care of young children. Early childhood professionals are becoming more involved and vocal in influencing policies that support the role of families and young children's development (Goffin, 1992). Thus, the role of advocacy by early childhood professionals is critical to sustained and increased interest in the care of young children.

Advocacy: Why and How?

An **advocate** is one who understands issues and concerns in a specific field and takes an active stand, whether defending the current status or supporting changes to better the field. In this case, advocacy is discussed as taking a stance in support of high-quality early childhood programs that promote the healthy growth and development of children and their families. The intent of this chapter is to look at the influences of political, economic, and social forces on early childhood programs. You will want to bring this perspective with you while you explore what the early childhood professional can do to influence political, economic, and social agendas.

Journal 12.8: Before you begin to read about advocacy, ask yourself: What can I do as an advocate? Begin a list of everyday actions you might take as an advocate, adding to the list as you read. ■

The Child Care and Development Block Grants, passed in 1990, are an example of the influence made by a large, coordinated number of early childhood advocates. Their combined influence has resulted in policy and economic decisions that affect a substantial number of children and programs. On the national and international level, membership in professional affiliations and active participation through conferences, shared stories, and active communication have the potential to create large-scale changes in early childhood policies. The National Association for the Education of Young Children, has developed and implemented guidelines and policies for ethical conduct, professional standards, and program accreditation. These policies are noted at the national, state, and local levels. Your involvement and voice in such an organization demonstrates your commitment to your profession and to quality care for young children. This is part of being an advocate.

Modeling Advocacy

The act of advocacy as an adult models important behavior for young children; that is, it is a commitment to beliefs or causes and consequent actions that support an important cause. If you truly wish children to be able to stand up for their rights and their beliefs, you must also model this behavior. When families see you taking a stance about early childhood issues, they will recognize your commitment and dedication to improving or extending the quality of services and resources for children and families. Marie is quite aware of Emily's dedication to her work with young children and families. She knows that Emily is an advocate of her family and the other families associated with the child care program and that Emily will help them find resources or services when needed. Marie and Angela saw Emily assist a new family when the parents needed help locating a nearby health clinic. Emily has developed a file and a directory of community resources to share with families.

Advocating for Children

When you share information with a parent that helps them learn a new way to communicate with their infant, you are also demonstrating your advocacy to young children. Let's return to the story of Jodie and listen to a conversation between her preschool teacher, Karla, and her parents. As you listen, think about the role of an advocate and identify where you notice Karla assuming a child advocacy position.

Karla: Child advocate

Lynn and Jerry are concerned about Jodie's language development. The 4-year-old has been using one-word responses most of the time at home and they are concerned about her progress. Lynn and Jerry wonder if it would be helpful to have the speech and language therapist come to the preschool and work with Jodie. Karla listens to their concerns. She tells them that she hears Jodie respond with two-word phrases occasionally, particularly when she is playing in the dramatic play area. Karla tells Lynn and Jerry that she will keep a checklist for a week and record some of Jodie's responses. She will then get in touch with them and help them decide if they would like to set up a meeting with the speech and language therapist.

Karla wants to follow up on Lynn and Jerry's observations and respond to their concerns. At the same time, she knows that Jodie becomes frustrated when she is pushed to increase her sentence length. Karla, wanting what is best for Jodie, will meet with the speech and language therapist to talk about options. She will then set up a meeting for Lynn, Jerry, the speech and language therapist, and herself to discuss ways to help Jodie.

The conversation ends with Lynn and Jerry making plans to call Karla next week and planning to keep track of any two- or three-word phrases that Jodie uses spontaneously. Karla also suggests that it might be helpful to ask Jodie to share stories about her friends at school instead of asking her to say more words. The conversational context seems like a good idea to Jerry and Lynn, and they leave feeling relieved and heard.

Journal 12.9: What was something that Karla did or said that showed her advocacy for young children? As a teacher, you may have to help parents see their child in a positive light, yet also respond to their concerns about the child. How did Karla do this? ■

Child advocacy assumes different shapes and roles. You can find many opportunities throughout a day to support the learning and development of young children, just as Karla did in her brief conversation with Jodie's parents. When you work with parents, you might think of ways to "educate and empower parents" about child development by sharing articles and news clippings (Patton, 1993). You will encounter opportunities in both your personal and professional life to advocate for children. At this point in your professional development, you may feel uncertain about how to fulfill that role. In the next section, you will find a discussion of specific actions you might take to declare yourself a children's advocate.

Becoming a Children's Champion

Throughout this book, you have seen numerous references to the National Association for the Education of Young Children and the policies and actions pursued by the organization to improve early childhood experiences for each and every child. NAEYC (1995) outlines five steps that anyone can take to advocate for children and become a children's champion.

1. The first step is to speak out on behalf of children by communicating information about the necessity for quality experiences for young children. You can do this with friends, colleagues, legislators, letters to the local paper, or community leaders. Your opinion and voice can carry important information to people in a position to make decisions, whether as a voter or a politician.

2. The second step looks at helping one child beyond your family. Perhaps you live in a neighborhood where several school-age children are home alone after school or in the early evening. This might be an opportunity for you to ask the family if you could plan an activity for their child one evening a week. Your time and energy with this child can make a difference to the child and to you as you participate in that child's development.

3. The third step takes you back to the focus on political forces influencing early childhood. Be an informed voter in your community—research the decisions and stances that different public officials advocate for young children. Legislative decisions affect the funding and availability of early childhood programs and services (e.g., welfare reform). Your vote and your voice is important to elected officials in making changes that support the growth and development of young children.

4. The fourth step asks you to explore the service opportunities within the organizations of which you are a member. Perhaps your church or club could raise funds for equipment for a child care center or volunteer to work two hours a month at a local school. Often, the suggestion of helping a neighborhood school, park, or child care center is enough to get others excited about the possibilities. These actions create a potential for new partnerships to benefit young children.

5. The last step asks you to encourage others to join you in supporting young children and the availability of services and resources for young children. When you watch volunteers at a natural disaster sight, such as setting up a water bucket line to put out fires, you can see how many hands help alter impossible circumstances. The same is true with joined efforts and voices working together to advocate for young children. When you gather a group of friends together to prepare a garden plot for a nearby preschool program, you will likely enjoy the experience of working together. Beyond that, you are making a contribution. Watching the children planting and tending their vegetable plants promotes an even greater satisfaction in your advocacy role.

Committing yourself to implementing these five steps creates more children's champions—people who are willing to stand up for the rights and welfare of children. Working together to "focus on a vision of high-quality learning opportunities for young children—and act individually and collectively to achieve that vision—the more our children and society will benefit" (NAEYC, 1995, p. 8). By following these steps, you will build a better world for yourself as well as for children, creating a stronger village.

Advocacy is an essential element of professionalism. What is professionalism? How do you become a professional? These questions are addressed in the next section.

Professionalism in Early Childhood Education

You have read about the political, economic, and social forces influencing young children and the priority given to their care and development in today's world. You have also learned of some ways to advocate for improved conditions for children and for the profession of early childhood education. Now let's take some time to discuss professionalism and how one continues to grow in this profession.

Professionalism

Attributes connected to someone considered to be a **professional** are educated, knowledgeable, committed to her profession, completion of a specialized course of study, and in possession of a knowledge base essential to her specialty area. These terms might be used when describing a doctor, accountant, counselor, or teacher. Whatever the profession, there are certain standards of criteria to be met prior to becoming a professional.

Perhaps one of the more critical criteria of a professional is that of possessing specialized skills and knowledge. The erroneous belief that most anyone can work with young children must be eradicated. This belief should be replaced with the knowledge that there is a strong relationship found between higher-quality programs for young children and early childhood providers who have received specialized training in their field (Bredekamp & Willer, 1993). Emily wants to continue to learn about helping toddlers with their language development. She has contacted the local community college and is taking a course this term called Language Acquisition. She found that many of the readings and course sessions relate directly to her interactions with her children, and she has made changes in her communication patterns to promote their language development.

Continued professional development. As you begin your journey into early childhood education, you might be wondering about the meaning of professionalism and how this relates to different careers in early childhood. In Chapter 1, we presented Figure 1.2, Definitions of Early Childhood: Professional Categories on page 22. This is a good time to review this figure, now that you have experienced the five early childhood programs and observed many different professionals interacting with children.

There are many different roles within the early childhood profession. As you noticed in Figure 1.2, practitioners might have a minimum of education in the profession at the entry level, in the role of teacher assistant. Each of the roles requires different levels of preparation and professionalism. At the same time that NAEYC is considering requirements for increased preparation for all professionals, individual states are also examining licenses and standards for those working with young children. You are apt to see many changes in the requirements for licensure in the coming years.

Child Development Associate credential. The National Association for the Education of Young Children has also developed a credential for those who meet specific criteria in their work in early childhood. When you have demonstrated that you have met the competency standards outlined by the Child Development Associate Consortium, you are eligible for the Child Development Associate (CDA) credential (see Table 12.1 on page 490). These competencies reflect important skills and a knowledge base necessary for those who work with young children. Many programs, including Head Start, require their professionals to hold a CDA credential.

■ TABLE 12.1 CDA Competency Goals and Functional Areas

CDA Competency Goals	Functional Areas
I. To establish and maintain a safe, learning environment.	**1.** *Safe:* Candidate provides a safe environment to prevent and reduce injuries. **2.** *Healthy:* Candidate promotes good health and nutrition and provides an environment that contributes to the prevention of illness. **3.** *Learning Environment:* Candidate uses space, relationships, materials, and routines as resources for constructing an interesting, secure, and enjoyable environment that encourages play, exploration, and learning.
II. To advance physical and intellectual competence.	**4.** *Physical:* Candidate provides a variety of equipment, activities, and opportunities to promote the physical development of children. **5.** *Cognitive:* Candidate provides activities and opportunities that encourage curiosity, exploration, and problem-solving appropriate to the developmental tasks and learning styles of children. **6.** *Communication:* Candidate actively communicates with children and provides opportunities and support for children to understand, acquire, and use verbal and nonverbal means of communicating thoughts and feelings. **7.** *Creative:* Candidate provides opportunities that stimulate children to play with sound, rhythm, language, materials, space and ideas in individual ways and to express their creative abilities.
III. To support social and emotional development and to provide positive guidance.	**8.** *Self:* Candidate provides physical and emotional security for each child and helps each child to know, accept and take pride in himself or herself and to develop a sense of independence. **9.** *Social:* Candidate helps each child feel accepted in the group, helps children learn how to communicate and get along with others, and encourages feelings of empathy and mutual respect among children and adults. **10.** *Guidance:* Candidate provides a supportive environment in which children can begin to learn and practice appropriate and acceptable behaviors as individuals and as a group.
IV. To establish positive and productive relationships with families.	**11.** *Families:* Candidate maintains an open, friendly, and cooperative relationship with each child's family, encourages their involvement in the program, and support the child's relationship with his or her family.
V. To ensure a well-run purposeful program responsive to participant needs.	**12.** *Program Management:* Candidate is a manager who uses all available resources to ensure an effective operation. Candidate is a competent organizer, planner, record keeper, communicator, and cooperative co-worker.
VI. To maintain a commitment to professionalism.	**13.** *Professionalism:* Candidate makes decisions based on knowledge of early childhood theories and practices. Candidate promotes quality in child care services. Candidate takes advantage of opportunities to improve competence, both for personal and professional growth and for the benefit of children and families.

Source: Reprinted by permission of the Council for Early Childhood Professional Recognition.
The Child Development Associate Assessment System and Competency Standards.

Becoming a Professional

So, you finish a course of study and are awarded a certificate or credential. Does this mean you are now a professional? And does this mean you have reached the end of your education?

When are you a professional? Becoming a professional takes dedication and commitment to the profession. This commitment begins during your course of study but becomes much more apparent when you begin your first career job with young children. Your learning from your courses and your field experiences will guide you in your planning, decision making, and interactions with children, families, and colleagues. But you will also develop many new questions. Perhaps this is the key to defining a true professional—one who considers herself "unfinished" and acknowledges that she has much more to learn. Your continued thirst for knowledge and your commitment to reading and reflecting on your work is part of being a professional.

Journal 12.10: As you think back to several of the early childhood professionals throughout this book, recall some of their professional activities and how their commitment to the profession translated into actions. Describe several ways that these professionals demonstrated their continued education or professional growth. ■

A look at one teacher's commitment to professionalism. Let's go back to Chapter 1, where you met Robin, the teacher of a multiage first/second-grade class, and take a look

These teachers model a commitment to lifelong learning as they participate in a college course for educators.

at professionalism through her work. Remember her dining room table that was covered with books, journals, and catalogs related to early childhood education? Recall her frequent conversations with other early childhood professionals about teaching, child development, and advocacy within the profession? Robin is committed to learning more and becoming the best teacher that she can be, even after 25 years of teaching. She is already considered an outstanding teacher and has received numerous awards and recognition for her teaching and dedication to her students.

Robin is not satisfied with the status quo; she wants to find more ways to reach her students and promote their successful learning. She enrolls in courses and workshops, and is a member of a study group that meets to share successful classroom practices as well as to help each other through struggles. Her students are fortunate. Not only do they have an exceptional teacher but they are also exposed to a model of lifelong learning. Robin brings innovative ideas to the classroom, shares her work with her students and their parents, and invites their input into her professional growth. You will want to remember some of her thoughts and priorities as you develop your own personal philosophy of early childhood education.

Developing and Assessing Your Personal Philosophy of Education

What do you think is important in developing a good environment for optimal learning and development for children in your care? What do you want these children to leave with at the end of their time with you? What are important characteristics of an effective early childhood professional? The answers to these questions will grow from your personal philosophy of working with young children, and your personal philosophy will evolve with your experiences and your continuing education.

Each day you work with young children, you are putting your philosophy into practice. Taking time to carefully think through your philosophy helps you make some tough decisions. Many professionals find it helpful to keep a journal to record their thoughts about their personal philosophy and their interactions with children and their families that emerge from their philosophy. Hopefully, your journal work here will begin a daily practice for you.

Articulating your thoughts or personal philosophy with someone you respect in your field is an excellent way to become more aware of your philosophy and to ensure that your actions really do reflect your beliefs. Working with young children is an important career—one that requires professionals who are willing to take the time and effort to examine their beliefs, biases, and goals for their work with children.

Taking time to reflect on your day also helps you make changes to improve your work and to congratulate yourself on good decisions that affect children in a positive way. You will also enjoy your work more when you add an intellectual dimension instead of merely reacting or going through an established routine. Making conscious choices and thoughtful decisions based on your personal philosophy of what is best for young children improves both your professional work and your programs for children. This is an essential element of both professional growth and professionalism. Another aspect of professionalism has been alluded to throughout these discussions. Continuing education provides new learning and extensions of your prior knowledge as you grow in your profession.

Continuing Education

The knowledge and experiences you bring to your first job in early childhood will form the foundation of your knowledge base. As you learn more from your experiences, you will also want to develop a continuing education plan for yourself. If you are employed at a large organization or a public school, topics of staff development might be selected by the school, with room for personal choices supported through tuition reimbursement programs. In smaller programs, such as Emily's child care program, you might need to actively seek further learning opportunities. These learning opportunities are available at national or local conferences, courses at a local community college, distance education programs through state agencies, or special programs offered on weekends.

Often, students of early childhood education have questions or interests in topics that were not included in their preparation. Perhaps you will find that you need more development in certain areas. Discussions about your personal development plans should occur with your supervisor or colleagues, helping you identify programs or courses that would assist you in gaining the knowledge you are seeking. Emily has a friend who is also involved in child care. She gets together with her friend about once a month to discuss their activities, plans, challenges, and changes they would like to make. Emily finds the interaction and support essential to her professional development. She appreciates having someone to share ideas with and to learn from in her career.

Remember Karla, Jodie's preschool teacher? Karla had limited experience working with children with special needs and wanted to learn more to help her be successful in teaching these children. She discussed her personal learning needs with her supervisor and found that the local community college offered two courses in special education that were of interest to her. The preschool agreed to pay 75 percent of the tuition for these courses, because they realize that Karla's knowledge would benefit the school. Karla also planned to visit two other preschools that were known to have model inclusion programs. Having Jodie in her class prompted Karla to create her professional development plan.

One word of advice: No one is expected to know everything all at once. You will have many years to continue learning and trying out new ideas with the children in your care. However, it is helpful to develop a written professional development plan that assesses your areas of strengths and the areas that you wish to strengthen. Sharing and discussing your plans with your colleagues and your supervisor will enable you to identify areas of professional development and will provide a format for exchanging ideas and knowledge.

Your continuing education will most likely focus on your professional development goals and result in an expanding knowledge base. Right now, as you begin your studies in early childhood education, you might wonder about expectations for ethical behavior within your profession as well as guidelines or standards that guide moral and ethical decisions.

Professional Ethics

In 1998, the National Association for the Education of Young Children Association approved a revised Code of Ethical Conduct, which provides guidelines for those who work with young children (see the appendix at the end of this book). These guidelines reflect a shared commitment of professional responsibility within the spirit of helping children and their families develop to their fullest potential.

One of the qualities or attributes expected of a professional is a commitment to ethical endeavors, as indicated in the Code of Ethical Conduct. The code establishes expectations or guidelines of professional responsibilities for early childhood professionals to follow within your relationships with children, families, colleagues, and the larger community and society (Spodek & Saracho, 1994).

Perhaps one of the more important guidelines to use in your work is to always consider the impact of your decisions on the child or children with whom you are working. Thinking in terms of what is best for the child helps you focus on each child's particular needs and shape your decisions to improve circumstances for that child. For example, let's say that during outside playtime, you find that Raul is "clingy" and wants to stay near you. You know that his parents are considering a separation and that life at home is tense for the family. Normally, you might encourage Raul to become involved in an activity with other children, but you sense that his clinging to you is a security need, as you represent a comforting adult in his life. Your decision to spend extra time with him right now and also to let his parents know that their interactions with him are important is based on what you think is best for Raul at this time in his life.

Journal 12.11: You are standing in line at a local fast-food restaurant. Behind you is a young mother with an infant and a toddler. The toddler is moving around the restaurant and the mother continually calls him back to her. She is growing agitated and sounds angry when she says, "Get back here now." What might you do in this situation? ■

As an early childhood education professional, you will face many ethical decisions on a daily basis. Having some guidelines and a framework to operate from in order to feel that you are doing your best at helping your children learn and develop will assist you greatly. The NAEYC Code of Ethical Conduct provides these important guidelines that should become part of your knowledge base as an early childhood professional. Another component of professionalism is becoming part of a professional organization, such as the NAEYC.

Professional Affiliations

Becoming an active member of a professional organization and having your voice heard is important in any profession. Early childhood education is in an evolving process of shaping programs and establishing certification and accreditation standards. Joining an organization that promotes thoughtful advancement of the state of young children demonstrates your commitment to children and to programs for children and their families. Most of the professional organizations sponsor conferences and publish journals with practical ideas for working with young children along with current research findings in the profession.

Professional organizations.   The National Association for the Education of Young Children is one of the largest organizations in early childhood education and is active in promoting high standards for program accreditation and for the quality of early childhood care. NAEYC also publishes two journals, *Young Children* and *Early Childhood Research Quarterly,* and sponsors an annual conference. Related regional conferences and workshops are offered across the country to promote professional development.

The World Organization for Early Education (also known as OMEP) works with the United Nations Educational, Scientific, and Cultural Organization (UNESCO) to support the improvement of young children's needs in the areas of education, development, health, and nutrition. This organization publishes *The International Journal of Early Childhood Education.*

The Association for Childhood International (ACEI) publishes two journals, *Childhood Education* and *Journal of Research in Childhood Education,* and sponsors an annual conference. This organization is concerned with improving education, programs, and practices for young children and supporting the professional development of teachers.

Each of these organizations provide numerous possibilities for learning more about early childhood, programs in early childhood, and professional growth opportunities. Joining one or more of these professional organizations is a way for you to stay informed in your profession and keep current with knowledge, issues, concerns, and research that affect early childhood. They are well worth your financial investment. The organizations keep the dues at a reasonable level to accommodate the varied range of salaries in the early childhood education profession.

Emily is a member of NAEYC and receives their journal, *Young Children.* She often finds ideas to use in her program, which means that Angela benefits from the articles in the journal. Even the professional association of NAEYC has become part of Angela's village.

Program accreditation.   Another area affected by professional organizations is accreditation of early childhood programs. Early childhood programs may seek accreditation from the NAEYC's National Academy of Early Childhood Programs. National accreditation is a voluntary process in which a center's administrators, staff, and parents join with representatives of the national Academy of Early Childhood Programs to determine whether the center's program meets the criteria for high-quality early childhood programs (Rutledge, 1995a).

You might be thinking, Why would a center want to spend the time and money to go through the accreditation process? Rutledge (1995b) presents several responses to this question:

1. National Accreditation provides recognition by our Early Childhood profession that the program is one of the best in the nation and meets high quality standards.

2. It is a staff development tool that helps staff recognize there their work is outstanding and areas where improvement it needed.

3. The center director is provided with effective ways to administer the program.

4. Accreditation confirms to the parents that their choice for their child's education was right.

These statements strongly support the rationale for working toward and attaining national accreditation.

Summary of Professionalism

There are high expectations of professionals in early childhood education—and there should be. You will be entrusted with the care of young children, along with the expectation that you will create and sustain a rich, nurturing environment. This is a significant role, and one that touches many young lives as it builds the future.

Professional organizations provide support, research, dissemination of knowledge, and implementation of guidelines for the profession of early childhood educators. Working together with other professionals also helps you expand your knowledge base and learn from others in the profession. Joining a professional organization is another avenue in voicing your support for the future of young children and their families.

PRINCIPLES AND INSIGHTS: A Summary and Review

The African proverb woven throughout this chapter. "It takes a village to raise a child," serves as a reminder that we all play an essential role in raising young children in a healthy environment. This proverb advocates for a society that values children and recognizes the importance of providing for the emotional, physical, and intellectual development of each and every child.

Federal, state, and local policies clearly have an impact on the availability of programs and resources for young children and their families. Your vote and your interest in politics can significantly affect young children. As national policy and control is shifted to local efforts, your voice can make a difference to the young children in your village.

A nation's economy is only as strong as its people and their work skills. At a very young age, children begin learning some of the basic principles and values needed in the workplace. As an early childhood professional, you will be creating environments where these skills can be practiced and valued. You will also have the opportunity to share with others the rationale for early childhood program on an economic level. Again, your active role with young children will contribute to strengthening and supporting your community or village.

Many of today's social issues have a direct impact on young children. Educational reform, need for health care, homelessness, and increasing diversity are some of the social issues we are currently experiencing. The early childhood professional who is knowledgeable about political, economic, and social issues and who advocates for resources and support for young children contributes to the well-being of his or her village.

When you enter the early childhood profession, you will be joining thousands of other professionals committed to improving their villages for the sake of young children. You've already begun the process of building that "best possible world" by choosing to study early childhood education. The more you learn about children and families, the better able you will be to contribute to the village goal: the well-being of children and of us all.

Becoming an Early Childhood Professional

Your Field Experiences

1. Interview a pediatric nurse or a pediatrician about the incidence of child abuse in your community. Some questions you might ask include the following:
   a. What are some signs or symptoms that alert you to the possibility of child abuse?
   b. What do you do if a child asks you to keep the abuse confidential?
   c. Have you had teachers or caregivers talk to you about suspected child abuse to confirm their suspicions?
   d. What recommendations do you have for early childhood educators regarding observing signs of child abuse?

2. Observe a program for teen parents in your community. How does this program help teen parents with their role as new parents as well as with their education? Where are the young children during the time the teens are in the program? What roles are there for volunteers in this program?

Your Professional Portfolio

1. In Journal 12.1, you were asked to find the names of your state representatives and legislators. Write a letter to one of these politicians, advocating for a personal area of interest within the field of early childhood education. Include a copy of this letter in your portfolio.

2. Interview a teacher or caregiver who you admire and who works with young children. Perhaps you could visit, write to, or call a teacher from your childhood. Ask that person about attributes or qualities that she or he associates with a professional in early childhood. What suggestions does this person have regarding steps a beginner can take when starting the journey of professionalism? Record the ideas gained from this early childhood specialist, along with your thoughts about what makes this person exceptional.

Your Professional Library

Books

Flaxman, E., & Parsow, A. (Eds.). (1995). *Changing populations, changing schools.* Chicago: University of Chicago Press.

Goffin, S., & Lombardi, J. (1988). *Speaking out: Early childhood advocacy.* Washington, DC: NAEYC.

Helfer, M., Kempe, R., & Krugman, R. (Eds.). (1997). *The battered child* (5th ed., rev. and expanded). Chicago: University of Chicago Press.

Koralek, D. (1992). *Caregivers of young children: Preventing and responding to child maltreatment.* Washington, DC: U.S. Department of Health and Human Services, Administration on Children, Youth, and Families, National Center on Child Abuse and Neglect.

Kozol, J. (1991). *Savage inequalities: Children in America's schools.* New York: Crown.

Tower, C. (1989). *Understanding child abuse and neglect.* Boston: Allyn & Bacon.

Ward, J., & Anthony, P. (1992). *Who pays for student diversity?* Thousand Oaks, CA: Corwin.

Whitcomb, D. (1992). *When the victim is a child: Issues and practices in criminal justice.* Cambridge, MA: Abt Associates.

Internet Addresses and World Wide Web Sites

www.ed.gov.
   Federal government web site, with numerous education topics

www.america-tomorrow.com/naeyc/pubaff.htm
   NAEYC Public Affairs: Latest Information to Strengthen Public Policy

www.ed.gov./legislation/GOALS2000/index.html
   Current reports and information on the Goals 2000 project

inet.ed.gov/Family/ParentCtrs/prevent.html
   Prevent Child Abuse, Parent Information and Resource Centers

www.nch.ari.net/edimpact.html
   Impact of Budget Cuts on Homeless Children

www.abacom.com/books/ab 0205120466.html
   Issues and Advocacy in Early Education

www.naeyc.org/naeyc
   National Association for the Education of Young Children

www.udel.edu/bateman/acei
   Association for Childhood Education International

The National Association for the Education of Young Children: Code of Ethical Conduct

PREAMBLE

NAEYC recognizes that many daily decisions required of those who work with young children are of a moral and ethical nature. The NAEYC Code of Ethical Conduct offers guidelines for responsible behavior and sets forth a common basis for resolving the principal ethical dilemmas encountered in early childhood education. The primary focus is on daily practice with children and their families in programs for children from birth to 8 years of age, such as infant/toddler programs, preschools, child care centers, family day care homes, kindergartens, and primary classrooms. Many of the provisions also apply to specialists who do not work directly with children, including program administrators, parent and vocational educators, college professors, and child care licensing specialists.

Core Values

Standards of ethical behavior in early childhood education are based on commitment to core values that are deeply rooted in the history of our field. We have committed ourselves to

- Appreciating childhood as a unique and valuable stage of the human life cycle
- Basing our work with children on knowledge of child development
- Appreciating and supporting the close ties between the child and family
- Recognizing that children are best understood and supported in the context of family, culture, community, and society
- Respecting the dignity, worth, and uniqueness of each individual (child, family member, and colleague)
- Helping children and adults achieve their full potential in the context of relationships that are based on trust, respect, and positive regard

Source: Copyright 1998 by NAEYC. Reprinted with permission from the National Association for the Education of Young Children.

Conceptual Framework

The Code sets forth a conception of our professional responsibilities in four sections, each addressing an arena of professional relationships: (1) children, (2) families, (3) colleagues, and (4) community and society. Each section includes an introduction to the primary responsibilities of the early childhood practitioner in that arena, a set of ideals pointing in the direction of exemplary professional practice, and a set of principles defining practices that are required, prohibited, and permitted.

The ideals reflect the aspirations of practitioners. **The principles** are intended to guide conduct and assist practitioners in resolving ethical dilemmas encountered in the field. There is not necessarily a corresponding principle for each ideal. Both ideals and principles are intended to direct practitioners to those questions which, when responsibly answered, will provide the basis for conscientious decisionmaking. While the Code provides specific direction for addressing some ethical dilemmas, many others will require the practitioner to combine the guidance of the Code with sound professional judgment.

The ideals and principles in this Code present a shared conception of professional responsibility that affirms our commitment to the core values of our field. The Code publicly acknowledges the responsibilities that we in the field have assumed and in so doing supports ethical behavior in our work. Practitioners who face ethical dilemmas are urged to seek guidance in the applicable parts of this Code and in the spirit that informs the whole.

Ethical Dilemmas Always Exist

Often "the right answer"—the best ethical course of action to take—is not obvious. There may be no readily apparent, positive way to handle a situation. One important value may contradict another. When we are caught "on the horns of a dilemma," it is our professional responsibility to consult with all relevant parties in seeking the most ethical course of action to take.

SECTION I:
ETHICAL RESPONSIBILITIES TO CHILDREN

Childhood is a unique and valuable stage in the life cycle. Our paramount responsibility is to provide safe, healthy, nurturing, and responsive settings for children. We are committed to supporting children's development respecting individual differences, helping children learn to live and work cooperatively, and promoting health, self-awareness, competency, self-worth, and resiliency.

Ideals:

I-1.1   To be familiar with the knowledge base of early childhood care and education and to keep current through continuing education and in-service training.

I-1.2   To base program practices upon current knowledge in the field of child development and related disciplines and upon particular knowledge of each child.

I-1.3   To recognize and respect the uniqueness and the potential of each child.

I-1.4   To appreciate the special vulnerability of children.

I-1.5   To create and maintain safe and healthy settings that foster children's social, emotional, intellectual, and physical development and that respect their dignity and their contributions.

I-1.6   To support the right of each child to play and learn in inclusive early childhood programs to the fullest extent consistent with the best interests of all involved. As with adults who are disabled in the larger community, children with disabilities are ideally served in the same settings in which they would participate if they did not have a disability.

I-1.7   To ensure that children with disabilities have access to appropriate and convenient support services and to advocate for the resources necessary to provide the most appropriate settings for all children.

Principles:

P-1.1   Above all, we shall not harm children. We shall not participate in practices that are disrespectful, degrading, dangerous, exploitative, intimidating, emotionally damaging, or physically harmful to children. *This principle has precedence over all others in this Code.*

P-1.2   We shall not participate in practices that discriminate against children by denying benefits, giving special advantages, or excluding them from programs or activities on the basis of their race, ethnicity, religion, sex, national origin, language, ability, or the status, behavior, or beliefs of their parents. (This principle does not apply to programs that have a lawful mandate to provide services to a particular population of children.)

P-1.3   We shall involve all of those with relevant knowledge (including staff and parents) in decisions concerning a child.

P-1.4   For every child we shall implement adaptations in teaching strategies, learning environments, and curricula, consult with the family, and seek recommendations from appropriate specialists to maximize the potential of the child to benefit from the program. If, after these efforts have been made to work with a child and family, the child does not appear to be benefiting from a program, or the child is seriously jeopardizing the ability of other children to benefit from the program, we shall communicate with the family and appropriate specialists to determine the child's current needs, identify the setting and services most suited to meeting these needs, and assist the family in placing the child in an appropriate setting.

P-1.5   We shall be familiar with the symptoms of child abuse, including physical, sexual, verbal, and emotional abuse, and neglect. We shall know and follow state laws and community procedures that protect children against abuse and neglect.

P-1.6 When we have reasonable cause to suspect child abuse or neglect, we shall report the evidence to the appropriate community agency and follow up to ensure that appropriate action has been taken. When appropriate, parents or guardians will be informed that the referral has been made.

P-1.7 When another person tells us of their suspicion that a child is being abused or neglected. we shall assist that person in taking appropriate action to protect the child.

P-1.8 When a child protective agency fails to provide adequate protection for abused or neglected children, we acknowledge a collective ethical responsibility to work toward improvement of these services.

P-1.9 When we become aware of a practice or situation that endangers the health or safety of children, but has not been previously known to do so, we have an ethical responsibility to inform those who can remedy the situation and who can protect children from similar danger.

SECTION II:
ETHICAL RESPONSIBILITIES TO FAMILIES

Families are of primary importance in children's development. (The term *family* may include others, besides parents, who are responsibly involved with the child.) Because the family and the early childhood practitioner have a common interest in the child's welfare, we acknowledge a primary responsibility to bring about collaboration between the home and school in ways that enhance the child's development.

Ideals:

I-2.1 To develop relationships of mutual trust with the families we serve.

I-2.2 To acknowledge and build upon strengths and competencies as we support families in their task of nurturing children.

I-2.3 To respect the dignity of each family and its culture, customs, and beliefs.

I-2.4 To respect families' childrearing values and their right to make decisions for their children.

I-2.5 To interpret each child's progress to parents within the framework of a developmental perspective and to help families understand and appreciate the value of developmentally appropriate early childhood programs.

I-2.6 To help family members improve their understanding of their children and to enhance their skills as parents.

I-2.7   To participate in building support networks for families by providing them with opportunities to interact with program staff, other families, community resources, and professional services.

Principles:

P-2.1   We shall not deny family members access to their child's classroom or program setting.

P-2.2   We shall inform families of program philosophy, policies, and personnel qualifications, and explain why we teach as we do—which should be in accordance with our ethical responsibilities to children (see Section I).

P-2.3   We shall inform families of and, when appropriate, involve them in policy decisions.

P-2.4   We shall involve families in significant decisions affecting their child.

P-2.5   We shall inform the family of accidents involving their child, of risks such as exposures to contagious disease that may result in infection, and of occurrences that might result in emotional stress.

P-2.6   To improve the quality of early childhood care and education, we shall cooperate with qualified child development researchers. Families shall be fully informed of any proposed research projects involving their children and shall have the opportunity to give or withhold consent without penalty. We shall not permit or participate in research that could in any way hinder the education, development, or well-being of children.

P-2.7   We shall not engage in or support exploitation of families. We shall not use our relationship with a family for private advantage or personal gain, or enter into relationships with family members that might impair our effectiveness in working with children.

P-2.8   We shall develop written policies for the protection of confidentiality and the disclosure of children's records. These policy documents shall be made available to all program personnel and families. Disclosure of children's records beyond family members, program personnel, and consultants having an obligation of confidentiality shall require familial consent (except in cases of abuse or neglect).

P-2.9   We shall maintain confidentiality and shall respect the family's right to privacy, refraining from disclosure of confidential information and intrusion into family life. However, when we have reason to believe that a child's welfare is at risk, it is permissible to share confidential information with agencies and individuals who may be able to intervene in the child's interest.

P-2.10   In cases where family members are in conflict, we shall work openly, sharing our observations of the child, to help all parties involved make informed decisions. We shall refrain from becoming an advocate for one party.

P-2.11   We shall be familiar with and appropriately use community resources and professional services that support families. After a referral has been made, we shall follow up to ensure that services have been appropriately provided.

SECTION III:
ETHICAL RESPONSIBILITIES TO COLLEAGUES

In a caring, cooperative workplace, human dignity is respected, professional satisfaction is promoted, and positive relationships are modeled. Based upon our core values, our primary responsibility in this arena is to establish and maintain settings and relationships that support productive work and meet professional needs. The same ideals that apply to children are inherent in our responsibilities to adults.

A—Responsibilities to Co-Workers
Ideals:

I-3A.1   To establish and maintain relationships of respect, trust, and cooperation with co-workers.

I-3A.2   To share resources and information with co-workers.

I-3A.3   To support co-workers in meeting their professional needs and in their professional development.

I-3A.4   To accord co-workers due recognition of professional achievement.

Principles:

P-3A.1   When we have concern about the professional behavior of a co-worker, we shall first let that person know of our concern, in a way that shows respect for personal dignity and for the diversity to be found among staff members, and then attempt to resolve the matter collegially.

P-3A.2   We shall exercise care in expressing views regarding the personal attributes or professional conduct of co-workers. Statements should be based on firsthand knowledge and relevant to the interests of children and programs.

B—Responsibilities to Employers
Ideals:

I-3B.1   To assist the program in providing the highest quality of service

I-3B.2   To do nothing that diminishes the reputation of the program in which we work unless it is violating laws and regulations designed to protect children or the provisions of this Code.

Principles:

P-3B.1   When we do not agree with program policies, we shall first attempt to effect change through constructive action within the organization.

P-3B.2   We shall speak or act on behalf of an organization only when authorized. We shall take care to acknowledge when we are speaking for the organization and when we are expressing a personal judgment.

P-3B.3   We shall not violate laws or regulations designed to protect children and shall take appropriate action consistent with this Code when aware of such violations.

C—Responsibilities to Employees

Ideals:

I-3C.1   To promote policies and working conditions that foster mutual respect, competence, well-being, and positive self-esteem in staff members.

I-3C.2   To create a climate of trust and candor that will enable staff to speak and act in the best interest of children, families, and the field of early childhood care and education.

I-3C.3   To strive to secure equitable compensation (salary and benefits) for those who work with or on behalf of young children.

Principles:

P-3C.1   In decisions concerning children and programs, we shall appropriately utilize the education, training, experience, and expertise of staff members.

P-3C.2   We shall provide staff members with safe and supportive working conditions that permit them to carry out their responsibilities, timely and nonthreatening evaluation procedures, written grievance procedures, constructive feedback, and opportunities for continuing professional development and advancement.

P-3C.3   We shall develop and maintain comprehensive written personnel policies that define program standards and, when applicable, that specify the extent to which employees are accountable for their conduct outside the workplace. These policies shall be given to new staff members and shall be available for review by all staff members.

P-3C.4   Employees who do not meet program standards shall be informed of areas of concern and, when possible, assisted in improving their performance.

P-3C.5 Employees who are dismissed shall be informed of the reasons for the termination. When a dismissal is for cause, justification must be based on evidence of inadequate or inappropriate behavior that is accurately documented, current, and available for the employee to review.

P-3C.6 In making evaluations and recommendations, judgments shall be based on fact and relevant to the interests of children and programs.

P-3C.7 Hiring and promotion shall be based solely on a person's record of accomplishment and ability to carry out the responsibilities of the position.

P-3C.8 In hiring, promotion, and provision of training, we shall not participate in any form of discrimination based on race, ethnicity, religion, gender, national origin, culture, disability, age, or sexual preference. We shall be familiar with and observe laws and regulations that pertain to employment discrimination.

SECTION IV:
ETHICAL RESPONSIBILITIES TO COMMUNITY AND SOCIETY

Early childhood programs operate within a context of an immediate community made up of families and other institutions concerned with children's welfare. Our responsibilities to the community are to provide programs that meet its needs, to cooperate with agencies and professions that share responsibility for children, and to develop needed programs that are not currently available. Because the larger society has a measure of responsibility for the welfare and protection of children, and because of our specialized expertise in child development, we acknowledge an obligation to serve as a voice for children everywhere.

Ideals:

I-4.1 To provide the community with high-quality (age and individually appropriate, and culturally and socially sensitive) education/care programs and services.

1-4.2 To promote cooperation among agencies and interdisciplinary collaboration among professions concerned with the welfare of young children, their families, and their teachers.

I-4.3 To work, through education, research, and advocacy, toward an environmentally safe world in which all children receive adequate health care, food, and shelter, are nurtured and live free from violence.

I-4.4 To work, through education, research, and advocacy, toward a society in which all young children have access to high-quality education/care programs.

I-4.5 To promote knowledge and understanding of young children and their needs. To work toward greater social acknowledgment of children's rights and greater social acceptance of responsibility for their well-being.

I-4.6 To support policies and laws that promote the well-being of children and families, to oppose those that impair their well-being. To participate in developing policies and laws that are needed, and to cooperate with other individuals and groups in these efforts.

I-4.7 To further the professional development of the field of early childhood care and education and to strengthen its commitment to realizing its core values as reflected in this Code.

Principles:

P-4.1 We shall communicate openly and truthfully about the nature and extent of services that we provide.

P-4.2 We shall not accept or continue to work in positions for which we are personally unsuited or professionally unqualified. We shall not offer services that we do not have the competence, qualifications, or resources to provide.

P-4.3 We shall be objective and accurate in reporting the knowledge upon which we base our program practices.

P-4.4 We shall cooperate with other professionals who work with children and their families.

P-4.5 We shall not hire or recommend for employment any person whose competence, qualifications, or character makes him or her unsuited for the position.

P-4.6 We shall report the unethical or incompetent behavior of a colleague to a supervisor when informal resolution is not effective.

P-4.7 We shall be familiar with laws and regulations that serve to protect the children in our programs.

P-4.8 We shall not participate in practices which are in violation of laws and regulations that protect the children in our programs.

P-4.9 When we have evidence that an early childhood program is violating laws or regulations protecting children, we shall report it to persons responsible for the program. If compliance is not accomplished within a reasonable time, we will report the violation to appropriate authorities who can be expected to remedy the situation.

P-4.10 When we have evidence that an agency or a professional charged with providing services to children, families, or teachers is failing to meet its obligations, we acknowledge a collective ethical responsibility to report the problem to appropriate authorities or to the public.

P-4.11 When a program violates or requires its employees to violate this Code, it is permissible, after fair assessment of the evidence, to disclose the identity of that program.

STATEMENT OF COMMITMENT

As an individual who works with young children, I commit myself to furthering the values and early childhood education as they are reflected in the NAEYC Code of Ethical Conduct.

To the best of my ability I will

- Ensure the programs for young children are based on current knowledge of child development and early childhood education.
- Respect and support families in their task of nurturing children.
- Respect colleagues in early childhood education and support them in maintaining the NAEYC Code of Ethical Conduct.
- Serve as an advocate for children, their families, and their teachers in community and society.
- Maintain high standards of professional conduct.
- Recognize how personal values, opinions, and biases can affect professional judgment.
- Be open to new ideas and be willing to learn from the suggestions of others.
- Continue to learn, grow, and contribute as a professional.
- Honor the ideals and principles of the NAEYC Code of Ethical Conduct.

REFERENCES

Advisory Committee on Head Start Quality and Expansion. (1994). Executive summary: The report of the advisory committee on Head Start quality and expansion. *Children Today, 22* (4), 5–8, 41.

Aeppli, W. (1986). *Rudolf Steiner: Education and the developing child.* Hudson, NY: Authroposophic Press.

American Association of University Women. (1992). *How schools shortchange girls.* Annapolis Junction, MD: Author.

American Psychiatric Association. (1994). *Diagnostic and statistical manual of mental disorders, fourth edition (DSM-IV).* Washington, DC: Author.

Armstrong, T. (1994). *Multiple intelligences in the classroom.* Alexandria, VA: ASCD.

Ashton-Warner, S. (1963). *Teacher.* New York: Simon & Schuster.

Bassuk, E. L., & Rosenberg, L. (1990). Psychosocial characteristics of homeless children and children with homes. *Pediatrics, 85,* 257–286.

Beatty, J. (1995). *Converting conflicts in preschool.* Ft. Worth, TX: Harcourt Brace.

Beatty, J. (1996). *Skills for preschool teachers* (5th ed.). Englewood Cliffs, NJ: Merrill.

Begley, S. (1996, February 19). Your child's brain. *Newsweek,* pp. 55–61.

Benson, C. S., Buckley, S., & Elliorr, A. M. (1980). Families as educators: Time use contributions to school achievement. In J. Guthrie (Ed.), *School finance policy in the 1980's: A decade of conflict.* Cambridge, MA: Ballinger.

Bereiter, C., & Engelmann, S. (1966). *Teaching disadvantaged children in the preschool.* Englewood Cliffs, NJ: Prentice-Hall.

Bergen, D. (1988). *Play as a medium for learning and development.* Portsmouth, NH: Heinemann.

Bergen, D., & Williams, J. (1991). Sex stereotypes in the United States revisited: 1972–1988. *Sex Roles, 24* (7/8), 413–423.

Berk, L. E. (1984). Development of private speech among low-income Appalachian children. *Developmental Psychology, 20,* 271–286.

Berk, L. E. (1985). Why children talk to themselves. *Young Children, 40* (5), 46–52.

Berk, L. E. (1992). Children's private speech: An overview of theory and the status of research. In R. M. Diaz & L. E. Berk (Eds.), *Private speech: From social interaction to self-regulation.* Hillsdale, NJ: Erlbaum.

Berk, L. E. (1994). Vygotsky's theory: The importance of make-believe play. *Young Children, 50,* 30–39.

Berk, L. E. (1996a). *Infants, children, and adolescents* (2nd ed.). Boston: Allyn & Bacon.

Berk, L. E. (1996b). *The young child: Development from prebirth through age eight.* Boston: Allyn & Bacon.

Berns, R. (1997). *Children, families, communities: Socialization and support.* Forth Worth, TX: Harcourt Brace Jovanovich.

Bernstine, N. (1997). Housing and homelessness. In Children's Defense Fund, *The state of America's children: Yearbook 1997.* Washington, DC: Children's Defense Fund.

Bianchi, S. M. (1990). America's children: Missed prospects. *Population Bulletin, 45* (1), 7–10.

Biber, B. (1988). The challenge of professionalism: Integrating theory and practice. In B. Spokek, O. N. Saracho, & D. L. Peters (Eds.), *Professionalism and the early childhood practitioner.* New York: Teachers College Press.

Biber, B., & Franklin, M. B. (1967). The relevance of developmental and psychodynamic concepts to the education of the preschool child. *Journal of the American Academy of Child Psychiatry, 6* (1–4), 5–24.

Birch, L. L., Johnson, S., & Fisher, J. A. (1995). Children's eating: The development of food-acceptance patterns. *Young Children, 50* (2), 71–78.

Black, J., & Puckett, M. (1996). *The young child: Development from prebirth through age eight.* Englewood Cliffs, NJ: Merrill.

Bloom, P. (1993). But I'm worth more than that: Addressing employee concerns about compensation. *Young Children, 48* (3), 65–68.

Bodrova, E., & Leong, D. (1996). *Tools of the mind: The Vygotskian approach to early childhood education.* Englewood Cliffs, NJ: Prentice-Hall.

Bomba, A. K., Oakley, C. B., & Knight, K. B. (1996). Planning the menu in the child care center. *Young Children, 51* (6), 62–67.

Boutte, G., LaPoint, S., & Davis, B. (1993). Racial issues in education: Real or imagined? *Young Children, 49* (1), 19–23.

Bowlby, J. (1962/1982). *Attachment and loss, Vol. 2. Attachment.* New York: Basic Books.

Bowman, B. T. (1993). *Head Start: Then and now.* Unpublished paper.

Bowman, B. T. (1994). The challenge of diversity. *Phi Delta Kappan, 76* (3), 218–224.

Bredekamp, S. (Ed.). (1987). *Developmentally appropriate practice in early childhood programs serving children from birth through age 8.* Washington, DC: National Association for the Education of Young Children.

Bredekamp, S. (1995). What do early childhood professionals need to know and be able to do? *Young Children, 50* (2), 67–69.

Bredekamp, S., & Copple, C. (1997). *Developmentally appropriate practice in early childhood programs* (2nd ed.). Washington, DC: National Association for the Education of Young Children.

Bredekamp, S., & Rosegrant, T. (1994). Learning and teaching with technology. In J. L. Wright & D. D. Shade (Eds.), *Young children: Active learners in a technological age* (pp. 53–62). Washington, DC: National Association for the Education of Young Children.

Bredekamp, S., & Willer, B. (1993). Professionalizing the field of early childhood education: Pros and cons. *Young Children, 48* (3), 82–84.

Brewer, J. A., & Kieff, J. (1996/1997). Fostering mutual respect for play at home and school. *Childhood Education, 73* (2), 92–96.

Bronfenbrenner, U., & Crouter, A. (1982). Work and family through time and space. In S. B. Kammerman & C. D. Hayes (Eds.), *Families that work: Children in a changing world.* Washington, DC: National Academy Press.

Bronson, M. B. (1995). *The right stuff: Selecting play materials to support development.* Washington, DC: National Association for the Education of Young Children.

Brophy, T., & Good, J. (1986). Teacher behavior and student achievement. In M. Wittrock (Ed.), *Handbook of research on teaching* (3rd ed., pp. 328–375). New York: Macmillan.

Brown, L., Branston-McLean, M. B., Baumgart, D., Vincent, L., Falvey, M., & Schroeder, J. (1979). Using the characteristics of current and subsequent least restrictive environments as factors in the development of curriculum content for severely handicapped students. *AAESPH Review, 4,* 407–424.

Bruce, J. (1995). Family policy: Supporting the parent-child link. In J. Bruce, C. Lloyd, & A. Leonard (Eds.), *Families focus: Perspectives on mothers, fathers, and children* (pp. 95–113). New York: The Population Council.

Bruner, J. S. (1951). Personality dynamics and the process of perceiving. In R. Blake & G. Ramsey (Eds.), *Perception: An approach to personality.* New York: Ronald Press.

Bruner, J. S. (1966). *Toward a theory of instruction.* New York: Vintage Books.

Bruner, J. S. (1971). *The relevance of education.* New York: Norton.

Bruner, J. S. (1985a). On teaching thinking: An afterthought. In S. F. Chipman, J. W. Segan, & R. Glasser (Eds.), *Thinking and Learning Skills* (vol. 2). Hillsdale, NJ: Erlbaum.

Bruner, J. S. (1985b). Vygotsky: A historical and conceptual perspective. In J. Wertsch (Ed.), *Culture, communication, and cognition* (pp. 22–34). New York: Cambridge University Press.

Bruner, J. S. (1990). *Acts of meaning.* Cambridge, MA: Harvard University Press.

Bruner, J. S., Goodnow, J. J., & Austin, G. A. (1956). *A study of thinking.* New York: Wiley.

Bullough, R. V., Jr. (1994). Personal history and teaching metaphors. *Teacher Education Quarterly, 21* (1), 107–120.

Bullough, R. V., Jr., & Gitlin, A. (1995). *Becoming a student of teaching.* New York: Garland.

Buskin, M. (1975). *Parent power: A candid handbook for dealing with your child's school.* New York: Walker & Co.

Caldwell, B. (1992). Head start. In L. Williams & D. Fromberg (Eds.), *Encyclopedia of early childhood education* (pp. 130–131). New York: Garland.

Cantor, N. (1990). From thought to behavior: "Having" and "doing" in the study of personality and cognition. *American Psychologist, 45* (6), 735–750.

Carey, S. (1978). The child as a word learner. In M. Halle, J. Bresnan, & G. Miller (Eds.), *Linguistic theory and psychological reality.* Cambridge, MA: MIT Press.

Carnegie Task Force on Meeting the Needs of Young Children. (1994). *Starting points: Meeting the needs of our youngest children.* New York: Carnegie Corporation.

Chaille, C., & Silvern, S. (1996). Understanding through play. *Childhood Education, 72* (5), 274–277.

Checkley, K. (1997). The first seven . . . and the eighth: A conversation with Howard Gardner. *Educational Leadership, 55* (1), 8–13.

Children's Defense Fund. (1991). *The state of America's children: Yearbook 1991.* Washington, DC: Author.

Children's Defense Fund. (1994a). *The state of America's children: Yearbook 1994.* Washington, DC: Author.

Children's Defense Fund. (1994b). *Wasting America's future.* Washington, DC: Author.

Children's Defense Fund. (1995). *The state of America's children: Yearbook 1995.* Washington, DC: Author.

Children's Defense Fund. (1996). *The state of America's children: Yearbook 1996.* Washington, DC: Author.

Children's Defense Fund. (1997). *The state of America's children: Yearbook 1997.* Washington, DC: Author.

Children's Services Division and the State Office for Services to Children and Families. (1995). *Recognizing and reporting child abuse and neglect: An explanation of Oregon's mandatory reporting law.* Salem, OR: Author.

Chilman, C. (1966). *Your child from 6–12.* Washington, DC: U.S. Department of Health, Education, and Welfare.

Clark, B. (1992). *Growing up gifted: Developing the potential of children at home and at school* (4th ed.). Englewood Cliffs, NJ: Merrill/Prentice Hall.

Clark, K., & Clark, M. (1947). Racial identification and preference in Negro children. In T. M. Newcomb & E. L. Hartley (Eds.), *Readings in social psychology.* New York: Holt, Rinehart & Winston.

Clifford, R. (1997). Welfare reform and you. *Young Children, 52* (2), 2–3.

Cline, D. B., & Ingerson, D. (1996). The mystery of Humpty's fall: Primary school children as playmakers. *Young Children, 51* (6), 4–10.

Clinton, H. R. (1996). *It takes a village and other lessons children teach us.* New York: Simon & Schuster.

Coleman, J. S., & Hoffer, T. (1987). *Public and private high schools: The impact of communities.* New York: Basic Books.

Committee for Economic Development. (1991). *The unfinished agenda: A new vision for child development and education.* New York: Author.

Coontz, S. (1992). *The way we never were: American families and the nostalgia trap.* New York: Basic Books.

Coontz, S. (1997). *The way we really are: Coming to terms with America's changing families.* New York: Basic Books.

Cost, Quality, and Child Outcomes Study Team. (1995). *Cost, quality, and child outcomes in child care centers: Executive summary.* Denver: Economics Department, University of Colorado at Denver.

Crain, W. (1980). *Theories of development: Concepts and applications.* Englewood Cliffs, NJ: Prentice-Hall.

Crockett, R. O. (1997, January 16). Mentor Graphics shores up top ranks. *The Oregonian,* p. C1.

Culkin, M., Helburn, S., & Morris, J. (1990). Current price versus full cost: An economic perspective. In B. Willer (Ed.), *Reaching the full cost of quality in early childhood Programs* (pp. 9–26). Washington, DC: National Association for the Education of Young Children.

Curran, D. (1985). *Traits of a healthy family.* Minneapolis, MN: Winston Press.

Currie, J., & Thomas, D. (1994). *Does Head Start make a difference? Labor and population program.* Working Paper No. 4406. Cambridge, MA: National Bureau of Economic Research.

Damon, W. (1988). *The moral child: Nurturing children's natural moral growth.* New York: Free Press.

Day, D. E., & Goffin, S. G. (1994). *New perspectives in early childhood teacher education.* New York: Teachers College Press.

Derman-Sparks, L. (1989). *Anti-bias curriculum: Tools for empowering young children.* Washington, DC: National Association for the Education of Young Children.

Derman-Sparks, L. (1992). "It isn't fair!" Antibias curriculum for young children. In B. Neugebauer (Ed.), *Alike and different: Exploring our humanity with young children.* Washington, DC: National Association for the Education of Young Children.

DeVries, R., & Zan, B. (1994). *Moral classrooms, moral children: Creating a constructivist atmosphere in early education.* New York: Teachers College Press.

Diffily, D., & Morrison, K. (1996). *Family-friendly communication for early childhood programs.* Washington, DC: National Association for the Education of Young Children.

Division for Early Childhood. (1993). *DEC Position on Inclusion.* Reston, VA: Council for Exceptional Children, Division for Early Childhood.

Dixon-Krauss, L. (1995). Partner reading and writing: Peer social dialogue and the zone of proximal development. *Journal of Reading Behavior, 27* (1), 45–63.

Dombro, A. L. (1995). Sharing the care: What every provider and parent needs to know. *Children Today, 23* (4), 22–25.

Dornbusch, S., & Gray, K. (1988). Single-parent families. In S. Dornbusch & K. Gray (Eds.), *Feminism, children, and new families.* New York: Guilford.

Douglass, A. (1996). Rethinking the effects of homelessness on children: Resiliency and competency. *Child Welfare, 75* (6), 741–751.

Driscoll, A. (1995). *Cases in early childhood education: Stories of programs and practices.* Boston: Allyn & Bacon.

Durkin, D. (1966). *Children who read early.* New York: Teachers College Press.

Earley, P. (1994). Goals 2000: *Educate America Act—Implications for teacher educators.* Washington, DC: AACTE Publications.

Edelman, M. (1989). Economic issues related to child care and early childhood education. *Teachers College Record, 90* (3), 342–351.

Edelstein, S. B. (1995). *Children with prenatal alcohol and/or other drug exposure: Weighing the risks of adoption.* Washington, DC: Child Welfare League of America.

Edwards, C., Gandini, L., & Forman, G. (1995). *The hundred languages of children: The Reggio Emilia approach to early childhood education.* Norwood, NJ: Ablex.

Eisenberg, N. (1992). *The caring child.* Cambridge, MA: Harvard University Press.

Eisenberg, N., & Harris, J. D. (1984). Social competence: A developmental perspective. *School Psychology Review, 13,* 266–277.

Elkind, D. (1981). *The hurried child.* Reading, MA: Addison-Wesley.

Elkind, D. (1987). *Miseducation: Preschoolers at risk.* New York: Knopf.

Elkind, D. (1994). *A sympathetic understanding of the child, birth to 16* (3rd ed.). Boston: Allyn & Bacon.

Epstein, J. L. (1992). *School and family partnerships.* Baltimore: Center on Families, Communities, Schools, and Children's Learning, Johns Hopkins University.

Epstein, J. L. (1995). School/family/community partnerships: Caring for the children we share. *Phi Delta Kappan, 76* (9), 701–712.

Erikson, E. H. (1968). *Identity: Youth and crisis.* New York: Norton.

Erikson, E. H. (1974). Once more the inner space: Letter to a former student. In J. Strouse (Ed.), *Woman and analysis* (pp. 320–340). New York: Grossman.

Evans, E. E. (1975). *Contemporary influences in early childhood education.* New York: Holt, Rinehart and Winston.

Fagot, B. I. (1978). The influence of sex of child on parental reactions to toddler children. *Child Development, 49* (2), 459–465.

Feeney, S., Christensen, D., & Moravcik, E. (1996). *Who am I in the lives of children?* Englewood Cliffs, NJ: Merrill.

Flavell, J., Miller, P., & Miller, S. (1993). *Cognitive development* (3rd ed.). Englewood Cliffs, NJ: Prentice-Hall.

Foster, S. W. (1984). An introduction to Waldorf education. *Clearinghouse, 57* (5), 228–230.

Franklin, M. B., & Biber, B. (1977). Psychological perspectives and early childhood education: Some relations between theory and practice. In L. G. Katz, M. Z. Glockner, S. T. Goodman, & M. J. Spencer (Eds.), *Current issues in early childhood education* (Vol. 1). Norwood, NJ: Ablex.

Freeman, E. B. (1990). Issues in kindergarten policy and practice. *Young Children, 45* (4), 29–34.

Frieberg, H. J., & Driscoll, A. (1996). *Universal teaching strategies.* Boston: Allyn & Bacon.

Frost, J. (1991). *Play and playscapes.* Albany, NY: Delmar.

Gage, J., & Workman, S. (1994). Creating family support systems in Head Start and beyond. *Young Children, 59* (1), 74–77.

Gallahue, D. (1982). *Developmental movement experiences for children.* New York: Wiley.

Gandini, L. (1993). Fundamentals of the Reggio Emilia approach to early childhood education. *Young Children, 49* (1), 4–8.

Garcia, E. (1991). *The education of linguistically and culturally diverse students: Effective instructional practices.* Santa Cruz, CA: National Center for Research on Cultural Diversity and Second Language Learning.

Garcia, E. (1994). *Understanding and meeting the challenge of student diversity.* Boston: Houghton Mifflin.

Garcia, E. (1997). The education of Hispanics in early childhood: Of roots and wings. *Young Children, 52* (3), 5–14.

Garcia, E., & August, D. (1988). *The education of language minority students.* Chicago: Charles C. Thomas.

Gardner, H. (1993a). *Educating the unschooled mind: A science and public policy seminar.* Washington, DC: American Educational Research Association.

Gardner, H. (1993b). *Multiple intelligences: The theory in practice.* New York: BasicBooks.

Garvey, C. (1977). *Play.* Cambridge, MA: Harvard University Press.

Garwood, S., Phillips, D., Harman, A., & Zigler, E. (1989). As the pendulum swings: Federal agency programs for children. *American Psychologist, 44* (2), 434–438.

Gerber, M. (Ed.). (1979). *A manual for parents and professionals: Resources for infant educators.* Los Angeles: Resources for Infant Educators.

Gerber, M. (1981). What is appropriate curriculum for infants and toddlers? In B. Weissbourd & J. S. Musick (Eds.), *Infants: Their social environments* (pp. 77–85).

Washington, DC: National Association for the Education of Young Children.

Gibbs, J. (1989). Biracial adolescents. In J. Gibbs & L. Huang (eds.), *Children of color*. San Francisco: Jossey-Bass.

Ginsberg, H., & Opper, S. (1969). *Piaget's theory of intellectual development: An introduction*. Englewood Cliffs, NJ: Prentice-Hall.

Ginsburg, H., & Opper, S. (1988). *Piaget's theory of intellectual development* (3rd ed.). Englewood Cliffs, NJ: Prentice-Hall.

Gnezda, M. (1996). Welfare reform: Personal responsibilities and opportunities for early childhood advocates. *Young Children, 52* (1), 55–58.

Goals 2000: Building on a decade of reform. (1996). [Online: web]. URL: http://inet.ed.gov/G2K/ProgRpt96/build.html

Goelman, H. (1992). *Visions of program revision: A report on the Early Childhood Education Review Project*. University of British Columbia: Center for the Study of Curriculum and Instruction.

Goffin, S. (1992). Federal legislation of importance to early childhood education: A chronology. In L. Williams & D. Fromberg (Eds.), *Encyclopedia of early childhood education* (pp. 58–64). New York: Garland.

Goffin, S. (1994). *Curriculum models and early childhood education*. New York: Macmillan.

Gonzalez-Mena, J., & Eyer, D. M. (1997). *Infants, toddlers, and caregivers* (4th ed.). Mountain View, CA: Mayfield.

Goodman, M. E. (1946). Evidence concerning the genesis of interracial attitudes. *American Anthropologist, 48*, 624–630.

Gordon, A., & Browne, K. (1993). *Beginnings and beyond: Foundations in early childhood education* (3rd ed.) Albany, NY: Delmar.

Gordon, I. (1968). The young child: A new look. In J. Frost (Ed.), *Early childhood education rediscovered*. New York: Holt, Rinehart and Winston.

Gordon, L. (1988). Job descriptions for infant care programs: Directors, teachers, and assistants. In P. Greenberg (Ed.), *Setting up for infant care: Guidelines for centers and family day care homes* (pp. 45–49). Washington, DC: National Association for the Education of Young Children.

Gowen, J. W. (1995). The early development of symbolic play. *Young Children, 50* (3), 75–84.

Grant, R. (1990). The special needs of homeless children: Early intervention at a welfare hotel. *Topics in Early Childhood Special Education*, 10 (4), 76–91.

Greenberg, P. (1990). Before the beginning: A participant's view. *Young Children, 45* (6), 41–52.

Greenberg, P. (1993). *Character development: Encouraging self-esteem & self-discipline in infants, toddlers, and two-year-olds*. Washington, DC: National Association for the Education of Young Children.

Greenspan, S. I. (1995). *First feelings: Milestones in the emotional development of your baby and child*. New York: Viking.

Gullo, D. F., & Clements, D. H. (1984). The effects of kindergarten schedule on achievement, classroom behavior, and attendance. *Journal of Educational Research, 78* (1), 51–56.

Haight, W. L., & Miller, P. J. (1993). *Pretending at home: Early development in a sociocultural context*. Albany: State University of New York Press.

Hartley, R. (1971). Play: The essential ingredient. *Childhood Education, 48* (2), 80–84.

Haugland, S., & Wright, J. (1997). *Young children and technology: A world of discovery*. Boston: Allyn & Bacon.

Hawkins, D. (1973). How to plan for spontaneity. In C. Silberman (Ed.), *The open classroom reader*. New York: Random House.

Head Start Bureau, Department of Health and Human Services. (1995). *Program information report*. Washington, DC: Author.

Heleen, O. (1992). *Is your school family-friendly?* Alexandria, VA: Association of Elementary School Principals .

Helen Gordon Child Development Center. (1996–97). *Parent handbook: Helen Gordon Child Development Center*. Portland, OR: Author.

Henderson, A. T. (1981). *The evidence grows*. Boston: National Committee for Citizens in Education.

Henderson, A. T. (1987). *The evidence continues to grow*. Boston: National Committee for Citizens in Education.

Henderson, A. T., & Berla, N. (1996). *The family is critical to student achievement: A new generation of evidence*. Washington, DC: Center for Law and Education.

Hendrick, J. (1990). *Total learning: Curriculum for the young child*. Columbus, OH: Merrill/Macmillan.

Hendrick, J. (1996). *The whole child: Developmental education for the early years*. Englewood Cliffs, NJ: Prentice-Hall.

Hersh, R., Paolitto, D., & Reimer, J. (1979). *Promoting moral growth: From Piaget to Kohlberg*. New York: Longman.

Hess, R. D. (1970). Social class and ethnic influences upon socialization. In P. H. Mussen (Ed.), *Carmichael's Manual of Child Psychology* (3rd ed., Vol. 2). New York: Wiley.

Hetherington, E. M. (1972). The effects of father absence on personality development in adolescent daughters. *Developmental Psychology, 7,* 313–326.

Hetherington, E. M. (1988). Parents, children, and siblings six years after divorce. In R. A. Hinde & J. Stevenson Hinde (Eds.), *Relationships with families.* Oxford: Oxford University Press.

Hetherington, E. M. (1989). Coping with family transitions: Winners, losers, and survivors. *Child Development, 60,* 1–4.

Hetherington, E. M., Cox, M., & Cox, R. (1976). Divorced fathers. *The Family Coordinator, 25* (4), 417–428.

Hetherington, E. M., Cox, M., & Cox, R. (1985). Long-term effects of divorce and remarriage on the adjustments of children. *Journal of American Academy of Psychiatry, 24* (5), 518–830.

Heward, W. L. (1996). *Exceptional children: An introduction to special education* (5th ed.). Englewood Cliffs, NJ: Prentice-Hall.

Hilgard, E., & Bower, G. (1975). *Theories of learning* (4th ed.). Englewood Cliffs, NJ: Prentice-Hall.

Hitz, R., & Driscoll, A. (1988). Praise or encouragement? New insights into praise: Implications for early childhood teachers. *Young Children, 43* (5), 6–13.

Hochschild, A. (1997, April 20). There's no place like work. *The New York Times Magazine.*

Hoffman, L. W. (1989). The effects of maternal employment in the two-parent family. *American Psychologist, 44* (2), 283–292.

Honig, A. S. (1983). Research in review: Sex role socialization in early childhood. *Young Children, 38* (6), 57–70.

Honig, A. S. (1985). High quality infant/toddler care: Issues and dilemmas. *Young Children, 41* (1), 40–46.

Honig, A. S. (1995). Singing with infants and toddlers. *Young Children, 50* (5), 72–78.

Howard, T. U., & Johnson, F. C. (1985). An ecological approach to practice with single-parent families. *Social Casework, 66,* 482–491.

Howes, C. (1988). Peer interaction of young children. *Monographs of the Society for Research in Child Development, 53* (1), Serial No. 217.

Hughes, F. P. (1991). *Children, play, and development.* Boston: Allyn & Bacon.

Huttenlocher, J., Haight, W., Bryk, A., Seltzer, M., & Lyons, T. (1991). Early vocabulary growth: Relation of language input and gender. *Developmental Psychology, 27* (2), 236–248.

Ijames-Bryant, D. (1997). *The state of America's children: Yearbook 1997.* Washington, DC: Children's Defense Fund.

Individuals with Disabilities Education Act, 20 U.S.C. § 1412(5)(B); 34 C.F.R. 300.551. (1990).

Isenberg, J., & Jalongo, M. (1993). *Creative expression and play in the early childhood curriculum.* New York: Macmillan.

Jabs, C. (1996, November). Your baby's brain power. *Working Mother,* pp. 24–28.

Johnson, D., Johnson, R., & Holubec, E. (1994). *The new circles of learning: Cooperation in the classroom and school.* Reston, VA: ASCD.

Johnson, J., & McCracken, J. (Eds.). (1994). *The early childhood career lattice: Perspectives on professional development.* Washington, DC: National Association for the Education of Young Children.

Johnson, J. E., Christie, J. F., & Yawkey, T. D. (1987). *Play and early childhood development.* Glenview, IL: Scott Foresman.

Jones, E. (1984). Training individuals: In the classroom and out. In J. Greenman & R. Fuqua (Eds.), *Making day care better: Training, evaluation, and the process of change.* New York: Teachers College Press.

Jones, E. (1986). *Teaching adults: An active learning approach.* Washington, DC: National Association for the Education of Young Children.

Jones, E. (1993). *Growing teachers: Partnerships in staff development.* Washington, DC: National Association for the Education of Young Children.

Jones, E., & Nimmo, J. (1994). *Emergent curriculum.* Washington, DC: National Association for the Education of Young Children.

Jusczyk, P. W. (1997). *The discovery of spoken language.* Cambridge, MA: MIT Press.

Kagan, S. L. (1994). Readying schools for young children: Polemics and priorities. *Phi Delta Kappan, 76* (3), 226–233.

Kamii, C. (1989). *Young children continue to reinvent arithmetic—2nd grade: Implications of Piaget's theory.* New York: Teachers College Press.

Kamii, C., & DeVries, R. (1978). *Physical knowledge in preschool education: Implications of Piaget's theory.* Washington, DC: National Association for the Education of Young Children.

Katz, L. (1992). *What should young children be learning?* Urbana, IL: ERIC Clearinghouse on Elementary and Early Childhood Education, University of Illinois, ED 290 554.

Katz, L. (1993a). Dispositions: Definitions and implications for early childhood practices. In *Perspectives from ERIC: EECE*. Monograph series No. 4. Urbana, IL: ERIC Clearinghouse on Elementary and Early Childhood Education.

Katz, L. (1993b). *Dispositions as educational goals*. Urbana, IL: ERIC Clearinghouse on Elementary and Early Childhood Education, University of Illinois, ED 363 454.

Katz, L. (1994). Perspectives on the quality of early childhood programs. *Phi Delta Kappan, 76* (3), 200–205.

Katz, L., & Chard, S. (1989). *Engaging children's minds: The project approach*. Norwood, NJ: Ablex.

Katz, L., & Raths, J. D. (1985). Dispositions as goals for teacher education. *Teaching and Teacher Education,* 1 (4), 301–307.

Katz, P. (1982a). Development of children's awareness and intergroup attitudes. In L. G. Katz (Ed.), *Current topics in early childhood education* (vol. 4). Norwood, NJ: Ablex.

Katz, P. (1982b). A review of recent research in children's attitude acquisition. In. L. Katz (Ed.), *Current topics in early childhood education* (vol. 4). Norwood, NJ: Ablex.

Kelman, A. (1990). Choices for children. *Young Children, 45* (3), 42–45.

King, E., Chipman, M., & Cruz-Janzen, M. (1994). *Educating young children in a diverse society*. Boston: Allyn & Bacon.

Kisker, E., Hofferth, S., Phillips, D., & Farquhar, E. (1991). *A profile of child care settings: Early education and care in 1990*. Washington, DC: U.S. Department of Education, Office of the Under Secretary.

Klein, T., Bittle, C., & Molnar, J. (1993). No place to call home: Supporting the needs of homeless children in the early childhood classroom. *Young Children, 48* (6), 22–31.

Knitzer, J., & Page, S. (1996). Young children and families: The view from the states. *Young Children, 51* (4), 51–55.

Kohlberg, L. (1976). The development of children's orientations toward a moral order. Sequence in the development of moral thought. In P. B. Neubauer (Ed.), *The process of child development* (pp. 143–163). New York: Jason Aronson.

Kohn, A. (1993). Rewards versus learning: A response to Paul Chance. *Phi Delta Kappan, 74* (10), 783–787.

Kohn, M. L. (1977). *Class and conformity: A study in values*. Chicago: Chicago University Press.

Kostelnik, M. J., Soderman, A. K., & Whiren, A. P. (1993). *Developmentally appropriate programs in early childhood education*. New York: Merrill.

Kramer, J. (1994). In D. E. Day & S. G. Goffin (Eds.), *New perspectives in early childhood teacher education* (pp. 31–33). New York: Teachers College Press.

Krashen, S. (1992). *Fundamentals of language education*. Torrence, CA: Laredo.

Krashen, S. (1996). *Under attack: The case against bilingual education*. Culver City, CA: Language Education Associates.

Krogh, S., & Nikko, A. (1994). Images of teaching held by beginning education students. *Journal of Early Childhood Teacher Education, 15* (3), 14–17.

Kuhl, P. K. (1992, October). *Infants' perception and representation of speech: Development of a new theory*. Paper presented at the International Conference on Spoken Language Processing, Banff, Alberta, Canada.

Lally, J. R. (1995). The impact of child care policies and practices on infant/toddler identity formation. *Young Children, 51* (1), 58–67.

Lally, J. R., Griffin, A., Fenichel, E., Segal, M., Szanton, E., & Weissbourd. B. (1995). *Caring for infants and toddlers in groups: Developmentally appropriate practice*. Washington, DC: Zero to Three.

Lamb, M. (1981). The development of father-infant relationships. In M. Lamb (Ed.), *The role of father in child development* (2nd ed.). New York: Wiley.

Lamb, S. (1991). The beginnings of morality. In A. Garrod (Ed.), *Approaches to moral development: New research and emerging theories* (pp. 9–29). New York: Teachers College Press.

Lazar, I., & Darlington, R. B. (Eds.). (1982). Lasting effect of early education: A report from the Consortium of Longitudinal Studies. *Monograph of the Society for Research in Child Development, 47* (2-3), Serial No. 195.

Lazarus, P. W. (1992). Developmentally delayed. In L. R. Williams & D. P. Fromberg (Eds.), *Encyclopedia of early childhood education* (pp. 319–321). New York: Garland.

Levine, R. (1997). *A geography of time*. New York: Basic Books.

Lombardi, J. (1990). Head Start: The nation's pride, a nation's challenge. *Young Children, 45* (6), 22–29.

Maier, H. (1978). *Three theories of child development* (3rd ed.). New York: Harper & Row.

Mamchur, C. (1983). Heartbeat. *Educational Leadership, 40* (4), 14–20.

Manfredi-Pettit, L. (1993). Child care: It's more than the sum of its tasks. *Young Children, 79* (1), 40–42.

Marchant, C., & McBride, S. (1994). Family stories. *Journal of Early Childhood Teacher Education, 15* (3), 7–11.

Marshall, H. (1995). Beyond "I like the way . . . ." *Young Children, 50* (2), 26–28.

Maslow, A. (1987). *Motivation and personality* (3rd ed.). New York: Harper & Row.

Maxim, G. W. (1989). *The very young child.* (3rd ed.). Englewood Cliffs, NJ: Merrill/Prentice-Hall.

Mazur, J. (1994). *Learning and behavior* (3rd ed.). Upper Saddle River, NJ: Prentice-Hall.

McBride, B. A., & Lee, M. (1995). *Child care on the community college campus: The relationship between teaching and service.* Presented at the National Organization of Child Development Laboratory Schools preconference, NAEYC annual conference, Dallas, TX.

McCall, K. P. (1990). *Educating homeless children and youth: A sample of programs, policies, and procedures.* Cambridge, MA: Center for Law and Education.

McCollum, J. A., & Maude, S. P. (1993). Portrait of a changing field: Policy and practice in early childhood special education. In B. Spodek (Ed.), *Handbook of research on the education of young children* (pp. 352–371). New York: Macmillan.

McCune, L. (1986). Symbolic development in normal and atypical infants. In G. Fein & M. Rivkin (Eds.), *The young child at play.* Washington, DC: National Association for the Education of Young Children.

McKey, R., Condelli, L., Ganson, H., Barrety, B., McConkey, C., & Plantz, M. (1985). *The impact of Head Start on children, family, and communities: Final report of the Head Start Evaluation, Synthesis, and Utilization Project.* Washington, DC: U.S. Government Printing Office.

McLean, M., Bailey, D. B., & Wolery, M. (1996). *Assessing infants and preschoolers with special needs.* Englewood Cliffs, NJ: Prentice-Hall.

McLean, S. V., Haas, N., & Butler, B. (1994). Kindergarten curriculum: Enrichment and improvishment. *Early Childhood Development and Care, 101,* 1–12.

McLoyd, V. C. (1990). The impact of economic hardship on black families and children: Psychological distress, parenting and socioemotional development. *Child Development, 61,* 190–198.

Meisels, S. J. (1989). Meeting the mandate of Public Law 99-457: Early childhood intervention in the nineties. *American Journal of Orthopsychiatry, 59* (3), 451–460.

Meisler, S. (1992, May 4). Gap between rich, poor now widest on record. *Washington Post,* p. A1.

Mentor Graphics Child Development Center. (1996). *Mentor Graphics parent handbook.* Wilsonville, OR: Author.

Miller, K. (1995). Caring for the little ones. *Child Care Information Exchange, 105,* 23–24.

Miller, K., & Gelman, R. (1983). The child's representation of number: A multidimensional scaling analysis. *Child Development, 54,* 1470–1479.

Moles, O. (1992). *Schools and families together: Helping children learn more at home.* Washington, DC: U.S. Department of Educational Research and Improvement.

Molnar, J., Rath, W., & Klein, T. (1990). Constantly compromised: The impact of homelessness on children. *Journal of Social Issues, 46* (4), 109–124.

Montessori, M. (1964). *The Montessori method.* (A. E. George, Trans.). New York: Schocker.

Morlund, J. K. (1966). A comparison of race awareness in northern and southern children. *American Journal of Orthopsychiatry, 36,* 22–31.

Morrison, G. (1995). *Early childhood education today.* Englewood Cliffs, NJ: Prentice-Hall.

Morrison, J. W., & Rogers, L. S. (1996). Being responsive to the needs of children from dual heritage backgrounds. *Young Children, 52* (1), 29–33.

Morrison, N. (1995). Successful single-parent families. *Journal of Divorce and Remarriage, 22,* 286–287.

Morrow, G. (1987). *The compassionate school: A practical guide to educating abused and traumatized children.* Englewood Cliffs, NJ: Prentice-Hall.

Morrow, L. (1990). Preparing the classroom environment to promote literacy through play. *Children's Quarterly, 5,* 537–554.

Nagel, N. G. (1996). *Learning through real-world problem solving: The power of integrative teaching.* Thousand Oaks, CA: Corwin.

National Association for the Education of Young Children. (1990a). *The demand and supply of child care in 1990: Joint findings from the National Child Care Survey 1990 and a profile of child settings.* Washington, DC: U.S. Department of Health & Human Services, Office of Policy and Planning, U.S. Department of Education.

National Association for the Education of Young Children. (1990b). NAEYC position statement on school readiness. *Young Children, 46* (1), 21–23.

National Association for the Education of Young Children. (1990c). *What are the benefits of high quality early childhood programs?* Washington, DC: Author.

National Association for the Education of Young Children. (1995). NAEYC—A community of learners. *Young Children, 51* (1), Annual Report.

National Association for the Education of Young Children. (1996a). NAEYC position statement: Technology and young children—Ages three through eight. *Young Children, 51* (6), 11–16.

National Association for the Education of Young Children. (1996b). *Responding to linguistic and cultural diversity: Recommendations for effective early childhood education.* Washington, DC: Author.

National Association for the Education of Young Children. (1997a). *Guidelines for appropriate curriculum content and assessment in programs serving children 3 through 8 years of age.* Washington, DC: Author.

National Association for the Education of Young Children. (1997b). NAEYC position statement on state implementation of welfare reform. *Young Children, 52* (2), 42–45.

National Center for Children in Poverty. (1995, April). *Number of poor children under six increased from 5 to 6 million, 1987–1992.* Washington, DC: Author.

National Education Goals Panel. (1995). *1995 National education goals report.* Washington, DC: Author.

National Institute of Child Health and Human Development. (1997). *Mother-child interaction and cognitive outcomes associated with early child care: Results of the NICHD study.* Bethesda, MD: Author.

Nelson, C. (1997). The new nuclear family: Grandparenting in the nineties. *Black Child, 2* (5), 9–11.

Neugebauer, B. (1992). What are we really saying to children? Criteria for the selection of books and materials. In B. Neugebauer (Ed.), *Alike and different: Exploring our humanity with young children.* Washington, DC: National Association for the Education of Young Children.

Neugebauer, R. (1991a, October/November). Churches that care: Status report #2 on church-housed child care. *Child Care Information Exchange,* pp. 41–45.

Neugebauer, R. (1991b). Status report #2 on employer child care. *Child Care Information Exchange,* (80), 5–9.

New, R. (1994). Culture, child development, and developmentally appropriate practices. In B. L. Mallory & R. S. New (Eds.), *Diversity and developmentally appropriate practices: Challenge for early childhood education.* New York: Teachers College Press.

Newberger, J. (1997). New brain development research—A wonderful window of opportunity to build public support for early childhood education! *Young Children, 52* (4), 4–9.

Newman, B., & Newman, P. (1991). *Development through life: A psychosocial approach* (5th ed.). Pacific Grove, CA: Brooks/Cole.

Olson, G. (1994). In D. E. Day & S. G. Goffin (Eds.), *New perspectives in early childhood teacher education* (p. 39). New York: Teachers College Press.

Olson, L. (1991, March 6). Social woes pose threat to reform, C.E.D. maintains. *Education Week,* pp. 1, 18.

Oregon Department of Education. (1995). *Oregon prekindergarten program requirements.* Salem, OR: Author.

Osborn, D. (1991). *Early childhood education in historical perspective* (3rd ed.). Athens, GA: Education Associates.

Paris, S. (1975). Integration and inference in children's comprehension and memory. In F. Restle, R. Shiffrin, J. Kastellan, H. Lindman, & D. Pisoni (Eds.), *Cognitive theory* (Vol. 1). Hillsdale, NJ: Erlbaum.

Parker, J. G., & Gottman, J. M. (1989). Social and emotional development in a relational context: Friendship interaction from early childhood to adolescence. In T. J. Berndt & G. W. Ladd (Eds.), *Peer relations in child development.* New York: Wiley.

Patton, C. (1993). What can we do to increase public knowledge about child development and quality child care? *Young Children, 49* (1), 30–31.

Peck, J. T., McCaig, G., & Sapp, M. E. (1988). *Kindergarten policies: What is best for children?* Research Monographs of the National Association of Young Children, V. 2. NAEYC #141, 31–60.

Pellegrini, A. D. (1988). Elementary school children's rough and tumble play. *Developmental Psychology, 24,* 802–806.

Pellegrini, A. D. (1989). So what about recess, really? *Play and Culture, 2,* 354–356.

Pellegrini, A. D., & Boyd, B. (1993). The role of play in early childhood development and education: Issues in definition and function. In B. Spodek (Ed.), *Handbook of research on the education of young children.* New York: Macmillan.

Pellegrini, A. D., & Perlmutter, J. C. (1988). Rough-and-tumble play on the elementary school playground. *Young Children, 44* (2), 14–17.

Perkins, D., Jay, E., & Tishman, S. (1993). New conceptions of thinking: From ontology to education. *Educational Psychologist, 28* (1), 67–85.

Phillips, C. B. (1994). The challenge of training and credentialing early childhood educators. *Phi Delta Kappan, 76* (3), 214–217.

Piaget, J. (1952). *The origins of intelligence in children.* New York: International Universities Press.

Piaget, J. (1962). *Play, dreams, and imitation in childhood.* New York: Norton.

Piaget, J. (1963). *The origins of intelligence in children.* New York: Norton.

Piaget, J. (1969). *Science of education and the psychology of the child.* New York: Viking.

Piaget, J., & Inhelder, B. (1969) *The psychology of the child.* New York: Basic Books.

Pinker, S. (1994). *The language instinct.* New York: Morrow.

Poulton, S., & Sexton, D. (1995/1996). Feeding young children: Developmentally appropriate considerations for supplementing family care. *Childhood Education, 72* (2), 66–71.

Powell, D. R. (1989). *Families and early childhood programs.* Washington, DC: National Association for the Education of Young Children.

Pratt, C. (1948). *I learn from children.* New York: Harper & Row.

Radke, M., & Trager, H. (1950). Children's perceptions of the social roles of Negroes and whites. *Journal of Psychology, 29,* 3–33.

Rafferty, Y., & Shinn, M. (1991). The impact of homelessness on children. *American Psychologist, 46* (11), 1170–1179.

Ramsey, P., & Myers, L. (1990). Salience of race in young children's cognitive, affective, and behavioral responses to social environments. *Journal of Applied Psychology, 11,* 49–67.

Ramsey, P. G. (1991). *Making friends in school: Promoting peer relationships in early childhood.* New York: Teachers College Press.

Replogle, E. (1994). Community: What two programs show us about the right focus for Head Start. *Children Today, 23* (2), 32–36.

Rice, A., Ruiz, R., & Padilla, A. (1974). Person perception, self-identity, and ethnic group preference in Anglo, black and Chicano preschool children. *Journal of Cross-Cultural Psychology, 5,* 100–108.

Richards, L. N., & Schmiege, C. J. (1993). Problems and strengths of single-parent families: Implications for practice and policy. *Family Relations, 42,* p. 278.

Rogers, C., & Sawyer, J. (1988). *Play in the lives of children.* Washington, DC: National Association for the Education of Young Children.

Rogoff, B., Mistry, J., Göncü, A., & Mosier, C. (1993). Guided participation in cultural activity by toddlers and caregivers. *Monographs of the Society for Research in Child Development, 55* (8, Serial No. 236).

Ross, H. S., & Lollis, S. P. (1987). Communication within infant social games. *Developmental Psychology, 23,* 241–248.

Rothlein, L., & Brett, A. (1987). Children's teachers' and parents' perceptions of play. *Early Childhood Quarterly, 5,* 495–512.

Rubin, K. H. (1980). Fantasy play: Its role in the development of social skills and social cognition. In K. H. Rubin (Ed.), *Children's play.* San Francisco: Jossey-Bass.

Rubin, K. H., Fein, G. G., & Vandenberg, B. (1983). Play. In E. M. Hetherington (Ed.), *Handbook of child psychology* (vol. 4). New York: Wiley.

Rubin, K. H., & Howe, N. (1986). Social play and perspective taking. In G. Fein & M. Rivkin (Eds.), *The young child at play.* Washington, DC: National Association for the Education of Young Children.

Russell, A. (1994). Our babies, our future. *Carnegie Quarterly, 39* (2), 1–11.

Rust, F. O. (1994). From a child's point of view. *Journal of Early Childhood Teacher Education, 15* (3), 3–6.

Rutledge, K. (1995a). National accreditation: What is it? *Oregon Association for Young Children Bulletin, 31* (1), 1, 8.

Rutledge, K. (1995b). Why should MY center become accredited? *Oregon Association for Young Children Bulletin, 31* (1), 8–9.

Safford, P. L. (1989). *Integrating teaching in early childhood: Starting in the mainstream.* New York: Longman.

Samuelson, R. J. (1996, January 8). Great expectations. *Newsweek,* p. 24.

Santrock, J. W. (1990). *Children.* Dubuque, IA: Brown.

Scales, B., Almy, M., Nicolopoulou, A., & Ervin-Tripp, S. (1991). *Play and the social context of development in early care and education.* New York: Teachers College Press.

Schneider, J., & Houston, P. (1993). *Exploding the myths: Another round in the education debate.* Washington, DC: American Association of Educational Service Agencies.

Schram, S. (1991). Welfare spending and poverty: Cutting back produces more poverty, not less. *The American Journal of Economics and Sociology, 59* (20), 129–140.

Schulman, M., & Mekler, E. (1985). *Bringing up a moral child.* Reading, MA: Addison-Wesley.

Schweinhart, L. J. (1994). Lasting benefits of preschool programs. *ERIC Digest,* EDO-PS-94–2.

Schweinhart, L. J., Barnes, H. V., & Weikart, D. P. (with Barnett, W. S., & Epstein, A. S.). (1993). *Significant benefits: The High/Scope Perry Preschool Study through age 27.* Ypsilanti, MI: High/Scope Press. Monographs of the High/Scope Educational Research Foundation, no. 10.

Schweinhart, L. J., Berrueta-Clement, J. R., Barnett, W. S., Epstein, A. S., & Weikart, D. P. (1985). The promise of early childhood education. *Phi Delta Kappan, 66* (8), 548–553.

Schweinhart, L. J., & Weikart, D. P. (1985). Evidence that good early childhood programs work. *Phi Delta Kappan, 66* (8), 545–551.

Seefeldt, C. (1987). *The early childhood curriculum: A review of current research.* New York: Teachers College Press.

Shade, D. D. (1996). Software evaluation. *Young Children, 51* (6), 17–21.

Shepard, L. A., & Smith, M. L. (1988). Escalating academic demand in kindergarten: Counterproductive policies. *The Elementary School Journal, 89* (2), 136–145.

Shulman, L. (1990, March 28). Teacher educators turn to case study method. *Education Week,* pp. 18–21.

Simons, R. L., & Associates. (1996). *Understanding differences between divorced and intact families.* Thousand Oaks, CA: Sage Publications.

Smilansky, S. (1968). *The effects of sociodramatic play on disadvantaged preschool children.* New York: Wiley.

Smith, P. K. (1989, April). *Rough and tumble play and its relationship to serious fighting.* Paper presented at the biennial meeting of the Society for Research in Child development, Kansas City, MO.

Snider, M., & Fu, V. (1990). The effects of specialized education and job experience on early childhood teachers' knowledge of developmentally appropriate practice. *Early Childhood Research Quarterly, 5,* 69–78.

Sobel, D. (1994). Authentic curriculum. *Holistic Education Review, 7,* 33–43.

Sommer, K., Whitman, T., Borkowski, J., Schellenback, C., Maxwell. S., & Deogh, D. (1993). Cognitive readiness and adolescent parenting. *Developmental Psychology, 29,* 389–398.

Spodek, B. (1986). *Today's kindergarten: Exploring the knowledge base, expanding the curriculum.* New York: Teachers College Press.

Spodek, B. (1988). Conceptualizing today's kindergarten curriculum. *The Elementary School Journal, 89* (2), 203–211.

Spodek, B. (1993). *Handbook of research on the education of young children.* New York: Macmillan.

Spodek, B., & Saracho, O. N. (1994a). *Dealing with individual differences in the early childhood classroom.* New York: Longman.

Spodek, B., & Saracho, O. N. (1994b). *Right from the start: Teaching children three to eight.* Boston: Allyn & Bacon.

Stainback, S., & Stainback, W. (1992). *Curriculum considerations in inclusive classrooms: Facilitating learning for all students.* Baltimore, MD: Paul H. Brookes.

Stone, J. (1993). Caregiver and teacher language—Responsive or restrictive? *Young Children, 48* (4), 12–18.

Stone, S. J. (1995/1996). Integrating play into the curriculum. *Childhood Education, 72* (2), 104–107.

Stott, F., & Bowman, B. (1996). Child development knowledge: A slippery base for practice. *Early Childhood Research Quarterly, 11* (3), 169–184.

Stroufe, L. A., Cooper, R., & DeHart, G. (1992). *Child development: Its nature and course.* New York: McGraw-Hill.

Sugawara, A. (1996, September). The child development center: An inclusive, collaborative community. *Collaborative Ties: Newsletter of the Oregon State University Child Development Center,* pp. 1–2.

Sullivan, S., & Birch, L. L. (1990). Pass the sugar: Pass the salt: Experience dictates preference. *Developmental Psychology, 26,* 546–551.

Swap, S. (1987). *Enhancing parent involvement in schools.* New York: Teachers College Press.

Tikunoff, W. J. (1985). *Applying significant bilingual instructional features in the classroom.* Rosslyn, VA: National Clearinghouse for Bilingual Education.

Uhrmacher, P. B. (1993). Coming to know the world through Waldorf education. *Journal of Curriculum and Supervision, 9* (1), 87–104.

United States Bureau of the Census. (1997). *Statistical Abstract of the United States: 1997* (117th ed.). Washington, DC: Author.

United States Department of Education. (1991). *A profile of child care settings: Early education and care in 1990.* Washington, DC: Author.

United States Department of Education. (1996a). *Community update.* Washington, DC: Author.

United States Department of Education. (1996b). *Eighteenth annual report to Congress on the implementation of the Individuals with Disabilities Education Act.* Washington, DC: Author.

United States Department of Education. (1996c, November). Teachers volunteer to train colleagues in using technology. *Community Update, 41,* 1.

United States Department of Education. (1997). *Digest of education statistics, 1997,* NCES 98-015, by Thomas D. Snyder. Production Manager: Charlene M. Hoffman. Program Analyst: Claire M. Geddes. National Center for Education Statistics. Washington, DC: Author.

United States Department of Health and Human Services. (1986). *Child sexual abuse prevention—Tips to parents.* Washington, DC: Author.

United States Department of Health and Human Services, National Center on Child Abuse and Neglect. (1996). *Child maltreatment 1994: Reports from the states to the National Center on Child Abuse and Neglect.* Washington, DC: U.S. Government Printing Office.

United States General Accounting Office. (1995). *Infants and toddlers: Dramatic numbers living in poverty.* Washington, DC: Author.

Van Scoy, I. (1995). Trading the three R's for the four E's: Transforming curriculum. *Childhood Education, 72* (1), 19–23.

Veatch, J. (1991). *Whole language and its predecessors: Commentary.* Paper presented at the annual meeting of the College Reading Association, Crystal City, VA.

Viadero, D. (1990, November 28). Battle over multicultural education rises in intensity. *Education Week,* pp. 1, 11, 13.

Villegas, A. M. (1991). *Culturally responsive pedagogy for the 1990s and beyond.* Trends and Issues Paper No. 6. Washington, DC: ERIC Clearinghouse on Teacher Education.

Vygotsky, L. S. (1962). *Thought and language.* Eugenia Hanfmann & Gertrude Vakar (Trans. & Eds.). Cambridge, MA: MIT Press. New York: Wiley (joint publishers).

Vygotsky, L. S. (1978). *Mind in society: The development of higher psychological processes.* Cambridge, MA: Harvard University Press.

Vygotsky, L. S. (1986). *Thought and language.* Cambridge, MA: MIT Press.

Waggoner, D. (1994). Language minority school age population now totals 9.9 million. *NABE, 18* (1), 24–26.

Wallerstein, J. S., & Kelly, J. B. (1980). *Surviving the breakup: How parents and children cope with divorce.* New York: Basic Books.

Wang, C., & Zollers, N. (1990). Adaptive instruction: An alternative service delivery approach. *Remedial and Special Education, 11* (1), 7–21.

Ward, C. (1996). Adult intervention: Appropriate strategies for enriching the quality of children's play. *Young Children, 51* (3), 20–24.

Washington County Community Action Organization. (1996). *Washington County Head Start parent handbook.* Hillsboro, OR: Author.

Washington, V., Johnson, V., & McCracken, J. (1995). *Grassroots success! Preparing schools and families for each other.* Washington, DC: National Association for the Education of Young Children.

Wasserman, S. (1990). *Serious players in the primary classroom.* New York: Teachers College Press.

Weitzman, L. (1985). *The divorce revolution.* New York: Free Press.

Wells, G. (1981). *Learning through interaction: The study of language development.* Cambridge: Cambridge University Press.

Whitebrook, M., Phillips, D., & Howes, C. (1993). *National Child Care Staffing Study revisited: Four years in the life of center-based child care.* Oakland, CA: Child Care Employee Project.

Whitehead, C. A. (1994). Seeking common ground: The family child care perspective. In J. Johnson & J. McCracken (Eds.), *The early childhood career lattice: Perspectives on professional development.* Washington, DC: National Association for the Education of Young Children.

Williams, J., & Best, D. (1990). *Measuring sex stereotypes: A multination study* (rev. ed.). Newbury Park, CA: Sage.

Wing, L. A. (1995). Play is not the work of the child: Young children's perceptions of work and play. *Early Childhood Research Quarterly, 10* (2), 223–247.

Winter, S. (1997). "SMART" planning for inclusion. *Childhood Education, 74* (4), 212–218.

Witherell, C. S. (1991). Narrative and the moral realm: Tales of caring and justice. *The Journal of Moral Education, 20* (3), 237–241.

Wittmer, D. S. (1996). Starting to share. *Scholastic Early Childhood Today, 11* (3), 28–29.

Wolery, M., & Wilbers, J. (1994). Introduction to the inclusion of young children with special needs in early childhood programs. In M. Wolery & J. Wilbers (Eds.), *Including children with special needs in early childhood programs* (pp. 1–22). Washington, DC: National Association for the Education of Young Children.

Wolfe, B. L. (1994). Effective practices in staff development: Head Start experiences. In J. Johnson & J. McCracken (Eds.), *The early childhood career lattice: Perspectives on professional development.* Washington, DC: National Association for the Education of Young Children.

Wong Fillmore, L. (1991). When learning a second language means losing the first. *Early Childhood Research Quarterly, 6* (3), 323–346.

Wood, D. J., Bruner, J. S., & Ross, G. (1976). The role of tutoring in problem solving. *Journal of Child Psychology and Psychiatry and Allied Disciplines, 17,* 89–100.

Woolfolk, A. E. (1995). *Educational psychology* (6th ed.) Boston: Allyn & Bacon.

Woolfolk, A. E. (1998). *Educational psychology* (7th ed.). Boston: Allyn & Bacon.

Zahn-Waxler, C., & Radke-Yarrow, C. (1984). Roots, motives, and patterns in children's prosocial behavior. In E. Stabb. D. Bar-Tal, J. Karylowski, & J. Reykowski (Eds.), *Development and maintainence of prosocial behavior: International perspecitves on positive behavior.* New York: Plenum.

Zahn-Waxler, C. & Radke-Yarrow C., & King, R. (1979). Child rearing and children's prosocial initiations toward victims of distress. *Child Development, 50,* 319–330.

Zeavin, C. (1997). Toddlers at play: Environments at work. *Young Children, 52* (3), 72–77.

Zigler, E., & Muenchow, S. (1992). *Head Start: The inside story of America's most successful educational experiment.* New York: BasicBooks.

Zigler, E., Styfco, S., & Gilman, E. (1993). In E. Zigler & S. Styfco (Eds.), *Head Start and beyond* (pp. 1–41). New Haven, CT: Yale University Press.

Zill, N., Collins, M., West, J., & Hausken, E. (1995). Approaching kindergarten: A look at preschoolers in the United States. *Young Children, 51* (1), 35–38.

AUTHOR INDEX

SUBJECT INDEX

A

Ability grouping, 437
Academics and kindergarten, 403–405
  increased pressure for, 395–396
Acceleration, definition of, 437
Accreditation of professional, 495–496
Actions songs, 297
Adaptation, Piaget's views, 78–79
Adaptive Learning Environments Model (ALEM),
  448
Adult education program, Head Start, 337–338
Adult roles in children's play, 147–156
  intervening, 151–154
  playful attitude, 154–156
  preparing the setting, 148–151
Advocating for children, 485–488
Affiliations, professional, 494–496
After-school care, 391–394
Aggression and rough and tumble play, 127–128
Aid for children in migrant families, 461
American Disabilities Act (ADA), 446
Anecdotal record form, 419
Antibias curriculum, 322–327
Anxiety-producing situations and
  play, 121–122
Arts-based curriculum, 184–186
Associative play, definition of, 146
Attachment:
  definition of, 44
  during middle childhood, 64–65
  sequence of, 45
Attention-deficit disorder, 435, 437
Au pairs as child care providers, 19
Auditory stimuli for infants, 270–271
Authentic curriculum, definition of, 162–164

Autonomy versus doubt and shame (Erikson), 92
Autosymbolic play, definition of, 128–129
Autotelic, definition of, 170

B

Babbling and language development, 49
Bank Street curriculum approach, 180–183
Behaviorism, Skinner's theory of, 100–102
Bilingual children, 314
Bilingual education, 346–347, 366–369,
  484–485
Binuclear family, definition of, 219
Biracial children, 227–228
Blended classes, 10–11
Blended family, definition of, 220
Blocks in curriculum (Pratt), 173–174
Bodily-kinesthetic intelligence (Gardner), 104
Body awareness:
  of preschoolers, 55
  of toddlers, 50–51
Books and materials promoting antibias,
  323–325
Brain development during infancy, 266
Bruner's theory of cognitive development, 84

C

Care giving, principles of, 267
Caring behavior in children, 69–70
Catch-up curriculum, 178–179
Categorization, teaching strategy, 104
Causal reasoning of preschoolers, 57
Centers, definition of, 8
Centration, definition of, 57
Challenges faced by families (*see* Families, and
  context for understanding children)